India Studies in Business and Economics

The Indian economy is considered to be one of the fastest growing economies of the world with India amongst the most important G-20 economies. Ever since the Indian economy made its presence felt on the global platform, the research community is now even more interested in studying and analyzing what India has to offer. This series aims to bring forth the latest studies and research about India from the areas of economics, business, and management science. The titles featured in this series will present rigorous empirical research, often accompanied by policy recommendations, evoke and evaluate various aspects of the economy and the business and management landscape in India, with a special focus on India's relationship with the world in terms of business and trade.

More information about this series at http://www.springer.com/series/11234

Lakhwinder Singh · Nirvikar Singh
Editors

Economic Transformation of a Developing Economy

The Experience of Punjab, India

Springer

Editors
Lakhwinder Singh
Department of Economics and Centre
for Development Economics
and Innovation Studies (CDEIS)
Punjabi University
Patiala
India

Nirvikar Singh
Department of Economics
University of California
Santa Cruz, CA
USA

ISSN 2198-0012 ISSN 2198-0020 (electronic)
India Studies in Business and Economics
ISBN 978-981-10-0196-3 ISBN 978-981-10-0197-0 (eBook)
DOI 10.1007/978-981-10-0197-0

Library of Congress Control Number: 2015958553

Printed on acid-free paper

This Springer imprint is published by SpringerNature
The registered company is Springer Science+Business Media Singapore Pte Ltd.

Foreword

Punjab is, in many ways, India's iconic state. A vast fertile land that marked the northwestern frontier of the Indian subcontinent, it bore the brunt of invasions through history, and, in 1947, the agony of one of the biggest migrations of uprooted people witnessed anywhere in the world, which it shared with Bengal in India's eastern flank, during India's independence and the partition of the sub-continent into India and Pakistan. Growing up in distant Bengal, I had watched with admiration Punjab's rise as it shook off its wrenching history, embraced the Green Revolution of the mid-1960s and strode ahead economically as one of India's most dynamic regions. By the early 1990s Punjab was India's third richest state in terms of per capita income, trailing behind only Maharashtra and Haryana, the latter having been carved out of the larger Punjab state in 1966. Punjab has continued to do well but it has not lived up to the enormous initial promise. By 2012 its rank had dropped to seventh, as it was overtaken by Kerala, Tamil Nadu, Gujarat and other states.

Punjab's history, both recent and distant, has been exciting, full of challenges and experiments. It was once an extremely egalitarian society, home to progressive ideology and religion; it was in the frontline of the radical movement for the nation's independence through the 1930s and 1940s. It was a region that saw the development of sophisticated canal irrigation dating back to colonial times; it made great strides in some light manufacturing sectors, such as textiles and bicycles. Its recent slowdown raises important questions in political economy about the causes of development and growth and the making of growth traps. Understanding these can enhance our understanding of Punjab and enable the state to restore its excellent earlier economic performance. But, in addition, given the iconic status of the Punjab economy, such an understanding can shed light on development in general from which we can learn and benefit wherever we are located in the world. This is what makes the book, *Economic Transformation of a Developing Economy: The Experience of Indian Punjab*, an important one.

The book's subject matter is the economic development of India's Punjab state, home to one of the most successful attempts to modernize agriculture, foster growth and eradicate poverty. The articles in the book—written by distinguished scholars —span the structural transformation of its economy, the education and health of its people, the fiscal policies of the state government, and the relations between the state and India's central government. The book concludes with thoughtful reflections on how Punjab's economy can be made vibrant once again.

The book teaches a lot—how irrigation in the state was extended from less than half of farmland at Independence to 98 % by 2010; how 100 % of Punjab's wheat and rice farmers now use high-yielding varieties, and how chemical fertilizer use per acre increased sixfold during the last five decades. You learn how the intensity of cropping increased from 125 % in the 1960s to almost 200 % today, how the share of wheat and rice has grown from half to more than three-quarters of cropped area while their yields have more than doubled since the 1970s. By the year 2000, Punjab's share in India's procured wheat and rice was more than half. With less than 1.5 % of India's land area, Punjab had become India's granary and as such provided the major impetus of India's subsequent rapid growth.

At the same time, as growth rates of agricultural output fell by half between 1970 and 2010—from 5 to about 2.5 % annually—industrial growth picked up from less than 7 to barely more than 8 %. The state's GDP has grown by more than 5 % per annum decade after decade, slowing down a little during the turbulent 1990s. But since 2005, when several Indian states began doing very well, Punjab's growth began to trail 11 other states. In the mid-1980s, Punjab's per capita output was the highest in the land. Since then, as India's economic growth picked up, Punjab started to slip in relative terms.

Analyzing the reasons for this recent trailing can gives us important insights into development in general. This book draws attention to several potential causes. As is pointed out in one of the chapters, inequality in Punjab has grown sharply, cutting into some of the state's earlier social cohesion and also resulting in the political capture of business. We know from standard growth theory that investment and savings are major drivers of growth. It therefore helps to look at investment-to-GDP ratios in Punjab and in the rest of India. In 1980, at about 15 %, this ratio was about the same. By 2010, it was 38 % in India but still 15 % in Punjab. Punjab is not nearly the best place for investors. An important part of investment and capital formation is the one that takes place in humans through education and the building up of human capital. Punjab, and for that matter all of India, need to pay more attention to this.

Another factor that has probably contributed to Punjab's relative slowdown, with several states, especially in southern India, overtaking it in the manufacturing and services sectors, is the subsidization of agriculture by the government, and the market distortion that this led to. The sheltering of the agricultural sector led to the huge success of the state's economy in this sector but the persistence of these interventions lulled the economy into a kind of complacency which robbed it of the incentives to develop the services sector where the rest of India has had huge successes. The articles in this book also show that Punjab's tenancy laws need to be reformed so that land can be leased with less worry. Massive fuel subsidies distort crop choices—making paddy more profitable and thwarting government efforts to diversify crops. Despite some improvement in access to bank credit, many farmers still rely on informal credit markets, paying onerous interest rates of 25 to 30 % and sometimes being driven to suicide to escape the humiliation of bankruptcy.

The potential for the Punjab economy is huge and Punjab is a great case study for many reasons. The state has shown not just how agriculture can be modernized quickly, but also the dangers of staying too long with agriculture as the leading edge of development. Punjab has shown the poverty reduction and improvements in living standards that come from large increases in productivity, but also the social and environmental risks that rapid economic transformations bring in their wake. It provides an inspiring example of the resilience of a progressive people.

Lakhwinder Singh and Nirvikar Singh have given us an excellent book that dissects the rich experience of Punjab from diverse angles and deserves to be read by those interested in Punjab, India, and even just development economics.

July 2015

Kaushik Basu
Senior Vice President and Chief Economist
of the World Bank

and

C. Marks Professor
Professor of Economics, Cornell University
Ithaca, USA

Preface

Punjab, after leading the way in India's Green Revolution, remained one of the nation's fastest growing states for some years. It was even pictured as a role model of economic development, to be emulated, particularly by other states in India, but also by other developing economies. However, an initial "golden period" (1966–1980) faded quickly during the political turmoil of the 1980s and even more dramatically after India's 1991 economic reforms. Since then, Punjab's growth has lagged quite badly, and its relative position in India's state income rankings has slipped dramatically. Meanwhile, concerns about ecological degradation—and even impending disaster—reflected in rapid deterioration of water quality and availability, have multiplied. Given these changes, the welfare of Punjab has become a concern not only within the state, but also among its relatively large diaspora, which had spread the population's reputation for entrepreneurial energy and economic success within and outside India. The state's waning economic position will also have far reaching implications for its political influence and stability.

All of these make it imperative to ask why Punjab faltered in transforming what were once high rates of economic growth and high levels of savings into successful industrialization of its economy. Despite the state's losing its initial opportunity to move on to a sustained path of economic development, finding answers to this question of 'why?' can be the first step in shaping policies to return Punjab's economy to economic prosperity and sustainable development. Indeed, it is arguable that Punjab needs a dramatic economic transformation for achieving an economically viable, ecologically sustainable, and socio-politically stable position within India. With these objectives in mind, the Centre for Development Economics and Innovation Studies (CDEIS), Punjabi University, in collaboration with the University of California, Santa Cruz, USA, organized an international conference on the theme, "Rejuvenation of Punjab Economy", which was held on 21–23 March 2014 at the Punjabi University campus. This volume is the outcome of this conference directed by Lakhwinder Singh and Nirvikar Singh. The 21 chapters included in this book are selected from the CDEIS-UCSC conference.

We express our gratitude to all the conference participants who contributed as presenters, session chairs, discussants and rapporteurs. We are grateful to the authors for accepting our invitation to write chapters, making detailed revisions and strictly observing deadlines. Organizing a conference and planning a volume from it requires considerable logistical support and teamwork. Punjabi University provided both. We particularly thank the higher level administration of the University and the excellent team of the Department of Economics and CDEIS. We especially appreciate the support of Profs. Inderjeet Singh, Anita Gill, Sukhwinder Singh, Kesar Singh Bhangoo, Jaswinder Singh Brar and Parmod Kumar Aggarwal. Thanks are also due to Mr. Baltej Singh Bhathal and Mr. Gurdeep Singh for their effective secretarial and administrative assistance in organizing the conference as well as during preparation of the manuscript. We are grateful to Ms. Sagarika Ghosh and Ms. Nupoor Singh for their support during the publication process. We express our deepest gratitude to Prof. Kaushik Basu, Senior Vice President and Chief Economist of the World Bank, for encouraging us to cooperate and also writing the foreword of the book.

The CDEIS gratefully acknowledges the financial contributions and support to the conference by Punjab Mandi Board, Mohali; Indian Council for Social Science Research (ICSSR), New Delhi; National Bank for Agriculture and Rural Development (NABARD), Mumbai; and Planning Commission Chair, Punjabi University.

Finally, we would like to thank our families for their encouragement and support during our work on this volume.

Lakhwinder Singh
Nirvikar Singh

Contents

Editors and Contributors

About the Editors

Lakhwinder Singh is a Professor at the Department of Economics, Centre for Development Economics and Innovation Studies (CDEIS), Punjabi University, India. Prior to this, he has been a faculty at the University of Delhi and National Institute of Public Finance and Policy, New Delhi. He has been a Ford Foundation Post-Doctoral Fellow in Economics at Yale University, USA and a Visiting Research Fellow, Seoul National University, South Korea. He has been awarded Asia Fellowship by the Institute of International Education, New York, 2001. His current research focuses on the national innovation system, international knowledge spillovers, patterns of development, globalization and agrarian distress in developing economies. Apart from publishing a number of research papers in journals of national and international repute, he is also the founding editor of the journal *Millennial Asia: An International Journal of Asian Studies*, published by Sage Publications and Association of Asia Scholars. He has co-edited the books *Economic and Environmental Sustainability of the Asian Region* (Routledge, 2010) and *Technology, Innovations and Economic Development: Essays in Honour of Robert E. Evenson*" (Sage Publishers, 2015).

Nirvikar Singh is a Distinguished Professor of Economics and Sarabjit Singh Aurora Chair of Sikh and Punjabi Studies at the University of California, Santa Cruz, where he is also the Director of the Centre for Analytical Finance. He is a member of the Advisory Group to the Finance Minister of India on G-20 matters, and has served as a consultant to the Chief Economic Adviser, Ministry of Finance, Government of India. His current research interests include entrepreneurship, information technology and development, business strategy, political economy, federalism and economic growth. He has authored over 100 research papers, including several on the East Asian and Indian economy and co-authored or edited four books, the most recent being *The Oxford Handbook of the Economics of the Pacific Rim* (Oxford University Press, 2014). He has also served as an advisor for several start-up and knowledge services firms in Silicon Valley and in India.

Contributors

Aradhna Aggarwal Department of International Economics and Business, Copenhagen Business School, Asia Research Centre, Frederiksberg Copenhagen, Denmark

Shayequa Zeenat Ali Centres for International Projects Trust, New Delhi, India

Jaswinder Singh Brar Centre for Research in Economic Change, Punjabi University, Patiala, India

Anita Gill Department of Distance Education, Punjabi University, Patiala, Punjab, India

Sucha Singh Gill Centre for Rural and Industrial Development (CRRID), Madhya Marg, Chandigarh, India

Varinder Jain Institute of Development Studies, 8-B, Jhalana Institutional Area, Jaipur, Rajasthan, India

K.N. Nair Centre for Development Studies, Trivandrum, Kerala, India

Rita Pandey National Institute of Public Finance and Policy, New Delhi, India

S. Pavithra National Institute of Agricultural Economics and Policy Research, Dev Prakash Shastri Marg, Pusa, New Delhi, India

Upinder Sahwney Department of Economics, Panjab University, Chandigarh, India

Tapas K. Sen National Institute of Public Finance and Policy, New Delhi, India

H.S. Shergill Emeritus Professor of Economics, Panjab University, Chandigarh, India

M.S. Sidhu Department of Economics and Sociology, Punjab Agricultural University, Ludhiana, India

R.S. Sidhu Punjab Agricultural University, Ludhiana, India

Gurpreet Singh Centre for Economic Studies and Planning, SSS, Jawaharlal Nehru University, New Delhi, India

Inderjeet Singh Department of Economics, Punjabi University, Patiala, India

Indervir Singh Central University of Himachal Pradesh, Dharamshala, India

Lakhwinder Singh Department of Economics and Centre for Development Economics and Innovation Studies (CDEIS), Punjabi University, Patiala 147002, India

Nirvikar Singh Department of Economics, University of California, Santa Cruz, CA, USA

Pritam Singh Department of Accounting, Finance and Economics, Oxford Brookes University, Oxford, OX33 1HX, UK

Sukhpal Singh Centre for Management of Agriculture, Indian Institute of Management, Vastrapur, Ahmedabad, India

Sukhwinder Singh Centre for Research in Economic Change, Punjabi University, Patiala, India

Shinder S. Thandi Global and International Studies, University of California, Santa Barbara, USA

Kamal Vatta Centres for International Projects Trust, New Delhi, India

List of Figures

List of Tables

Chapter 1
Economic Transformation and Development Experience of Indian Punjab—An Introduction

Lakhwinder Singh and Nirvikar Singh

The historical experience of economic transformation of the world's advanced economies has included significant structural change, both of production and workforce structure, over time. The pace of this transformation differed across economies and over time, but an important common feature has been shifting from a low-productivity–low-wage economy to one with high productivity and wages. This has involved shifting economic activities from rural/agricultural to urban/industrial activities. The dynamic force behind this change has been innovation. The innovative process has also generated opportunities for institutional change and cultural transformation of societies along with economic transformation.

Historically, the transformation of the industrially advanced countries of the world was never smooth, but rather faced several roadblocks. Arguably, the state during this economic transformation phase played a leading role, not only in removing roadblocks but also in actively guiding, directing or planning the pathways of transformation. This process did not necessarily involve direct state action, but could be through enabling suitable incentive systems for private economic agents of production to succeed (Kuznets 1966). Research on this transformation experience in the post second world war period conducted by Chenery (1960) examined the relationship between the level of economic prosperity (measured through per capita income) and the structure of the economy. He established the importance of the industrial sector in achieving higher levels of per capita income and economic well-being. However, Chenery and subsequent scholars who have examined the role of accumulation of capital in economic transformation have

L. Singh (✉)
Department of Economics and Centre for Development Economics and Innovation Studies (CDEIS), Punjabi University, Patiala 147002, India
e-mail: lakhwindergill@pbi.ac.in

N. Singh
Department of Economics, University of California, Santa Cruz, CA 95064, USA

L. Singh and N. Singh (eds.), *Economic Transformation of a Developing Economy*, India Studies in Business and Economics,
DOI 10.1007/978-981-10-0197-0_1

neglected the institutional and cultural aspects of transformation, which was an integral part of Kuznets's analysis of structural transformation (Syrquin 1988).[1]

The recent successful transformation experience of the newly industrializing economies of East Asia has re-ignited interest among scholars in understanding the interlinked processes of economic development and structural transformation.[2] The engine of growth in East Asia remained the industrial sector. An important feature of this transformation was in developing unique innovation capabilities through systems of innovation specialized in 'short cycle technologies' that allowed South Korea and Taiwan to pass through the middle-income trap (Lee 2013). Furthermore, the sustained economic growth experience of China since the 1980s and India's high growth experience in the first decade of the twenty-first century have generated interest in examining the path of structural change that may occur in the future of the global economy. The engine of growth in the Chinese economy has been manufacturing, but it has arguably been the services sector in India (e.g., Singh 2006; Nayyar 2013). In this respect, the economic transformation and catch-up of China and India have followed different pathways.

The reasons for the relative stagnation of manufacturing and industry in India and the importance of services have something to do with the specifics of the country's policy environment, as well as the emergence of information technology services as a source of innovation and economic dynamism. Nevertheless, the sustained accumulation of capital and transformation of developing economies like India can only be expected to occur if systemic constraints can be removed, with the active support of the state in nurturing innovation capabilities and building synergies across and within sectors, whatever the relative importance of manufacturing and services in this process.

When considering the possible future economic trajectory of India, one has to recall that it is a country of continental size, and the level of economic development differs substantially across Indian states. Of course China is even larger, and has also seen diversity in economic development among its regions, but it has a much more centralized political system, which provides very different mechanisms for managing this diversity.

In India's case, the state of Punjab, due to its historical importance, strategic location and significant religious minority, is an important example of the challenges of the nation's diversity. Economic growth and transformation of the Punjab economy through the Green Revolution in the pre-reform period gave leading status to Punjab, in terms of economic prosperity, among India's states. According to per capita income rankings, Punjab remained number one among the Indian states for over three decades, that is, the 1970s, 1980s and 1990s. This rise was mainly due to the ushering in of the Green Revolution in Punjab from about 1966, which emerged

[1]The role of institutions in economic development has received wide attention, of course, including Acemoglu et al. (2005) and North et al. (2009).

[2]A basic empirical analysis of the relationship between growth and structural change in India is performed by Cortuk and Singh (2011, 2015).

from the promotion of much-needed food security for the country, as well as a political consensus on a state-led model of economic development. Punjab, with the help of the Union government, developed a physical and institutional infrastructure that supported and nurtured private economic agents in realizing the full potential of their investments. Modern production methods, supported by an effective research and extension system and assured markets, allowed the agriculture sector to thrive. Agricultural productivity increased manifold and generated substantial employment opportunities, while a remunerative procurement system of food grains led to the emergence of economic surpluses (Dhesi and Singh 2008). Private investment, due to this conducive economic environment, flourished, and as a consequence, economic prosperity spread in multiple dimensions. Complementary economic activities, such as an agricultural machinery industry, transport and services, also started flourishing (Bhalla 1995). As a consequence of these developments, Punjab achieved another distinction, of having the lowest incidence of poverty among India's states (Ahluwalia 1978).

The agriculture sector emerged as an engine of growth and structural transformation of the Punjab economy very early in the Green Revolution period. In 1966–67, the share of agriculture in the state domestic product was 52.85 and increased to 54.27 in 1970–71 (Singh and Singh 2002). The importance of the agriculture sector in the economy of Punjab can further be seen from the employment structure. The agriculture sector provided employment to 62.67 % of the workforce in the year 1971 (Singh et al. 2016). In the subsequent decade, the agriculture sector dominated both in terms of income and employment generation. At the same time, the cropping pattern moved towards concentration, changing from more diversified to less diversified, in what is commonly known as a wheat–paddy rotation. The structure of the Punjab economy remained highly skewed towards agriculture, and the agriculture sector further concentrated on these two crops, which were targeted to provide food security for the nation. As is well known, agriculture is subject to diminishing returns, and agricultural productivity growth started showing signs of slowing as early as the late 1970s and early 1980s. This in turn contributed to escalating costs of production and a decline in the surpluses from farm production. The high degree of dependence of the population on agricultural income, combined with a declining number of man-days due to an increasing use of agricultural machinery in farm operations, put pressure on earning income from farm labour. Furthermore, capital-intensive agriculture increased investment requirements per unit of agriculture production, rendering small and marginal sized land holdings non-viable. These trends, which evolved into a crisis of structural stagnation of Punjab economy, started to appear in the late 1970s and early 1980s. However, instead of addressing this looming crisis through economic transformation of the Punjab economy, one can argue that the political leadership, both at the national and state level, diverted the focus to other issues, contributing to political turmoil that lasted more than a decade.

At the same time, new economic policy initiatives of the Indian government that began in the 1980s relaxed internal and external constraints, allowed expansion of capacity of the industrial sector and helped to raise the growth of the national economy. Meanwhile, the Punjab economy during the 1980s was suffering from extreme political and social turmoil. The functioning of democratic government at the state level was completely disrupted, and there was no avenue to use the opportunity provided by the national economic policy reform. In fact, turmoil in the state completely diverted the government from engaging in developmental activities to tackling law and order problems instead. The heavy expenditure incurred on the security forces, including large investments on enhancing the capabilities of the police in Punjab, acted as a drain on the public exchequer. The normal functioning of the state government was derailed, making the institutions for collecting revenue and providing health and educational services, dysfunctional. To cover revenue shortfalls, the state government began borrowing heavily from the central government. As a result, the burden of debt on the state government increased dramatically.

Beyond the significant financial costs of the turmoil, there were enormous and long-lasting human costs. The state's social overhead capital suffered in multiple ways, and the impact of this was visible in the subsequent decades. For example, there was an elimination of the kind of political opposition required for a well-functioning democracy. Several prominent social workers and important political leaders were killed in this period, silencing the voice of democracy through the channel of social movements.

Against the backdrop of Punjab's turmoil, it is now almost forgotten that a significant economic transformation agenda and programme had been contemplated and laid down in an industrial policy resolution of the government of Punjab in 1978. This programme was expected to be implemented during the 1980s, but was completely sidelined by the disruption of democratically elected governments. Instead, the Punjab economy remained locked into an equilibrium that was dominated by an agricultural system which remained oriented towards fulfilling the needs of national food security.

When the Indian government initiated full-fledged liberalization and globalization of the economy in July 1991, Punjab's economy and society were characterized by this situation of disrupted developmental institutional arrangements and extreme fragility. At the same time, Punjab's turmoil was being reduced, and achieving peace with a restoration of democratically elected government was the primary item on the political agenda. During the first half of the 1990s, Punjab returned to some level of peacefulness, and a democratic government did begin to function, but with a fragile fiscal policy and huge debt burden. In this situation, there was little scope for the state political leadership to restore the kinds of institutional arrangements and capacity needed to catalyse an economic transformation.

Arguably, there were possibly compelling arguments for reducing government intervention in economic activities, both directly and indirectly, thereby giving market forces a greater role in the economy. However, this was taken as an opportunity by some of the state's political leadership to change their character from statesmen-politicians to businessmen-politicians. This leadership has adopted a strategy to gain political legitimacy by using populist measures on the one hand, and promoting their business interests through state power on the other. Their engagement in business activities, especially in rent-thick sectors, has added tremendously to their wealth. Meanwhile, weak institutional arrangements, a dysfunctional fiscal policy and a rising debt burden have continued to characterize the state. The consequence of this process has been a deceleration of economic growth in the 1990s (Singh and Singh 2002) and emergence of agrarian distress, including farmer and agricultural labourer suicides (Singh et al. 2016).

The post-reform period performance of Punjab compared with other Indian states was examined by Ahluwalia (2002) with a view to identifying the factors that contributed to differential economic performance among major Indian states. This study brought out the fact that Punjab remained at the bottom among the major Indian states in its investment–SDP ratio, in the post-reform period. It is well recognized that investment is fundamental to determining economic growth. Punjab's investment–SDP ratio declined sharply, from 24.06 in 1995 to 13.40 in 1999–2000 (Singh 2014). This fall included the agriculture sector, which has served as the backbone of the Punjab economy. Contrary to the accelerated growth experience of the Indian economy in the first decade of the twenty-first century, the Punjab economy decelerated and regressed relative to the national economy. Punjab slipped from ranking first in per capita income after the Green Revolution to second in the late 1990s and now ninth after a decade-and-a-half of the twenty-first century.

Instead of attending to the structural problems faced by the Punjab economy, the political leadership engaged in populist fiscal profligacy through subsidies and other giveaways, further increasing state government indebtedness and weakening the capacity for economic governance. Social sectors such as health and education, which are central to human development, suffered severely due to a lack of investible public resources. Arguably, the institutional arrangements for delivering development have become even more dysfunctional, even after a succession of democratically elected governments. The self-interested behaviour of the political leadership likely has contributed to a drying up of investment opportunities in the state and consequently intensified its economic crisis.

The process of turning from a relatively successful economic development experience to derailment of economic development surely needs to be reversed. Punjab occupies a strategic position in the country, in terms of food security and national security, and therefore its economy requires early attention to arrest its downward spiral. To explore policy measures for the revival, rejuvenation and transformation of the Punjab economy, a conclave of researchers, policy makers and policy implementation agencies was organized jointly by the Centre for Development Economics and Innovation Studies (CDEIS), Punjabi University and the University of California, Santa Cruz, USA, on March 21–23, 2014, at the Punjabi University campus. Selected papers presented and discussed in the conference were revised by the authors after incorporating comments and suggestions made by the discussants and participants. Furthermore, the papers were again read by both the editors and detailed comments were given to the authors for further revisions. The 20 final selected, revised papers are collected in this volume, keeping in view thematic unity, and are organized into seven sections as follows.

1.1 Understanding the Crisis of Agrarian Transition

The agrarian economy of Punjab has undergone dramatic changes in the post-independence era. It has transformed from traditional to technologically "modern," and from modern to highly capital- and resource-intensive. Punjab's agriculture now has high productivity relative to developing countries, as well as to other Indian states, as measured by per hectare yield of two crops, wheat and rice. The contribution of Punjab to India's central pool of buffer food stocks in 2013 was 29.3 % in rice and 43.4 % in wheat (GOP 2013). Not only has agriculture in Punjab contributed to the food security of the country but generating this surplus also helped reduce poverty in the state.

However, the specifics of this agrarian transformation generated their own problems. Increasing agrarian distress for farmers with small and marginal sized holdings and for rural labour has followed from declining returns and rising costs, and the resultant reduced surpluses. Lack of alternative remunerative employment opportunities has reduced the state economy's capacity to generate sustainable livelihoods. This is further being reflected in high rates of suicides among marginalized farmers and agricultural labourers. The current pattern of highly specialized agriculture has also generated a high degree of environmental stress through the use of high levels of chemical fertilizers, pesticides and groundwater resources. The sustainability of Punjab agriculture is now seriously in question, both in terms of ecological and human health, and in remunerative occupations for the state's people. The four chapters in this section shed light on the emerging crisis of agrarian transformation of the Punjab economy as well as attempts to provide possible alternative ways forward.

K.N. Nair and Gurpreet Singh, in Chap. 2, have traced the evolution of the process of agriculture transformation from the colonial period to the present. The authors use institutional and technological perspectives in explaining the differential performance of the agriculture sector across Indian states. The superior performance of agriculture in Punjab during the colonial period is attributed to three factors, that is, land rights, modernization of the canal system and the revenue collection system. Clear property rights of ownership of land title were granted to cultivators. This generated relatively efficient land markets, and land prices increased manifold. Canal irrigation improved land productivity and evidence shows that wheat productivity was higher on irrigated versus non-irrigated land. Land revenue was collected through relatively rich landowners, who passed the collected revenue to the administration while retaining some part of the revenue. These surpluses also generated an informal credit market in Punjab agriculture. Rich landowners were engaged in lending money, although at high rates of interest.

The interaction of technological progress in agriculture, generating a supportive research and extension system along with other institutional changes, and a network of rail transportation worked together to enable superior agriculture performance as well as higher revenue for the colonial administration. However, the evolution of interlinked agrarian markets for credit, land and produce within this system allowed surpluses from the farmers to be squeezed, which contributed to large-scale alienation of land and consequently forced the British to pass the Land Alienation Act in 1901. This Act pushed moneylenders out of the land market. The authors argue that canal irrigation was the main factor in triggering institutional and technological changes, which led to economic prosperity but also increased socio-economic divisions within and across various regions of India.

Nair and Singh further argue that the post-independence agriculture of Punjab was conditioned by the food insecurity of the country, so that institutional and technological changes were devised both by the union government and the state government to fulfil the nation's food security requirements. The success of the Green Revolution is essentially attributed to the evolution of institutions that governed the agriculture sector, accompanied by technological innovations, and supported by subsidies to electricity, water, fertilizer, plus assured government procurement of the output at minimum support prices. Now, however, agriculture productivity has reached a plateau due to environmental and over-mechanization constraints, and the institutional arrangements which facilitated and enabled high productivity agriculture have turned into roadblocks for further progress. The authors conclude that the crisis of agrarian transition faced by the state urgently needs to be resolved. Their well-founded opinion is that the agrarian crisis is complex and its extent is large; therefore, the state government will not be able to overcome it without the support of the Union government.

R.S. Sidhu, Kamal Vatta and S.Z. Ali examine the wheat revolution and its economic consequences for agriculture development in Chap. 3. The authors note that agricultural productivity variations across India's states are quite large. Agricultural productivity, which increased manifold during the early Green Revolution period in Punjab, is now stagnating. Can agricultural productivity be increased with the same combination of factors through which productivity was increased earlier? This question is put to the test by the authors by employing a simultaneous equation econometric model to determine factors affecting productivity growth of wheat in India as a whole as well as in Punjab specifically.

A significant result is that wheat productivity is highly correlated with availability of water for irrigation. Irrigation emerges as the most important determinant of increase in wheat production among non-price variables. It is argued by the authors that to achieve the targeted agriculture growth of 4 %, the area under irrigation needs to be increased across Indian states and the efficiency of the existing irrigation infrastructure needs significant improvement.

While examining the factors behind the rise of wheat productivity and production in Punjab, the authors also test the role of the agriculture research and extension system through the creation of new HYVs seeds over the time period 1970–2011. The major conclusion emerging from this empirical investigation is that the factors that increased wheat productivity included non-price, price and institutional variables. They also examine the question of who benefitted more—small or large farmers—from the rise in wheat productivity. Their methodology involves using frontier production function approaches for estimation of the coefficients of technical efficiency. The variations in productivity of wheat across farm size categories turn out to be quite small. The average level of technical efficiency relative to the estimated frontier achieved by different categories of farms ranged between 85 and 95 %. However, 57 % of large sized farmers achieved the highest (90 %) frontier level of productivity compared with relatively low proportions of small and medium sized farmers. On the whole, the authors conclude that irrigation is vitally important for agriculture productivity growth, and therefore water use efficiency needs substantial improvement. They also stress the need for rationalization of cropping patterns, while keeping in view the groundwater situation of particular regions of the state and the country as a whole.

In Chap. 4 Sukhpal Singh provides an overview of existing thinking on diversification strategy for agriculture, identifies flaws in that thinking and suggests alternative ways to tackle the agrarian crisis of Punjab. The author discusses in detail the Johl committee reports—one (1986) and two (2002)—on diversification of Punjab agriculture, and connects this discussion to the Kalkat committee report of 2013. He finds many similarities in the approaches of the earlier committee reports and notes their ineffectiveness in leading to any significant diversification of agriculture in Punjab. These diversification reports generated considerable academic debate, but failed to change the ground realities of Punjab agriculture. Singh identifies flaws in the policy of diversification, including the fact that it targeted, directly and indirectly, support for farmers with large sized holdings, but failed to provide recommendations for the crisis-ridden small peasantry of Punjab.

It is also a well-recognized fact that the quasi-mono-culture of the wheat–paddy rotation of Punjab agriculture is a highly specialized cropping pattern, which is adversely affecting the groundwater balance and has severe environmental consequences. For this reason, the sustainability of Punjab agriculture is seriously under question. The other very important factor underlined by the author is non-remunerative agriculture for small holders and agricultural labour. The rationale of subsidies, especially of free supply of electricity for exploitation of groundwater, which is contrary even to the diversification policy of the state government, is challenged by the author. He suggests an alternative strategy to develop community-based solutions and farmer (cooperative) companies for sustainability of the diversification of Punjab agriculture, based on the success stories of farmer companies thriving in other states of India. He suggests several alternative solutions such as contract farming and environmentally safe crops, but all this will need innovative new institutional arrangements, which may have to be provided by the state government.

As indicated in the three important contributions mentioned above, water is the lifeline of agriculture, and given innovations in new seed varieties, fertilizers and institutional arrangements, the productivity of crops is dependent on assured irrigation. Rita Pandey, in Chap. 5, examines the state of groundwater balance in Punjab and suggests strategies to make it sustainable. The author notes that the net irrigated area is predominantly under tube well irrigation, that is, 71 %. Therefore, the pressure on groundwater for fulfilling irrigation needs in Punjab is very high. The groundwater table is receding at a rapid rate. Out of 137 developmental blocks, 112 are over-exploited so far as groundwater is concerned. These blocks belong to the central part of Punjab. The author notes two significant factors that have determined the over-exploitation of groundwater: one, the scarcity of surface water, especially canal water for irrigation and two, groundwater has advantage in terms of control over the timing and amount of water. The welfare implications in terms of rising costs of lifting water from the aquifer and falling water table are having negative effects on agricultural production.

The increasing awareness among policy makers and political leaders regarding the critical importance of groundwater is a positive development. This is reflected in the new agriculture diversification programmes devised by the state of Punjab and enactment of Punjab Preservation of Subsoil Water Act of 2009, which has restricted the unmindful pumping of water from the aquifer during dry spells. The act has allowed transplantation of the paddy crop only from June 10 onwards, which roughly coincides with the start of the rainy season. There is growing evidence that in a normal monsoon the delayed paddy planting reduces pressure on the groundwater table. The author examines the practices of other Indian states, and the laws passed by the Union government, which could have been used in managing groundwater, but have not been employed by the state of Punjab. There are several options available for sustainable use of groundwater on both the supply side and demand side. To accomplish sustainable water use, the author identifies regulatory instruments and economic instruments. However, the state of Punjab has not been able to use the available regulatory instruments; to the contrary, it has encouraged over-exploitation of groundwater by subsidizing electricity and providing other capital subsidies too. In conclusion, Rita Pandey provides nine guiding principles to support informed interventions by the state government for sustainable use of groundwater. An important suggestion given by the author, based on a successful experiment in the Moga district of Punjab, is that of artificial recharging of aquifers through harvesting rainwater. This can not only recharge the aquifer but also save electricity use by reducing the cost of lifting groundwater for irrigation purposes.

1.2 Agrarian Markets and Distributive Outcomes

It is a widely known fact that there is a positive relationship between well-functioning agrarian markets and economic development. In developing countries, either these markets are missing or they are imperfect. Imperfect markets either lead to inefficiencies and underperforming agriculture, or generate high rents and transactions costs, over-exploitation of resources, and under-pricing of outputs or over-pricing of inputs. Therefore, the contribution of well-functioning agrarian markets is substantial in terms of its effects on the economic development process and transformation of a developing economy. The five chapters included in this section examine issues pertaining to the functioning of agrarian input and output markets and the consequences for distributive justice.

In Chap. 6, H.S. Shergill provides an overview of the functioning of land lease markets and its impact on undermining the efficiency of the agriculture production system in Punjab. While comparing the extent of cash rent tenancy across Indian states, the author marshals evidence to show that Punjab is distinct in terms of leasing the area operated: more than 80 % of the total area covered by modern cash rent tenancy is leased in. He examines the transformation of cash rent tenancy since the inception of the Green Revolution and finds that the area under cash rent tenancy was even higher in Punjab than the all-India average (29 % in 1971–72 compared with an all-India level of only 15.42 %). However, the major form of tenancy in the early Green Revolution period was not cash rent tenancy. During the period of the Green Revolution, these trends dramatically changed in favour of cash rent tenancy in Punjab, but the all-India proportion increased at a very slow pace and remained marginal. Modern cash rent tenancy has increased in Punjab at a fast rate and reached 90.42 % in 2010–11, a phenomenon popularly called 'reverse tenancy'. The author also shows that there are only small variations in cash rent tenancy across various regions of Punjab. And this testifies that Punjab is a leading state in terms of structural transformation that has occurred in the system of agrarian tenancy practices.

An important question asked by the author is why has the rest of India been sticking to the traditional systems of tenancy, while Punjab dramatically altered the course of its tenancy system. He provides an answer to this question in terms of unravelling the underlying factors responsible for this change. He argues that the character of the land lessors and tenants has completely changed in Punjab due to the adoption of a capitalist farming system. Land lessors are mostly small owners and absentee medium and big farmers. The lessees are medium and big farmers who are using modern capital-intensive techniques of production and have acquired appropriate expertise and capabilities to reap the highest benefits from attaining high productivity from those plots of land. The existing law, which was enacted to protect the tenant in a traditional tenancy system, is now ineffective for attaining equity in the land market, due to the very existence of modern cash rent tenancy. Therefore, the author proposes enactment of an alternative modern tenancy law for overcoming current inefficiencies and inequities both in the specific functioning of the land market and the agriculture production system overall.

M.S. Sidhu, in Chap. 7, examines the nature and extent of the food grains market and its relationship to agricultural development. The food grains market has revolved around the food security needs of the nation. It is regulated through legislation including the widely implemented APMC Act of 1961. This act declares any sale of wheat and paddy made other than in regulated food grains markets as illegal. The government of India has been procuring all the output that comes to the regulated markets and does so at assured minimum support prices. The author points out that 99 % of the wheat and 100 % of the paddy in Punjab are being sold through the regulated markets, which have reduced the role of informal agriculture output markets in the state. In the year 2012–13, 250.92 lakh tons of wheat, which was 43.43 % of the total wheat procured by the government of India, and 85.58 lakh tons of paddy, which was 25.15 % of the total paddy procured in India, were transacted in the food grains market of Punjab. To handle such a large food grain output, the government of Punjab had set up total of 1795 purchase centres by the year 2013–14. The author estimates that farmers on average travel only 7–8 km to transport food grains to market. This shows that the infrastructure laid down by the state government, not only setting up purchase centres, but also covering each village with metalled road networks, facilitated easy access to food grains procurement centres. This system of a network of purchasing centres and road connectivity has facilitated the efficient post-harvest clearance of agricultural output. The Punjab Mandi Board has been entrusted with the duty of regulating the market and creating the infrastructure, while generating revenue through collection of fees levied on the sale purchase of the agriculture output. This organization has played a key role in developing and maintaining rural link roads and developing markets.

The other important feature of the output market pointed out by the author is that the storage capacity for the food grains, both covered and open, was 234 lakh tonnes in the year 2013–14. Sidhu also provides evidence regarding how the regulated market assigned a special role to commission agents as intermediaries. These agents are often involved in the moneylending business and trap the farmers in this interlinkage to extract farmers' surplus. These commission agents are thriving because the APMC Act of 1961 prohibits direct sale of food grains. However, the author also notes the lack of modern food grain storage facilities as a contributory factor in this situation. He suggests that the government should develop, perhaps through public–private partnerships, new safe storage capacity (such as silos), so that wastage of food grains can be prevented in the future.

It is well established, both theoretically and empirically, that there is a positive relationship between access to finance and agricultural development. Well-functioning financial markets can reduce inefficiencies in economic transactions and can also leverage surpluses for investment in productive economic activities. However, developing economies typically have imperfect financial markets that reduce investment opportunities and squeeze surpluses from productive economic agents.

In this vein, Anita Gill, in Chap. 8, has examined the nature, extent and evolution of the credit market and its relationship with agricultural development in Punjab. While analysing the overall development experience of the Punjab economy, the author documents the relative decline of the agriculture sector in the state's economy. The agriculture sector has gone from a very high to a low growth rate in value addition. The rate of growth has declined in the 1990s at a sharp rate, recovering a little bit in the first decade of twenty-first century, but remaining quite low compared to the early Green Revolution period. This has reduced the relative importance of agriculture as an income generating sector, but one which continues to support a large proportion of the workforce. The slow rise in agricultural output prices compared with input prices has in fact squeezed the income of agriculture-dependent households and pushed the small and marginal peasantry of Punjab into a crisis-like situation.

While tracing the history of agrarian credit markets of Punjab, the author argues that credit markets in Punjab were comprised of both formal and informal sources of finance. Institutional intervention in the credit market started with the enactment in 1904 of a cooperative society act, and subsequently, commercial banks' entry into the credit market in the 1970s. The institutional credit market has undergone structural transformation. The cooperative banks were providing more than 82 % of total institutional finance in the year 1970, but a complete shift has occurred since then, with commercial banks' contribution to agricultural credit in Punjab being more than 78 % in 2012–13. Despite institutional intervention in the agriculture credit market in Punjab, informal lenders' presence in extending credit declined, but continued to be very high, that is, more than 40 %.

An important feature of this study is that the author has conducted two surveys of the same households with a gap of 20 years (1993–94 and 2012–13), for understanding the change in the agrarian credit market. On the basis of evidence, it is argued that there is a marked shift in the agrarian credit market from informal lenders to formal sources of finance. But the extent of the existence of informal lenders still continued. Even the extent of linking credit with other markets has declined but still persists. The requirement in the informal credit market for collateral underwent a change and now land is being asked for as collateral, suggesting that commission agents seek to appropriate land from borrowers. The credit raised by rural households has been spent largely on productive purposes (67 %), while cross-household variations have been observed in terms of uses of credit.

Why was there a decline in the extent of informal lending in the agrarian credit markets in the study villages? The author argues that when the agrarian crisis became pervasive, the government of India and the Reserve Bank of India announced several measures designed to increase the inflow of institutional credit. Low-cost and flexible programmes such as Kisan Credit Card, Agriculture Debt Waiver and Debt Relief Scheme, and One Time Settlement schemes were announced. For rural labour, the MGNREGA remained quite effective in terms of reducing linkages of credit with the labour market. However, to save the farmers from the clutches of exploitative interlinked informal agrarian markets, much still needs to be done by the state.

Complementary to Gill's analysis of the functioning of the informal and interlinked agrarian credit markets, Indervir Singh, in Chap. 9, reports on a primary survey of commission agents, spread over four developmental blocks, designed to examine their business conduct. Drawing lessons from the economic theory of interlinked agrarian credit markets, Singh reaches the conclusion that imperfect information makes the rural credit market oligopolistic. Under such a situation, the interest rates charged are higher than the marginal cost of lending and this also inhibits expansionary formal credit public policy.

Singh provides new evidence, based on his carefully conducted survey of 30 commission agents, on risk minimization by the commission agents through spending time and resources to screen and monitor lenders and to enforce contracts. Commission agents develop social relations with client farmers and continue to fulfil their needs while linking credit provision with services in other markets. Commission agents also ask the most trusted client farmers to certify new clients and verify the clearance from other commission agents in case of a shift from a previous lending agent.

An important piece of empirical evidence brought out by Singh is that the rate of default is very low, and in cases where default occurs, legal recourse is the least preferred remedy. Recent high default rates have occurred due to repeated crop failures and farmers turned to new commission agents, who with an eye on the land of borrowing farmers have started lending without much screening and monitoring. When commission agents used unfair practices to recover loans from defaulters, civil society organizations appeared on the scene to rescue the farmers. However, the involvement of these civil society organizations (farmer unions) triggered further defaults. According to the author, this benefitted medium and large farmers rather than small and marginal farmers. In fact, small and marginal farmers have high dependence on commission agents for meeting their credit needs and they suffered due to the credit rationing that came about.

Kamal Vatta and Pavithra S., in Chap. 10, provide analysis on one of the most pressing issues of recent times, that is, economic inequality. As pointed out by the authors, land is the most productive asset available in the countryside. While examining household inequality of productive assets, based on two primary surveys conducted in 2005–06 and 2010–11, the authors find that access to land has increased for the top 10 % of farm households, from 46.67 to 51.74 %. However, access to land decreased from 17.78 to 9.53 % between 2005–06 and 2010–11, for the bottom decile of farming households. The estimated value of the Gini coefficient has increased.

An important piece of evidence provided by Kamal Vatta and Pavithra is that the relationship between level of education and size of land asset holdings is one of high positive correlation. The authors conclude that new opportunities of employment require education, and those are concentrated in the larger sized farming categories, which indicates further the concentration of income from sources other than agriculture.

The most significant finding that emerged from the empirical exercise done by the authors is that across various sources of income in rural Punjab, the value of the Gini coefficient increased. A similar increase in inequality of income emerges from considering the income shares of the poorest quintile and the richest quintile households over time. These inequalities were also strongly present in educational outcomes. These empirical observations and calculations bring out the stark reality of the situation in rural Punjab, where poverty has also returned, along with increasing inequality. Thus, the authors suggest that this trend of rising inequality and poverty is a cause for concern and needs urgent attention from the state's policy makers to arrest it.

1.3 Structural Transformation of Punjab Economy: Emergence of Industry and Services

Punjab's economy has witnessed some, but not all, of the structural transformation that has been observed in other developing economies. The agriculture sector constituting agriculture and allied activities has progressively been reduced and contributed 28.70 % to the state domestic product in 2012–13. The secondary sector-manufacturing, construction and electricity-provided 24.41 % of state domestic product. However, the tertiary sector emerged in 2012–13 as the most dominant sector of Punjab economy with its contribution to the state domestic product being 46.89 % (GOP 2013). There has been a sharp decline in the agriculture sector's contribution to the state domestic product, and the secondary sector is maintaining its share but tertiary services are fast gaining in share. In terms of workforce structure, the agriculture sector, according to the 2011 population census, employed more than 35 % of the workforce, while manufacturing just employed 10.24 % of the workforce (GOI 2011). The long-term sustainability of a developing economy is determined by the rate of its structural transformation and the dynamics of its emerging productive sectors. For understanding the dynamics of structural change and sustainability of the emerging development path of the Punjab economy, three contributions analysing the nature and growth of emerging sectors, that is, industry and services, are included in this section.

Aradhna Aggarwal, in Chap. 11, has investigated in a comparative framework the relationship between economic growth and structural change during the post-reform period. Structural change entails expansion of value added and employment in higher productivity sectors. This process of transformation, accompanied by economic growth, has a capacity to make a dent in the poverty rate. While subdividing the whole period into slow and fast growth periods of the Indian economy after reforms, the author finds that Punjab has lagged behind in its economic growth and slipped in its relative ranking. Employment growth also declined to 0.5 % between 2004–05 and 2011–12, which was a fast growth period for the Indian economy.

The empirical exercise carried out by Aradhna Aggarwal shows that structural change occurred both in terms of gross state domestic product and employment structure. On the basis of Shapley's decomposition analysis, it is argued that productivity effects, both inter- and intra-sectoral, have driven growth during the fast and slow growth periods. The construction sector is an exception and employment creation programmes focused on the construction sector are growth reducing, according to this analysis.

The author suggests that policy makers have to simultaneously emphasize achieving high growth rates of gross state domestic product and increasing the employment elasticity to realize the possibility of sustainable growth. Furthermore, it is argued that the state should take initiatives to strengthen the skill-oriented educational system, and that economic growth and manpower planning need to be integrated for solving the unemployment problem. The system of flexibility in the labour market should be combined with income security of workers, and the state should provide assistance in retraining and relocation of the workers. The author outlines five principles for devising and implementing a comprehensive employment policy to draw the full benefits from any structural transformation of the economy.

Varinder Jain, in Chap. 12, examines the nature, character and evolution of the manufacturing sector of Punjab from colonial times to the present. To trace the evolution of the industrial sector in an agrarian economy, the author reviews both theoretical and empirical literature dealing with the relationship between agriculture development and industrial dynamics. The linkages between the agricultural and industrial sectors, at an early stage of industrialization, had remained very high. Taking a cue from classical economic theory, Jain analyses the factors used by the colonial rulers to develop agriculture in otherwise barren areas of Punjab. An irrigation network, a railway network and commercialization of agriculture were the three factors that generated economic surplus to fulfil the needs of the British administration. This also generated an intermediary class of moneylenders that started squeezing the surpluses from the peasantry and started usurping agriculture land. These conditions forced the colonial authorities to enact the Land Alienation Act of 1901, which prevented moneylenders from investing in landed property. However, as argued by the author, this act sowed the seeds of investing some of the surpluses in industrial establishments. This process was even boosted by the independence struggle in the case of handloom cloth, and the policy environment was reasonably favourable for industrialization. However, the partition of greater Punjab to West and East Punjab disrupted the linkages of trade, finance and industrial raw materials. Large number of industries and the well-developed agriculture of West Punjab went to Pakistan with Partition.

An important finding emerges from the analysis of policies to resurrect the industrial sector in the post-independence period. Well-designed rehabilitation programmes of the Indian and Punjab governments, by extending institutional and financial support, helped in firmly rooting small-scale industrialization in the East Punjab. The division of East Punjab in 1966 into three parts, which roughly coincides with the Green Revolution, almost again disrupted the progress of industrialization due to raw material sources going to other two states. However, the Green Revolution generated huge demand for agriculture-related inputs and a rise in incomes led to a higher demand for consumption goods, and again boosted the industrial development in Punjab.

The comparative empirical analysis mentioned in this chapter clarifies that Punjab's industrial sector progressed better than the other states in the 1980s but performed poorly in the 1990s and lagged much behind the neighbouring states of Himachal Pradesh and Haryana. During the first decade of the twenty-first century, there was some revival of industrial growth, but the dominant role of the unorganized industrial segment in Punjab's manufacturing growth highlights the weak industrial base and vulnerabilities of this segment in the current competitive environment. Such an industrial base is unable to provide dynamic and sustainable growth momentum. For rejuvenation of the industrial sector of Punjab, Jain has suggested a strategy to provide a supportive policy framework, one which will enable the industrial sector not only to overcome structural weaknesses but also to graduate from small and inefficient to large, efficient and competitive in the increasingly globalized world economy.

In Chap. 13, Inderjeet Singh presents a systematic account of the structural transformation of Punjab economy from the onset of the Green Revolution to the present. An important feature of this chapter is that the author divides the whole period of analysis into four meaningful sub-periods, that is, the rise of the primary sector during the early Green Revolution phase, the period of social turmoil, the post-social turmoil period and the recovery period.

From the analysis of the growth of the primary, secondary and tertiary sectors and the shifting of sectoral shares, the author draws the conclusion that, in terms of contribution to the gross state domestic product, the primary sector is losing importance and both the secondary and tertiary sectors are gaining ground. The tertiary sector has become a dominant sector, but in comparison to the all-India average as well with respect to other states, Punjab is way behind in this shift.

Factors that contributed to the slow growth of the service sector in Punjab, as pointed out by the author, are the social turmoil in the state during the 1980s and the early 1990s which helped put the economy into a crisis. Investors and entrepreneurs in trade, hotels, restaurants, real estate, ownership of dwelling and business services lost interest in the state and capital flight took place in the 1980s and early 1990s. Activities complementary to these services, professional services and supporting services also followed the same path. The social turmoil period witnessed a sharp rise in the share of 'public administration' due to heavy public expenditure on police and paramilitary forces. Another important finding of this chapter is that Punjab experienced a greater shift in workforce to the non-agricultural sectors as compared to the country as a whole.

The sub-period wise disaggregated analysis of the service sectors reveals that developed regions, with better economic and social infrastructure, have a higher share of tertiary sector in domestic product and vice versa. Much of the tertiary sector development as well as overall development has taken place in the already developed regions of Punjab, while the relatively backward Malwa region continues to be dominated by the agricultural sector and remained low on the ladder of the service sector.

An important conclusion that emerges from the inter-sectoral linkage analysis is that the service sector has very weak linkages with the primary sector, whereas it has relatively strong linkages with the secondary sector and with itself. Therefore, it is suggested by the author that to draw full benefit from the service sector for economic growth and transformation of the Punjab economy, the efficiency of the workforce needs substantial improvement. Investment in human capital and infrastructure is required to exploit the potentialities of service sector growth. Since the investment–SDP ratio is very low in Punjab, the author argues that the Union government should shoulder some responsibility in helping the state government to overcome investment deficiencies in the state.

1.4 Human Development in Punjab's Economic Transformation

Education and health are the two pillars of human development. It is now a widely accepted argument in economic thinking that there is a positive relationship between human development and the level of economic growth. However, this relationship is not unidirectional. The level of human development is relatively low in the developing countries but is improving. These improvements in human development are not the automatic consequence of economic growth, but rather, reflect the conscious decisions of the state and households to invest. Due to significant positive externalities in the case of basic health and education, households in developing countries arguably may under-invest in human development, creating a role for the state in developing human resources. When the state falters in investing in basic human development, there can be distortions in the economic transformation process and lower economic growth. Arguably, Punjab has been facing this issue of state failure in providing adequate support for basic education and health. Two chapters included in this section provide comprehensive analyses on the state of human development in Punjab and its interrelations with economic growth and transformation of the Punjab economy.

Jaswinder Singh Brar, in Chap. 14, has examined intensively the trends of education in the state over the last two decades. He has identified the dichotomy between the high-income and low educational achievements of Punjab state. To capture the political economy of this dichotomy, the author has analysed in a comparative framework the literacy achievements, educational level of workforce, exclusion of have-nots and quality of education. Punjab, compared with major states of India in terms of literacy indicators, has been moving towards the bottom in terms of rates of improvement. It has been lagging behind in terms of female literacy and literacy of the scheduled caste population. The gap between low literacy districts and high literacy districts has also widened in Punjab. This gives a sufficient idea of the underperformance of a relatively high-income state with low levels of human capital.

Brar has also provided evidence regarding the level of the skill base (measured by specific reading and arithmetic skill levels) in the relevant age group of the workforce, since the skill base ultimately allows the workforce to participate in economic activities. He had also made comparisons with high skill base states such as Kerala and Himachal Pradesh and shown that the position of Punjab is relatively low in terms of its skill base. The disaggregate analysis across farm size categories brings out the fact that small and marginal farmers are less skilled compared with the large size categories of farmers. The landless workforce also has a low skill base, reinforcing the impression that human capital planning has not been adequate. The chapter highlights that the quality of education in terms of abilities to reading, writing and solving arithmetic problems was slightly better than the national average, but much lower than the better performing states of India. There are also wide gaps between sexes and between the rich and the poor.

The dismal picture of Punjab's education sector, as pointed out by the author, certainly owes something to deficiencies in public investment in education. The state government's policy has included keeping teaching and administrative positions vacant in schools, neglecting infrastructural requirements in public schools and transferring efficient teaching staff from well-functioning public schools—allegedly in some cases due to pressure from private school operators. These policies, according to the author, have increased the burden of bearing the cost of education on households forced to rely on private schools of unreliable quality. The author has suggested a major reversal of policy towards public education in order to build Punjab's human capital more effectively.

In Chap. 15, Sukhwinder Singh has scrutinized the relationship between economic development and the health status of the Punjabi population. On the basis of empirical evidence, the author argues that the adoption of the new economic policy in 1991 reduced public investment support to the health sector and increased the involvement of international agencies such as the World Bank. These agencies provided investment with a condition of allowing greater participation of the private sector in health and medical services. Consequently, the rise of private health and medical services has increased out-of-pocket health expenditure of households, which has made it difficult for the poor to access health and medical services.

Furthermore, the author has provided new evidence regarding the changing patterns of diseases in Punjab. The rate of growth of the population with documented ailments has increased in the post-reform period compared with the pre-reform period. A rise in the aged population, and modern lifestyle diseases reflect aspects of Punjab's health situation that are similar to a developed society. The development pattern of Punjab has also been reflected in the emergence of deadly diseases like cancer and HIV AIDS. It is emphasized by the author that the public health infrastructure has fallen behind due to deficiencies of public investment, non-appointment of doctors, and withdrawal of free medicines and other supporting services in public hospitals. The decline in rural hospitals and deterioration of public health facilities have greatly affected the rural population in general and the rural poor in particular. An important finding that is reported by the author is that a lack of accountability of public health service providers has also contributed to these problems.

To make Punjab's health sector more effective and equitable, the author has suggested an alternative approach to public policy based on three pillars, that is, raising the demand for 'improved health', improving the quality of public health services and making the health system more accountable to its users.

1.5 External Factors in Punjab's Economic Development

Theories of long-run economic growth and transformation have considered a range of exogenous and endogenous factors that determine the nature and rate of development. In the case of Punjab, two mostly external factors, namely, the position of Punjab as a state in the Union of India, and substantial migration resulting in a significant diaspora population, have both been important. Papers assessing the impact of each of these factors on the long-run growth and transformation of the Punjab economy are included in this section.

Shinder S. Thandi, in Chap. 16, has examined the diaspora–development nexus with a view to seeking answer to the question of whether Punjabi diaspora has the capacity and potentialities to arrest the downturn of Punjab economy. An important contribution of this study is in terms of identifying the factors that have contributed to the relative regression of Punjab economy vis-à-vis other dynamic states of India. The author has explained the falling contribution of agriculture in the income and employment of the economy of Punjab. The crisis of agriculture is shown to have been reflected in the extreme form of suicides committed by the farmers in Punjab. Agricultural growth remained heavily dependent on natural resources that have been over-exploited, resulting in an ecological crisis. The paucity of investment for a desirable path of economic transformation was attributable to international border issues and the militancy movement of the 1980s. The nature of the Indian federation and resultant tenor of Centre–State relations have also impinged on the economic transformation of Punjab. Furthermore, Thandi has underlined the importance of factors such as the nature of economic and political governance that have led to the emergence of high state government indebtedness.

Drawing on various academic and policy debates, Thandi has outlined the potential contribution of diasporas to economic transformation. He has argued that diasporas can provide four kinds of capital—intellectual, socio/cultural, financial and political—to a nation state, which can be used for supplementing developmental activities. Furthermore, he has emphasized that the benefit of diaspora can be reaped in terms of raising productive capacity in terms of harnessing resources (FDI) and entrepreneurial capabilities.

The author has traced the progress and spread of the Punjabi diaspora both in developed countries and newly rich Gulf nations. According to him the estimated number of the Punjabi diaspora is around two million and out of that number, 75 % live in three highly developed countries, that is, Canada, USA and UK. The Punjabi diaspora in these countries has thrived in professional, business and entrepreneurial activities and has achieved considerable influence in economic and political spheres. Therefore, the Punjabi community has a substantive scope for contributing to the process of economic transformation of the Punjab economy if engaged through innovative policy initiatives. Thandi, while characterizing the past limitations of the Punjabi diaspora in its contribution to rejuvenation of the Punjab economy, has emphasized two significant channels—remittances and philanthropic—that each has enormous potential to contribute to successful transformation of the Punjab economy. He provides a road map for positive engagement of the diaspora and suggests a suitable policy framework for the government of Punjab to consider.

In Chap. 17, Pritam Singh has analysed the relationship between the role of central government and economic development of a sub-national/state economy. Firstly, the author has attempted to identify the external factors that shape the long-run pattern of economic development. Centre–State relations that shape the channel of engagement of the central government with the state government are considered by the author as a prime external factor in determining the evolution of Punjab's economy.

The agricultural orientation of Punjab's economy goes back to the colonial period. During the period of British colonial rule in Punjab, the needs of the British government determined the rate and direction of economic development of Punjab. The post-colonial economic development of Punjab has similarities with the British colonial period, mainly because of national food requirements. The emphasis on agriculture, while directing government investment and enacting suitable institutional arrangements, was meant to fulfil the nation's need for attainment of self-sufficiency in food grain production.

The author has argued that if Punjab's economy is to improve the rate of economic progress and change the structure of its economy, it has to dramatically shift its strategy and policy for a non-agrarian economic transition. To achieve this non-agrarian transformation of the Punjab economy, a reshaping of Centre–State relations is urgently required. Singh has suggested that Punjab would benefit from a more decentralized federal structure, allowing more flexibility in its path of economic development. While citing various international experiences of defying the force of global capitalism that promotes more dependent paths of economic development, the author suggests that decentralization within India will better support a path of development that is better suited to the internal needs of the Punjab, including the urgent concern of environmental sustainability.

1.6 Fiscal Policy of Punjab in Comparative Perspective

Fiscal policy is one of the most important dynamic policy instruments for developing countries, affecting public investment for economic growth and influencing the rate and direction of economic activities. It is a major policy for sub-national economies as well. The fiscal policy of Punjab played an important role in the development of the state's economy during the early stage of Green Revolution but was disrupted during the period of political turmoil in the 1980s and early 1990s. Once fiscal policy became dysfunctional it remained so, despite the restoration of democratically elected governments. Two contributions included in this section discuss the state of Punjab's fiscal policy, compare it with other states of India and draw lessons for revival of fiscal policy.

Tapas Sen, in Chap. 18, outlines the relationship between fiscal policy and economic development and notes that good fiscal policy can support growth. He empirically examines Punjab state's fiscal position and compares it with other Indian states. While taking various indicators of fiscal health of the state's economy and comparing it with other states, he finds that in general Punjab's performance is poor given its higher level of per capita income and low level of poverty. The author argues that Punjab presents an odd combination of a relatively high-income state with public finances that have been under stress for a long time. This chapter looks at the trends in broad fiscal aggregates and a limited amount of disaggregated information to establish the pattern and locate the causes of the persistent stress. It examines fiscal balances, including receipts and expenditures, the link between fiscal balances and indebtedness, and the link between the stock of debt and revenue expenditures through interest liabilities. To establish a context, it also assesses the fiscal performance of Punjab in relation to other major states of India. It concludes with policy imperatives that have implications not only for the fiscal balances of the state, but also for the development of the real economy of Punjab.

In Chap. 19, Upinder Sawhney analyses the fiscal deterioration in Punjab since the early 1980s and the factors responsible for it. According to her, the fiscal crisis of Punjab state was caused by political, economic and administrative failure during the period of political turmoil in Punjab. The administration became non-functional, non-transparent and non-accountable, resulting in deterioration of tax collection and distorted expenditure patterns. She presents empirical evidence that Punjab state continues to falter on fiscal indicators and to borrow heavily to finance its liabilities. The rising debt burden and falling capital expenditure have reduced the capacity of the state government to direct economic activities and to provide basic social overhead capital, resulting in decline in the economic growth of Punjab's economy.

The analysis of fiscal imbalances of Punjab shows how the fiscal performance of the state is lacking: except for fiscal deficit targets, the state has failed to achieve the targets recommended in its own fiscal responsibility legislation. Punjab achieved the debt targets in the last 2 years of the study period but only by excluding the share of contingent liabilities from the total debt. If contingent liabilities are included in the total outstanding debt the picture changes completely and debt including contingent liabilities was 50.74 and 49.75 % of GSDP for the years 2010–11 and 2011–12, respectively.

The continued deterioration in the finances of Punjab's government is a worrisome feature and the author identifies the root cause in populist measures of successive governments such as irrational subsidies and discretionary distribution of grants. The author has suggested policy measures to fix the fiscal crisis of the Punjab government such as revenue augmentation, expenditure rationalization and inclusion of the revenue generated by the government from various fees and taxes in the consolidated fund. The suggestions made in the study are significant and show possibility for improvements in the state's fiscal policy.

1.7 Perspectives on Rejuvenation of Punjab Economy

For quite a long period of time, Punjab's economy has displayed a range of problems, including slowing growth, greater inequality and environmental degradation. Policy makers suggested dramatic changes in public policy to arrest the downturn of Punjab's economy, especially after the mid-1980s. A major component of the suggested strategy was diversification of agriculture, but there have been other aspects of change that have been considered. The debate has involved economists across the spectrum and the government of Punjab has also sought the advice of experts from think-tanks and research institutes for economic policy innovation. However, these reports and individual suggestions have tended to gather dust in the corridors of power in the state. Twenty-two independent economists, who had been intensively involved in the economic analysis of problems of Punjab's development experience, gathered at Punjabi university several years ago, arrived at a minimum consensus and suggested public policy measures for the rejuvenation of the Punjab economy (CDEIS 2012). But Punjab is a typical case of public policy paralysis. It is trapped in a vicious cycle. It seems that more forceful attempts are required to break this vicious cycle. In this vein, two contributions are included in this section, both of which seek to provide some strategic vision for reshaping policy and overcoming public policy paralysis.

Sucha Singh Gill, in Chap. 20, has examined the ineffectiveness of economic policy, identified obstacles and provided a strategy and vision for successful transformation of the Punjab's economy. Firstly, the contribution of this chapter is that it brings out the factors responsible for agrarian distress. Both internal and external factors have been identified that have made the agriculture sector distress-prone. It is argued that frequent natural calamities, breakdowns of market clearing mechanisms, price volatility and absence of distress redressal mechanisms for the population engaged in agriculture have been the root causes of persistent agrarian crises. The existing system of compensation in terms of subsidies does not reach the distressed small and marginal farmers, but rather it is being captured either by well-to-do sections of rural society or by intermediaries.

Secondly, the author gives an account of the policy for diversification of agriculture recommended by three committees (Johl 1986, 2002; Kelkat 2013), shows how this policy was flawed and provides some reasons why it has not succeeded. The long-term involvement of the government and experts to fine-tune the public policy of diversification of agriculture of Punjab, combined with its ineffectiveness in delivering any tangible results, has been perceived by societal stakeholders as rhetoric. This resulted in credibility loss of both the experts who recommended the policy, as well as the government.

Thirdly, the chapter traces the history of the farmers' movement for social mobilization to confront the problems faced by agricultural development and the articulation of the movement's leadership to provide a vision for future of agriculture. An important finding that emerges from this discussion is that there has been a high-level consciousness of the farmers' movement in innovating an agenda for farmers to involve themselves in production, processing and marketing of agricultural produce, and in linking agriculture with industrialization of the Punjab economy. The farmers' organization (Bhartiya Kisan Union) has also been aware of the fact that it has to involve private sector firms and multinational corporations in the process of linking industry with agriculture. It has proposed that these agribusiness firms should be located in rural areas and provide employment to the local rural workforce. However, although this proposal was in consonance with national policy, local interests both in government and the bureaucracy did not create a supportive institutional framework and the proposed vision of the farmers' organization could not be tried out.

Finally, the contribution of this chapter is in providing a strategic vision for future agriculture development policy. The author has argued that while formulating a future agriculture diversification strategy, farmers' organizations should be treated as partners in formulation and implementation of policy and in designing supportive institutional mechanisms. It is, thus, suggested that the state's political parties should awaken to the agrarian agenda, while farmers' organizations must engage themselves in a strategy of struggle and reconstruction. To realize the goal of transformation of Punjab economy, it is imperative to build linkages between agriculture and industry while involving all the stakeholders in the state economy.

Nirvikar Singh, in Chap. 21, has provided a framework for envisioning Punjab in the twenty-first century. In his chapter, Nirvikar Singh suggests that Punjab is trapped in a political and economic equilibrium that, if not broken, will lead to environmental disaster and economic stagnation or worse. He discusses possibilities for creation of new industries and services in Punjab, and the role of some form of industrial policy. Any such path will require heavy investments in education. The discussion includes a consideration of the state's political economy, including societal and cultural fault lines, which increases the practical challenges of formulating and implementing economic policies that may lead to positive changes.

In considering the possible future of Punjab's economy, however, it is also important to consider the changing national context. For example, the national focus on "Make in India" and avowed goals of improving the environment for doing business might give Punjab's state government some opening for changing how it addresses the problems that businesses in Punjab, whether manufacturing or services, have in getting started, growing, and reaching national and international markets. The new NITI Aayog, which has replaced the Planning Commission, might be able to provide additional expertise for infrastructure project planning. The explicit commitment in the last budget to creating a national agricultural common market may signal a willingness to change the system which supports, but also limits Punjab's agrarian economy.

Nirvikar Singh's chapter emphasizes the negative effects of recent (as opposed to Green Revolution-era) interactions between the Center and the Punjab government, but the new regime may provide political space for a less adversarial future. For example, the current Chief Minister of Punjab is heading a NITI Aayog committee to look at the question of making skill acquisition a fundamental right for everyone. There are obvious problems with this goal, but the participation of the Punjab CM in the national push for skill development is a potential positive signal. Similarly, the CM's daughter-in-law, who is Minister for Food Processing Industries at the Center, is trying to spur a previously stalled effort to create large-scale food processing parks nationwide, including in Punjab. It is possible that these kinds of efforts will also just degenerate into the kind of rent-seeking that has plagued the Punjab economy over the past two decades, but there is also a possibility that national resources and expertise can be used more to aid in Punjab's needed economic transformation.

Nirvikar Singh's chapter suggests that radical and urgent policy actions are needed, and the two examples of Punjab politicians acting on the national stage may not be enough to represent the kind of significant change that is needed, of course. The apparent prevalence of drugs and alcohol in the state, and the cushion of remittances from non-resident Punjabis may also work against positive change. If the experience of other Indian states is a guide, however, more effective political competition at the state level, and a better articulated demand for economic progress from the state's population may be the necessary condition for radical change in governance and in economic performance.

1.8 Conclusion

Punjab's economy, for a significant period of time, has been trapped in relative economic stagnation, political apathy and public policy paralysis. The 20 following chapters in this volume present an authoritative assessment of the complex and multidimensional challenges of the Punjab economy. Each contribution provides scholarly analysis and offers policy solutions relevant to the ground realities. Overall, this volume articulates a consensus on the need for affirmative policy actions for an economic revival of Punjab, with ecological sustainability and political stability. This consensus envisions a Punjab for the twenty-first century and suggests the nature of the needed transformation of its economy and polity. However, the magnitude of the necessary changes is such that the state government alone is unlikely to have the requisite capacity. Therefore, the involvement of the Union government, private sector, civil society and even the diaspora is likely to be required. On its own, however, the state government can improve economic governance by removing destructive subsidies and rationalizing fiscal policy. It is also to be hoped that this book provides some more general perspectives on the challenges of overcoming roadblocks to economic transformation of a developing economy and that it will generate wider debate in some areas of development economics.

References

Acemoglu D, Simon J, Robinson JA (2005) Institutions as a fundamental cause of long-run growth. In: Philippe A, Durlauf SN (eds) Handbook of economic growth, vol 1A. Elsevier BV, Amsterdam

Ahluwalia MS (1978) Rural poverty and agricultural performance in India. J Develop Stud 14(2):298–323

Ahluwalia MS (2002) State level performance under economic reforms in India. In: Krueger A (ed) Economic policy reform and Indian economy. University of Chicago Press, Chicago, pp 91–128

Bhalla GS (1995) Agriculture growth and industrial development in Punjab. In: Mellor JW (ed) Agriculture on the road to industrialization, Chapter 3, pp 67–112. International Food Policy Research Institute (IFPRI), Johns Hopkins University Press, Baltimore

CDEIS (2012) Rejuvenation of Punjab economy: a policy document, policy paper no. 1. Centre for Development Economics and Innovation Studies, Punjabi University, Patiala

Chenery HB (1960) Patterns of industrial growth. Am Econ Rev 50(4):624–654

Cortuk O, Singh N (2011) Structural change and growth in India. Econ Lett 110:178–181

Cortuk O, Singh N (2015) Analysing the structural change and growth relationship in India: state-level evidence. Econ Polit Wkly 50(24):91–98

Dhesi AS, Singh G (eds) (2008) Introduction. In: rural development in Punjab: A success story going astray. Rutledge, New Delhi

GOI (2011) Population census 2011. Ministry of Home Affairs, Government of India, New Delhi

GOP (2013) Statistical abstract. Economic and Statistical Organization, Government of Punjab, Punjab, Chandigarh

Johl Committee I (1986) Report of expert committee on diversification of agriculture in Punjab. Government of Punjab, Chandigarh

Johl Committee II (2002) Agricultural production pattern adjustment programme in Punjab for productivity growth: a report. Government of Punjab, Chandigarh

Kalkat Committee (2013) Agriculture policy for Punjab. Government of Punjab, Chandigarh

Kuznets S (1966) Modern economic growth: rate, structure and spread. Yale University Press, New Haven. New Haven and reprinted by Oxford and IBH Public Co, New Delhi

Lee K (2013) Schumpeterian analysis of economic catch-up: knowledge, path-creation, and the middle-income trap. Cambridge University Press, Cambridge

Nayyar D (2013) Catch up: developing countries in the world economy. Oxford University Press, New Delhi

North D, Wallis JJ, Weingast B (2009) Violence and social orders. Cambridge University Press, Cambridge

Singh L (2014) Economic governance and Punjab's economic growth. In: Singh I, Singh S, Singh L (eds) Punjab's economic development in the era of globalisation. LG Publishers Distributors, Delhi

Singh L, Bhangoo KS, Sharma R (2016) Agrarian distress and farmer suicides in north India. Routledge, New Delhi

Singh L, Singh S (2002) Deceleration of economic growth in Punjab: evidence, explanation and a way-out. Econ Polit Wkly 37(6):579–586

Singh N (2006) Services-led industrialization in India: assessment and lessons. In: O'Connor D (ed) Industrial development for the 21st century: sustainable development perspectives. UN-DESA, New York, pp 235–291

Syrquin M (1988) Patterns of structural change. In: Chenery HB, Srinivasan TN (eds) Handbook of development economics, vol 1. North Holland, Amsterdam, pp 203–214

Part I
Understanding the Crisis of Agrarian Transition

Chapter 2
The Role of Technological and Institutional Changes in the Growth and Transformation of Agriculture in Punjab

K.N. Nair and Gurpreet Singh

2.1 Introduction

Uneven performance of agriculture across regions in India and the factors shaping it has been a subject of interesting debate among academic researchers and policy makers in recent decades. Differences in the pace and patterns of technological change, institutional setting and environmental conditions have been identified as the crucial factors causing uneven patterns of agricultural growth.[1] Those who base their arguments on the crucial role of institutions state that it was the property right regimes created during the colonial period that contributed to the differences in the pace and pattern of agricultural growth across regions in the post-independence period. It is argued that in the regions where land rights were created and taxes were collected directly from the peasants by the colonial administration showed greater

[1]There exist a large number of studies on regional dimensions on agricultural growth in India. A few of the important contributions are as follows: Vaidynathan (2010), Bhalla and Singh (2010) and Birthal et al. (2014).

G. Singh (✉)
Centre for Economic Studies and Planning, SSS, Jawaharlal Nehru University, New Delhi 110067, India
e-mail: preet.cds@gmail.com

K.N. Nair
Centre for Development Studies, Trivandrum, Kerala, India

L. Singh and N. Singh (eds.), *Economic Transformation of a Developing Economy*, India Studies in Business and Economics,
DOI 10.1007/978-981-10-0197-0_2

dynamism in agricultural growth compared with other regions.[2] Those who critique this argument substantiate their position by focusing on the fact that even before the British rule, considerable differences existed in the pattern of agricultural development within the Indian subcontinent.[3] Those who consider technological change as the main driving force behind agricultural growth base their argument on the fact that irrespective of the differences in the institutional settings, agricultural technology has spread, during the green and post-green revolution periods making the growth process spatially broad based and dynamic and hold the view that technological progress is more important than institutional reforms in accelerating the pace of agricultural growth.[4] While recognizing the importance of technology and institutions in shaping agricultural growth, another view is that the sources of disparity is also rooted in the variations in the environmental conditions. Some region could succeed in spreading the green revolution due to the policies and programmes for removing the environmental constraints (Roy 2007).

It appears from the various empirical and analytical studies that for a coherent explanation of the differential process of growth across regions, institutions, technology and environment need to be treated as part of the factors that shapes agricultural growth. However, unravelling the relative role of these factors is a challenging task due to the continuous interaction between technology and institutions in a given environment affecting the path ways of development.[5] There are other exogenous and endogenous factors that have to be taken into consideration in providing explanations for the nature of interaction between technology and institutions. One of the significant factors to be taken into account is the linkage between population growth and technological change. In traditional agriculture with primitive or low level of technical change like shift in cultivation from short fallow to long fallow and to more intensive forms of cultivation for sustaining productivity and per capita output required labour-intensive investment in the creation of irrigation facilities, land development, soil conservation, etc. In societies characterized

---

[2]An important contribution in this respect is by Banerjee and Iyer (2005). There are also other interesting papers on the effect of colonial legal systems in shaping the present-day institutions such as Acemoglu et al. (2001, 2002), Engerman and Sokooff (1997, 2002) and Sokooff and Engerman (2000). In this paper, we follow North and Thomas (1973) in conceptualizing institutions in terms of rules, norms and values that include both formal and informal institutions, and organizations as institutions.

[3]See for details Weintraub (2005).

[4]The writings of Shultz (1964) have dominant influence in this line of thinking: his point was that it is the missing knowledge base that contributed stagnation in agriculture and what the state should do is to invest in agricultural research and technology generation and facilitate its rapid diffusion.

[5]Historical experiences of various countries show that (i) institutional arrangements hamper or discourage development or dissemination of new technology, (ii) institutional arrangements encourage or assist the developments and dissemination of new technology, (iii) the type of technology and its pattern of dissemination either hamper or discourage institutional changes and (iv) the type of technology and its pattern of dissemination either encourage or assist institutional changes.

by higher levels of population densities, the choice would be towards more labour-intensive and yield increasing technology.[6] In the evolution of technology, it is also argued that technological innovation would be determined by the changes in relative factor prices intended to overcome resource constraints by generating a sequence of innovations leading to the substitution of technical inputs for the limiting factors.[7] Historical experience of USA, Japan and Western Europe provide evidence to support the induced innovation hypothesis. While in Japan, both land-saving and labour-saving technological change had taken place, in the USA and Western Europe, it was largely labour-saving technologies. It was also seen that in societies where capacities for endogenous technical changes do not exist, it could take place through diffusion and adaption of technologies imported from other countries.

An important insight we could derive from the various analytical and empirical studies is that for understanding the role of technology and institutions in shaping agricultural growth it would be useful to adopt a historical approach by bringing in exogenous factors like population growth and endogenous factors like the capacity to innovate. Though there had been a number of studies that attempted to examine the contemporary developments in various facets of the agrarian economy with its historical roots, studies that explicitly treat the role of technology and institutions in shaping agricultural growth are very few.[8] The present paper is an attempt to contribute to this literature. It is done in the context of the state of Punjab.

The case of Punjab will be insightful from a number of perspectives: Punjab has been the forerunner in the agriculture-induced economic growth in the country. The driving force behind the growth of agriculture in the state has been the modern biophysical technology that led to rapid increase in productivity of crops, faster income growth, decline in poverty, and structural changes in the economy. The technological changes also have brought in institutional changes not only in relation to the agricultural sector, but also for the entire state and society. However, the agricultural sector in the state is confronted with deceleration in productivity and output growth; the growth in agriculture in the past has witnessed a negative impact on the environment and ecology. Since, the state is the main producer of food grains for the country, the deceleration of agricultural growth is of major concern for the entire country. Given this background, it may be of interest to examine the interaction between technology and institutions in Punjab agriculture and its implications for sustaining the growth process.

The rest of this chapter is organized as follows. Section 2.2 will review some of the salient aspects of agriculture in Punjab during the colonial period. This is followed by a review of the growth process in agriculture, especially from the

[6]The main contributor to this argument is Boserup (1965). See her pioneering notes on conditions of agricultural growth.

[7]See Hayami and Ruttan (1971).

[8]A number of papers put together in this perspective are available in Narayana and Mahadevan (2011). An important contribution in this context is also by Boyce (1987).

perspective of technological change in Sect. 2.3. Section 2.4 will examine the changes in the institutional structure of agriculture. Section 2.5 will highlight the implications of technological and institutional changes on the wider development of the state.

2.2 Agriculture in Punjab: Some Historical Insights

The present state of Punjab was part of the erstwhile Punjab province of British India. Most of the studies done by economic historians for the colonial period related to Punjab Province. In this section, we plan to draw from the works of few scholars who did pioneering research on this region.[9]

The British annexed Punjab in the year 1849. They found the region with vast potential for development, contribution to the revenue base and consolidation of the political power of the British Empire. There existed already a prosperous irrigated agriculture in the northern parts of the province. The canals existed were the inundation canals along the Jamuna River and the Hosely canal constructed to provide perennial waters from the river Ravi to the city of Lahore and Amritsar. The hard working peasants of Punjab were exporting agricultural products such as sugar and indigo to Sind and Kabul. The main reasons cited for the colonial investment in canal irrigation were (1) to mobilize revenue by promoting irrigated agriculture and (2) many regions were affected by a series of famines during the first half of the nineteenth century. Where ever agriculture development based on canal irrigation the famines did not occur or its incidence was lighter. By investing in irrigated agriculture, the expectation was to save expenditure on the famine relief.[10] (3) With the expansion of agriculture, it would be possible to export wheat, cotton, indigo and other agricultural commodities, and horses and mules to the British Empire. (4) By developing agriculture and bringing in economic prosperity, the Empire expected to gather support of the people to sustain the colonial regime. The scope for expansion in irrigated agriculture was enormous due to low cost in the development of canal irrigation due to the topography of the region and the perennial supply of water from the Himalayan Mountains. Population density was very low and plenty of unoccupied crown land was available. It was possible to move people from other regions to settle down there without disturbing traditional property rights. The sale of the crown land also offered the scope for mobilizing additional revenue to the state. The development of agriculture in the region would lead to the growth of cities and towns and could broaden the base of taxation of the State. The

---

[9]This section has been drawn largely from the works of Paustan (1930) and Hirashima (1978).

[10]The region was visited by famines in 1802, 1812, 1817, 1824, 1833 and 1837. Rainfall was low and unpredictable. The causes of famine were (i) lack of rainfall which precluded the possibility of producing food for subsistence during periods of drought and (ii) lack of transportation facilities and means of communication. Famines created a balance between population and food supply; see Paustan (1930) for details.

mutiny of 1857–58 prompted the British to expand the construction of Railways to the region for the faster movement of troops; but it also helped the transport of agricultural commodities to the market towns and export destinations and paved the way for the rapid commercialization of agriculture. The Bari Doab canal that was already yielding some revenue at the time of annexation was modified during the first year of the British rule. Sikh soldiers who were retrenched after the mutiny were used in the construction of canals of Bari Doab between river Ravi and river Bias. Colonization started first in the Sind canal system where considerable extent of waste lands (more than 2.3 lakh acres) was available. Population from the adjacent districts were moved to Sind. Government constructed main canals, and the own farm development was left to the settlers. Colonization in the lower Chenab canal started in 1892, where people from the densely populated districts and the nomadic tribes were encouraged to come and settle.

The impact of the colonial policy of encouraging agricultural development was evident from a number of indicators. Area under cultivation had increased at a faster rate along with the increase in the percentage of canal-irrigated area to total cultivated area during the period 1861–1921. Cultivated area increased from 20 million acres in 1861–29 million acres by 1921. The percentage of canal-irrigated area increased from 6.3 % in 1861 to 36 % in 1921. The pace of irrigation expansion took place at a faster rate during the first two decades of the twentieth century. Compared to the area expansion, the growth of population was at a much slower rate: the size of the population was about 16 million in 1861 and it increased to 21 million by 1921. In other words, the per capita land available for cultivation had increased along with improvements in its quality due to the rapid expansion of irrigation. The expansion of irrigation was accompanied by attempts to improve the yields of crops by developing improved seed varieties in the Lyallpur Research Station by the Imperial Council of Agricultural Research. The expansion of irrigated agriculture resulted in significant increase in productivity of crops, especially that of wheat. The yield of irrigated wheat was considerably higher than unirrigated wheat as evident from the yield data compiled for the early parts of the last century by Paustan (1930) (see Table 2.1). There were no evidences that showed significant impact of agricultural research on crop yields. The link between the research centre

Table 2.1 Average yield of wheat in irrigated and unirrigated crops in Punjab province in British India (pounds/acre)

District		1901	1912	1923
Lahore	Irrigated	752	660	1000
	Unirrigated	382	520	520
Lyallpur	Irrigated	–	1000	1200
	Unirrigated	–	480	500
Multan	Irrigated	960	960	960
	Unirrigated	720	750	600

Source Paustan (1930)

and the peasants were mainly through the large farmers.[11] As revealed by Paustan's estimate, the value of output per acre of irrigated land and per capita agricultural output showed substantial improvement. His estimates showed that the value of production per acre of irrigated land in 1926–27 as Rs. 45 and the estimated per capita production as Rs. 20.

Until the annexation of Punjab by the British, land rights were exercised on the basis of leases by the rulers. During the period of Mughal rule in the sixteenth and seventeenth centuries, land revenue was collected by non-hereditary, transferable state officials (the Mansabdari system introduced by Emperor Akbar). After the collapse of Mughal rule in the early eighteenth century, these local officials gained power in several areas and often became de facto hereditary landlords and petty chiefs in their local areas. Later, the British had succeeded in replacing the customary system of land tenure by a more legally based one, in which land rights were defined and recorded through courts. These resulted into creation of private saleable property rights. With recording of titles, land began to achieve a trading value and frequent changes in land ownership took place. According to Paustan's estimate, the value of land per acre in 1869–70 was Rs. 10 and by the year 1919–20 it increased to Rs. 275. He attributed the acquisitive ethos of the Punjab peasant as one of the strongest reason for the increase in land prices. Another study, the structural disparities and irrigation development in Punjab during the British period, by Hirashima (1978) showed that the creation of private property rights on land during the colonial period accompanied by expansion of irrigated agriculture had resulted in the expansion of the land market, with land prices moving at a higher rate than the product prices.

> After the land market was established, land prices started to increase. It was found that deflated price of land or land value in real terms increased at a compound rate of 6.43 per cent per annum during 1862-1900 and 4.86 during 1901 to 1928. It was also found that during the period 1891 to 1942, the annual growth rate of gross agricultural product at current prices was 1.34 per cent and land prices 4.92 per cent (Hirashima 1978).

With the development of the land market, peasants began to use their land as equity capital for raising credit from the informal credit market. The rich land owners also acted as intermediaries to the revenue administration in the collection of land revenue from the peasantry. They could retain a part of the revenue collected with them in addition to income from cultivation. This constituted their sources of capital to lend money to the peasants by taking land as the mortgage at exorbitant rates of interest. Thus, along with the prosperity created by irrigated agriculture, and the development of the land market, credit markets began to develop, and the uncontrolled activities of the money lenders resulted in large-scale alienation of land. The British passed the Land Alienation Act in the Punjab in 1901 that pushed the money lenders out of the land market. Wealthy farmers with sufficient initial capital began to invest their surplus in the purchase of land and land

[11]For an insightful discussion of the impact of Agricultural Research in British India, see Pray (1984). His data suggest that the impact of research on crop yield was small.

prices continued to increase. The outcome of this process was the widening of structural disparities in agriculture, especially the increasing concentration of land. In sum, development of irrigation as a leading input in agriculture had resulted in economic prosperity: but it also contributed to the development of the land and credit markets and widening of the socio-economic disparities.

2.3 Technological Change and Agricultural Growth Since Independence

Partitioning of British India into two independent nations, namely India and Pakistan, resulted in the division of Punjab province. Major part of the canal-irrigated area formed parts of the Pakistan Punjab. Given the immense potential of agricultural development in the Indian Punjab, Government of India, in the first Five Year Plan, gave considerable importance to the development of canal irrigation in the state by investing in the Bhakra Nangal Project with multiple goals of expansion of irrigated area and generation of electricity. The use of other technologies to improve yield levels was largely based on the traditional technology. In the 1950s, the districts of Punjab recorded higher rates of agricultural output growth (Minhas and Vaidyanathan 1965) compared to most other regions in the country. As it is well known that the food crises in the early 1960s forced the policy makers in the country to initiate the new strategy for agricultural development. This strategy was based on the use of high yielding variety of seeds and fertilizers in the districts well-endowed with irrigation facilities. The strategy also contained the provision of cheap credit and assured procurement of output by the state. The state of Punjab immensely benefited from this strategy. There exist a large number of studies that had examined the various dimensions of the green revolution. For the purpose of developing our argument in this paper, we shall draw our insights from this literature.

One of the most significant technological changes in Punjab agriculture since the early spread of green revolution had been in the quality irrigation. The percentage of area under irrigation to the net sown area was about 40 % in the mid-sixties, with canal irrigation accounting for about 60 % and the rest largely with wells and tube wells. However, over the last five decades, the irrigation coverage increased from about 75 % in the early 1970s to nearly 98 % by 2009–10. During this period, much of the expansion in irrigation took place in the development of wells and tube wells (see Table 2.2). This is evident from the sharp fall in the percentage of area irrigated by the canal system and sharp increase in the percentage of area irrigated by wells and tube wells.

In the mid-1960s, about 85 % of the total land area was already brought under cultivation. The expansion of irrigation has contributed to the rapid increase in cropping intensity from about 126 in the early sixties to 140 by seventies and further to 190 by 2009–10 (see Table 2.3). Along with the expansion of the leading

Table 2.2 Percentage of area under irrigation in Punjab

Year	Area irrigated as percentage of net sown area	Source-wise irrigated (percentage of area)			
		Government canals	Tube wells and wells	Others	Total
1960–61	54.00	58.00	41.00	1.00	100.00
1965–66	59.00	57.00	39.00	4.00	100.00
1970–71	71.10	44.53	55.09	0.38	100.00
1980–81	81.00	42.28	57.33	0.38	100.00
1990–91	93.00	42.97	57.12	0.41	100.00
2000–01	95.00	23.82	76.13	0.05	100.00
2008–09	97.20	27.31	72.59	0.10	100.00

Source Calculated from statistical abstract of Punjab, various issues

Table 2.3 Selected indicators of agricultural development in Punjab

Year	Cropping intensity (%)	Proportion of area under HYV (%)		Consumption of NPK (kg/ha)	No. of tractors per 1000 NSA in hectares
		Rice	Wheat		
1965–66	129	5.41[a]	35.00[a]	–	0.35
1970–71	140	33.33	69.03	37.51	1.33
1980–81	161	92.64	98.04	112.67	28.36
1990–91	178	94.17	99.97	162.62	68.53
2000–01	187	95.98	100	165.34	102.13
2008–09	190	100	100	223.46	118.01

Source Calculated from statistical abstract of Punjab, various issues
[a]Figures for the year 1967–68 are taken from Sidhu (Sidhu and Byerlee 1991)

input, the other components of the technology, namely high yielding varieties, and use of chemical fertilizers also expanded at a rapid rate. The green revolution that took place initially in wheat has been rapidly accompanied by rice in the recent decades. The percentage of area under high yielding varieties of rice and wheat recorded 100 % coverage by 2009–10; the use of chemical fertilizer showed a sixfold increase per acre in the past five decades. The spread of agro-mechanical technology in agriculture began to take place at a rapid rate in the post-green revolution phase. The number of tractors that was roughly about one per 1000 ha of net sown area, in 1970–71, increased to 28 by 1980–81, and further to 68 in 1990–91, and reached a level of more than 100 by 2000–01. Along with tractors, other complimentary equipments, harvesters and thrashers also showed a similar trend. It is to be noted that the technological change in Punjab agriculture followed the classical sequence of irrigation technology followed by biochemical technology and subsequently the agro-mechanical technology.

What has been the impact of technological change on the long-term growth of agriculture in the state? To answer this question, it is useful to highlight briefly its

Table 2.4 Trend growth rate of area, yield and production of major crops in Punjab (%)

Period	Wheat	Rice	Maize	Bajra	Barley	Pulses	Oilseeds
Area							
1970–80	2.31	12.37	−3.54	−9.71	−3.42	−1.23	−5.11
1980–90	1.26	5.39	−5.49	−18.86	−8.09	−7.84	−3.08
1990–2000	0.19	2.42	−1.9	−8.81	−3.55	−5.63	−0.97
2000–09	0.42	0.51	−0.91	−2.01	−6.79	−10.15	−3.92
Yield							
1970–80	2.3	5.5	0.21	−0.68	4.94	−0.46	−0.32
1980–90	3	1.28	−1.26	−3.28	5.45	3.61	2.95
1990–2000	2.06	0.08	2.62	−3	2.34	−1.28	0.06
2000–09	−0.28	1.54	2.22	2.05	0.87	2.13	2.4
Production							
1970–80	4.67	18.55	−3.34	−10.32	1.35	−1.68	−5.41
1980–90	4.3	6.74	−6.68	−21.52	−3.08	−4.51	−0.22
1990–2000	2.26	2.5	0.67	−11.55	−1.29	−6.83	−0.92
2000–09	0.14	2.06	1.29	0	−5.98	−8.23	−1.62

Source Calculated from statistical abstract of Punjab, various issues

impact on the growth of output of crops and the component elements. The production of wheat and rice, the crops that benefited largely from the new technology had shown high rates of growth in the 1970s and 1980s (see Table 2.4). However, the rates of growth began to show deceleration in the 1990s, and in the first decade of the present century. Looking at the contribution of changes in area and yield of these crops, it becomes evident that (i) in the case of wheat, its area contribution was significant in the 1970s (since area increased by about 2.3 % per annum); in the subsequent decades, the contribution of area expansion has become insignificant. (ii) As far as rice is concerned, the expansion of area has been significant in the early decades, but it began to decelerate sharply in the last two decades. Coming to the rates of growth in yield levels, it is seen that (i) the productivity of wheat has increased by about 2–3 % in the decades from 1970 to 2000, and in the subsequent decade, it showed a falling trend. (ii) In the case of rice, productivity growth was very high in the 1970s but in the subsequent decades, it has increased but at a much lower rate. The performance of large number of other crops including coarse grains, pulses and oilseeds has been very dismal. The production of these crops has declined. In all these crops, area under cultivation has shown decline overtime. However, yield growth has shown a revival in the last decade.

A much better picture on the emerging pattern of agriculture in the state becomes evident, if we look at the contribution of various crops to the total share of gross cropped area (GCA) (see Table 2.5). Rice and wheat contributed to roughly half of the GCA in the early 1970s, with wheat accounting for 40 %, rice 11 % to GCA. Overtime, the area under these crops increased; they now account for about 77 % of GCA. The contribution of rice has also increased, but that of wheat remained around 41–44 %. From the changes in the share of various crops in GCA, it is

Table 2.5 Percentage share of various crops in gross cropped area in Punjab (%)

Crop share (in percentage) in gross cropped area (GCA)												
Period	Rice	Wheat	Rice and wheat	Bajra	Maize	Barley	Oilseeds	Pulses	Sugarcane	Cotton	Other	GCA
1970–80	10.88	40.45	51.33	2.19	8.39	1.27	4.85	6.32	1.79	8.89	14.98	100
1980–90	22.27	43.38	65.65	0.52	3.97	0.78	2.74	3.08	1.29	9.03	12.92	100
1990–00	28.99	42.7	71.69	0.11	2.26	0.5	2.36	1.28	1.46	8.42	11.92	100
2000–09	33.09	43.77	76.86	0.08	1.97	0.28	1.02	0.51	1.41	6.74	11.15	100

Source Calculated from statistical abstract of Punjab, various issues

evident that there has been a decline in the diversification of agriculture. The state has been concentrating its resources in the production of rice and wheat as high-valued commercial crops. These trends in the cropping pattern can be linked with the scale of production, input subsidies and the policies of the government. The procurement policies of government have remained limited to rice and wheat which has encouraged the farmers to opt for these specific crops. Moreover, high intensity of agricultural mechanization combined with input subsidies such as electricity, water and fertilizers facilitate farmers to have large-scale farming operations where wheat and rice suit the best under present agro-climatic conditions. However, due course of time, productivity of these crops have reached at a plateau (see Table 2.4) due to reasons related to environment and over-mechanization. The declining productivity of these crops has severely affected the overall growth of agricultural sector of the state.

The overall growth of agriculture in the state was high in the 1970s and 80s with a rate of growth of about 4–5 % per annum (see Table 2.6). However, it has decelerated to around 2.6–2.7 % in the subsequent decades. In comparison, industry output has shown some improvement in the rate of growth in the last two decades; the service sector also showed a marginal increase in the growth. The overall growth in NSDP was about 5.3 % for all the decades except in the 1990s, where it had shown a rate of growth of 4.5 %. In terms of the composition of output, the contribution of agriculture (including the allied sectors) to NSDP was 50 % in the early 1970s (see Table 2.7). Though it has shown a decline in the recent decades, compared to the other states and for the country as a whole, the share is still high: about 35 % in 2009–10. The share of manufacturing sector has increased from 13.8 to 43 %. The shift in the sectoral composition of NSDP has been accompanied by

Table 2.6 Trend growth rate of each sector in Punjab, 1970–71 to 2000–10 (%)

Period	Agriculture	Industry	Services	NSDP
1970–71/1979–80	4	6.7	6.9	5.2
1980–81/1989–90	5.1	6.9	4.5	5.3
1990–91/1999–00	2.7	7.1	5.1	4.5
2000–01/2009–10	2.6	8.4	5.9	5.3

Source Calculated from statistical abstract of Punjab, various issues

Table 2.7 Sectoral share of agriculture in net state domestic product in Punjab 1970–80 to 2000–10 (%)

Period	Agriculture	Industry	Services	All
1970–71 to 1979–80	49.9	13.8	36.3	100.0
1980–81 to 1989–90	45.5	15.3	39.2	100.0
1990–91 to 1999–00	42.5	19.6	37.9	100.0
2000–01 to 2009–10	35.0	22.3	42.7	100.0

Source Calculated from EPW Research Foundation, 2009, and CSO, 2010
Note Series are constant at 1999–00 prices

Table 2.8 Percentage distribution of workers in each type of activity in Punjab during 1961–2001 (%)

Years	Cultivators	Agricultural labourers	Agricultural workers	Workers in household industries	Other workers	Total
I	II	III	IV (II + III)	V	VI	VII
1971	42.6	20.1	62.7	3.2	34.2	100
1981	35.9	22.2	58.1	2.6	39.4	100
1991	31.4	23.8	55.2	1.3	43.4	100
2001	23	16.4	39.4	3.4	57.3	100
2011	22.62	16.32	38.94	3.65	57.39	100

Source Census of India, various years

shifts in the distribution of workers across different sectors (see Table 2.8). The percentage of cultivators declined from 42.6 % in 1971 to 23 % by 2001 and maintained the same level by 2011. The share of workers in the household industry was very negligible in the state, and the share of "other workers" increased from 34 % in 1971 to 57 % by 2011, with the significant increase taking place between 1981 and 2011. Such transfer of population from agriculture to non-agriculture has taken place due to a variety of factors; the most significant among such factors has been the overcapitalization of agriculture that resulted in decline in the viability of small and marginal farms and shift of farmers to the non-farm sectors for their employment and livelihood. The mechanization of agriculture has resulted in decline in labour use per unit of cultivated area and reduction in the employment prospects in agriculture. Consequently, it appears that the younger generation is moving away from agriculture labour to the other sectors. The agricultural induced non-farm sector growth has provided opportunities for labour from the farm sector to gradually shift from agriculture to the non-agricultural sectors. However, the question being debated is whether such shifts have resulted in improvement in their levels of living. As we argue in the next section, this process has implications for institutional transformation in the agricultural sector.

2.4 Institutional Changes and Agricultural Growth

Technological changes in agriculture and its impact on agricultural growth and development has induced a number of changes in the property rights relating to the ownership and access to land and other natural resources in the state. In this context, analysis of the data from various rounds of the National Sample Survey showed the following trends. (i) There has been a gradual increase in the percentage of households owning land in the marginal size class of holding. This has taken place due to the downward mobility of households from the higher size categories. The share of owned land of the small and marginal size groups has shown gradual increase overtime. Obviously, the increase in the share of these categories has been due to the decline in the share of the higher size groups. However, it is not possible to see uniform pattern in the higher size groups. Interestingly, since 1990–91, the semi-medium and medium size class showed a fall in their percentage share, but that of the larger size group showed an increase from 12.2 to 15.3 % (see Table 2.9). (ii) A comparison of the trends and patterns in the distribution of ownership and operational holdings showed the higher size groups, as the gainers from the distributional changes. It occurred largely through the operation of the land lease market (see Tables 2.9 and 2.10). (iii) The fact becomes evident from a look at the percentage of holdings leasing in land by size groups holdings (see Table 2.11 for details).

The fact that the changes taking place in the land market has been favourable to the higher size groups of holdings is also evident from the directional changes in the index of land concentration as well as the percentage share of various household size groups in both owned and operated area. The Gini coefficient of land

Table 2.9 Percentage distribution of households and area owned by size class in Punjab, 1971–72 to 2002–03 (%)

Size class of ownership holding[1]	Percentage of households				Percentage of area owned			
	1971–72	1981–82	1992–93	2002–03	1971–72	1981–82	1991–92	2002–03
Marginal (0.002 to ≤1.000 ha)	67.5	66.8	69.6	76.3	4.4	5.5	7.1	9.1
Small (1.001–2.000 ha)	8.3	10.0	9.9	9.5	8.8	10.7	12.3	15.6
Semi-medium (2.001–4.000 ha)	12.7	11.6	12.2	7.9	25.0	22.8	30.2	25.3
Medium (4.001–10.000 ha)	9.1	9.9	7.1	5.1	37.9	42.2	38.0	34.5
Large (>10.01 ha)	2.2	1.4	1.0	1.0	23.6	18.5	12.2	15.3
All classes (ha)	100.0	100.0	100.0	100.0	100.0	100.0	100.0	100.0

Source NSSO 59th round, household ownership holdings in India, report No. 491
Note ha indicates hectares
[1]The size classification of land holdings has been adopted from National Sample Survey Organization (NSSO). NSS report No. 492, some aspects of operational land holdings in India, 2002–03, Chap. 3, can be referred for further details

Table 2.10 Percentage distribution of operational holdings and area operated by size categories of operational holdings in Punjab 1971–72 to 2002–03 (%)

Operational holding	Percentage of holdings				Percentage of area operated			
	1971–72	1981–82	1992–93	2002–03	1971–72	1981–82	1991–92	2002–03
Marginal (≤1.000 ha)	11.7	59.0	63.2	66.3	1.5	3.9	6.2	7.3
Small (1.001–2.000 ha)	19.1	10.4	11.4	11.2	7.1	8.9	10.7	11.7
Semi-medium (2.001–4.000 ha)	32.7	14.0	13.9	12.9	24.3	21.8	26.7	26.2
medium (4.001–10.000 ha)	30.5	14.2	9.8	7.8	45.1	45.9	40.6	36.4
Large (>10.000 ha)	6.0	2.5	1.7	1.9	22.1	19.6	15.8	18.5
All classes	100.0	100.0	100.0	100.0	100.0	100.0	100.0	100.0

Source NSSO, 59th round, some aspects of operational land holdings in India, report no. 492

Table 2.11 Percentage distribution of operated area by type of possession for each size class of operational holding in Punjab for 2002–03 (%)

Operational holdings	Owned	Leased-in	Others	All
Marginal (≤1.000 ha)	95.38	3.79	0.83	100.00
Small (1.001–2.000 ha)	89.92	10.08	0.00	100.00
Semi-medium (2.001–4.000 ha)	81.14	18.87	0.00	100.00
Medium (4.001–10.000 ha)	80.17	19.83	0.00	100.00
Large (>10.000 ha)	85.44	14.56	0.00	100.00
All classes	83.16	16.83	0.01	100.00

Source NSSO 59th round, some aspects of operational land holdings in India, report No. 492
Note
1. Calculated only for kharif season
2. Includes the categories otherwise possessed and operated but not possessed on the date of survey

Table 2.12 Distribution of owned and operated area by household size groups 1961–62 and 2002–03

Household size groups	Distribution of owned area		Distribution of operated area	
	1961–62	2002–03	1961–62	2002–03
Bottom 60 %	6.1	2	23.5	4.9
Middle 30 %	43.4	36.7	43	40.6
Top 10 %	50.5	61.3	33.5	54.5

Source Nair and Banerjee (2011)

ownership for Punjab was estimated 0.717 for 1961–62 and it increased to 0.800 for 2002–03 (Nair and Banerjee 2011). The change becomes more evident from the distribution of owned and operated area by household groups for 1961–62 and 2002–03 (see Table 2.12). This land concentration has taken place in spite of the fact that the state had done legislation on the tenancy act and introduced ceiling on land holdings.

The changes in the direction of land concentration will have to be seen in the larger background of the nature and direction of technological change. To be more specific, the following relationship and process needs to be taken into account in explaining this; firstly, the changes in the composition of irrigation and its technological base. As we noted earlier, the dominance of canal irrigation has been significantly reduced in recent decades as a result of rapid increase in wells and tube wells that required considerable own farm investment. Since well- and tube well-irrigated lands are more productive than canal-irrigated area, there has been faster adoption of this technology. The density of well irrigation began to increase rapidly resulting in decline in the water table leading to further investment in the deepening of well. The capacity created in well irrigation required a minimum size of holding to make it viable. From this perspective those who have excess capacity, leasing in land from others or selling water had become an option. On the other hand, those without access to well irrigation, leasing out their land had become another option to be followed. The outcome of these processes has been the increase in the land lease market and also the development of the water market. Secondly, a similar process seems to have taken place in the other components of the agro-mechanical equipments, namely tractors, harvesters and thrashers. In the early phase of green revolution, the intensity of labour use per unit of cultivated area has increased, and in the absence of local labour, large-scale in-migration of labour from other states began to occur. The scarcity of local labour began to increase with shift of labour from farm to non-farm sectors. The rapid diffusion of agro-mechanical technology in the post-green revolution period has contributed to the saving of labour in ploughing, land preparation, sowing, transplanting, harvesting, thrashing, and transportation. As demonstrated by the data from the cost of cultivation studies, the expansion of farm mechanization has resulted in the decline in labour use per unit of cultivated area. Since, the density of machinery and equipments has increased overtime, those with excess capacity in relation to their owned area began to rent out their machinery and equipments or lease in land to make use of the economies of scale. Conversely, those who could not afford this, it was possible to hire the equipments or lease out their land. Development of a rental market for machinery and equipments and further development of the lease market has been the outcome of this process. The intensification and expansion of cultivation has also changed the traditional property rights relating to the grazing rights for landless and marginal farmers who own livestock. Since, there are standing crops in the fields for most parts of the year; grazing of animals after the harvest season has become highly restricted.[12] However, the sharp reduction in the work animal stock as a result of mechanization has contributed to the prospects for raising more animals for milk production. The development and expansion of dairy cooperatives, and marketing and processing of milk have induced farmers to take dairying as a source of employment and income.

The institutional changes noted above in response to the technological changes needs to be viewed in the context of the changes in the commercialization of input and output markets. The government control over input and output prices of wheat and rice promoted a certain degree of specialization in production with various institutional linkages (both public as well as private). These institutions facilitated the commercialization of agriculture during the early years of green revolution (Ladejinsky 1969; Ghosh 1979). The farmers started selling a major part of their output in the market. Not only the product market got commercialized, they also started participating in the input markets on regular basis due to considerable increase in the use of inputs like high yielding varieties of seeds, chemical fertilizers, and mechanized tools such as pumping sets, electric motors, threshers, tractors and harvest combines (Bhalla et al. 1990; Satish 2006; Sidhu and Byerlee

[12]According to a recent survey on the practice of keeping livestock in India, the percentage of households sending their animals for grazing is negligible in the states of Punjab and Haryana. However, in the neighbouring states of Rajasthan and Uttar Pradesh, the practice is still widespread. See DRS (2013) for details.

1991). In this way, the prices (both input and output) became the direct concern for the farmers. To boost the benefits of green revolution and to encourage the farmers, substantial resources were transferred to Punjab for infrastructural investment and agricultural subsidies. However, credit supplied by formal institutional agencies (commercial banks and cooperatives) were not sufficient to meet the increasing need of credit (both short and long terms). Since the new inputs were purchased with cash, the farmers of Punjab had to invariably invest a substantial amount of cash in every crop (Gill 1996; Jodhka 2006). Given that their own resources were limited, they invariably had to borrow, either directly from the informal credit market, or via commission agents through whom they sold their marketed surplus. Subsequently, the existence of Arhtias (money lenders) became very crucial since they fulfilled the gap in availability of credit from institutional sources and the total demand for credit in the rural Punjab. Historically there has been slow expansion of banking system in the rural areas of Punjab. The slow penetration of bank branches in the agrarian society has led to low level of availability of institutional finance and to high dependency on money lenders (Gill 2004). The role of money lenders were not confined to the credit market alone but to various other input and product markets. The above arguments are evident from the data available from the All India Rural Debt and Investment Surveys. The latest round of published data for 2002–03 showed that more than 2/3rd of the borrowings by farmers were for meeting these production credit needs and purchase of farm assets (see Table 2.13). The data also show that in spite of the progress made in the expansion of formal credit institutions, more than 60 % of the outstanding debt by farmers was to the money lenders (see Table 2.14). Available data also showed that the situation remained without much change over a long period. In order to bring out the role of money lenders and commission agents in the credit market, it would be useful to elaborate more on this. As we noted, the private ownership of land was established in Punjab during the British period (Hirashima 1996). It was not the farmers who judged the value of the land but the money lenders. They played their big role in setting up the land market. Through the process of accounting of both input and output markets, they managed to value the price and rent of lands (Hirashima 2000). Up to the time when the famous Punjab Land Alienation Act of 1900 was enforced, it was the money lenders who participated in land market transactions. The money lenders realized that the land transactions were more profitable than traditional money lending and grain marketing. Therefore, the formalization of land markets started after the intervention of money lenders into the market. The rising land ceiling had also given the signal to large farmers and the professional money lenders to acquire more land. It was the small and marginal farmers and landless labourers in villages who did not participate in the land market (Hirashima 2008). However, inflation of land prices seemed to be benefiting the small chronically deficit farmers, as they sold their smaller area to repay their debts (Shergill 1986).

The land lease market emerged formally after green revolution. The heavy indebtedness of small and marginal farmers forced them to leave agriculture and lease out their lands to the large farmers. The phenomenon of "reverse tenancy" seemed to occur when the small farmers left agriculture and joined the ranks of

Table 2.13 Percentage distribution of outstanding loans by purpose of loan for each size class of land possessed of farmer household in Punjab in 2003 (%)

Size class of possessed holding	Capital exp. in farm business	Current exp. in farm business	Non-farm business	Consumption exp.	Ceremonies	Edu.	Medical	Other exp.	All	Percentage of indebted HHS
Marginal	13.3	7.0	7.9	20.9	21.5	0.1	8.8	20.5	100	**56.7**
Small	12.0	49.6	10.1	12.0	7.6	0.3	0.0	8.4	100	**75.8**
Semi-medium	28.9	49.1	4.9	1.6	6.3	0.0	1.2	8.1	100	**82.7**
Medium	33.4	38.6	0.7	9.6	10.9	0.0	2.9	4.0	100	**83.6**
Large	27.5	30.4	0.0	3.9	4.0	0.0	0.0	34.2	100	**83.9**
All classes	26.4	36.0	4.4	8.5	10.2	0.0	2.6	12.0	100	**65.4**

Source NSSO 59th round, indebtedness of farmer households, report no. 498

Table 2.14 Percentage distribution of outstanding loans of farmers' households by source of loan in Punjab in 2003 and 1971 (%)

Sources of debt/years	1971[1]	2003[2]
1. Government	6.9	1.9
2. Cooperative society	32.0	17.6
3. Commercial bank	4.9	28.4
Institutional credit (1+2+3)	**43.8**	**47.9**
4. Agricultural/professional money lenders/landlord	25.1	36.3
5. Traders	12.3	8.2
6. Relatives and friends	14.8	6.3
7. Others	3.0	1.13
Non-institutional credit (4+5+6+7)	**56.2**	**52.1**
All	100.0	100.0

Source(s)
[1]Adopted from Satish (2006)
[2]NSSO 59th round, indebtedness of farmer households, report no. 498

proletariat (Gill 1989; Singh and Grewal 2001; Vyas 1994). Tenancy at will was very prominent during the land reforms in Punjab due to the labour-intensive techniques in agriculture. When the tenancy reforms happened in the state, the official data showed a sharp decline in the incidence of tenancy. However, in reality magnitude of tenancy did not change much. It was after the inception of green revolution that the self-cultivation experienced a sudden increase due to the labour-saving techniques in agriculture, and thus, the decline of actual tenancy was witnessed (Singh 1989). This is how the technological changes have altered the land institution in Punjab since green revolution.

Further, impact of technological diffusion in the state has been seen through the inception of informal channels of commercialization. The moneylenders are playing their roles in a much bigger way than they did in the past. The phenomenon of multiple roles of the moneylender was first introduced by Malcolm Darling in his classic work *The Punjab peasant in prosperity and debt* in 1925 (Darling 1928). A money lender may be a landlord who finances his tenants and workers engaged on land; he may be a trader who finances the cultivator only to obtain exclusive rights to purchase his crop; or he may be an input dealer who lent money on the condition that inputs for cultivation must be purchased only from him (Gill 1996). A number of empirical studies have established the existence of interlinked contracts. A variety of interlinkages including those in land, labour, inputs and output markets in which credit is the central part can be found. Interlinked credit contracts were used as a mechanism to alleviate screening, incentive and enforcement problems (Gill 2004). In this way, the commission agents had displayed a greater foresight in the credit market than the formal institutional sources, by not insisting on land as collateral. Exorbitant rates of interest were charged and the cultivators were forced to pay it, because institutional credit was just not in adequate supply.

However to support the farmers, various policy measures of each successive government were directed towards the promotion of their interests (Jodhka 2006). This lead to the diversion of public investment and subsidized inputs from urban to rural areas; this included provision of essential inputs such as water and power at highly subsidized rates; stabilization of agricultural prices; availability of cheap credit, availability of subsidized agricultural inputs such as fertilizers and insecticides. Therefore, dependency of farmers on government increased over time.

With due course of time, peasantry became the central question of the political interest. Dominant leadership of Akali Dal came out of capitalist farmers (Puri 1983). During the late 1960s to late 1980s, the Akali Dal expanded its base among the peasantry. Its mobilization capacity is also based on the peasantry. With the modernization of agriculture, expansion of education and with experience to rule Akali party produced a mature leadership from the upper layers of peasantry (Singh 1984). Various political parties of the states had supported the farmers' lobby and demanded the special provisions to entire state and farmers in particular (Gill and Singhal 1984). The demand of special provisions first came out from the Anandpur sahib Resolution that clearly demanded the economic advantages for the peasantry. These demands were for raising the level for land ceiling, cheap inputs and abolition of excise duty on tractors, and remunerative agricultural prices. Such demands basically served more the capitalist farmers (Corsi 2006). The development in recent past showed that the technological changes had not only altered the institutions concerning land but also the political agenda of the state. The present-day political situation proves the nexus of political powers with landlords and commission agents. The small farmers are either operating on the mercy of commission agents or in the process of leasing out land to the large farmers.

2.5 Technology and Institutions: Wider Implications

In the preceding sections, we have made an attempt to provide an overview of the evolution of technology and institutions in Punjab. Linking the developments since the green revolution with its historical roots prior to independence provides interesting insights, it is seen that agricultural developments in both the periods, while bringing prosperity has resulted in institutional changes in the land market, and its functioning was mediated by the interlinked markets. The interlinked markets did result in the accumulation of surplus in the hands of large farmers, who ploughed it back into money-lending activities, and in trade and commerce that further reinforced their economic dominance. Though all the sections of the peasantry could participate in the process of technology-driven agricultural development, given the scale bias of the technologies, the large size groups of holdings could realize higher productivity and returns from investment. The marginal and small farmers whose profit margins were squeezed by various intermediaries in the interlinked market appear to be moving out of crop production into other non-agricultural activities, by either leasing out or selling their land to the higher size groups of holdings. It is to be noted that the growth process in agriculture resulted in significant increase in income levels of the population and contributed to rapid reduction in the incidence of poverty.[13]

It is also useful to highlight briefly the changing role of the state (both at the centre and the state of Punjab) in creating an enabling policy environment for the rapid promotion of agricultural development in the state of Punjab. Coming to the role of the Government of Punjab, the following policy interventions formed part of the framework for stimulating the growth process (1) the consolidation of land holding, creation of infrastructure for transport, power, irrigation, development of market towns (2) investment of agricultural research and extension service and (3) provision of input subsidies of various types like, almost free canal irrigation and electricity for irrigation pumps; for the rapid diffusion and adoption of technology. Though, agriculture is a state subject, the role of the central government has been equally or more important in deciding the direction of changes in the agriculture of Punjab. A few points worth mentioning in this context were as follows: (1) the investment in the creation of irrigation and power projects (2) provision of input subsidies (especially for chemical fertilizer) and (3) procurement of the surplus grains produced in the state at minimum support price and moving it to the grain-deficit regions in the country for the public distribution system. Questions have been raised often regarding the effectiveness of the procurement policy in providing remunerative prices to the farmers. Enough has been written on this subject by experts, but it is sufficient to note that production has been increasing even when the profit margins were squeezed with rising input costs. (4) Economic liberalization initiated from the early 1990s followed by India signing the WTO agreement in 2000, provided both opportunities and threats for Punjab's agriculture. The domestic liberalization has resulted in the removal of trade barriers within India and the free movement of grains contributing to the rapid development of interstate grain trade. In the post-WTO period, the scope for export of rice and wheat to the world market has improved with more access to the importing countries. Since the cost of production is high in India as compared to many other exporting countries, the exporting surplus grain to the world market required subsidy from the central government. However, it required keeping domestic subsidies to less than 10 % of the agricultural GDP. Indian domestic market has been given market access to other exporting countries. With the integration to the world market, Indian domestic prices have become sensitive to the movement of food grain prices in the international market.

From a historical perspective, one could see that as agricultural growth and development expanded, older institutions have undergone change, and number of new institutions have evolved endogenously or introduced exogenously. Such a process has evolved not only in the state of Punjab, but also in the neighbouring

[13]There exist a large number of studies that examined the impact of agricultural growth on the reduction of rural poverty. An interesting study covering the experiences of selected state in the country is by Jones and Sen (2003).

state of Haryana and other regions of the country that witnessed technology-driven agricultural growth. The allocation of resources, and its utilization in the production process, and efficiency of production, has been shaped not only by the interaction between technology and institutions, but also among the institutions and institutional arrangements. The deceleration in the productivity growth of food grains, or falling factor productivity in agriculture, or degradation of the natural resource base witnessed is a product of these interactions. Reversing these trends is no more a development challenge that could be resolved by the state alone: many of the key decisions affecting the performance of agriculture has been taken by the national government, and therefore, realizing the goal of sustaining the agricultural growth process would require a collaborative effort between the national government and the state governments. How to realize this in a centre–state federal framework is a major challenge.

At the analytical level, it is interesting to comment on the viewpoints and theories we have drawn attention in the introductory section of this paper. The experience of Punjab is a definite pointer to the role of historical forces in shaping agricultural growth in the post-independent period at the regional level. The initial property right regime on land created by the British, and the investment in the expansion and modernization of canal irrigation combined with investment in railways contributed to the development of agriculture in the Punjab. The peasants got exposure to the management of irrigated agriculture with the technologies prevalent. The outcome that emerged was exploitative since there had been siphoning of the peasant's income by the money lenders and commission agents. The agricultural development since independence in the state of Punjab continues to persist with some of the institutions and institutional arrangements inherited from the past. On the positive side, the institutional setting that existed in the state before independence facilitated the peasantry to absorb the new technology in agriculture. The environmental conditions in Punjab with adequate supply of water could result in realizing higher levels of agricultural productivity.

The deceleration in the growth of agriculture in recent decades calls for further explanations at the analytical level. The quality of institutions that has emerged overtime could be one of the important factors to be taken into account in explaining the emerging situation of Punjab agriculture. Recent theoretical developments on institutions and economic performance argued that, where the institutions are grabber friendly it would pull down growth performance and where they are producer friendly, it would sustain growth (Mahlum et al. 2006). If we go by this argument, it would appear that the deceleration in productivity and output growth could be due to the decline in the quality of agrarian institutions that has emerged over time. The most striking aspects in this context are as follows: (i) the interlinked markets and (ii) institutions that are meant to regulate the use of natural resources. As we argued in the previous section, the interlinked markets have been working to the advantage of the large farmers, commission agents and money lenders and they could grab a good part of the income generated by the peasantry. So long as, the formal credit system do not succeed in reaching out to the credit requirements of the farmers and the state do not succeed in reforming the product and input markets, the dominance of the money lenders and commission agents would continue to prevail. Reforming these institutions is essentially a political process in which political leadership would be in a position to construct coalition that gives legitimacy in policy making (Grabowski 2012). In a state like Punjab, where political coalitions derive their sources of strength from large farmers, money lenders and commission agents, political coalitions would always weigh their short-term political gain or loss to the long-term development needs of the state. If the political benefits flowing out of the development needs outweigh the short-term political loss, then ruling coalitions may incorporate in their development agenda "the development needs of the agricultural sector". However, this would occur only if there exists an accumulated technological backlog for accelerating the growth in productivity. Unfortunately, the accumulated technological backlog for increasing productivity at the quickest possible time on a mass scale needs to be perfected for widespread diffusion and adoption which calls for well-informed decision-making by the national government.

References

Acemoglu D, Johnson S, Robinson JA (2001) The colonial origins of comparative analysis of poverty and agricultural growth in rural India. J Dev Stud 40(1):1–31

Acemoglu D, Johnson S, Robinson JA (2002) Reversal of fortune: geography and institutions in the making of the modern world income distribution. Quart J Econ 117(4):1231–1294

Banerjee A, Iyer L (2005) History, institutions and economic performance: the legacy of colonial land tenure systems in India. Am Econ Rev 95(4):1190–1213

Bhalla GS, Singh G (2010) Growth of Indian agriculture: a district level study. http://planningcommission.nic.in/reports/sereport/ser/ser_gia2604.pdf. Accessed 15 Mar 2014

Bhalla GS, Chada GK, Kashyap SP, Sharma RK (1990) Agricultural growth and structural changes in the Punjab economy: an input-output analysis. Research report 82, International Food Policy Research, Washington, DC

Birthal Pratap S, Joshi Pramod K, Negi Digvijay S, Agarwal Shaily (2014) Changing sources of growth in Indian agriculture: implications for regional priorities for accelerating agricultural growth. IFPRI discussion paper no. 1325. International Food Policy Research, Washington, DC

Boserup E (1965) The conditions of agricultural growth the economics of agrarian change under population pressure. George Allen & Unwin Ltd., London

Boyce J (1987) Agrarian impasse in Bengal, institutional constraints to technological change. Oxford University Press, Oxford

Corsi M (2006) Communalism and the green revolution in Punjab. J Dev Soc. Accessed from http://jds.sagepub.com/content/22/2/85

Darling ML (1928) The Punjab peasant in prosperity and debt, 2nd edn. Oxford University Press, London

DRS (2013) External monitoring and evaluation of national dairy plan phase I (National Dairy Support Project). Baseline study final report 2013, Development and Research Services Pvt. Ltd, New Delhi

Engerman SL, Sokoloff KL (1997) Factor endowments, institutions, and differential paths of growth among new world economies: a view from economic historians of the United States. In: Haber S (ed) How Latin America fell behind. Stanford University Press, Stanford

Engerman SL, Sokoloff KL (2002) Factor endowments, inequality and paths of development among new world economies. Economia 3(1):41–109

Ghose AK (1979) Institutional structure, technological change and growth in poor agrarian economies: an analysis with reference to Bengal and Punjab. World Dev 7(4–5):385–396
Gill SS (1989) Changing land relations and implications for land reforms. Econ Polit Wkly 24(25): A79–A85
Gill A (1996) Interlinked agrarian credit markets in Punjab: exploitative, yet growing. Econ Polit Wkly 31(10):586–588
Gill A (2004) Interlinked agrarian credit markets: case study of Punjab. Econ Polit Wkly 39 (33):3741–3751
Gill SS, Singhal KC (1984) The Punjab problem: its historical roots. Econ Polit Wkly 19(14):603–608
Grabowski R (2012) The politics of rapid growth, Asia pacific economic literature Crawford School of Public Policy, The Australian National University and Wiley Publishing, Australia
Hayami V, Ruttan VW (1971) Agricultural development: an international perspective. John Hopkins University Press, Baltimore
Hirashima S (1978) The structure of disparity in developing agriculture: a case study of Pakistan Punjab. Institute of developing economics, Tokyo
Hirashima S (1996) Asset effects in land price formation in agriculture: the evidence from South Asia. Pak Dev Rev 34(4):963–976
Hirashima S (2000) Issues in agricultural reforms: public investment and land market development. Econ Polit Wkly 35(43/44):3879–3884
Hirashima S (2008) The land market in development: a case study of Punjab in Pakistan and India. Econ Polit Wkly 43(42):41–47
Jodhka SS (2006) Beyond 'crises': rethinking contemporary Punjab agriculture. Econ Polit Wkly 41(16):1530–1537
Jones RP, Sen K (2003) What has luck got to do with it? A regional analysis of poverty and agricultural growth in rural India. J Dev Stud 40(1):1–31
Ladejinsky W (1969) The green revolution in Punjab: a field trip. Econ Polit Wkly 4(26):A73–A82
Mahlum HKM, Tarvik R (2006) Institutions and the resource curse. Econ J 116(508):1–20
Minhas BS, Vaidyanathan A (1965) Growth in crop output in India, 1951–54 to 1958–61: an analysis by component elements. J Indian Soc Agric Stat 17(2):230–252
Nair KN, Banerjee A (2011) Structural changes in land distribution and implications for improving access to land. In: Narayana D, Mahadevan R (eds) Shaping India: economic change in historical perspective. Routledge, New Delhi
Narayana D, Raman M (eds) (2011) Shaping India, economic change in historical perspective. Routledge, New Delhi
North DC, Thomas RP (1973) The role of the western world: a new economic history. Cambridge University Press, New York
Paustan PW (1930) Canal irrigation in Punjab: an economic enquiry relating to certain aspects of the development of canal irrigation by the British in the Punjab. Cambridge University Press, New York
Pray CE (1984) Impact of agricultural research in British India. J Econ Hist 44(2):429–440
Puri HK (1983) The Akali agitation: an analysis of socio-economic bases of protest. Econ Polit Wkly 18(4):113–118
Roy T (2007) A delayed revolution: environment and agrarian change in India. Oxf Rev Econ Policy 23(2):239–250
Satish P (2006) Institutional credit, indebtedness and suicides in Punjab. Econ Polit Wkly 41 (26):2754–2761
Schultz TW (1964) Transforming traditional agriculture. University of Chicago Press, Chicago
Shergill HS (1986) Land sales and land prices in Punjab: 1952–53 to 1978–79. Econ Polit Wkly 21(38–39):125–128
Sidhu DS, Byerlee D (1991) Technical change and wheat productivity in post-green revolution Punjab. Econ Polit Wkly 26(52):A159–A166
Singh G (1984) Socio-economic bases of the Punjab crisis. Econ Polit Wkly 19(1):42–47

Singh I (1989) Reverse tenancy in Punjab agriculture: impact of technological change. Econ Polit Wkly 24(25):86–92

Singh RP, Grewal SS (2001) Tenancy pattern in post green revolution Punjab. In: Gill SS (ed) Land reforms in India, vol 6. Intervention for agrarian capitalist transformation in Punjab and Haryana, Sage Publications, New Delhi

Sokoloff KL, Engerman SL (2000) History lessons: institutions, factors endowments, and paths of development in the new world. J Econ Perspect 14(3):217–232

Vaidynathan A (2010) Agricultural growth in India: technology and institutions. Oxford University Press, New Delhi

Vyas VS (1994) Agricultural policies for the nineties: issues and approaches. Econ Polit Wkly 24 (26):A54–A63

Weintraub ER (2005) Autobiographical memory and the historiography of economics. J Hist Econ Thought 27(1):1–11

Chapter 3
Growth Pattern and Economic Impacts of Wheat Productivity on Punjab Agriculture

R.S. Sidhu, Kamal Vatta and Shayequa Zeenat Ali

3.1 Introduction

In recent years, the agriculture sector in India is beset with many problems. The growth in the sector, especially of crops, has stagnated since mid-1990s (Chand 2005). The growth in the agriculturally developed regions like Punjab, Haryana, etc., too has slowed down (Sidhu et al. 2005). The productivity growth of important foodgrains like wheat and rice has stagnated. Consequently, the profitability of farming has deteriorated even in the developed pockets due to which very serious problems like indebtedness and farmers' suicides have emerged (Sidhu and Gill 2006). Many factors are considered responsible for these developments, which make it a compelling case to investigate the story of growth (and deceleration) in terms of its processes, so that futuristic road map for its growth is developed to meet the challenge of growing food demand in the country.

The most important and feasible method of increasing agricultural output in future would be through raising the productivity of land by increasing the irrigated area, higher use of fertilizers, adoption of input use efficient practices, development of infrastructure and institutions such as agricultural research, extension, input delivery, credit, etc. Within India, there are large disparities in the state-wise area under irrigation, cultivation of high yielding seeds and consumption of fertilizers. The proportion of net sown irrigated area ranges from less than about 30 % in Orissa and Chhattisgarh and Madhya Pradesh to 98 % in Punjab and the fertilizer consumption varies from about 56–88 kg/ha of gross cropped area in Assam, Madhya Pradesh and Orissa to 243 kg in Punjab (GOI 2012). There is also skewed pattern of

R.S. Sidhu
Punjab Agricultural University, Ludhiana 141001, India

K. Vatta (✉) · S.Z. Ali
Centres for International Projects Trust, 910-11, Pragati Towers,
Rajendra Place, New Delhi 110008, India
e-mail: kamal@cipt.in

L. Singh and N. Singh (eds.), *Economic Transformation of a Developing Economy*, India Studies in Business and Economics,
DOI 10.1007/978-981-10-0197-0_3

fertilizer consumption towards irrigated areas as well as *rabi* season (winter season). This variability points towards an enormous scope that exists to boost agricultural production through increase in the use of fertilizers along with other complementary inputs and positive input–output price policy. It was the package of irrigation-high yielding seeds-chemical fertilizers during the late-1960s, 1970s and 1980s which shifted the agricultural production system of the country on a high growth path and transformed it from food deficit to food self-sufficient nation. The question arises whether it will again be the same package, which will ensure 4 % growth of the agriculture sector as well as food security through increasing production of wheat.

3.2 Growth in Input Use and Production of Wheat in India

The pattern of growth in fertilizer use, area under high yielding seeds and irrigated area in different time periods was different but was strongly associated with one another. With the introduction of high yielding seeds of wheat on irrigated areas during late-1960s and early-1970s, fertilizer use picked up with a growth rate of 9.4 % during 1970s. As the growth in irrigated area slowed down during 1980s and 1990s, the growth in area under high yielding seeds as well as fertilizer use decelerated (Table 3.1). The growth in wheat production was strongly associated with these variables, which was facilitated by favourable input–output price policy and availability of cheap institutional agricultural credit. The growth has, however, been sluggish since mid-1990s, which became stagnant during 2000–01 and 2009–10. It appears that the stagnation in the expansion of irrigated area caused stagnation in the area under high yielding seeds and associated fertilizer use and even the greater availability of institutional credit and relative fall in fertilizer prices with respect to wheat price could not encourage production. It is thus argued that slow/no growth in irrigated area and consequent slowdown/stagnation in growth in area under improved seeds as well as fertilizer use were primarily responsible for slowdown in the growth of wheat productivity and production in the country and may have had serious implications for achieving the targeted growth of 4 % in the agriculture sector.

Table 3.1 Growth rates of fertilizer use and other related variables in India, 1970–71 to 2009–10

Period	Yield	Production	NPK use	Area under HYVs	Irrigated area	Price ratio	Short-term credit
1970–71 to 1979–80	1.87	4.31	9.39	11.62	2.67	1.20^{ns}	14.43
1980–81 to 1989–90	3.10	3.58	5.47	3.28	1.01	0.48^{ns}	13.10
1990–91 to 1999–2000	1.82	3.57	1.93	2.21	0.59	−4.59	18.88
2000–01 to 2009–10	0.69	1.90	1.26^{ns}	0.71^{ns}	−0.54^{ns}	−0.13^{ns}	24.30

Note ns means non-significant, all the other figures are significant at 5 % level

3.3 Determinants of Wheat Production in India

The pattern and growth of fertilizer use, high yielding varieties and irrigation of wheat in India during 1970–71 to 2009–10 indicated complementarities to increase wheat production. Irrigation triggers adoption of high yielding seeds, which are more responsive to fertilizer application. The combination of this package in a sequential manner helps raising productivity and production. This analysis capturing such relationships is carried out by using the following simultaneous equation models for wheat production to estimate their contribution towards growth. The error terms are assumed to be serially independent and identically distributed in such estimation. The equations were identified and subsequently estimated by using the software STATA.

$$Q_t = f\,(\mathrm{NPK}_t, \mathrm{HYV}_t)$$
$$\mathrm{NPK}_t = f\,(P_t, \mathrm{HYV}_t, \mathrm{Credit}_t)$$
$$\mathrm{HYV}_t = f\,(\mathrm{Irri}_t)$$

where:

Q_t Wheat production (million tonnes) in period t
NPK_t Fertilizer consumption in wheat (thousand nutrient tonnes) in period t
P_t Ratio of fertilizer price to the wheat minimum support price (MSP) for period t
HYV_t Area under high yielding varieties of wheat (million ha) in period t
Irri_t Percentage of wheat area under irrigation.

The relative contribution of each determinant of production, fertilizer use and area under high yielding varieties as well as their derived impact estimated with the help of simultaneous equation model is given in Table 3.2. The adjusted R^2 was very high in all the equations of the model, indicating the robustness of the relationships. Irrigation was seen as the main driver of promoting high yielding seeds,

Table 3.2 3SLS estimates of the determinants of wheat production and related factors, India, 1970–71 to 2009–10

Particular	Production	NPK use	Area under HYVs
NPK consumption	0.24**	–	–
Price ratio	–	−0.04**	–
Area under HYVs	0.73**	1.35**	–
Short-term credit	–	0.12**	–
Area irrigated	–	–	1.08***
R-square	0.95	0.95	0.96

Note The figures are the elasticities estimated for each coefficient. ** and *** represent the significance at 5 and 1 % levels, respectively

which in turn helped increasing production of wheat directly and through promoting higher use of fertilizers. Fertilizer application was also facilitated by favourable fertilizer/output price regime, which showed a declining trend due to fertilizer subsidies, and institutional agricultural credit growth. The elasticity of area under high yielding wheat varieties to irrigation was as high as 1.08 and that of production to area under high yielding varieties as 0.73. The fertilizer use was also very elastic to high yielding seeds. The institutional credit and fertilizer price (real) also helped increasing use of fertilizers but the impact of non-price factors was stronger than that of price factors in increasing wheat production.

The process of growth and stagnation in wheat production derived through its determinants led to the same conclusions. Expansion in irrigated area resulted in a larger area under high yielding varieties of wheat in order to realize higher production and profits. Since high yielding varieties were high nutrient consumers and were thus highly responsive to chemical fertilizers, the use of chemical fertilizers increased. Recognizing the potential of high yields of wheat, the Government of India put in place the institutional and policy frame in the shape of higher output prices, fertilizer subsidies and greater access to institutional credit to encourage the use of chemical fertilizers and other modern production inputs for obtaining higher foodgrain production and meeting food demand. All these factors in combination raised wheat productivity and production in the country. This process was replicated in all the potential areas of the country. The success of this package was high in those areas, where groundwater resources were also exploited to increase the irrigation scope and intensity. Punjab represents a classic case of such policy.

3.4 Growth in Wheat Production in Punjab: A Success Story

History of agriculture is the history of evolution of mankind as well as evolution of agriculture. Human beings selected plants and animals which met their requirements. History of agriculture is replete with uncertainty due to the vagaries of weather such as floods, droughts and famines. India is also vulnerable to crop failures and famines. There were 19 famines in India between the eleventh and twentieth century and the Bengal famine of 1943 was the last one. After the era of Green Revolution that began in 1960s, India never experienced a famine-like situation, though it experienced the worst drought of the century in 1987. Punjab and Northwestern India are equally prone to crop failures, and famines recorded in the pre-partition Punjab were in 1802, 1812, 1817, 1824, 1834, 1837, 1851–52, 1860, 1868–69 and 1877–78. Despite these constraints, the region emerged as the food basket of India. This was possible due to the irrigation, land, social, legislative and institutional reforms. Punjab, with 1.53 % geographical area, contributes about 39 % wheat and 27 % rice to the central pool of foodgrains (2010–11). It was the result of technological developments in agriculture and their rapid dissemination and adoption backed by Government policy support in market, prices, input delivery and credit.

3.5 Crop Improvement Programme in Wheat

The scientific crop improvement efforts were made with thrust in increasing production of the foodgrains. Collective efforts were made by crop breeders, geneticists, biochemists, crop physiologists, agronomists, plant pathologists, entomologists, soil scientists and farm engineers to achieve transformation of the farm technology from traditional to the current levels of productivity and production. Systematic crop breeding efforts for yield increase and incorporating other desirable traits, testing of the suitable types at multi-locations and the new seeds thus developed in adaptive trials were carried out in collaboration with the state directorate of agriculture and at farmers' fields for adaptability before recommending for cultivation in the state.

Punjab Agricultural University (PAU) is a State Agricultural University (SAU), but is well knit with the National Agricultural Research System (NARS) in the Indian Council of Agricultural Research (ICAR) through All India Coordinated Research Projects (AICRP) for the development of wheat varieties for the state and the NWPZ (North West Plains Zone comprising eight states). The materials are tested in the all-India crop improvement projects in zonal evaluation by PAU and those which appear to be promising for Punjab are further tested in local adaptive trials as is done for the indigenously developed varieties at PAU. After being found suitable, these varieties are released for cultivation in Punjab or in specified areas of the state. Similarly, PAU varieties, which have the advantage in other zones, are released nationally for the benefit of the farmers of other states. Materials received from international nurseries in the collaborative programmes and found suitable are also used in the breeding programmes and the varieties thus developed or improved are recommended for cultivation in the state after adaptive trails to maximize the farmers' benefits.

Wheat research is not only focused on yield enhancement but also on plant production and protection technologies to ensure efficient resource utilization and crop protection from the incidence of diseases, weeds and pests. The priority of the research agenda continues to undergo changes depending upon the emerging issues and problems being faced by the production system. During 1960s, 1970s and 1980s, the breeding programme largely emphasized yield enhancement through improved genotypes, which were responsive to higher use of inputs. Weed management was another issue in wheat cultivation due to predominance of the weed called *Phlaris minor*. Production practices like sowing time, fertilizer application, spacing, irrigation schedule, etc., were also fine-tuned in order to maximize production. Incidence of diseases, especially rusts, is also an unending process in wheat cultivation. It is often said that rust never sleeps in wheat. During 1990s, as rice–wheat production system caused degradation of natural resources, especially soil and water, the research aimed at developing resource-efficient practices and technologies while maintaining productivity growth. Continued emphasis on natural resource conservation technologies along with yield and quality improvement in wheat is the thrust area of research in the past more than one decade. Recently, wheat research programme is also being geared up to address the challenge of heat stress, which is adversely influencing wheat productivity under ensuing climate changes. Genetic engineering, molecular biology and biotechnology tools in wheat research are currently being applied to shorten the varietal development programme of desirable traits.

Since its inception, PAU has released 33 varieties of bread wheat, 6 of durum wheat and 3 of *triticale* for sowing under different ecological conditions of the State. Out of these, 22 bread wheat varieties and 5 of durum wheat were released at the national level. The cultivation of varieties developed by PAU is spread across all the wheat-growing zones of the country from Himachal Pradesh to Karnataka as illustrated in Fig. 3.1.

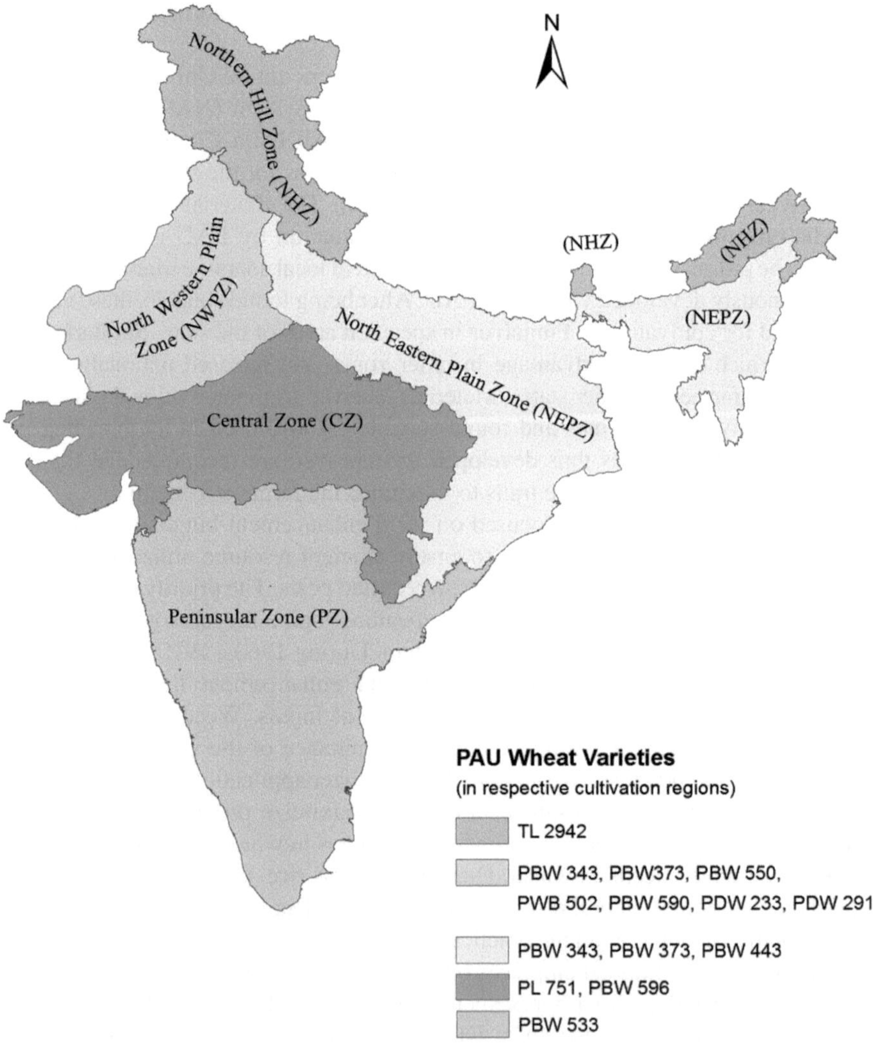

Fig. 3.1 PAU wheat varieties and the regions of their cultivation. *Source* PAU (2009a)

During 1960–61, the area under wheat cultivation in Punjab was only 1.4 million ha with the total production of 1.74 million tonnes and productivity of 1244 kg/ha. However, the area under wheat increased to approximately 3.5 million ha and the productivity increased manifold to 4693 kg/ha during 2010–11. In 1965, the first improved variety, named C 306, was released and the average yield of state was 1244 kg/ha against the yield potential of this variety at 3370 kg/ha. The release of wheat variety Kalyansona in 1970 enhanced the yield potential to 4200 kg/ha, which was further enhanced to 4680 kg/ha with the release of WL 711 in the year 1975 (Figs. 3.2 and 3.3). During the course of time, WL 711 developed susceptibility to Karnal bunt. Another wheat variety, named PBW 343, with an average yield potential of 5.42 t/ha, which was resistant to Karnal bunt and yellow as well as brown rust, was released in 1995. During 2010, a new wheat variety PBW 621 was developed by PAU, which gives around 8 % higher yield than PBW 343 and is highly resistant to yellow rust and moderately resistant to stem rust (Ug 99).

As the adoption rate of these high yielding varieties increased, the average productivity in the state went up from 2.2 t/ha in 1970–71 to 4.5 t/ha in 2000–01 due to higher use of complementary inputs like fertilizers, chemicals for control of diseases and pests as well as adoption of recommended cultivation practices in sowing, irrigation, spacing, etc. These wheat varieties, especially WL 711 and PBW 343, also became popular in other states due to their better potential. PBW 343 occupied almost 90 % of the area in the State and about 70 % (7 m ha) in North Western Plains Zone and was spread even to the Eastern parts of India. On the whole, the average annual gain in production through the genetic upgradation and higher use of complimentary inputs during the period 1965–95 was estimated to be

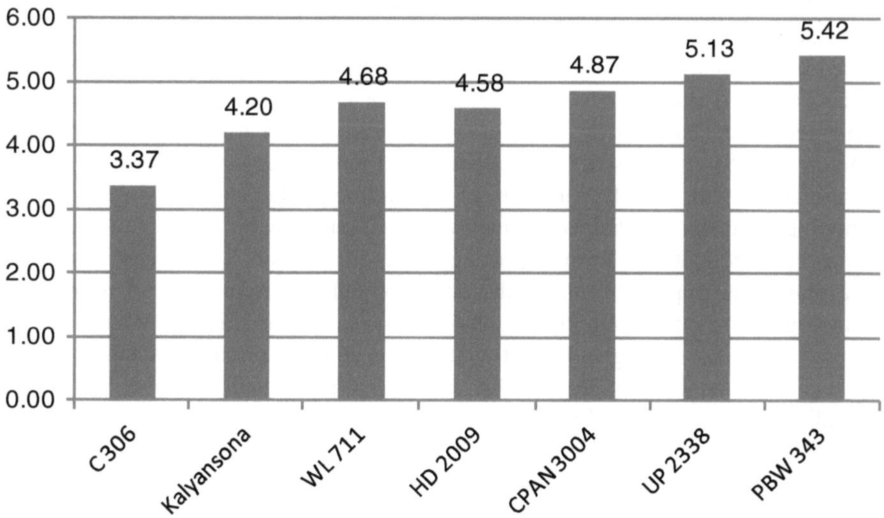

Fig. 3.2 Genetic gain for yield in North West Plains Zone yield (tonnes/ha). *Source* PAU (2009b)

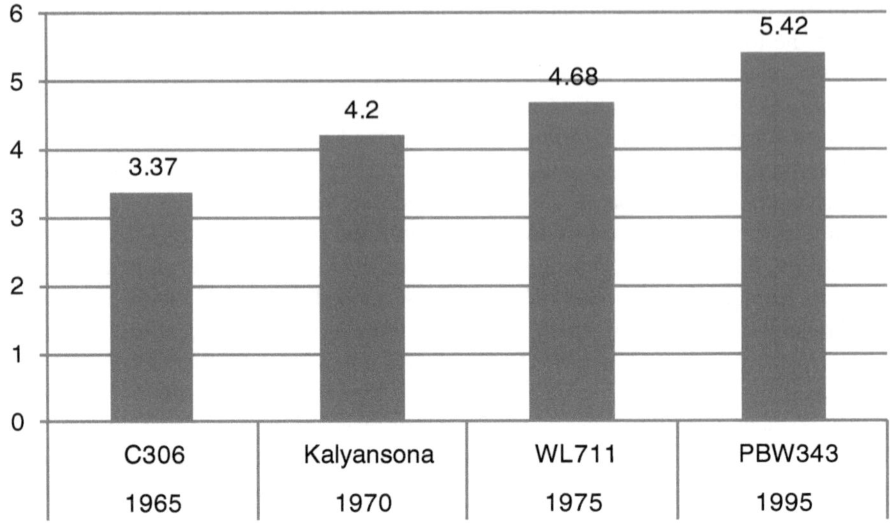

Fig. 3.3 PAU wheat varieties—Yd tonnes/hec

38 kg/ha. Presently, the variety PBW 550, released in 2007 for cultivation in the state, is resistant to yellow rust and is performing exceedingly well in the farmers' fields.

3.6 Dissemination and Adoption of New Technology

Development of technology and its dissemination is one of the important mandates embedded in the agriculture research system and state policy. This task is assigned to the Punjab Agricultural University and State Department of Agriculture. PAU implements its technology transfer model through Farm Advisory Service Scheme (FASS) at all district headquarters and Krishi Vigyan Kendras (KVKs) in collaboration with the Department of agriculture. The extension network for technology transfer has helped in achieving fast-paced adoption of new technologies and consequent transformation of agriculture in Punjab. The extension services have played an important role in the development and refinement of need-based technologies by providing continuous feedback on the field problems to the research scientists. Strong and effective interface between researchers and extension workers is ensured through monthly meetings, participation of subject matter specialists in field days and workshops and training camps. During field days and workshops, the researchers come face to face with the farmers and highlight production and protection technology to the farmers and receive the feedback on technology-related difficulties and problems for seeking solutions. Extension wing of the university also organizes monthly interactions with progressive farmers to highlight cutting-edge technologies and their adoption in the state.

To create awareness about the developed technologies and impart education about their benefits, regular workshops and training are organized for the personnel/extension workers of the Department of agriculture. Another important extension activity to disseminate new agriculture technology by the university is holding Kisan Melas (Farmers' Fairs) twice (for kharif and rabi season) at Ludhiana and six times at Regional Stations during each year. More than 5 lakh farmers visit these melas every year, where they personally see the new technologies and interact with the scientists on their economic, natural resource conservation, production and protection implications. The improved seed of newly developed varieties is also sold to the farmers in these fairs. The seed is distributed in small quantities so that a large number of farmers have access to it and develop their own seed for next year crop. Live and intimate links with the growers have paid dividends in the adoption of new technologies at the farmers' fields very quickly. The enterprising and innovative behaviour of farmers has also resulted in quick adoption of new technology.

In addition, extension education also identifies potential stakeholders, fosters partnerships, pools competence and sources from conventional and non-conventional sources to build human capital of rural men and women for their sustainable development. Literature pertaining to farm technologies is compiled and printed and sold at nominal cost to disseminate the information and educate the growers about farm recommendations. The following discussion indicates the degree of adoption of recommended package of production and protection techniques in the case of wheat crop in the Punjab state. These recommendations emerge from rigorous testing of new technologies first at experimental stations and then at farmers' fields in the form of adaptive trials. Two cases on the level of adoption of improved seeds and fertilizer use according to the university's recommendation are discussed here, which are based on a sample survey of 700 farmers in the year 2009–10.

3.7 Variety Coverage Area and Sowing Time

The Punjab Agricultural University has recommended many wheat varieties for cultivation in the State (Table 3.3). The most popular wheat varieties grown are PBW 343 and PBW 502, which occupied 64 and 14 % of the total wheat area in

Table 3.3 List of recommended varieties of wheat in Punjab

Particulars	Name of the variety	Where recommended
Timely sowing	PBW 502, PBW 343, WH 542 and TL 2908	Whole of Punjab
Late sowing	PBW 509	Whole of Punjab except sub-mountainous regions
	PBW 373, TL 1210	Whole of Punjab
Rainfed sowing	PBW 527 and PBW 175	Whole of Punjab
Durum wheat	PDW 274, PDW 291 and PDW 233	Whole of Punjab

Table 3.4 Variety-wise sowing time of wheat on sample farms in Punjab, 2009–10 (area in %)

Variety	End of October	1–15 November	16–30 November	1–15 December	After 15 December	Total	% area under variety
Recommended varieties							
Early sown varieties							
DBW 17	13.12	74.93	11.95	–	–	100.00	1.65
PBW 343	11.81	49.31	30.33	7.70	0.85	100.00	63.64
PBW 502	9.36	61.30	27.81	1.53	–	100.00	14.06
PBW 550	6.23	49.29	40.19	4.29	–	100.00	5.59
WH 542	10.33	55.30	34.37	–	–	100.00	1.86
All early sown	11.05	51.86	30.30	6.17	0.62	100.00	86.80
Late sown varieties							
PBW 373	–	–	54.33	43.97	1.70	100.00	3.39
PBW 509	–	–	45.65	28.26	26.09	100.00	0.44
All late sown	–	–	53.32	42.16	4.52	100.00	3.83
Unrecommended varieties							
HD 2733	–	81.82	18.18	–	–	100.00	0.63
HD 2687	31.94	60.35	5.51	–	–	100.00	4.36
WL 711	–	38.71	61.29	–	–	100.00	1.04
HD 2329	6.57	82.35	11.08	–	–	100.00	2.78
HD 2338	–	40.00	60.00	–	–	100.00	0.10
HD 2851	12.77	61.70	17.02	8.51	–	100.00	0.45
Vikram	–	–	100.00	–	–	100.00	0.01
All unrecommended	17.42	65.68	15.37	1.43	–	100.00	9.37
All varieties	11.22	51.17	29.79	7.10	0.71	100.00	100.00

Note The estimates are based on the sample size of 700 farms spread throughout Punjab
Source PAU (2009a)

2009–10. Around 91 % of the wheat area was under the recommended high yielding varieties of wheat while around 9 % area was under unrecommended wheat varieties (Table 3.4). These unrecommended varieties too are high yielding, developed mostly by the Indian Agricultural Research Institute (IARI) and Wheat Research Institute (WRI), Karnal but are not recommended by PAU for cultivation in the state due to their non-suitability in Punjab due to their vulnerability to diseases and pest attack. Farmers procure their seeds from private seed dealers and cultivate. Even some PAU varieties (WL 711) have also been included in the list of non-recommended varieties because over time these have become more prone to diseases.

Time of planting is another important parameter impacting the crop productivity. The normal sowing time for wheat is from 4th week of October to 4th week of November. Since rice is cultivated on a large proportion of cultivated area, which is harvested by the first week of October, plenty of time is available for timely sowing of wheat as wheat follows the rice crop in the rice–wheat crop rotation. Thus, around 63 % of wheat area was sown by the first fortnight of October, 2010. Yet, due to limited supply of surface water in southern districts of Punjab some of the wheat area (around 30 %) was planted in the second fortnight of November. Around 11 % of wheat area was planted in the first fortnight of December due to irrigation constraint and cultivation of cotton but a large proportion of this area was under late sown recommended varieties which perform equally good even under late sown conditions.

3.8 Fertilizer Application

As per recommended fertilizer dosage for wheat by PAU, 50 kg of nitrogen, 25 kg of phosphorus and 12.5 kg of potash per acre are applied. This recommendation is based on the crop requirement of different nutrients for the given productivity potential under normal soil health conditions. It is evident from Table 3.5 that the majority of farmers in the state were using higher than recommended dosage of nitrogenous fertilizers in order to realize higher productivity. While use of phosphorus was at the recommended level of 76 % of the sampled farms, about 20 % of them were applying more than the recommended dose of phosphorus on their farms.

Application of potassium K is very less in Punjab soils because its soils are rich in illite minerals supplying potash to plants and hence no application of potash on more than 96 % farms. Zinc and manganese deficiencies have also been shown in soils in the state due to monoculture of wheat–rice and high crop productivity. Yet, its application is not widely prevalent. The inefficient fertilizer application may be attributed to fertilizer subsidies being largely biased towards the nitrogenous fertilizers. More focused extension efforts are required to generate awareness among the farmers on the benefits of balanced fertilizer application in agriculture.

Table 3.5 N, P, K, Zn and Mn application on sample farms for wheat in Punjab, 2009–10 (frequency distribution in percent)

N (kg/acre)	%	P (kg/acre)	%	K (kg/acre)	%	Zinc (kg/acre)	%	Mn (kg/acre)	%
15–25	0.14	Nil	1.00	Nil	95.71	Nil	93.43	Nil	90.86
25–35	0.71	<10	0.14	5–10	0.57	0–1	1.14	1–2	5.00
35–45	2.29	10–20	2.28	10–15	2.00	1–2	0.86	2–3	2.71
45–55	15.43	20–30	76.72	15–20	0.86	2–5	0.71	3–4	0.86
55–65	38.14	30–40	15.29	20–25	–	5–10	1.14	>4	0.57
65–75	35.86	40–50	4.57	25–30	0.43	10–15	2.43	Total	100.00
75–85	6.00	Total	100.00	30–35	0.43	15–20	0.29		
>85	1.43			Total	100.00	Total	100.00		
Total	100.00								

Note The estimates are based on the sample size of 700 farms spread throughout Punjab
Source PAU (2009a)

3.9 Minimum Support Price Policy

The government intervention in foodgrain marketing in India began in a big way in the mid-1960s with a view to encourage widespread adoption of new technology based on high yielding varieties (HYVs) of wheat and rice combined with intensive use of chemical fertilizers under assured irrigation conditions resulting in a comparatively much higher productivity than before. There has been a substantial increase in the MSP (nominal terms) of wheat in the past, with the MSP of wheat increasing from Rs. 117 per quintal during 1980–81 to Rs. 1350 per quintal in 2013–14 (Table 3.6). The highest growth in the MSP was witnessed at 10.72 % per annum during 1990–2000. It owed to the politico-economic situation in the country. During 1980s (Period I), the MSP grew at 4.37 % per annum and it was higher at 6.86 % per annum during 2000–10 and even higher at 7.60 % per annum during 2000–13. The rise in MSP might not have been above the inflation rate during all the years but the extent of rise coupled with effective procurement made it the most remunerative and least risky (production and marketing risk) crop of the winter season.

The role of MSP is to ensure reasonable profits to the producer after covering his cost of production. Ideally, prices in the harvest season should hover around the minimum support prices following an increase (w.r.t. MSP) in the later period due to storage costs and time involved. The positive deviations of farm harvest prices over MSP (FHP > MSP) indicate the effectiveness of MSP for farmers, while negative

Table 3.6 Trends in minimum support price for wheat during 1980–2013 (in Rs/quintal)

Year	MSP	Year	MSP	Year	MSP
1980–81	117	1990–91	215	2000–01	580
1981–82	130	1991–92	225	2001–02	620
1982–83	142	1992–93	275	2002–03	620
1983–84	151	1993–94	330	2003–04	630
1984–85	152	1994–95	350	2004–05	640
1985–86	157	1995–96	360	2005–06	650
1986–87	162	1996–97	380	2006–07	750
1987–88	166	1997–98	475	2007–08	1000
1988–89	173	1998–99	510	2008–09	1080
1989–90	183	1999–00	550	2009–10	1100
				2010–11	1120
				2011–12	1220
				2012–13	1285
				2013–14	1350
Compound growth rate (% per annum)					
Period	CGR		Period	CGR	
1980–1990	4.89		2000–10	6.86	
1990–2000	10.72		2000–13	7.60	

Source GOI (2012)

Table 3.7 Deviations of FHP vis-à-vis MSP of wheat in Punjab state (1980–2010)

State	Period	Negative deviations		Positive deviations	
		Frequency	% difference	Frequency	% difference
Punjab	I(1980–1989)	1	0.70	8	5.00
	II(1990–1999)	0	–	10	6.00
	III(2000–2010)	2	2.39	9	4.89
	IV(1980–2010)	4	3.68	27	5.15

Freq frequency; *% difference* percentage of average positive or negative deviations over average MSP
Source Ali (2009)

deviations (FHP < MSP) reflect the prevalence of distress sale of the produce harming the producer's interest. In Punjab, the farm harvest prices of wheat ruled higher than the MSP in 27 years out of 31 years during 1980–2010 (Table 3.7). On an average, the positive difference between the FHP and MSP was 5.15 % while the negative difference was 3.64 %. These small deviations indicate that that the MSP policy for wheat was highly successful in Punjab showing that whatever produce was offered for sale in the market got purchased at MSP or little above. The farmers earned profits. These results reinforce the argument that due to large public procurement of grains, the price policy was more effective in surplus states.

3.10 Determinants of Wheat Production in Punjab

The production choices in Punjab state have undergone significant changes over time. The production of wheat has increased from 5.15 million tonnes in 1970–71 to 17.90 million tonnes in 2011–12. Both, increase in the wheat area and productivity, contributed towards this growth. The area under wheat increased from 2.30 million ha in 1970–71 to 3.51 million ha in 2011–12 and the productivity from 2238 to 5096 kg/ha during the same period. Increase in cropping intensity also helped growth in area under the crop leading to higher production (Table 3.8).

Various factors, price and non-price, are considered to be responsible for growth in yield and production of wheat. Higher relative prices of a commodity in comparison to competing crops result in the transfer of resources under that commodity. On the other hand, increase in irrigated area brings larger area under high-yielding varieties, which are more responsive to the use of chemical fertilizers and consequently, higher yield and higher production are realized. Therefore, apart from better profitability of the crop (derived from combination of price and yield), increase in irrigated area, high use of fertilizers, etc., contributed to growth in wheat production. This section tends to estimate the impact of these factors on area and productivity of wheat in the Punjab state.

For this purpose the data pertaining to the period of 1970–71 to 2011–12 was used. To work out the yield and acreage response, a simultaneous equation model

Table 3.8 Trends in wheat production and other related variables in Punjab

Year	Area ('000 ha)	Production ('000 tonnes)	Yield (kg/ha)	Fert use (kg/ha of GCA)	NIA as % of NAS	Number of electric tubewells (Lakhs)	Cropping intensity (%)
1970–71	2299	5145	2238	38	71	0.91	140
1975–76	2439	5788	2373	47	75	1.46	150
1980–81	2812	7670	2730	113	81	2.80	161
1985–86	3112	10988	3531	153	88	4.41	171
1990–91	3273	12159	3715	163	93	6.00	178
1995–96	3221	12510	3884	164	93	7.25	186
2000–01	3408	15551	4563	165	95	7.88	187
2005–06	3464	14476	4179	214	97	9.05	188
2010–11	3510	16472	4693	242	98	11.42	189
2011–12	3513	17902	5096	243	98	11.57	190

was estimated. The functional form of the simultaneous equation model is given below. The error terms are assumed to be serially independent and identically distributed in such estimation. The equations were identified and subsequently estimated by using the software STATA.

$$A_t = f(A_{t-1}, Y_{t-1}, \mathrm{FHP}g_{t-1}, \mathrm{CI})$$
$$\mathrm{CI} = f(\mathrm{Ipc}_{t)}$$
$$Y_t = f\left(\mathrm{Ipc}_t, \ F_{qt},\right)$$
$$F_{qt} = f\left(F_{pt}, \ Y_{t-1}\right)$$

where:

A_t Area under wheat ('000 ha) in year t
A_{t-1} Area under wheat ('000 ha) in year $t-1$
Y_{t-1} Yield of wheat (kg/ha) in year $t-1$
$\mathrm{FHP}g_{t-1}$ Ratio of output price (FHP) of wheat to gram (competing crop) in year $t-1$
CI_t Cropping intensity in year t
Y_t Yield of wheat (kg/ha) in year t
Ipc_t Percentage of irrigated area in year t
F_{qt} Fertilizer consumption (N + P + K in '000 nutrient tonnes) in wheat in year t
F_{pt} Ratio of price of fertilizer to price of wheat in year t.

Elasticities were calculated to examine the contribution of different factors to wheat acreage and productivity over time. The cropping intensity was found to be the most significant factor influencing acreage under wheat, which in turn was boosted by increase in irrigated area. The elasticity of wheat area with respect to cropping intensity was very high at 0.68 and that of irrigation was about 0.6

Table 3.9 Short-run elasticities of the determinants of area, productivity and related factors of wheat in Punjab

Particular	Area	Cropping intensity	Yield	Fertilizer consumption
FHP (Lag) (SR)	0.04**	–	–	–
Cropping intensity (SR)	0.68**	–	–	–
Yield (Lag) (SR)	–	–	–	1.5***
Percent irrigated area (SR)	–	0.88***	0.72*	–
Fertilizer consumption (SR)	–	–	0.43***	–
Fertilizer–output price ratio	–	–	–	−0.2*

Note The long-run elasticity of FHP (lag) was 0.15 and was significant at 5 % level. *, **, *** mean significance at 10, 5, 1 % levels, respectively

(through cropping intensity). Thus expansion in irrigation helped significantly in raising wheat production in the state through cropping intensity. The impact of price on wheat acreage was significantly positive but was much lower than non-price factors. The short-run price elasticity of wheat area was estimated to be 0.04, while that of long run was 0.15 (Table 3.9). Further, the use of fertilizers and irrigation significantly raised productivity in the state. The respective elasticity coefficients were 0.43 and 0.72. Lower fertilizer prices relative to wheat prices helped in raising fertilizer use and consequently the crop productivity. Yet, the impact of prices was lower (elasticity coefficient of 0.2) than that of irrigation.

3.11 Wheat Revolution and Small Farmers

The foregoing analysis has shown that wheat productivity and production in the state has increased substantially over time due to modern production technology including improved seeds, chemical fertilizers and irrigation complemented by agricultural marketing and price policy, institutional credit and input delivery system. The average income from wheat cultivation to the farmers also rose significantly due to increase in productivity and improvement in input use efficiency. Movements in input and output prices also reflected in the profitability. However, it is imperative to examine whether all farm categories benefitted from this revolution or small farmers' gains were smaller than those of other farmers due to structural constraints in the adoption of new technology because of their poor access to capital and other resources. There was almost no difference in the average productivity of wheat among different farm size categories in the year 2006–07. Small and medium size farms recorded 4.14 and 4.16 t/ha wheat yield while large size farms recorded 4.23 t/ha wheat yield (Table 3.10). This exhibits that technological gains in terms of wheat productivity percolated almost equally to all farm size categories. The use of modern production technology was almost similar on all farms, except the

Table 3.10 Costs and returns from wheat production in Punjab during 1981–82 and 2006–07 (Rs/ha)

Costs/returns	Category of farms		
	Small	Medium	Large
1981–82			
1. Yield (qtl/ha)	28.99	27.91	28.67
2. Gross value of output	4599	4371	4489
3. Cost of cultivation	3509	3273	2849
4. Returns to land and mgt.	1090	1098	1640
5. Cost of production (Rs/qtl)	121	117	99
2006–07			
1. Yield (qtl/ha)	41.39	41.58	42.29
2. Gross value of output	41356	40361	40453
3. Cost of cultivation	16880	17081	15836
4. Returns to land and mgt.	24476	23280	24617
5. Cost of production (Rs/qtl)	408	411	374

differences in the use of large capital equipments (combine harvesters) and labour (Table 3.11). Both sets of farm situations were maximizing their returns by employing more intensively the available resources. For instance, use of labour was high on small farms while machinery was used more intensively on medium and large farms. For other inputs there was hardly any difference. Small farmers therefore had the same level of access to new technology as other farmers had. Similar were the results on average productivity and use of inputs in wheat cultivation in the year 1981–82, which shows that the benefits of new technology were more or less equitably distributed among different farm size categories even in the year 1981–82, when green revolution was getting stabilized (Table 3.12). Yet, profits to the producers (returns to land and management) were higher on large farms as compared to small and medium farms due to size efficiency. However, the differences in profits among different categories got levelled in the year 2006–07. Small farms were using wheat straw to raise gross value of output and to optimally utilize their family labour.

The proportion of large farmers realizing productivity in the range of 4.0–4.5 t/ha was the highest at 58 % while this proportion was around 46 % in small farmers and 45 % in medium farmers in the year 2006–07. The range of highest productivity of 4.5–5.0 t/ha was recorded on medium farms, whose proportion was higher by about 5 % than on small and large farms. Yet, the highest level of productivity was witnessed on small farms though their number was very less, which shows that some small farmers realize very high levels of productivity to compensate for their small holdings (Fig. 3.4).

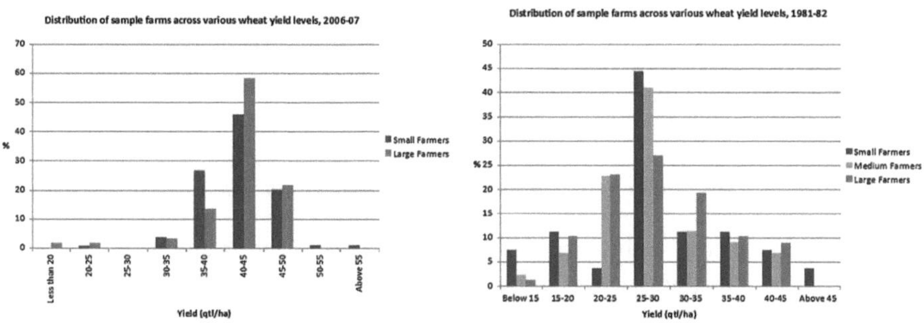

Fig. 3.4 Distribution of farmers across different levels of wheat productivity 1981–82 and 2006–07

3.12 Technical Efficiency of Wheat Across Different Farms

The concept of technical efficiency in a broad sense is used to characterize the utilization of resources on farm. The basic concept is formalized through frontier production function defined as one that maximizes output for given level of inputs. The available literature suggests that stochastic frontier model with a composed error is a more appropriate model to estimate technical efficiency in agriculture production. The technical efficiency of all farms was therefore estimated to study their relative position with respect to the most efficient farm situation(s) by employing this technique. The data set from cost of cultivation scheme for the year 2006–07 was used for measuring the technical efficiency of wheat for different farm size categories. Under this scheme, data is collected from 300 farms spread over the whole state comprising 120 farmers operating less than or equal to 2.0 ha (small farmers), 120 farmers operating area of 2.01–6.0 ha (medium farmers) and 60 farmers operating more than 6.0 ha of land (large farmers). Wheat is grown on all farms in the state. The model is given as under:

$$Y = aX_1^{b1}\, X2_2^{b2}\, X_3^{b3}\, X_4^{b4}\, X_5^{b5}\, e^E$$

where:

Y Wheat production in quintals
X_1 Human labour in man-hours
X_2 Tractor use in hours
X_3 Nitrogen use in kg
X_4 Phosphorus use in kg
X_5 Expenditure on plant protection in rupees
a Intercept
E Error term

The b_1–b_5 are the elasticity coefficients and the farm-specific error $E_i = v_i - u_i$. V_i is the symmetric component which permits random error having zero mean associated with random factors and u_i is the one-sided component, which reflects technical inefficiency relative to stochastic frontier.

$$\sigma^2 = \sigma^2 u + \sigma^2 v \text{ and variance ratio } \gamma = \sigma^2 u / \sigma^2 v$$

The γ parameter is estimated, which has value between 0 and 1, where $\gamma = 0$ implies full technical efficiency and a value close to 1 implies that one-sided error term u_i dominates the symmetric error v_i and the shortfall of realized output from the frontier is largely due to technical inefficiency. In the present paper, Frontier 4.1 computer program was used to estimate the maximum likelihood parameter of the stochastic production frontier model, and the indices of the farm-specific technical efficiency (TE) were estimated as:

$$\mathrm{TE}_i = \exp(-E[u_i/E_i]), (i = 1, 2, 3, \ldots, n) \text{ so that } \mathrm{TE}_i \text{ varies from 0 to 1.}$$

The observed variance parameters σ^2 and γ were found to be significantly different from zero, which statistically confirms the differences in technical efficiency in wheat production among different farm situations. The value of γ at 0.54 indicates that more than half of the total variation in wheat production from the frontier was attributed to technical inefficiency (Table 3.13). Therefore, the shortfall of realized output from the frontier was within the control of individual farmer. The mean TE on sample farms in wheat was estimated at 89 %, which indicates that with the given level of input use and technology, there is still 11 % unexploited potential in wheat production in the Punjab state and production can be increased to that extent without any additional input use. TE was also measured for small and other farm categories. It was seen that there were very few farms which operated at less than 80 % technical efficiency and these were almost equally distributed among small (2.53 %), medium (3.34 %) and large (3.33 %) farm categories. Around 45 % of the small holders had the realized output of more than 90 % of the frontier production while such farmers were 49 % in medium farm size category and 57 % in the large farm size category. In brief, most of the farmers in each size-category were able to reach 85–95 % of the frontier levels of productivity, reflecting that the farmers were highly efficient. The realization of higher technical efficiency can be attributed to a highly effective extension system in the state, access and use of improved inputs such as seeds, fertilizers and agrochemicals (Fig. 3.5).

3.13 Conclusion and Policy Implications

The productivity and production of foodgrains at the national level too is largely dependent upon irrigation in combination with high yielding varieties and use of fertilizers. The growth/stagnation in the production of wheat is therefore determined

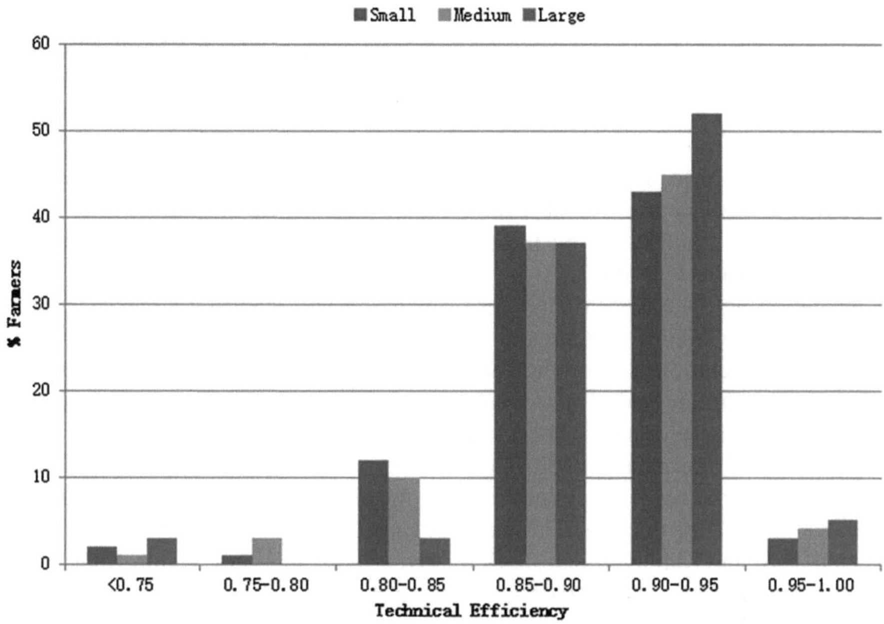

Fig. 3.5 Distribution of sample farms by technical efficiency levels, 2006–07

by the availability of irrigation water, fertilizer-responsive HYVs of crops, its price in relation with input prices and availability of credit for purchasing fertilizers and other inputs. The growth pattern of wheat output in relation to these determinants in India was similar during the last three and a half decades. The adoption of HYVs of wheat on irrigated areas along with higher use of fertilizers turned out to be the prime mover for its production. The prices of fertilizers in relation to wheat prices along with institutional credit facilitated this process. After registering significant growth in 1970s and 1980s, the growth slowed down and almost stopped after mid-1990s. When the area under irrigation stagnated due to fall in public investments in irrigation, the whole process of growth in wheat production got blunted and ultimately stagnation set in threatening the food security of the country.

The foregoing estimates on elasticities derived from the three and a half decades of experience in wheat production in India can be used to build the scenario of its 4 % growth. It is assumed that the net irrigated area grows at the rate of 1.5 % per annum, which roughly comes to one million hectare. The past data shows that 40 % of additional irrigated area goes under wheat due to its relative technology and price advantage compared to competing crops, which comes to 3.32 % increase in wheat irrigated area. Taking the elasticity of area under HYVs of wheat to irrigated area at 1.12, the increase in wheat area under HYVs will be 3.59 %. Since the elasticity of wheat production to area under HYVs is 0.73, the production is expected to increase by 2.6 % due to rise in area under HYVs. Similarly, fertilizer use is very responsive to coverage of area under HYVs, which will go up by about 4.85 % on the basis of 1.35 elasticity coefficient. Higher use of fertilizers by 5.2 % will further enhance wheat production by 1.16 %. Further, as experienced in the past, the fertilizer–wheat price ratio and institutional agricultural credit supply are assumed to be maintained at current level. Therefore, annual increase in irrigated area by one million ha will significantly push the wheat production to ensure food security of the country in the long run.

Irrigation will act as a 'trigger' for growth and will lead to a larger area under high yielding varieties and greater demand for fertilizers under the supportive institutional backup in price policy and credit. Irrigation investments therefore can bring the agriculture sector out of morass of stagnation. To start with, irrigation investments may be made in the most potential unirrigated areas, the rest of the components of the strategy will automatically start working and the agriculture sector will get the required momentum and move on to a higher growth path. The net sown area is less than 10 % in Jharkhand and less than about 30 % in Orissa and Chhattisgarh and Madhya Pradesh. Similarly, a large chunk of area in Bihar, West Bengal and eastern Uttar Pradesh is unirrigated where the scope of irrigation expansion is immense. The average productivity of wheat in these areas is less than 2 t/ha, which can be raised by irrigation. The All India Coordinated Research Project on Wheat has indicated that the difference in productivity between front-line demonstrations and farmers' fields is almost 52 %, which needs to be bridged by targeted extension activities to encourage adoption of modern technologies including high yielding seeds, fertilizers and other inputs. The policy should therefore lay emphasis on the development of irrigation potential in these areas on priority. Secondly, the already created irrigation potential must be exploited fully through the maintenance of old irrigation infrastructure. While there is a strong case for expanding the irrigation potential, it is also emphasized that the focus should also be there to improve the water use efficiency in agriculture. Apart from that, the cropping patterns should be planned as per the natural resource endowments of the regions (especially the groundwater) and should not lead to the over-exploitation of the resources in the long run. The pricing policy (not only for output but also for inputs such as electricity, irrigation water and fertilizers) should also focus to encourage the optimal water use in the scenario of enhanced irrigation potential.

Appendix

See Tables 3.11, 3.12 and 3.13.

Table 3.11 Pattern of input use in wheat production in Punjab during 2006–07

Input	Unit	Category of farms		
		Small	Medium	Large
1. Human labour	Man hours			
• Owned		118.25	73.14	51.11
• Hired		176.42	120.90	87.13
• Total		294.67	194.04	138.23
2. Animal labour	Hours	2.59	0.66	0.54
3. Tractor use	Hours			
• Owned		1.72	10.64	12.80
• Hired		13.47	5.24	2.74
• Total		15.19	15.88	15.54
4. Combine harvester use	Hours	0.64	1.09	1.39
5. Seed value	Rs	1086.96	1090.46	1038.32
6. FYM				
• Quantity	qtl	9.99	13.41	1.49
• Value	Rs	53.93	75.92	8.55
7. Fertilizer nutrients				
• N	kg	158.51	160.77	161.47
• P	kg	65.72	64.23	65.94
• K	kg	0.81	0.75	0.66
• Total value	Rs	2730.09	2729.35	2761.83
8. Insecticides and fungicides	Rs	146.67	156.41	160.91
9. Weedicides	Rs	798.58	776.06	806.53
Main product	qtl	41.39	41.58	42.29
Av. farm size	Ha	1.32	3.98	8.60
% area under wheat (%)	% of GCA	40.01	40.94	38.92

Table 3.12 Pattern of input use in wheat production in Punjab during 1981–82

Input	Unit	Category of farms		
	Per ha	Small	Medium	Large
1. Human labour	Man hours			
• Owned		319.74	236.36	137.40
• Hired		149.35	189.86	206.62
• Total		469.09	426.22	344.02
2. Animal labour	Hours	62.48	43.54	10.03
3. Tractor use	Hours			
• Owned		3.01	6.31	9.83
• Hired		1.89	1.76	0.29
• Total		4.90	8.07	10.12

(continued)

Table 3.12 (continued)

Input	Unit	Category of farms		
	Per ha	Small	Medium	Large
4. Combine harvester use	Hours	–	0.07	0.16
5. Seed				
• Quantity	kg	153.31	173.46	163.48
• Value	Rs			
6. FYM				
• Quantity	kg	6.25	9.21	2.30
• Value	Rs	6.25	11.07	2.68
7. Fertilizer nutrients				
• N	kg	102.21	108.09	105.95
• P	kg	48.11	45.94	47.85
• K	kg	5.66	8.26	8.05
• NPK	kg	150.32	162.29	161.85
• Total value	Rs	1089.04	868.05	872.13
8. Insecticides and fungicides	Rs	19.07	43.75	92.02
9. Weedicides	Rs	1092.25	931.02	773.33
10. Main product	Qtl	28.99	27.91	28.67
11. Average farm size	Ha	2.20	4.69	10.48
12. % area under wheat	% of NAS	70.00	76.33	71.56

Table 3.13 Maximum likelihood estimates of stochastic frontier production function for wheat in Punjab, 2006–07

Particular	Coefficient	Standard-error	*t*-ratio
Intercept	−0.6686	0.1240	−5.3926
Human labour (hours)	0.0413	0.0189	2.1877
Tractor labour (hours)	0.1689	0.0405	4.1749
N-kg	0.6138	0.0430	14.2806
P-kg	0.1593	0.0219	7.2790
Chemicals (Rs)	0.0100	0.0082	1.2289
σ^2	0.0405	0.0073	5.5519
γ	0.5444	0.1530	3.5569
Log-likelihood function	118.1320		

Note All values are significant at 5 % level. Log-likelihood is significant at 10 % level

References

Ali SZ (2009) Effectiveness of price policy for foodgrains in India with special reference to Punjab State. Unpublished thesis. Punjab Agricultural University, Ludhiana

Chand R (2005) Exploring possibilities of achieving four percent growth rate in Indian agriculture. Working paper, National Centre for Agricultural Economics and Policy Research. New Delhi

GOI (2012) Agricultural statistics at a glance. Ministry of Agriculture, Government of India, New Delhi

PAU (2009a) Prospects of wheat crop: 2009–10. Department of Economics and Sociology, PAU, Ludhiana

PAU (2009b) Status report on PAU. Punjab Agricultural University, Ludhiana

Sidhu RS, Gill SS (2006) Agricultural credit and indebtedness in India: some issues, keynote paper. Indian J Agric Econ 61:11–35

Sidhu RS, Bhullar AS, Joshi AS (2005) Income, employment and productivity growth in the farming sector of Punjab: some issues. J Indian Sch Polit Econ 17:59–72

Chapter 4
Rethinking Diversification of Agriculture in the Indian Punjab: An Examination of Strategy and Mechanisms

Sukhpal Singh

4.1 Introduction

The issues of agricultural or crop diversification and specialization have attracted attention of researchers over the last decade in the context of South Asian region including Punjab—both the Indian and the Pakistan (Kurosaki 2003; Singh 2004; Akanda 2010; Shergill 2013). Given the climatic factors, resource constraints especially water, changing food habits, and policy and economic environment, it is expected that more diversified cropping patterns are needed and they will be more sustainable (Akanda 2010; Sidhu and Vatta n.d.).

The concept of diversification has been defined differently in the literature. It can include the following: (a) a shift of resources from farm to non-farm activities; (b) use of resources in a larger mix of diverse and complimentary activities within agriculture; (c) a movement of resources from low-value agriculture to high-value agriculture (Sharma and Singh 2013); and (d) a change in the mix of crops in a season or year growing more number of crops per unit area of land. The link between agricultural diversification and long-term structural change in the economy occurs mainly because diversification is a bridge between the declining income opportunities from growing food crops and an exit from agriculture altogether (Ahmad and Isvilanonda 2003).

Diversification could also be of livelihoods or occupational involving two usually related components: (1) multiplicity, i.e. multiple livelihoods (jobs, incomes, etc.) requiring several part-time and concurrent activities and (2) change, transformation or adaptation: usually from an essentially subsistence agricultural sector to non-subsistence, non-agricultural sectors, part of which could be the rural non-farm economy (Start n.d.). The benefits of farm diversification include high and more stable

S. Singh (✉)
Centre for Management of Agriculture, Indian Institute of Management, Vastrapur, Ahmedabad 380015, India
e-mail: sukhpal@iimahd.ernet.in

L. Singh and N. Singh (eds.), *Economic Transformation of a Developing Economy*, India Studies in Business and Economics,
DOI 10.1007/978-981-10-0197-0_4

farm incomes and employments, greater long-term prospectus for farm income growth and more environmentally sustainable farming system. The simplest interpretation of farm diversification is that farmers seek to generate a portfolio of income from activities with different degrees of risk, expected returns, liquidity and seasonality and adjust their output mix accordingly. Farm diversification is different from village-level diversification where households become more specialized overtime, but village economy offer a wide range of goods and services for sale under commercialized rural economic development process (Delgado and Siamwalla 1997).

This chapter examines the logic of diversification, its rationalization in the state agricultural programmes and policy (first agricultural policy of the state) in Sect. 4.2 and mechanisms identified and used to bring about diversification in Sect. 4.3. Section 4.4 discusses the way forward in terms of reorientation of policy and institutions to move towards achieving more sustainable farm and rural sector from a livelihood perspective as a strategy, and Sect. 4.5 concludes the paper.

4.2 Strategy for Diversification: What and Why

Punjab's farm sector which was known for its crop diversity until the Green Revolution (GR) is today completely dominated by wheat in *Rabi* (accounting for 86 % of *Rabi* area with 2 % for potato and 12 % for other crops) and paddy in *Kharif* (accounting for 63 % of *kharif* area with cotton another 14 % and other crops 23 %). Wheat and paddy account for almost 80 % of gross cropped area (GCA) and 85 % of the gross value of crop output (Sidhu and Vatta n.d.). Further, cereal crops account for 95 % of cropped area and within that wheat and paddy account for 55 and 42 %, respectively (Sodhi and Singh 2013). Therefore, there is no doubt that crop diversity in Punjab has declined over the years and across regions (Singh and Sidhu 2004).

The Johl Committee report on diversification of Punjab agriculture (1986) recommended that at least 20 % of the area under wheat and paddy should be brought under new crops such as oilseeds, pulses and fruits and vegetables which accounted for only less than 2 % of the GCA at that time as they were not, like many other crops, competitive with wheat or paddy in terms of their relative profitability. It was thus realized that the economic condition of a vast majority of farmers, especially marginal and small, could not be improved unless there were changes in the cropping pattern and the technology of production. Diversification, intended to stabilize incomes and employment in the farming sector, could either be in terms of variety of crops grown or technologies used. The processing and marketing activities were necessary to bring dynamism to the agricultural sector by way of either reduction in cost of cultivation through productivity improvement or cutting costs directly, or raising returns to the producers by value addition or diversification.

It is only an irony that the Johl Committee had to recommend as strategy for diversification in 2002 what it had recommended 15 years ago (in 1986) for the first time. Despite these reports and many attempts at diversification, the state's farm sector is yet to see any perceptible change. The diversification strategy suggested by the second Johl Committee report was that one million hectares of paddy and wheat cultivation should be replaced with high-value crops such as oilseeds and pulses. It proposed a crop adjustment programme (CAP) to compensate farmers who were willing to make the switch. This amount came to Rs. 12,800 million which was less than the cost incurred on procuring and storing 8 million tonnes of paddy/rice and wheat, i.e. Rs. 70,000 million for procurement and Rs. 20,000 million for handling storage and transport including wastage.

After the first Johl Committee report (1986), there was not much academic analysis of the farming crisis in the state except a seminal paper by Gill (1988) which examined the contradictions of Punjab model of growth and attempted alternatives to it. The second Johl Committee report (2002) evoked more academic analysis of policy and mechanisms in the form of papers by Sidhu (2002) and Singh (2002). That was followed by some more research such as Singh (2004) and Shergill (2007), the latter opposing crop diversification. More recently, there has been some more policy analysis, i.e. Singh (2012) and Shergill (2013), the latter once again reasoning why paddy area will not reduce.

4.2.1 Diagnosis and Diversification

The Committee for Formulation of Agricultural Policy for Punjab State submitted its draft report to the state government which was published by the State Farmers Commission in March 2013. This report was accepted soon after and is being implemented since 2013–14. The policy report documents the performance of the farm sector in the state, identifies the challenges and sets policy objectives and measures and strategies to achieve them. It has chapters on the crop sector, livestock sector and the institutional framework besides an introduction and a summary of recommendations.

The policy document recognizes the emerging food grain production in other states, especially of paddy, and, therefore, underlines the need to move away from paddy not only for the reasons of natural resource conservation but also for demand-side changes. Therefore, the challenge identified is to sustain farmer incomes without degrading natural resources such as soil and water and still produce for the market, such crops and products which are in demand and remunerative. It identifies the aims of the policy as addressing various interlinked concerns of sustainability of the current cropping pattern and stagnating farm incomes through a simultaneous and multi-pronged action with an emphasis on the improvement in production technology and infrastructure pushing up capital formation, restructuring incentives and streamlining the institutions to achieve a long-term growth rate of 3 % in the primary sector (farming and dairying).

The policy report talks of tenancy laws and the size of landholding constraint forgetting that Punjab has the largest size of operated holding in India (4 h against 1 h in India). It fails to recognize that it is not the size of land but what you do on it which matters—small can be prosperous and there are millions of such small and prosperous farmers in India. It recognizes the poor state of small farmers, but does not say anything specific about them in recommendations. Rather, it talks of promoting corporate dairy farms (large) which is already happening due to the Punjab government policy. That trend in policy is not good for small farmers as there will be exclusion of small dairy farmers even from (cooperative) dairy sector.

The policy still is focused on yield enhancement even in new crops, citing yield gaps, but market orientation which is much needed is lacking though it talks of demand-driven agriculture. It views diversification in terms of new crops being grown using old ways which are not desirable. The policy document recommends intercropping only in agroforestry. Why intercropping is not possible in mainstream crops is not explained. Further, the most important production risk management strategy—crop insurance—is not even mentioned. The report forgets to recognize that the two pressing problems of farmers are production risk and market risk.

The policy paper recognizes the need for diversification within the crop sector, shifting of area from paddy to other crops, such as maize. But, if one is also worried about crop diversity for other than groundwater reasons, and for enhancing income of farmers, then wheat also becomes a candidate for diversification though policy does not target it at all. Further, summer crops take only less than 5 % of the summer area which is surprising in a state like Punjab which can easily take third crop. Additionally, rice–wheat cycle takes place on 54 % of area and cotton–wheat on another 12 % area. A good 20 % area is put to other crops—wheat cycle (Bal et al. n.d.). Pearl millet and many vegetables easily fit into summer cropping cycle and maize and vegetables as alternative to wheat in Rabi.

In fact, the policy needs to go beyond crop diversification. There is a need to diversify the entire rural economy as most of the rural population and workers are still dependent (directly or indirectly) on agriculture and allied agricultural activities. Diversification of entire rural economy would entail: (i) shifting of surplus workforce in agriculture and allied agricultural activities to non-agricultural activities, (ii) development of rural non-farm sectors, which in turn would require (iii) integration of agricultural and rural planning with overall economic planning (Ghuman 2013).

The policy paper has very conveniently ignored the issue of power subsidy to agriculture. The crop diversification (as being emphasized in the policy paper), depleting water table and free electricity to the farm sector, does not go well with each other. The free electricity to the farm sector goes against the argument for crop diversification. If other measures were taken, perhaps paddy would not be grown as much as it is. But, why shy away from measures like systems of root intensification (SRI) or microirrigation systems (MIS) to save water and cut cost of production which are gaining ground everywhere? In fact, many states and agencies in India are now looking at SRI across crops and enterprises. It misses many upcoming and innovative methods and technologies on water saving like *khettalavadis* (farm ponds) and does not learn from other states such as Andhra Pradesh or Gujarat which have special purpose vehicles (SPVs) or projects for promotion of MIS. The policy document is still shy of sustainable agricultural practices like organic and

mentions lack of organic matter as the reason for not recommending organic practices. This, despite the fact that a private agency has been helping the state in going organic for the last many years and there is a organic farming council existing as a special purpose vehicle (SPV) since the mid-2000s.

Another argument made is that paddy and wheat crops have the lowest yield risk and market/price risk, but it is a case of low-level equilibrium in terms of net returns. Should one continue farming paddy as it is less risky—both in production and marketing?

Interestingly, the policy talks of the need and plans for diversification but does not touch upon the previous experience of this strategy and why it failed during 2002–2007 and how it will be done differently now. The last attempt at diversification (2002–2007) could not go beyond 0.25 million hectares against a target of diversion of 1 million hectares from that under paddy despite all kinds of perverse incentives and schemes. Now, the target is 12 million hectares diversion away from paddy without any specific mechanisms. It still asks for assured markets and prices for new crops which may not be possible and may not be sustainable. That is the minimum support price (MSP) culture. It has been well established that the present wheat–paddy system has been mainly the outcome of the GR and the MSP regimes. The policy paper, while suggesting alternative crops, emphasizes the system of remunerative MSP for alternative crops. It does not take into account the changing national scenario rapidly heading towards market-driven economy, including agriculture. The emerging contradictions between market-determined prices and the administered prices (such as MSP) need to be taken care of by any agricultural policy in the presence of changing position of Punjab in India's food provision especially rice and wheat and the multiple stakeholders and considerations in determination of MSP (Ghuman 2013). The MSP and procurement already exist for many alternative crops, but how can it be done for perishables, especially procurement, without which MSP has little meaning?

The policy proposes tripling of area under sugarcane but without any reference to the functioning of the sugar mills—cooperative and private—in the state and assessment of their competitiveness and performance especially when the sugar sector is likely to be decontrolled. Maize area is targeted to be increased four times of the existing area without any assessment of its demand and mechanisms of procurement. Surprisingly, potato—a very important and well-established crop with plenty of state support including a Potato Development Board, and infrastructure in place like cold storages and processing units, is not even mentioned in the new crop plan other than seed potato. Similarly, barley is missing from the list of new crops though in practice, it is a major crop for diversification of cropping pattern. Other than small area under groundnut in a couple of districts proposed by the policy document, the oilseeds, including sunflower, are completely missing from the list of crops proposed for diversification and no explanations are given for this bias.

The policy is still in traditional farmer cooperative mode and not even aware of producer companies (PCs) provision and other institutions such as Joint Liability Groups (JLGs), Multi-State Co-operative Societies (MSCS) which can be set up at local level with plenty of support from the Union government institutions like Small

Farmer Agribusiness Consortium (SFAC) or National Bank for Agriculture and Rural Development (NABARD). Similarly, SFAC has launched many programmes to promote farmer producer organizations (FPOs) which are essentially PCs. In the 2013–14 Union budget, SFAC has been provided Rs. 500 million to provide matching equity grants to registered PCs up to a maximum of Rs. 10 lakh per PC to enable them to leverage working capital from financial institutions. It has also been allocated Rs. 1000 million for credit guarantee fund for PCs (SFAC 2013). Besides this, SFAC is also procuring pulses at MSP from various producer agencies and has replaced National Co-operative Agricultural Marketing Federation (NAFED) for this role.

On promoting more affordable farm mechanization, it sticks to only agroservice centres for machinery, managed largely by Primary Agricultural Co-operative Societies (PACS). What about PCs, Self Help Groups (SHGs), agribusiness centres and private entrepreneurs like *Zamindara* Farm Solutions, with the latter already doing a good job in this field and promoting co-ownership model? It talks only of farmer income and not of landless labour and recommends mechanization which can hit the labour interest hard. The large subsidies given on paddy transplanters and other equipment in the recent past are not even mentioned. For example, action plan for diversification provides 75 % subsidy on mechanical cane harvesters costing more than Rs. 10 million each. On the other hands, small cotton-picking machines which can increase efficiency or reduce labour drudgery are not even mentioned in the action plan. Today, even value chains talk of labour interest for sustainability. Then, how can a state policy on a sector ignore farm and allied labour interest? The mechanization needed is one which provides for proactive and creative involvement of workers, not their displacement. Is it that farmers continue with paddy and wheat as it sustains combine harvesters which are used more for custom hiring in other states? Is there a political economy to supporting mechanization in the name of the average farmer? Earlier, under the agricultural marketing infrastructure (AMI) scheme of the Union government, 92 % of the projects sanctioned and 66 % of the subsidy sanctioned were for combine harvesters alone. Further, four districts accounted for 60 % of these subsidies. Due to this bias, the combine harvesters were removed from the scheme in 2006 (Singh 2012a).

In agricultural extension which is central to any diversification attempt, no new models are proposed. There are public–private partnerships (PPPs) and franchise models in operation in India which should have been studied for their value and relevance while planning for high-value crops. Just relying on existing public extension mechanisms may not do. The policy proposes the creation of an agricultural research development fund by charging a cess from farmers at the time of sale of their produce. If so far, the largest gainers from agricultural business/trading have been non-farmers, i.e. traders and processors, why should not the technology fund/cess be charged from buyers and *arthiyas* instead of farmers? This is suggested as farmers are in dire crisis already, whereas other stakeholders are doing well and should not mind paying it. If farmers are being asked to fund their own technology development, why support other sectors with public funds?

The policy recommends in great detail the promotion of dairy sector as a diversification of income strategy since it is growing well, but asks for milk price stabilization fund. If that is the state of affairs in the cooperative dairy sector after a few decades of its existence, and in the presence of MNCs in the milk sector, then where is the sustainability of the sector? Demand-driven agriculture should be investment based, not subsidy based.

Though the state has seen contract farming (CF) practice for 20 years, the APMC Act has still not been amended. But, the state government has already passed the Regulation of Contract Farming Act, 2013. That leaves out two important aspects of APMC reform—direct purchase and private wholesale markets. The report should have examined the said contract farming Act and the experience of CF in the state in various forms for the last two decades to make specific suggestions to leverage CF for demand-driven diversification. Similarly, it recommends *Apnimandis* (farmers' markets) but does not mention or analyse why they did not work in the past as Punjab was the pioneer in this innovation. The recently politically proposed and advocated denotification of perishable produce from the APMC Act is also not discussed at all and is being attempted without a thought to leverage it for incentivizing CF and direct purchase. Untargeted waivers are no good.

It was also recognized quite early that it was important to move farmers with investible surpluses from the GR period to the industrial sector. But, that has never been attempted. On the other hand, private agribusiness firms have been thought to be harbingers of change since the late 1980s. There are also doubts being raised whether the state (provincial) is serious about diversification given its back and forth and contradictory policies on the agricultural sector over the years (Shergill 2013).

4.2.2 The New Diversification Agenda

Punjab government plans to reduce area under paddy by about 1.2 million hectares from 2.8 million hectares to 1.6 million hectares during next five years because of excessive exploitation of natural resources including groundwater depletion and depleting soil fertility due to paddy sowing. It has proposed to shift this area to maize (0.4 million hectare), cotton and Basmati paddy (0.2 million hectares each), sugarcane (0.26 million hectares), agroforestry (0.14 million hectares), pulses (0.05 million hectares) and fruits and vegetables (0.08 million hectares). For 2013–14, it has planned to shift paddy area towards maize (40,000 ha), cotton (50,000 ha), Basmati (50,000 ha), pulses (10,000 ha) and sugarcane (17,000 ha), totalling 1.67 lakh hectares. Basmati paddy buyers have been exempted from payment of market fee (2 %), rural development cess (2 %) and infrastructure cess (3 %), reducing their purchase costs by half. Financial assistance of Rs 10,000 per hectare is provided to farmers for seeds, insecticides and other inputs with Union government provided funds for diversification accounting for 30 % of total expenditure in the annual diversification plan. The state government has approved Rs. 1980 million for setting up of a Center of Excellence under the Crop Diversification Program to carry out the research work at the Punjab Agricultural University in a phased manner during the next five years. Furthermore, one litchi estate will be established at Pathankot and one pear estate at Amritsar at a cost of Rs. 38 million each besides establishing subestate for litchi at Gurdaspur. Punjab Agricultural Marketing Board will set up 20 big dryers across the state at a cost of Rs. 1600 million to facilitate the farmers in getting remunerative price of their produce.

The Union government has also stepped in with additional funds of Rs. 2240.5 million for the state as part of its Rs. 5000 million crop diversification plan in original GR states (of Punjab, Haryana and West UP) under Rashtriya Krishi Vikas Yojana (RKVY) during 2013–14 (Table 4.1). The activities under the Union diversification plan include alternate crop demonstrations, farm mechanisation and value addition, site-specific activities, awareness training and incentives for effective implementation (Table 4.2). There are specific tasks at farmer level which can be supported from this funding (Table 4.3). But, unfortunately, even the Union scheme does not provide any funds for facilitating marketing of new crop produce.

The alternate crops proposed are direct-seeded Basmati, cluster bean, *kharif* pulses (green gram, black gram and pigeon pea), oil seeds and maize. Cluster demonstration units (one unit = 10 ha) of identified alternate crops in each district will be organized through identified beneficiary groups by State Department of Agriculture (SDA). One progressive farmer will be designated as group leader for organization of cluster demonstration. Honorarium of Rs. 2000 per cluster demonstration of 10 h is provided on one-time basis for organization of cluster demonstration. Assistance át the rate of Rs. 10,000 per hectares for maize, *kharif* pulses (*arhar, mung* bean, *urd* bean, cluster bean) and oilseeds (soya bean, *til*) and Rs. 10,000 per hectares for poplar-based agroforestry system for sole crop is provided. The financial assistance of Rs. 10,000 per hectares, except poplar-based agroforestry system, is given in the form of Rs. 5000 for critical inputs including honorarium and other activities, Rs. 2500 for land development and Rs. 2500 for marketing support. An amount of Rs. 5000 per hectares for intercropping of pulses and wheat is provided to the farmers, in terms of critical inputs, for organization of demonstrations. The District Programme Management Group (PMG) is responsible for arrangement of critical inputs for organizing cluster demonstrations. All critical

Table 4.1 Distribution of paddy area for diversification across states

State	No. of districts	Total paddy area ('000' ha, 2011–12)	% share of respective state of paddy area to all three states' paddy area	Targeted area of paddy for diversion ('000' ha)
Punjab	20	2759.20	50.25	140.00
Haryana	10	1194.00	21.75	60.00
West UP	15	1537.20	28.00	80.00
All	45	5490.40	100.00	280.00

Source GoI (2013)

Table 4.2 State-wise and activity-wise allocation of funds for crop diversification across states during 2013–14

S. No	State	% share of respective state to total rise area of all three states	Allocation of funds (Rs. million)					
			Alternate crops demonstrations (60 %)	Farm mechanization and value addition (23 %)	Site-specific activities (15 %)	Contingency for awareness training, implementation and monitoring (2 %)	Incentives for implementation of programme (10 %)	Total
1	Punjab	50.25	1347.0	516.3	336.7	45.0	0	2245.0
2	Haryana	21.75	591.0	226.5	147.7	19.8	0	985.0
3	West UP	28.00	753.0	288.6	188.2	25.2	0	1255.0
4	National level		0	0	0	15.0	0	15.0
State total		100.00	2691.0	1031.4	672.6	105.0	0	4500.0
National level		0	0	0	0	0	500.0[a]	500.0
Grand total		100	2691.0	1031.4	672.6	105.0	500.0	5000.0

[a]The amount is earmarked as incentive which will be disbursed to any state depending on the performance against the indicators developed by NCAP irrespective of their entitled allocation

Source GoI (2013)

Table 4.3 Crop and component-specific pattern of assistance (Rs./ha)

S. No	Components	Crops/systems	
		Maize, *kharif* pulses *(arhar, mung* bean, *urd* bean, cluster bean), oilseeds (soya bean, *til*)	Poplar-based agroforestry system (sole)
A	Cost of critical inputs (seeds, micronutrients, seed treating chemical and PP chemical)	4500	7500
	Production technology and publicity materials	150	150
	Honorarium and mobility to group leader of cluster demonstration	200	200
	Visit of GOI/state officials for hiring of vehicle or POL	150	150
	Subtotal	5000	10,000
B	Land development charges[a]	2500	–
C	Marketing support (store bin, etc.)[b]	2500	–
D	Intercrops with poplar (critical inputs)	–	5000
	Grand total	10,000	15,000

[a, b]Land development charge and marketing will be paid to the farmers in cash to support the losses incurred due to diversion of area from paddy to alternate crops
Source GoI (2013)

inputs are ensured by the SDA well in advance before the sowing/transplanting of the crops. State will decide crop-specific cluster demonstrations as per the availability of quality seeds of identified alternate crops.

23 % of total state allocation is earmarked for farm machinery, processing and value addition activities. The crop-specific farm machinery is provided to the farming groups (of 10 farmers each) on custom hiring basis. An assistance át the rate of 50 % cost of machine limiting to Rs. 25,000 for maize sheller, Rs. 0.5 million for portable maize dryer, Rs. 3000 for powered sprayer, Rs. 25,000 for multi-crop thresher, Rs. 0.2 million for portable cleaner-cum-grader for pulses and Rs. 1 million for maize processing unit is made available. 15 % of total state allocation is earmarked for site-specific activities which are to a part of the action plan submitted by the state. 10 % of total state allocation is earmarked and kept at Union Ministry of Agriculture level for incentive to the state governments for implementation of the programme of diversion of paddy area to alternate crops as per target fixed. This amount is released separately after monitoring and evaluation of the programme by designated agency.

State Department of Agriculture is mandated to organize awareness trainings for farmers for diversification of paddy to other alternate crops for additional income generation, restoration of soil fertility, agroprocessing and value addition of crop produce to make farming as a profitable enterprise. The SDA is also required to develop training material with the help of other line departments like Forest and

State Agricultural Universities (SAUs). Assistance át the rate of 50 % Rs. 5000 for a group of 50 beneficiary farmers for cluster demonstration is provided for awareness training program. 2 % of the total state allocation is earmarked for awareness trainings, implementation and monitoring of the programme out of which an amount of Rs. 0.2 million for state level and Rs. 0.2 million per district is provisioned for publicity, organization of review meetings, implementation and monitoring visits, contingencies, etc. (GoI 2013).

4.3 Mechanisms Planned and Used (The How) and Performance

The contract farming arrangement with the growers by the private domestic and multinational agribusiness interests has been central to all the diversification reports and attempts since the Johl Committee Report (1986) and was to achieve both the objectives of cost reduction and value addition by providing farmers better seeds and other inputs, and better markets and prices (Singh 2002, 2004). The increasing cost of cultivation was the reason for the appearance of CF in villages of Japan and Spain also during the 1950s (Singh 2004).

The percentage share of contract farmed area in total in 2002–03 was merely 0.12 %. It increased to 0.96 % in 2003–04 and 1.2 % in 2004–05. The area under CF remained almost same, hovering around 1 % during 2004–05 to 2008–09 and declined to 0.97 % in 2009–10 (Table 4.4). The extent of contract farmed area shows that CF as scheme has not done much to change the scenario of agricultural sector of the state. Thus, during 2002–03, the actual area under CF as against targeted was only 5.6 % with some crops reaching 100 % or 2/3 but others only 10–20 % each of the respective targets. But, by 2009–10 when targets were lowered instead of raising them, the actual achieved area under CF reached 71.5 % of targeted but no crop achieved more than 60 % with the exception of Basmati paddy (Table 4.5). In 2002–03, out of 13 crops targeted, CF was undertaken only in

Table 4.4 Extent and share of contract farming in Punjab (area in 000 ha)

Year	Area under CF	GCA	% share of CF
2002–03	09	7826	0.12
2003–04	76	7905	0.96
2004–05	99	7932	1.2
2005–06	87	7868	1.1
2006–07	96	7861	1.2
2007–08	96	7870	1.2
2008–09	94	7912	1.2
2009–10	76	7900	0.97
2010–11	34	7900	0.4
2011–12	4.8	7900	0.06

Source Sharma and Singh (2013); PAFC website

Table 4.5 Target area and actual area under contract farming in Punjab (area in hectare)

Year	2002–03			2009–10			2010–11
Crop	Targeted area	Actual area	Actual as % of target	Targeted area	Actual area	Actual as % of target	Targeted area
Hyola	30,000	3919.20	13.06	24,281	7412	30.5	–
Barley	2000	328	16.40	6070	3315	54.6	6070
Winter maize	1200	1261.20	105.10	–	–	–	–
Durum wheat	40,000	–	–	–	–	–	–
Sunflower	5000	3416.40	68.63	–	–	–	–
Spring corn	2000	–	–	16,188	9710	59.9	–
Basmati	10,000	–	–	24,281	30,317	124.8	–
Kharif corn	60,000	–	–	40,469	23,705	58.6	–
Guar gum	2000	–	–	–	–	–	–
Castor	2000	–	–	–	–	–	–
Groundnut	400	–	–	–	–	–	–
Organic Basmati	400	–	–	–	–	–	–
Vegetables	800	–	–	–	1122	–	–
Others	4200	–	–	–	4062	–	–
Total	160,000	8924.80	5.58	111,287	79,643	71.5	6070

Source Sharma and Singh (2013)

4 crops. Moreover, actual area for CF in three crops was very low as compared to the targeted area, i.e. in *hyola,* it was 13.06 % of the targeted area, barley 16.4 % and sunflower 68.63 %, but in maize actual area was more than the targeted area, i.e. 105.10 %. In later years, very few crops were selected for CF namely Hyola, barley, spring corn, Basmati and *Kharif* corn. Actual area under CF for these crops was very low as compared to the targeted area with the exception of Basmati. However, in 2010–11, only barley was selected to be undertaken for CF which again points to the poor performance of the CF scheme. It is worth mentioning here that initially many companies operated through PAFC (indirect CF), but by 2012, only one company was involved in indirect CF, i.e. United Breweries. As per the information from PAFC, the major driving force for the companies to do indirect CF was the concession given by the Punjab State Agricultural Marketing Board in market fee (0.25 % instead of 2 %) and Rural Development Cess (0.25 % instead of 2 %). Thus, aggregate reduction of 3.5 % made the procurement of agricultural produce very attractive for the processors. But this concession was later withdrawn by the Government of Punjab. Therefore, either companies had quit CF or were involved in direct CF. After that, the programme was shelved until recently when it has been revived with new targets and mechanisms under a new agricultural policy.

Table 4.6 Area of different crops under contract farming in Punjab during the second phase of diversification (area in acres)

Year	Crop							
	Hyola	Barley	Durum wheat	Basmati	Maize	Mint	Potato seed	Total
2007–08	33,812	7550	–	84,034	113,513	–	–	228,279
2008–09	35,324	6220	–	84,016	107,530	1121	–	234,211
2009–10	18,315	8192	–	74,914	82,750	1122	4062	189,175
2010–11	–	7627	1500	70,806	–	635	4178	84,746
2011–12	–	11,961	–	–	–	–	–	11,961

Source PAFC Website

The targets were lowered in the second phase, and the achievements thus seem higher in % age terms, but are very low in absolute terms (Tables 4.5 and 4.6).

In April 2013, the Punjab assembly enacted the Punjab Contract Farming Act, 2013. It should be noted that Punjab has still not amended the APMC Act despite the fact that it was the first state to undertake and promote CF in the 1990s and then during the last decade for bringing about diversification in the crop sector. Direct purchase from farmers and setting up of private wholesale markets to give choice to farmers to sell wherever and whoever they would like to are two major aspects of the model APMC Act besides the legalization of CF. The CF Act of Punjab deals only with CF, and the other two reforms are still pending as they are to do with amendment of the APMC Act though CF also did not need a separate legislation as many other states, including neighbouring Haryana, have legalised CF by amending the APMC Act. Therefore, it is important to understand why Punjab took the route of a separate legislation on this aspect instead of doing all the required reforms in the APMC Act and the implications of this Act for various stakeholders. The major reason for Punjab going for a separate Act on CF can be found in the political economy of the state's agribusiness sector wherein the farming and the trading interests are at loggerheads in protecting their interests. There has been a constant battle on direct payments to farmers for their produce by buying agencies between the two lobbies, and the issue has been hanging fire since over a decade now. Whereas the farmer lobby would like to have direct payments, the *arthiya* (Commission Agent) lobby opposes it tooth and nail. This is so as direct payments hit the business of interlocking of credit, input and output markets run by *arthiyas* where a *parchi* (slip) system prevails for lending in kind to farmers and recovery of payments at the time of sale of produce. The direct purchase (when permitted with the APMC Act amendment) will reduce volumes in APMC *mandis,* and therefore, *arthiyas'* and traders' hold on farmer produce and the private wholesale markets (again under APMC Act amendment) will create competition for *arthiyas*/traders operating from APMC *mandis* and the *Mandi* Board itself. This is perhaps the reason that instead of amending the APMC Act which would involve allowing direct purchase and setting up of private wholesale markets and, therefore, upset the applecart of the *arthiyas* and the *Mandi* Board itself, the separate Act route has been taken.

Under the new CF Act, the state government will declare control over purchase, sale, storage and processing of agricultural produce to be covered under CF. The buyer has to register with the local registering authority by paying a fee as specified in the by-laws. A company as per the Act means public limited company under the Companies Act. Duration of contract can be one crop season to three years, and 108 crops are notified under the Act. The buyer will have to submit reports of the contract transactions to the registering authority as well as the Commission.

Contract farmed produce can be sold in the APMC market, or at the farm itself or as specified in the agreement. The net weight of the packing unit has to be as per APMC Act and the buyer will have to make arrangements for packing and weighing of the produce in advance of delivery and give a receipt to the farmer as proof of delivery of produce. There can be no rejection of produce after delivery to buyer. Payment will be made by cheque/demand draft or electronic clearing system (ECS) on the spot at the time of delivery, otherwise with interest for delay up to 30 days, failing which the Contract Farming Commission can recover it as land revenue with interest. If there is a deliberate delay by the buyer in payment, produce bought by the contract farming agency can be seized by the Commission. Crop loss or damage will be recovered from the buyer if it supplied inputs and extension as per Commission's decision. Only temporary structures on farmer land for the duration of the contract can be put up by the buyer, and if not removed immediately after the expiry of the contract duration, it will become property of the producer. No recoveries of any dues or penalties can be made from the producer by way of sale or mortgage of his/her contracted land. This provision is in line with the Model APMC Act and removes the perceived fears about contracting companies staking claims on contract growers' land.

The district collector will be responsible for CF dispute resolution and give decision within 30 days, and no civil court can entertain such cases. Decisions of the Commission will be like a decree of a court. A contracting party can appeal after payment of 50 % of dues of disputed amount. Buyers can be fined up to one month in prison and/or Rs. 0.1–1 million for a violation of the Act and át the rate of 50 % Rs. 500 per day for violation of first conviction, and the farmer is liable for one month jail and/or Rs. 5000 fine for violation of the Act and át the rate of 50 % Rs. 100 per day for violation of first conviction.

It is interesting to note that the provisions of the Act are very different from the provisions for CF in APMC Acts of other states. For example, Gujarat or Haryana amended APMC Acts have bank guarantees from buyers/contracting agencies (5–15 % of the value of the contracted produce, respectively, in the two states) to protect farmer interest in case of company/buyer default. The Haryana APMC Act even prescribes that, wherever applicable, the contract price will not be lower than the MSP of the crop. In Gujarat, only processors and exporters are eligible to purchase the commodity from the farmer grown under CF. The Gujarat APMC Act also specifies that market fee will not be charged more than once for a given produce within the state and it will be 50 % of the normal for contracting agencies and nil in tribal areas of the state for CF agencies. The Gujarat Act also allows contracts for up to 5 years and even beyond with mutual agreement. In both the states, the State Agricultural Marketing Board is the arbitrator for CF disputes.

There are many missing elements in the Punjab Act. The state is promoting agroforestry as part of its diversification plan but how can three year contracts work in agroforestry? Surprisingly, the Act notified crops also include *gur*, *shakkar* and *khandsari* which are never contract produced generally as they are value-added products from sugarcane. Another important crop being contract produced in the state, baby corn, is missing from the list, as is garlic.

4.3.1 Mechanism of Diversification (Contract Farming) and Issues

Though CF is an important mechanism for diversification, it is more about who does CF, why and how that it can help or hinder diversification. Though the state has enacted the new contract farming Act, it has not been operationalized and an agency with direct interest in the matter has been entrusted to look after it until the Commission is in place. In order to ensure better farm incomes from new crops, it is important to ensure that contracts are fair and balanced and reduce farmer's market and production risks of new crops. This is not fully provided for in the Act.

Further, since resource conservation such as water and soil is central to diversification agenda, it is also important to examine how CF influences these resources and sustainability. Contract farming influences the direction of ecological change through two actors. One, the contracting agency lays down the production schedule for the farmers at the farm level. By determining the crop to be grown and the husbandry practice the farmer has to follow, the contracting agency influences the impact CF will have on the environment. The government is the second actor as the main source of conservation measures, i.e. advisory, financial and material. The farmer's access to these measures is, to a large extent, is determined by the government policy. Thus, the contracting agency and the government have a larger role to play in environmental/ecological change than the farmer, since they occupy a 'privileged' position in the realm of decision-making.

Contracts tend to be concerned with land management measures which ensure crop growth and quality and production levels only in the short-term agricultural cycle, except in organic CF situations. Land management measures geared to maintain resource quality over the long term are not specified. The grower is responsible for decisions about investment in the long-term maintenance of land quality and productive capacity in conditions where contracting companies influence the land use practices through contracts which tie growers to larger markets and encourage production growth. Environment is also impacted through rejection of some produce of the grower by the contracting agency as the cost of not harvesting results in soil loss through tillage and excessive use and wastage of chemicals causing nutrient depletion (Singh 2010).

The environmental implications of CF include monocultures leading to depletion of soil quality and effect of fertilizers and pesticides on natural resources, environment, humans and animals. The contracting firms tend to aggravate the environmental crisis as most of the contracts are short term (one or two crop cycles) and the firms tend to move on to new growers and lands after exhausting the natural potential of the local resources, particularly land and water, or when productivity declines due to some other reason. The overexploitation of groundwater, salination of soils, decline in soil fertility and pollution are examples of environmental degradation due to CF. The firms do not pay heed as the costs of such effects are externalized so far as the firm is concerned (Singh 2010).

During the last phase of diversification attempt (2002–2007), it was found that CF led to less water consumption on contract farms as against non-contract farms. The water consumption for paddy was 265.71 h per acre compared with only 183.86 h for Basmati paddy promoted and grown under the CF arrangement. Similarly, maize cultivation under CF led to water use of the order of only 18.35 h per acre. This meant that crops being grown under CF arrangement were water saving. That was so due to the provincial government plan to promote those crops. Overall, contract growers' weighted water consumption per acre was 120.49 h compared with 129.58 h in case of non-contract growers. But, reduced water consumption on contract farms was due to greater area devoted to the new crops (Basmati and maize) and not due to any new agricultural practices promoted by the contracting agencies. In fact, the contract farmers were practicing more intensive agriculture than the non-contract farmers and were devoting significantly higher number of water hours to Basmati and maize than that by non-contract farmers across all crops. Thus, increased commercialization of the various crops under CF propelled these contract farmers to use various inputs more intensively. Further, crop combination of potato and sunflower promoted under CF was more water intensive, though more remunerative than wheat (the alternative traditional crop) and therefore defeated the very purpose of CF in the state (Singh 2007).

In fact, the crops chosen for diversification do not score well on water use as number of irrigations is quite high in case of Basmati (15), sugarcane (14) spring maize (12) and winter maize (8) and they account for a major chunk of power subsidy after paddy, even higher than wheat (Singh 2012). On the other hand, crops which could have helped save water such as bajra, pulses, barley, mustard and soya bean have been left out.

4.4 Rethinking Diversification

Diversification is not just about changing from one set of crops to another but about its purpose, i.e. sustainability of farming systems and enterprises. It is also about doing same thing differently, i.e. following different crop practices for the same crop/s or doing altogether different things like growing new crops in new ways, i.e.

organic castor which Punjab has never grown. Unless practices and incentives for certain practices are changed, the present policy will not cut much ice.

Choices involved in promoting technological progress and providing rural infrastructure are likely to remain critical for providing the incentives for successful diversification of farmers faced with a structural need to adjust their output patterns away from exclusive dependence on cereals. The major requirements for diversification into non-traditional activities include (1) transfer, adaptation and extension of technology for cost reduction, (2) investment at farm level with some lag before pay back, (3) availability of specialized inputs, (4) heavy investment at processing level, (5) availability of infrastructure, (6) a conducive regulatory environment and (7) thorough knowledge of markets and established reputation in markets. The major institutions for lowering transaction cost in new crops and activities include CF and producer collectives, but monopolistic approaches to institutions of collective actions are not desirable. Actions taken need to encourage the use of markets, not to replace them (Delgado and Siamwalla 1997).

Delgado and Siamwalla (1997) emphasize that where technologies are available, infrastructure and institutions become constraints. Private marketing initiatives can help diversification in the presence of infrastructure and a trading class. It is also the experience of many countries like Denmark in dairy and Japan in sericulture that a combination of technological innovations in the new activity and non-monopolistic institutions of collective action such a cooperatives were critical to diversification away from cereals. The need for institutional innovations for farm diversification is the greatest in economies which have not gone through agricultural transformation and where agricultural markets do not work. Therefore, rural production and marketing institutions are key to farm diversification.

Since, diversification is about larger questions of resources and livelihoods, it is important to look beyond crops. In Punjab, still 25 % tube wells are run with diesel engines (Perveen et al. 2012), and central Punjab alone accounts for 70 % of all tube wells in the state. The owner farmers have been deepening them over the years with 90 % at least once, around 55 % twice and 20 % thrice during the last 10 years. Measures like putting cap on tube wells (Shergill 2013) have equity dimension which cannot be ignored. For example, in 2010–11, each electric tube well farmer, on an average, obtained power subsidy of Rs 50,000 per year (ranging from Rs. 19,184 to 42,671 and 1,12354 across semi-medium and medium to large farmers, respectively) with average subsidy of Rs. 10,000 per h per year assuming 20 % tube wells were diesel based and average operated holding size of non-small farmers was 5 h each (Singh 2012) and those with diesel could avail nothing. Thus, paddy cost would go up by 47 % and wheat cost by 13 % if power subsidy is withdrawn (Singh 2012).

Diversification in the farm sector was achieved successfully in Thailand through private initiatives where the state played an essential role in setting the investment climate and investing infrastructure and supporting small farmers with farm credit. In partnership with private sector, the state agencies, i.e. Bank for Agriculture and Agricultural Co-operatives (BAAC) and the Department of Agricultural Extension (DOAE), provided credit and extension support, respectively, to the contract growers working with private companies in high-value crops (Singh 2005). The

Board of Investment (BOI) provided incentives to CF agencies in the form of exemption from import duties on machinery, exemption from income tax for certain activities for five to eight years, 50 % deduction in normal income tax rates on net profits from certain operations for five years after the income tax exemption for first five years and a deduction of an amount equal to 5 % of the increased income over previous year for ten years. The Ministry of Commerce also actively promoted organic agriculture providing training and funding to food chain actors, i.e. producers, processors and exporters (Ellis 2011). The Thai success in diversification in agri-food sector was jointly determined by the synergy of government actions and private sector initiatives. Stable policies supported by continuity in programmes and competent bureaucracy were also major factors (Dyster 2014).

The private sector can play an important role in moving the state's agriculture out of the existing crisis. Contract farming can come handy to rectify the situation as export-oriented firms which need chemical-free raw materials due to international market pressure and can make contract growers switch to less environmentally harmful/more environmentally friendly production processes as they have the resources, including technologies and markets, to promote this kind of farming. It makes both business and development sense. These firms can also help farmers adopt good agricultural/farm practice (GAP/GFP) as the international market is increasingly demanding this kind of system in agroproducts. Further, PPPs can be explored as individually neither state nor private sector can attend to the problems which are so deep-rooted and require institutional structures and innovations. There are many examples of successful PPPs in agribusiness in India including one in the form of Mahagrapes (a grape growers' cooperatives' company created through PPP for export of grapes) and Asia which can be learned from (Singh 2011, 2013).

It is also important to remember that modern high-value crops whether for export or domestic markets are prone to high production and market risks. Therefore, there is need to bring in modern risk reduction arrangements like warehouse receipt systems and crop insurance already in place in India to help farmers manage risk better. Unfortunately, the state has not looked at the crop insurance issue seriously as the present dominant crops (wheat, paddy and cotton) all have MSP and yields are more or less assured.

4.5 Conclusions

Agricultural diversification is also about technological and institutional diversification. The state should not depend on its own apparatus only and the private sector to deliver the diversification agenda. New and more innovative institutions need to be created and supported such as SHGs, PCs and franchises. There are hundreds of PCs in India across states, crops and services with plenty of support being provided by various agencies but hardly any in Punjab (Singh and Singh 2014). Given that subsidized provision of irrigation water is one of the main incentive factors of the GR, diversification away from paddy may be hard to achieve in the absence of tradable property rights in water that match social and private cost in water used. Therefore, one needs to be careful about assuming that markets alone will insure a smooth adjustment out of over reliance on cereals. Also, other sources of energy like solar need to be explored and water sharing arrangements encouraged especially for small farmers. Further, when it is larger farmers who devote higher proportion to paddy and wheat crops compared with small farmers (Perveen et al. 2012), there is no logic in providing free electricity to all farmers irrespective of farm size.

What comes out from the analysis of the CF situations as mechanism of diversification is that increasingly environmental concerns are dictated by the market demand, e.g. the case of chemical residues or organic practices. However, markets may not signal the importance of ecological concerns in all situations and all times due to various imperfections in the market and externalities in the presence of weak monitoring. For example, in Kenya, soil erosion was not attended to by the contracting agencies as that was not reflected in the product quality and was an externality of the contract production. It continued to be seen as the responsibility of the farmer and the government. Similarly, price premiums for environmentally friendly food may not encourage genuineness due to incentive to cheat and mislabel due to information asymmetry. Therefore, it is important to proactively provide for ecological concerns into CF programs and policies. This can be done by way of land use planning based on soil depth, soil quality, land slope and suitable water availability. It is also important to understand previous land use and make it mandatory to follow crop rotation, if necessary (Singh 2010).

Further, from a smallholder perspective, the crop choice for diversification is very important. For example, Kinnow will not fit the bill as it has large gestation time and needs large investments. On the other hand, maize or baby corn is good choice but may not compete with Maharashtra and Karnataka unless alternative export markets are explored. But, if there are already private enterprises which are able to export Global GAP-certified fresh produce from Punjab, there is no reason to doubt that it cannot be scaled up and done even better with enabling support from the state and other development agencies.

References

Ahmad A, Isvilanonda S (2003) Rural poverty and agricultural diversification in Thailand. Paper downloaded from: lup.lub.lu.se/record/1387047/file/206004 on March 6 2014

Akanda AI (2010) Rethinking crop diversification under changing climate, hydrology and food habits in Bangladesh. J Agric Env Int Dev 104(1–2):3–23

Bal SK, Choudhury BU, Sood A, Bains GS, Mukherjee J (n.d.) Cropping pattern analysis for the Punjab state using low resolution remote sensing data, Department of agricultural meteorology, PAU Ludhiana. A presentation, downloaded from: hau.ernet.in/coa/seminar09/skbal.pd on March 6 2014

Delgado CL, Siamwalla A (1997) Rural economy and farm income diversification in developing countries. MSSD discussion paper no. 20, IFPRI, Washington, DC

Dyster RT (2014) Agri food exports; why Thailand is a model of diversification, Philippine Daily Inquirer, Jan. 26. Downloaded from http://business.inquirer.net on March 06 2014

Ellis W (2011) The strategic role of the private sector in agriculture and rural development, platform knowledge piece 3. Global Donor Platform for Rural Development (GDPRD), Bonn

Ghuman RS (2013) Brief view on the proposed Punjab state agricultural policy paper (first draft), unpublished paper. CRRID, Chandigarh

Gill SS (1988) Contradictions of Punjab model of growth and search for an alternative. Econ Polit Wkly 23(42):2167–2173

GoI (2013) Crop diversification program in Haryana, Punjab and Western Uttar Pradesh, 2013–14. Crops Division, DoAC, MoA, GoI, New Delhi

Kurosaki T (2003) Specialisation and diversification in agricultural transformation: the case of West Punjab, 1903–92. Am J Agric Econ 85(2):372–386

Perveen S, Krishnamurthy CK, Sidhu RS, Vatta K, Kaur B, Modi V, Fishman R, Polycarpou L, Lall U (2012) Restoring groundwater in Punjab, India's Breadbasket: finding agricultural solutions for water sustainability, Columbia Water Center (CWC) white paper. Earth Institute, Columbia University, New York

Sharma N, Singh SP (2013) Agricultural diversification and contract farming in Punjab. J Econ Soc Dev 9(1):38–51

Shergill HS (2007) Diversification of cropping pattern: a re-examination. IDC, Chandigarh

Shergill HS (2013) Why area under rice will not be reduced in Punjab. IDC, Chandigarh

Sidhu HS (2002) Crisis in agrarian economy in Punjab-some urgent steps. Econ Polit Wkly 37:3132–3138

Sidhu RS, Vatta K (n.d.) Risk in Punjab agriculture: current status and emerging issues, unpublished paper, PAU Ludhiana

Singh S (2002a) Multinational corporations and agricultural development: a study of contract farming in the Indian Punjab. J Int Dev 14(2):181–194

Singh S (2002b) Contracting out solutions: political economy of contract farming in the Indian Punjab. World Dev 30(9):1621–1638

Singh S (2004) Crisis and diversification in Punjab agriculture—role of state and agribusiness. Econ Polit Wkly Rev Agric 39(52):5583–5590

Singh S (2005) Role of the state in contract farming in Thailand: experience and lessons. ASEAN Econ Bull 22(2):217–228

Singh MP (2007) Contract farming and emerging agrarian structure: the case of Punjab, PhD thesis, CSRD, JNU, New Delhi

Singh S (2010) Globalisation and sustainability issues in agriculture in Asia—a case of India. In: Gill SS, Singh L, Marwah R (eds) Economic and environmental sustainability of the Asian region. Routledge, New Delhi, pp 23–44

Singh S (2011) Public-private partnerships for agribusiness development in Thailand and India: experience, issues, and strategies. In: Da Silva CA, Mhlanga N (eds) Innovative policies and institutions to support of agro-industries development. FAO, Rome, pp 41–62

Singh K (2012a) Electricity subsidy in Punjab agriculture: extent and impact. Indian J Agric Econ 67(4):617–632

Singh S (2012b) Institutional and policy aspects of Punjab agriculture: a smallholder perspective. Econ Polit Wkly Rev Rural Aff 47(4):51–57

Singh S (2013) Governance and upgrading in export grape global production networks in India: Capturing the Gains Working paper no. 33, University of Manchester, Manchester

Singh J, Sidhu RS (2004) Factors in declining crop diversification-case study of Punjab. Econ Polit Wkly 39(52):5607–5610

Singh S, Singh T (2014) Producer companies in India: organisation and performance. Allied, New Delhi

Sodhi MS, Singh S (2013) Analysing the potential of increase in acreage for kinnow, maize, wood, turmeric and moong as per the draft agriculture policy for Punjab 2013. MIGM, Indian School of Business, Mohali

Start D (n.d.) Rural diversification: what hope for the poor? www.odi.org.uk/publications/4818. Accessed 6 Mar 2014

Chapter 5
Groundwater Irrigation in Punjab: Some Issues and a Way Forward

Rita Pandey

5.1 Background

5.1.1 Concerns in Agriculture

Punjab located in the northwestern part of India comprising a mere 1.54 % of the total geographical area, and little over 2 % of the total population in the country accounts for 12 % of the national food grain production. It is the largest contributor of wheat (around 55 %) and second largest contributor of paddy (around 42 %) to the central pool of the country, though its relative contribution in central pool of food grains for both wheat and paddy has been declining during the last few years (Singh et al. 2012; Tiwana et al. 2007). Sustainability of agriculture in Punjab is thus important for the state's economy and also for food security in India.

Thrust on agriculture in Punjab started during the green revolution period. Supported by a mix of institutional and technological factors, 85 % of the area in the state is under agriculture. The area sown more than once has increased by 250 % since the late sixties. Consolidation of landholdings, reclamation of new agricultural lands, development of irrigation, and use of biochemical inputs comprising high-yielding variety seeds, chemical fertilizers, insecticides, and mechanical inputs were among the important factors which helped agriculture in the state in making rapid strides.

The emerging scene of agriculture in Punjab is facing some serious concerns. Green Revolution sustained till the eighties, after which the agricultural production in the state showed the signs of stagnation.[1] This has been largely attributed to

[1]Signs of stagnation in agriculture were not limited to Punjab alone.

R. Pandey (✉)
National Institute of Public Finance and Policy, 18/2 Satsang Vihar Marg,
Special Institutional Area, New Delhi 110067, India
e-mail: rita@nipfp.org.in; rita_pandey@yahoo.com

L. Singh and N. Singh (eds.), *Economic Transformation of a Developing Economy*, India Studies in Business and Economics,
DOI 10.1007/978-981-10-0197-0_5

continuous cultivation of rice–wheat cropping system[2] having negative implications for soil quality (nutrient balance) and infestation of weeds and pests. In the nineties, increase in the cost of inputs (increased application of fertilizer and insecticides was necessary to address soil health and pests issues; falling water tables required additional investment for irrigation) further aggravated the situation through squeezing the profitability of agriculture adversely affecting the socioeconomic condition of farmers in the state. According to (GoP 2013), the agriculture in state has reached a plateau making it very hard to make further progress under available technologies and the natural resource base, and the very sustainability of rice–wheat production system is under threat and climate change is posing new challenge on future agricultural growth.

5.1.2 Concerns in Groundwater

Groundwater has played a key role in success of green revolution in India in Punjab, Haryana, and western Uttar Pradesh (UP). Data from minor irrigation census 2011 show that these states account for 55 % of the tube wells in India. On an average, there are 28 tube wells per sq. km. of net sown area in Punjab alone. Punjab has 85 % of its area under cultivation with an average cropping intensity of 188 %. The water demand from agriculture in the state is therefore very high.

High water demand is also attributed to the water-intensive commercial crop models promoted during the green revolution. This was further incentivized by, among others, procurement and price support policies leading to massive surge in groundwater development for irrigation in Punjab.

The net area irrigated by wells covers 71 % of the total irrigated area of the state, while the remaining 29 % is irrigated by government canals.[3] Punjab's water table has been reducing at an alarming rate, with most of the demand coming from irrigation. The rate of fall in water table was 18 cm during 1982–87, which increased to 42 cm during 1997–2002 (Hira et al. 2004) and further to 75 cm during 2002–2006 (Singh 2006). The current situation of groundwater development in Punjab is the most critical in the country as 80 % of the monitored wells are considered overexploited (CGWB 2012). Annual groundwater extraction in Punjab is 31.16 billion m^3 as opposed to 21.44 billion m^3 availability. Very high level of groundwater is being extracted in Amritsar, Fategarh Sahib, Jalandhar, Kapurthala, Mansa, Ludhiana, Moga, Nawanshahr, Patiala, and Sangrur Districts. Out of the 137 blocks in the state, only 25 are safe; 103 are overexploited, 5 critical, and 4

[2]Almost no rice was grown in Punjab prior to 1950. According to Johl 2002, 35 % of gross cropped area was under rice in the state.

[3]Punjab hosts three main perennial rivers-Sutlej, Beas, and Ravi; and a seasonal river Ghaggar. This water is mainly supplied through a vast canal network of about 14, 500 km. The canal water supply is more extensive in the south-western zone of the state which receives less rainfall and has high salinity in soils and ground water. http://www.pbirrigation.gov.in

semi-critical (IDFC 2013). Area identified by CGWB for groundwater recharge is 2.275 m ha. The issue of overexploitation of groundwater is concentrated mostly in central Punjab. Other areas have waterlogging and salinity and poor water quality issues.[4]

This clearly is resulting in significant and increasing social and economic costs. Farmers are being confronted with the need to move to deeper wells with inevitable increase in cost of farming, making it especially difficult for small and marginal farmers. This also has implications for intersectoral distribution and equity. Subsidized agricultural power supply is putting an additional and unsustainable burden on state budgets.

This precarious situation calls for an integrated approach including a mix of regulatory, technological, and economic instruments to address groundwater management in Punjab besides high-level policy reform.

5.1.3 The Questions Asked in This Paper

This paper therefore aims to ask and assess three questions: Why groundwater? what has been done in Punjab and other states to address decline in groundwater levels? and What evidence and insights does a selective review of empirical literature provide on water demand and supply dynamics? Based on these analyses, the paper identifies the main issues and suggests a way forward in this context.

5.2 The Nature, Magnitude, and Drivers of Decline in Groundwater in Punjab

5.2.1 Understanding the Nature and Magnitude of the Problem

The aquifers underlying Punjab are characterized by alluvial deep systems which lead to higher specific yield relative to shallow hard rock formations in some other parts of India. In general, the major sources of inflow into the aquifers are precipitation in addition to other sources of recharge including that from irrigation recharge. The term 'aquifer overexploitation' applies to a physically unsustainable situation in which the extraction of groundwater exceeds the recharge within a given area over a given period of time. Recharge rates that are low relative to

[4]In about 20 % area of Punjab especially in South-West, ground water is of poor quality which led to liberal allocation of canal water. Poor efficiency of canal system covering 70 % area in South-West Punjab as compared to 14 % in Central Punjabhas contributed to fast rise in water table in south west causing poor land productivity.

storage, combined with the common occurrence of saline groundwater at greater depths, or at the same level in other parts (as is the case especially in south-west Punjab), can put these large alluvial aquifers at risk of aquifer mining and irreversible overexploitation as well as contamination of water. The hydrogeological systems and other dynamics underneath the earth are much more complex; however, this simple definition of overexploitation provides a physical indicator for the purposes of classification of groundwater blocks and helps in making an assessment of the environmental and socioeconomic costs of groundwater exploitation (This Para draws from World Bank 2010).

Other indicators of overexploitation of groundwater would be decreasing well yields and frequent well failures, deeper drilling depths, and use of advanced and expensive technology. Also, as the depth to water table deepens, the amount of energy required to pump a unit of water is likely to increase. These indicators not only help make an assessment of economic costs of overexploitation but also distributive aspects.

The water tables in Punjab have been in continuous decline on a widespread basis, with aquifer depletion rates currently in the range 0.7–1.2 m per year (approximately equivalent to a net 100–200 mm per year of excessive extraction) (World Bank 2010). The cost of extracting groundwater depends on the depth of water table. The fixed cost of extracting groundwater at around 8 m shows sharp increase. At 8 m, surface pumps become infeasible to extract water and farmers have to invest in more expensive technologies such as submersible pumps to extract groundwater. Punjab had the largest area experiencing such decline (Sekhri 2012a). What is alarming is that the decline has accelerated over time.

An important aspect of groundwater management is the analytics of water ownership. In India, including Punjab, land owners have the right to dig wells on their land and access and own water underneath (private property right) (Singh 1992). Given the physical and the hydrogeological attributes of the groundwater, it cannot be compartmentalized such that it coincides with the landholding pattern. This unique feature of the resource can potentially constrain the private property right to the extent the wells of neighboring farmers/density of wells in village/block/area interfere with the yield/life of a given/set of well(s).[5] Since only the landowners can own groundwater, it cannot be characterized an open access resource. Further, interactive effects of wells make it difficult to assign common property rights to groundwater (Chandrakanth et al. 2011). This study however notes that a number of studies have attributed common property rights to the groundwater resource.[6]

[5]The density of wells per unit area as well as the number of wells per million cubic meter of groundwater which determine the degree of interactive effects of wells is increasing over time in Hard Rock Areas (Chandrakanth et al. 2011).

[6]See Moench (1995).

5.2.2 Why Groundwater: The Drivers

Groundwater use is strongly contextual and intersectorally linked. It is important to emphasize that in India, in general, the primary driver of private groundwater use is neither resource availability nor well yield potential (Shah 2007), but the inadequacy and unreliability of water provided through the public water supply systems.

In agriculture, for example, groundwater use depends significantly on the availability of surface irrigation, energy options and costs of pumping, and cropping choices. In the elevated alluvial areas of central Punjab, water tables are deeper and coverage of irrigation canals is less extensive than in the lower plains.[7] The primary driver in this case was absence of surface water and the abundance of groundwater. Government support for developing wells however (subsidies on well construction and equipment) contributed to this significantly.

Secondary drivers: Groundwater has advantages like farmers can control the timing and amount of water. Supportive policies that provided flat rate/subsidized/free electricity for irrigation well pumping; cheap diesel; support in terms of assured prices; and procurement for some crops with very high consumptive use of water, such as paddy, wheat, and sugarcane facilitated groundwater extraction.

Being a largely private activity, the groundwater use went unregulated. This led to instances of water 'Landlords' selling surplus water from under their land to small and marginal farmers and for other use.

5.2.3 Welfare Implications

From a welfare perspective, rapid decline in water tables can result in significant social cost. Sekhri (2011) uses groundwater data in conjunction with annual agricultural output data at the district level to show that a 1 m decline in groundwater from its long-term mean can reduce food grain production by around 8 %. Using village level data from UP and the fact that there is a nonlinearity in cost to access groundwater at 8 m, Sekhri (2012b) shows that poverty rate increases by around 11 % as groundwater depth falls from over 8 m to below 8 m. In some parts of Gujarat, where the water tables are falling almost at a rate of 3 m a year, it is estimated that water savings of 30 % can free up 2.7 billion units of electricity for non-agricultural use. Department of drinking water supply, Government of India, estimates that in 2010, approximately 15 % of the total habitations in the country went from full coverage of drinking water to partial coverage due to drying up of groundwater sources.

[7]Central Punjab provides the most significant and illustrative example for considering the issues and approaches for addressing excessive groundwater exploitation (World Bank, 2010).

5.2.4 The Main Issues

The groundwater situation in central Punjab can be characterized by overexploitation (largely attributed to crop intensification and unsustainable crop mix), negative externalities (due to interactive effects of wells), inefficiencies (low productivity of water), and inequities (initial and premature well failure). Both the primary and secondary drivers coupled with weak or absent water management policies and institutions are said to be responsible for much of the problem. Incentives and penalties are thus crucial in bringing about sustainability, efficiency, and equity in water use.

5.3 Policy and Programmes for GroundWater Management in India

Legislative provisions: The Indian Constitution provides the states jurisdiction over the groundwater within their boundaries. Also, state governments have the primary responsibility for water supply and irrigation with powers to devolve these functions to up to village level institutions.

At the central government level, the Ministries of Water Resources (MoWR) and of Environment and Forests (MoEF) are responsible for evolving policy guidelines and for enforcing protection of surface and groundwater resources both in terms of quality and quantity. Since water is a state subject, the policy guidelines are mostly of an advisory nature with the implementation left to the state governments.

In the recent times, the Courts have played a proactive role in evolving policy guidelines and enforcement. The Supreme Court of India on the basis of public interest litigation passed several orders in 1996 and issued directions to the Government of India for setting up the Central Groundwater Authority (CGWA) under the Environment Protection Act, 1986 (EPA 1986), for the purposes of regulation and control of groundwater development. The Court further directed that the CGWA should regulate indiscriminate boring and withdrawal of groundwater in the country and issue necessary directions with a view to preserving and protecting the groundwater.

The CGWA in consultation with the Ministry of Law has opined that though the states are competent to make their own laws pertaining to groundwater and constitute state groundwater authorities, the provisions of the EPA (1986) would override the state under Article 253. The CGWA has notified sixty-five areas in various parts of the country for registration of groundwater abstraction structures. Based on data thus generated, vulnerable areas are notified for the purpose of groundwater regulation.

In an effort to control and regulate the development of groundwater, the MoWR prepared and passed a model Bill in 2005 for adoption by all the states and UTs. The main thrust of the Bill is to ensure that all the states and union territories form their own state groundwater authorities for proper control and regulation of groundwater resources. Some of the states (see Planning Commission 2007) have already enacted groundwater legislation, although at various stages of development. The Planning Commission's Expert Group on Groundwater Management and Ownership has argued that the legislative framework is reasonably robust, in that in principle, it enables the groundwater management practices that are likely to be pragmatic and effective in India. The priority lies in the enforcement of existing measures, supported by innovative approaches such as an expansion of community-based management.

Administrative and organizational set up: Management of groundwater suffers from fragmentation of responsibility at both central and state levels. Many agencies in various sectors have mandates relevant to groundwater, but there is little coordination among them and a lack of regulatory oversight. Not all states have dedicated groundwater authorities, and in almost, all cases groundwater-related agencies suffer from under-staffing, lack of capacity, marginalization, and outdated mandates that prioritize survey and development ahead of resource management.

Although the CGWA and Central Groundwater Board (CGWB) have the potential to become champions of sustainable groundwater management in India, the continued lack of clarity over their status and chronic under-staffing means central government institutions cannot properly fulfill their functions and effectively support state agencies (World Bank 2010).

5.3.1 Policy and Programmes for Groundwater Management in Punjab

The Punjab state government is yet to formulate groundwater legislation despite serious depletion of groundwater levels (particularly in central Punjab). Also, Punjab does not mandate rainwater harvesting. However, recent initiatives such as (i) incentives for changing cropping pattern, (ii) regulation mandating delayed paddy nursery and sowing activities (The Punjab Preservation of Sub Soil Water Act 2009), (iii) considering reforms in agricultural power sector, and (iv) other demand- and supply-side measures are significant positive steps.

5.3.1.1 Crop Diversity Programmes in Punjab, Haryana, and Western Uttar Pradesh

The purpose of this program (Government of India designed and funded program)[8] is to motivate farmers in Original green revolution States to divert the area of paddy

[8]Crop Diversity Programme in Punjab, Haryana, and western Uttar Pradesh(2013-14), Ministry of Agriculture, Government of India.

to alternate crops (maize, *kharif* pulses, oilseeds, cultivation of *rabi* and *kharif* intercrops) from ensuing *kharif* season. Through this program, the following is expected to be achieved:

(i) To demonstrate and promote the improved production technologies of alternate crops for diversion of paddy cultivation;
(ii) To restore the soil fertility through cultivation of leguminous crops that generates heavy biomass and consumes less nutrient intake.

The program will be implemented in the notified overexploited and critical blocks based on the recommendation of CGWB. At least 5 % of area under paddy in identified blocks will be diverted toward alternate crops. The program provides for assistance for land development, farm mechanization, and establishment of agro-based processing units for value addition and marketing support to generate additional income and restore soil fertility. The program will be implemented by the central government through a Central Steering Committee constituted for the purpose. An amount of Rs. 500 crore has been earmarked under *Rashtriya Kisan VikasYojana* for the year 2013–14.

5.3.1.2 The Punjab Preservation of Subsoil Water Act, 2009

It is encouraging that the Government of Punjab has recognized that overexploitation of groundwater is an issue of serious concern and has recently implemented this Act to contain it. The main purpose of the Act is to save groundwater by prohibiting sowing and transplanting paddy before specified dates in hot and dry summer[9] period. The Act prohibits farmers from sowing nursery of paddy before 10 May and transplanting paddy before 10 June in a year. Any farmer, who contravenes the provisions of the Act, shall be liable of penalty of rupees ten thousand for every month or part thereof, per hectare of the land till the period such contravention continues.

The authorized officer, either *suo motto* or on the information brought to his notice regarding the violation of any provision of the Act, shall be competent to issue directions to the farmer, who has violated any provision of this Act to destroy the nursery of paddy or sown or transplanted before the notified date. In case, a farmer does not act as per the directions of the authorized officer given under the Sect. 5.5 and the authorized officer shall cause such nursery of paddy, or sown or transplanted paddy, as the case may be, to be destroyed at the expenses of such farmer.

According to, Singh (2009), the fall in water table can be checked by about 30 cm by delaying the transplanting with the effective implementation of the Act.

[9]There is hardly any rainfall up to 15th June in Punjab and the relative humidity is lowest, wing speed is highest and temperature is maximum, due to which water evaporates very fast (Singh, 2009).

The savings in electricity have been estimated at 276 million units.[10] In contrast to these findings, a recent study (Sekhri 2012a), which evaluated the impact of this Act, finds that the annual ground level situation worsened in rice-growing areas after the policy change. The intuitive reason for this could be in farmers' response to policy in increased number of irrigation applied or more water used per irrigation. The study observes that in the absence of farm level data on number of irrigation applied and water use, it is not possible to establish the mechanism.

5.3.1.3 Introducing Reforms in Agricultural Power

Based on personal communication with government officials in Punjab, the following insight into current deliberations in Punjab in this context can be summarized as follows:

- All tube wells would be electrified by 2015 although there are no plans of metering of electricity at the tube well level which is estimated to cost Rs. 700 crores.
- Electricity consumption is currently monitored only at the feeder level. It appears that the government is open to learn from experiences based on the Gujarat model of separate feeders for agriculture and 24 × 7 electricity provisions.

5.3.1.4 Other Measures

Policy on use of technological solutions such as happy seeders, laser levelers for promoting water use efficiency, and other resource conservation technologies (RCTs) for water saving and increasing productivity is under consideration. Some of these technologies are already in use although there is no government policy yet on promoting the same.

Artificial recharge project in Moga district

As per the available estimates, all the blocks in Moga district are categorized as overexploited where groundwater withdrawal has exceeded natural recharge by more than 200 %. The decline of water levels has severely impacted the farmers of the area especially those having land less than 2 ha. It was reported that in this area many farmers started migrating to non-farming activities such as dairy farming or even selling off their lands to big landlords having adjoining farmlands. In order to augment the dwindling groundwater resources, a project for artificial recharge was taken up for augmenting the depleted aquifer through artificial charge in Bassian

[10]These estimates are based on simulations using historic data from central Punjab and does not account for selection issues (Sekhri, 2012a).

Drain in Moga district. The project is reported to have shown encouraging results. In an area of 11 km^2, the observed rise in water level was 0.20 m that could also save 15 MW of energy due to reduced lift of pumps. The farmers of the area also reported that there is appreciable increase in the discharge of their shallow tube wells due to artificial recharging of aquifer system of the area. This project can potentially be replicated (Gupta and Marwah 2012).

5.4 Potential Measures and Instrument for Promoting Sustainable Use of Groundwater

Significant social and economic consequences of overexploitation of groundwater in Punjab require a focused approach for effective intervention. A mix of regulatory, economic, and institutional options with focus on irrigation efficiency in general and economic efficiency in the use of irrigation water in particular can be used. In this context, two broad categories of intervention are water demand management measures and supply management measures that would target resource enhancement.

5.4.1 Supply-Side Measures

These measures target resource enhancement as a means of recovery in water tables (which is a very complex phenomenon) mainly through measures which would enhance the recharge of the aquifer through infiltration. This can be done by: (i) retaining runoffs (by building physical structures, forest conservation, afforestation, plantations, rainwater harvesting, etc.), (ii) artificial recharge (uses surface water and runoff)[11] practices, and (iii) adopting agricultural practices including RCTs such as laser levelers, tensiometers, and happy seeders[12] which promote infiltration and/or reduce loss of irrigation water. Alluvial settings in Punjab with abundant excess runoff as well as groundwater storage capacity required for recharge provide good potential for recharge (World Bank 2010). It appears that these measures have not yet received the desired attention. It is important to note here that there is little or no public investment on groundwater development/resource enhancement. While surface water is provided by public

---

[11]A project was taken up for augmenting the depleted aquifer through artificial recharge in Bassian Drain in Moga district. In an area of 11km2 the rise in water level observed was 0.20m. See Gupta and Marwaha (2012).

[12]As per the personal conversation with officials of farmers' associations in Punjab some progress has been made in this direction by promoting and improving farmers' access to these technologies.

investment on tanks, dams, and reservoirs, groundwater has to be extracted and used by farmers' private investment.

Delhi was the first state to mandate rainwater harvesting. Many states followed the suit. In Gujarat, concentrated efforts to recharge groundwater began in the Saurashtra region after the 1987 drought. Initial efforts to divert runoff to groundwater wells led to widespread adoption of the practice by farmers throughout Saurashtra without government intervention. Over time, farmers experimented with new technologies and farmers began constructing check dams in streams and rivers to reduce water speed and to allow the river water to seep into the ground and replenish the groundwater supply (Mehta 2006). Farmers continued constructing check dams through the 1990s with the assistance from NGOs who also bore some of the costs. In January 2000, the Gujarat government introduced the Sardar Patel Participatory Water Conservation Project in response to the work of farmers and NGOs in the Saurashtra, Kachchh, Ahmadabad, and Sabar Kantha regions. The program initially funded 60 % of the estimated cost of new check dams, and beneficiaries/NGOs financed the remaining 40 %. In 2005, the government increased its financing to 80 % of the estimated cost, and the pace of construction increased outside of the Saurashtra region.

5.4.2 Demand-Side Measures

While broader interventions in groundwater management through groundwater legislation and other sectoral policies will certainly be needed to bring down groundwater extraction/use in the state within the sustainable limits, in this section we explore suitability of some demand management measures with potential to make a difference in Punjab situation.

Broadly speaking, demand-side measures can be categorized into three types of instruments: regulatory instruments, economic instruments, and other instruments—a residual category.

5.4.2.1 Regulatory Instruments

In the present context, such measures would include metering and rationing of water/electricity, prohibiting nursery and planting of identified crops before specified dates, promoting substitution of less water consuming crops for water-intensive crops, and farming practices for improving water use efficiency.

Effective regulation in general requires not only sound legislation but also the administrative capacity to monitor and enforce rules. Moreover, metering water/electricity will involve significant transaction costs when there are very large numbers of small users, as in the case of Punjab due to fragmentation of land. Standard environmental economics theory tells us that a price-based instrument is expected to be potentially more successful in such a setting unless it is a case of severely threatened resources/blocks[13] which would require urgent focus on the quantity of water.

The Punjab state government is yet to formulate groundwater legislation. As discussed before, measures such as crop diversity program for promoting alternate crops in paddy areas and Punjab Preservation of Subsoil Water Act, 2009, for promoting water saving are being implemented.

According to Kulkarni and Shah (2013), in many ways trajectory of water resource development in Punjab has been following a simple principle of 'developing' which in the case of groundwater means extracting more water to produce more grain. The consequences of intensive water resource mobilization, in the absence of systematic groundwater management backed by robust water governance mechanisms, have been extreme depletion of groundwater resources on the one hand and a rising water level, leading to waterlogging and soil salinity on the other (Kulkarni and Shah 2013; Perveen et al. 2012).

5.4.2.2 Economic Instruments

These can be categorized into price-based instruments and quantity-based instruments.

Price-based instruments

These would include pricing in the form of a tax, cess, user fee, etc. These can act as incentives to conservation of water. Actual impact will depend on the price elasticity of demand for water/electricity for pumping groundwater. In designing, these instrument issues such as the equity considerations of the groundwater-dependent farmers vis-à-vis those who have access to surface irrigation[14] and equity and affordability of small and marginal farmers will need to be addressed. However, implementation and transaction cost issues are similar as in the case of regulatory instruments. Although if designed well, due to inherent static cost minimization and dynamic efficiency, price-based instruments will result in more efficient allocation and use of water resources.

Tradable groundwater rights

While a well-defined rights regime helps water users to reach optimal outcomes, the measure can involve very high transaction costs of implementation. However, if this instrument is implemented in a framework of shared/community/public well and is appropriately mixed with regulatory and/or price-based instrument, this can

[13]A regulatory instrument or a quantity based economic instrument such a tradable permits is recommended in such settings.

[14]Surface irrigation has huge subsidies. Fixed costs do not enter the price; only a small fraction of operating cost is recovered.

overcome the scale and public monitoring constraints and thus result in lower transaction costs.

Shared/community/public wells concept may be tried as a pilot. Sekhri (2011) shows that public wells provision can reduce the rate of depletion, and if an optimal price is charged, it can also reverse depletion. But this can work only where cost of groundwater extraction is high, or in areas where water tables are deep. Foster and Sekhri (2008) find evidence that bilateral trade arrangements between farmers who sell and buy groundwater also decelerate depletion rates. Malik et al. (2008) show that in a shared well situation in Bist Doab area of Punjab under conditions of rationed water allocation, the farmers have high motivation to allocate more water to crops that are economically more efficient and also use it more efficiently for the chosen crops than the farmers who have unrestricted access to groundwater by virtue of having wells under individual ownership. In this case, their access is limited in terms of number of hours per day access to pumps which is linked to the size of shareholding (land/crop). The benefit of promoting such arrangements is that these do not require top-down monitoring. It has been argued that water rights without tradability will lead to wasteful use (Frederick 1993). On the contrary, Rosegrant and Ringler (1998) indicate that tradable water rights would lead to farmers allocating their water for high-value crops. A clear understanding on this can contribute to designing appropriate institutions and policies for sustainable use of groundwater.

Internationally, the only developing country where evidence of positive efficiency and equity impacts of tradable property rights in groundwater is seen in Chile (Rosegrant and Gazmuri 1994; Thobani 1997).

5.4.2.3 Other Instruments

This category, in the present, context would include the following:

- Subsidies/user charges for promoting investment in/leasing of water-saving methods/equipment.
- Public disclosure of information on receding resource and potential medium and long-run risks associated with it. Groundwater literacy and sensitization.
- Measures such as supporting environment for uptake/marketing of alternate crops to encourage farmers gradually reduce cropping of water-intensive crops.
- Technology, research, and extension support.

The Andhra Pradesh Farmer Managed Groundwater Systems Project (APFAMGS) shows that sustainable management of groundwater is feasible only if users understand its occurrence, cycle, and limited availability. Preliminary findings in the project area have shown that the project has achieved a closer alignment of water availability and water use, and reductions in groundwater use have been realized through, for example, crop diversification (with an increase in low-water-use crops) and water-saving irrigation methods. Importantly, farmers have not sacrificed profitability to reduce water use. The reductions in groundwater draft in APFAMGS are not coming from altruistic collective action, but from the individual risk management and profit-seeking decisions of thousands of farmers (World Bank 2010).

Another success story in Andhra Pradesh is the system of rice intensification (SRI). Several factors such as depleted water resources, stagnated rice productivity, the growing importance of organic agriculture, increased production costs, and the need for better utilization of family labor among small and marginal farmers called for a shift in cultivation practice. SRI offered a way to not just reduce the demand for water while growing irrigated rice, but also of simultaneously increasing rice production. SRI was introduced in Andhra Pradesh in kharif 2003 in all 22 districts of the state by Acharya N.G. Ranga Agricultural University (ANGRAU). Since 2003, ANGRAU has taken several initiatives to promote SRI in Andhra Pradesh.

RCTs such as zero tillage, laser land leveling, and furrow bed planting have received attention in the context of increasing the productivity of the rice–wheat cropping pattern in south Asia (food security issues) and saving of increasingly scarce water resources. While the impacts of RCTs on yields are easy to measure, impacts on water savings are not well understood beyond the field scale because of the complex movement of water. Ahmad et al. (2014), using both physical measurements and farmer survey data from the rice–wheat cropping system in Punjab in Pakistan shows that the primary drivers for adopting of RCTs were reduced cost of production and labor requirements, higher yield, and reduced field scale irrigation water application. However, the study indicates that the field scale reduction in water application did not always result in real savings due to rebound effect, suggesting that without regulations and policies to regulate the use of saved water, adoption of RCTs can result in overall increased water use. Nevertheless, RCTs can potentially lead to increase in productivity of water. However, a more realistic and practical approach would be to weigh the technical solutions along with behavioral and incentive issues (Singh 2011). This is supported by the findings of a recent study by Columbia Water Center (2012) which using farmer survey and field-level data in Punjab and Gujarat show that in conjunction with other measures RCTs such as tensiometer and direct or dry seeding of rice can potentially lead to increase in productivity of water and that the farmers are open to reliable and cost-effective strategies for saving water in irrigation applications for rice.

5.4.2.4 Energy Subsidy-Irrigation Nexus: A Contentious Issue

This is an important policy question for at least two reasons:

One, electricity subsidies are widely perceived to be one of the main causes of groundwater overexploitation. A general argument against energy subsidies is that they encourage farmers to extract groundwater at unsustainable rates which causes lowering of water tables requiring more energy to extract groundwater, thus raising the cost of agricultural production. Further, use of free/cheap electricity may make electricity more expensive to non-farm users. In Punjab, development of groundwater is preceded by crop choices which, in turn, have been distorted by central government policies rooted in achieving the objectives of food security. Clearly, this is not an energy pricing issue alone and requires that the larger policy issues embedded in demand for water are appropriately addressed. Empirical studies on pricing of irrigation water seem to support this view.

Before we discuss some of these studies, let us put this question in the larger context of irrigation subsidies. In the case of surface water-based irrigation, the entire cost of development is borne by the state. A very small portion of operational expenses are recovered from the farmers. In groundwater irrigation, most of the development cost is borne by the farmers. Chandrakanth (2002) shows that the farmers using groundwater bear a much higher proportion of irrigation cost (77 %) compared to surface water irrigation farmers and that the negative externalities faced by the farmers due to cumulative interference of irrigation wells are largely responsible for well failures in hard rock aquifers. Also, groundwater situation varies across districts/basins, etc.; therefore, the question of subsidy on energy, cost of groundwater irrigation, and water table situation should be considered together and not in isolation.

More scientific studies are required to get a better idea of the costs of the two sources of irrigation to the state and the farmers. Moreover, it can also be argued that the increase in the power subsidy costs in recent decades is the result of the increasing inability of farmers to bear the full costs of pumping from decreasing groundwater levels (Shah 2009; Dubash 2007).

Detailed scientific studies are required to study the impact of reduction in energy subsidies on cropping pattern, and land and water productivity. There is also need to put some basic data in order. For instance, Chandrakanth et al. (2011) indicate that there are conflicting estimates of use of electricity for irrigation and also on proportion of land irrigated by groundwater and surface water at the country level. Data at more disaggregated level pose further problems.

Meenakshi et al. (2013) measure the impact of metering agricultural tube wells (from a flat rate to a metered tariff) on groundwater users (pump owners and water buyers) and informal groundwater markets in West Bengal. Overall, the findings do not show any significant impact on any of the outcomes assessed. On the contrary, Badiani and Jessoe (2011) show that reducing electricity subsidies can potentially affect groundwater extraction rates. A recent study in Gujarat shows that voluntary shift to metering and billing is possible; however, no evidence of response to the price signal was seen (Fishman et al. 2014).

A low flat tariff and the resulting electricity subsidy have also been criticized from an equity perspective because much of the agricultural electricity subsidy goes to big farmers who own a major proportion of the water extraction mechanisms fitted with electric pumps (Howes and Murgai 2003). This, however, is aligned more with targeting of subsidy than subsidy per se.

Two, subsidized/free agricultural power supply is putting an unsustainable burden on state budgets and is the prime cause of bankruptcy of the state boards in India.

As the number of tube wells increased manifold in 70 and 80s, prevalence of unmetered tube wells and flat rate electricity tariff became a norm which was entirely a result of conscious policy decisions made by various levels of government for administrative ease and keeping a check on transaction costs of metering, measuring, and charging the consumers.[15] Slowly it became a potent instrument for appeasement of voters, thus keeping the rate perpetually low or supplying it free of any charge. As a result, the quality of power deteriorated. This affected the small farmers more as, like big farmers, they could not afford to substitute diesel and generators for free electricity. There were equally serious implications for the groundwater sector. Since the marginal cost of extracting groundwater was close to zero, it provided an incentive for overpumping. In many areas, this spawned active groundwater markets. These markets emerged in response to unmet demand for irrigation and the flat tariff system (Meenakshi et al. 2013). It may be argued that the emergence of active groundwater markets would be a positive outcome from economic efficiency point of view. The price at which water would be traded will reflect the opportunity cost for using water. Such transfers can promote access equity and efficiency in use. Moreover, such markets can provide extremely useful information price elasticity of demand for irrigation by crops and size of holdings.

However, the main drawback of the flat tariff system/free electricity has been the total lack of energy accounting, no accurate estimates of the total electricity consumed by the agricultural sector, and the subsidy provided by the electricity utilities. The total annual economic cost of subsidized power remains contested (mainly due to varying assumptions of transmission and distribution losses, the use of off-peak power, and the unreliability or intermittence of the supply (Shah 2007)). Then, there are equity issues in subsidy. Free electricity has implications for poor quality and rationed supply of electricity.

The problems facing the electricity sector due to unmetered supply to agriculture and the consequent lack of incentives among farmers to make efficient use of electricity and among the utilities to do robust energy accounting are now widely acknowledged and are at the top of the policy agenda (Planning Commission, 12th Plan Strategy Challenges).

5.4.2.5 Evidence from Literature: Drawing Inference on Instrument Choice

The context here is the debate on measures for promoting efficient, equitable, and sustainable use of groundwater for irrigation. In other words, we are broadly looking at measures to promote:

Inter-temporal efficiency—reducing overexploitation;
Allocative efficiency—cropping mix;

[15]Unmetered electricity supply also became a convenient garb for state electricity boards to hide their inefficiencies in terms of transmission and distribution losses (Sant and Dixit 1996). Electricity Act of 2003 has made metering mandatory for all categories of electricity consumers (GoI, 2003).

Efficiency in use of water—farming practices; irrigation and farm machinery; Externalities—equity issues

The vast body of literature focusing on regulations and market instruments including the potential linkage between electricity pricing and groundwater use for irrigation and the implication of electricity prices for access to equity, efficiency, and sustainability in groundwater use (see Malik et al. 2008; Kumar 2005; Moench 1995; Chandrakanth et al. 2011 for detailed review) provides empirical evidence and/or insights into approaches such as state regulation on groundwater withdrawal; cooperative management of groundwater; tradable property rights in groundwater[16]; rationing of electricity to farm sector; prorata power tariff in agriculture[17]; community-based ownership and management of groundwater; volumetric rationing in groundwater allocation; and its positive impact on cropping pattern and land and water productivity in Punjab (Malik et al. 2008). These and other studies referred in earlier sections in the chapter point toward differing, often opposite views/empirical results on the equity and productivity impacts of these instruments.

No consensus exists about appropriate tariff structures either, which generate efficiency in resource use, equity in access to groundwater, and sustainability of resource use. Saleth (1997) argues that power tariff policy alone cannot be an effective tool for achieving efficiency, equity, and sustainability in groundwater use and opines that even an imperfect system of groundwater rights will have more sustainable benefits than a most perfectly designed power tariff structure.

The argument is that when tradable property rights are enforced, efficient water markets would develop (Kumar 2005).

In the context of Gujarat, several scholars and institutions have argued for establishing tradable property rights in groundwater (Kumar and Singh 2001). However, there is an absolute paucity of sufficient empirical data to compare and analyze the differential impacts of different levels of pricing of electricity and groundwater rights allocations on water and energy productivity (Kumar 2005).

Since 2004–05, agricultural sector has been recovering—this recovery, however, was associated with renewed dynamism in rain-fed areas in Jharkhand, Chhattisgarh, Andhra Pradesh, Karnataka, Rajasthan, Gujarat, and Madhya Pradesh. Rain-fed area crops mainly cereals *Bajra*, *Jawar*, maize, cotton, and oilseeds had higher yield growth—which came mainly from use of better seeds and better practices, where agricultural extension services primarily driven by civil society, farmer producer organic, and agricultural business companies helped in adoption of better practices. This indicates that different solutions will emerge in different situations. Farmers have valuable knowledge and capacity to assess both the potential and the risks of supportive environment and positive incentives

The question then is how does this literature help inform the policy making? And what inferences can we draw for the policy making/design of instruments that may

[16]Argue that pro rata pricing would have positive impact on equity, efficiency and sustainability in semi-arid and aid regions. Metering has been criticized on account of its negative welfare effects.

[17]It has been argued that water rights will be more effective than evolving energy pricing policy.

encourage sustainable use of water. A modest assessment would be that it provides at least the following broad guidance for interventions. These are listed in the following section.

5.5 Some Suggestions

(i) Understanding groundwater overexploitation/use is complex and very much influenced by numerous natural, economic, and political factors at play, and these factors vary a lot across and within natural, social, economic, and political boundaries and interact in many different ways among themselves. Therefore, no one solution/success story can be successfully implemented/replicated in entirety.

(ii) There is urgent need to put a strategy in place to 'manage' the resource for which the necessary condition is that we know the resource; credible estimates of total consumption of irrigation water, electricity, and diesel disaggregated by crops, regions etc. Similarly, credible information on productivity of water under different crops and other local conditions. This will help identify different aspects (technology, seeds, and other farming practices) which need to be targeted.

(iii) Implementation and enforcement of existing laws is weak. For instance, Electricity Act 2003 made metering mandatory, but to no avail. West Bengal is the only state which has been able to meter agricultural tube wells. Punjab is yet to formulate a groundwater policy. Water harvesting is not mandated in Punjab although some states have made good progress on this.

(iv) Economic rewards and penalties are required for management of groundwater as these can potentially help provide signal to users about economic/opportunity cost of water. This can be achieved by implementing price-based and/or quantity-based instruments. Evidence of some success of implementing various measures in Gujarat, West Bengal, Punjab, western UP, and Andhra Pradesh provides useful reference points.

(v) It would be prudent to involve the stakeholders in decision making for both valuable inputs on local socioeconomic dynamics and environmental and economic risks perceived by them of the status quo, as well as to garner the buy-in for the new approaches/instruments.

(vi) Supply-side measures have the potential to succeed in Punjab. Role of public investment in groundwater should be examined. Although not yet systematically practiced, there is great potential for exploring various resource-enhancing measures including conjunctive use of surface water and groundwater to meet rising demand in both rural and urban settings. In this context, it is important to mention that Punjab has a good number of ponds. This valuable source of water is being lost due to water quality and other issues. Ponds can be revived/developed into a source of irrigation water, among others, and catchment areas as a source of recharge of groundwater table. This however needs to be examined further in detail.

(vii) Since the objective is sustainable groundwater management, the focus should be on water in designing the policy instruments. A policy on number of functioning irrigation wells and provision of water flow meters (with an eye on gradual pricing of water and regulation of water draft from wells) may be introduced in a gradual manner. These initiatives on their own may give rise to different types of institutional arrangements and thus markets. This is likely to be more efficient than top-down approach in promoting institutional arrangements. Till the time, water meters are installed a flat charge on water may be introduced taking cue from the water markets in the informal sector.[18] This should go hand in hand with awareness and sensitization campaigns through extension services.

(viii) Cooperative/shared well framework should be promoted. This is also akin to/sets favorable ground for transferable permits.

(ix) Strong focus on gradual shift in cropping pattern through innovative farming and irrigation methods/technology (examples of AP and other states which are sowing millets and other crops). Enabling environment such as price and procurement support for alternate crops, support for RCTs should be examined in a holistic manner.

References

Ahmad MD, Ilyas M, Giordano M (2014) Constraints and opportunities for water savings and increasing productivity through resource conservation technologies in Pakistan agriculture. Ecosyst Environ 187(6):106–115

Badiani R, Jessoe KK (2011) Electricity subsidies for agriculture: evaluating the impact and persistence of these subsidies in India. Working Paper, University of California Davis, USA

CGWB (2012) Ground water year book, ministry of water resources. Government of India, New Delhi

Chandrakanth MG (2002) Valuation of natural and environmental resources: methodology and estimation, summaries of group discussion. Indian J Agric Econ 57(1):23–30

Chandrakanth MG et al (2011) Groundwater conservation and management in India: application of IoS and wade frameworks. University of Agricultural Sciences, Bangalore

Columbia Water Center (2012) Restoring groundwater in Punjab India's breadbasket. White Paper, Columbia Water Center, Columbia University, USA

Dubash N (2007) The electricity-groundwater conundrum: case for a political solution to a political problem. Econ Polit Weekly XLII(52):45–55 (Dec 29)

Fishman R, Lall U, Modi V (2014) Can energy pricing save India's groundwater? Evidence from a pilot in Gujarat. Paper presented at the 11th annual meeting of the international water resource economics consortium, Sep 7–9, Washington DC, USA

[18]This is aligned to twelfth Five-Year Plan which proposes a paradigm shift in the management of water resources in India, a crucial element of which is the shift in emphasis from development to management, with the empowerment of water users and improved water efficiency (Shah 2013).

Foster A, Sekhri S (2008) Expansion of markets for groundwater in rural India? Working paper. Brown University, USA
Frederick KD (1993) Balancing water demand with supplies: the role of management in a world of increasing scarcity. Technical Paper 189. World Bank, Washington, DC
Government of Punjab (2013) Report of the Committee set up for formulation of agriculture policy for Punjab State. Government of Punjab
GoI (2013-14) Crop diversification program in Haryana, Punjab and Western Uttar Pradesh. Ministry of Agriculture, New Delhi
Gupta S, Marwaha S (2012) Ground water exploitation and food security issue—a case study of Moga District, Punjab State, India. Abstract volume, world water week in Stockholm
Hira GS, Jalota SK, Arora VK (2004) Efficient management of water resources for sustainable cropping in Punjab. Department of Soils, Punjab Agricultural University, Ludhiana
Howes S, Murgai R (2003) Karnataka: incidence of agricultural power subsidies, an estimate. Econ Polit Weekly 38(16):1533–1535
IDFC (2013) India Rural Development Report 2012/13. New Delhi
Kulkarni H, Shah M (2013) Punjab water syndrome-diagnostics and prescriptions. Econ Polit Weekly XLVIII(52):64–73
Kumar MD (2005) Impact of electricity prices and volumetric water allocation on energy and groundwater demand management: analysis from Western India. Energy Policy 33(1):39–51
Kumar MD, Singh OP (2001) Market instruments for demand management in the face of scarcity and overuse of water in Gujarat, Western India. Water Policy 5(3):387–403
Malik AK, Junaid M, Tiwari R, Kumar D (2008) Towards evolving groundwater rights: the case of shared well irrigation in Punjab. Institute of Rural Management, Anand
Meenakshi JV, Banerji A, Mukherji A, Gupta A (2013) Impact of metering of tube wells on groundwater use in West Bengal, India. Project report submitted to 3ie by International Water Management Institute www.iwmi.org/iwmi-tata/apm2012
Mehta A (2006) The rain catchers of saurashtra, Gujarat. In: Okonski K (ed) The water revolution: practical solutions to water scarcity. International Policy Press, London, p 226
Moench M (1995) Ground water management: simply dominated focus of traditional, NGO, and government efforts. VIKSAT, Ahmedabad
Perveen S, Krishnamurthy CK, Sidhu RS, Vatta K, Kaur B, Modi V, Fishman R, Polycarpou L, Lall U (2012) Restoring ground water in Punjab: finding agricultural solutions for water sustainability. Columbia Water Centre white paper: agriculture, India 2012, Earth Institute, Columbia University, USA
Planning Commission (2007) Expert group on groundwater management and ownership. Planning Commission, Government of India
Rosegrant Mark W, Renato Gazmuri Z (1994) Reforming water allocation policy through markets in tradable water rights: lessons from Chile, Mexico, and California, EPTD discussion paper 2. International Food Policy Research Institute, Washington
Rosegrant MW, Ringler C (1998) Impact on food security and rural development of transferring water out of agriculture. Water Policy 1:567–586
Saleth RM (1997) Power tariff policy for groundwater regulation: efficiency, equity and sustainability. Artha Vijnana XXXIX(3):312–322
Sant G, and Dixit S (1996) Beneficiaries of IPS subsidy and impact of tariff hike. Economic and Political Weekly, 31(51):3315–3321
Sekhri S (2011) Missing water: agricultural stress and adaptation strategies in. University of Virginia, Mimeo
Sekhri S (2012a) Sustaining ground water: role of policy reforms in promoting conservation in India. Paper presented in India policy forum 2012, IIC New Delhi
Sekhri S (2012b) Wells, water and welfare: impact of access to groundwater on rural poverty (Mimeo). University of Virginia, USA
Shah T (2007) The groundwater economy of South Asia: an assessment of size, significance and socio-ecological impacts. In: M Giordano, Villholth KG (eds) The agriculture groundwater

revolution: opportunities and threats to development. Comprehensive assessment of water management in agriculture series. CABI Publishing, Wallingford

Shah T (2009) Taming the anarchy: groundwater governance in South Asia. Res Future, Washington, DC

Shah M (2013) Water: towards a paradigm shift in the twelfth five year plan. Econ Polit weekly XLVIII(26 and 27):40–52

Singh C (ed) (1992) Water law in India. The Indian Law Institute, New Delhi

Singh K (2006) Fall in water table in central Punjab: how serious. The Punjab State Farmers Commission, Government of Punjab, Chandigarh

Singh K (2009) Agrarian crisis in Punjab: high indebtedness, low returns and farmers suicides. In: Reddy DN, Mishra S (eds) Agrarian crisis in India, Chapter 10, Oxford University Press, New Delhi, pp 261–284

Singh N (2011) Federalism and water management in India, mimeo. UC Santa Cruz, USA

Singh J, Grover DK, Dhaliwal TK (2012) State agricultural profile-Punjab. AERC Study no. 30, Agro-economic Research Centre, Punjab Agricultural University, Punjab

Thobani M (1997) Formal water markets: why, when and how to introduce tradable water rights. World Bank Res Observer 12(2):161–179

Tiwana NS, Jerath N, Ladhar SS, Singh G, Paul R, Dua DK, Parwana HK (2007) State of environment: Punjab-2007. Punjab State Council for Science and Technology, Chandigarh, Punjab 243

World Bank (2010) Deep wells and Prudence: towards pragmatic action for addressing groundwater overexploitation in India. Report 51676. The International Bank for Reconstruction and Development/The World Bank 1818 H Street, NW, Washington, D.C. 20433, USA (http://siteresources.worldbank.org/INDIAEXTN/Resources/295583-1268190137195/DeepWellsGroundwaterMarch2010.pdf)

Part II
Agrarian Markets and Distributive Outcomes

Chapter 6
Growth of Cash Rent Tenancy and Modernisation of Land Lease Market in Punjab

H.S. Shergill

The main objective of this chapter is to show that nature of farm tenancy and land lease market in Punjab has completely changed over the Green Revolution period. The traditional share tenancy has been almost completely replaced by modern cash rent tenancy. The profile of lessors and lessees and nature of land lease market transactions has completely changed, and a competitive modern land lease market has become firmly established. But the tenancy laws of the state have not changed in line with the development of modern tenancy over this period. The tenancy laws of the state enacted in the 1950s, suitable and relevant for a regime of share tenancy and small weak tenants, are still in operation. These tenancy laws have become not only outmoded and irrelevant in the new complexion of land lease transactions, but also a major impediment in the full flowering of modern land lease market and structural change in agriculture. The existing tenancy laws of the state, therefore, need to be modernised to bring these in line with the new realities of land lease market transactions. The evidence on the changed nature of tenancy in Punjab is presented and evaluated in Sects. 6.1 and 6.2, profitability of cash renting is evaluated in Sect. 6.3, the factors responsible for the growth and dominance of cash rent tenancy in Sect. 6.4, and the need for and elements of modern tenancy laws are discussed in Sects. 6.5 and 6.6, that is followed by conclusions.

6.1 Growth of Cash Rent Tenancy in Punjab: The Evidence

Farm tenancy is a universally prevailing institutional mechanism through which land owners not wanting to or able to cultivate their own land rent it out to others to cultivate it for a specified period in exchange for a pre-agreed payment. Farm tenancy as an institution is very old and has existed in pre-modern as well as in modern societies, though its nature and form changes in response to the level of

H.S. Shergill (✉)
Emeritus Professor of Economics, Panjab University, Chandigarh 160014, India
e-mail: profshergill@gmail.com

L. Singh and N. Singh (eds.), *Economic Transformation of a Developing Economy*, India Studies in Business and Economics,
DOI 10.1007/978-981-10-0197-0_6

agricultural technology, commercialisation of agriculture and level of development of the country. In pre-modern traditional agriculture, share tenancy is the dominant form of farm tenancy, and rent payed to the landlord takes the form of a fixed share of farm produce. In modern agriculture, on the other hand, fixed cash rent tenancy prevails and rent paid to the landlord is a fixed amount of cash per unit of land. In the evolution of agriculture in developed capitalist countries, this has been the universally observed pattern; however, the rate and shape of shift from share tenancy to fixed cash rent tenancy has varied from country to country.

6.1.1 Growth of Cash Rent Tenancy in Punjab: Comparison with Other States

The modernisation of agriculture is occurring in all the regions of India, albeit at different rates and in different patterns. Among the states of India, the modernisation of agriculture has been the fastest in Punjab, and by now it has reached an advanced stage, whatever the indicator of modernisation one uses; degree of commercialisation, degree of mechanisation, yield rates, level of production efficiency, evolution of farm size structure or any other. The modernisation of agriculture being the most advanced in Punjab among states of India, the growth of cash rent tenancy has also been the fastest. By now, cash rent tenancy has become dominant in Punjab, and share tenancy has been almost completely eliminated. The comparative information on the proportion of fixed cash-rented area in total leased in area for major states of India for the year 2002–2003 (from NSSO 59th Round) presented in Table 6.1 clearly shows how advanced is Punjab agriculture in the prevalence of cash rent tenancy. In 2002–2003 (the latest year for which comparative state-wise NSSO data are available), 80 % of total leased in area in Punjab was leased in on fixed cash rent basis; compared to 30.17 % in India as a whole. In fact, except for the neighbouring State of Haryana, the growth of cash rent tenancy has not yet crossed even the one-third share of total leased area in most of the other states of India. The uniqueness of the fast growth of cash rent tenancy in Punjab is highlighted by the fact that in seven out of the 20 major states of the country the fixed cash-rented area in total leased in area is less than 20 %. Not only cash renting of land is much more developed in Punjab compared to other states, but also land leasing itself has grown at a fast rate. In Punjab, in 2002–2003 about 18 % of cultivated area was leased out to tenants (the highest among major states), compared to just 6.6 % in the country as a whole, and less than 3 % in 5 major states. The information given in Table 6.1 leaves little doubt about the complete dominance of fixed cash rent mode of leasing land and quite high development of land leasing itself in Punjab.

Table 6.1 Extent of land leasing and cash rent tenancy: Punjab and other major states of India (2002–2003)

Sr. no.	State	Proportion of leased in area in total operated area (%)	Proportion of cash-rented area in total leased in area (%)
1	Punjab	17.83	80.30
2	Haryana	14.38	73.72
3	Kerala	4.18	40.11
4	Rajasthan	2.82	36.39
5	Karnataka	3.68	33.26
6	Tamil Nadu	6.11	32.59
7	West Bengal	9.39	30.16
8	Maharashtra	4.59	28.91
9	Andhra Pradesh	10.02	28.45
10	Madhya Pradesh	2.80	27.71
11	Himachal Pradesh	2.87	24.67
12	Uttar Pradesh	9.77	24.15
13	Uttaranchal	3.49	24.07
14	Assam	5.04	16.51
15	Chhattisgarh	5.41	14.50
16	Bihar	11.75	12.94
17	Orissa	13.15	10.96
18	Gujarat	5.08	9.45
19	Jammu & Kashmir	0.32	7.82
20	Jharkhand	2.08	2.18
	All India	6.60	30.17

Source NSS Report No. 492: some aspects of operational land holdings in India, 2003

6.1.2 Evolution of Cash Renting in Punjab over Green Revolution Period

The growth of cash rent tenancy in Punjab over the Green Revolution period is pictured in Table 6.2 on the basis of NSSO data. In 1971–1972, about 29 % of leased in area in Punjab was contracted on fixed cash rent basis, compared to about 15.42 % in the country as a whole. Between 1971–1972 and 1981–1982 (the early phase of green revolution), cash-rented area in total leased in area rose to 42.13 % in Punjab; whereas in India as whole it declined to 10.86 %. The growth of cash rent tenancy in Punjab in the next 10 years (1981–1982 to 1991–1992) was slower, from 42.13 to 49.20 % of the total leased in area. The maturing of green revolution in Punjab gave a further push to the growth of cash rent tenancy, the cash-rented area proportion in leased in area reaching 80.30 % by 2002–2003. The NSSO

Table 6.2 Growth of cash rent tenancy in Punjab agriculture

State	Percentage of fixed cash-rented area in total leased in area		Source of information
	Punjab	All India	
1971–1972	29.08	15.42	NSS, 26th round
1981–1982	42.13	10.86	NSS, 37th round
1991–1992	49.20	19.00	NSS, 48th round
2002–2003	80.30	30.17	NSS, 59th round
2010–2011	90.42	–	Primary survey of 300 farms conducted in May–July 2011, Institute for Development and Communication, Chandigarh

information is available right now only up to 2002–2003, but a random survey of 300 farms conducted by the author in connection with a Punjab Government project indicated that by 2010–2011 the share of cash-rented area in total leased in area in Punjab has reached 90.42 %. The information displayed in Table 6.2 clearly suggests the following conclusions: (i) the growth of cash rent tenancy in Punjab over the Green Revolution period has been quite fast and much faster than in the other states of India; (ii) by now, cash rent tenancy in Punjab has almost completely replaced the traditional share tenancy; (iii) the growth of cash rent tenancy over this period has not been at the same pace throughout; it has been faster in the early phase and the mature phase of green revolution, but slower in the middle phase.

6.1.3 *Regional Variations in Growth of Cash Rent Tenancy*

In spite of Punjab's small size and compact structure, some regional variation in the development of cash rent tenancy is also observable. The information from the 2010–2011 survey referred to earlier presented in Table 6.3 indicates that cash rent tenancy is more developed in the central and Northern Malwa zones of the state where 93.23 and 96.55 % of leased in area, respectively, is contracted on cash rent basis. Even in the Eastern Malwa zone, share of cash-rented area in total leased in area was more than 90 %. The share of cash-rented area in total leased in area was lower in the foothills zone (87.65 %) and the southern western Malwa zone (82.35 %) of the state. It may be mentioned that in both these zones rice–wheat rotation cultivation is less dominant than in the Central zone and the two Malwa zones of the state; maize and sugarcane being the important crops in foothills zone, and cotton in the southern western zone. It may also be emphasised that the regional variations in the development of cash rent tenancy in Punjab being moderate (the range being 82.35–96.35 %), one can say that cash renting is the dominant mode of land leasing throughout the state.

Table 6.3 Regional variations in extent of cash rent tenancy (2010–2011)

Zone	Districts in the zone	Main crops	Percent of cash-rented area in total leased in area
Punjab	All	Wheat, rice, cotton, sugarcane and maize	90.42
Foothills	Gurdaspur, Pathankot, Hoshiarpur, Roop Nagar, Nawan Shaher, SAS Nagar	Wheat, rice, maize and sugarcane	87.65
Central	Amritsar, Tarn Taran, Jalandhar, Kapurthala	Wheat and rice	93.23
Northern Malwa	Ludhiana, Moga, Fatehgarh Sahib	Wheat and rice	96.55
Eastern Malwa	Patiala, Sangrur, Barnala	Wheat and rice	91.35
Southern western Malwa	Bathidna, Mansa, Faridkot, Ferozepur, Mukatsar, Fazilka	Wheat, rice and cotton	82.35

Source Primary survey of 300 farms conducted in May–July 2011, Institute for Development and Communication, Chandigarh

6.2 Changed Profile of Land Lessors and Tenants

6.2.1 Profile of Land Lessors

One of the factors responsible for the shift to cash rent tenancy is the completely changed profile of land lessors. In the pre-green revolution traditional agriculture, the typical land lessor was a big semi-feudal landlord living in the village and dominating the rural sector. But now it is mostly the small land owners who are renting out land or the big owners who have left the village for good and have settled in the urban sector. The information on the relevant features of land leasing out households for the year 2002–2003 (NSSO, 59th Round) is presented in Table 6.4. Out of the 14.65 lakh land-owning households in the state, 5.22 lakh households (35.63 % of total) were not cultivating any land; obviously they were leasing out their land to others for cultivation. Out of these 5.22 lakh land leasing out households, 48.73 % resided in rural areas and 51.27 % in the urban sector. The owned land size-wise distribution of these non-cultivating land owners shows that 87.17 % of them owned less than 1 ha of land; another 4.98 % of these owned between 1 and 2 ha. So, more than 90 % of land leasing out households were small owners having less than 2 ha of land. It may also be observed that most of the bigger land owners (owning 4 ha or more) leasing out land were absentee owners living in the urban sector. All the 100 % owners of 10 ha or more leased out land were living in the urban sector, and 75 % of lessors leasing out 4–10 ha were resident of urban sector. More than 50 % of even small owners (owning less than 2 ha) leasing out land were resident in the urban sector. On the basis of information

Table 6.4 Non-cultivating land owners of Punjab: owned land amount and residential location (2002–03)

Owned land size class (ha)	Number of land-owning households (lakh)			Residential location of non-cultivating land owners (per cent of all non-cultivating)	
	Total	Not-cultivating any land	Non-cultivating as per cent of total land owning	Rural	Urban
Up to 1.0	8.24 (4.28)	4.55 [87.17]	55.22	51.08	48.92
1.0–2.0	2.74 (7.27)	0.26 [4.98]	9.55	18.33	81.67
2.0–4.0	2.15 (11.29)	0.27 [5.17]	12.61	58.93	41.67
4.0–10.0	1.27 (13.76)	0.11 [2.10]	8.76	24.03	75.97
10.0 and above	0.25 (6.25)	0.03 [0.58]	12.13	0.00	100.00
All	14.65 (42.85)	5.22 (100.00)	35.63	48.73	51.27

Notes (1) *Source* NSS, 59th round, 2003
(2) Figures in round brackets indicate area owned (lakh hectare) by each size class
(3) Figures in square brackets are percentages

given in Table 6.4, it can be safely concluded that most of the land lessors in Punjab are small owners, and absentee big owners who have left the rural sector are living in the urban sector. It is the completely changed profile of land lessors that is responsible for growth of cash rent tenancy. As will be discussed in detail latter, share tenancy for being profitable to the land lessor requires his close monitoring of the inputs used and outputs produced by the tenant. But effective monitoring is possible only if the land lessor is more powerful than the tenant and is also present on the scene of farm production. The small land lessors cannot monitor the inputs used by the big farm tenants even when they are resident in the village; the absentee big land lessors are prevented by the distance factor and lack of farming experience from monitoring the inputs used by the tenants. Consequently, such lessors prefer to rent out on a fixed cash rent basis in which no monitoring by the lessor is necessary and the rent amount can be obtained without visiting the village.

6.2.2 *Profile of Tenants*

The profile of tenants has also completely changed in Punjab over the Green Revolution period. The ubiquitous small weak tenant farmer of the pre-Green

Table 6.5 Tenant farms and pure owned land operators: size, technology and productivity differences (2010–2011)

Sr. no.	Feature description	Tenant farms	Pure owned land operating farms
1	Share in total operated area (%)	54.52	45.48
2	Share of leased in area in operated area (%)	47.67	0.00
3	Size of operational holding (ha)	6.69	3.30
4	Size of owned land (ha)	3.53	3.30
5	Per cent owning tractors	83	55
6	Per cent owning power-operated tube wells	78	61
7	Per cent employing permanent farm servants	56	27
8	Fertilizer used in paddy (kg/ha)	220	195
9	Fertilizer used in wheat (kg/ha)	263	233
10	Paddy yield (kg/ha)	4881	4245
11	Wheat yield (kg/ha)	4505	4148

Source Primary survey of 300 farms conducted in May–July 2011, Institute for Development and Communication, Chandigarh

Revolution era has almost completely disappeared and has been replaced by the bigger enterprising farmer having a sizeable owned land of his own, and also the complete paraphernalia of modern farm machinery and a number of hired permanent farm servants. The changed profile of tenants in Punjab agriculture is clearly visible from the information presented in Table 6.5. The size of operational holding of tenants is more than double of the pure owned land operating farms, and a significantly higher proportion of them are owning tractors and power-operated tube wells compared to the pure owner operators. The mean size of their own land is also higher than that of the pure owned land operating farms, and the proportion of tenant farms employing permanent farm servants was more than double of the pure owned land operating farms. In the use of chemical fertilizers, also the tenant farms were ahead of pure owners' operators, and so was the case in getting higher rice and wheat yields. So the information presented in Table 6.5 fully supports the generally prevalent impression about the enterprise and efficiency of present-day tenant farmers of Punjab. They not only operate bigger sized holdings, but also have a sizeable owned area of their own, and they are the leaders in the adoption of modern machinery and biochemical technology and operate their farms with the help of regularly hired permanent farm servants. Their better expertise in modern farming is clearly reflected in the significantly higher yield per acre they are able to get in the two main crops of the state—rice and wheat. It may also be noted from Table 6.5 that these more enterprising more efficient and big tenant farms now operate more than half of the cultivated area of the state.

Table 6.6 Share in leased in area of various farm size classes (2010–2011)

Farm size class (acres)	Sample information (2010–2011)		Total number of farms in Punjab (2010–2011)	Total area leased in by the size group of farms (acres)	Share of size group in total leased in area (%)
	Number of sample farms	Area leased in per farm (acres)			
Marginal (Up to 2.50)	50	0.16	16,4431	26,309	0.88
Small (2.50–5.00)	63	0.52	195,439	101,628	3.38
Medium (5.00–10.00)	87	1.25	324,515	405,644	13.49
Big (10.00–25.00)	75	4.85	298,451	1,447,487	48.13
Large (25.00 and above)	25	14.72	69,718	1,026,249	34.12
All	300	2.86	1,052,554	3,007,317	100.00

Note Information on sample farms is from primary survey of 300 farms conducted in May–July 2011, Institute for Development and Communication, Chandigarh. Information on total number of farms in Punjab in various size groups is from *Statistical Abstract of Punjab*, 2012

Of course even now there are some enterprising marginal and small farmers who are leasing in land. But their presence in the land lease market is inconsequential, as their share in the total leased in area is very small. The distribution of total leased in area by farm size classes presented in Table 6.6 shows that the marginal and small farmer tenants' share in total leased in area is bare 4.26 %, compared to 95.74 share of the medium and bigger farm size groups. In fact, the land lease market of Punjab is now completely dominated by big farms (operating 10 acres or more), who control and operate about 82 % of the total leased in area of the state. They dominate the land lease market and set its tone and tenor in terms of cash rent rates and other terms and conditions of lease. The marginal and small tenant farmer is barely surviving in some obscure niches of the land lease market; leasing in pieces of land that probably do not suit the bigger tenants due to their location and other factors.

6.3 Tenant's Earnings from Cash-Rented Land

The fast growth of cash rent tenancy in Punjab and the dominance of big farmers (who are quite profit conscious) in land lease market suggests that cash renting of land must be a profitable business in the prevailing technological, productivity and

Table 6.7 Economics of cash renting: tenant's earnings compared with cash rent paid and owner-operator's earnings (average for triennium ending 2010–2011)

Sr. no.	Variable description	Variable value
1	Crop rotation system	Rice–wheat
2	Gross value of output per hectare (rupees)	120,509
3	Paid out costs per hectare (rupees)	31,134
4	Net return per hectare (rupees) (2–3) = (owner-operator's earnings)	89,375
5	Proportion of paid out costs in gross value of output (%)	25.84
6	Proportion of net return in gross value of output (%)	74.16
7	Cash rent rate per hectare (%)	36,322
8	Tenant's net earnings per hectare after paying cash rent (4–7) (rupees)	53,053
9	Share of cash rent in net value of output (%)	40.64 (30.14)
10	Share of tenant in net value of output (%)	59.36 (44.02)

Notes (1) Estimated from the information given in cost of cultivation scheme reports of CACP (2) Figures in brackets indicate share of cash rent and cash renting tenant's earnings, respectively, in gross value of output

price conditions of rice and wheat farming in Punjab. For a share tenant, operating in traditional agriculture profitability of rented in land does not matter much; as his prime motive for leasing in land is to use surplus family labour to eke out a living. But a big farmer operating in modern agriculture will lease in land only if it is profitable, because profit motive dominates farmers' behaviour once agriculture is modernised and commercialised. To what extent cash renting of land in Punjab is profitable for the tenant requires a comprehensive study it its own right that cannot be attempted here. However, a preliminary evaluation of its profitability is attempted on the basis of cost of cultivation data of CACP for the year 2010–2011. The details of this evaluation are presented in Table 6.7 and indicate that a cash renting tenant earned a net income of Rs. 53,053 per hectare after meeting the paid out costs and paying the cash rent. This estimate is based on the assumption that cash renting tenants' per hectare yield of rice and wheat is equal to the overall state average. But we have seen (Table 6.5) that the rice and wheat yield obtained by cash renting tenants is significantly above the average. Consequently, the net earnings of a tenant from cash-rented land must be higher than the average figure of Rs. 53,053 mentioned above. It may be seen from Table 6.7 that paid out costs eat up about 26 % of the gross return per hectare from rice–wheat rotation system; and out of the remaining amount above 41 % goes to the landlord as rent and 59 % is retained by the tenant as reward for his management, labour and capital services. Even as a share of gross return per hectare, tenants' net earnings come to about 44 % and landlords' cash rent to 30 %; the remaining 26 % being spent on purchased inputs. In addition to its profitability per se, the attractiveness of cash renting to medium and big farms is enhanced by the existence of considerable excess capacity in tractor and other machinery owned and the team of permanent farm servants employed by them. The fixed per unit cost of using this excess capacity on additional rented in land is virtually zero. For example, the marginal cost of using tractor on additional rented in land is only the expenses incurred on diesel used to operate it for this purpose.

6.4 Growth of Cash Rent Tenancy: Causal Factors

The growth of cash rent tenancy with the modernisation of agriculture is a universally observed phenomenon in the development of agriculture in capitalist countries. In all the developed countries, cash renting of land is the rule, and share renting a rare exception produced by peculiar conditions of the lessor and lessee. So the basic cause of fast growth of cash rent tenancy in Punjab is the fast pace of modernisation of agriculture compared to other states. Even by the historical standards of modernisation of agriculture in the present-day developed countries, the pace of modernisation of agriculture in Punjab has been fairly fast. Just in a span of four-decades agriculture in the state has been modernised, fully commercialised and attained productivity level comparable to developed countries. How modernisation of agriculture created favourable conditions for the growth of cash renting in the specific historical context of Punjab is briefly described and discussed in this section

6.4.1 Heightened Production Inefficiency of Share Tenancy

The production inefficiency of share tenancy in modern conditions has been emphasised by all the classical economists from Adam Smith onwards. A very neat statement of the classical position is given by Marshall in his *Principles of Economics* (1949, p. 535), which is reproduced for ready reference: "when the cultivator has to give his landlord half of the returns to each dose of capital and labour that he applied to the land, it will not be to his interest to apply any doses the total return of which is less than twice enough to reward him. If, then he is free to cultivate as he chooses he will cultivate less intensively than on the English plan". The English plan referred to by him is leasing on fixed cash rent basis; at that time, share renting prevailed in France and many other countries on the continent, but cash renting was the rule in England. The basic economic principle that producer's net returns will be maximised when he uses inputs up to the point of equality of his share of the marginal product with the opportunity cost of the inputs, results in share tenant using smaller amount of variable inputs, compared to cash rent tenant and owner—operator. So, under similar production conditions, the variable inputs used and the output produced per unit of land by a share tenant will be smaller compared to a cash rent tenant or owner operator. This inbuilt disincentive and production inefficiency of share tenancy remains dormant in traditional agriculture, but manifests with full force once the agriculture is modernised. In traditional agriculture, share tenancy is kept production-efficient by the operation of many factors such as:

(i) Share tenant is a small weak farmer who cannot dare to disobey landlords' directions regarding the intensity of input use, whatever his own disincentive and inclination.
(ii) The landlord is a big powerful owner resident and dominant in the village, who can easily monitor the inputs used by the share tenant.
(iii) The tenant is a tenant-at-will having no legal security of tenure and can be easily evicted by the landlord if he cultivates land less intensively.
(iv) The technology being traditional and stagnant, the optimal dose of inputs per unit of land gets standardised and known to everyone in the village; so the tenant cannot easily shirk using that amount of inputs.
(v) The rational element in tenant's consciousness is very weak and he is not very particular in equating his share of marginal product with opportunity cost of variable inputs used. His sole aim is to eke out a living by using his family labour.
(vi) The most important variable input used by tenant is family labour, that has almost zero opportunity cost in traditional agriculture due to non-availability of non-farm work. So even half of the marginal product of labour is positive and greater than the zero opportunity cost of tenant' family labour. He uses family labour, under such conditions, up to the point of zero marginal product to maximise his share of output.

All these factors combine to check the inbuilt disincentive of the share tenant to use variable inputs less intensively, and his production efficiency remains comparable with the owner operator and cash rent tenant in traditional agriculture.

The modernisation of agriculture makes all these checks on the share tenant in operative, and his inherent tendency to use variable inputs less intensively manifests and makes share tenancy an inefficient production arrangement from the landlord point of view, as well as for society as a whole. This is exactly what has happened in Punjab with the fast modernisation of agriculture. The profile of both tenant's and lessors has radically changed and the power equation between them has been completely reversed. Like modern agriculture everywhere, tenant in Punjab is no longer a small weak farmer; rather, he is an economically sound enterprising farmer having the full paraphernalia of modern machinery and sizeable owned land of his own. In terms of production efficiency and agricultural expertise, he is among the best farmers in the village. The land lessor, on the other hand, is no longer a big powerful land owner resident and dominant in the village. In most cases, he is a small owner not residing in the village or if resident in the village not in a position to dictate the big tenant farmer the input use on his share rented out land. The medium and big owners who are leasing out land in Punjab today are almost all absentees, residing in the urban sector or NRI's. So, due to small size of the land rented out and his weak position in the village or/and absence from the village due to settlement in the urban sector, the modern lessor of land in Punjab is no longer in a position to dictate the share tenant the dose of inputs to be used per unit of land; nor he is in a position to monitor whether or not such an amount of variable inputs has been actually used. The big quantity and great variety of variable inputs used in modern agriculture (casual labour, fertilizers, weedicides and insecticides, diesel and electricity, etc.) also makes such monitoring impossible even if the lessor is a big owner resident in the village. The tenant's position vis-a-vis the lessor is strengthened by the modernisation of agriculture by two other factors also. The enactment of tenancy laws that precedes modernisation of agriculture provides security of tenure to the tenant; he cannot be easily ejected if in occupation of leased in land for a specified number of years. Secondly, the farm labour becomes scarce with the modernisation of agriculture, and the opportunity cost of tenant's family labour becomes positive and sizeable because of the non-farm work being available. So, the share tenant has a choice either to use the additional dose of family labour on share rented in land, or hire it out for non-farm work. So, he is neither willing nor can be compelled to use family labour on share rented in land beyond the point of equality of market wage rate with one-half of the marginal product of labour on share rented in land. Under such a scenario, the lessor suffers a substantial loss if he rents out his land on a share rent basis; hence, a strong preference emerges among the lessors to rent out land on a fixed cash rent basis. By doing that he not only gets an assured rent per acre, but also avoids the monitoring costs and botheration of keeping track of the inputs used and output produced on share rented out land.

6.4.2 Heightened Tenant Preference for Cash Renting

A strong preference for fixed cash rent leasing in also emerges in the tenant once agriculture is modernised. The completely changed profile of the tenant (a medium/big land owner having full paraphernalia of farm machinery) is the main cause of emergence of this preference. The reasons for this preference for cash rent leasing in are many and varied; more important of these are described and discussed. The modern tenant being among the most enterprising and efficient farmers of the village is confident of reaping a good return by fully intensifying cultivation on the cash rented in land. Secondly, since cash rent rate per acre adjusts to growth of farm productivity slowly with a time lag, so in a regime of continuous growth of farm productivity (as has been the case in Punjab over the Green Revolution period), the entire increment of natural growth of productivity is also pocketed by him. The comfortable economic position of the tenant also results in his developing a strong dislike for the interference of the lessor in production decisions on the leased in land; and that produces in him a strong dislike for share renting land. In share tenancy, the lessor has a right to participate in production decisions about his share rented out land; but on cash rented out land, the lessor becomes a virtual non-owner for the lease period and is debarred from inferring. The preference for cash renting and dislike of share renting by a modern relatively well-off tenant is also strengthened by the subordinate social position of the share tenant vis-a-vis the lessor in village society; it was a stark fact in traditional agriculture, but that taint lingers to some extent even after modernisation of agriculture. Somehow, in these days almost no tenant wants to rent in on a share basis, if he can afford to pay the cash rent in advance; share tenancy has gone out of fashion in Punjab rural side.

6.4.3 Sharp Reduction in Yield and Price Risk

The great reduction in yield and price risk with the emergence of rice–wheat rotation system in Punjab also accelerated the growth of cash rent tenancy. One of the major factors in tenants preferring share renting over cash renting was their strong desire to reduce production and price risk (Cheung 1969; Stiglitz 1974). In share tenancy, the production and price risk are proportionately shared by the landlord–lessor with the tenant; so tenants' risk is greatly reduced. The rent being a share of the produce falls proportionately when yield falls. On the other hand, in cash renting the entire production and price risk is borne by the tenant. So long as production and price risk was big and the tenant's risk-bearing capacity very low (as was the case in pre-green revolution agriculture), the tenant was not willing to rent in on fixed cash rent basis. He had neither the desire nor the capacity to bear the entire production and price risk; that is why share renting was the rule in pre-green revolution agriculture in Punjab. After the Green Revolution, the production risk was sharply reduced in the case of rice and wheat crops because of the great stability of yield of new high-yielding varieties (HYVs) of rice and wheat. The price risk in rice and wheat farming was simply eliminated by the introduction of an effectively functioning minimum support price and assured purchase programme after 1966. The sharp reduction in production and price risk in HYV of rice and wheat farming created a strong incentive among the tenants to rent in on cash rent basis, and reap the entire benefit of continuously growing rice and wheat yields and minimum support prices. Moreover, the changed profile of the tenant (he being now a medium/big owner and a relatively well-off farmer), also enhanced his risk-bearing capacity and he was quite willing to rent in land on cash rent basis. The higher proportion of leased in area rented on share basis in the foothills zone and south-western zone may be due to maize and cotton (which are more risky) being important there.

6.4.4 Improved Financial Position and Credit Availability to Tenants

Another factor that worked to make cash renting popular among tenants was their enhanced financial capability to pay the advance instalment of cash rent. In share tenancy, rent is paid by the tenant after harvesting the crop; it being a certain share of the produce. But in cash rent tenancy, the cash rent has to be paid in advance in the beginning of every crop season. A small weak farmer is debarred from cash renting in land simply by his inability to muster enough cash to pay the advance instalment of cash rent; he neither has cash of his own, nor he can get credit from anywhere to do so. The modern relatively well-off tenant in most cases has sufficient cash of his own to pay the advance instalment of cash rent; in some cases, when he does not have sufficient cash of his own, the local commission agent is keen enough to give him credit for it on the condition that he will market his produce through his commission agency. This factor also gave considerable impetus to the growth of cash rent tenancy in Punjab over the Green Revolution period and the increasing dominance of medium and big farmers in leasing in land. The hassle-free receipt of cash rent also made cash renting of land more attractive to lessors. In many cases, the Commission Agents transfer the cash rent online to the lessors on behalf of the tenants, and this mode of rent payment is found very convenient by NRI lessors and others living in the urban areas.

6.4.5 Impact of General Monetisation of Rural Economy

As a result of the constellation of many factors and processes, the monetisation of rural economy has become almost complete in Punjab. Almost the entire farm production is sold in the market, most of the farm inputs are now purchased by the farmers, most of the goods consumed by farm families are purchased from the market, (even Deshi ghee is not produced at home by most peasant households), and the traditional Jajmani system of payment in kind to artisans is completely gone, and almost all the permanent farm servants and casual labourers hired by them are paid in cash. So, almost complete monetisation of the rural economy and life has occurred in Punjab over the Green Revolution period. This complete shift towards use of cash in all economic transactions also accelerated the shift from share tenancy to cash rent tenancy. In a regime characterised by universal use of cash in economic transactions, persistence of the older form of exchange in kind in particular activities becomes odd and untenable even if it is profitable. The people simply lose the habit of thinking and exchanging in kind, once the use of money in economic transactions becomes all pervasive. But when the exchange in kind is not even profitable (as became the case of share tenancy once agriculture was modernised), its survival becomes impossible.

So the overall drift of rural economy towards monetisation of exchange also contributed in making cash rent tenancy more popular both among tenants as well as lessors.

6.5 Tenancy Laws and Imperfection in Land Lease Market

Although a sizeable land lease market has developed and cash rent tenancy has become almost universal, yet many imperfections in the land lease market exist and persist. The main source of these imperfections in the land lease market is the existing tenancy laws of the state. These tenancy laws were enacted mostly in the 1950s to protect the small weak tenant farmers from the exploitation of big semi-feudal landlords who were the main lessors of land at that time; share tenancy was the prevailing node of land leasing. The main objective of these tenancy laws was to provide security of tenure to the tenants and ensure fair rent to them. These laws were need of the hour in the agrarian conditions prevailing in Punjab on the eve of independence, and they have served their purpose. But in the totally changed agrarian conditions of today, these tenancy laws have become not only irrelevant, but also a major hindrance in the further development of productive forces and structural change in agriculture. These laws are responsible for creating many imperfections and negative tendencies in the land lease market that obstructs the free flow of land for cultivation among rural households. As a result leased in area remains sub-optimal and production from existing area is not maximised, many inefficient farmers persist in self-cultivation on account of the fear of land loss created by these laws.

The main imperfections in the land lease market of Punjab are:

1. The high risk of lessor losing land to the tenant if land is leased out for a long time on a formally written/registered lease contract. There is a clause in the existing tenancy laws whereby if a tenant has been cultivating a leased in plot continuously for 3 years or more and there is sufficient proof of that in the land records, then he cannot be evicted by the landlord. The tenant then becomes a virtual occupancy tenant; and the landlord being merely entitled the fair rent as fixed by law.
2. The virtual village-wise segmentation of land lease market because potential lessees from other villages are not able to enter on account of the practice of renting out for one year to a particular tenant. But renting in for only one year is not economically viable for non-residents who have to create a new establishment in the village. Moreover, lessors do not trust such non-resident tenants, information on their reliability not being available. The fear in the minds of lessors of such tenants usurping the leased in land by invoking the tenancy laws gets exaggerated because of lack of information about their character.

3. The refusal of lessors to enter into written lease contracts and long-term lease contracts, to protect their ownership right against the possibility of tenant grabbing the rented in land by invoking the provisions of the prevailing tenancy laws.
4. The practice of advance payment of cash rent has created a huge barrier that prevents many enterprising efficient small farmers from leasing in land.
5. The non-availability of cheap institutional credit to tenant farmers on account of absence of any written proof of their having rented in land.

These imperfections in the land lease market result in many undesirable economic consequences such as:

1. Persistence of inefficient big land owners in self-cultivation owing to fear of losing land to tenants.
2. The virtual absence of long lease contracts and the practice of annual rotation of tenants to prevent them from availing the protection of tenancy laws. This dissuades the tenants from making land improvements that impact production only after a time lag and in a staggered manner over time.
3. The tenants are not able to get credit from formal sector credit agencies for cultivation of leased in land, because they cannot show any documentary proof of their having leased in land; it being leased in on an oral contract. Consequently, they have to borrow from Commission Agents at high interest rates.
4. The exclusion of many efficient and enterprising small farmers from the demand side of land lease market because they cannot pay advance cash rent from their own sources, and formal sector credit agencies do not provide them credit to pay advance rent.
5. The undue inflation of land rents due to annual bidding among tenants for leasing in land. The uncertainty of availability of leased in land for next year makes tenants offer unduly high rents, and as a result rent rate per acre continuously rises.

In view of the above imperfections and negative consequences, and the completely changed character of lessors and lessees in Punjab, the existing outmoded tenancy laws need to be replaced by modern tenancy laws.

6.6 Modernisation of Tenancy Laws

The tenancy laws are the rules and regulations enacted and enforced by the government to regulate the relations between lessors and lessees of land. The main objective of tenancy laws in traditional agriculture has been to protect the small weak tenant farmer from the exploitation of big semi-feudal landlords. The exploitation of small weak tenant farmers takes the form of rack renting, insecurity of lease tenure and many other direct/indirect excesses committed by the landlords.

The first and basic tenancy law of Punjab was enacted by the British government in 1887. After independence, a number of tenancy laws were enacted during the 1950s when land reforms occupied the centre stage of the state-induced agrarian change in the country. The tenancy laws in operation at present in Punjab are:

1. Punjab Tenancy Act, 1887.
2. Punjab Occupancy Tenants Act, 1952.
3. Punjab Security of Land Tenure Act, 1953.
4. Pepsu Tenancy and Agricultural Act 1955.

Of course, amendments and modification in these basic laws have been made from time to time. The main objective of the tenancy laws passed in the 1950s was to provide ownership rights to occupancy tenants, and security of tenure and fair rent to tenants-at-will. These laws were need of the hour in the agrarian conditions prevailing in the Punjab on the eve of independence; the tenants were mostly small weak farmers and lessors were mostly big semi-feudal landlords who dominated the rural side. These tenancy laws did play a significant role in providing relief to the tenants and in making a large number of occupancy tenants' owners of land. But in the totally changed technological and economic conditions of Punjab agriculture today these tenancy laws have become not only irrelevant, but the main source of imperfections in the land lease market discussed in the previous section. As a result, the free flow of land between those land owners who do not want to self-cultivate and others who want to cultivate more land than what they own is obstructed. The leased in area, therefore, remains at a sub-optimal level, and production from the existing area is not maximised.

Modernisation of Tenancy Laws: An Outline of Objectives

The main objectives of the modernisation of tenancy laws should be:

1. The risk of land owner losing land to the tenant should be completely eliminated. The laws should ensure the inviolability of owner's right to his land, irrespective of the length of occupancy by the tenant.
2. Easy and costless registration of lease contracts at the village level itself.
3. Speedy and hassle-free enforcement of lease contracts; particularly in lessor getting the leased in plot vacated immediately after the expiry of lease period.
4. Acceptance of lease contracts as collateral for borrowing by tenants from the banks and other credit suppliers.
5. Special incentives, financial as well as in enforcement of lease contract, for the development of long lease contracts.

The changes in tenancy laws on these lines will:

1. Facilitate smooth flow of land from the less efficient to more efficient farmers and maximisation of leased in area.
2. Result in maximisation of output from the existing area under cultivation.
3. Induce many big owner—cultivators to leave farming by renting out their land, and shift to some non-farm occupation or activity.

4. Result in rise in the average size of operational holdings, and more economical use of tractors and other machinery and consequently lower unit cost of production.
5. Improve the relations between lessors and lessees because of the disappearance of the lurking fear in lessors' mind of the lessee usurping his land by invoking the legal provision in the existing tenancy laws. The lesssors will not be afraid of leasing out their land to the same tenant on a long-term basis, once the tenancy laws are modernised on the above lines.

Such a change in tenancy laws will be Pareto optimal; as everyone will gain and no one will lose. The country will gain from increased production from the same area; more efficient farmers will gain by expanding their operational holdings to the level of their managerial ability and paraphernalia of machinery; the small owners and inefficient big owners will gain by earning a handsome cash rent per acre without any fear of losing their land; the per unit cost of production will fall by the elimination of under utilisation of machinery, and relations between lessors and tenants will improve once the fear of lessor losing his land is gone. Moreover, it has no financial cost to the state, and the enforcement costs of these new modern tenancy laws will be much smaller than the existing tenancy laws. A beginning in this direction has already been made by Punjab Government by enacting Punjab Security of Land Tenure (Amendment Act, 2011). According to this amendment, the protection to tenant from ejectment (provided by the existing laws) will not be available where the tenancy is for a fixed period, lease deed between lessor and tenant has been properly registered, and the lease period has expired. The beginning has been made, but much more needs to be done to make leasing out land absolutely risk free for the lessors. The security of tenure to the tenants should be guaranteed till the expiry of the lease period; the absolute unencumbered right of land owner to get his land back after the expiry of the lease period should be enforced quickly and hassle-free.

6.7 Conclusions

The main conclusions of the empirical evidence and analysis presented in the proceeding pages are now summarised:

1. The traditional share tenancy has been almost completely replaced by modern cash rent tenancy in Punjab.
2. The lessors are now mostly small owners and absentee (urban resident, NRI) medium and big owners, and the lessees are mostly medium and big farmers having the complete set of modern machinery and better farming expertise to get highest crop yields.
3. Owing to the completely changed nature of tenancy, the existing tenancy laws of the state have become not only irrelevant, but also a big hindrance in the free

flow of land between lessors and lessees and in the further development of productive forces and structural change in agriculture.

4. The existing tenancy laws have created many imperfections in land lease market such as high risk of lessor losing his land (to the tenant), if leased out on a long-term basis on a formal written contract, prevalence of short-term oral lease contracts and the annual rotation of tenants, advance payment of the entire cash rent, and village-wise segmentation of lease market.
5. These imperfections have resulted in the persistence of many inefficient big owners in self-cultivation, sub-optimal production from the existing cultivated area, exclusion of efficient-enterprising small farmers from leasing in land, disincentives to tenants in making land improvements and inflation of land rent rate.
6. The tenancy laws should be modernised to eliminate the risk of owner losing his leased out land, to ensure easy and costless registration and enforcement of lease contracts, and acceptance of lease contracts by banks to lend to the tenants.
7. The modernisation of tenancy laws will maximise production from the existing cultivated area, reduce the unit cost of production by fuller utilisation of farm machinery on big tenant farms, and speed up the structural change in agriculture by inducing big inefficient owners to leave agriculture by renting out their land.

References

Cheung SNS (1969) The theory of share tenancy. University of Chicago Press, Chicago
Govt. of Punjab (2011) The punjab security of land tenures (Amendment Act, 2011). Chandigarh
Marshall A (1949) Principles of economics, 8th edn. MacMillan and Co., London
NSSO Govt. of India (1972, 82, 92, 2003) Reports for 26th, 37th, 48th and 59th rounds. New Delhi
Stiglitz JE (1974) Incentives and risk sharing in share cropping. Rev Econ Stud 41:126

Chapter 7
Marketing System and Agricultural Development in Punjab

M.S. Sidhu

7.1 Introduction

Agriculture sector is the backbone of developing countries like India. It is a major source of employment and income in the rural areas. This sector also provides food to its expanding population and raw material to the industry; it provides potential for exports to earn foreign exchange necessary for import of capital goods for industrial development and economic growth. In order to sustain/increase the rate of economic growth, agricultural surplus has to be increased and mopped up for capital formation. An efficient marketing system can also mop up surplus farm production, both of food grain and industrial raw material. In developing countries, agricultural market policies are trusted as an integral part of development policies and their functioning has remained an important part of public policy in India (Chand 2012).

The studies conducted earlier have found that as regard to market infrastructure, some states like Punjab, Haryana, Tamil Nadu, Kerala and Gujarat have better infrastructure facilities whereas in the states like Madhya Pradesh, Rajasthan, Bihar, Assam and West Bengal, a lot of needs to be done (Deshpande and Gopalaappa 2003). Another study revealed that agricultural marketing in Punjab is in an advanced stage as compared to Bihar where it is still evolving (Kumar 2011). The Agricultural Produce Markets Act (APMC), despite all its flaws, provides an assured price and market to the farmers (Sharma 2014). This Act mandates the sale and purchase of agricultural commodities at specific market yards or sub-yards. Prices are determined by open auction, conducted in a transparent manner in the presence of designated officials. The regulation of markets helped the Punjab farmers to sell their produce efficiently and peak marketing season of crops like

M.S. Sidhu (✉)
Department of Economics and Sociology, Punjab Agricultural University, Ludhiana 141004, India
e-mail: mssidhu_pau@yahoo.co.in

L. Singh and N. Singh (eds.), *Economic Transformation of a Developing Economy*, India Studies in Business and Economics,
DOI 10.1007/978-981-10-0197-0_7

Table 7.1 Categorization of different farm size groups, 2007–08 (Area in ha)

Farm category/district	Ludhiana	Patiala	Sangrur
Small	Up to 2.6	Up to 2.12	Up to 2.22
Medium	2.06–5.80	2.12–5.74	2.22–5.40
Large	5.80 and above	5.74 and above	5.40 and above

wheat and paddy is over in just 40–45 days. The public procurement of wheat and paddy at the Minimum Support Price (MSP) has played an important role in making the country self-sufficient in food grains. Rather, India has become a big exporter of these two commodities in the recent past. In this chapter, an attempt has been made to study marketing and agricultural development in Punjab.

7.2 Database

The study is mainly based on the data taken from secondary published sources. The farmers were categorized into small, medium and large categories on the basis of their size of operational holdings using cube root frequency method (Sidhu and Singh 2009). The small, medium and large farmers in Ludhiana, Patiala and Sangrur districts had the operational holding as obtained by the cumulative cube root frequency method given in Table 7.1.

7.3 Contribution of Punjab to the Central Pool of Food Grain

Punjab is the major contributor of wheat and rice to the central pool. The public procurement of these two crops commenced in an organized method in the state during 1960s. During the year 1967–68, Punjab contributed about 59 % of wheat and 7 % of rice to the central pool (Table 7.2). In absolute terms, the wheat contribution has increased from about 14 lakh tonnes in 1967–68 to 128 lakh tonnes in 2011–12 but declined to 109 lakh tonnes in 2012–13. The wheat contribution was as high as 72 % during the year 1987–88. In the recent years, this figure varied between about 38 and 43 %.

Over time, the contribution of rice to the central pool has increased from 2.38 lakh tonnes in 1967–68 to 7.54 lakh tonnes in 1972–73, 22 lakh tonnes in 1977–78, 34 lakh tonnes in 1987–88, 61 lakh tonnes in 1997–98 and 86 lakh tonnes in 2010–11 but declined to 77 lakh tonnes in 2011–12 and again rose to 86 lakh tonnes in 2012–13. In percentage terms, there had been variation in rice contribution from 7 % in 1967–68 to 49 % in 1987–88. In recent years, the percentage share of Punjab in rice procurement has declined due to its procurement on a large scale in other states like

Table 7.2 Contribution of Punjab to the central pool of food grains, 1967–68 to 2012–13 (lakh tonnes)

Crop year	Procurement of wheat			Procurement of rice		
	India	Punjab	% share of Punjab	India	Punjab	% share of Punjab
1967–68	22.98	13.58	59.09	32.33	2.38	7.36
1972–73	45.31	27.07	59.74	27.06	7.54	27.86
1977–78	54.77	32.06	58.54	48.53	21.90	45.13
1982–83	82.92	51.77	62.43	70.47	32.52	46.15
1987–88	65.81	47.49	72.16	69.02	33.65	48.75
1992–93	128.35	64.94	50.60	130.53	49.05	37.58
1997–98	126.52	61.46	48.58	155.91	60.59	38.86
2002–03	158.01	89.38	56.57	164.22	79.39	48.34
2007–08	260.43	99.41	38.17	287.36	79.81	27.77
2010–11	283.35	109.58	38.67	341.98	86.35	25.25
2011–12	381.48	128.34	33.64	350.60	77.31	22.05
2012–13	250.92	108.97	43.43	340.28	85.58	25.15

Source (i) Agricultural Statistics At A Glance, various issues
(ii) Statistical Abstract of Punjab, various issues

Andhra Pradesh, Chattisgarh, Orissa, West Bengal, Uttar Pradesh, etc. Besides, the area under basmati rice has increased in Punjab and there is no levy system on basmati rice and it is not contributed to the central pool. They levy rate is 75 % on the non-basmati rice purchased by the millers/traders. They are free to sell 25 % of rice at the market price within or outside the state. But this is not the case for wheat. There is no levy system on the wheat purchased by the traders. They are free to sell it anywhere. The levy on wheat was there for a short period of time during early 1970s (Ghuman et al. 2010). Due to various difficulties faced at that time, the levy system on wheat was withdrawn very soon.

In brief, we can say that marketed surplus of paddy with the Punjab farmers is more than 90 %, whereas this figure is around 70 % for wheat. It is a testimonial to the fact that Punjab has largely been producing for the market, both in the case of wheat and rice (Ibid). The assured marketing of these two crops has played an important role in the overall agricultural development of the state in the post-green revolution period.

7.4 Share of Punjab in the GDP from Agriculture Sector in India

The information regarding share of Punjab in the GDP from agriculture sector in India from 1970–71 to 2011–12 is shown in Table 7.3. It may be stated that Punjab's share in the geographical area of the country is just 1.53 %. Similarly,

Table 7.3 Share of Punjab in the gross domestic product from agriculture sector in India at factor cost (at current prices), 1970–71 to 2011–12 (Rs. crores)

Year	India	Punjab	% share of Punjab
1970–71	18,352	863	4.70
1975–76	29,077	1,364	4.69
1980–81	46,332	2,422	5.23
1985–86	76,571	4,259	5.56
1990–91	145,734	8,231	5.65
1995–96	277,846	16,503	5.94
2000–01	423,522	26,449	6.25
2005–06	536,822	32,992	6.15
2006–07	604,672	37,614	6.22
2007–08	716,276	45,626	6.37
2008–09	806,646	52,431	6.50
2009–10	928,586	57,402	6.18
2010–11	1,132,048	63,553	5.61
2011–12	1,268,081	70,879	5.59

Note Agriculture sector includes livestock also
Source (i) Agricultural Statistics At A Glance, various issues
(ii) Statistical Abstract of Punjab, various issues

Punjab has 2.29 % of India's population but its share in the GDP from agriculture sector was 4.70 % in 1970–71 which increased to 6.50 % in 2008-09 but declined to 5.61 % in 2010–11 and 5.59 % in 2011–12 due to fast agricultural development in other states also. Punjab is one of the agriculturally developed states of the country. The yield of different crops is high in Punjab as compared to rest of the country. Similarly, the input use is also quite high. The irrigated area is 98 % of the net area shown in Punjab as against 45 % at the national level. Similarly, the cropping intensity in the state is about 190 % in comparison to about 140 % in the country. Due to all these factors, the share of Punjab in the GDP from agriculture sector of India has been high in spite of small size of the state. The public procurement of food grains particularly wheat and paddy at the MSP has economically benefitted the Punjab farmers and it played an important role in overall agricultural development with high share in the GDP from agricultural sector of India.

7.5 Number of Regulated Markets

The information regarding the number of regulated markets in Punjab is given in Table 7.4. Their number was 108 in 1976–77 which increased to 149 in 2011–12. At present, 294 sub-yards are also attached with the regulated markets. The number of villages served per regulated market has declined from 113 in 1976–77 to 82 in 2011–12. Similarly, the area served per regulated market declined from 466 to 338 km^2 in the corresponding period. In the peak marketing season of wheat and paddy, the Punjab Mandi Board set up purchase centres in the villages. In this way,

Table 7.4 Number of regulated markets in Punjab, 1976–77 to 2011–12

Year	No. of regulated markets	No. of sub-yards attached with regulated markets	Average number of villages served per regulated market	Average area served per regulated market (km^2)
1976–77	108	214	113	466
1981–82	123	503	99	409
1986–87	141	519	88	352
1991–92	143	519	86	352
1996–97	144	519	86	350
2001–02	144	519	86	350
2006–07	145	294	85	347
2010–11	146	294	84	345
2011–12	149	294	82	338

Source Statistical Abstract of Punjab, various issues

the total number of markets including principal yards, sub-yards and purchase centres was 1795 during the year 2013–14. Such an efficient market infrastructure resulted in smooth public procurement of wheat and paddy and farmers of the state do not have to travel more than 7–8 km for the sale of wheat and paddy crops. The study conducted at Punjab Agricultural University has revealed that 99 % of wheat and cent per cent of paddy was sold by the farmers in the regulated markets in Punjab (Sidhu and Singh 2009).

7.6 Income and Expenditure of Punjab Mandi Board

The income of the Punjab Mandi Board was Rs.408 crore in 2011–12 which increased to Rs. 503 crore in 2012–13 (Table 7.5). The major source of income of the Board has been from the market fee followed by sale of plots in the mandis and interest received. The market committees with an annual income of market fee up to Rs. 20 lakh contribute of the market fee to the Punjab Mandi Board, for the next slab of Rs. 20–40 lakh, this share increases to 40 % and it goes upward to 50 % and income of more than 40 lakh per annum. The other sources of income are licence fee from market committees, rent of Kisan Bhawan, sale of tender forms, etc. As far as the expenditure is concerned, the maximum share was of the rural link road which was 26.81, 46.85 and 26.63 % in 2010–11, 2011–12 and 2012–13, respectively. About one-tenth of the expenditure was on the development of mandis. The expenditure of salary to staff was around one-fifth. The share of interest of bank loans varied between 6.45 and 8.13 % in the period under reference. Another important item of expenditure was pension and leave salary which accounted for about 4 %. The expenditure on gratuity and death compensation was less than 2 %. The Board had utilized its expenditure on office, Apni Mandi,

Table 7.5 Income and expenditure of Punjab Mandi Board, 2010–11 to 2012–13 (Rs. in crores)

Sr. no.	Particulars	2010–11	2011–12	2012–13
A	Income	407.62	424.66	503.19
(i)	Contribution from market committees	293.18 (71.93)	289.76 (68.23)	384.80 (76.47)
(ii)	Sale of plots in mandis	103.94 (25.50)	116.70 (27.48)	101.14 (20.10)
(iii)	Interest received	7.49 (1.84)	13.31 (3.13)	13.86 (2.75)
(iv)	Other income[a]	3.01 (0.73)	4.89 (1.16)	3.39 (0.68)
B	Expenditure	407.62	424.66	503.19
(i)	Rural link roads	109.30 (26.81)	198.92 (46.85)	134.02 (26.63)
(ii)	Development of mandis	41.14 (10.09)	41.69 (9.82)	44.71 (8.89)
(iii)	Salary to staff	69.13 (16.96)	87.21 (20.54)	114.16 (22.69)
(iv)	Interest of bank loans	29.26 (7.18)	34.50 (8.13)	32.47 (6.45)
(v)	Pension/leave salary	14.56 (3.57)	15.49 (3.65)	18.99 (3.77)
(vi)	Post-harvesting scheme	15.88 (3.90)	4.12 (0.92)	6.22 (1.24)
(vii)	Gratuity and death compensation	7.98 (1.96)	7.63 (1.81)	7.39 (1.47)
(viii)	Other expenses[b]	17.02 (4.18)	20.49 (4.83)	85.64 (17.02)
(ix)	Excess of income over expenditure	103.35 (25.35)	14.61 (3.45)	59.59 (11.84)

[a]Income from licence fee from market committees, rent of KisanBhawan, sale of tender forms, etc.
[b]Expenditure on office, ApniMandi expenses, Travelling Allowance, Medical expenses, running and maintenance of vehicles, acquisition of land, etc.
Note Figures in parentheses are percentages to income (A) and expenditure (B)
Source Punjab Mandi Board, Chandigarh

travelling allowance (TA), medical expenses, running and maintenance of vehicles, acquisition of land, etc. The Punjab Mandi Board had taken loan for development purpose only, therefore, it had to pay interest on these loans.

7.7 Road Connectivity in Punjab

The information about districtwise road length per unit of area and population and villages linked with roads in Punjab from 1977–78 to 2011–12 is shown in Table 7.6. The total road length was 28,556 km in 1977–78 which increased to 46,701 km in 1994–95 and 81,808 km in 2011–12. The roads per lakh of population were 184 km in 1977–78, which increased to 230 km in 1994–95 and 291 km in 2011–12. The roads per 100 km^2 of area increased from 57 km in 1977–78 to 93 km in 1994–95 and 291 km in 2011–12. The villages linked with roads were 85 % in 1977–78, 97 % in 1994–95 and 100 % in 2011–12. Punjab is second state after Haryana to link each and every village with metalled link road. The road infrastructure in the central districts is better as compared to other districts. The

Table 7.6 Districtwise road length per unit of area and population and villages linked with roads in Punjab, 1977–78 to 2011–12

S. no.	Districts	Total roads (km)			Roads per 100 km^2 of area (km)			Roads per lakh of population (km)			Percentage of villages linked with roads		
		1977–78	1994–95	2011–12	1977–78	1994–95	2011–12	1977–78	1994–95	2011–12	1977–78	1994–95	2011–12
i	Gurdaspur	2538	3188	4282	71	89	120	180	181	185	84	100	100
ii	Pathankot	@	@	1556	@	@	@	@	@	@	@	@	100
iii	Amritsar	2693	4016	5394	54	79	204	128	160	213	70	97	100
iv	Tarn Taran	@	@	3080	@	@	126	@	@	270	@	@	100
v	Kapurthala	1024	1603	2395	63	100	147	208	248	291	86	87	100
vi	Jalandhar	2527	4083	5812	74	120	221	152	201	264	89	100	100
vii	S.B.S. Nagar	@	@	2471	@	@	195	@	@	400	@	@	100
viii	Hoshiarpur	2351	3564	5529	60	94	164	195	247	347	70	98	100
ix	Rupnagar	1659	3410	2591	80	162	189	259	374	376	95	97	100
x	S.A.S. Nagar	@	@	2396	@	@	219	@	@	236	@	@	100
xi	Ludhiana	2428	6064	10,099	64	160	268	149	250	286	94	97	100
xii	Firozpur	2816	4012	3562	48	68	67	235	250	173	71	87	100
xiii	Fazilka	@	@	2384	@	@	@	@	@	@	@	@	100
xiv	Faridkot	2442	4389	1947	42	77	133	185	254	310	100	100	100
xv	Shri Muktsar Sahib	@	@	4140	@	@	158	@	@	452	@	@	100
xvi	Moga	@	@	3354	@	@	151	@	@	335	@	@	100
xvii	Bathinda	2181	2293	3824	39	67	113	86	234	271	100	100	100
xviii	Mansa	@	1134	2339	@	52	108	@	196	301	@	99	100

(continued)

Table 7.6 (continued)

S. no.	Districts	Total roads (km)			Roads per 100 km^2 of area (km)			Roads per lakh of population (km)			Percentage of villages linked with roads		
		1977–78	1994–95	2011–12	1977–78	1994–95	2011–12	1977–78	1994–95	2011–12	1977–78	1994–95	2011–12
xix	Sangrur	2646	3620	5393	52	72	149	202	215	322	100	100	100
xx	Barnala	@	@	1746	@	@	124	@	@	289	@	@	100
xxi	Patiala	3251	3481	5544	70	97	172	237	228	288	95	98	100
xxii	Fatehgarh Sahib	@	1844	1970	@	168	167	@	408	325	@	99	100
	Punjab	28,556	46,701	81,808	57	93	162	184	230	291	85	97	100

@: District was not formed in the particular year

Source Statistical Abstract of Punjab, Various issues

widespread road connectivity in rural Punjab has played an important role in the agricultural development. The road connectivity along with its rural electrification has totally transformed the scenario of rural areas of the state.

7.8 Storage Capacity in Punjab

Food grain production is generally seasonal in nature but its consumption is spread all over the year. Therefore, storage of food grains adds time utility. The peak procurement period of wheat in general during April and May in Punjab. Similarly, October and November are peak procurement months for paddy. Storage of food grains is as important as its production. The information about agencywise storage capacity in Punjab from 1980–81 to 2011–12 is shown in Table 7.7. The storage capacity was about 112 lakh tonnes in 1980–81 which was more than doubled to about 234 lakh tonnes in 2011–12. It included both hired as well as open storage capacity. It may be stated that about 51 % and about 49 % of this storage capacity were covered and open, respectively. Due to financial constraints, covered storage capacity has not been added in the recent past in Punjab. It is a fact that marketing infrastructure in the developing countries like India cannot be at par with the infrastructure available in the developed countries like USA. The maximum storage capacity during 2011–12 was with the FCI (about 36 %) followed by Markfed (19 %), PUNSUP (about 14 %), PAIC (about 13 %), Food and Supplies Department (about 10 %), PSWC (about 8 %), CWC (0.31 %) and Punjab Mandi Board (0.09 %). The FCI is the national-level nodal agency for the public procurement of wheat and paddy. Therefore, it has the maximum storage facilities in Punjab because state-level public procurement agencies procured wheat and paddy on behalf of the FCI. Ultimately, the whole produce is handed over to the FCI in due course of time. The storage infrastructure in Punjab has played an important role in food security of the country.

7.9 Production and Market Arrival of Paddy and Wheat

The arrival of paddy and wheat was 8.46 lakh tonnes and 31.21 lakh tonnes, respectively, during the year 1970–71 (Table 7.8). The arrival was about 82 and 61 % of paddy and wheat production, respectively, in this year. The assured public procurement of these two crops at the MSP encouraged the Punjab farmers to bring more area under these crops. Consequently, the production and market arrival of paddy and wheat increased significantly during the last four decades or so. The record arrival of paddy was 143 lakh tonnes in 2005–06. This figure in case of wheat was 129 lakh tonnes in 2011–12. The market arrival as percentage of production has been more for paddy in comparison to wheat. The latter is the staple food of the Punjabis. Therefore, the farmers keep it in more quantity for family

Table 7.7 Agencywise Storage Capacity in Punjab[a], 1980–81 to 2011–12 (Lakh tonnes)

Year	Food Corporation of India	Food and Supplies Deptt.	Markfed	Punjab State Warehousing Corporation	Central Warehousing Corporation	Punjab State Civil Supply Corporation	Punjab Mandi Board	Punjab Agro-Industries Corporation	Total
1980–81	51.81 (46.36)	26.07 (23.33)	12.83 (11.48)	8.60 (7.70)	4.05 (3.63)	8.38 (7.50)	–	–	111.73 (100.00)
1985–86	45.99 (39.10)	22.20 (18.87)	17.97 (15.28)	14.20 (12.07)	5.52 (4.69)	11.75 (9.99)	–	–	117.63 (100.00)
1990–91	49.62 (45.17)	4.10 (3.73)	16.05 (14.61)	22.21 (20.22)	6.06 (5.52)	9.41 (8.56)	2.41 (2.19)	–	109.86 (100.00)
1995–96	59.76 (39.14)	8.64 (5.66)	27.63 (18.10)	35.66 (23.36)	3.84 (2.52)	16.60 (10.87)	0.54 (0.35)	–	152.67 (100.00)
2005–06	71.05 (36.92)	7.69 (3.99)	36.10) (18.76	36.06 (18.73)	7.00 (3.64)	20.91 (10.87)	0.54 (0.28)	13.10 (6.81)	192.45 (100.00)
2009–10	76.30 (36.41)	18.70 (8.92)	41.52 (19.81)	19.54 (9.32)	2.28 (1.09)	31.59 (15.08)	0.12 (0.06)	19.50 (9.31)	209.55 (100.00)
2010–11	83.22 (36.77)	18.38 (8.12)	44.34 (19.59)	16.57 (7.32)	1.29 (0.57)	32.37 (14.30)	0.24 (0.11)	29.92 (13.22)	226.33 (100.00)
2011–12	83.96 (35.87)	23.36 (9.98)	43.30 (18.50)	19.24 (8.22)	0.68 (0.31)	33.36 (14.25)	0.22 (0.09)	29.92 (12.78)	234.04 (100.00)

[a]Includes hired storage capacity and open capacity
Note Figures in parentheses indicate percentages
Source Statistical Abstract of Punjab, Various issues

Table 7.8 Production and market arrival of paddy and wheat in Punjab, 1970–71 to 2012–13 (Lakh tonnes)

Crop year	Production of paddy	Market arrival of paddy	Production of wheat	Market arrival of wheat
1970–71	10.27	8.46 (82.38)	51.45	31.21 (60.66)
1980–81	49.75	44.32(89.09)	76.77	39.41 (51.34)
1990–91	100.11	78.94 (78.85)	121.59	63.67 (52.36)
1995–96	105.07	73.37 (69.83)	125.17	59.84 (47.81)
2000–01	136.67	115.42 (84.48)	155.51	105.79 (68.03)
2005–06	152.34	143.10 (93.93)	144.97	81.74 (56.38)
2010–11	161.74	131.36 (81.22)	164.72	110.94 (67.35)
2011–12	157.33	120.17 (76.38)	179.82	129.35 (71.93)
2012–13	169.76	133.75 (78.79)	166.09	111.16 (66.93)

Note Figures in parentheses indicate arrival of paddy and wheat as percentage of production
Source Agriculture At A Glance (2013–14), Department of Agriculture, Punjab, Chandigarh

consumption. Besides, the seed requirement of wheat is high (about 100 kg per ha) as compared to paddy (about 20 kg per ha). Above all, the wheat is also used as cattle feed by the farmers. Such a practice is not there in case of paddy.

7.10 Cost of Production (C_2) of Paddy Vis-à-Vis MSP

The information regarding cost of production (C_2) of paddy in Punjab vis-à-vis MSP from 1981–82 to 2010–11 is given in Table 7.9. The C_2 cost includes all paid-up costs and imputed value of family labour and rent of owned land. The margin of MSP over C_2 cost varied from about 19 % in 1986–87 to as high as 53 % in 2007–08. Over time, the MSP of paddy (superfine/A grade) has increased from Rs. 123 per qtl in 1981–82 to Rs. 1030 per qtl in 2010–11. The favourable price policy of paddy encouraged the state farmers to bring more area under paddy and it is about 36 % of the total cropped area. Paddy is the most important crop next to wheat in the state. The rice area is about 28 lakh hectares. Wheat occupies about 35 lakh hectares of area.

7.11 Cost of Production (C_2) of Wheat Vis-à-Vis MSP

The C_2 cost of wheat was Rs. 61 per qtl in 1970–71 which increased to Rs. 880 per qtl in 2010–11 (Table 7.10). Similarly, the MSP of wheat increased from Rs. 76 per qtl to Rs. 1170 per qtl during the same period. The margin of MSP over C_2 cost was as low as 4.25 % in 1975–76. It was the highest (54.33 %) in 2007–08. In the recent

Table 7.9 Cost of production (C_2) of paddy in Punjab vis-à-vis minimum support price, 1981–82 to 2010–11 (Rs. per qtl)

Crop year	Cost of production (C_2)	MSP fixed by the Union Govt. (superfine/A grade)	Margin of MSP over C_2 cost
1981–82	102.31	123.00	20.69 (20.22)
1986–87	129.23	154.00	24.77 (19.17)
1991–92	206.77	250.00	45.23 (21.87)
1996–97	344.81	415.00	70.19 (20.36)
2001–02	392.91	560.00	167.09 (42.53)
2005–06	487.28	600.00	112.72 (23.13)
2006–07	477.42	650.00	172.58 (36.15)
2007–08	505.92	775.00	269.08 (53.19)
2008–09	669.86	930.00	260.14 (38.83)
2009–10	773.18	1030.00	256.82 (33.21)
2010–11	836.46	1030.00	193.54 (23.14)

Note (i) MSP of paddy fixed by the Union Government included bonus
(ii) Figures in parentheses indicate margin of MSP in percentage terms over C_2 cost
Source CACP, Ministry of Agriculture, Govt. of India, New Delhi

Table 7.10 Cost of production (C_2) of wheat in Punjab vis-à-vis minimum support price, 1970–71 to 2010–11 (Rs. per qtl)

Crop year	Cost of production (C_2)	MSP fixed by the Union Government	Margin of MSP over C_2 cost
1970–71	61.04	76.00	14.96 (24.51)
1975–76	99.45	105.00	5.55 (5.58)
1980–81	124.70	130.00	5.30 (4.25)
1985–86	129.29	162.00	32.71 (25.30)
1990–91	190.79	225.00	34.21 (17.93)
1995–96	342.83	380.00	37.17 (10.84)
2000–01	432.06	610.00	177.94 (41.18)
2005–06	556.27	700.00	143.73 (25.84)
2006–07	617.11	850.00	232.89 (37.74)
2007–08	647.95	1000.00	352.05 (54.33)
2008–09	804.80	1080.00	275.20 (34.19)
2009–10	816.89	1100.00	283.11 (34.66)
2010–11	880.26	1170.00	289.74 (32.92)

Note (i) MSP of wheat fixed by the Union Government included bonus
(ii) Figures in parentheses indicate margin of MSP in percentage terms over C_2 cost
Source CACP, Ministry of Agriculture, Govt. of India, New Delhi

years, the margin of MSP was about one-third over C_2 cost. The favourable price regime of wheat encouraged the state farmers to bring more area under wheat and the state is recorded as the largest wheat producer after Uttar Pradesh in the country.

About 44 % of the total cropped area in Punjab is under wheat. The development of dairy sector is also linked to the crop farming. The wheat bhusa is used by the farmers as dry fodder for their milch animals. At present, the share of agriculture and livestock sector (at current prices) in the Gross State Domestic Product (GSDP) of Punjab is about 28 % as compared to about 14 % in the country. This shows that agricultural development is dependent on efficient marketing.

7.12 Area, Production and Yield of Rice in India and Punjab

The data regarding area, production and yield of rice in India and Punjab from 1960–61 to 2011–12 have been shown in Table 7.11. Perusals of the table show that Punjab had just 0.64 % rice area of the country in 1960–61. It increased to 0.82 % in 1965–66 and 1.04 % in 1970–71. At present, about 6 % of rice area of India is in Punjab and the state's share in rice production is about 10 %. The rice production in absolute terms increased from 0.23 million tonnes in 1960–61 to 0.67 million tonnes in 1970–71, 3.23 million tonnes in 1980–81, 6.51 million tonnes in 1990–91, 9.15 million tonnes in 2000–01 and 10.54 million tonnes in 2011–12. The marketing support to the farmers has played an important role for this achievement. It may be stated that rice is not a traditional crop of Punjab but its public

Table 7.11 Area, production and yield of rice in India and Punjab, 1960–61 to 2011–12

Year	Area million ha		Production million tonnes		Yield (kg/ha)		
	India	Punjab	India	Punjab	India	Punjab	Difference between Col. 7 and 6
1960–61	34.13	0.23 (0.64)	34.58	0.23 (0.67)	1013	1009	(−) 4
1965–66	35.47	0.29 (0.82)	30.59	0.29 (0.95)	862	1000	(+) 138
1970–71	37.59	0.39 (1.04)	42.22	0.67 (1.59)	1123	1765	(+) 642
1975–76	39.48	0.57 (1.44)	48.74	1.45 (2.97)	1235	2553	(+) 1318
1980–81	40.15	1.18 (2.94)	53.63	3.23 (6.02)	1336	2733	(+) 1397
1985–86	41.14	1.71 (4.16)	63.83	5.49 (8.60)	1552	3200	(+) 1648
1990–91	42.69	2.02 (4.73)	74.29	6.51 (8.76)	1740	3229	(+) 1489
1995–96	42.84	2.18 (5.09)	76.98	6.84 (8.89)	1797	3132	(+) 1335
2000–01	44.71	2.61 (5.84)	84.98	9.15 (10.77)	1901	3506	(+) 1605
2005–06	43.66	2.65 (6.05)	91.79	10.21 (11.12)	2102	3856	(+) 1754
2010–11	42.86	2.83 (6.60)	95.98	10.84 (11.29)	2239	3828	(+) 1589
2011–12	43.97	2.81 (6.39)	104.32	10.54 (10.10)	2372	3741	(+) 1369

Note Figures in parentheses indicate area and production of Punjab in % terms of India
Source (i) Agricultural Statistics At A Glance, various issues
(ii) Statistical Abstract of Punjab, various issues

procurement at the MSP encouraged the farmers to increase the area and production. There is no doubt that large-scale cultivation of rice crop has depleted the ground water resources and created problems related with soil health and environment. Under the diversification plan of Punjab agriculture, there is a proposal to shift 12 lakh ha rice area to other crops by the year 2017. The yield of rice in Punjab is quite high as compared to the national average. In early 1960s, the yield was just about 1000 kg per ha in the state but increased to 3856 kg per ha in 2005–06. It increased in the country also but at a slow rate. During the year 2011–12, India's rice yield was 2372 kg per ha as compared to 3741 kg per ha in Punjab.

7.13 Area, Production and Yield of Wheat in India and Punjab

The information regarding area, production and yield of wheat in India and Punjab from the years 1960–61 to 2011–12 is shown in Table 7.12. During this period, the wheat area of Punjab has remained about 11–13 % of the country although in absolute terms, it increased from 1.40 million ha in 1960–61 to 2.30 million ha in 1970–71, 2.81 million ha in 1980–81, 3.27 million ha in 1990–91, 3.41 million ha in 2000–01 and 3.53 million ha in 2011–12. The wheat production in Punjab has

Table 7.12 Area, production and yield of wheat in India and Punjab, 1960–61 to 2011–12

Year	Area (million ha)		Production (million tonnes)		Yield (kg/ha)		
	India	Punjab	India	Punjab	India	Punjab	Difference between Col. 7 and 6
1	2	3	4	5	6	7	8
1960–61	12.93	1.40 (10.83)	11.00	1.74 (15.82)	851	1244	(+) 393
1965–66	12.57	1.55 (12.33)	10.40	1.92 (18.46)	827	1238	(+) 411
1970–71	18.24	2.30 (12.61)	23.83	5.15 (21.61)	1307	2237	(+) 930
1975–76	20.45	2.45 (11.98)	28.84	5.79 (20.08)	1410	2373	(+) 963
1980–81	22.28	2.81 (12.61)	36.31	7.68 (21.15)	1630	2730	(+) 1100
1985–86	23.00	3.11 (13.52)	47.05	10.99 (23.36)	2046	3531	(+) 1485
1990–91	24.17	3.27 (13.53)	55.14	12.16 (22.05)	2281	3715	(+) 1434
1995–96	25.01	3.22 (12.87)	62.10	12.52 (20.16)	2483	3886	(+) 1403
2000–01	25.73	3.41 (13.25)	69.68	15.55 (22.32)	2708	4563	(+) 1855
2005–06	26.48	3.47 (13.10)	69.35	14.50 (20.91)	2619	4179	(+) 1560
2010–11	29.07	3.51 (12.07)	86.87	16.47 (18.96)	2988	4693	(+) 1705
2011–12	29.90	3.53 (11.81)	93.90	17.98 (19.15)	3140	5097	(+) 1957

Note Figures in parentheses indicate area and production of Punjab in % terms of India
Source (i) Agricultural Statistics At A Glance, various issues
(ii) Statistical Abstract of Punjab, various issues

increased from 1.74 million tonnes in 1960–61 to 5.15 million tonnes in 1970–71, 7.68 million tonnes in 1980–81, 12.16 million tonnes in 1990–91, 15.55 million tonnes in 2000–01 and 17.98 million tonnes in 2011–12. The wheat production in the country has increased from about 10 million tonnes in 1965–66 to about 94 million tonnes in 2011–12. It is worth noting here that Punjab produces about one-fifth of wheat production of India. It is a big achievement of the small state with just 1.53 % geographical area of the country. The wheat yield of Punjab has increased from around 12 qtl per ha in 1960–61 to about 51 qtl per ha in 2011–12. The state produced about 4 qtl per ha more in 1960s in comparison to India. Now, the gap has increased to about 20 qtl per ha. The credit in this regard goes to high yielding varieties, irrigation, use of chemical fertilizers, farm machinery, agricultural credit, marketing support, etc. Above all, the state farmers are progressive one and they had adopted the new farm technology in a short period of time due to strong extension support.

7.14 Pattern of Sale of Wheat by the Farmers in Punjab

The information regarding pattern of sale of wheat by the selected farmers during the year 2007–08 is shown in Table 7.13. A perusal of the table reveals that selected farmers sold about 96 % of their marketed surplus in the post-harvest period and the rest about 4 % in the lean period. The small farmers sold the maximum quantity (97.66 %) in the post-harvest period followed by large farmers (96.70 %) and medium farmers (95.56 %). Almost similar trend was observed in the sale pattern of wheat by all three categories of farmers (Sidhu and Singh 2009). This happened on account of minimum support price (MSP) of wheat and its public procurement by public procurement agencies like Food Corporation of India, PUNGRAIN, PUNSUP, MARKFED, Punjab State Warehousing Corporation and Punjab Agro-Industries Corporation. Therefore, it was the rational economic decision of the selected farmers to sell their marketed surplus in the post-harvest period. Due to insufficient storage facilities and other economic reasons, they were unable to spread their sale over a period of months in the lean period.

The districtwise analysis of the sale pattern of wheat showed that 98.44 % of the marketed surplus was sold in the post-harvest period by the farmers of Ludhiana district. This figure was 98.39 % for Sangrur district and 93.22 % in case of Patiala district. The medium farmers of Patiala district sold about 89 % of their produce in the post-harvest and 11 % in the lean period. For all other categories of farmers of three districts, this figure was more than 95 % for sale of wheat in the post-harvest period. In the lean period, the wheat was sold generally to the traders, chakki owners, landless agricultural and other labourers in the village.

Table 7.13 Pattern of sale of wheat by the selected farmers in Punjab, 2007–08 (Figures in qtl)

Particulars	Marketed surplus[a]	Quantity sold in post-harvest period[a]	Quantity sold in lean period[a]
Ludhiana district			
Small	34.99	33.99 (97.14)	1.00 (2.56)
Medium	123.74	121.24 (97.98)	2.50 (2.02)
Large	213.80	212.47 (99.38)	1.33 (0.62)
Average	97.39	95.87 (98.44)	1.52 (1.56)
Patiala district			
Small	29.49	28.79 (97.63)	0.70 (2.37)
Medium	127.04	112.82 (88.81)	14.22 (11.19)
Large	387.21	366.13 (94.56)	21.08 (5.44)
Average	130.28	121.45 (93.22)	8.83 (6.78)
Sangrur			
Small	37.62	37.00 (98.35)	0.62 (1.65)
Medium	94.61	94.61 (100.00)	–
Large	333.93	325.51 (97.48)	8.42 (2.52)
Average	119.68	117.75 (98.39)	1.93 (1.61)
Overall			
Small	33.79	33.00 (97.66)	0.79 (2.34)
Medium	113.08	108.06 (95.56)	5.02 (4.44)
Large	311.64	301.36 (96.70)	10.28 (3.30)
Overall average	115.79	111.70 (96.47)	4.09 (3.53)

[a]Per holding
Note Figures in parentheses indicate percentage of the marketed surplus
Source Sidhu and Singh (2009)

7.15 Pattern of Sale of Paddy by the Farmers in Punjab

It is interesting to note that all the selected farmers of three districts sold cent per cent of their marketed surplus of paddy in the post-harvest period (Table 7.14). It was on account of public procurement of paddy at the MSP all over Punjab (Sidhu and Singh 2009). In the lean period, the public procurement of paddy was not there. By keeping paddy for long periods, its moisture content also declines which results in economic loss to the farmers. Moreover, the paddy is a bulky crop as compared to wheat, therefore, the farmers could not store it for long period at their houses. Above all, the storage facilities available with the selected farmers were inadequate to store the produce. Therefore, it was a rational economic decision of the selected farmers to sell the paddy crop in the post-harvest period.

Table 7.14 Pattern of sale of paddy by the selected farmers in Punjab, 2007–08 (Figures in qtl.)

Particulars	Marketed surplus[a]	Quantity sold in post-harvest period[a]	Quantity sold in lean period[a]
Ludhiana district			
Small	70.62	70.62 (100.00)	–
Medium	267.12	267.12 (100.00)	–
Large	505.37	505.37 (100.00)	–
Average	216.51	216.51 (100.00)	–
Patiala district			
Small	64.91	64.91 (100.00)	–
Medium	190.04	190.04 (100.00)	–
Large	562.71	562.71 (100.00)	–
Average	202.00	202.00 (100.00)	–
Sangrur			
Small	79.68	79.68 (100.00)	–
Medium	157.82	157.82 (100.00)	–
Large	505.03	505.03 (100.00)	–
Average	196.00	196.00 (100.00)	–
Overall			
Small	71.10	71.10 (100.00)	–
Medium	200.37	200.37 (100.00)	–
Large	526.64	526.64 (100.00)	–
Overall average	205.30	205.30 (100.00)	–

[a]Per holding
Note Figures in parentheses indicate percentage of the marketed surplus
Source Sidhu and Singh (2009)

7.16 Methods of Sale of Wheat

The information regarding various methods of sale of wheat crop by the selected farmers during the year 2007–08 is given in Table 7.15. A perusal of the table indicated that about 99 % of the produce was sold in the regulated markets, 0.65 % in the village itself to the landless agricultural and non-agricultural labourers, village shopkeepers, etc., and 0.32 % to the *chakki* owners. The medium and large farmers sold more than 99 % of their marketed surplus in the regulated markets whereas the figure was about 98 % in case small farmers. It is worthwhile to point out here that Punjab Mandi Board set up more than 1600 purchase centres in the State for the purchase of wheat and paddy in the post-harvest period (Sidhu and Singh 2009). Therefore, the farmers of Punjab do not have to cover more than 7–8 km of distance for sale of their produce, i.e. wheat and paddy. The districtwise analysis also revealed a similar trend for the method of sale of wheat adopted by the selected farmers. The selected farmers of Patiala district sold 98.05 % of the

Table 7.15 Methods of wheat sale adopted by the selected farmers in Punjab, 2007–08 (Figures in qtl.)

Farm Category	Marketed surplus	Sale in regulated market	Sale to *chakki* owner	Sale in village
Ludhiana district				
Small	34.99	33.76 (96.48)	0.90 (2.57)	0.33 (0.95)
Medium	123.74	121.85 (98.47)	0.89 (0.72)	1.00 (0.81)
Large	213.81	210.22 (98.32)	0.92 (0.43)	2.67 (1.25)
Average	97.39	95.49 (98.05)	0.90 (0.92)	1.00 (1.03)
Patiala district				
Small	29.49	29.06 (98.54)	0.10 (0.34)	0.33 (1.12)
Medium	127.04	126.32 (99.43)	0.33 (0.26)	0.39 (0.31)
Large	387.21	384.88 (99.40)	–	2.33 (0.60)
Average	130.28	129.38 (99.31)	0.15 (0.11)	0.75 (0.58)
Sangrur				
Small	37.62	37.20 (98.89)	0.17 (0.45)	0.25 (0.66)
Medium	94.61	94.61 (100.00)	–	–
Large	333.93	331.93 (99.40)	–	2.00 (0.60)
Average	119.68	119.11 (99.52)	0.07 (0.06)	0.50 (0.42)
Overall				
Small	33.79	33.08 (97.90)	0.40 (1.18)	0.31 (0.92)
Medium	113.64	112.30 (99.31)	0.37 (0.33)	0.41 (0.36)
Large	311.64	309.00 (99.15)	0.31 (0.10)	2.33 (0.75)
Overall average	115.79	114.67 (99.03)	0.37 (0.32)	0.75 (0.65)

Note Figures in parentheses indicate percentage of the marketed surplus
Source Sidhu and Singh (2009)

produce in the regulated markets as compared to 99.31 % for Patiala and 99.52 % for Sangrur district. The sale of wheat in the regulated markets ensured MSP to the farmers (Sidhu and Singh 2010). Therefore, they had preference for sale of produce in the regulated markets (Ibid). It may be stated that no non-official intermediary handles the sale of wheat and paddy in the regulated markets in Punjab. Such non-official intermediaries may be active in the markets of agriculturally less developed states like Bihar, Orissa, Jharkhand, etc.

7.17 Methods of Sale of Paddy

It is interesting to note that 100 per cent of the marketed surplus of paddy was sold by different categories of the selected farmers in the regulated markets (Table 7.16). Since paddy has to be milled for rice, therefore, there was no direct sale to the buyers in the village. None of the selected farmers sold it directly to the rice millers.

Table 7.16 Methods of paddy sale adopted by the selected farmers in Punjab, 2007–08 (Figures in qtls.)

Farm Category	Marketed surplus	Sale in regulated market	Sale to *chakki* owner	Sale in village
Ludhiana district				
Small	70.62	70.62 (100.00)	–	–
Medium	267.12	267.12 (100.00)	–	–
Large	505.37	505.37 (100.00)	–	–
Average	216.51	216.51 (100.00)	–	–
Patiala district				
Small	64.91	64.91 (100.00)	–	–
Medium	190.04	190.04 (100.00)	–	–
Large	562.71	562.71 (100.00)	–	–
Average	202.00	202.00 (100.00)	–	–
Sangrur				
Small	79.68	79.68 (100.00)	–	–
Medium	157.82	157.82 (100.00)	–	–
Large	505.03	505.03 (100.00)	–	–
Average	196.00	196.00 (100.00)	–	–
Overall				
Small	71.10	71.10 (100.00)	–	–
Medium	200.37	200.37 (100.00)	–	–
Large	526.64	526.64 (100.00)	–	–
Overall average	205.30	205.30 (100.00)	–	–

Note Figures in parentheses indicate percentage of the marketed surplus
Source Sidhu and Singh (2009)

As already discussed, the farmers got MSP for sale of the produce in the regulated markets. Due to competition, even the millers/traders offered slightly higher price over MSP of paddy to the farmers (Sidhu and Singh 2010). Therefore, the selected farmers preferred to sell their produce in the regulated markets to get MSP or even higher price. It may be stated that as per Agricultural Produce Markets Acts (APMC), 1961, it is illegal to buy and sell directly. The farm produce can only be sold in the regulated markets set up by the Punjab Mandi Board/State Government. The price offered by the millers/traders was just Rs. 3–4 per quintal higher than the MSP of paddy fixed by the Union government. The public procurement agencies all over India cannot offer even 1 paisa over and above the MSP of wheat and paddy.

The commission agents system is there in Punjab in the regulated markets. They charge 2.5 % commission ad valorem from the buyers for the sale/purchase of crops like wheat and paddy in Punjab. The farmers are not required to pay and commission to the commission agents for the services rendered by them. It is a fact that almost all the farmers receive MSP for the sale of wheat and paddy crop in the state for sale through commission agents provided the produce fulfils prescribed grade specifications fixed by the Food Corporation of India (FCI).

It is a fact that farmers of Punjab take credit from institutional and non-institutional sources. Among the non-institutional sources, the commission agents are the most popular source of credit. The payment of farmer's produce is made through the commission agents. A recent study conducted at PAU has brought out that the average debt of each farm household was Rs. 2.18 lakh during the year 2012–13 (Singh et al. 2014). Although the banking system is highly developed in the state but 35.25 % of the total credit was advanced by the commission agents (*Ibid*). The rate of interest charged by them from the farmers varied between 12 and 36 % per annum. From the farmer's point of view, it is easy method of taking credit without doing any paper work. Besides the farmers and commission agents have long social and economic relations, therefore, the farmers also have faith in them in spite of high rate of interest.

7.18 Strategy for Efficient Marketing

It is a well-known fact that income of the farmers is mainly dependent on the fixed farm resources owned by them. The notable among these are land and farm machineries, i.e. tractors, tube wells and other farm equipments. Higher the size of land holding, the higher is the level of farm income and vice versa. There are 10.53 lakh operational holdings in Punjab, out of which about 34 % comprises of marginal and small farmers operating less than 2 ha of area. In spite of the prevailing scenario of farm holdings, the need of hour is to enhance their income through various measures particularly efficient marketing. Some of these measures are as under.

7.19 Grain Storage

The Union Government has already formulated a plan to modernize grain storage facilities or silos in the country. The storage facilities with a capacity of 2 million tonnes would be put up under the Public–Private Partnership (PPP) route initially. The development of silos would be through the design, build, finance, operate and transfer (DFOT) modes. The private players would put up the money to set up the storage infrastructure while the FCI would take these on rent for grain storage for 30 years. Silos with 50,000 tonnes and 25,000 tonnes capacities are proposed to be built at 42 locations across 10 states including Punjab, Haryana, Uttar Pradesh, Madhya Pradesh, Gujrat, Bihar and Assam. For creation of 50,000 tonnes capacity silos, around 7 acres (2.8 ha) of land is required while the 25,000 tonnes capacity silos would need 5 acre land (2 ha).

Already in the year 2008, under a pilot project, the FCI had entered into a built–own–operate (BOO) agreement for 20 years with Adani Agri. Logistics for setting up two silos with a capacity of more than 5 lakh tonnes at Moga in Punjab and Kaithal in Haryana. Adani has invested Rs. 650 crore for building two base silos and five field depots at Chennai, Coimbatore, Bangalore, Navi Mumbai and Hugli. It may be stated that Government of India and State Governments are aware about the storage problems of wheat and rice in the country. Therefore, it has been decided to create additional covered storage capacity all over India. The storage capacity of the state agencies was 34.14 million tonnes as on 31 December 2012 which increased to 36.68 million tonnes as on 31 December 2013. The total storage capacity of the FCI and State agencies is 74.35 million tonnes. The construction of godowns with a total capacity of 20.40 million tonnes was approved in 19 states under the Private Entrepreneurs Guarantee (PEG) scheme. For Punjab, 4.3 million tonnes of additional storage capacity is being built up. This measure of the government will address the shortage of covered godowns space to some extent and quantitative and qualitative losses will also come down and our exports of wheat and rice will fetch high price in the international market.

7.20 Farmer Producer Organizations (FPOs)

There are 138 million operational holdings in India with an average holding size of 1.16 ha. About 84 % of the holdings comprise of marginal and small farmers with low level of production and marketed surplus. Only about 1 % of the holdings consist of large farmers operating more than 10 ha of area. The scenario in Punjab in this regard is comparatively better with the average size of holdings of 3.77 ha. Keeping in view such a scenario, an individual farmer cannot sell his produce in the distant markets where they can get high price of their produce. There are 53 cities in the country, which has population of 10 lakh and above each. All these 53 markets are big consuming centres of the farm produce. Therefore, the farmers may prefer group/cooperative marketing for sale of the produce in these big markets. The Government of India has also formulated a scheme of Farmer Producer Organization (FPO) for achieving inclusive agricultural growth during the 12th Five Year Plan.

The Small Farmers' Agribusiness Consortium (SFAC) has been nominated as a central procurement agency for undertaking price support operations under MSP for pulses and oil seeds. The SFAC will operate only through FPO at the farm gate. Member-based FPOs would act as aggregators and provide greater bargaining power to producers, especially small holders, and enable their integration in the value chain, generating higher incomes and employment (Government of India 2014). It is a praise worthy measure taken by the Union Government for the promotion of group marketing of farm produce by the farmers. The farmers of Punjab may take benefit of this scheme for efficient marketing of farm produce.

7.21 Food Processing and Value Addition

Punjab is an agriculturally developed state of the country and surplus in wheat, rice, cotton, fruits, vegetables, meat and poultry, mushrooms, honey, etc. In spite of surplus production of various agricultural and allied commodities, the level of processing and value addition is too low resulting in about 25–40 % of losses in case of perishables like fruits and vegetables (Gupta 2012). The processing of fruits and vegetables is hardly 2 % in India as against 70–75 % in developed countries. Over all, the processing of all the perishables is around 6 % which is proposed to be increased to 20 % by the end of this decade. At present, the value addition is 20 % which is proposed to be increased to 35 %. The population of the country is about 1250 million at present. It is growing at the rate of about 1.6 % per annum. India is a large and growing market for food products. Its 350 million strong urban middle class with its changing food habits poses a huge market for farm products and processed foods. As such, the food processing sector is one of the larger sectors in India in terms of production, growth, consumption and export. The turnover of the total food market is approximately 2.50 lakh crores, out of which value-added food products comprise Rs. 80,000 crores (Gupta 2012).

Some estimates suggest that in developed countries, up to 14 % of the total work force is engaged in agroprocessing sector directly or indirectly. However, in India, only about 3 % of the workforce finds employment in this sector revealing its underdeveloped state and vast untamed potential for employment. Properly developed agroprocessing sector can make Punjab and other parts of the country a major player at the global level for marketing and supply for processed food. Already, the State Government has earmarked 100 acres (40 ha) of land for setting up food park at Laddowal, near Ludhiana. The Punjab Agro Industry Corporation has been designated as nodal agency for building required infrastructure at the food park and to attract private investment on a large scale there. Besides, there is proposal to set up mini food park in 25 acres (10 ha) of land in different parts of the state. The Union Ministry of Food Processing will provide subsidy for all the projects related to food processing investment. All these measures of the State and Union Government are right step in the right direction for the promotion of diversification of agriculture and enhancement of farm income particularly of marginal and small farmers.

7.22 Conclusions

Agriculture sector is the backbone of developing countries like India. It is a major source of employment and income in the rural areas. This sector also provides food to its expanding population and raw material to the industry, it provides potential for exports to earn foreign exchange necessary for import of capital goods for industrial development and economic growth. In order to sustain/increase the rate of economic growth, agricultural surplus has to be increased and mopped up for capital formation. An efficient marketing system can also mop up surplus farm production, both of food grain and industrial raw material. In developing countries agricultural market policies are trusted as an integral part of development policies and their functioning has remained an important part of public policy in India.

The AMPC despite all its flaws provides an assured price and market to the farmers. The number of regulated markets has increased from 108 in 1976–77 to 149 in 2011–12. At present, 294 sub-yards are also attached with the regulated markets. In the peak marketing season of wheat and paddy, the state farmers do not have to travel more than 7–8 km for sale of their produce. The main source of income of the Punjab Mandi Board is market fee. The Board utilizes its funds mainly for the rural link roads and development of mandis. The road connectivity in rural Punjab is one of the best in the country and all villages are linked with metalled roads. The efficient marketing system has encouraged the farmers to produce more and the state is now known as grain bowl of the country. Punjab produces about 10 % rice and 20 % wheat of the country. The favourable marketing support in the form of MSP and public procurement of wheat and paddy has made the country self-sufficient. Rather, India has become the largest exporter of rice in the world last year. Similarly, the country is the third largest exporter of wheat now. The agricultural development is mainly dependent on the marketing support although we are facing a number of problems in the farm sector in Punjab.

The other states of the country are also following the Punjab model of agricultural development based on marketing support in the form of public procurement of farm produce at the MSP. There is need for additional scientific grain storage capacity to reduce quantitative and qualitative losses. Besides, processing and value addition of farm produce is meagre at present. It may be increased to create employment for the rural youth and enhance income of the farming households.

References

Chand R (2012) Development policies and agricultural markets. Econ Polit Wkly 47(52):53–63

Deshpande RS, Gopalappa DV (2003) Administrative reforms in the field of agricultural marketing in the context of WTO. Indian J Agric Mark 17(a):1–13

Ghuman RS, Rangi PS, Sidhu MS (2010) National food security: the strategic role of Punjab. J Agric Dev Policy 20(2):1–16

Government of India (2014) Economic survey—2013–14. Ministry of finance, department of economics affairs, economic division, New Delhi

Gupta BC (2012) Convocation address delivered at the college of agriculture engineering and technology. Punjab agricultural university, Ludhiana, January 27, pp 1–12

Kumar P (2011) Structure of markets and prices in agriculture: empirical evidence from Punjabs and Bihar margin. J Appl Econ Res 5(2):183–220

Sharma D (2014) Leaving farmers to reap the bitter harvest. Hindustan times, Jalandhar IV(17), January 20, p 10

Sidhu MS, Singh G (2009) A study on staggered public procurement of wheat and paddy in Punjab. Research Report, department of economics and sociology, PAU, Ludhiana, pp 1–52

Sidhu MS, Singh G (2010a) A study on staggered public procurement of wheat in Punjab. Agric Econ Res Rev 23(2):325–334

Sidhu MS, Singh G (2010b) A study on staggered public procurement of paddy in Punjab. Indian J Agric Mark 24(2):122–135

Singh S, Bhogal S, Singh R (2014) Magnitude and determinants of indebtedness among farmers in Punjab. Indian J Agric Econ 69(2):243–256

Chapter 8
Agricultural Credit in Punjab: Have Policy Initiatives Made a Dent in Informal Credit Markets?

Anita Gill

8.1 Introduction

Most developing countries have the common characteristic of having a predominantly agrarian economy. It is, therefore, imperative that any development strategy in such economies should devote substantial effort at agricultural development. A major constraint in agricultural development being non-availability of finance, the need for affordable, sufficient and timely supply of institutional credit to agriculture cannot be overlooked.

In India, agriculture has always been the most important economic sector, currently accounting for above 17 % of GDP but a dependence of 51 % population on it (World Bank 2012). It was recognized long back that the plight of majority of the population could be improved only by increasing agricultural productivity. A very important input to achieve this is credit—in fact, an assessment by the Reserve Bank of India had pointed out that every 1 % increase in real agricultural credit results in an increase in real agricultural GDP by 0.22 % with a one-year lag (Subbarao 2012). Public policy in India has thus always been directed towards ensuring adequate credit with focus on institutionalization of rural credit. However, despite adoption of a multi-agency system, and the tremendous expansion of branch network in rural areas, credit situation in agricultural sector has seen limited success, which is amply evident from the persistence of the informal lenders with all their exploitative practices even after several decades of administered allocation of credit to agriculture. In fact, rising costs of cultivation and declining productivity increased credit needs but eroded the incomes and hence repaying capacity of farmers, which, combined with inadequate, untimely institutional finance led to a situation of high levels of indebtedness from informal lenders and ultimately triggered farmers to take the extreme step of committing suicides. This was especially

A. Gill (✉)
Department of Distance Education, Punjabi University, Patiala 147002, Punjab, India
e-mail: anitagill@pbi.ac.in

L. Singh and N. Singh (eds.), *Economic Transformation of a Developing Economy*, India Studies in Business and Economics,
DOI 10.1007/978-981-10-0197-0_8

so in the immediate post-economic reform era, when both the state and the banks backtracked on their commitments of investment and lending in agriculture. Recently, efforts towards better flow of institutional credit to agriculture in the form of lower interest rates, doubling the credit flow, and schemes such as Kisan Credit Cards, have been initiated, which is expected to bring some respite to the crisis ridden agricultural sector.

Like the rest of the country, Punjab's agrarian economy too has been reeling under a severe crisis characterized by stagnating productivity, falling incomes and increasing costs of production. This despite the fact that Punjab had played a pioneering role in ushering in Green Revolution that saw India's transition from a food-importing country to a food surplus economy. Institutional credit had complemented the agricultural sector in Punjab to achieve a landmark progress (Singh 1990). But since the late 1980s, waning of the initial prosperity of farmers due to increasing farm costs and input prices has put heavy pressure on the farmers to borrow more from the informal lenders in the absence of access to adequate formal finance. Informal loans entail exorbitant rates of interest and interlinked credit transactions (sale of crop/labour to the lender), but their persistence and magnitude in the agrarian credit market raise concerns regarding the adequacy and efficacy of credit policy for agriculture.

The present paper is an attempt at reexamining the agrarian credit structure and situation in Punjab especially since the beginning of the present century, so as to assess the recent policy initiatives for strengthening the quality as well as quantity of the agrarian credit delivery system. The paper is divided into six sections. The introductory section is followed by a section on the methodology adopted for sample size for the two surveys carried out with a twenty-year gap. The structural changes in Punjab economy are examined in Sect. 8.3. The agricultural credit market structure and situation in Punjab will be taken up in Sect. 8.4. Apart from making use of secondary sources of data, particularly for the formal credit situation, and results of independent primary surveys, observations from a primary survey and a revisit study of the survey area carried out after a twenty-year time period for assessing the changing situation in informal credit market will also be made use of in this section. Section 8.5 will dwell on the public policy initiatives in improving the credit delivery mechanism and also suggest some further possible remedial measures. Concluding remarks are presented in Sect. 8.6.

8.2 Methodology

The present paper draws its results and conclusion on the basis of a revisit study that was carried out after a twenty-year gap, in six villages of Patiala district of Punjab. In an attempt to capture the persistence of informal lenders and the characteristics of informal lending, a primary survey had been carried out in the immediate post-reform period, i.e. in 1993–1994 in Patiala district (Gill 2000). The district at that time was divided into nine development blocks (now eight, with the exclusion of Dera Bassi), which were officially classified into three agro-climatic zones. One block from each zone was selected. Thus, from the undulated plain region Ghanour block, from the upland plain region Patiala block, and from the flood plain region Samana block were selected. Two villages from each block were selected. The study region thus consisted of six villages—Ramgarh and Roargarh from the Patiala block; Chappar and Sogalpur from the Ghanour block; and Dodra and Retgarh from the Samana block. Around forty households from each village were sought to be contacted for the collection of required information, but non-response from certain households limited the actual sample to be 181 households. The field investigation was carried out with the help of a detailed questionnaire through the method of personal interview. Data were collected for two crop seasons.

The survey was followed up again after a twenty-year gap, in 2012–2013. Attempt was made to re-examine the same households regarding their borrowing situation. However, since the time gap was immense, a few households could not be contacted as they had either shifted out of the village, or left cultivation. Hence, new households were added in the same land size group wherever possible. Despite this, the total sample size turned out to be 173 for the revisit study. However, this sample was sufficient to study the credit situation regarding interlinked transactions and make comparisons with the previous survey.

8.3 Punjab Economy-Structural Changes

Punjab state has an area of 50,362 km^2 comprising 48,256 km^2 (95.84 %) of rural area. Its total population according to 2011 census was 277.04 lakhs, of which 62.50 % was rural population. Its per capita income stood at Rs. 78,594 at current prices (Rs. 46,422 at 2004–2005 prices) in 2011–2012, with the states of Gujarat, Maharashtra, Kerala, Sikkim, Tamil Nadu, Haryana, Uttrakhand and Himachal Pradesh[1] ahead of it (Statistical Abstract of Punjab 2012). The average annual growth rate of net state domestic product (NSDP) of the Punjab economy was 3.66 % during 2000–2001 and 2005–2006 which increased to 7.25 % during 2006–2007 and 2011–2012 (Table 8.1). In sharp contrast to this, agricultural NSDP, which grew at a high rate of 5.15 % per annum during 1980–1981 and 1990–1991, slipped to a low of 0.9 % per annum from 2000–2001 to 2005–2006 and recovered marginally to 1.50 % per annum during 2006–2007 and 2011–2012. These low growth rates are indicative of a grave crisis like situation.

The gravity of situation is further highlighted if the share of agriculture sector in NSDP is observed (Table 8.2). This share was 54.27 % in 1970–1971, which declined sharply to 27.32 % in 2012–2013, a decline of nearly 27 % points. The share of manufacturing sector doubled from around 8 % to nearly 17 %, i.e. an

[1]States not mentioned rank wise. Union territories have been excluded in this comparison

Table 8.1 Average annual growth rates of NSDP and agricultural NSDP of Punjab (% per annum)

Year	Agricultural NSDP	NSDP of Punjab
1980–1981 to 1990–1991	5.15	2.39
1991–1992 to 1998–1999	2.16	2.55
2000–2001	0.69	3.40
2001–2002	−0.18	1.32
2002–2003	−5.79	2.57
2003–2004	7.79	4.94
2004–2005	1.78	5.24
2005–2006	1.11	4.52
2000–2001 to 2005–2006	0.90	3.66
2006–2007	2.70	10.78
2007–2008	3.7	8.67
2008–2009	1.82	5.54
2009-2010	−1.30	6.4
2010–2011 (P)	1.14	6.5
2011–2012 (Q)	0.96	5.6
2006–2007 to 2011–2012	1.50	7.25
2012–2013 (A)	0.22	5.20

Source Estimated from NSDP at factor cost by sectors in Punjab; Economic and Statistical Organisation, Government of Punjab: Statistical abstract of Punjab (1980, 1995, 2012)
Note (i) Figures till 1998–1999 are at 1980–1981 prices, till 2005–2006 at 1999–2000 prices and 2006–2007 onwards at 2004–2005 prices
(ii) *P* implies provisional; *Q* implies quick estimates; *A* implies advance

increase of 9 % points. Services sector improved its share. The deceleration of the growth rate has reduced the relative income share of the agricultural sector.

This structural shift, however, is in contrast to the high degree of dependence of population on agriculture in Punjab. In 1971, workforce engaged in agriculture (cultivators and agricultural workers) was 62.67 %, which dramatically fell to 35.6 % in 2011 (Table 8.3). However, it is still high compared to the sectoral share of agriculture in NSDP. Simultaneously, the cultivator population declined by more than half, although that of agricultural workers did not decline as much. The share of industrial workers too declined slightly, while the gain of workforce in the services sector was dramatic—from 26 to 54 % over the period 1971–2011. This is indicative of the curious phenomenon of Punjab economy having bypassed the usual path of structural transformation and becoming service oriented prematurely. Agriculture income has been squeezed much more than the lift of workforce from this sector. A substantial portion of the workforce still dependent on agriculture for livelihood is facing the problem of being gainfully employed elsewhere.

Another difficult situation confronting the cultivators relates to the tardy growth of minimum support prices (MSPs) for wheat and paddy which are the two major crops of Punjab. Table 8.4 clearly brings out that the real rise of MSP was negative

Table 8.2 Sectoral distribution of NSDP at factor cost in Punjab (%)

Sector	Year						
	1970–1971	1980–1981	1990–1991	2000–2001	2010–2011 (P)	2011–2012 (Q)	2012–2013 (A)
Agriculture and livestock	54.27	48.46	47.63	37.79	29.43	28.28	27.32
(a) Agriculture	38.51	32.22	30.69	26.45	19.98	19.06	18.40
(b) Livestock	15.76	16.24	18.94	11.34	09.45	09.22	8.92
Manufacturing	08.04	11.00	16.27	12.93	16.62	16.60	16.79
Electricity, gas and water supply	00.84	01.31	02.45	02.24	01.30	01.17	1.13
Construction	09.21	06.15	03.74	05.16	07.79	07.73	6.79
Trade, hotel and restaurants	10.96	14.58	11.33	15.53	12.47	12.29	12.40
Transport, storage and communication	01.73	02.05	02.32	04.19	04.91	04.88	4.56
Banking and insurance	01.80	02.55	04.67	04.56	05.58	05.74	6.07
Real estate and business services	04.79	04.26	03.20	03.69	04.41	04.48	4.58
Public administration	01.79	02.81	03.28	04.27	04.50	04.54	4.55
Others	06.57	06.81	05.11	9.14	10.68	11.66	12.86

Source Economic and Statistical Organization, Statistical Abstract of Punjab (1960, 1995 and 2012), Government of Punjab
Note: *P* implies provisional; *Q* implies quick estimates; *A* implies advance

Table 8.3 Structure of workforce in Punjab (%)

Sector	Year				
	1971	1981	1991	2001	2011
Agriculture	62.67	58.02	56.07	38.95	35.60
(a) Cultivators	42.56	35.86	31.44	22.62	19.55
(b) Agricultural workers	20.11	22.16	24.63	16.32	16.05
Industrial workers	11.30	13.50	12.28	08.43	10.24
Other workers	26.03	28.47	31.65	52.63	54.16
Total	100.00	100.00	100.00	100.00	100.00

Source Calculated from Economic and Statistical Organization, Statistical Abstract of Punjab (1980, 1995 and 2012), Government of Punjab

during the period 1980–1981 and 2005–2006, while there was a marginal increase from 2005–2006 to 2011–2012. This is in the face of greater increase in the total operational costs of paddy and wheat as compared to increase in yield, which substantially lowers the margins of cultivators (Singh 2009). Besides, there is expenditure to be made on machinery and its maintenance/replacement, apart from the mandatory consumption expenditures.

The above factors have proved to be an ever-increasing financial burden on the farmers, leading them more and more towards indebtedness for fulfilling production as well as consumption needs. Their repayment capacity too has been severely

Table 8.4 Minimum support prices for wheat and paddy (in Rs.)

Year	MSP of wheat at current prices	MSP of wheat at constant prices	MSP of paddy at current prices	MSP of paddy at constant prices
1980–1981	130	399.63	105	322.78
1985–1986	162	336.06	142	294.54
1990–1991	225	307.04	205	279.75
1995–1996	380	317.86	360	301.13
2000–2001	610	393.17	510	328.71
2005–2006	640	598.13	570	532.71
2011–2012	1285	709.94	1080	596.68
Average annual growth rate (1980–1981 to 2005–2006 (1993–1994 prices)	−0.69		−0.33	
2005–2006 to 2011–2012 (2004–2005 prices)	2.67		1.72	

Source (i) Rangi and Singh (2007) quoted in Gill (2010)
(ii) Government of India, Economic Survey 2012–2013

jeopardized. Institutional credit had seemingly not been enough to keep farmers away from the informal lenders, resulting in their exploitation and distress-driven suicides.

8.4 Credit Market Situation in Agriculture

Rural credit market in India has always been characterized by the coexistence of both formal and informal sources of finance. Before the beginning of the First Plan in 1951, almost the entire credit needs of the rural sector were provided by the money lenders (Pradhan 2013). The evolution of institutional credit to agriculture can be broadly classified into four distinct phases (Golait 2007):

(i) 1904–1969 (dominance of cooperatives, setting up of Reserve Bank of India (RBI));
(ii) 1969–1975 (nationalization of commercial banks and setting up of Regional Rural Banks (RRBs)); Priority sector norms (1972);
(iii) 1975–1990 (setting up of NABARD);
(iv) 1991 onwards (financial sector reforms, microfinance and SHG-Bank Linkage).

The enactment of the Cooperative Societies Act in 1904 laid the ground for the institutional involvement in agricultural credit. The decade of 1970s marked the entry of commercial banks into the arena of agricultural credit. The setting up of RRBs in 1975 and the formation of National Bank for Agriculture and Rural

Development (NABARD) in 1982 were commendable efforts by RBI to institutionalize the credit channel for rural sector.

These efforts have culminated into a multi-agency approach for purveying credit to agriculture, comprising of cooperative banks, scheduled commercial banks and RRBs. The spread of this institutional machinery led to a considerable increase in the share of institutional credit for agriculture, from around 7 % in 1951 to more than 60 % in 2002. The share of non-institutional sources accordingly declined from 93 to 39 % during the same period (All India Debt and Investment Survey and NSSO, quoted in Subbarao 2012). Institutional share wise, the share of commercial banks in 2011–2012 was the maximum (72.4 %), followed by cooperative banks (16.9 %) and RRBs (10.6 %). The break-up of this share in 1991–1992 was 43, 52 and 5 %, respectively (NABARD Annual Reports).

The agriculture credit market structure in Punjab too comprises of both the institutional and the non-institutional sources. The institutional sources, such as the rest of India, are multi-agency, comprising of scheduled commercial banks (29), RRBs (3) and cooperative banks. The cooperative credit structure has two constituents—short-term agricultural credit institutions and long-term agricultural credit institutions. The former are a three-tiered structure with the Punjab State Cooperative Bank at the apex level, the Central Cooperative Banks (CCBs) at the district/tehsil level and the Primary Agricultural Credit Societies (PACS) which disburse loans to the ultimate borrowers. At present, there are 20 CCBs with 827 branches, and 3968 PACS (Statistical Abstract of Punjab, 2012). The long-term agricultural needs are met by the Agricultural Development Banks, with the Punjab State Cooperative Agriculture Development Banks (SCADS) at the apex and the Primary Cooperative Agricultural Development Banks (PCADB) at the grassroot level. At present, there are 89 branches/offices of the PCADBs. There are three RRBs in the State—Sutlej Gramin Bank, Malwa Gramin Bank and Punjab Gramin Bank, sponsored by Punjab and Sind Bank, State Bank of Patiala, and Punjab National Bank, respectively.

Table 8.5 gives the institutional credit flow to agriculture in Punjab. It can be observed that while in the immediate post-reform era, the share of cooperative banks in institutional credit was the maximum; their share has been declining over the years, especially till 2010–2011, after which the share of cooperatives picked up only slightly. The share of commercial banks, on the other hand, increased tremendously.

Table 8.6 gives an indication of banks' reach out to rural areas and the use of rural deposits for rural credit (credit–deposit, i.e. C-D ratio) in Punjab. While the rural branches increased in absolute numbers, their share in total bank branches decreased from 2000 till 2012, with only a non-descript improvement in 2013. The rural C-D ratio, on the other hand, increased over the same period, although till 2005, the bank branches had not even maintained the RBI stipulated mandatory C-D ratio of at least 60 %. At present, it is around 68 %. Also, while deposits had increased nearly 4.5 times during this 13-year period, credit had increased by nearly 6.5 times. However, if we consider rural C-D ratio for scheduled commercial banks only, it was 57 % in 2012, as compared to 72.73 % for rural India for the same year. (RBI, Quarterly Statistics on Deposits and Credit of Scheduled Commercial Banks).

Table 8.5 Institutional credit flow to agriculture in Punjab (Rs. in lakhs)

Year	Commercial banks	Cooperative banks	RRBs	Total
1970–1971	1799.39 (17.62)	8410.45 (82.38)	–	10,209.84 (100.00)
1980–1981	14,458.14 (37.54)	24,058.45 (62.46)	–	38,516.59 (100.00)
1995–1996	76,380 (38.99)	115,612 (59.02)	3908 (1.99)	195,900 (100.00)
2000–2001	260,990 (50.67)	240,795 (46.75)	13,286 (2.58)	515,071 (100.00)
2004–2005	769,593 (60.15)	468,125 (36.59)	41,698 (3.26)	1,279,416 (100.00)
2010–2011	3,031,032 (80.83)	553,062 (14.75)	165,666 (4.42)	3,749,760 (100.00)
2011–2012	2,759,569 (78.62)	547,840 (15.61)	202,755 (5.78)	3,510,164 (100.00)
2012–2013	3,052,976 (78.11)	618,748 (15.83)	237,073 (6.06)	3,908,797 (100.00)

Source (i) EPW Research Foundation 2007–2008: agricultural credit in India: changing profile and regional imbalances—special tabulations provided by NABARD
(ii) Controlling Heads of Banks, Chandigarh
(iii) Satish (2006)
Note (i) Figures are for direct agricultural advances
(ii) Figures in parentheses are percentages to total

Against this backdrop of institutional finance, a disturbing feature of the post-reform period in Punjab, as in the rest of the country, is the persistence of the informal lenders. In 1962, non-institutional credit agencies accounted for 89 % of outstanding cash debt, which decreased to 22 % in 1992. But in 2002, informal sources again increased their share to around 44 % (Table 8.7). The challenge of lowering non-performing assets and meeting other prudential norms in the wake of financial sector reforms translated into fewer favours for agriculture. This combined with backtracking of public expenditure on health, education and rural development forced greater borrowings from informal sources. Independent surveys carried out after this period also highlight the hold of informal lenders who mainly operate in the garb of commission agents (Table 8.8). These are the lenders, who finance cultivators to obtain exclusive rights to purchase their crop, and/or force them to purchase inputs only from the lenders. This apart from the exorbitant rates of interest charged on the loan amount. Such dual transactions, technically called interlinked credit transactions, are an important aspect of the informal indebtedness.

In an attempt to capture the persistence (or otherwise) of informal lenders and changing (if any) characteristics of informal lending, a survey that had been carried out in the immediate post-reform period, i.e. 1993–1994 in six villages of Patiala district of Punjab (Gill 2000), was followed up again after a twenty-year gap, i.e. in 2012–2013. The change in source-wise borrowings of these households over the two points of time is presented in Table 8.9. The table gives some startling results in

Table 8.6 Bank branches, deposits and credit in rural areas in Punjab

Year (as on March)	Branches (number)	Deposits (Rs. in lakhs)	Credit (Rs. in lakhs)	Credit-Deposit (C-D) ratio
2000	1699 (51.66)	1,111,047	564,272	0.51
2001	1706 (51.40)	1,225,428	666,586	0.54
2002	1713 (51.16)	1,524,893	885,446	0.58
2003	1754 (51.12)	1,662,521	922,893	0.55
2004	1748 (50.19)	1,799,049	954,890	0.53
2005	1751 (48.31)	1,905,518	1,088,003	0.57
2006	1723 (48.48)	2,027,228	1,235,520	0.61
2007	1732 (46.82)	2,338,668	1,542,670	0.66
2008	1770 (45.94)	2,631,617	1,649,177	0.63
2009	1817 (45.23)	3,158,440	1,898,232	0.60
2010	1882 (4443)	3,521,932	2,125,737	0.60
2011	2008 (43.36)	4,007,040	2,539,315	0.63
2012	2140 (43.25)	4,466,595	2,906,282	0.65
2013	2389 (43.96)	5,221,820	3,576,069	0.68

Source Controlling Heads of Banks, Chandigarh
Note (i) Figures are total of scheduled commercial banks, RRBs and cooperative banks
(ii) Figures in parentheses are percentages to total bank branches in Punjab

Table 8.7 Share of institutional and non-institutional agencies in outstanding cash debt in rural areas in Punjab (%)

Year (as on June)	Government	Cooperatives	Commercial banks	Informal
1962	3.6	7.1	–	89.3
1972	5.2	24	3.1	67.7
1982	8.9	21.4	43.8	25.5
1992	2.5	20.1	55.3	22.1
2002	1.2	19.0	28.6	43.7

Source Compiled from All India Debt and Investment Survey: quoted in Pradhan 2013

Table 8.8 Estimates of agency-wise share in credit flow to agriculture in Punjab (%)

Credit Agency	1997 (Shergill)	2002 (P. Satish)	2003 (NSSO)	2005–2006 (Sukhpal et al.)	2008 (Shergill)
Commercial banks	19.42	24.43	28.40	44.65	31.78
Cooperatives	27.14	30.12	17.60	17.28	18.91
Commission agents	46.32	45.45[a]	44.50	31.98	43.36

Source Field Surveys of Authors, NSSO 59th Round, 2005
[a]Credit from all informal sources

the sense that although borrowings from cooperatives registered some change, commercial banks found immense favour, save for the landless and extra large cultivators (whose preference for commercial banks was the same). At the same time, percentage of households borrowing from informal lenders had gone down for all size groups of holdings, except the extra large farmers. The reasons, as reported by the respondents, were policy initiatives undertaken since the last few years, such as lowering interest rates (under the interest subvention scheme) of institutional loans, increasing the limit of collateral-free loans, Kisan Credit Card (KCC) scheme, the debt waiver, debt relief and one-time settlement (OTS) schemes, and debt swap schemes to bring farmers into the institutional fold. The landless, who had to compulsorily borrow from landlords by providing their labour as collateral, had found relief in schemes such as MGNREGA. Overall, the percentage of households of all size groups' borrowings from commercial banks was 44.5, 54.33 % from cooperatives and 42.2 % from informal sources, as compared to 24.3, 62.4 % and a staggering 86.2 %, respectively, in 1993–1994. Interestingly, an intensive survey of three of the most distressed districts of Punjab—Sangrur, Mansa and Bathinda—also pointed out a somewhat similar decline in the percentage of households borrowing from non-institutional sources (Singh et al. 2013). Another study revealed that for rural labour households in Punjab, the debt by source of borrowing registered the percentage shares of formal and informal debt as 19 and 81, respectively, in 2004–2005, which changed to 35 and 65 %, respectively, in 2009–2010, a clear shift towards institutional finance (Chandrasekhar 2014).

It is also pertinent to note that the percentage of non-borrowers had decreased. This was mainly in households where alternative sources of income had been generated because some member of the family, a child in 1993–1994, had grown up and found work as a driver, mechanic, watchman, army, etc., or in schemes such as MGNREGA. The minimum numbers of non-borrower households were from the category of large and extra large farmers. It was just the extra large cultivator size group that continued to rely heavily, rather more, on the informal lenders.

Despite the decline, it cannot be denied that borrowings from informal sources persist for all size class of households. Tables 8.10 and 8.11 present and compare the main types of informal lenders and the way in which credit transactions are interlinked with other transactions as a form of collateral. In 1993–1994, it was the commission agent ('arhtiya' in local parlance) who was the dominant informal lender, and whose

Table 8.9 Number of household borrowing from different sources: changing trend from 1993–1994 to 2012–2013

Size group of holding (Acres)	Commercial banks		Cooperatives		Informal lenders		Non-borrower from any source		Total	
	1993–1994	2012–2013	1993–1994	2012–2013	1993–1994	2012–2013	1993–1994	2012–2013	1993–1994	2012–2013
Landless	5 (13.89)	6 (13.64)	4 (11.11)	9 (20.45)	21 (58.33)	14 (31.82)	6 (16.67)	15 (34.10)	36 (100)	44 (100)
Up to 2.5	2 (4.65)	14 (24.14)	17 (39.53)	24 (41.38)	23 (53.49)	16 (27.58)	1 (2.33)	4 (6.90)	43 (100)	58 (100)
2.51–5.00	8 (11.11)	27 (33.75)	30 (41.67)	31 (38.75)	31 (43.05)	18 (22.50)	3 (4.17)	4 (5.00)	72 (100)	80 (100)
5.01–10.00	10 (12.66)	19 (30.65)	29 (36.71)	19 (30.65)	37 (46.83)	16 (25.81)	3 (3.80)	8 (12.90)	79 (100)	62 (100)
10.01–25.00	14 (18.18)	10 (35.71)	27 (35.07)	10 (35.17)	36 (46.75)	7 (25.00)	– (0.00)	1 (3.57)	77 (100)	28 (100)
Above 25.00	5 (26.32)	1 (25.00)	6 (31.58)	1 (25.00)	8 (42.10)	2 (50.00)	– (0.00)	– (0.00)	19 (100)	4 (100)

Source Field survey
Note (i) Figures in parentheses are percentages
(ii) – implies nil
(iii) Households borrowing from multiple sources have been counted in each group

Table 8.10 Number of households involved in various types of interlinked credit transactions in the informal credit market 1993–1994

Size group of holding (Acres)	No. of HHs in the group	Source of borrowing	Types of linkage with					Not borrowed from informal source
			Land	Labour	Output	Both input and output	None/personal surety	
Landless	29	Landlord C.A. cloth merchant	–	17	2	1	1	8
Up to 2.5	25	C.A., Landlord	–	1	16	5	1	2
2.51–.00	39	C.A., Landlord	–	–	25	5	2	7
5.01–10.00	41	C.A., Landlord	1	–	32	3	1	4
10.01–25.00	38	C.A.	1	–	35	1	–	2
Above 25	9	C.A.	–	–	8	–	–	1
Total	181	–	2 (1.27)	18 (11.46)	118 (78.16)	15 (9.55)	5 (3.18)	24

Source Field survey, Gill (2000)
Note (i) Figures in parentheses are percentages to total borrowers from informal sources i.e. 181 − 24 = 157 borrowers
(ii) C.A. implies commission agent
(iii) – implies nil

thrust was on crop as collateral. 75 % credit transactions were interlinked with output, i.e. sale of crop only through the lender–arhtiya. In some cases (9.55 %), credit was linked with both input and output, i.e. the lender doubled up as arhtiya as well as input supplier. For the landless, labour acted as collateral to obtain credit from landlords, i.e. the borrower and/or his family member(s) work for the landlord till repayment of loan. Only a small percentage could borrow without (or personal) surety.

Table 8.11, presenting the results of the survey in 2012–2013, revealed that although the arhtiya was still the dominant source, the linkage with output had declined (to around 59 %) and so had the linkage with labour. Apparently, land found greater favour with the lenders due to its high price, as a form of collateral (12.33 %)—more so in case of marginal farmers. But it was the commission agent who was demanding land as collateral either because he was also a landlord wanting to grab land or simply because land seemed better than the collateral than the crop (which could fail and give him nothing for sale). Interestingly, the percentage of households borrowing without interlinked contracts went up (around 25 %) in the later survey. The main households in this group belonged to the landless class or the marginal farmers, as they had borrowed from shopkeepers and relatives also and hence could escape providing collateral in those cases. Nearly 58 % households had

Table 8.11 Number of household involved in various types of interlinked credit transactions in the informal credit market 2012–2013

Size group of holding (Acres)	No. of HHs in the group	Source of borrowing	Types of Linkage with					Not borrowed from informal source
			Land	Labour	Output	Both input and output	None/personal surety	
Landless	35	C.A. shopkeeper landlord	1	3	1	–	9	21
Up to 2.5	40	C.A., relative	5	–	5	–	6	24
2.51–5.00	47	C.A.	2	–	13	–	3	29
5.01–10.00	35	C.A.	–	–	16	–	–	19
10.01–25.00	14	C.A.	1	–	6	–	–	7
Above 25	2	C.A.	–	–	2	–	–	–
Total	173	–	9 (12.33)	3 (4.11)	43 (58.90)	–	18 (24.66)	100

Source Field survey
Note (i) Figures in parentheses are percentages to total borrowers from informal sources
i.e. 173 − 100 = 73 borrowers
(ii) C.A. implies commission agent
(iii) – implies nil

not borrowed from informal sources, mainly because they were borrowing from both commercial banks and cooperatives.

A purpose-wise analysis of the loans revealed that around 67 % (i.e. 115) of households had used the loan taken from either source for productive expenditures, while 54 % (94 in numbers) households had utilized their borrowings for unproductive purposes. However, a larger number of households (87) used their formal loans on productive purposes, while informal loans were used for unproductive purposes by a bigger number (47) of households. The unproductive purposes were mainly house construction/repair and marriages, a result which is in consonance with not only our earlier survey (Gill 2000), but also of surveys carried out by other economists (Shergill 2010; Singh et al. 2007). Healthcare expenses did not figure very prominently in the present survey, save for a few instances. Again, it can be argued that house construction/repair expenditure cannot justifiably be called unproductive, while strong demonstration effect is responsible in a big way for expenditure on marriages.

A noticeable difference that came to light was that the rate of interest charged by the informal lender had declined in 2012–2013, as compared to 1993–1994. While during the earlier survey it was between 24 and 36 %, it varied between 18 and 24 % in the revisit study. The lowering of formal rates of interest ostensibly had played a role in this decline. Despite this, informal rates of interest continued to be much higher than the formal interest rates which vary between 4 and 10–12 %, which is why 98 of the 173 households registered a clear preference for formal borrowings, while only 37 households favoured informal lenders on account of easy access and availability.

To sum up, the informal lenders in the agricultural credit market of Punjab who had returned with a vengeance in the post-reform period are still persisting, although they seem to be losing ground, albeit at a slow pace. A number of factors seem to be working against their once all powerful existence. The 'wake-up call' policies of the government adopted in the light of distressingly high numbers of suicides could be an important factor behind this trend. It is in the fitness of things to examine the recent policy initiatives in this regard.

8.5 Policy Initiatives

In response to the glaring agrarian crisis in the post-reform era, and recognizing short falls in institutional credit flow to agriculture as one of the culprits, the government of India and the RBI announced a plethora of measures to improve access to finance from formal institutions in the rural India. A number of committees and task forces were set up to examine the issue and make recommendations. The outcomes of these efforts were a number of schemes related to indebtedness and to improve flow of institutional credit.

It is pertinent to mention here that the policy makers in India have always emphasized the role of rural financial institutions not only for making investments in agriculture, but also for freeing the farmers from the clutches of moneylenders. Some of the efforts in this direction have been mentioned in the beginning of Sect. 8.3. There is no denying that even prior to 1990, banks suffered from a number of maladies ranging from large non-performing assets to organizational weaknesses. However, post-1990, the banking sector faced formidable challenges in a reform-zest environment imposed through regulatory and prudential norms. Non-farm activities became the favoured ones on account of these being more profitable, and in the process banks faltered on their social commitments including the all important one of providing credit for agriculture. The already inadequate agricultural credit situation became worse, and it was ultimately realized that tardy credit was a major player in worsening the plight of farmers. Many committees (Government of India 2005, 2007, 2010, 2013; Reserve Bank of India 2004) examined the various aspects of institutional agricultural finance and came up with a number of schemes. Some of these have been taken up in this section.

In 1998–1999, Kisan Credit Card (KCC) scheme was introduced to provide flexible and cost-effective credit support to farmers from the banking system. The scheme is being implemented by commercial banks, cooperative banks and RRBs. The scope of the scheme was enhanced in 2004–2005 to include investment credit and some consumption requirement. An interest subvention of 2 % (later enhanced to 3 %) was added as an incentive for prompt repayment of production loans so that farmers who promptly repaid their crop loans receive loans at an effective rate of 4 % per annum. The limit of collateral-free farm loans was also increased to Rs. one lakh. Punjab has recorded the highest coverage of KCCs (ratio of number of cards to operational holdings)—77.53 % (Samantara 2010). Up to March 2013, commercial banks had disbursed 1,930,697 cards with an amount of Rs. 4,003,660 lakhs, while cooperatives had disbursed 958,097 cards with a total amount of Rs. 735,033 lakhs. Total disbursement was of 2,888,825 cards (Controlling Heads of Banks). The scheme has proved to be a mechanism of cutting down transaction costs for farmers. There is no processing fee up to a limit of Rs. 3 lakhs. However, despite this impressive performance, it is being feared that farmers in small villages of border areas are still deprived of this facility (Haque 2014).

In 2004, the Government of India had announced a package for doubling the credit flow to agriculture, from Rs. 80,000 crore in 2003–2004, in three years. This target was achieved in two years (Satyasai 2008) and is looked upon as a measure to increasing adequacy so as to bring a greater number of farmers into the institutional fold.

The government had implemented an Agricultural Debt Waiver and Debt Relief Scheme (ADWDRS) in 2008 which aimed at bringing defaulter farmers back into the institutional fold. The scheme covered all direct agricultural loans disbursed to farmers between 31 March 1997 and 31 March 2007, and overdue as on 31 December 2007 remaining unpaid till 29 February 2008. Under this, the entire eligible amount was to be waived in case of small and marginal farmers (up to 2 hectares). For other farmers, there was to be a one-time settlement (OTS) scheme under which farmers were to be given a rebate of 25 % of eligible amount provided they paid the balance of 75 % (Govt. of India 2008). Since this scheme was for formal loans only and hence came under heavy criticism, a scheme was designed especially to free farmers from the clutches of informal lenders—the Debt Swap Scheme—which facilitates farmers in swapping the loan taken from informal sources, for redemption of debt from such sources and hence make them 'moneylender free'. However, this scheme has reported limited success, especially in Punjab. The fault lay partly with the banks, several of these having not extended any loan under this scheme, although the stipulation is that 3 % of total disbursements for agriculture are to be earmarked for extending loans under this scheme. Till March 2013, Rs. 23,724 lakhs had been extended under this scheme in Punjab, which was just 16 % of the target (Controlling Heads of Banks). Also, the reluctance shown by farmers to disclose the names of their moneylenders or their financial liabilities with them, or even having repaid their informal loan out of their KCC limit, has slowed down the progress of this scheme.

These policy initiatives have obviously not gone unnoticed and did have a positive impact however small, especially in reducing reliance on informal sources. Since most of these measures were announced less than a decade back, it is yet to be seen how far these will be successful. However, it must be admitted that there is also a need to look beyond numbers and focus on some practices that are deterrent in freeing farmers from informal lenders. One such practice, widely prevalent (especially in Punjab), is the practice of interlinking informal loans with sale of produce through the lender–arhtiya, and indirect payment to farmers through him (Gill 2000, 2010; Satyasai 2008). If farmers can sell their produce directly to the procurement agencies, or even just receive direct payment for sale of produce, it would considerably mitigate farmers' exploitation. Unfortunately, the response of both the State and the farmers on this issue has been bleak due to vested political interests and lack of enthusiastic response to the direct payment scheme, on the part of farmers (Singh 2014). Registration and licensing of money lenders is another step has to be aggressively implemented to keep an eye on their lending policies. The cooperative credit system needs to be strengthened further to increase their share in institutional loans, given the commercial banks' tendency to avail the opportunities thrown up by para-banking activities.

8.6 Concluding Remarks

Beginning from Pandit Nehru's exhortation soon after independence that everything else can wait, but not agriculture, agricultural growth has all along been at the centre of policy interventions. Though public policy has always recognized the role of finance in achieving this and has always attempted at ensuring adequate and cheap credit vide its institutionalization, to agriculture, there is room for improvement. The economy of Punjab, which once enjoyed the status of being the grain bowl of the country and the most prosperous state, fell on bad days characterized by agrarian distress and distress-driven suicides. Indebtedness, especially from informal lenders had a contributory role in this grim situation. The zeal of reforms post 1991 had to be subsequently toned down to introduce schemes and measures which did bring some improvement, in thwarting informal lenders and bringing farmers into the institutional fold. This achievement has been noticed in Punjab. But it is also true that what has been reaped is what can be called just the lowest hanging fruits, and there is need to look beyond. The role of the State government is vital, not merely because agriculture (and hence its problems) is a state subject, but also because it is important that the corrective measures be translated into more effective contributions through proper implementation.

References

Chandrasekhar S (2014) Reading the tea leaves on financial inclusion: the case of rural labour households. Econ Polit Wkly XLIX(3):43–51

EPW Research Foundation (2007–2008) Agricultural credit in India: changing profile and regional imbalances, Mumbai

Gill A (2000) Rural credit markets: financial sector reforms and the informal lenders. Deep and Deep Publishers, New Delhi

Gill A (2010) Punjab peasantry: a question of life and debt. In: Deshpande A (eds) Agrarian crisis and farmers suicides. Sage Publications, New Delhi, pp 292–311

Golait R (2007) Current issues in agricultural credit in India: an assessment. Reserve Bank India Occas Pap 28(1):79–99

Govt. of India (2008) Implementation of the agricultural debt waiver and debt relief scheme. Press Information Bureau, May 23. Available at http://www.pib.nic.in/newsite/printrelease.aspx. Accessed 6 Mar 2014

Government of India (2005) Indebtedness of farmer households-Situation assessment survey of farmers. NSSO 59th Round, Ministry of Statistics and Programme Implementation, New Delhi, May

Government of India (2007) Report of the expert group on agricultural indebtedness. Department of Economic Affairs, Ministry of Finance, New Delhi, July

Government of India (2010) Report of the task force on credit related issues of farmers. Ministry of Agriculture, New Delhi, June

Government of India (2013) State of Indian Agriculture 2012–13. Directorate of Economics and Statistics, Department of Agriculture and Cooperatives, Ministry of agriculture, New Delhi

Govt. of Punjab, Statistical Abstract, 1980, 1995 and 2012, Chandigarh

Haque T (2014) Ensure credit for farmers from banks. The Sunday Tribune, 23 Feb, p 14

Pradhan NC (2013) Persistence of informal credit in rural India: evidence from all India debt and investment survey and beyond. Department of Economic and Policy Research, RBI Working Paper Series, April

Reserve Bank of India (2004) Report of the advisory committee on flow of credit to agriculture and related activities from the banking system, Mumbai, June

Samantara S. (2010) Kisan credit card—a study. Occasional paper no. 52, NABARD, Mumbai

Satish P (2006) Agricultural institutional credit, indebtedness and suicides in Punjab. Econ Polit Wkly XLI(26):2754–2761

Satyasai KJS (2008) Rural credit delivery in India: structural constraints and some corrective measures. Agri Econ Res Rev 21:387–394

Shergill HS (2010) Growth of farm debt in Punjab 1997 to 2008. Institute for Development and Communication, Chandigarh

Singh K (2009) Agrarian crisis in Punjab: high indebtedness, low returns, and farmers' suicides. In: Reddy and Misra (eds) Agrarian crisis in India, Oxford University Press, New Delhi, pp 261–284
Singh K (1990) Case studies of successful farmers, societies and private entrepreneurs: experience and issues. Keynote Paper Indian J Agri Econ 45(3):347–354
Singh L, Kesar SB, Rakesh S (2013) Agrarian crisis in Punjab: study of suicides of farmers' and agricultural labourer's. A report submitted to ICSSR, Centre for Development Economics and Innovation Studies, Punjabi University, Patiala
Singh S (2014) Making direct payments to farmers. The Tribune, 8 Feb, p 20
Singh S et al (2007) Flow of funds to farmers and indebtedness in Punjab. The Punjab state farmers commission, Govt. of Punjab, February
Subbarao D (2012) Agricultural credit-accomplishments and challenges. Speech delivered at the thirty years anniversary celebrations of NABARD, Mumbai, 12 July
World Bank (2012) World development indicators. World Bank, Washington DC

Chapter 9
Imperfect Information and Contract Enforcement in Informal Credit Market in Rural Punjab

Indervir Singh

9.1 Introduction

Rural credit markets, in developing countries, are dominated by informal credit and have been a major policy issue due to high interest rate charged in these markets. Rural credit markets in India have also been dominated by informal credit with high interest rate as one of their important features. These markets have been a major policy concern in India. The problems related to the informal nature of rural credit market in India got noticed by the end of the nineteenth century during the British rule (Mohan 2006; Shah et al. 2007). This recognition of credit problem in rural areas led to passing of Co-operative Societies Act in 1904. The Maclagan Committee's recommendations further resulted in the establishment of cooperative banks in all provinces by 1930. The Reserve Bank of India Act that led to the institution of Reserve Bank of India (RBI) in 1935 also had specific provisions to attend to the credit needs of the agricultural sector. However, these interventions were of little help, and the share of institutional credit was just 7.3 % of the total in 1951 (Pradhan 2013). The low share of institutional credit in 1951 led to more efforts to further strengthen the corporate credit societies. However, the increase in share of cooperative societies from 3.1 % in 1951 to 20.1 % in 1971 was considered much less than what was required to improve the situation in the rural credit market. In addition, the faulty system of identifying beneficiaries led to high losses along with poor quality of service. It was felt that the increase in the share of institutional credit would require the participation of the commercial banks in this effort. The nationalization of commercial banks helped to substantially increase the share of institutional credit in the next 10 years from 29.2 % in 1971 to 61.2 % in 1981. However, the share of institutional credit did not improve much after 1981. The share of formal credit in 1991 was estimated at 64 %, which was just 2.8 % higher

I. Singh (✉)
Central University of Himachal Pradesh, Dharamshala 176215, India
e-mail: indervirs@gmail.com

L. Singh and N. Singh (eds.), *Economic Transformation of a Developing Economy*, India Studies in Business and Economics,
DOI 10.1007/978-981-10-0197-0_9

than the 1981 figure. The next decade saw a decline of 6.9 % points in the share of formal lending to 57.1 % in 2002.

Despite the efforts to increase access to institutional credit and control informal credit, the policy interventions have not generated the expected results and the prevalence of informal lending in the rural credit market has remained a major concern in India. The share of agricultural moneylenders, traders, landlords and commission agents (though declined from 76.7 % in 1951 to 33.2 % in 2002) remained significant, and the interest rate in the informal markets is still higher compared to the interest on formal credit. The large share of informal credit does not pertain to underdeveloped areas, even agriculturally developed states like Punjab suffer from a large share of informal loans and high interest rate.

One of the main reasons for the lower levels of achievement of formal credit institutions is inadequate understanding of the functioning of the rural credit market (see Bell 1990; Bell and Srinivasan 1989). The main limitation of formal credit is imperfect information, which makes screening of borrowers difficult. In comparison, the local moneylenders spend time and money to screen the borrowers. Further, the possibility of linking the loan with transactions in other markets, such as product or rental market, lowers their cost of enforcement. These factors lower the cost of screening, monitoring and enforcement, and provide the local moneylenders some monopoly power over their clients. However, the ease of entry and exit in the informal credit market has led many researchers to point out that the market may be monopolistically competitive rather than a monopoly (see Aleem 1990).

Though there are number of studies that have explained the working of rural credit market based on imperfect information, there is still a limited understanding on the use of formal and informal institutions in screening, monitoring and enforcement of a contract by rural moneylenders. The role of civil societies, such as farmer unions, has also received less scholarly attention. To fill this gap, the present study analyses the rural credit market in the state of Punjab, which is one of the most agriculturally developed states in India. As per the National Sample Survey (2005), Punjab had the highest per capita indebtedness in 2003, and 44.5 % of the total loan on farmers for the same year in Punjab was from agricultural/professional moneylenders or traders, in comparison with 30.9 % of all India. Majority of the informal moneylending in the rural areas of Punjab is done by the commission agents, who are intermediaries between farmers and purchaser of the crop. Most of the loans extended by them are interlinked to output market (Gill 2004).

The present study analyses the issues of screening, monitoring and enforcement of the credit contract in informal credit market under imperfect information. It has been argued that the lender spends significant amount of time and resources on information. The screening and monitoring is very important part of their strategies. The screening process is also designed in such a way that it helps enforcing the contract in case of default. However, a large number of defaults may increase the cost of monitoring and enforcement of a contract. The problems may be further exaggerated due to interference of civil societies. The study points at the possible higher cost of non-legal remedies.

The paper is divided into six sections. After the introduction, Sect. 9.2 discusses the framework in which issue of contract enforcement is analysed. Section 9.3 provides the methodology of data collection. Section 9.4 tries to provide a brief introduction on relationship between farmer and commission agent and changes over time. Section 9.5 examines the strategies adopted by commission agents for screening, monitoring and enforcement. It analyses the role of law, social norms and civil societies in contract enforcement and renegotiation of the contract. Section 9.6 concludes the study.

9.2 Analytical Framework

The analysis of rural informal credit markets is often based on the assumption that lenders are monopolists. The basic reason for the monopoly assumption is high interest (often called as usury rate of interest) charged in these markets and credit rationing. However, the presence of many lenders and free entry into those markets raise another question, what are the reasons for the absence of competition in them?

The studies try to answer the puzzle by pointing out that information is imperfect in the credit market. Stiglitz and Weiss (1981) argue that imperfect information leads to credit rationing and may result in considerable monopoly power over their existing customers. The study points out that a bank's decision to lend depends not only on interest rate but also on its riskiness. The riskiness of the project is due to adverse selection (selecting a high-risk borrower) and moral hazard (lender's inability to monitor borrower's action to maximize the probability of repayment). Both effects are the result of imperfect information, where lender has less information than borrower. Due to the imperfect information in the credit market, the lender prefers to screen the borrowers. The interest rate is one of the possible screening instruments. The high-risk borrowers are more likely to agree to a high interest rate if uncertainty regarding the repayment of loan is high. On the other hand, low-risk borrowers are less likely to borrow at a high interest rate. The high interest rate will increase the average riskiness of the pool of borrowers by excluding the low-risk borrowers. The increase in interest rate may increase expected returns of banks but at a diminishing rate, and the expected pay-off may start declining beyond a point. As a result, the bank may prefer to lend at an interest rate at which its expected pay-off is maximum rather than at a demand–supply equilibrium and credit will be rationed. The imperfect information may give lenders a certain level of monopoly power over their existing customers. For example, if a bank has better information of its customers than any other bank, then it can always outmatch the offers made by other banks to any of its good customers. Other banks in the presence of informational disadvantage can only attract bad borrowers, and hence, they will have no incentive to steal other bank's customers, and the banks may have monopoly power over their customers, depending on the extent of information asymmetry or cost of acquiring information.

The above argument can be used to explain the rural credit market, where the lender may have some control over its clients due to his informational advantage.[1] Hoff and Stiglitz (1990) analysed the information asymmetry problem in rural credit markets. The study argues that the rural credit market can be better explained if one considers that the information, in these markets, is imperfect. A lender extends a loan to receive the principal and interest in the future. Since there is a time lag between receiving the loan and repaying it, there are lots of uncertainties regarding the repayment of debt. Therefore, a lender faces three problems: screening (or adverse selection), incentive (or moral hazard problem) and enforcement (also see Bell 1990). The screening problem is related to separating the risky borrowers (with more probability of default) from less risky borrowers. It is also difficult for lender to ensure that a borrower will take action which will maximize the likelihood of repayment, and this is called incentive problem. In addition, it is costly to compel repayment, which creates enforcement problem.

To solve these three problems, lenders use both direct and indirect methods. The indirect method is related to designing the terms of the loan in such a manner that probability of repayment of loan could be maximized. The classical theory predicts that increase in demand for loan will raise the interest rate and market will clear. However, increase in interest rate also increases the average risk on a pool of loans, and therefore, the careful designing of loan terms may lead to credit rationing (see Stiglitz and Weiss 1981). The direct method, often used by local moneylenders, is spending time and money to screen the borrowers and linking the loan with transactions in other markets, such as product or rental market. The use of threat to cut down credit, geography and kinship relations also plays an important role in solving the problem of imperfect information and influencing the borrower to increase the possibility of repayment. All of these factors lower the cost of screening, monitoring and enforcement. The direct method also gives the local moneylenders some monopoly power over their clients, which makes a case for monopoly in informal credit market. However, ease of entry and exit in the informal credit market points out that the market may be monopolistically competitive, rather than monopoly.

Thus, the credit market, unlike other competitive markets with no externality, fails to achieve efficient outcome due to imperfect information and high cost of legal enforcement. The actual lending, under imperfect information and weak enforcement, will be less than under perfect information and costless enforcement, and a lender may not lend even when it is beneficial for both lender and borrower. However, the lower level of lending due to imperfect information can still be considered as constrained Pareto efficient (Besley 1994). The rural credit market in developing countries, which is often dominated by informal moneylenders and characterized by high interest rates, suffers acutely from imperfect information

[1]Basu and Bell (1991) analysed the rural credit market as a fragmented duopoly, where two lenders have some common customers. The lenders, in this case, are neither monopolist (with clearly distinct set of customers) nor oligopoly (with same set of customers); rather, the market structure will be between a monopoly and an oligopoly and called it fragmented duopoly.

resulting in failure of public policy aimed to provide loans at low interest rate to reduce dependency of the borrowers on informal sector and increase investment in rural areas (mainly agricultural sector).

A number of empirical studies have found imperfections in credit market due to asymmetric information and established that the informal rural credit markets are monopolistically competitive markets rather than monopolies. Aleem (1990) studies the informal credit market operated in villages linked to town of Chambar, Sind, Pakistan, during 1980–81. Asymmetric information is a major problem in the credit market of Chambar. It is also costly to legally enforce the credit contracts. Therefore, moneylenders invest considerably in screening out bad borrowers. Screening improves their information about borrowers, and solves the problem of adverse selection and moral hazard. Since screening is costly, the credit from each moneylender is a differentiated product. Free entry into the market coupled with product differentiation leads to a situation where the average cost of lending is close to market rate of interest in Chambar but higher than the marginal cost of lending. Based on the findings, the study argues that the rural credit market has monopolistic competition rather than a monopoly as often argued. Similarly, Siamwalla et al. (1990) find the asymmetric information as the major reason for failure of formal credit institutions in Thailand, where the formal sector had high default rate and failed to drive out informal lending. The low interest rate on formal credit could also not affect the interest rate in the informal sector which remained high and stable. The study argues that informal lenders are not monopolist and high interest rate is the result of high cost of information.

The low interest rate and less likelihood of rationing in credit markets with negligible information asymmetry further prove the argument. Udry (1990) based on his study in northern Nigeria argues that the collateral requirement and interlinkage of markets are less likely in the absence of information asymmetry in the credit market. The study in a survey conducted in villages of northern Nigeria finds that 97 % of the total informal credit was from relatives, friends or residents of the same village. The close relation between a lender and a borrower reduced the information asymmetry. The repayment of a loan was based on production and consumption shocks, and the lenders were willing to extend another loan during shock period.

The presence of imperfect information with significant enforcement problems led many studies to argue for policies like improving the information base in formal sector and increase in rate of interest in formal sector. The studies also point out that banning of informal lending may not solve the problem. Bell et al. (1997) argue that informal credit existed due to rationing of credit in formal sector and banning informal lending may adversely affect the agricultural output. The study based on the analysis of the rural credit market in Punjab finds that banning informal credit may lower the credit availability in rural areas by 35 %.

The above studies point out that the strategies of the lenders and borrowers as well as the presence of high interest rate in informal credit market can be best understood with asymmetric information. A successful lender must solve three problems associated with lending: (1) screening of borrowers, (2) monitoring of the borrower and (3) enforcement of contract. With costly enforcement, a lender tries to lower the risk of selecting bad borrower by acquiring information on borrowers and ensuring that lender's action maximizes the likelihood of repayment. Once the default happens, the lender and borrower adopt strategies that maximize his expected pay-offs.

The strategies, adopted by the lenders and the borrowers after the default, and their interaction have attracted less attention of the researchers. Nonetheless, a number of studies point out various mechanisms used by parties to enforce a contract and their impact on economic activities. These studies mostly deal with contracts among manufacturers, traders and customers. The instruments of contract enforcement can be broadly divided into four categories: (1) loss due to termination of future transactions, (2) fear of loss of reputation in the market, (3) law, (4) social norms and (5) harassment or other criminal activities. Among the five instruments, loss due to termination of future transactions makes a repeated contract self-enforcing if the short-run pay-off from cheating is less than the discounted long-run pay-offs (see Telser 1980). However, self-enforcing contracts requires that no party should know when the relationship is going to end, and none should have a discount rate high enough to make the short-run benefits more attractive. If the parties know when the relation is going to end, one of the parties will have incentive to defect in the last round. Expecting default in the last round, the second party will have incentive not to play the last round. Seeing the second party's move, the first party may default in the second last round, and therefore, the second party will not play the second last round too. If this argument is extended, the parties will have no incentive to enter into the contract even in the first round. High discount rate of a party will lead to defection by the party, as it will make the short-run pay-off (from default) higher than discounted long-run pay-offs (from continuing relation).

The possibility of loss of reputation in the market can compel a party to perform, as it may deprive a party from any beneficial transaction with other parties. To know the trustworthiness of a party, people often rely on signals originated from his past behaviour. In this regard, expected discount rate can be used to separate the honest people from dishonest ones. Honest people expect long-time relations, and therefore, their discount rate for future pay-offs will be less compared to the dishonest who are interested in short-time relationship. The default acts as a signal for potential partners about the trustworthiness of the defaulting party. If the potential partners doubt the trustworthiness of a party, they are less likely to enter into a contract with that party (see Klein and Leffler 1981). Therefore, a party will perform if the present value of possible benefits is greater than the benefits of default. However, the reputation to work as an instrument of enforcement, the potential parties must have information about the default (if any) and its reason. In the absence of information about the default, the potential parties may not know whether a party has defaulted on his previous promise. The reputation may also not be effective in preventing default, if the potential parties cannot distinguish between a genuine (or unavoidable) default and an intentional default. Unlike intentional default, the unavoidable default is not the result of an opportunistic behaviour rather it is the outcome of circumstances that have made performance impossible or extremely costly. Hence, there must be an information sharing mechanism for fear of loss of reputation to work. Though the aggrieved party may share the information about the default, it is often costly (especially when the number of parties is large) for the concerned party to do so without any possible direct benefits. Therefore, the parties may find themselves in a prisoner's dilemma situation, where all will benefit by sharing information, but each party may benefit by not sharing information. Here, business associations and civil societies may play an important role in providing credible information and may also lower the cost of information sharing by keeping records of the firms. A number of studies argue that reputation-based private ordering enforced by business associations may prove more flexible and less costly than public legal system (Bernstein 2001).

The loss of future transactions with the aggrieved party and other potential partners prevents default in a large number of cases, and nonetheless, the default may still occur if the requirements necessary for these instruments to work are not met. In such cases, third-party punishment may ensure the performance as per promise. Law and social norms act as an important third-party enforcement mechanism. Social norms are the informal rules of the society, which govern the behaviour of the people. Society uses punishments such as social stigma, guilt and feeling of shame to induce its members to follow the rules (Elster 1989; Basu 2000). It should be mentioned that the people who punish someone for not following the norm do not directly benefit from it, unlike the previous two cases where a party refuses to do business with other expecting a default. The feeling of guilt works when the party has internalized the norm, that is, his utility depends on his keeping the promise. Therefore, the default lowers his utility. The criticism of the defaulting party by others also lowers the utility of defector if he values their views about him.

Ellickson (1991) based on the survey of cattlemen, in Shasta County, California, shows that the cattlemen solve their conflicts of cattle trespassing and sharing of fencing cost on the basis of the existing social norms and, most of the time, are unaware of the existing legal provisions. The study points out that social norms in the county are based on mutual cooperation. The punishments, such as gossips and mild physical reprisals, are the main instruments to discipline the deviants. However, following social norms in any activity by an individual depends on monetary incentives, shortness of future relationship and probability that cost can be transferred to a third party. People follow informal control because of their lower transaction cost as compared to the legal procedure. A similar line of argument is provided by Posner (2000). He argues that people usually do not rely on formal law to ensure coordination and rather do it through informal rules because legal suits are costly and time-consuming. It is observed that in most of the cases, people do not know about existing legal provisions. Even when people know about the legal rules, they often do not let law influence their relationships with others.

Law or court action is one of the most important enforcement mechanisms. In a country, the contracts are governed by a set of formal rules enforced by the state. An important feature of the law is that it provides clear rules regarding the rights of the parties and the compensation in the event of default. The clear rules help parties to form ex ante expectations. The contracting parties often organize economic activities around those set of rules. Although people often prefer to use social norms due to their lower cost of enforcement, they are less likely to work when the parties are members of a large group. In this context, Cross (2002) argues for the superiority of formal institutions over the informal ones and points out that in many cases, the informal enforcement may be more costly, difficult to monitor, create violence and inhibit change from inefficient to efficient rules. Since informal arrangements happen mostly among relatives, friends and small networks, they may limit the transactions to small group. Further, the cost of not following a social norm declines with the increase in the number of rule breakers, as the rule breakers are less likely to punish other rule breakers and the cost of punishing rule breakers also increases. Moreover, the society also requires information to form a view about the rule breaker, and social norms may not work with if the information is incomplete. Therefore, the cost imposed by informal institutions on borrower may change with circumstance. For example, an unavoidable circumstance, which increases the default rate, may lower the social stigma attached to default, thereby increasing the possibility of default further. However, the legal rules may differ among countries, and a set of rules may be better in facilitating the economic activities than others. Further, the cost of enforcement may differ considerably among countries despite having similar legal rules. Inefficient rules and high cost of legal enforcement compel people to resort to alternatives to the legal action. Since there are limits to the use of social norms, fear of losing reputation and termination of any future transactions, other alternatives, such as harassment and criminal activities, are often used by people.

These alternatives often prove costly and have negative impact on the economic activities. Hay and Shleifer (1998), in their study of former Soviet Union countries, point out that the quality of the legal system is bad in Russia. People use the legal system much less than their actual need, and instead, the private (criminal) enforcement of the contract is common. However, private enforcement of law need not be always efficient. Private enforcement often fails to provide clear rules to govern all cases, making people unable to build their future expectations and organize their economic activities on the basis of those rules. As a result, the arbitrary solutions of private enforcers of contract do not lead to a better situation.

Fafchamps (1996) studies the enforcement of commercial contracts between supplier of intermediate goods, manufacturers, traders and customers in Ghana. Business in sub-Saharan Africa faces the problem of delayed supply, late payments and unreliable quality, which increases the cost of conducting business. It is argued that a contract requires both parties to expect net gain from the transactions. If the cost of breaching is too low, the probability of breach will be high and the creditor may not enter into a contract. On the other hand, the debtor may not enter into a contract if the cost of breach is very high since the most successful debtors face risk. Therefore, the contract must be flexible enough to accommodate genuine defaulters, and punishment must be severe enough to discourage opportunistic behaviour. The study lists four types of costs for debtors for non-payment: (1) cost due to feeling of guilt, (2) cost due to the use of coercive force, such as harassment, threats and court action, (3) loss due to suspension of future transactions and (4) loss of reputation in the market. The likelihood of repayment may be increased with adopting a contract that requires legal security. However, these types of contracts, due to their high cost, may not be practical for small debts. Therefore, the creditor adopts a contract, which maximizes his pay-offs rather than the one that ensures the payment. The study finds that the desire for preserving the relationship (to avoid suspension of future transactions) is the main reason for the compliance with commercial contracts in Ghana. Harassment is an important way of debt collection, as it imposes high cost on debtor. Regular visits to debtors and harassment are also used to separate genuine defaults from non-genuine defaults. The legal enforcement is generally not a preferred remedy as it destroys the relationship between the parties. Only a few firms, among the total surveyed firms, have used the service of a lawyer or gone to the court. The formal contracts are also not popular among the firms, and the signature of the debtor is taken in the account books. The signature in account book is not for legal enforcement but to avoid any dispute regarding the amount of debt. Reputation effect is not an effective enforcement mechanism due to the absence of any information sharing mechanism among firms. The use of illegitimate force and use of police to put pressure are less preferred enforcement mechanisms among creditors. In addition, rescheduling of date of delivery of goods or payment of debt is common among firms. There are also cases when a debtor shifts to another business or moves to another city or just disappears, making it hard to enforce contract. The paper argues that the growth of firms is limited by the absence of an efficient legal system and lack of reputation as an enforcement mechanism.

The literature on contract enforcement provides a deep understanding of various instruments that can be used to enforce contract; however, most of these studies (with the exception of Fafchamps 1996) do not deal with the combination of strategies that may be adopted by a party to enforce a contract. For example, the studies, which examine the use of reputation to enforce contract, do not study the use of social norms, law and harassment in relation to reputation. Further, the possibility of renegotiation after default is often not discussed when the legal enforcement is weak, which is not uncommon in the informal credit markets, where the lender may be successful in getting a significant share of his lending amount back. The legal system may also facilitate renegotiation. For instance, the legal provisions in India facilitate the renegotiation of the contract by allowing it under Indian Contract Act. The Section 63 of Indian Contract Act allows the promisee to grant a concession or waive wholly or in part the performance of the promise made by the promisor without requiring any type of compensation in exchange (Singh 2013).[2]

To understand the issue of renegotiation better, let us suppose that a borrower defaults on his loan. Under this situation, lender can either enforce the contract using one of the available methods or choose not to take any action and, thereby, bear the loss of the loan. There is a cost attached to each of the alternative enforcement mechanisms. The lender will choose an alternative which minimizes

[2]Indian law differs significantly from English law on this provision.

his loss, that is, the one where the difference between expected debt recovered and the cost of recovery is the highest. The borrower will benefit from non-payment, but he may have to face legal or social sanctions. The default may also result in the loss of reputation of the borrower and deprive him of any future loan. On the other hand, the high loss of borrower due to repayment of loan increases the probability of default. Therefore, the borrower will also choose an action that maximizes his expected benefits. If the partial payment reduces the cost of sanction, then the borrower may use the renegotiation as a strategy to maximize his benefits. Since it is costly to enforce the contract with low probability of success through formal mechanism, the lender may be ready to renegotiate the contract and accept an amount that minimizes his loss. Thus, both lender and borrower may find renegotiation as the best solution. The renegotiation is more likely when the enforcement cost is high and the borrower values his reputation high. In India, the Section 65 of Indian Contract Act also enables renegotiation by reducing the risk of any strategic behaviour and making it even more likely.[3]

Another aspect, not addressed in the literature, is the possibility of harassment by borrowers and involvement of civil societies. The studies do talk about harassment of borrower by lender, and it is assumed that borrower has no incentive to harass the lender. The lender uses harassment to increase the likelihood of repayment. However, the borrower may also harass the lender if the borrower wants the lender to consider renegotiation of the contract. The harassment increases the bargaining power of the borrower (who is already at an advantageous position) and helps him to maximize his pay-off from renegotiation. The act of harassment may include the use of criminal activities, filing false complaints under different (mostly criminal) laws and the use of a civil society to pressurize the lender. The use of these instruments is more likely when their cost is low. For example, the harassment may be more prevalent when the legal system fails to punish for criminal activities, and it is more likely to use a highly active and politically influential civil society if the cost of doing so is less.

Though the civil societies may aim to protect the borrowers when the default is genuine or unavoidable, their interference may prove costly to the society.[4] It is because civil societies often deal with a large number of people and have limited knowledge about the type of borrower (i.e. honest or dishonest), and therefore, they are less likely to know whether the default is genuine or intentional. This leads to the problem of asymmetric information, where the borrower knows his type, but the civil society does not. Now, the civil society may invest in obtaining the information to identify genuine defaults before pursuing the case of a defaulter with the lender.

---

[3]However, the borrower may use the Section 63 to his benefit if the lender has high opportunity cost of non-payment in time.

[4]Santhakumar (2003) studies the role of civil societies in environment conservation in Kerala. The study argues that the civil society chooses to oppose the economically beneficial projects due to the failure of the legal system and state to enforce the environmental law. Though the active role, played by the civil societies, prevents degradation of environment, it also hinders the economic growth, which could have avoided if the enforcement of environmental law was efficient.

If the information is costly, the civil society may choose not to pursue the case or may pursue the case without knowing the type of the borrower. When the number of defaults is less, it may be less costly to know the type of defaulter. Though less costly, the benefits of interference may also be less with fewer defaults. As the number of defaults increases, the cost of distinguishing between genuine and intentional defaults also increases. The cost further increases when an unavoidable shock is also present in the economy. If civil society chooses to interfere without the knowledge of type of the borrower, a number of intentional defaulters may also benefit. The problem may further exaggerate, as a number of intentional defaulters may choose to default and seek the help of civil society. With the increase in the number of defaults, the social norms may not remain an effective enforcement mechanism. Also, the fear of losing reputation may not work as a credible threat, since the potential partners are less likely to be able to distinguish between genuine and intentional defaulters under these circumstances. Since the lender does not know the change in cost imposed by social norms and loss of reputation on borrower under the new circumstances, he may not be able to use his previously acquired knowledge about the type of the borrower. The interference by a civil society may make it more difficult for the lender to get information. For example, pressure from the civil society may prevent the regular visits of lender to the borrower's workplace or home, which is one of the important methods to acquire information. As a result, the lender is likely to respond by rationing credit for all. The borrowers, who are hurt by this credit rationing the most, often belong to the weakest section of the society and have few alternative sources of credit. For example, the rationing of informal credit in agricultural sector is likely to hurt marginal and small farmers more than the medium and large farmers. The higher income of the medium and large farmers shields them against any greater negative impact of credit rationing. Also, large farmers have better access to the alternative sources of credit. The cost of screening and monitoring is generally same for small and large farmers, whereas credit requirements of small farmers are low. Therefore, the average cost of lending to a small farmer (compared to a large farmer) is higher in the initial phase. As the studies point out that high rate of interest also increases the risk of default, the small farmers may face both high rate of interest and credit rationing.

The above discussion points out that in addition to adverse selection and moral hazard problem, the enforcement may also take a complex form with various parties trying to maximize their own benefit. Thus, the default cases may be categorized as successfully enforced, unenforced and renegotiated.

9.3 Data Collection

The commission agents, who act as the middlemen between farmers and government agencies or private parties in the sale of the crop, and commonly known as arhtia, are one of the main sources of informal loan to the farmers in the state of Punjab. These commission agents mainly operate at block level. Therefore, four blocks are selected for the purpose of the study. Stratified random sampling is used to select these blocks.

The Economic and Statistical Organisation of Punjab has ranked all 138 blocks on the basis of 16 socio-economic indicators (which include indicators related to education, health, banking and agricultural infrastructure) in 1997–98. Since the ranking is old and ranking for a recent year is not available, an alternative method is used to check the validity of the ranking. First, the districts were ranked based on average ranking of their blocks (district with lowest average is given first rank). Then, this ranking was compared with the ranking of districts based on their human development index in 2001 and per capita income in 2008–09 provided by Punjab Planning Board. The ranking of the district does not show any major change over the years (some difference in district ranking is expected as the three rankings are based on different indicators). Comparing districts does not prove that the ranking of blocks shall remain the same especially when the ranking of blocks involves a much larger number of variables, and however, it increases the probability that the ranking of the blocks may not have changed considerably and hence can be used to draw sample. Four blocks are selected out of these 138 blocks using stratified random sampling. The whole sample frame is divided into 4 strata with first 3 strata having 34 blocks each and the last stratum having 36 blocks. Since the blocks are listed as per the development level, each stratum represents a different level of development. Here, the first stratum includes the most developed blocks, and each next stratum represents lower development level than previous with last stratum representing the least developed regions. From each stratum, one block is selected for the survey.

To select the blocks for survey, blocks, in each stratum, are numbered from 1 to 34 (1 to 36 in case of the last stratum), and one block, from each stratum, is selected using random number tables. Four blocks that are selected for the survey are Banga (in district of Nawan Shehar presently known as Sahid Bhagat Singh Nagar), Malout (in district of Mukatsar), Samrala (in district of Ludhiana) and Mansa (in district of Mansa). All these blocks are situated in different districts and represent areas with different development levels. In second stage, the 30 commission agents are selected using random sampling from each block. In addition, one village is selected randomly from each block. The four villages selected are Boota (in block of Banga), Jhad Sahib (in block of Samrala), Sarava Bodla (in block of Malout) and Kokhar Khurad (in block of Mansa). From each village, 25 randomly selected farmers are interviewed to know about existing rate of interest and any problem related to enforcement. Though the farmers provided information on rate of interest and amount of loan, no farmer with any loan-related problem was found. It may be due to the small sample size, since the loan defaults are a small percentage of the total. Another possible reason is the reluctance of farmers to disclose any information on the default as it often creates a bad image of the defaulter in the society. To solve this problem, the interviewed farmers were asked about their views on defaults and their impact in general. In addition, the discussions were organized with small groups of farmers on the issue of default and enforcement by informal moneylenders in their village and area. The data collection was done between April 2011 and July 2011.

9.4 Relationship Between Farmers and Commission Agents

Commission agents, commonly known as arhtia, are the intermediaries who facilitate the sale of crop of the farmers to government agencies or private parties. For their assistance, they are paid a commission by the buyer, which is calculated as certain percentage of the value of crop. The arhtias require a licence to operate. The activities of commission agents are regulated and monitored by the market committee. With the start of government purchase of crops like wheat and rice, their major business became the facilitation of government procurement. In addition, some arhtias (called as pakka arhtias) also help farmers to sell their crop to mills or traders. These arhtias bid for the crop on behalf of a mill or a trader (Banerji and Meenakshi (2004) analyse incentives of pakka arhtias in bidding). Singh and Dhaliwal (2011) estimated the actual number of commission agent families in Punjab at 20232, and there are 20.29 commission agent families per 1000 farmer households.

In addition to facilitating sale of crops, they used to provide loans to the farmers. There are many factors which facilitate the lending activities. Arhtias had the resources to lend money to the farmers. Lending to farmers also insured that they would sell the produce through him. These loans were less risky for the arhtias, since they knew the paying capacity of the farmers, and loan along with its interest could be easily adjusted from the value of the crop. On the other hand, it was easier for the farmer to borrow from an arhtia than from anyone else. In other words, the interlinked markets reduced the information asymmetry. In fact, lending became the integral part of arhtia's business. If an arhtia refuses to lend the money, the farmers start selling their crop through another arhtia. It means that there is hardly any option for an arhtia to choose between lending and not lending if he wishes to continue his business.

Here, one point should be made clear that commission agents are not professional financers. As per Punjab Registration of Money Lenders Act, 1938, a person is not allowed to provide financing services without a licence from the collector of the district. However, the act does not prohibit friendly loans advanced to the people. Arhtia's loan to a farmer is often proved as a friendly loan in the court due to two reasons. First, court does not consider a person moneylender just because he has advanced loans to some people (see *Gurdeep Singh vs. Gopal Singh*).[5] Proving them as moneylenders becomes even more difficult, since they do not lend to people who do not sell their crop through them, and many loans are given on the trust bases. Second, a farmer, being in contact with the commission agent, can be easily considered as a known person, and the loan can be regarded as a friendly loan. Therefore, arhtias continue to lend to the farmers, where a large number of loans are given without any proper written agreement. Nonetheless, they keep regular

[5]*Gurdeep Singh vs Gopal Singh*, RSA No.871, High Court of Punjab and Haryana, 1 (2010) [URL: http://indiankanoon.org/doc/325494/] accessed on 20 August 2011.

account of transactions and take the signature of the farmer on account book. It is mainly to keep the record of transactions and prevent any dispute.

Though lending by arhtias is often considered as the reason for many problems of farmers, it exists as it serves the needs of the farmers. Arhtias know the financial condition of the farmer better than any other financers and hence can calculate the risk better. It is easier for the farmer to borrow from the arhtias. Bell et al. (1997) in their study in Punjab showed that banning the informal lending will result in 35 % less credit to farmers.

The relationship between farmers and arhtias has undergone many changes and shocks over the years. Between mid-1990s and early 2000s, a large number of farmers lost cotton crop for many consecutive years due to bollworm. The failure of crop, in the absence of any insurance, results in a large number of defaults in cotton belt of Punjab (Mansa and Malout being one of them). A large number of defaults lowered the social stigma related to default. High default rate and poor condition of farmers due to crop failure lead to a tensed relationship between farmers and commission agents, which also increased the role of farmer unions in their relationships. Despite the increased tension in the relationship of farmer and commission agents, the lending remained an important part of arhtia's business.

The survey data show that average value of crop sold through them varies between Rs. 27.14 million in Mansa and Rs. 44.40 million in Samrala, with an average of Rs. 37.37 million for the four markets (Table 9.1). The average number of customers are also different in each block. Samrala (with 175.2 farmers per firm) had much higher average than any other block. The average number of customer in Smarala is more than double as compared to Malout, which had just 84.1 customers per firm (the lowest average). Total lending in a season is a significant share of the value of crop of that season. The survey shows that the per firm lending was about 38.9 % of total value of rabi crop. The lending as the percentage of value of crop sold was the highest for Mansa (58.7 %) and the lowest for Banga (14.5 %). Malout and Samrala with 43.5 and 45.5 % share had similar pattern in lending as the share of crop value. Here, it should be mentioned that one must be cautious in making any conclusion from the lending data due to the possibility of reporting error.

Table 9.1 The main features of surveyed firms for 2010–11

Block	Average age of firm (in years)	Average agricultural land operated by commission agents (in hectare)	Value of rabi crop per firm (in millions)	Value of crop sold per firm in one year (in millions)	Number of farmers per firm	Per firm lending in rabi season (in millions)	Total lending as the percentage of value of rabi crop
Mansa	44.8	0.0	11.78	27.14	119.8	6.91	58.7
Malout	22.9	16.8	17.53	38.73	84.1	7.63	43.5
Samrala	28.1	2.52	19.76	44.40	175.2	8.99	45.5
Banga	38.6	2.08	18.17	39.22	126.1	2.63	14.5
Total	33.6	5.36	16.81	37.37	126.3	6.54	38.9

Source Primary survey

However, assuming that the possibility of error is much lower in patterns, the dependency of farmers on commission agents seems to be lower in developed Banga, which is the most developed block among the four.

9.5 Screening, Monitoring and Enforcement

The commission agents use various mechanisms to reduce the risk of default. Although the mechanism available for screening, monitoring and enforcement may be the same for all the commission agents, yet the extent of their use may vary among regions depending on the risk of default. The present section, divided into three subsections, discusses the various mechanisms used for screening, monitoring and enforcement in the four surveyed markets.

9.5.1 Screening of Contracts

Screening is the most important step among the three, as the riskiness of the pool of loans depends on the decisions taken at this stage. The lender's control over the situation decreases once the loan is extended, and he faces monitoring and enforcement problem. Screening of the contract does not necessarily negate the role of monitoring and enforcement in ensuring repayment, and instead, screening (or avoiding adverse selection) lowers the cost of monitoring and enforcement by selecting the low-risk borrowers.

The commission agents use the screening for two decisions. First decision is related to take a farmer as a regular customer. Second decision is regarding the size of the loan. The regular customer gets small loans for his cultivation and consumption needs and is often based on the value of crop brought by farmer for sale. A non-regular customer does not create any problem, as the commission agents generally do not extend him a loan. A commission agent does not expect a long-term relation with non-regular customer; therefore, it is difficult for him to

Table 9.2 Criterion used to screen potential customers

Block	Percentage of commission agents		
	Require someone to vouch for new customer	No-objection letter/clear slip from previous commission agent	Ask from old customers
Mansa	100	100.0	100
Malout	100	100.0	100
Samrala	100	73.3	100
Banga	76.7	0.0	100
Total	94.2	68.3	100

Source Primary survey

enforce the loan in case of default. On the other hand, it is very difficult to refuse a loan to a regular customer. The change of commission agent is, though not a common phenomenon, not rare as about 2–5 % farmers change their commission agent every year (the figure is provided by most of the commission agents). Therefore, a commission agent has to decide about his criterion of taking up a new customer. The commission agent must draw a line for each customer as far as the size of the loan is concerned. Each borrower due to imperfect information has a risk of default attached to it. The possibility of default increases when the borrower is not an efficient spender and the size of the loan is large. Therefore, the commission agent has to decide the limit of loan for each customer and avoid any risky lending.

The commission agents base their first decision on the information collected from their sources from the village and their old trusted customers. They often spend significant time and resources to keep good relationship with the people who can provide them information. Even when the commission agent is from the same village, inquiring about the potential customer is considered important. The commission agent also compels the new applicant to provide him with important information about his past record, thus shifting the significant share of cost of information to the farmer. The commission agents ask the farmer to fulfil three criterions. First, the farmer must be recommended by an old customer of the commission agent. All the commission agents in four markets use this criterion (see Table 9.2). Second, the farmer must ask one or two persons with good reputation in that area to vouch for him (it also helps in contract enforcement, which will be discussed in the next subsections). It again compels the farmer to disclose the information about his riskiness, as a person with good reputation due to fear of losing credibility would not vouch for a farmer without having sufficient information about him. All commission agents in Mansa, Malout and Samrala and 76.7 % commission agents in Banga impose this condition on new customers.

Third, the famers are often asked to get no-objection letter (or clear chit) from the previous commission agent. The information on clearing of previous dues indicates that the farmer is not a defaulter and can be trusted. In addition, the commission agent by asking no-objection letter also signals others to coordinate their activities. All commission agents in Mansa and Malout, where the default rate is very high (see, Tables 9.4 and 9.7), reported the use of this criterion. However,

Table 9.3 Criterion used to decide the size of lending

Block	Number of commission agents using criterion of			
	Value of crop sold	Only income of household	Only past experience	Income and past experience
Mansa	0	0	3.3	96.7
Malout	0	0	0.0	100.0
Samrala	0	0	0.0	100.0
Banga	0	0	0.0	100.0
Total	0	0	0.8	99.2

Source Primary survey

Table 9.4 Average number of defaults, bad loans and court cases filed in last 10 years

Block	Number of defaults per firm (1)	Total bad loans per firm (in millions) (2)	Amount recovered per firm (in millions) (3)	Net loss per firm (in millions) (4)	Amount recovered as share of total bad loans (5) = (3)/(2) × 100	Number of court cases filed per firm (6)
Mansa	10.4	2.17	0.53	1.64	24.6	1.2
Malout	11.8	4.01	1.33	2.69	33.2	5.1
Samrala	3.4	0.76	0.36	0.40	47.4	0.1
Banga	2.0	0.44	0.25	0.19	56.8	0.0
Total	6.9	1.85	0.62	1.23	33.5	1.6

Source Primary survey

they also point out that some of the commission agents do not follow the practice and often use different ways to avoid taking no-objection letter. For example, a commission agent instead of the farmer can take his son as customer. In some cases, a farmer may also sell his crop in the name of his friend and then becomes the regular customer of the commission agent. No-objection letter is also less prevalent in Samrala, where only 73.3 % reported to use it as a criterion. No commission agent from Banga reported to use this as a screening method. The no-objection letter as a screening mechanism is more important in high default region. One unsuccessful commission agent (who has lost most of his extended loan and does not have any customer at present) from Mansa (high default region) told that the main reason for his failure is to engage with bad customers who had earlier defaulted on their previous commission agents. He was a new entrant and was aggressively pursuing the goal to attract customers. Due to his negligence, he ended up with bad borrowers.

As far as the size of the loan is concerned, most of the commission agents give importance to both income and past experience. Among these two, they often give more preference to past experience than income(see Table 9.3). In Mansa, 3.3 % commission agents said that they only look at past experience. One of the commission agents during the interview told that there are a few marginal and small farmers whom he can loan a large amount without any written agreement. However, he is not willing to extend a similar loan to most of the large farmers even with a written agreement. The loans extended to farmers are often without any formal contract, and a formal contract is only used for a larger sum of money or when a farmer fails to pay the loan for two or three consecutive seasons.

Though the net loss per firm is relatively larger in default rate areas, there is no clear-cut division between high default region and low default region as per the screening process is concerned. For example, the loss per firm in Samrala and Banga is not very different (see Table 9.4). The difference between the two is even lesser, given that average lending per firm is much higher in Samrala than in Banga (Tables 9.1 and 9.4). In addition, neither Samrala nor Banga experienced a shock similar to that in Mansa and Malout. Therefore, the perception of commission agents of risk seems to be also based on the development level of the region and the present default rate. The development of the region may lower the risk of default if it reduces the risk of agricultural shock. Therefore, the cost of screening may also decline with the development of the region.

The above discussion shows that the informal lending puts a great emphasis on the screening process. The screening criterion is made tough to avoid any potential defaulter. This is especially harder in less developed and high default rate regions. The experience of commission agents indicates that those who disregard the screening process are more likely to end up in high loss. As the literature suggests, the high screening cost provides a commission agent certain level of monopoly power over the farmer (at least in the short run). The monopoly power is especially high for marginal and small farmers, since the commission agent has less incentive to incur (due to low value of their crop which results in low income from commission and lending) screening cost. The high screening cost (which is almost the same for all customers) increases the cost of lending to a marginal or small farmer. Some commission agents mentioned that marginal and small farmers are less likely to move to other commission agents or default.

9.5.2 Monitoring the Borrower's Action

The studies argue that the borrower may not always take decisions that maximize the likelihood of repayment. For example, a farmer who has bought a farm machinery may not use it optimally. Therefore, the ability to monitor borrower's actions becomes very important to ensure repayment. Monitoring the borrower's action, to solve moral hazard problem, is a highly costly activity. The commission agents often have many years of experience with the farmer and know his work and his consumption behaviour. Nonetheless, they continue to gather information on the farmer's activities. The main method used by the commission agent to get information about the farmer is frequent visits to the farmer's house and inquiring from other customers. The commission agents often attend social and family functions of the borrowers to gather information about his spending habits. A large unproductive expenditure of the farmer is seen as a worrying signal for the commission agent.

The commission agents often face difficulty with respect to monitoring, as it does not require just observing the behaviour of the farmer but also the actions of his family members. The unreasonable consumption and bad work routine of a farmer's family are recognized as an important reason for the farmer's loss. Many commission agents blame the high expenditure on consumer durables, lack of commitment towards work and lack of proper care in the use of farm machinery as some of the main reasons behind indebtedness and, subsequently, default. The commission agents have little direct control on the use of loan already extended; however, they do control it indirectly by controlling the supply of future loans.

The data on the visits of commission agents could not be collected due to their reluctance to reveal information, possibly due to the fear that it may be understood as harassment of the farmers. Another problem is that a significant share of the commission agents in some of the markets is engaged in agricultural activities and lives in the same village. It is easy for a commission agent to monitor the actions of other farmers if he himself is engaged in agriculture and lives in the same village. Under this situation, it is difficult to know the real cost of monitoring because the monitoring activities of the farmer commission agents are not be clearly defined unlike their non-farmer counterparts. However, the general observations from discussions with commission agents point out that the commission agents in Banga and Samrala are less worried about the monitoring. Especially in Banga, the commission agents are much less concerned with keeping a closed look at expenditure of the farmers. On the contrary, most of the commission agents from Mansa and Malout (underdeveloped blocks) specifically told that monitoring the expenditure pattern is very important in calculating the risk of default.

A few commission agents may also have an alternative motive of acquiring land as pointed out by Bell and Clemenz (2006). In this case, monitoring is not required, as the loan is secured on farmer's land. However, these loans are highly risky, and only those commission agents that can ensure the enforcement of contract may get into this type of contract. The alternative motive may also hurt the reputation of the commission agent by proving him untrustworthy and depriving him of business from other parties. Further, the farmer may still sell the land to a higher bidder than the commission agent and pay the debt. There is also social opposition to these motives. The influence of social opposition was observed during the interview when all commission agents tried to distinguish themselves from those who adopt these strategies. Some of the commission agents indicate that the alternative motive of lending may also make a commission agent less trustworthy among other commission agents.

9.5.3 Enforcement of Contract

The lending of money is always associated with the risk of default by borrowers, and the farmer-and-commission-agent relationship is not free from this problem. In case of default, the legal system is the most efficient way to solve the dispute. A weak enforcement by the legal system adversely affects the economic activity and compels people to use costly alternatives (see Chemin 2009). The literature on weak legal enforcement points out that the high cost of legal enforcement (due to delay in decision of the court and its enforcement) may render the law ineffective and is the main reason for inefficiencies (see Fabbri 2001). The high cost of legal enforcement may also lead to the use of alternative methods of enforcement, such as social norms, harassment and other criminal activities. Among these, social norms may also be used due to their lower transaction cost. The interference of a civil society may also influence the enforcement. Further renegotiation is also possible, when enforcement is costly for the lender and the default also costs dearly to borrower due to the loss of reputation, social norms and fear of court action. In this context, the present section examines the role of law, social norms, civil societies and other criminal activities in informal credit market. The next subsection discusses the default by farmers on loans from arhtias and analyses the problems of legal enforcement.

9.5.3.1 Legal Enforcement of Contract

Table 9.4 provides information on average number of default cases, loss of firm and court cases filed in last 10 years. The reason for taking 10-year data is that it is difficult to pinpoint a date of default, since the non-payment of loan is considered default only if a farmer falls short of his payments for more than one season. Also, the relationship between farmer and commission agent may continue for many seasons if the farmer keeps paying a minimum amount each year. Therefore, the commission agents often find it difficult to call a non-payment as default for many years. In addition, a longer period is required to know the impact of legal action. Though combining 10-year data on defaults does not allow us to calculate their loss as the ratio of total lending, it is less likely to have any serious implication on the present study which aims to understand the lender's strategies in informal credit market. The use of 10-year period also helped to understand the variety of strategies adopted by the commission agents over time.

The average number of defaults and loss per firm is the highest in Malout followed by Mansa. Samrala and Banga have much lower number of defaults and per firm losses. The number of court cases filed per firm is also highest in Malout followed by Mansa. The average number of court cases in Samrala is negligible, whereas no court case was found in the case of Banga. Here, Malout and Mansa are clearly the region with the highest risk of default. As far as the loss per firm and number of court cases are concerned, Malout is much ahead of other three. The commission agents in Malout lost about Rs. 2.69 million and have filed a court case in about 43.1 % cases of default (see Tables 9.4 and 9.7). On the other hand, the commission agents in Mansa, which have almost similar average number of defaults, filed a court case in 9.6 % cases of default. The data also show that the total loss of a commission agent is not the same as amount due to farmer. The commission agents in case of default are often successful in renegotiating the contract and getting back a portion of the loan. The amount recovered by the commission agents in the four blocks ranges between 24.6 and 56.8 % of total bad loan.

Interestingly, the share of the loan recovered through renegotiation increases with the increase in the level of development, whereas the numbers of court cases filed per firm are much less in the developed blocks. It may be due to the reasons that the shocks in developed blocks are farmer specific rather than region specific. Therefore, the impact of a shock in developed region might be less than an underdeveloped region, which may allow farmers to pay larger share of their loans.

Tables 9.5 and 9.6 show success of court cases in ensuring repayment of loan. The information about Malout and Mansa, which have larger number of court cases, points out that winning a case does not ensure repayment. Only 0.7 % of court cases

Table 9.5 Number of court cases and their present status

Block	Number of cases filed (1)	Present status of the court cases (in percentage)						
		Status after winning the court cases					Pending cases (7) = % of (1)	Compromise after court case but before judgment (8) = % of (1)
		Full payment (2) = % of (1)	Partial payment (3) = % of (1)	Total compromises and full payment after winning (4) = (2) + (3)	No payment (5) = % of (1)	Total won (6) = (4) + (5)		
Mansa	30	23.3	13.3	36.6	6.7	43.3	46.7	10.0
Malout	152	0.7	25.7	26.4	35.5	61.8	6.6	31.6
Samrala	2	0	0	0.0	50	50	50	0
Banga	0	NA	NA		NA	NA	NA	NA
Total	184	4.3	23.4	27.7	31.0	58.7	13.6	27.7

Source Primary survey

Table 9.6 Repayment status of loan after winning court case (in percentage)

Block	Full payment after winning (1)	Partial payment (2)	Payments after winning the case (3) = (1) + (2)	No payment (4)	Total cases won (5) = (3) + (4)
Mansa	53.8	30.8	84.6	15.4	100.0
Malout	1.1	41.5	42.6	57.4	100.0
Samrala	0.0	0.0	0.0	100.0	100.0
Banga	NA	NA	NA	NA	NA
Total	7.4	39.8	47.2	52.8	100.0

Source Primary survey

in Malout result in full repayment of the debt. The figure is relatively better for Mansa, where 23.3 % of court cases result in full payment. While the full payment is about 53.8 % of the winning cases for Mansa, it is just 1.1 % for Malout. In addition, the partial payment as the share of won cases is 30.8 and 41.5 % for Mansa and Malout, respectively. Overall, 84.6 % of cases in Mansa and 42.6 % of cases in Malout resulted in full or partial repayment after winning. There are a larger number of pending cases in Mansa and Malout (46.7 and 6.6 %, respectively). There were also a significant number of compromises before the judgment of the court. The number of cases in which the debt was not paid even after winning the case is about 57.4 and 15.4 % for Malout and Mansa, respectively.

The above discussion seems to indicate that Mansa has outperformed Malout with much better recovery rate through court cases. However, considerable doubts are raised about this success, if one takes into account the fact that only a small percentage of default cases in Mansa go to court. Looking at the repayments after winning a court case as the share of total defaults shows that the number of cases, in which full payment is received after winning, is just 2.2 % of the total default cases in Mansa and total repayments (full and partial) make 3.5 % of the total defaults (Table 9.7). Here, the record of Malout with 11.3 % full and partial repayments (of total default cases) seems to be performing better than Mansa. It is because the number of defaults that result in a court case is much larger in Malout (43.1 %) than in Mansa (9.6 %). As a result, the actual number of repayments is larger despite their lower success rate. The large number of cases in Malout compared to Mansa despite the less probability of repayment in former block suggests that the commission agents may also be using court cases as a strategy to secure partial repayment by compelling the borrower to renegotiate the contract (this point is again discussed in the next section). The data on compromises after the court case but before the judgment also point towards this direction (see Table 9.5). The share of the cases in which compromises happened before the judgment is much higher in Malout (31.6 %) than in Mansa (10 %). It points out that the alternative motive of the court case may be much stronger in Malout than in Mansa, where chances of recovery after winning may be the prime motive of a court case.

Table 9.7 Court cases filed and number of repayments after winning the case as the percentage of total default cases

Block	Total number of default cases (1)	Percentage of default for which the case was filed (2) = % of (1)	Percentage of repayments after winning the court case		
			Full (3) = % of (1)	Partial (4) = % of (1)	Total (5) = (3) + (4)
Mansa	312	9.6	2.2	1.3	3.5
Malout	353	43.1	0.3	11.0	11.3
Samrala	101	2.0	0.0	0.0	0.0
Banga	61	0.0	NA	NA	NA
Total	827	22.2	1.3	5.2	6.2

Source Primary survey

Table 9.8 Average time taken by courts to decide the cases and average expenditure

Block	Average number of years taken by court case	Average fee of lawyer (in '000 Rs.)
Mansa	4.2	23.66
Malout	5.0	23.49
Samrala	3.0	–
Banga	–	–
Total	4.9	23.50

Source Primary survey

Despite the high success rate of court cases in Mansa, the large number of cases where no case was filed shows that the legal remedies are less popular among commission agents. Even in Malout where litigation is relatively common, no court case was filed in about 57 % of the default cases. On an average, a court case takes 3–5 years (Table 9.8). The cases where payment was done by a cheque reported to take less time due to clear evidence of payment. The average fee of a lawyer is about Rs. 23,000. In addition, the plaintiff also has to pay a court fee, which increases with the increase in the amount involved in litigation.

The commission agents often consider delay in court case and other costs as a deterrent to filing a lawsuit. In addition, non-payment even after winning the case, which requires further litigation and may lead to other conflicts, makes litigation less attractive. However, a number of other reasons were also mentioned for not filing a court case, which are sometimes more important than cost of litigation. The commission agents have more than one reason for not filing a lawsuit in case of default (Table 9.9). The inefficiency of the legal system is a major reason for not filing a court case in all blocks, with 73.3 % of commission agents in Mansa and 60 % in other markets reporting it as the main reason for not filing the case. The second important reason is the fear of interference by kissan unions (is discussed in the later section). The fear of kissan union is reported by 70 % of commission agents in Mansa and 43.3 and 40 % of commission agents in Malout and Samrala. No commission agent in Banga reported this reason.

Table 9.9 Reasons provided by commission agents for not filing the court case

Block	Reasons for not filing court case (in percentage)					
	No proof	Inefficient legal system	Interference of kissan unions	Threat by farmer	Fear of more defaults	Criticism of the people
Mansa	36.7	73.3	70.0	16.7	46.7	0.0
Malout	13.3	60.0	43.3	26.7	13.3	0.0
Samrala	6.7	60.0	40.0	0.0	3.3	13.3
Banga	10.0	60.0	0.0	0.0	3.3	36.7
Total	16.7	63.3	38.3	10.8	16.7	12.5

Source Primary survey

No proof of loan and fear of more defaults are other reasons provided by significant number of commission agents. The commission agents often do not enter into a proper contract with the farmer, merely recording most of the transactions in their account book. Though the farmer is asked to sign on the account book, it is just to avoid any conflict at later stage [a similar trend was observed by Fafchamps (1996) in Ghana]. The commission agents cannot use these account books in court, as it may prove them moneylenders making their loan illegal and claim invalid. Though they can seek a licence for lending money, they often choose not to do so. Even when they may possess a moneylending licence, they choose not to keep proper accounts as required by the law. They seem to be doing it because they have to pay tax on the interest earned without any significant improvement in the cost of legal enforcement. A formal agreement is only written in case of a large loan or non-payment of loan amount for more than one season. Hence, the lawsuits cannot be filed in the absence of an admissible proof of loan. The commission agent who has a lesser number of defaults also fears that the defaults may increase if more farmers know about the defaults. The commission agents believe that an unsuccessful recovery of a loan will make other farmers doubt their ability to enforce the contract leading to more defaults. The belief is especially stronger in Mansa where about 47 % of commission agents reported this reason. Other reported reasons are threat by farmer and criticism by people, where the former reason is important only in Mansa and Malout, and the latter reason is given by commission agents in Samrala and Banga. The difference in the pattern of reasons for Mansa and Malout from Samrala and Banga, where the former group is less developed and has high default rate, seems to indicate that the nature and extent of problem faced by high and low default regions regarding litigation may be different.

The pattern found in the four blocks is in line with the literature, which argues that the people do not prefer the legal remedy due to its high enforcement cost. Besides, other factors such as interference of the civil societies, fear of more defaults and no admissible proof may add to the cost of legal enforcement. The cost of enforcing the court's decision is also significant; therefore, the renegotiation of the contract is common even when the commission agent has won the case.

9.5.3.2 Social Norms, Reputation and Contract Enforcement

Social norms are the law of society, which are enforced by a group of people on their own members, and deviation from the law brings punishment (see Elster 1989; Basu 2000). These norms decide the nature of interaction with people from own society and people from other societies, activities which one can perform and what people think as fair. Thus, social norms can also ensure cooperation, even when a contracting party has incentive in not doing so. Also, the fear of reputation loss, as pointed by the literature, provides an incentive to a party to perform as per its promise.

Social norms are an important enforcer available to the lenders in informal credit market. Social norms due to the low cost of enforcement may prove more efficient in a number of cases. Nonetheless, social norms are effective only if the enforcers have information on both the parties. The availability of account book with farmer's signature proves handy in this regard. Here, the social norms related to default may lead to shame, criticism by society and loss of cooperation of other people. Fear of reputation loss also plays an important role in the enforcement. The commission agents often employ the use of social norms to enforce a contract.

Some of the commission agents' strategies at the time of screening are also linked to enforcement through social norms. The most important conditions of the commission agent at the time of screening are recommendation of old customer and asking the famer to get someone to vouch for him. Due to this condition, the farmer in case of default also loses relationship with the fellow farmer as well as the person who vouched for him depriving him from any possible gains from the association. The bad relationship with previously associated people again hurts a person's reputation in society. Thus, the fear to lose reputation becomes a powerful incentive to repay the loan. The impact of this strategy is clear from the fact that all commission agents in Mansa, Malout and Samrala and 76.7 % of the commission agents in Banga said that asking someone to vouch for farmer proves useful in contract enforcement (Table 9.10).

About 60 % of the commission agents said that using an influential person or another customer to pressurize the borrower increases the likelihood of repayment. The effectiveness of these methods can be observed in large number of settlements without any court case in the all the blocks (Table 9.11). The partial payments

Table 9.10 The use of social norms and reputation to prevent default or renegotiate contract

Block	An influential person helped in recovery	Used other customers to approach farmer	Farmers avoid court cases due to fear of reputation loss	Asking farmer to get someone to vouch for him
Mansa	63.3	63.3	50	100
Malout	73.3	73.3	68.2	100
Samrala	53.3	60.0	50	100
Banga	36.7	46.7	NA	76.7
Total	56.7	60.8	62.5	94.2

Source Primary survey

Table 9.11 Out-of-court settlements as the percentage of total defaults

Block	Compromises as the percentage of total number of defaults			
	After court case but before judgment	After winning the case	Without court case	Total
Mansa	1.0	3.5	30.4	34.9
Malout	13.6	11.3	34.3	59.2
Samrala	0.0	0.0	76.2	76.2
Banga	0.0	–	93.4	93.4
Total	6.2	6.2	42.3	54.7

Source Primary survey

without litigation in Mansa, Malout, Samrala and Banga are 30.4, 34.3, 76.2 and 93.4 % of the total default cases, respectively. The low percentage of settlement without a lawsuit in Mansa and Malout, which has relatively larger number of defaults, is also consistent with the argument that the effect of social norms declines with the increase in the number of rule (or norm) breakers (see Basu 2000).

The court case is also considered as an effective way to compel the borrower to repay the loan. The repayment in a significant number of default cases is the result of renegotiation of contract after filing the case or after winning it. The percentage of commission agents who think that the farmers avoid the court case due to fear of reputation loss is 68.2 % in Malout and 50 % in both Mansa and Samrala. A large number of settlements before and after the court judgment indicate that the commission agents may be using litigation to ensure repayment. The farmer respondent also points out that normally farmers do not like to default as they value their reputation very high, and a court case does not go well with their credibility in society. Due to the fear of reputation loss, most of the farmers try to renegotiate contract if they are unable to pay full amount.

The data indicate an association between level of development and renegotiation strategies and success. While the likelihood of successful renegotiation increases with the increase in level of development, the usefulness of involving third party in renegotiation declines with the increase in the level of development (see Tables 9.10 and 9.11). The court cases as a means to pressurize the farmers to repay are used to a much lesser extent by the commission agents in the developed regions. It might be due to higher cost of reputation loss in the developed areas as compared to the underdeveloped ones. The people in developed areas are likely to benefit more from their association with other parties; therefore, they may value their reputation more. The high cost of reputation loss may compel the borrowers to renegotiate without involving the third party.

Social norms and reputation are also popular as they provide flexibility to the contract, making it easy to renegotiate in case of unavoidable default. The people associated with the farmer and the commission agents also help in renegotiation in a number of cases. The commission agents may also prefer a flexible contract. Fafchamps (1996) points out that the borrower may not enter into a contract if the cost of default is too high. Therefore, a contract must allow for genuine default.

The survey results conform with the literature that points out that social norms and fear to lose reputation play much important role than the fear of court action in contract enforcement. The major reason for the popularity of these instruments is their expediency and flexibility.

9.5.3.3 Civil Societies, Violence and Contract Enforcement

The commission agents told that the default rate in Malout and Mansa was high between mid-1990s and early 2000s when a large number of farmers lost cotton crop due to bollworm.[6] The higher rate of defaults also increased the opportunistic behaviour among the farmers. Social norms do not penalize a person when the default is due to genuine reasons, such as the crop failure. An unavoidable default entails lower reputation loss, thereby allowing considerable decline in the cost of default for the defaulters. However, this came as an opportunity for some of the farmers to fake the information and default on the grounds of crop loss. The problem was accentuated with concentration of crop failure in some areas. The large number of genuine defaults concentrated in some villages increased the monitoring cost of commission agents by making it difficult to identify the opportunistic behaviour. It also made it difficult for them to prove the opportunistic behaviour in front of others, which is required for social norms and fear of reputation loss to work. Even when the opportunistic behaviour was proved, the cost of breaking norm was much less as a large number of farmers were defaulting. Since the commission agents were unable to separate out justifiable defaults from dishonest defaults, many of them started pursuing all defaulters with same force using tactics, such as regular visits to farmer's home and humiliating him in front of others. As a large number of genuine defaulters felt unreasonably harassed, the social opposition of commission agents' tactics increased in the society, which in turn reduced the likelihood of reputation loss of a non-payer.

The whole scenario increased pressure on the commission agents. As a result, a large number of commission agents preferred to renegotiate the contract and accept a lower amount in the settlement. The situation also led to increased activity of farmer unions, which were highly critical of tactics used by commission agents. There were 17 farmer unions active in the region, out of which three were large unions and rest 14 had a small member base. These farmer unions started defending the defaulted farmers and made the recovery difficult. The commission agents also reported that some members of farmer unions also started to use their position to compel commission agents to accept a much lower amount and make some money in the process. The interference of farmer unions increased the cost of recovery so much that the commission agents in a number of cases had to accept a much lower amount or let go off the loan altogether. The tension between farmers and

[6]The crop failure coupled with large debt is considered as the reason for farmer suicide in this region (see Gill and Singh 2006; Gill 2010).

Table 9.12 Percentage of commission agents who reported the use of pressure or threat

Block	Threat by farmer	Did any violent activity happened	If kissan union created problem in recovery
Mansa	16.7	6.7	50.0
Malout	26.7	3.3	53.3
Samrala	0.0	0.0	23.3
Banga	0.0	0.0	0.0
Total	10.8	2.5	31.7

Source Primary survey

commission agents with interference of farmer unions even led to violent activities in some cases. For example, a clash between the farmer union members and the commission agent in Beero Ke Khurd, Budhlada, on 11 October 2010 during the auctioning of the agricultural land of a defaulter farmer on the court order led to the death of a farmer union leader and two others sustained serious injuries. Both commission agents and farmers reported many similar incidents. However, the farmer unions did not establish any system to identify genuine defaults. Consequently, the defence of a farmer was hardly ever based on the genuineness of a farmer's problem, and a large number of farmers who benefited from it were medium and large farmers who did not face loss of crop. Marginal and small farmers who had to face maximum difficulty due to crop failure did not benefit due to their high dependency on commission agents. As discussed earlier, the cost of screening and monitoring, which is the same for all borrowers, leads to higher cost of lending to marginal or small farmers, who take small loans. The high screening cost increased the monopoly power of the commission agents, making it difficult for a marginal or small farmer to move to any other commission agent. The screening and monitoring cost further increased with the increase in default rate and higher interference of civil societies. As a result, marginal and small farmers, with increased interference of civil societies, often face both high rate of interest and rationing of credit.

Table 9.12 provides the data on the number of commission agents who faced interference of kissan unions or threat by farmers. More than 50 % of the commission agents in Mansa and Malout reported the interference of kissan unions. The interference was relatively less in Samrala, and no interference was reported in Banga. Mansa and Malout have a large cotton belt and were among the most affected regions due to crop failure. There were also some incidences where farmers were reported to use threat or false criminal case to avoid repayment. 26.7 and 16.7 % of the commission agents in Malout and Mansa, respectively, reported to have faced threat by a farmer. The conflict between farmer and commission agent had also turn violent in some cases. The percentage of commission agents who were involved in any violent activity were 6.7 and 3.3 % in Mansa and Malout, respectively. Though many of these activities may be aimed to defend the disadvantaged farmers, the experience of most of the farmers and commission agents indicates that these tactics may have proved costly. The above discussion points out that inefficiency of legal system may result in the use of many costly alternatives. The problem of default started declining with relatively stable crop production after 2005–06. With decline in default cases, the commission agents reported a substantial drop in interference of farmer unions.

9.6 Conclusions

The existence of informal credit in rural India has been a major concern since British rule. The informal moneylenders due to high interest rate charged by them are often considered monopolist. A number of studies have pointed out that the credit market does not behave like a competitive market due to imperfect information. The imperfect information in rural credit market makes the market monopolistically competitive. The imperfect information also results in the low success rate of policies seeking expansion of formal credit in those areas. The present study analyses screening, monitoring and enforcement of contract under imperfect information in rural credit market of Punjab. The results show that the commission agents, who are a major source of informal credit to farmers, spend considerable time and resources to screen the potential borrowers. Main methods employed by the commission agents for screening are recommendation from an old customer, asking the farmer to get a person with good reputation to vouch for him and a no-objection letter from his previous commission agent. Monitoring the behaviour is also costly and involves getting information about the borrower and his family's activities. It is often done by making frequent visits to the farmer and enquiring about the farmer from other customers. Once the default happens, the commission agents use both formal (law) and informal (social norms) institutions to ensure repayment. The lawsuits, however, are a less preferred way of enforcement due to its high cost, whereas fear of reputation loss and pressure from the person who had vouched for the farmer often prove useful in enforcement of contract. The renegotiation of contract facilitated by legal provisions under Indian Contract Act is common. However, the large number of defaults (which happened in two of the surveyed blocks) triggered by a shock seems to increase the monitoring and enforcement cost by making information costly and reducing the cost of reputation loss. The large number of defaults may also lead to increase in the interference of civil societies. Though the interference of the civil societies may be aimed at helping the borrower affected by shock, the most beneficiaries may be the well-off borrowers. The experience of Punjab shows that while the medium and the large farmers benefitted more from the interference of farmer unions, the problems of marginal and small might have been aggravated from such interference due to credit rationing by the commission agents.

Based on the present understanding of the informal credit market, the following policy suggestion can be made. As pointed out by Bell et al. (1997), banning the informal credit market may lower the credit availability. There is also a need to look at interlinked markets as a means of enforcement of credit contracts rather than an instrument of exploitation, because the credit availability may decline in its absence. Therefore, the policy must aim at changing the rules and regulation to create conditions where both farmers and commission agents can benefit from their relationship.

There are three main problems of informal credit markets. First, the interest rate charged is high in many cases. Second, the enforcement is often costly and the default often leads to harassment or other criminal activities. Third, it is difficult to distinguish between genuine and intentional defaults. It is clear from the previous studies that interlinked markets are going to persist, and banning these is not likely to improve the situation. Therefore, the solution to these problems lies in developing a system that compels the commission agents to disclose information, lowers the cost of legal enforcement and provides reputation-based enforcement. One of the possible solutions to this problem is to formalize the lending activities (some of the commission agents also expressed similar views). Formalizing the interlinked markets will benefit both sides by bringing more clarity about the nature of their relationship and making it easier to monitor their activities. For example, the lending by commission agents to farmers can be legalized, and interlinked markets can be recognized as a valid security for the debt. To prevent any foul play, the commission agents can be asked to submit details of their lending activities to a regulating agency on a regular basis. To induce commission agents to disclose this information, any undisclosed loan can be declared illegal (including friendly loans). To provide flexibility in the contract and safeguard farmer against shocks, law may allow delayed payment in case of any proven shock. The commission agents will have an incentive to shift to the new system, only if it lowers their cost of legal enforcement. Therefore, there must provide a less costly system to resolve any conflict. Also, arbitration instead of court action can be used to lower the transaction cost and provide greater flexibility.

The banks and other formal lending institutions can also use the information provided by commission agents to know the credit history of a farmer for extending the loan. Information sharing may serve dual purpose. First, this will help formal institutes to solve adverse selection problem, thereby making it easy for a farmer with good record to move to other sources. This will also increase competition among the lenders. Second, it will reduce the possibility of default by increasing the value of reputation providing an incentive to commission agents to disclose information and lowering the possibility of intentional defaults. The commission agents may still avoid disclosing their lending activities to evade the tax. The stringent tax collection may prevent this tendency. Alternatively, they may be provided some tax concession in the initial years of the shift.

The major reason for the high default rate is economic shocks, where unavoidable circumstances, such as crop failure, may lead to default. However, asking the commission agents to bear the whole burden of shock may negatively affect the credit availability in shock-prone areas. Majority of the commission agents deals with 100–150 farmers from two or three villages. The agricultural shock, which affects the whole village or many nearby villages, may put a heavy burden on the commission agents. Therefore, the government must facilitate the development of market for crop insurance.

The present study aims to provide the overview of the issues in rural informal credit market, and a better understanding requires further detailed examination of the working of legal system, administration, social norms and reputation.

References

Aleem I (1990) Imperfect information, screening, and the costs of informal lending: a study of a rural credit market in Pakistan. World Bank Econ Rev 4(3):329–349

Banerji A, Meenakshi JV (2004) Millers, commission agents and collusion in grain markets: evidence from basmati auctions in North India. Working papers #129, Centre for Development Economics, Delhi School of Economics

Basu K (2000) Prelude to political economy: a study of the social and political foundations of economics. Oxford University Press, New York

Basu K, Bell C (1991) Fragmented duopoly: theory and applications to backward agriculture. J Dev Econ 36:145–165

Bell C (1990) Interactions between institutional and informal credit agencies in rural India. World Bank Econ Rev 4(3):297–327

Bell C, Clemenz G (2006) The desire for land: strategic lending with adverse selection. J Dev Econ 79:1–25

Bell C, Srinivasan TN (1989) Interlinked transactions in rural markets: an empirical study of Andhra Pradesh, Bihar and Punjab. Oxford Bull Econ Stat 51(1):73–83

Bell C, Srinivasan TN, Udry C (1997) Rationing, spillover, and interlinking in credit markets: the case of rural Punjab. Oxford Econ Pap 49:557–585

Bernstein L (2001) Private commercial law in the cotton industry: creating cooperation through rules, norms, and institutions. Mich Law Rev 99(7):1724–1790

Besley T (1994) How do market failure justify interventions in rural credit market? World Bank Res Observer 9(1):27–47

Chemin M (2009) Do judiciaries matter for development? Evidence from India. J Comp Econ 37 (2):230–250

Cross FB (2002) Law and economic growth. Tex Law Rev 80(7):1737–1775

Ellickson RC (1991) Order without law: how neighbors settle disputes. Harvard University Press, Cambridge

Elster J (1989) Social norms and economic theory. J Econ Perspect 3(4):99–117

Fabbri D (2001) The legal enforcement of credit contracts and the level of investment. Working Paper No. 57, Centre for Studies in Economics and Finance, University of Naples, Italy

Fafchamps M (1996) The enforcement of commercial contracts in ghana. World Dev 24(3): 427–448

Gill A (2004) Interlinked agrarian credit market: case study of Punjab. Econ Polit Weekly 39 (33):3741–3751

Gill A (2010) Punjab peasantry: a question of life and debt. In Deshpande RS, Arora S (eds) Agrarian crisis and farmer suicides. Sage Publication, New Delhi

Gill A, Singh L (2006) Farmers' suicides and response of public policy: evidence, diagnosis and alternatives from Punjab. Econ Polit Weekly 41(26):2762–2768

Hay JR, Shleifer A (1998) Private enforcement of public laws: a theory of legal reform. Am Econ Rev 88(2): 398–403 (Papers and Proceedings of the Hundred and Tenth Annual Meeting of the American Economic Association)

Hoff K, Stiglitz JE (1990) Introduction: imperfect information and rural credit markets: puzzles and policy. World Bank Economic Review 4(3): 235–250 (A Symposium Issue on Imperfect Information and Rural Credit Markets)

Klein B, Leffler KB (1981) The role of market forces in assuring contractual performance. J Polit Econ 89(4):615–641

Mohan R (2006) Agricultural credit in india: status, issues and future agenda. Econ Polit Weekly 41(11):1013–1021

National Sample Survey (2005) Situation assessment survey of farmers: indebtedness of farmer households. Report No. 498 (59th Round), National Sample Survey Organisation, Government of India

Posner EA (2000) Law and social norms. Harvard University Press, Cambridge

Pradhan Narayan Chandra (2013) Persistence of informal credit in rural india: evidence from 'All-India Debt and Investment Survey' and beyond. WPS (DEPR):05/2013. RBI Working Paper Series, Reserve Bank of India, India

Santhakumar V (2003) Citizens' actions for protecting the environment in developing countries: an economic analysis of the outcome with empirical cases in India. Environ Dev Econ 8:505–528

Shah M, Rao R, Shankar PSV (2007) Rural credit in 20th century India: overview of history and perspectives. Econ Polit Weekly 42(15):1351–1364

Siamwalla A, Chirmsak P, Poapongsakorn N, Satsanguan P, Nettayarak P, Mingmaneenaking W, Tubpun Y (1990) The thai rural credit system: public subsidies, private information, and segmented market. World Bank Econ Rev 4(3):271–295

Singh I (2013) Economics of contract law in India. In: Santhakumar V, Gangopadhyay S (eds) Law and economics, vol 2: Practice. Sage Publication, New Delhi

Singh S, Dhaliwal TK (2011) The status of commission agent system in Punjab agriculture. Indian J Agric Econ 66(4):662–675

Stiglitz JE, Weiss A (1981) Credit rationing in markets with imperfect information. Am Econ Rev 71(3):393–410

Telser LG (1980) A theory of self-enforcing agreements. J Bus 53(1):27–44

Udry C (1990) Credit markets in northern nigeria: credit as insurance in a rural economy. World Bank Econ Rev 4(3):251–269

Chapter 10
Household Income Inequality and Asset Distribution: The Case of Rural Punjab

Kamal Vatta and S. Pavithra

10.1 Introduction

10.1.1 Inequality: Why Does It Matter?

Economic growth, poverty reduction and inequality are central to the development policy of any economy. Rising income inequalities not only affect the rate of poverty reduction but also have an impact on living standards, health and the general welfare of the population. In India, the income shares of top and bottom 10 % of the population were found to be 29 and 4 %, respectively during the year 2010 (World Bank). The World Bank database shows that the Gini coefficient of inequality increased from 33.4 in 2005 to 33.9 in 2012. Such trends raise serious questions as to: Which section of the population has actually been benefiting from the economic growth? How to apportion the gains of developments to the downtrodden sections of the society? Disparities in the distribution of income and assets is one face of inequality however, there are other dimensions of the inequality as well such as inequalities of power, prestige, status, gender, job satisfaction, condition of the world, degree of participation, freedom of choice, etc., which are considered to be the issues of higher significance than inequality itself. Persistent income inequalities might lead to differences in opportunities and may hinder the socio-economic mobility (Todaro and Smith 2007; IMF 2014).

K. Vatta (✉)
Centers for International Projects Trust, 910-11, Pragati Towers,
Rajendra Place, New Delhi 110008, India
e-mail: kamal@cipt.in

S. Pavithra
National Institute of Agricultural Economics and Policy Research,
Dev Prakash Shastri Marg, Pusa, New Delhi, India

L. Singh and N. Singh (eds.), *Economic Transformation of a Developing Economy*, India Studies in Business and Economics,
DOI 10.1007/978-981-10-0197-0_10

10.1.2 Driving Factors Behind Rising Inequality

A review of the past studies shows that industrialization, modernization, education levels and asset distribution have been identified as the broad drivers of inequality. Globalization, technological change, regulatory and institutional changes triggered the inequalities in wages and salaries across the OECD countries (OECD 2011). According to Lopez (2011), education infrastructure and macroeconomic stability positively affect both growth and income distribution. Wells (2014) observed that education had a negative impact on inequality and found that the level of development showed a nonlinear relation with the extent of inequality. Based on the study on urbanization and inequality in Asia, Kanbur and Zhuhang (2013) concluded that the effect of urbanization and its impact on inequality was country specific. However, in the case of India urbanization explained less than 15 % of the increase in inequality. Koechlin and Leon (2007) identified an inverted U-shaped relation between migration and inequality. Mukhopadhya (2013) found that property income increased the inequality in China. Sicular (2013) opined that the faster rise in the incomes of the rich, as compared to the poor, led to a persistent inequality in China, also the private ownership of wide range of assets, especially urban housing, contributed to the rising inequalities. Birdsall and Londono (1997) concluded that unequal distribution of assets, especially of human capital, leads to disproportional distribution of income among the households. In Northern Vietnam, non-agricultural income was found to contribute more to inequality (Adger 2006). Adams (1996) examined the impact of remittances on inequality and concluded that internal remittances had a negative impact on inequality while the external remittances had positive impact on household inequality (see also, Koechlin and Leon 2007). Pal and Ghosh (2007) identified the macroeconomic policies which could have possibly led to inequality in India as fiscal tightening, regressive tax policies and expenditure cuts; financial sector reform that reduced institutional credit flow to small producers and agriculturalists; liberalization of rules for foreign and domestic investment, which led to more regional imbalance and skewed investment patterns, and trade liberalization.

10.1.3 The Trends in Inequality

Wide disparities between the rural and urban areas and within urban areas have been reported in India. An evidence of increasing regional disparities and widening inequality in India was provided by Deaton and Dreze (2002), wherein increasing disparities were reported between the urban and rural areas in terms of per capita expenditure, the extent of inequality being higher in the urban areas of most of the states. Dev and Ravi (2007) showed that the extent of inequality either increased or increased at a slower rate in 13 of the 17 states in India and the Gini coefficient for urban area increased in 15 states during the post reform period. Decomposition results also showed that inequality component was positive in 13 states, wide disparities were observed between the rural and urban areas (see also, Sen and Himanshu 2004; Vakulabharanam 2010; Vakulabharanam and Motiram 2012).

Mohanty (1999), concluded that modernisation of agriculture has increased the dominance of large farmers leading to higher inequality in rural areas especially in the modernized villages. Chattopadhyay (2005) found that the improvement in the income distribution in West Bengal during the impressive agricultural growth could not be sustained in the periods of declining agricultural growth phase thus leading to inequality. Paul (1990) analysed the disparity in income and land distribution in Haryana between the periods of 1969–70 to 1982–83 and found that the Gini coefficient for income disparity increased at about 4 % per annum among the farm families and there was a persistent decline in the per capita land holding.

10.1.4 A Review of Inequality and Household Asset Distribution

Income inequality is a widely debated issue; however, there has been a shift in the emphasis from income poverty to asset poverty to address the problems of poverty reduction and the inequality at household as well as individual levels. The recent report from the IMF indicates that inequality of wealth (gini 0.68) is higher than that of income inequality (gini 0.36) in many countries of the world. Inequality in non-financial assets has shown significant rise in countries like India and Indonesia (Ostray et al. 2014). For the poor households, assets are not just the consumables but in fact act as inputs which they can use as securities or collateral during sudden income shocks or downturns (Deere and Doss 2006; Dick et al. 2011).

Chopra (1986) examined the extent of inequality in the access to and distribution of assets in Punjab. The extent of inequality in the access to the use of assets such as land, tractors and machinery was high among the small farmers than the large farmers which in turn could affect the adoption of agricultural technology and could deprive the small farmers from the benefits of development policies. Swaminathan (1988) found extreme disparities in land ownership in the Gokilapuram village of Tamil Nadu. The extent of inequality worsened between the periods of 1977 to 1985 with the concentration of land ownership being the major contributor to inequality. It is found that agricultural support and production were highly concentrated on large farms. Large farms accounted for about 45–85 % of the production and received 35–75 % of all support representing 50–75 % of the of farm income higher than that of the other classes (Moreddu 2011).

10.2 The Study on Asset Distribution and Income Inequality in Rural Punjab

10.2.1 Background of the Study

The performance of Punjab's economy has not been very encouraging in the recent years and the state has lagged behind in many parameters of economic development. The agriculture sector in Punjab has shown significant slowdown in the crop production and productivity with the rate of growth in Punjab falling far below the national averages (Vatta et al. 2013). Without any significant progress in crop diversification towards high value crops and with constant decline in crop profitability, the crisis in the agrarian sector has been deepening in the recent times. The mechanization of agriculture sector contributed to an annual decline in farm sector employment by 50 million man-days from 1983–84 to 2000–01, rendering livelihoods of the rural landless even more vulnerable (Sidhu and Singh 2004). The decline in farm incomes during 1999–00 to 2004–05 caused a corresponding increase in rural poverty from 6.2 to 8.4 %. The uneven sharing of growth benefits in Punjab agriculture have led to widening of farm income gaps across various land holding categories (Joshi 2004) with farm income of a large farmer being witnessed to be as high as 16 times that of a small farmer (Vatta et al. 2008). Though, rural non-farm sector comprising various industrial and service sector activities provides some hope to absorb the growing rural labour force, there has not been any significant progress in employment generation in these sectors during the recent times (Vatta and Sato 2012).

Further, less than expected impact of growth of non-farm sector on poverty alleviation and reduction in income inequality has been witnessed due to highly skewed distribution of endowments of productive assets (Reardon et al. 2000; Lanjouw and Shariff 2004). The assets not only act as consumables but also as securities or collateral during sudden income shocks or downturns. The impacts of asset ownership are not only observed significantly at the household levels, but also at the individual levels. Reardon et al. (2000) observed that the non-farm activities, which were skill or capital intensive, were more accessible to the wealthier households than the poor. Such unequal access to non-farm activities was mainly triggered by the limited investment capacity of the households and the lack of low capital entry barrier activities.

With more remunerative employment opportunities being apportioned largely by the workers with better education and endowments, the current changes in the labour markets in India in general and in Punjab in particular, are expected to have contributed towards an increase in income and asset inequality. The present study is thus an attempt to examine the extent of income and asset inequality in rural Punjab. Apart from throwing light on the reasons for such changes in inequality, it also provides some options which can help in reducing such gaps in the future.

10.2.2 Data and Methodology

The present study is based on the data collected from two primary surveys conducted at two different points of time in rural Punjab. The first survey was conducted during the year 2005–06 and pertained to 315 rural households spread across different size categories, while the second survey was conducted during the year 2011–12 pertaining to 290 rural households across different size categories. The sample selection was based on probability proportional to size criterion and the distribution of samples at two points is given in Table 10.1. The households were further classified into the landless (operating no land), marginal farmers (operating less than 2.5 acre), small farmers (operating 2.5–5 acre), medium farmers (operating 5–15 acre) and large farmers (operating 15 acre and above).

Both the datasets are not exactly comparable to each other, and hence, all the differences during the two points of time may not be attributed to the changes happening over time. While the sample in the first survey was spread over 20 villages in 10 districts, that in the second survey pertained only to 3 villages in 3 districts of Punjab. In the first survey, ten districts were Amritsar, Sangrur, Kapurthala, Hoshiarpur, Ropar, Ludhiana, Ferozepur, Mansa, Faridkot and Gurdaspur. In the second survey, the selected districts were Ludhiana, Amritsar and Sangrur. Despite all that the comparison of various parameters of inequality over time will throw significant light on the broad changes occurring in rural income and asset distribution in Punjab during the period of comparison which corresponds to the period of high economic growth in India.

10.2.3 Data Limitations and Issues

The study attempts to compare two distinct datasets which differ in the sample size and the study locale. Both the sets have been generated based on probability proportional to size criterion and the difference in the sample size was not very huge. While the base study conducted in 2005–06 had the study areas in the districts which represented high, medium and low intensity of non-farm employment in Punjab, the criterion for the second study was to select the villages based the nature

Table 10.1 Distribution of the study samples across different size categories during 2005–06 and 2011–12

Household category	Sample size	
	2005–06	2011–12
Landless	142	177
Marginal farmers	41	22
Small farmers	44	16
Medium farmers	57	33
Large farmers	31	42
Total	315	290

of the economy such as dominance of agriculture and level of industrial development. Hence, one village each was selected in areas characterized by well-developed industrial linkages, dominance of productive agrarian economy and intermediate industrial development with dominance of remittances. The criteria in both the studies are different however, given that an area with well-developed industrial linkages implies the high intensity of the non-farm employment in the region and the ones with intermediate industrial development and agricultural dominance might act as a proxy for the medium and low non-farm employment regions some important policy implication might be derived from the comparative study of the regions over the time. However, it is emphasized that results have to interpreted with due caution considering these variations in the two studies.

In order to measure inequality in land distribution and income from various sources, Gini coefficient was estimated by using the following formula:

$$G = \frac{2}{n\mu}\mathrm{cov}(y, r)$$

where

n Number of rural households
μ Average value of land/income
y Series of land/income, and
r Series of corresponding land/income ranks

Relative concentration coefficient was estimated to ascertain whether a particular source of income was increasing or decreasing inequality. A value above unity reflected that the source was contributing towards overall income inequality and vice versa. The measure is an extension of the Gini coefficient and was calculated in the following manner:

$$g_i = R_i * \frac{G_i}{G}$$

where

g_i Relative concentration coefficient
G_i Gini coefficient for the ith income source, and
G Gini coefficient for the total income

$$R_i = \frac{\mathrm{cov}(y_i, r)}{\mathrm{cov}(y_i, r_i)} = \frac{\text{covariance between source income amount and total income rank}}{\text{covariance between source income amount and source income rank}}$$

10.3 Findings of the Study

10.3.1 Distribution of Owned and Operational Land

Ownership and access to assets determine the household participation in various income generating activities. Land is considered as the most important asset in the rural areas and its distribution has a significant influence on the income inequality. The distribution of land is highlighted in Table 10.2. The average size of owned land has increased for the marginal and small farmers and has declined for the medium and large farmers. For the marginal farmers, the size of owned land increased from 1.19 to 1.45 acre and for small farmers it increased from 3.56 to 3.73 acre. On the other hand, it declined from 7.74 to 7.63 acre and from 24.58 to 23.67 acre for the medium and large farmers, respectively. However, a further look into the proportion of land owned by the bottom 70 % households reveals an increase in inequality in the land distribution during 2005–06 to 2010–11. While the share of bottom 70 % households was 17.78 % in 2005–06, it declined considerably to 9.53 % in 2010–11. Correspondingly, the share of top 10 % households in the owned land increased from 46.67 to 51.74 % during this period. It indicates an increase in inequality in land distribution and has adverse implications for the distribution of rural income as farming is an important source of rural livelihoods.

10.3.2 Education Amongst Rural Households

Education is an important component of human resource which strongly influences the earnings of an individual in the long run. While inequality in access and extent of education is influenced by the asset ownership and income levels of the household, it also influences the level of asset ownership and household income. The pattern of education in Table 10.3 reveals such inequality. The average number of years of schooling was 3.5 for the poorest quintile in 2005–06 and it increased continuously to 7.3 for the richest quintile of rural households. The corresponding education in 2010–11 was 3.6 and 8.1 years. The level of education amongst the richest quintile of households was more than double at both the points of time. The extent of inequality in education is also visible from the proportion of illiterate individuals in various quintile groups during 2005–06 and 2010–11. The proportion

Table 10.2 Distribution of owned land in rural Punjab (acre)

Farm size category	2005–06	2010–11
Marginal	1.19	1.45
Small	3.56	3.73
Medium	7.74	7.63
Large	24.58	23.67
Land share of bottom 70 % households (%)	17.78	9.53
Land share of top 10 % households (%)	46.67	51.74

Table 10.3 Pattern of education among rural households in Punjab (%)

Quintile group	2005–06			2010–11		
	Schooling	% illiterate	Secondary and above (%)	Schooling	% illiterate	Secondary and above (%)
First (poorest)	3.5	55.7	3.2	3.6	44.8	2.3
Second	4.6	47.4	5.9	4.3	41.7	2.8
Third	5.0	38.8	6.1	5.0	40.6	3.9
Fourth	6.9	26.8	16.4	5.8	27.2	14.7
Fifth (richest)	7.3	25.1	21.9	8.1	22.2	15.6

Note The education level pertains to the age group of 15 years and above. Schooling is education in number of years completed

of illiterates amongst the poorest quintile was more than double when compared to the richest quintile group, indicating the disadvantaged situation of the poor. This trend is further strengthened by the proportion of individuals who were educated to the senior secondary level or above, as the proportion was several times higher amongst the richer quintile groups. While the individuals educated to the senior secondary or above level of education was just 3.2 and 2.3 % amongst the poorest quintile, it was as high as 21.9 and 15.6 % amongst the richest quintile group, during 2005–06 and 2010–11, respectively.

10.3.3 Access to Income Sources and Income Distribution

There have been large inter-sectoral differences in productivity of employment activities in rural economy of Punjab. The differences have been documented to have existed even within a given sector. The factors such as ownership of land and extent of education apart from many other factors (age, caste, nearness to urban areas) have been the major determinants of access to employment in more productive employment activities (Vatta and Sidhu 2010; Vatta et al. 2008). As large inequality in the land ownership and education has been highlighted before, the access to various sources of income is also expected to differ significantly across various income groups. The access to various sources of income has been highlighted in Table 10.4. It is clear that there has been a significant decline in

Table 10.4 Pattern of access to various income sources among rural households in Punjab (% households)

Source of income	% households with access	
	2005–06	2010–11
Crop and dairy farming	62.3	56.9
Agricultural labour	28.7	11.7
Non-farm income	69.7	65.5
Transfer income	35.8	11.7
Rental income	12.1	5.9

access to various income sources during 2005–06 to 2010–11. The proportion of households having access to agricultural income declined from 62.3 to 56.9 %. There was a sharp decline in the proportion of households having access to agricultural labour from 28.7 to 11.7 % to transfer income from 35.8 to 11.7 % and to rental income from 12.1 to 5.9 % during this period. The decline in access to non-farm income was to a lower extent from 69.7 to 65.5 %. In overall, the access has declined and it corresponds to the recent NSS estimates that the rural areas lost the employment opportunities and even the urban areas could not generate much employment and the period of 2004–05 to 2009–10 turned out to be the period of jobless growth in India (Vatta and Sato 2012).

In order to examine the income inequality, it is important to examine the share of different income quintile groups in total income from a given source. This information has been presented in Table 10.5 and gives the share of the poorest and richest quintile groups during 2005–06 and 2010–11. It is worth noting that the poorest quintile group earned less than 5 % of most of the different categories of income earned by the rural households in 2005–06. The share was just 2.5 % in the total household income during 2005–06, which increased to 3.3 % in 2010–11. The share of richest households in the overall income declined from 56.5 to 53.7 % during this period. The share of the poorest households in income from agricultural wages increased tremendously from 24.4 to 66.2 % and that of non-farm income increased from 4.0 to 11.2 %. The share of richest quintile of households increased in almost all the income categories except in transfer income where it declined from 59.8 to 52.0 %. Despite an increase in the share of the poorest quintile group in income sources, it is clear that there is a huge gap in income distribution, with the richest households earning several times higher than their poorest counterparts. It is highlighted by the gini ratio provided below. It is clear that the non-farm income, rental and transfer income is even more unequally distributed than the farm income. The gini value for agricultural wage labour is also very high but it is due to the reason that most of the poor households get employed in this activity due to it being relatively less remunerative and non-regular employment activity. The overall Gini coefficient has shown a small increase from 0.46 to 0.49 during 2005–06 to 2010–11.

Table 10.5 Share of the poorest and richest quintile groups in various income sources in rural Punjab (%)

Source of income	Poorest quintile		Richest quintile		Gini ratio	
	2005–06	2010–11	2005–06	2010–11	2005–06	2010–11
Farm income	1.5	3.5	62.4	65.7	0.52	0.64
Agri labour	24.4	66.2	7.8	–	0.77	0.91
Non-farm income	4.0	11.2	46.9	47.7	0.73	0.65
Transfer income	0.7	8.6	59.8	52.0	0.90	0.85
Rental income	–	3.9	63.6	65.8	0.58	0.94
Overall	2.5	3.3	56.5	53.7	0.46	0.49

Note The figures are % shares in the total income from a given source across all the sample households

Table 10.6 Relative concentration coefficient for various income sources in rural Punjab

Income source	2005–06	2010–11
Farm income	1.06	1.18
Agri labour	0.74	0.68
Non-farm income	0.82	0.72
Transfer income	1.20	1.15
Rental income	0.93	1.07

Note The value of relative concentration coefficient above unity reflects that the income source contributes to an increase in overall income inequality and vice versa

Gini coefficient for farm income, agricultural wage income, and rental income registered an increase over time but declined for the non-farm income and transfer income. However, the extent of inequality still seems to be quite high.

A further look at the relative concentration coefficient throws a light on whether the income source contributes towards increasing the overall income inequality or otherwise. Farm income and transfer income were found to be inequality increasing sources with the relative concentration coefficient for these sources being more than unity. The relative concentration coefficient has shown an increase over time for the farm income (Table 10.6). This is obvious given that farm income accrues to the households having either the ownership of land or the access to it through lease in. The coefficient registered a decline for non-farm income and transfer income, while it increased for rental income. These results are in line with the earlier observations on income shares and inequality.

10.4 Conclusions and Policy Implications

There exists a widespread inequality in land ownership in rural Punjab, which is the most important asset in a rural economy. The share of land owned by the bottom 70 % households declined considerably during 2005–06 and 2010–11. Correspondingly, the share of top 10 % households increased from 46.67 to 51.74 % during this period. The inequality in education was reflected by the proportion of illiterates amongst the poorest quintile being more than double of the richest quintile group. The proportion of more educated individuals was 7–8 times higher for the richest quintile group. There has been a significant decline in access to various income sources during 2005–06 to 2010–11, which is in line with the overall jobless experience of the Indian economy during 2004–05 to 2009–10. The poorest quintile group earned considerably less amongst different categories of income earned by the rural households and the share of richest quintile of households increased in almost all the income categories except in transfer income. The overall Gini coefficient has shown a small increase from 0.46 to 0.49 during 2005–06 to 2010–11. Finally, farm income and transfer income were found to be inequality increasing sources with the relative concentration coefficient for these sources being more than unity. Relative concentration coefficient has shown an increase over time for the farm income and rental income and declined for non-farm income and transfer income. In nutshell, there exists a widespread inequality in land ownership along with unequal access to education in rural Punjab, which strongly influences the rural income distribution as revealed by large income inequality. A further increase in such inequality in the recent times is a matter of concern for more careful planning towards an egalitarian society in the long run.

References

Adams Jr RH (1996) Remittances, income distribution, and rural asset accumulation, FCND Discussion Paper No. 17. International Food Policy Research Institute, Washington, DC, USA

Adger WN (2006) Income inequality in former centrally planned economies: results for the agricultural sector in Vietnam. CSERGE Working Paper GEC 97–06

Birdsall N, Londono JL (1997) Asset inequality matters: an assessment of the world bank's approach to poverty reduction. Am Econ Rev Pap Proc 87:32–37

Chattopadhyay AK (2005) Distributive impact of agricultural growth in rural West Bengal. Econ Polit Wkly 40:5601–5610

Chopra K (1986) Dimensions of inequality in a high growth region. Econ Polit Wkly 12:491–496

Deaton A, Dreze J (2002) Poverty and inequality in India: a re-examination. Econ Polit Wkly 37:3729–3747

Deere CD, Doss CR (2006) The gender asset gap: what do we know and why does it matter? Feminist Econ 12:1–50

Dev MS, Ravi C (2007) Poverty and inequality: All-India and states, 1983–2005. Econ Polit Wkly 42:509–521

Dick RM, Johnson N, Quisumbing A, Njuki J, Behrman J, Rubin D, Peterman A, Waitanji E (2011) Gender, assets, and agricultural development programs: a conceptual framework. CAPRi Working Paper No. 99. International Food Policy Research Institute, Washington, DC. http://dx.doi.org/10.2499/CAPRiWP99

IMF (2014) Fiscal policy and income inequality. International Monetary Fund, Washington, DC, USA. http://www.imf.org/external/pp/ppindex.aspx

Joshi A (2004) Punjab: farm household income, investment and consumption. Econ Polit Wkly 39:321–323

Kanbur R, Zhuang J (2013) Urbanization and inequality in Asia. Asian Dev Rev 30:131–147

Koechlin V, Leon G (2007) International remittances and income inequality: an empirical investigation. J Econ Policy Reform 10:123–141

Lanjouw P, Shariff A (2004) Rural non-farm employment in India: access, incomes and poverty impact. Econ Polit Wkly 39:4429–4446

Lopez JH (2011) Pro-poor growth: a review of what we know (and of what we don't). Paper prepared in the context of "Pro-poor Growth" program sponsored by the World Bank's PREM Poverty Group. The World Bank, Washington DC, USA

Mohanty BB (1999) Agricultural modernisation and social inequality. Case Study of Satara District, Econ Polit Wkly 34:A50–A61

Moreddu C (2011) Distribution of support and income in agriculture, OECD Food, Agriculture and Fisheries. Working Papers No. 46, OECD Publication. http://dx.doi.org/10.1787/5kgch21wkmbx-en

Mukhopadhaya P (2013) Trends in income inequality in China: the effects of various sources of income. J Asia Pac Econ 18:304–317

OECD (2011) Growing income inequality in OECD countries: what drives it and how can policy tackle it?. OECD Forum on Tackling Inequality, Paris, France

Ostray JD, Berg A, Tsangarides CG (2014) Redistribution, inequality, and sustainable growth: reconsidering the evidence. IMF Staff Discussion Note, SDN/14/02

Pal P, Ghosh J (2007) Inequality in India: a survey of recent trends. DESA Working Paper No. 45, ST/ESA/2007/DWP/45, United Nations, New York, USA

Paul S (1990) Green revolution and income distribution among farm families in Haryana, 1969–70 to 1982–83. Econ Polit Wkly 25:A154–A158

Reardon T, Taylor EJ, Stamoulis K, Lanjouw P, Balisacan A (2000) Effects of non-farm employment on rural income inequality in developing countries: an investment perspective. J Agric Econ 51:266–288

Sen A, Himanshu (2004) Poverty and inequality in India–II, widening disparities during the 1990s. Econ Polit Wkly 39:4361–4375

Sicular T (2013) The challenge of high inequality in China. Poverty Reduction and Equity Department, The World Bank, Washington DC, USA

Sidhu RS, Singh S (2004) Agricultural Wages and Employment. Econ Polit Wkly 39:4132–4135

Swaminathan M (1988) Growth and polarization: changes in wealth inequality in Tamil Nadu village. Econ Polit Wkly 21:491–496

Todaro MP, Smith SC (2007) Poverty, inequality and development. In: Economic development, 8th edn., Chap. 6. Pearson Education, pp 229–291

Vakulabharanam V (2010) Does class matter? class structure and worsening inequality in India. Econ Polit Wkly 45:67–76

Vakulabharanam V, Motiram S (2012) Understanding poverty and inequality in urban India since reforms bringing quantitative and qualitative approaches together. Econ Polit Wkly 47:45–52

Vatta K, Sidhu MS, Kaur A (2013) Pattern of growth and emerging challenges for Punjab agriculture. In: Report submitted to the United Nations Environment Programme. Punjab Agricultural University, Ludhiana, India, p 46

Vatta K, Garg BR, Sidhu MS (2008) Rural employment and income: the inter-household variations in Punjab. Agric Econ Res Rev 21:201–210

Vatta K, Sato T (2012) Indian labour markets and returns to education: 1983 to 2009–10, DP 2012–33. Discussion Paper Series, Research Institute for Economics and Business Administration, Kobe University, Japan

Vatta K, Sidhu RS (2010) Rural non-farm employment, income distribution and poverty: micro level evidence from the Punjab state. Indian J Agric Econ 53:693–709

Wells R (2014) Education's effect on income inequality: an economic globalisation perspective. Globalisation, Soc Educ 4:371–391

World Bank, World Data Bank; World Development Indicators. http://databank.worldbank.org/data/views/reports/tableview.aspx

World bank data base. http://data.worldbank.org/indicator/SI.DST.05TH.20

Part III
Structural Transformation of Punjab Economy: Emergence of Industry and Services

Chapter 11
Growth, Employment and Structural Change: Punjab Versus 16 Major States of India

Aradhna Aggarwal

11.1 Introduction

There is a general consensus that the unprecedented growth in GDP in India in the post 1990 period has not been accompanied by commensurate growth in employment. It is termed as "jobless growth". There is emphasis in the policy debate that jobless growth has been responsible for the disappointing results in reducing poverty. However, according to an emerging economic thinking, emphasis should be placed not only on increasing employment levels per se but also on its sectoral composition (Wang and Szirmai 2008; Timmer and Szirmai 2000; Macmillan and Rodrik 2011; Aggarwal and Kumar 2012 for a detailed survey). The 'New Structural Economics', as it has come to be known as, emphasises that the basic cause of low growth–low growth circle is that the labour force is trapped into low-productivity sectors. An expansion of more productive and dynamic sectors can push the economy into a virtuous circle in which the growth of productive employment, productive capacities and earnings mutually reinforce each other to accelerate growth and reduce poverty. Thus, labour flows from low-productivity activities to high-productivity activities are a key driver of sustained economic growth and development. Following the emergence of this thinking, there has been growing interest in the analysis of structural change in the economy as a mechanism of sustained growth (Dietrich 2009; Cortuk and Singh 2011; Macmillan and Rodrik 2011). The advent of this thinking within the realm of the "New Structural Economics" has prompted a stream of empirical literature which focuses on systematically unpacking the relationship between economic growths on the one hand and, employment and structural change in employment on the other (see, for

A. Aggarwal (✉)
Department of International Economics and Business, Asia Research Centre, Copenhagen Business School, Porcelenshaven 24A, 1-4.sal, 2000 Frederiksberg Copenhagen, Denmark
e-mail: aa.int@cbs.dk; aradhna.aggarwal@gmail.com

L. Singh and N. Singh (eds.), *Economic Transformation of a Developing Economy*, India Studies in Business and Economics,
DOI 10.1007/978-981-10-0197-0_11

instance, Gutiérrez et al. 2009).[1] This literature discards the traditional employment elasticity approach of analyzing the relationship between growth and employment (i.e. the percentage change in employment in response to 1 % change in output) because the latter says nothing about the changes in the structure of labour force. While contributing to this line of the literature, the present study uses Shapley decompositions to analyse the structural change in employment over the period from 1993–94 to 2011–12 and its contribution to economic growth in 16 major states with special reference to Punjab. By structural change in employment we mean inter-sectoral movement of labour.

The Indian economy has witnessed two different policy regimes since independence. The first policy regime which characterised the first 30 years of planning period, i.e. from 1950–51 to 1979–80 was associated with the "state-led growth model". The centerpiece of this model was the promotion of import-substitution-based industrialization with a particular emphasis placed on the basic and heavy industries. The public sector was assigned the commanding heights of the economy. A turning point in the Indian economy occurred in 1980–81 when the "state-led model of growth" was abandoned in favour of a "market-led growth strategy". Gradual reforms were introduced to de-regulate industries, foreign direct investment, technology transfers and imports. In the early 1990s, however sweeping reforms were introduced to assign the private sector commanding heights of the economy. It has come to be known as the "Liberalisation, Privatization and Globalization (LPG) regime". The present study focuses on the LPG regime and analyses the relationship between growth and structural change in employment across 16 major states for the period 1993–94 to 2011–12 with a special focus on Punjab. It also outlines the growth experience of 16 states in terms of GSDP and the changes in sectoral shares of GDP and investigates whether the structural change in employment is commensurate with that in GSDP.

The rest of the study is organized into three sections. Section 11.2 provides the theoretical underpinning for the analysis. Section 11.2 analyses economic growth and structural change in GSDP across 16 major states with a special reference to Punjab. It also focuses on employment growth and structural change in employment. Section 11.3 disentangles the relationship between growth and structural change in employment, and finally, Sect. 11.4 concludes the analysis and draws on policy implications.

11.2 Economic Growth and Structural Change in Employment: A Theoretical Framework

Economic growth in developing countries is intrinsically tied to dynamics of its production structures, which bring about growth through the expansion of value-added and employment in higher productivity sectors at the cost of lower

[1]See, Kucera and Roncolato (2012) and Aggarwal and Kumar (2012) for literature review.

productivity sectors. When labor and other resources move from less productive to more productive activities, the economy grows even if there is no productivity growth within sectors (Mcmillan and Rodrik 2011).[2] Structural change thus removes constraints from productivity growth. The primary sector is considered to be a low-productivity sector. Labour productivity gaps between different sectors are very large in developing countries. Typically, labour productivity in primary sector is relatively much lower than in non-primary sectors. Within non-primary sectors, manufacturing is typically more productive than services. It means that shifts from primary to non-primary sectors in particular manufacturing is growth enhancing. This type of structural change can also contribute significantly to poverty reduction by raising income levels of those absorbed in the more productive sectors. Moving out of the less productive sectors (generally primary sector) where poverty rates are often much higher to more productive sectors may also relieve some of the pressure put on agricultural productivity and have some direct poverty reducing effect through raising agricultural incomes. Such change in the structure of employment can have very large effects on poverty, as it may enable people to escape poverty traps. Economic growth accompanied by structural change in income and employment should therefore have positive effects on poverty reduction. Therefore, production structures should be the starting point for economic analysis and the design of appropriate policies.

It is instructed to note that the structural change in the economy (sectoral share of GDP) alone may not produce desired sectoral structure of employment. It may actually be associated with a rise in poverty unless it is matched by a desired structural change in employment. For instance, an expansion in the more productive sectors at the cost of the less productive sectors (in terms of value added) may result in a net reduction in employment. Where the displaced workers go can have an important impact on poverty outcomes. If it generates unemployment and informality, it can put downward pressure on wages. This in turn can have poverty enhancing effect in terms of both absolute and relative poverty. In an influential study McMillan and Rodrik (2011) show that since 1990 structural shifts in employment has been in favour of low productive sectors in Latin America and Africa. While in former the labour absorbing sectors have been non-tradable sectors such as personal and community services and wholesale and retail trade; in the latter, the employment share of relatively unproductive agriculture has increased significantly. In Asia on the other hand, there are indications of shift in the structural employment in favour of more productive sectors which is likely to have positive impact on poverty. Clearly, the structural change in GDP needs to be accompanied with critical expansion of the high-productivity sectors to have

[2]Timmer and Szirmai (2000) coined the term 'structural change bonus' for this (see also, Bosworth et al. 1995; Fagerberg and Verspagen 2002, 2007; Timmer and de Vries 2009). McMillan and Rodrik (2011) show that the bulk of growth in Asia and developing countries in Latin America and Africa can be explained by the contribution of structural change to overall labor productivity whereas the contribution of trend productivity growth to total productivity growth remains rather limited.

substantial impact on employment creation in these sectors. In so much as the labor market clears and higher productivity sectors have higher returns, this structural change in employment will ensure sustained growth and reduction in poverty. A large number of studies have appeared worldwide analysing structural change in employment as a mechanism of sustained growth (see for example, Islam 2004; Melamed et al. 2011; Mcmillan and Rodrik 2011; Naudé et al. 2014). The present study deals with the state-level analysis for the period 1993–94 to 2011–12.

11.2.1 Economic Growth and Structural Composition of GDP in Punjab

While analysing the trend rates of growth of State domestic product from 1993–04 to 2011–12 of Punjab vis-à-vis 15 other major States, data on aggregate and sectoral GDP at the state level are drawn from the Centre for Statistical Organization (CSO), Ministry of Statistics and Program Implementation sources. For analysing the growth patterns of Punjab in the LPG regime, we identify two sub-periods within this regime: 1993–94 to 2004–05 and 2004–05 to 2011–12. While acceleration in growth started from 1992–3, it was in the post 2003–04 periods that the economy witnessed unprecedented growth (Aggarwal and Kumar 2012). While the period of 1993–94 is termed as a "moderate growth phase", the period thereafter is referred to as "high growth phase" in the rest of the analysis.

11.2.1.1 Economic Growth

Punjab achieved remarkable growth since independence and emerged as one of the richest states of India in terms of per capita income in the 1960s. This growth and prosperity are primarily the result of Punjab's adoption of new technology in agriculture. Its cultivators were the first to adopt the Borlaug seed-fertilizer technology during the mid-1960s. This could be because during the post-independence period Punjab was helped by a large inflow of resources from the national government for both rehabilitation and infrastructure development. This enabled Punjab to make substantial investments in infrastructure mainly in irrigation, power and communication which in turn might have enabled farmers to adapt the HYV technology to local conditions and exploit it successfully. Whatever may be the reasons, the state has become a symbol of green revolution in India and rapid growth of agriculture has had a large impact on the entire economy. Between 1961–62 and 1990–91 Punjab was in the topmost quartile, and it tended to move further and further away from the national mean.

However, it could not sustain this momentum and started slipping after liberalisation. In 1993–94 it ranked third (after Maharashtra and Haryana) in terms of per capita income among major Indian states; its rank slipped to 7 by 2011–12.

Table 11.1 Growth in income per capita: Punjab vis-à-vis other states

States	GSDP per capita (Rs)				Average annual growth rate (%)			
	1993–94	Rank	2011–12	Rank	1993–2005	Rank	2005–2012	Rank
Punjab	**24,024**	**3**	**55,780**	**7**	**8**	**8**	**8.8**	**15**
Maharashtra	27,598	1	70,363	1	7.2	11	13.4	2
Haryana	26,883	2	69,043	2	9.2	5	12.4	4
Kerala	21,965	4	60,293	5	7.4	10	10.9	7
Orissa	20,615	5	31,737	11	6.4	12	9.7	12
Himachal Pradesh	18,333	6	61,051	4	12.9	2	10.6	9
Gujarat	17,805	7	66,548	3	14.6	1	13.7	1
Andhra Pradesh	17,460	8	47,297	9	7.8	9	11.5	5
Karnataka	17,374	9	47,629	8	9.4	4	10.3	10
Tamil Nadu	16,871	10	58,694	6	11.4	3	12.9	3
West Bengal	15,088	11	37,556	10	8.5	7	9	14
MP	14,772	12	28,663	13	5	16	11.1	6
Rajasthan	13,976	13	31,079	12	8.6	6	9.7	13
Assam	12,080	14	25,866	14	5.1	15	7.2	16
Uttar Pradesh	11,946	15	22,370	15	5.5	14	9.8	11
Bihar	9,037	16	18,056	16	5.8	13	10.6	8

Source Central Statistical Organisation

Table 11.1 presents the GSDP per capita of the 16 major states. The growth rate of the combined GSDP of all 16 states taken together increased from 7.9 % during 1993–05 to over 11 % during 2005–12. In the moderate growth phase, the GSDP varied from a low of 5.1 % per year for Madhya Pradesh to a high of 12.9 % in HP, which gives a ratio of 2.6 between the highest and the lowest. In the high growth phase, the growth rate accelerated in all the states except Himachal Pradesh. The GSDP variation had been from a low of 7.2 % per year for Assam to a high of 13.4 % for Tamil Nadu, contracting the ratio to 1.6. Interestingly In this scenario, Punjab also improved its growth rate from 8 to 8.8 %. But this rate of growth pulled it down from the 8th to 15th rank in terms of growth rate. Two states at the upper end of the spectrum (in terms of growth), namely Gujarat and Tamil Nadu maintained high growth rates and their ranking over time. The growth rate accelerated in Haryana, AP, Kerala, Maharashtra, Bihar, Madhya Pradesh and UP so much so that their rankings in terms of growth of GDP also improved significantly. Punjab, HP, Karnataka, Rajasthan, West Bengal and Assam on the other hand slipped in terms of the rate of growth.

In terms of GSDP per capita, Punjab along with Orissa lost their rankings drastically. On the other hand, Gujarat, HP and TN significantly improved their rankings over time. Change in the relative ranking of other states had been marginal. Of the 5 BIMARU states namely, Bihar, Madhya Pradesh, Rajasthan and UP, the first two accelerated their growth rates and improved their ranking but growth was not high enough to push their ranking in terms of GSDP per capita.

11.2.1.2 Structural Change in GDP

Figure 11.1 depicts GSDP shares of the three sectors: agriculture, industry and services for the period of 18 years from 1993–94 to 2011–12 for each state covered in the analysis. It is observed that in all the states, there had been a shift in the share of GSDP generated in the agricultural sector to other economic sectors namely industry and services. It may be seen that Punjab has been the leader in terms of structural change in the economy away from primary to non-primary sectors. The share of agriculture in GSDP has declined by 20 % over the past two decades in Punjab. Orissa is the only other state which almost equaled the performance of Punjab in this regard.

Figure 11.2 presents the share of each sector in total structural change where the latter is estimated using the index of 'Norm of Absolute Values' (NAV). It is one-half the sum of the absolute value of the sectoral share differences of each sector between the beginning and ending year of the period, and captures the amount of value added shares transferred from declining to growing sectors during the period (Dietrich 2009). It takes on a value of zero when no change occurs and 100 when 100 % of share is shifted from one group to another. It is represented by

$$\mathrm{NAV} = 1/2\left(\sum_i Y_{it} - Y_{ik}\right)$$

where NAV is the index of 'Norm of Absolute Values' (NAV), Y_{it} and Y_{ik} represent the share of ith sector in GSDP in time t and k, respectively where $t > k$.

It shows that the decline in the share of agriculture in total structural change varies between 40 and 50 % in almost all states including Punjab. However, there

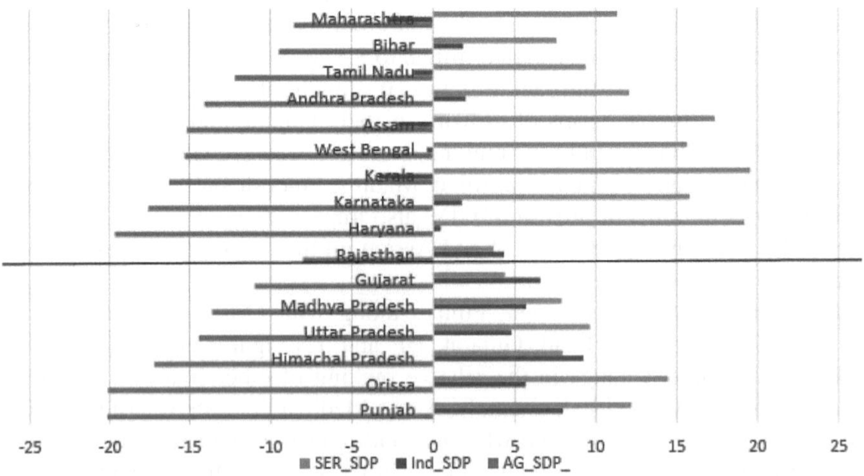

Fig. 11.1 Changes in the sectoral shares: 1993–94 to 2011–12 (*Source* Own calculations based on Central Statistical Organisation, Ministry of Statistical Planning and Implementation, India)

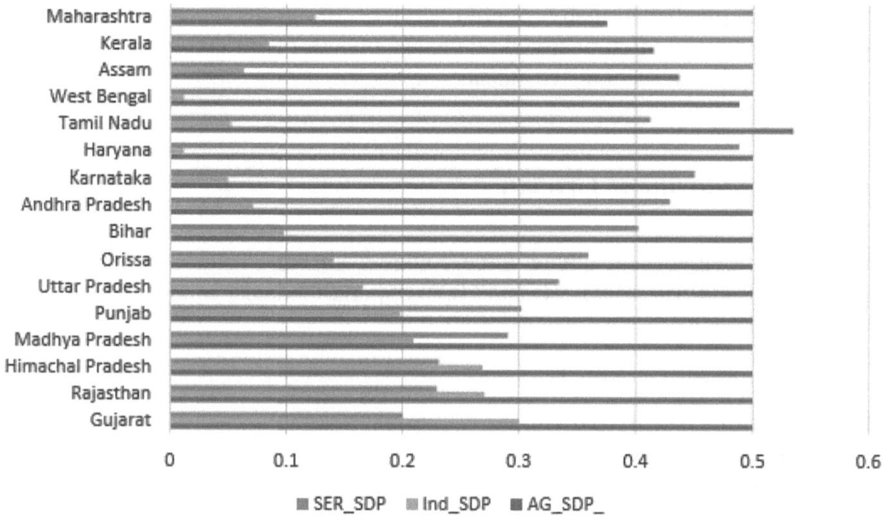

Fig. 11.2 Sectoral shares in structural change in income per capita: Punjab versus other states (*Source* Central Statistical Organisation)

are only six states where the share of non-agricultural shares was fairly distributed between industry and services. These are Gujarat, Rajasthan, HP, Punjab, MP and UP. Thus, Punjab witnessed a fairly balanced diversification of the economy. In 10 states structural shift in GSDP has been heavily biased in favour of services. In at least 5 states, the share of industry declined between 1993–94 and 2011–12 (Fig. 11.2). These are W. Bengal, Kerala, Maharashtra, Assam and Haryana. In the remaining 6 states, the share of both manufacturing and services rose but the former had been marginal.

Within industry, Punjab along with Gujarat has been the only state where both construction and manufacturing improved their shares. In Bihar, MP, TN, Karnataka and UP, it was the share of construction that rose significantly. In HP, Rajasthan and Orissa, manufacturing improved its share with that of construction remaining almost constant. In all other states, the composition of the industrial sector has remained fairly stagnant with no significant changes in the shares of manufacturing, construction, mining and utilities.

Within the service sector, there has been a clear trend of shifts towards transport and communication and business (including ICT) and financial services in most states. In Punjab, however all the service sectors witnessed expansion in their shares.

Clearly, Punjab emerges as one of the fastest diversifying economy in India. While it lagged behind in terms of growth acceleration (despite increase in the rate of growth) and hence slipped in relative ranking among Indian states, it emerged as a leader in terms of structural shifts in the composition of GDP. The share of agriculture declined sharply while that of the industry and services increased. Within industry the share of both manufacturing and construction grew while that of utilities declined marginally. Within services, the share of all the sub-sectors increased. The distribution of structural change outside of agriculture is most highly diversified for Punjab among 16 states.

11.2.2 Employment Growth

Data on employment and labour force comes from three rounds of the National Sample Survey (NSS), 1993–94, and 2004–05; and the latest round of 2011–12 to cover the LPG regime.

11.2.2.1 Employment Growth

Figure 11.3 presents employment statistics based on the quinquennial NSS Rounds undertaken since 1993–94. The UPSS-based worker population (WPRs), labour participation and unemployment rates have been applied to the population census data to arrive at the levels of work- and labour-force and also to derive the growth rates. The population estimates are based on the compound annual population growth rates between the relevant census years. All population estimates are as on 1st March of the relevant round.

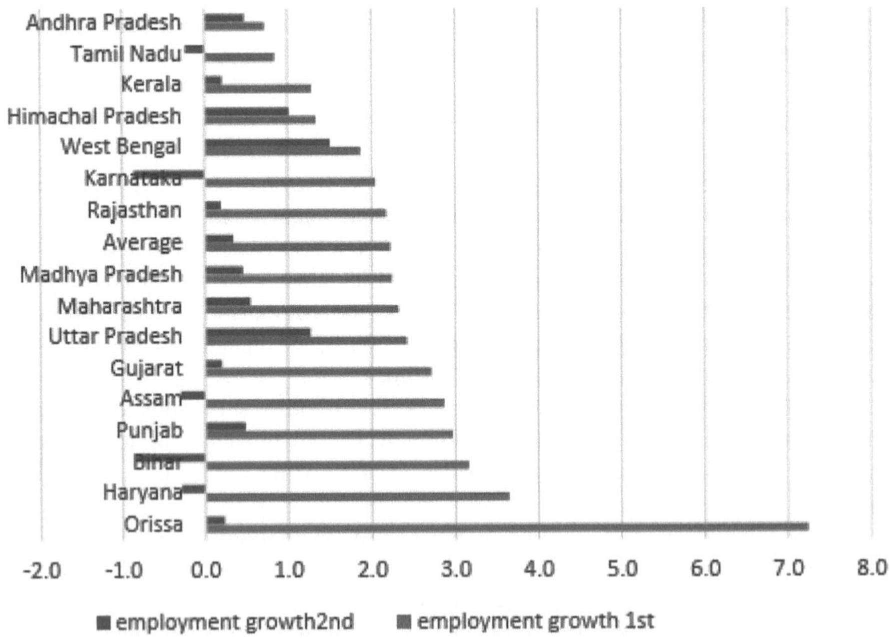

Fig. 11.3 Employment growth rates: Punjab versus other states (*Source* Authors calculations based on NSS rounds)

It may be observed that in the first phase of moderate growth, employment grew at a compound annual rate of above 2.2 % per annum for the 16 major states combined. In the high growth phase of 2004–05 to 2011–12, the employment growth rate declined to 0.5 %.

The employment growth rate declined in all the states with no exception. In Punjab, employment grew at the above average rate of 3 % in the first phase; it declined to 0.5 % in the second phase. This means the decline of 2.5 % point in the employment growth rate. The states which witnessed more pronounced fall in employment growth rate are: Orissa, Haryana, Bihar, Assam and Karnataka. This means that Punjab has been among the top six states where decline in employment growth has been the most pronounced. However, it is encouraging that the employment growth still remained positive and slightly above the average of the 16 major states covered under the study.

11.2.2.2 Structural Change in Employment

Table 11.2 shows that the composition of employment has changed markedly over the past two decades in Punjab. In the early 1990s, 51 % of the workers worked in the agricultural sector of the economy; another 17 % were employed in the secondary sector consisting of mining, manufacturing, electricity, water and gas, and construction; and about 31 % were employed in services. Over time as the economy developed the share of agriculture declined to 36 % while that of industry increased to 31 %. Interestingly, the share of services increased marginally to 32 %. The rising importance of non-primary sectors in employment and the relative decline of

Table 11.2 Employment growth by sector: Punjab versus other major states (%)

	Growth rate between 1993–94 and 2011–12		Share in 1993–94		Share in 2011–12	
	Punjab	15 major states combined	Punjab	15 major states combined	Punjab	15 major states combined
Agriculture	−0.088	0.04	50.8	63.0	36.5	49.8
Mining	–	−1.41	0.0	0.8	0.0	0.5
Manufacturing	5.778	2.81	11.3	10.6	16.8	12.5
Utilities	1.837	2.10	1.6	0.4	1.5	0.5
Construction	15.810	15.87	4.7	3.5	13.2	10.6
Trade and hotels	1.759	4.21	11.8	7.8	11.3	10.8
Transport and communication	3.146	3.69	4.2	3.1	4.8	4.0
Financial and business services	8.712	6.91	1.2	1.0	2.2	1.8
Community services	1.665	1.39	14.5	9.8	13.7	9.6
Overall	2.063	1.52	100.0	0.0	100.0	0.0

Source NSS Rounds 1993–94 and 2011–12

primary sector is a natural consequence of economic growth, an experience shared by most other states. However, it is interesting to note that in Punjab almost entire labour force released from agriculture was absorbed in the secondary sector. The service sector employment remained almost stable. In 15 states combined, the share of services also grew though marginally.

Further, within the secondary sector (Fig. 11.4), construction has emerged as a major absorber of employment. Its share in total employment increased from 4.7 % in 1993–94 to 13.2 % by 2011–12. This experience was shared by most other states. However, unlike most other states, in Punjab manufacturing also increased its share substantially by 6 % points from almost 11 to 17 %.

Finally, within services, financial services recorded an impressive growth in Punjab, a pattern that is shared by other states as well (Fig. 11.5). This was followed by transport and communication. Other sectors showed only marginal changes. For the combined 15 states, increase in employment share was recorded in all the services except community services. In Punjab, however financial services, and transport and communication recorded a marginal increase in employment shares which was almost offset by the declining share of other services. Overall, the share of services in employment remained almost stable.

In sum, while GDP growth is highly diversified across sectors in Punjab, employment was created essentially in construction and manufacturing. However, as a result of the structural change, the Punjab economy which was least diversified in 1993–94 improved its diversification index significantly both in employment and GSDP. GSDP has been more diversified than employment but the gap is reducing. Overall, while inter-sectoral changes have been taking place in 16 major economies of the country, Punjab emerges as a leader in particular in employment diversification (Fig. 11.6).

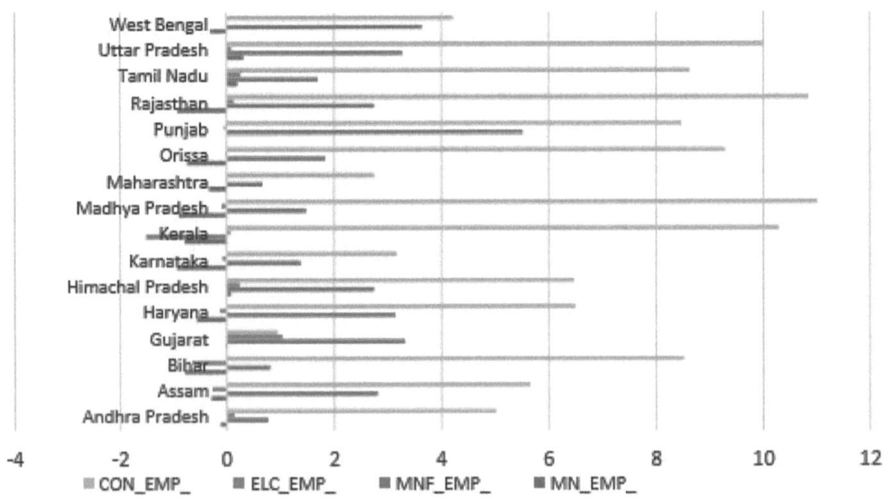

Fig. 11.4 Structural change in industry employment: Punjab versus other major states (*Source* NSS Rounds 1993–94 and 2011–12)

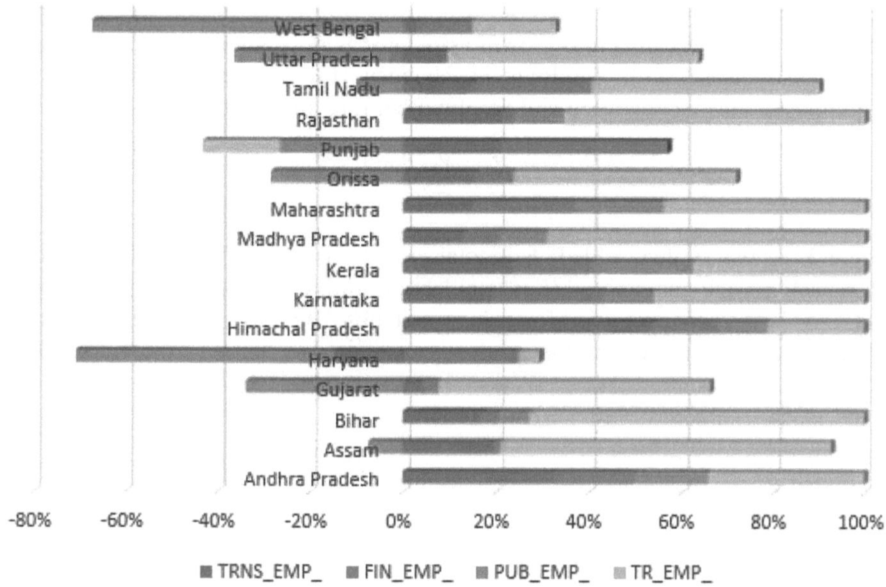

Fig. 11.5 Structural change in service employment: Punjab versus other major states (*Source* NSS Rounds 1993–94 and 2011–12)

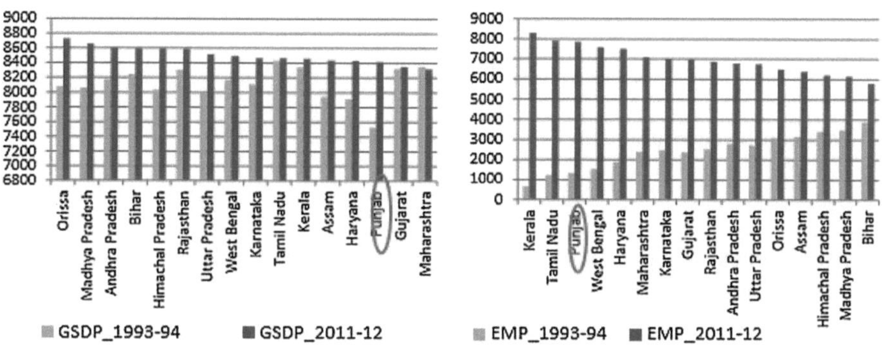

Fig. 11.6 Diversification index of GSDP and employment: Punjab versus other major states (*Source* Central Statistical organisation and National Sample Surveys)

11.3 Decomposition: Understanding the Employment Profile of Growth

11.3.1 The Methodology

To understand how growth has been translated into increases in productivity and employment at the aggregate level and by sectors (or regions), we use Shapley decompositions of per capita GDP growth. Using this methodology, we decompose growth in GDP per capita into growth associated with changes in productivity and growth associated with employment changes. Employment effect is further decomposed into labour force and employment rate effects. Thus

$$\frac{Y}{N} = \frac{Y}{E} * \frac{E}{N}. \tag{11.1}$$

where Y is total Value Added, E is total employment and N is total population. Thus, Y/N is GDP per capita, Y/E is total labour productivity or labour productivity, and E/N is the share of workforce in population (workforce participation rate). While the former represents the productivity effect, the latter is the employment effect. But

$$\frac{E}{N} = \frac{E}{L} * \frac{L}{N}. \tag{11.2}$$

In (11.2) L is the labour force. Thus, E/L is the employment rate, i.e., the share of work force in total labour force and L/N is the labour force participation rate.

This means that GDP per capita can be decomposed into three components: growth associated with GDP per worker, growth associated with changes in employment rates and growth associated with changes in the size of the labour force. Per capital income $Y/N = y$ can thus be expressed as:

$$\frac{Y}{N} = \frac{Y}{E} * \frac{E}{L} * \frac{L}{N}. \tag{11.3}$$

This can be rewritten as,

$$y = \omega * e * a$$

This implies that the total change in per capita GDP will be the sum of the growth attributed to each of its components ω, e, and a, i.e.,

$$\frac{\Delta y}{y} = \bar{\omega}\frac{\Delta y}{y} + \bar{e}\frac{\Delta y}{y} + \bar{a}\frac{\Delta y}{y}$$

Or

$$\Delta y = \bar{\omega} * \Delta y + \bar{e} * \Delta y + \bar{a} * \Delta y \tag{11.4}$$

while $\omega * \Delta y$ represents growth linked to productivity change, $e * \Delta y + a * \Delta y$ is the employment effect on growth. $\omega * \Delta y$ will reflect the amount of growth that would be consistent with a scenario in which labour productivity, had changed as observed but employment rate and the share of labour force a had remained constant. In the same way $e * \Delta y$ will be the amount of growth consistent with a scenario in which

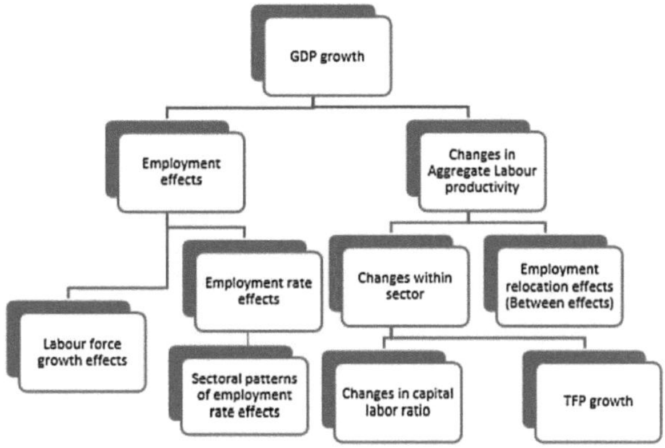

Fig. 11.7 Decomposition of GDP per capita (*Source* Author's conceptualization based on the Shapley decomposition)

labour productivity ω, and the share of labour force in population a, remains 'unchanged'. The amount of per capita growth linked to labour force changes will be $a * \Delta y$. There may be several ways in which this equation can be estimated depending upon the assumption regarding the base year of the three parameters. Shapley decomposition considers all possible alternatives, and then makes a weighted average of each.

Each component of Eq. 11.4 can further be disaggregated. For instance, $\omega * \Delta y$ can be disaggregated into the productivity growth due to inter-sectoral relocation of labour and intra-sectoral changes in capital labour ratio or total factor productivity. Similarly employment effect can also be disaggregated at the sectoral level. The decomposition plan used in the study is presented in Fig. 11.7.

11.3.2 Employment and Growth: Decomposition Results

11.3.2.1 Decomposition of Growth in Per Capita Income

Figure 11.8 shows results for the Shapley decomposition of per capita growth into two main components: one, growth linked to labour productivity; two, growth linked to employment changes at the aggregate level. It shows that the labour productivity has been the dominant driver of growth per capita value added across all the states. However, its contribution to growth has varied across states. It varied between as high as over 200 % for Orissa to 78 % for Punjab. Interestingly Punjab had the lowest contribution of labour productivity to its growth in the moderate growth phase of 1993–94 to 2004–05 among 16 Indian states. On the other hand, employment contributed 27 % point to growth which was the highest among 16 states. In the high growth period of 2005–12, the contribution of labour productivity to growth increased significantly for all the states including Punjab. Punjab improved its relative ranking also. On the other hand, the employment effect turned

(a)

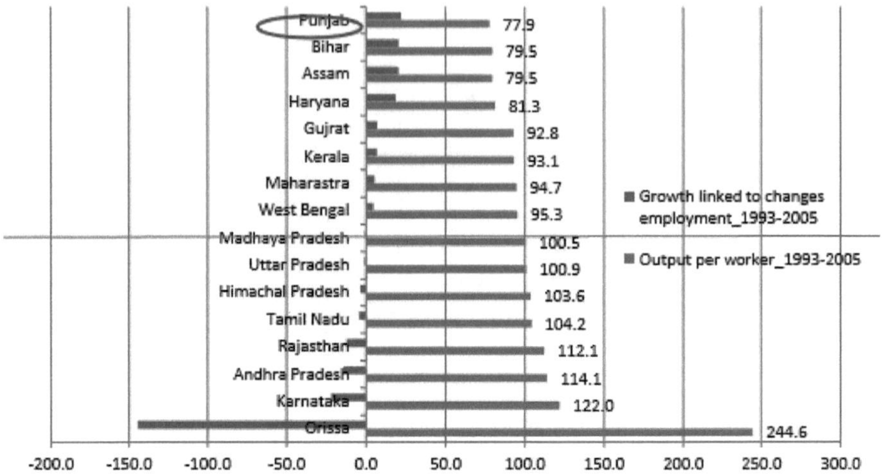

(b)

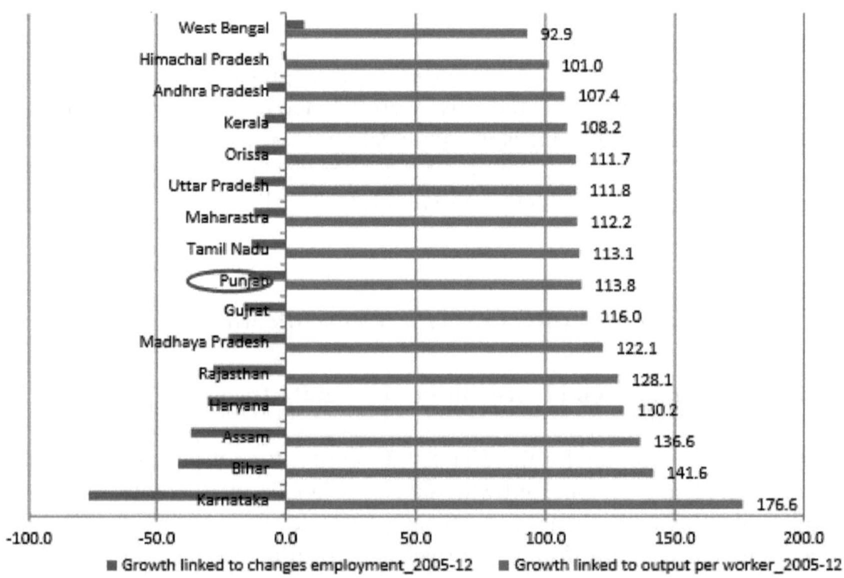

Fig. 11.8 Decomposition of growth in per capita value added: **a** 1993–05 and **b** 2005–12 (*Source* NSS surveys and Central Statistical Organisation)

negative. Punjab was not alone. The employment induced effects turned out to be negative in all the states with the only exception of West Bengal during this phase. Clearly, the growth-employment (work-force) link weakened with increasing liberalisation of the economy. This substantiates our earlier findings.

11.3.2.2 Decomposition of Labour Productivity

To further explore the employment-growth link, we decomposed the employment effect into: employment rate effect and labour force effect in Fig. 11.9. It may be seen that a large positive labour force effect was instrumental in a positive employment effect in Punjab during 1993–05. This experience was shared by most other states during this period with the only exception of Assam, Bihar, and Madhya Pradesh and to some extent Gujarat. As the growth accelerated in the post 2005 period, the employment rate effect became positive along with a few other states, namely Kerala, Orissa, Andhra Pradesh, Himachal Pradesh, Gujarat and Maharashtra. However, as it happened in all other states, the negative labour force effect more than offset the positive employment rate effect leaving the overall employment effect negative. West Bengal remains the only exception where both employment rate and labour force effect remain positive during the high growth period.

11.3.2.3 Decomposition of the Employment Effect

Theoretically, during the low income growth phases, labour force is likely to expand as more and more people; in particular, females enter the work force to earn livelihood. This is because at low levels of income, survival instincts dictate that the women work gainfully. As income increases, women feel less pressured to work and therefore withdraw from the workplace. In the Indian context, this could also be due to family status purposes (Bhalla and Kaur 2011; Olsen and Mehta 2006). As a family's income improves, it tends to withdraw its women from manual labour. Typically in developing countries, there is a U-shaped relationship between women's LFPR and the level of development (Boserup 1970). Our analysis shows that in India, the female participation rates have exhibited a tendency to decline since the early 1980s affecting the labour force participation rates. This is manifested in the contracting labour force effect.

It is however worrisome that after the income levels reaches a certain high level and women re-enter the work force which is commensurate with their family status, there will be an increasing demand for high quality jobs.

Labour productivity is decomposed into two components.

$$\Delta\frac{Y}{E} = \sum i\Delta\Theta_{it}\, y_{it} + \sum i\Delta y_{it}.\Theta_{it},\, \Theta_{i,t-k}$$

Y/*E* refers to aggregate labour productivity, y is sectoral labour productivity, θ is employment share, Δ is the first-difference operator, i indexes sectors, $t-k$ and t stand for initial and final years. The first term in the decomposition is the weighted sum of productivity growth within individual sectors, where the weights are the employment share of each sector at the beginning of the time period. This is termed as the 'within' component of productivity growth. The second term captures the productivity effect of labor relocation across different sectors. It is essentially the

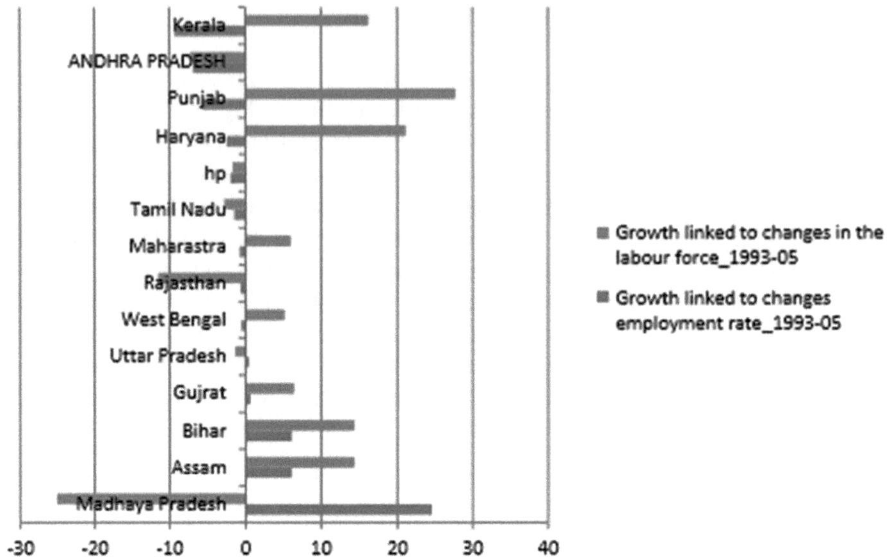

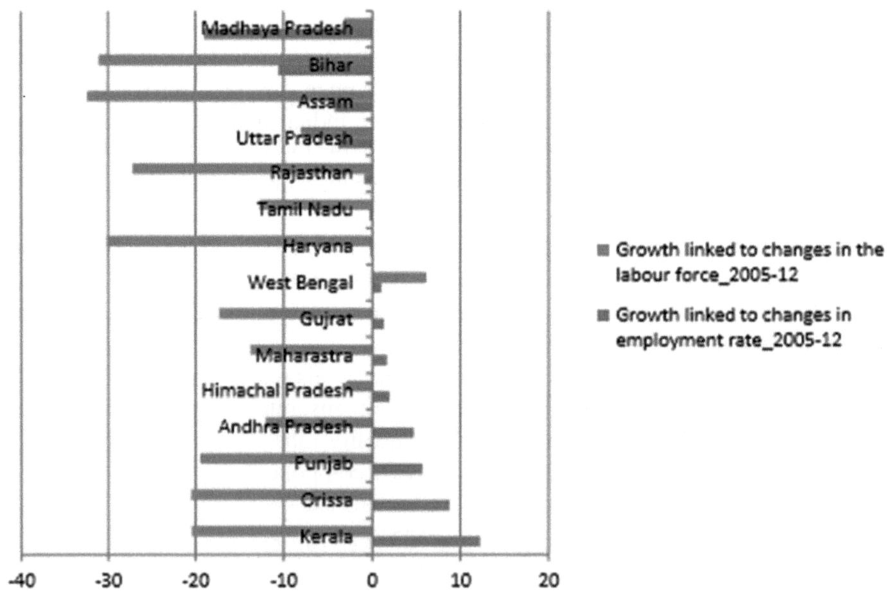

Fig. 11.9 Decomposition of the employment effect: **a** 1993–05 and **b** 2005–2012 (*Source* Author's calculations based on the NSS data)

inner product of productivity levels (at the end of the time period) with the change in employment shares across sectors. This second term is called the 'structural change' term. The structural change component indicates how sectoral shifts in employment affect overall productivity. Relocation of jobs from bad jobs sectors (low productivity) to good jobs sector (high productivity is productivity enhancing while the opposite is true for the shift of labour from good to bad sectors.

Figure 11.10 presents decomposition results of the productivity effects. It may be observed that intra-sectoral productivity dominated the productivity effects in Punjab in both the periods. Interestingly its contribution to total labour productivity also remained at over 91 %. However, Punjab's relative ranking changed as the inter-sectoral productivity effects declined in other many states. It is a manifestation of retrogression in the inter-temporal movement of labour in other states vis-à-vis Punjab. In Punjab, that inter-sectoral shifts in labour continued to have positive effect on GSDP per capita. This implies that labour released from agriculture is being absorbed by higher productivity sectors in particular manufacturing.

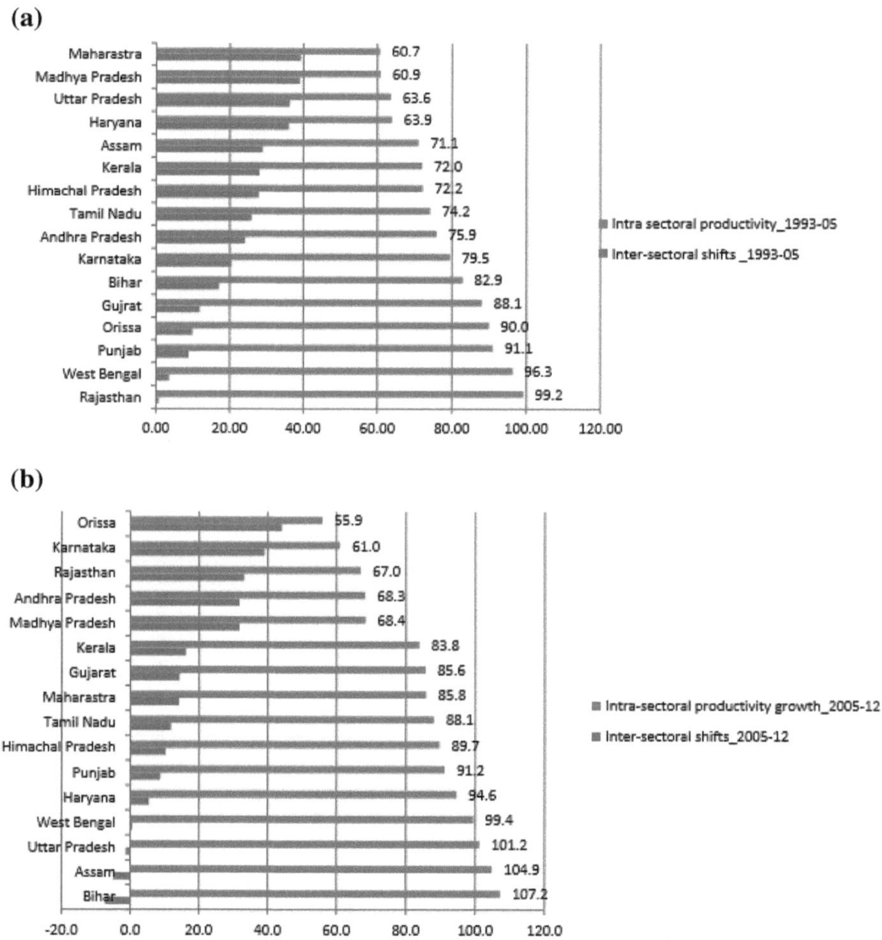

Fig. 11.10 Decomposition of productivity effect: **a** 1993–05, **b** 2005–12 (*Source* Author's estimates based on NSS data)

Table 11.3 Decomposition of labour productivity into intra- and inter-sectoral

Sector	Change in employment share (% points)	Inter-sectoral productivity 1993–05	Intra-productivity 1993–05	Change in employment share (% points)	Inter-sectoral productivity 2005–12	Intra-productivity 2005–12
Agriculture	−0.07	46.8	25.1	−0.076	63.5	19.2
Mining	0	0.0	0.0	0.000	0.0	0.0
Manufacturing	0.023	13.7	9.4	0.032	13.3	22.5
Utilities	−0	−12.4	5.2	0.003	6.9	1.1
Construction	0.026	−8.5	5.9	0.059	−48.9	−1.1
Trade and hotels	0.029	−18.0	14.5	−0.034	3.0	20.4
Transport and communication	0.021	−7.6	10.2	−0.015	−10.3	13.1
Business service	0.005	98.8	3.1	0.005	62.3	13.0
Community services	−0.03	−12.8	26.5	0.026	10.1	11.9
Total		100.0	100.0		100.0	100.0

Source Author's estimates based on NSS and CSO data

11.3.2.4 Decomposition of Inter-and Intra-Sectoral Productivity Effects by Sector

Inter-sectoral productivity effects: Table 11.3 shows that the shift in employment from agriculture to other sectors has a productivity enhancing effect. It has enhanced the productivity of agriculture itself. Shifts of labour in favour of construction have also been negatively related with productivity growth. A massive increase in construction employment has had a negative effect on GDP per capita growth. Government initiated programmes which create employment opportunity in this sector appear to have a negative effect on productivity and hence growth and poverty. Apparently, a shift of labour from agriculture to construction will have dampening effects on productivity growth in the Punjab economy.

Trade is another sector which appears to be a low-productivity sector in Punjab. A shift in employment away from this sector too seems to have productivity enhancing effects in Punjab. In all other sectors employment rate changes are positively related with productivity growth. As a matter fact, any shift of labour from agriculture to manufacturing and finance and business services can result into substantial increase in productivity in Punjab.[3]

Intra-sectoral productivity growth: In the first period, productivity growth was essentially concentrated in agriculture, trade and community services; it was diversified in the second period. Thus manufacturing, transport and communication, and financial services also made substantial contribution to productivity growth in the second period. The economy seems to be moving to higher value addition activities in these sectors. Enhanced within—sector productivity in agriculture is notable in the context of Punjab.

11.4 Conclusions

In the 1990s, sweeping reforms were introduced in the Indian economy. However, the growth impact of these reforms in the 1990s was moderate. It was the period of 2004–5 to 2011–2012 which witnessed unprecedented growth in the Indian economy. Our state-level analysis indicates that almost all the states contributed to this growth experience. Punjab was no exception but its growth was outpaced by other states pushing its relative ranking down in terms of GSDP per capita. The employment growth was not impressive either, in a comparative framework.

However, Punjab economy witnessed unprecedented structural change in GSDP and employment. The share of agriculture declined significantly by 20 % point in GSDP and 14 % point in employment. While the decline in the share of agricultural GSDP was offset by a diversified incremental changes in other sectoral shares, that in agricultural employment was absorbed essentially in manufacturing and

[3]As a matter of fact, this is noticed in most states with a few exceptions.

construction. Increasing share of manufacturing has been a notable feature of the economy which it shares with Gujarat, Rajasthan, and Himachal Pradesh. More importantly, these changes resulted into a well diversified structure of GSDP and employment in Punjab in a comparative framework of 16 states.

Economic diversification has paid off in terms of productivity and economic growth gains in the economy. Both inter- and intra-sectoral productivity effects have contributed to the productivity effects of growth. Inter-sectoral productivity has been complemented by intra-sectoral productivity in most sectors. In general, intra-sectoral productivity has increased in all the sectors except construction. Inter-sectoral productivity has also been positive through all the sectors except construction indicating that labour relocation in favour of construction has had productivity–reducing effects. The social programmes on employment creation that focus on construction sector may have growth reducing effects. It may be noted, however that shifts of labour away from agriculture and trade and hotels has had productivity enhancing effects.

Labour can be limited in its ability to move between sectors due to adjustment costs as it moves across the economy. Costs are associated with acquiring new skills and qualifications, relocation and finding new employment. Sometimes, displaced workers take on lower paid jobs as they move across sectors, particularly if the cost of vertical movement is high. Well-designed labour market policies can facilitate adjustment by reducing the costs of labour mobility across occupations. This requires improved access to quality education and training. Education is often a crucial precondition for adjustment of labor market towards more profitable economic activities. Further, the state needs to make a transition to entrepreneurial economy which is driven by entrepreneurship and innovation. Finally, there is a need to conceptualize new models of labour management systems to address labour market rigidities. The state needs to introduce a system that combines flexibility in labor market with income security of workers and assistance in their retraining and relocation.

References

Aggarwal A, Kumar N (2012) Structural change, industrialization and poverty reduction: the case of India. ESCAP South and South-West Asia Office, Development paper 1206

Bhalla S, Kaur R (2011) Labour force participation of women in India: some facts, some queries. Working Paper 40, Asia Research Centre, London School of Economics and Political Science, London, UK

Boserup E (1970) Woman's Role in Economic Development. George Allen and Unwin Ltd, London

Bosworth B, Collins SM, Chen Y (1995) Accounting for differences in economic growth. Brookings Discussion Papers in International Economics, No. 115 (October): 1–63

Cortuk O, Singh N (2011) Structural change and growth in India. Econ Lett 110(3):178–181

Dietrich A (2009) Does growth cause structural change, or is it the other way round? A Dynamic Panel Data Analyses for Seven OECD Countries. Jena Economic Research Papers 2009-034, Friedrich-Schiller-University Jena, Max-Planck-Institute of Economics

Fagerberg J, Verspagen B (2002) Technology-gaps, innovation-diffusion and transformation: an evolutionary interpretation. Res Policy 31:1291–1304

Fagerberg J, Verspagen B (2007) Innovation, growth and economic development: have the conditions for catch-up changed? Int J Technol Learn Innov Develop 1(1):13–33

Gutierrez C, Orecchia C, Paci P, Serneels P (2009) Does employment generation really matter for poverty reduction? In: Kanbur R, Svejnar J (eds) Labor markets and economic development. Routledge, New Delhi

Islam R (2004) The nexus of economic growth, employment and poverty reduction: an empirical analysis. Recovery and Reconstruction Department, Geneva, ILO

Kucera D, Roncolato L (2012) Structure matters: sectoral drivers of growth and the labour productivity-employment relationship. ILO Research Paper No. 3, December

McMillan M, Rodrik D (2011) Globalization, structural change, and productivity growth. NBER working paper 17143. Cambridge, NBER

Melamed SR, Grant HU (2011) Jobs, growth and poverty: what do we know, what don't we know, what should we know?. ODI Background Note, Overseas Development Institute

Naudé W, Szirmai A, Haraguchi N (2014) Structural change and industrial development in the BRICS (eds). Oxford University Press, Oxford

Olson W, Mehta S (2006) The right to work and differentiation in indian employment. Indian J Labour Econ Sept/Oct

Timmer MP, de Vries GJ (2009) Structural change and growth accelerations in Asia and Latin America: a new sectoral data set. Cliometrica, J Histor Econ Econ History, Association Française de Cliométrie (AFC), 3(2):165–190

Timmer MP, Szirmai A (2000) Productivity growth in Asian manufacturing: the structural bonus hypothesis examined. Struct Change Econ Dyn Elsevier, 11(4):371–392

Wang L, Szirmai A (2008) Productivity growth and structural change in Chinese manufacturing, 1980–2002. Industrial and Corporate Change, Oxford University Press, 17(4):841–874

Chapter 12
Manufacturing Sector in Punjab: Evolution, Growth Dynamism, Key Concerns and Rejuvenation Strategy

Varinder Jain

12.1 Introduction

Historically, the large-scale development of an irrigation network by the British played a key role in transforming the barren lands into fertile fields capable of producing agrarian surpluses. The expansion of railway network contributed to commercialisation of agriculture. These two major interventions along with many other developments that took place in due course facilitated the emergence of a manufacturing sector in Punjab. However, the trajectory of growth has not been smooth and since its inception, it passed through various hard phases when the manufacturing segment went almost to the brink of collapse. During such times, the state played a key role in providing a conducive environment that facilitated its revival and growth (Tewari 1998, 1999). There emerged numerous industries which besides catering to the domestic needs made a mark in export markets. Despite such robust performance in the past, there is an emerging evidence that indicates decelerated pattern of growth (Singh 2005), most often related with state's apathetic attitude towards industry (Singh and Jain 2007). It is also observed that the enterprises are trying to strive and survive in competitive business environs through intensive and extensive usage of labour, which have implications for the quality of employment generated by these enterprises (Jain 2010a).

Amidst such evidence, it is noteworthy that the growth dynamism of Punjab's manufacturing sector is often examined per se and there has been a limited effort to decipher its growth performance in a comparative perspective. It is suggested that there would emerge a more vivid picture of industrial stagnation if the growth profile of Punjab's manufacturing sector is matched by that recorded by its counterparts in

V. Jain (✉)
Institute of Development Studies, 8-B, Jhalana Institutional Area,
Jaipur 302004, Rajasthan, India
e-mail: vjain2007@gmail.com

L. Singh and N. Singh (eds.), *Economic Transformation of a Developing Economy*, India Studies in Business and Economics,
DOI 10.1007/978-981-10-0197-0_12

Haryana and Himachal Pradesh.[1] This study focuses on this aspect by way of examining the growth performance of manufacturing sector in the states of Punjab, Haryana and Himachal Pradesh. It also provides a thorough account of the evolution of manufacturing sector in Punjab during the pre-independence period. Along with this, it documents the key concerns which are followed by various policy suggestions that may help in rejuvenating the dilapidated industrial economy of Punjab.

12.2 Theoretical Perspectives on Industrial Evolution in an Agrarian Economy

Available theoretical literature on agriculture–industry relationship strongly advocates the interdependence between the two sectors. This interdependence is said to be so significant that one is often held crucial to the growth of the other and vice versa. In fact, the development of agriculture sector serves a prerequisite for a sound growth of industrial sector as the agriculture sector contributes to manufacturing sector growth by (1) supplying various raw materials, (2) releasing surplus labour for industrial sector, (3) maintaining low wage rates through supply of food items (to industrial workforce), (4) procuring imported machinery through earnings from agricultural exports and so on. Similarly, the industrial sector supports agriculture by (1) supplying inputs (like fertilisers, insecticides, agricultural tools, etc.), (2) generating adequate infrastructure for agricultural development, (3) providing market for the farm produce and so on.

In economic theory, this agriculture–industry relationship got recognised since the early beginnings of Classical Political Economy. Bharadwaj (1987) points out, "In Petty's time when different sorts of activities were carried on within the same enterprise, neither social nor intra-enterprise division of labour had progressed much so that the producers, mostly in possession of their own means of production, employing also family labour, catered to a variety of their own needs, the distinction between 'agriculture' and 'industry' did not emerge sharply. It was in the works of the Physiocrats that such a sectoral separation emerges significantly, although 'industry' was perceived more as an appendage to agriculture, and constituted predominantly artisan households" (p. AN-15).

It is observed that the Physiocrats' model of the economy portrayed agriculture as such sector which not only generated major production but also the surplus. This model conceived agriculture as the only productive sector and the rent (appropriated by landed proprietors) as the only form of surplus generated. It was believed that the artisan (manufacture) sector do not produce any surplus. So, the demand for its products was to be met through rental revenues of the proprietors (Bharadwaj 1987, p. AN-16). Despite considering the industry merely as an appendage and

[1]With the enactment of *Punjab Reorganisation Act, 1966,* the Greater Punjab was trifurcated into three states, viz. Punjab (current), Haryana and Himachal Pradesh.

sterile (without surplus), the Physiocrats' first macro-modelling of the economy facilitated thinking over agriculture–industry relationship.

However, the advancement of capital relations in agriculture and industry led to the transformation in their interrelation. Adam Smith, in contrast to Quesnay, considered that the manufacturing sector is contributing to 'net product'. Though Smith's analysis assigned significance to the agriculture sector for the provision of subsistence (food items), it also considered the industrial sector relatively more advantageous to the economy due to its scope for greater division of labour, which may lead to further subdivisions and expansions in industrial employment along with the achievement of higher productivity through the invention of superior machinery. Smith opined that an economy having substantially developed industrial sector enjoys relatively better terms of trade between agricultural produce and manufacturers. For Smith, the agriculture–industry linkage was the symbiotic relation between the 'country' and the 'town'. He emphasised that the country supplies the town with necessary subsistence and the materials of manufactures and the town repays by sending back a part of the manufactured produce for the inhabitants of the country. He further emphasised that in any civilised society, the great commerce is carried on between the inhabitants of the country and the town (Eltis 1988).

Overall, the industry, in its primitive form, remained an appendage to agriculture and there had not arisen much possibility for interlinkages. But, the growing specialisation and increasing division of labour caused spatial and organisational separation between industry and agriculture. Simultaneous progress in technology and product diversification in input and output markets had resulted in the emergence of interlinkages between industry and agriculture, which became stronger over the period of time (Eapen 2003). Hirschman (1958) was the first to consider 'production linkages' as inducement mechanisms for stimulating economic activities through backward and forward linkages. He considered backward linkages as those related with input provision and the forward linkages as those related with the utilisation of output. Similarly, Nurkse (1961) based on the idea of 'linked progress' advocated the simultaneous movement of both farming and manufacturing sectors irrespective of the temporal differential in their equilibrium rates of growth. Kuznets (1968) opined that industrialisation facilitates agricultural transformation as a coincident revolution in agricultural productivity releases human resources to industry and therefore, technological advancement should support both. Kalecki (1960) too observed that the rapid development of industry requires investment and technological advances in agriculture. So a revolutionary upsurge in agricultural production becomes the basic prerequisite for rapid industrialisation of an underdeveloped economy.

Though the theoretical models such as Hymer and Resnick (1969) and Ranis and Stewart (1993) focused attention on agriculture–industry interaction, a pioneering attempt to specify, empirically and quantitatively, the agriculture–industry linkages was made by Harriss (1987a, b). Harriss conceptualised the linkage of small industries with agriculture in two ways: first, by exploring the nature of their linkage in terms of forward, backward or consumption links besides exploring whether these links are direct or indirect; second, by interpreting the linkages in terms of (three types of) flows, viz. commodity flows, flows of finance (private investment capital, wages, interest, state revenue and expenditure) and labour (location, migration and wages). In this line, the macro-economic models have examined the impact of growth in the agricultural sector on the industrial segment. The empirical studies, for example in case of India, had found that 1 % growth in the agricultural output increases industrial output by 0.5 % and national income by 0.7 % (Rangarajan 1982).

Given these theoretical insights into the relation between agriculture and industrial sector, it is interesting to notice that the Punjab's economy due to its plain fertile lands, vast irrigation canals and transportation network has remained primarily an agricultural economy for a long time. However, there emerged various conditions that contributed to the emergence of sound manufacturing sector. These conditions are discussed below.

12.3 Conditions Shaping the Evolution of Manufacturing Sector in Punjab

12.3.1 Public Investment and the Commercialisation of Agriculture

In 1849, the British annexed Punjab. However, the ruling groups were not replaced but confirmed as useful intermediaries between state and people and this partnership got further consolidated with their vital support to the British for suppressing the first war of independence in 1857. This cooperation continued with Punjab's contribution of manpower and logistic support to help British subdue and police territories both in South Asia and overseas. Over half of the British Indian army was recruited from Punjab and the people of this province were called (by the British) the 'Martial Races' of India (Ali 1988). By the early 1860s, the British desired the extension of cultivation to hitherto barren inter-fluvial tracts, or *doabs* of western Punjab. This region was sparsely populated by semi-nomadic pastoralists and was much underdeveloped. By mid-1880s, these barren lands got irrigation by way of tapping the water resources of western rivers with perennial canals, their branches and distributaries.

The canalisation of this region was done at such a massive scale that by 1947, there emerged one of the largest irrigation systems of the world. A total of nine projects were accomplished. The largest irrigation system was of the Lower *Chenab* whose irrigated land was over 2,000,000 acres. The irrigation system of Lower *Bari Doab* and *Nili Bar* irrigated over 1,000,000 acres each. Other irrigation systems were Lower *Jhelum* (450,000 acres), *Sidhnai* (250,000 acres), *Chunian* (100,000 acres), *Sohag Para* (90,000 acres), Upper *Doab* (80,000 acres) and Upper *Jhelum*

Table 12.1 Financial record of the productive irrigation canals of the Punjab in 1926–27

Particulars	Rs.
1. Total capital outlay at the end of 1926–27	291,548,419
2. Total accumulated surplus revenues	582,701,089
3. Total area irrigated and assessed to water rates	10,466,574
4. Direct revenue assessed during the year 1926–27	40,001,726
5. Indirect receipts	19,237,637
6. Total assessed receipts (4 + 5)	59,239,363
7. Working expenses for the year 1926–27	17,316,353
8. Net assessed revenue for the year 1926–27	41,923,010
9. Percentage earned over total capital outlay in the year 1926–27 (8 as percentage of 1)	14.38 %

Source Paustian (1930, p. 145)

(40,000 acres) colonies[2] (Ali 1987, p. 114).[3] This investment in irrigation remained much profitable to the British. By 1926–27, the total accumulated surplus revenues of the canals were approximately twice as large a sum as the total capital cost of the productive irrigation canals combined. For the year 1926–27 alone, these canals earned a net surplus equivalent to 14.38 % of the total capital investment in these canals (Table 12.1). With the completion of various works in the later years, the net revenue as a percentage of total capital invested increased further to 16.3 % for the period 1937–46 (Islam 1997).

Another major public investment was made in extension of transport facilities, especially railways. Table 12.2 provides the chronology of railway expansion in British Punjab. The railway mileage, which was 410 in 1872–73 increased to 5,500 in 1932–33—a more than 13 times increase. By 1936, when Calvert wrote his *Wealth and Welfare of the Punjab*, the railway network was so well-developed that there were "very few places more than 25 miles from a line. The 660 stations were served on an average 50 villages apiece" (p. 109). Both these interventions by the British proved significant. The canal irrigation made possible the reclamation of large tracts of waste land and the railways gave an added impetus.

Improvements in general communication facilitated the cultivation of crops like wheat, cotton, other cash crops, cereals and pulses, etc., and there took place an extension in acreage under various crops. Table 12.3 indicates that cereals and pulses retained a major share of cultivated area. Wheat occupied second place as it was cultivated over more than one-sixth of total cultivated area. It was mostly grown in canal colonies and was exported to different European markets, particularly after the opening up of Suez Canal in 1869. The cultivation of cash crops also gained significance over time. The decennial acreage under cash crops became

[2]A large chunk of this canal-irrigated area came to the share of Pakistan at the time of India's independence in 1947.

[3]See, Footnote 9.

Table 12.2 Chronology of railway expansion in British Punjab

Period	Details of railway expansion
1861–70	By 1861, the first railway line was opened between Karachi and Kotri
	By 1862, Lahore was connected to Amritsar
	By 1870, this line was extended to Ghaziabad (in east) and Multan (in south)
1871–80	By 1873, line from Lahore to Jhelum was constructed
	By 1878, a line from Kotri to Lodhran and Multan was opened
1881–90	By 1883, line from Lahore to Peshawar was constructed
1891–00	By 1891, Delhi-Ambala-Kalka railway line was opened
	By 1896, the canal colonies were linked by extending railway line to Lyallpur
	Between 1895–00, the Wazirabad-Sangla Hill-Khanewal line was opened
	By 1897, Delhi-Bhatinda-Samasata line was opened and then brought to Lahore
1901–10	By 1903, Malakwal-Shorkot Road line was opened
	By 1907, Shahdara was linked to Sangla Hill
1911–20	By 1911, line from Shorkot Road to Chichoki Mallian was opened

Source Calvert (1936, pp. 107–108)

Table 12.3 Decennial acreage under different crops ('000 acres)

Crops	1906–15		1916–26		1927–36		1937–46	
	Acres	%	Acres	%	Acres	%	Acres	%
Cereals and pulses	7,214	25.70	8,024	27.13	8,656	27.61	10,031	30.7
Wheat	4,446	15.84	4,912	16.61	5,183	16.53	5,843	17.88
Minor cereals	1,940	6.91	1,917	6.48	2,059	6.57	2,638	8.07
Cash crops	1,739	6.20	2,549	8.62	3,180	10.14	3,350	10.25
Cotton	1,035	3.69	1,588	5.37	2,163	6.90	2,458	7.52
Fodder	1,614	5.75	2,289	7.74	2,794	8.91	3,483	10.66
Others	10,083	35.92	8,299	28.06	7,321	23.35	4,875	14.92
Total sown area	28,071	100	29,578	100	31,356	100	32,678	100

Source Based on Islam (1997, p. 69)

almost twice in 1937–46 period than that in 1906–15 period. Besides other cash crops, it was cotton that gained significance during this period. Its acreage became more than double. It is learned that various economic incentives along with availability of canal irrigation, transport and communication facilities led to increased cultivation of various crops in the province.[4]

[4]Banerjee (1982, pp. 47–76) provides a detailed account of the growth of commercial agriculture in Punjab during the British rule.

Nonetheless, the state failed to provide a determined developmental stimulus and as a consequence, Punjab remained an underdeveloped region. It is noteworthy that under the colonisation policy of the state, the land distribution by the state was governed by the need of the British to consolidate their political position for fulfilling military requirements and to maintain an extractive system for financing their administration. The studies like Ali (1988) have found no evidence of state's utilisation of significant proportion of its surplus on developmental activities in the province.[5] A major part of the revenue from canal colonies was sent to the Centre where it was utilised for military expenditure and for the maintenance of imperialist political and administrative superstructure and the rest was used for administrative expenses within the province, largely on irrigation, revenue and police departments.

12.4 Capital Accumulation and the Transformation of Agrarian Surpluses

The agriculture sector generated economic surplus—a large part of which was appropriated by the state as land revenue. The land revenues were based on initial assessment and were to remain in effect for some years. Afterwards, they were revised (generally upwards). Such mechanism was generally inelastic to economic fluctuations and bad harvest. As a result, there remained little possibilities for capital accumulation by the peasantry; rather the farmers had to approach *Sahukars* for meeting their land revenue obligations and other crop and non-crop related expenses. These *Sahukars* were largely engaged in the profession of money-lending and their rates of interest were generally usurious.

As far as the rights over land were concerned, the British conferred occupancy rights of land in canal colonies to the cultivating classes, mostly *Jats*. These rights were converted automatically into the proprietary rights after 10 years of cultivation. Such a provision provided easy (and profitable) collateral against which the money-lenders provided credit to the peasantry.[6] The widespread indebtedness led to the displacement of Zamindars' ancestral holdings to the money-lenders at a large scale. Having observed such massive mortgages and being alarmed by the impending political and economic crisis, the field officer Thorburn published his monograph *Musalmans and Money-Lenders in the Punjab* in 1886.[7] This attracted

[5]Similar has been the observation made by Mukherjee (1985, p. 65) as she points out "Yet in spite of all these 'advantages', there is no evidence of a progressive transformation of agriculture along capitalist lines, either by the index of a rapid increase in productivity through investment of capital in agricultural production, or by that of a growth of capitalist relations in agriculture".

[6]Such a choice by the money-lenders was also guided by the fact that they were not granted any rights over the land.

[7]An Indian reprint of this monograph got published in 1983, see, Thorburn (1983).

the attention of the British authorities and subsequently, the state passed the 'Punjab Alienation of Land Act' in 1901. Under this act, the alienation of land among the members of agricultural tribes was permitted but the sales by agriculturists to persons not belonging to the agricultural tribes were prohibited. It also prohibited village artisans and menials (*dalits*) to possess land.

As a consequence, the position of agriculturist money-lender got strengthened with the elimination of *Sahukars* from the land market. But, this Act did not result in the virtual withdrawal of the *Sahukars* from the rural economy as they continued to extend credit to the Zamindars. But they took care in making advances by keeping in mind the circumstances and position of the client. Besides this, they also learned to manipulate the law. They devised a new type of *benami* mortgage by which they used to get rich agriculturists buy land and then transfer the property (informally) to them. Thus, the overall accumulation of agrarian surplus remained confined to the land market.

12.5 Evolution of Manufacturing Segment

The non-cultivating classes, in response to the Punjab Alienation of Land Act, 1901, sought other alternatives for investing their surplus money. There was a diversion of capital from money-lending to trade and commerce. It marked a new chapter in Punjab's rural economy. The industry being a lucrative option due to inbuilt talents of artisans (like *Ramgarhias*) resulted in the growth of numerous cottage and small-scale industries. Various manufacturing activities in these industries were pursued and the people got skilled in cloth weaving, utensil making, basket weaving, ivory carving, wood carving, metal inlay work, etc. (Latifi 1911).

The *Khaddar* industry gained prominence. Owing to moderately cold climate, there was a demand for coarse clothing and the *Khaddar* was well suited to peoples' needs. The raw material was obtained locally and the industry was pursued as a home industry. Similarly, the mill yarn hand-loom weaving was also dominant and the most important centres were Hoshiarpur, Jalandhar, Ludhiana, Amritsar, Gurdaspur and Sialkot districts (Chitra 1948, p. 155). A number of Momins or Julahas were engaged in this industry and a variety of cloth articles like dhoties, sarees, chaddars, coatings, shirtings, towel, lungis, shawls and carpets were manufactured.

Woollen industry also got significance as the famous woollen weaving centres were Ludhiana, Dera Gazi Khan, Bhera, Amritsar, Panipat and Dhariwal. Most of the wools were produced locally and the finest material came from Hissar. The products of this industry were rugs, shawls, namdas (coloured felts), hosiery goods, serges and pile carpets. The pile carpets of Amritsar and Multan were famous. Similarly, the silk looms employing thousands of workers were located at Amritsar, Lahore, Multan and Jalandhar. Earlier the raw material was imported from China but with passage of time, it was produced locally. This industry produced articles such as turbans, waist bands, sarees, fringes, tassels and pyjama strings. The embroidery units emerged as a significant branch of this industry. The embroidery

Table 12.4 Registered factories and workers in undivided Punjab during 10 years preceding the partition

Year	Number of factories	Number of working factories	Number of workers
1937	862	798	69,473
1938	887	780	72,268
1939	917	800	78,302
1940	927	780	81,197
1941	1,032	906	1,07,321
1942	1,107	998	1,32,728
1943	1,191	1,110	1,43,166
1944	1,253	1,157	1,47,732
1945	1,343	1,206	1,55,990
1946	1,450	1,255	1,57,584

Source Anwar (1953)

work was done on cotton, wool and silk. The *Phulkari* (flower) work flourished and was adopted as a domestic industry done mostly by the females in the household.

It was only with the recommendations of the Fiscal Commission (appointed in 1921) that there emerged an era of significant industrial evolution in the state. The number of industries rose to 673 in 1932–33 from 296 in 1921.[8] The cotton textile industry was the prime manufacturing industry of Punjab. It produced yarn and piece-goods. This industry got stimulus during the World War I due to increased military requirement of government and the shrinking of imports from Lancashire. The non-cooperation movement also provided some stimulus but the industry had to suffer due to Japanese competition in the subsequent years. The suffering got accentuated to such an extent that the government had to exempt excise duty in addition to various other measures.[9]

Punjab was also a major producer of sugarcane but there was non-existence of refined sugar industry. The Indian Tariff Board remarked in 1931, "although the Punjab grows about half a million acres of sugarcane, the prospects so far as the white sugar industry is concerned are limited to a small proportion of that acreage". There were seven sugar factories but all were suffering from competition from sugar produced in the United Provinces and imports from Java, Mauritius and Germany. Similarly, the government designed a cement factory in 1920 to fulfil its demand for irrigation and other civil works. The number of factories increased to 3 in 1933 and 6 in 1939 which employed 561 and 835 persons, respectively. There were few other large-scale industries like paper industry, glass industry, foundry industry, breweries and distilleries.

Table 12.4 indicates that there were a considerable number of registered factories in undivided Punjab before partition that employed thousands of workers. There

[8]It increased further to 887 in 1939 (as per the Annual Report on the Working of the Indian Factories Act in the Punjab, as quoted in Saini (1975)).

[9]For a detailed protection to the industry, see Saini (1975, pp. 263–265).

was a spurt in the evolution of registered factories during the war years of 1941–44. The number of registered factories during this period increased considerably. In 1946, the total number of existing factories recorded an increase of 68 % over those of 1937 while the workers employed were more than double the number of 1937.

12.6 Event of Partition and the Shattering of Punjab's Industrial Economy

At the eve of Independence, Punjab was a well-balanced economic region possessing economic resources in such a way that every sub-region was vital for the prosperity of the other. Nonetheless, there were marked disparities in the development of various sub-regions within the province. Industrially, the East Punjab got little attention and there was a high concentration of industrial activity in western districts.[10]

With the end of British rule in 1947, another nation, viz. Pakistan was formed and the greater Punjab was bifurcated—the Pakistani and Indian sides were called West Punjab and East Punjab respectively. Following the partition, there was a large-scale migration and displacement of non-Muslims and Muslims from West and East Punjab, respectively. It was not a peaceful resettlement of the population; rather there took place widespread communal disturbances and massive blood-shed on both sides of the border.

As far as the industrial economy is concerned, it is learned that the partition disturbed raw material sources, markets and finance mechanisms. The East Punjab emerged as a great loser as it used to depend more on West Punjab not only for its supplies of raw materials like wheat, cotton, lime, coal, gypsum, salt and wool, etc., but also for its markets.[11] Moreover, the wealth and development resources that came to the share of East Punjab were considerably small.[12] A large number of factories at important city centres such as Lahore, Multan, Lyallpur, Gujranwala, Sialkot and Wazirabad which had flourished on the account of generations-long sunk capital and finance of non-Muslims, were left in Pakistan. The industrial centres of Rawalpindi, Sialkot, Lahore, Wazirabad and Gujranwala were built largely by non-Muslims and in these industrial centres, about 400 industrial establishments, valued at nearly Rs. 40 crores, belonged to non-Muslims (Rai 1965, p. 137). The Muslims in East Punjab left about 1,000 establishments which were of

[10]Anwar (1953) points out that at the eve of independence, 40 % of the industry of the Punjab was located in Lahore alone.

[11]For example, 30 % of the output of the hosiery industry was readily consumed in the markets of West Punjab.

[12]In the agricultural sector, the refugees in East Punjab had to bear the net loss of about 20 lakh acres of land besides their compromise with the land quality. Moreover, the East Punjab got only three million canal-irrigated acres out of a total of over fourteen million acres.

Table 12.5 Status of industry in East and West Punjab at the time of independence

Industry type	East Punjab		West Punjab	
	No. of factories	No. of workers	No. of factories	No. of workers
Textiles	106	14,071	16	20,074
Engineering	79	6,437	154	24,135
Minerals and metals	67	3,691	75	7,666
Food, drink and tobacco	40	3,562	39	4,295
Chemicals, dyes, etc.	18	1,548	36	2,816
Paper and printing	8	1,733	42	3,899
Wood, stone and glass	14	1,067	38	7,789
Tanneries	2	106	3	1,954
Gins and presses	72	4,155	178	14,843
Miscellaneous	9	6,654	21	22,000
Total	415	43,024	602	1,09,471

Source Vakil (1950, p. 151)

very poor nature. Similarly, a number of famous industrial institutions were lost in West Punjab.[13] Out of the total number of factories in Punjab, East Punjab received 415 factories (employing 43,024 workers) whereas West Punjab got 602 factories (employing 1,09,471 workers) (Table 12.5).

The exodus of Muslim skilled labour from East Punjab crippled industries like hosiery, metal works, tanning and leather and lac industry in which Muslims formed a majority of skilled and semi-skilled labours.[14] Being already backward in industrial development, the East Punjab suffered greatly as most of factories and workshops were closed. The carpet and basket weaving, foundry and engineering industries which were mostly run by Muslims suffered seriously. A survey conducted by the East Punjab Board of Economic Inquiry revealed that in border districts of Amritsar, Jalandhar, Gurdaspur, Firozpur and Ludhiana, most of the industries had to remain understaffed due to the migration of Muslims which formed 54 % of the total workers. The shortage of labour led to a sharp increase in wage rates which rose from Rs. 48 per month in 1946–47 to Rs. 63 per month in 1947–48. The total gross value of industrial output also fell from Rs. 12.5 crores in 1946–47 to Rs. 10 crores in 1947–48 (Vakil 1950, pp. 146–147).

[13]Prime among them had been the Craik Technical Institute, the Dyeing and Calico Printing Institute, the Weaving Demonstration Factory, the Central Pottery Agency, etc.

[14]As many as 18,54,188 Muslims belonging to 22 different tribes of artisans and menials migrated to Pakistan. They constituted 38.6 % of the total Muslim population of the Punjab (GoP 1950, p. 159).

Textile and hosiery industry suffered due to shortage of raw materials and markets. The woollen industry which was one of the best organised industries in East Punjab was considerably dislocated. Earlier, it used to get a good supply of its long staple wool from Pakistan but now, the inadequacy of this raw material affected its output significantly. Similarly, a majority of skilled workers employed by this industry were Muslims and their migration to Pakistan caused scarcity of skilled workmen, which led to a decline in its value added.[15] Similar had been the plight of hosiery industry, which was mainly concentrated in Ludhiana (East Punjab). There had been a loss of business confidence and there took place a flight of capital from East Punjab. The banking facilities also got dislocated. The fear and panic of partition discouraged investment and the availability of adequate capital became a major problem. Moreover, the locational disadvantage of the state having a border along a hostile country could not attract capital from other states.

12.7 Rebuilding from the Wrecks of Partition

After partition, the East Punjab was left as an industrially backward region and the damage caused was so wide and rampant that it was not possible to rehabilitate the dislodged industrial economy without strenuous effort by the state. The state government without losing time took the help of central government in providing liberal financial assistance, raw materials, new sites for industrial establishments and the training facilities in different lines to the displaced persons and others. A significant proportion of migrated Hindus and Sikhs were not used to rural life and farming occupation and there was a little scope of accommodating them in agricultural sector. So, new townships and industrial areas near the principal cities were established. There were very few persons who could bring their wealth and after losing their hoards, the erstwhile rich had to make a fresh start in their struggle for existence. The state aptly modified the 'State Aid to Industries Act, 1935' to help the small industrialists.[16] Table 12.6 informs about the financial help provided by state to industrialists during 1948–49 to 1950–51 period. This liberal financial assistance inspired confidence among worn-out industrialists.

Owing to the difficulty in accommodating large number of refugees and the simultaneous demand for skilled labour, the state drew up schemes for providing short-term training courses to displaced persons. It provided accommodation, raw materials, etc. By the end of 1949–50, 17 demonstration parties trained 1,570

[15]Vakil (1950) points out that for India, the value of products manufactured got increased from Rs. 6.9 crores in 1946 to Rs. 8.2 crores in 1947 but for East Punjab, it has fallen from Rs. 2.2 crores in 1946 to Rs. 1.4 crores in 1947. Similarly, the value added by manufacture in East Punjab decreased from Rs. 86 lakhs in 1946 to Rs. 59 lakhs in 1947.

[16]Earlier the loans advanced under this Act needed some immovable property as security but after partition, it provided loans up to Rs. 2000 merely on two good personal securities without their having to pledge any property for the purpose.

Table 12.6 Financial help (in Rs.) provided by the state to industrialists

	1948–49	1949–50	1950–51
Loans	3,72,500	4,26,450	2,99,200
Subsidies	1,24,246	83,561	33,300
Grants-in-aid	–	8,000	1,000
Total	4,96,746	5,18,011	3,33,500

Source GoP (1952)

persons. State also awarded a number of scholarships and stipends to encourage training.[17] Nonetheless, their effort remained inadequate. So, the Industries Department undertook the task of establishing various vocational training centres to provide short-term courses with intensive training in various small-scale industries. Through these centres, training in carpentry, smithy, foundry, moulding and welding, oil pressing, manufacture of surgical instruments, utensil making, hosiery, leather goods, cycle repairs, etc. was provided in almost every important city of Punjab. Moreover, the state also arranged special training programmes for the widows living in widow homes. The state also opened up cotton and wool spinning and weaving centres at several places. These centres provided work to 14,000 spinners and 1,400 weavers. Moreover, in 1949, the state stopped giving free rations to displaced persons in refugee camps to force them to work. Many centres were closed and the important refugee camps were turned into 'Work Centres' for providing training facilities and the gainful employment.[18] By the end of 1950, there were 15 work centres[19] left with a total capacity of 1400 workmen.

All this gave a fillip to the revival of manufacturing sector. Soon came the era of planned economic development. Although the First Five Year Plan laid special emphasis on agriculture, the efforts of state government were also directed towards industrial development in the state. During this plan period, the vacuum created due to migration of skilled labour was filled up and most of uprooted small-scale industries were rehabilitated. Six industrial areas at Jalandhar, Ludhiana, Jagadhari, Panipat, Sonepat and Bahadurgarh (covering a total area of 1,576 acres) were established. Jalandhar and Batala emerged as centres of sports good industry; Ludhiana started gaining significance for cycles and sewing machine parts industry; Jagadhari started producing high-class plywood and Sonepat started manufacturing cycles. Similarly, the textile industries of Amritsar started working at their full capacity and the manufacturing of machine tools and agricultural implements in Ludhiana had become known throughout the country.

[17]Significant among these have been 29 Gandhi Memorial Scholarships for students specialising in various crafts. Five of these scholarships valued £300 each for training abroad. The rest carried Rs. 100 per month each for training within the country.

[18]Initially, the state started forty two such centres to teach a number of crafts. The state also paid, for the first 3 months, stipends to facilitate them during the initial training period but thereafter, the trainees were paid standard daily wages.

[19]These work centres operated at Jalandhar, Ludhiana, Abdullapur, Panipat, Sonepat, Rohtak and Hissar.

An Industrial Finance Corporation was set up. It provided liberal loans to various industries. By the end of 1964–65, it provided cumulative loans worth Rs. 71,588 since its inception in 1953–54 (GoP 1968). A vigorous drive was also carried out for integrating various small-scale industries on cooperative lines for increasing their efficiency and economic functioning. Moreover, the state made provision for marketing facilities and raw materials, quality marketing for industrial goods, testing, finishing, heat treatment and other common facility services. It was also thought that there should be a diversification of current industrial nature and thereby a move for the establishment of some large and medium industries like the newsprint mill, a cement factory, a large factory for steel production and structural machine tools was made but these initiatives could not be implemented due to Chinese aggression in 1962. There was another setback of Indo-Pak conflict in 1965 to Punjab's industrial economy, which caused a flight of capital from the state.

Nonetheless, the state set up industrial estates at Ludhiana, Malerkotla, Batala, Nilokheri and Sonepat at a total cost of Rs. 74.97 lakhs and consequently, by the end of third Five Year Plan, there were 13 urban and 34 rural industrial estates. The efforts made during the first three Five Year Plans helped Punjab in achieving some progress, notably in the field of small-scale industries. The contribution from the industries to the total state income has increased progressively over the years and rose from 10.2 % in 1952–53 to 16.4 % in 1964–65. By 1964, the number of registered working factories alone increased by 111.7 % over 1956 and the number of workers engaged increased by 84.8 % over the same period.

This period also witnessed a series of agitations by the Hindus and the Sikhs to assert their demand for a separate state—as a consequence of which, there took place Punjab's reorganisation on a linguistic basis. Three states, viz. Punjab, Haryana and Himachal Pradesh, were formed. It gave shock to industrial economy that had just started to recover. All the registered paper and glass factories had gone to Haryana. Similarly, the developing industrial complex around Delhi came to the share of Haryana and whatever mineral and forest resources were available had gone to either Haryana or Himachal Pradesh. As a result, the new state of Punjab was left with 8 urban and 20 rural estates. There were only 4,069 factories registered under the Factories Act in 1965. Out of them, 3,544 were actually working and were employing 1,03,654 workers. Only 7 of these factories employed 1,000 or more workers and none exceeded 5,000 workers. There were 14,589 units registered with the Industries Department for the purpose of getting loans and the supply of scarce raw material, etc. These units provided employment to 1,26,058 workers. Thus, at the eve of Green Revolution, Punjab became once again a less important state in terms of its industrial development. It remained primarily an agricultural state with more than 70 % of its population dependent on agriculture.

12.8 Industrial Evolution During Post-green Revolution Period

Owing to the adoption of Borlaug seed-fertiliser technology during the mid-1960s, the state of Punjab made remarkable achievement in the production of food grains. Such an advent has been aptly known as the Green Revolution (Wolf 1969). The agriculture sector became more productive. The rapid growth of agriculture had a large impact on the entire economy. As far as the industrial sector is concerned, the increasing use of new agricultural technology stimulated the demand for intermediate inputs like fertilisers, pesticides, power, diesel, capital goods (like electric motors, diesel engines, tractors, threshers, etc.) and other consumption goods. In response to this newly emerging demand, there emerged vibrant engineering and hand-tool industries.

There also emerged industries processing agricultural products. Increasing per capita income levels of large rural population provided a push to all sorts of consumption goods industries. The food processing industries like dairying, grain mills, edible oil manufacturing, breweries and beverage industry recorded rapid expansion. Similarly, a big spurt took place in the production of textiles and durable consumer goods like sewing machines, radios, bicycles, television sets, etc. (Bhalla 1995). This period also witnessed a significant urbanisation of Punjab in response to agricultural marketing cum trading activities. The urban population grew by 44.5 % during 1971–81 period, which was higher than 25 % growth during the previous decade. As a consequence of growing urbanisation and agricultural prosperity, there emerged a clustering of numerous large and small-scale industries in large cities. Much of this clustering took place in those cities which were situated on the 'Grand Trunk' road from Delhi to Amritsar.

During the post-1980 period, the Punjab economy passed through the difficult phase of militancy when the life and livelihoods became insecure. It had an adverse impact on industry as well. Table 12.7 indicates that there has been an overall deceleration in industrial output and employment during the 1980–81 to 1990–91 period. The cotton textile industry was the major victim. However, the major growth in output was recorded mainly by industries such as beverages, tobacco and tobacco products, paper and paper products, rubber, plastic, petroleum and coal products and chemical and chemical products.

During 1990–91 to 2000–01 period, the overall industrial output grew by 31.61 % per annum and all the industries except beverages, tobacco and tobacco products recorded positive growth—the major growth was recorded by cotton textiles. Similarly, there has been a rise in employment in all the industries. It has been the post 2000–01 period when the output growth has been negative in almost all the industries. Such pattern indicates dismal performance of the manufacturing sector during recent times.

However, in order to gain a vivid picture of Punjab's industrial performance, it would be better to locate its growth experience vis-à-vis Haryana and Himachal Pradesh. It may be observed from Table 12.8 that the growth rate of Punjab's

Table 12.7 Industry-wise CAGR (%) of output and employment, 1980–81 to 2009–10

Industry type	Output			Employment			Employment elasticity of output		
	I	II	III	I	II	III	I	II	III
Food products	6.58	5.17	−21.33	11.37	2.97	33.22	1.73	0.57	−1.56
Beverages, tobacco and tobacco products	74.87	−32.55	−26.40	5.37	3.43	39.93	0.07	−0.11	−1.51
Cotton textiles	−11.24	29.53	−7.29	3.94	0.25	51.47	−0.35	0.01	−7.06
Woollen textiles, silk synthetics	2.95	9.59	−31.07	7.96	3.18	4.29	2.70	0.33	−0.14
Leather and fur products	2.31	0.51	−4.55	14.55	1.31	1.99	6.29	2.56	−0.44
Wood and wood products	6.03	3.49	−11.18	13.37	2.59	13.90	2.22	0.74	−1.24
Paper and paper products	17.11	7.02	−21.24	11.27	3.72	27.88	0.66	0.53	−1.31
Rubber, plastic, petroleum and coal products	15.43	6.40	−20.88	10.96	4.06	30.94	0.71	0.63	−1.48
Chemical and chemical products	15.08	2.74	−32.81	8.43	3.13	45.40	0.56	1.14	−1.38
Non-metallic mineral products	6.64	4.15	−6.55	10.73	3.47	20.33	1.62	0.84	−3.10
Basic metal and alloy industry	9.89	4.50	−22.66	5.42	3.86	38.21	0.55	0.86	−1.69
Metal products	4.01	5.49	−9.98	6.05	2.17	13.71	1.51	0.40	−1.37
Machinery except electrical machinery	1.98	8.67	−13.47	6.46	15.77	11.58	3.26	1.82	−0.86
Electrical machine apparatus, appliances supplies and parts	12.13	0.84	−22.10	10.35	18.27	−0.82	0.85	21.80	0.04
Transport equipments and parts	9.08	7.44	−20.50	5.61	20.86	8.72	0.62	2.80	−0.43
Other	3.60	5.18	−6.79	11.51	10.15	24.17	3.19	1.96	−3.56
Repair and personal services	28.68	3.88	−3.11	29.64	−1.95	−2.07	1.03	−0.50	0.67
All	−13.27	31.61	−17.95	−13.72	2.96	27.87	1.03	0.09	−1.55

Note 1 CAGR implies compound annual growth rate; output values are at constant prices (base 1993–94)
Note 2 Period I, II and III refer to 1980–81 to 1990–91 period, 1990–91 to 2000–01 period and 2000–01 to 2009–10 period
Note 3 Employment elasticity is estimated as the ratio of the growth rate of employment and output
Source GoP (2013)

Table 12.8 Trend growth rate (%) of manufacturing sector NSDP, (base 1993–94)

Period	Duration	Punjab	Haryana	Himachal Pradesh
Overall				
I	1970–71 to 1979–80	9.94	8.23	4.62
II	1980–81 to 1989–90	8.29	9.74	11.69
III	1990–91 to 1999–00	4.32	7.24	10.29
IV	2000–01 to 2009–10	10.28	7.20	11.69
Registered segment				
I	1970–71 to 1979–80	9.87	8.39	4.82
II	1980–81 to 1989–90	8.44	7.51	17.76
III	1990–91 to 1999–00	5.84	9.49	12.34
IV	2000–01 to 2009–10	8.67	6.49	12.01
Unregistered segment				
I	1970–71 to 1979–80	10.01	7.88	4.45
II	1980–81 to 1989–90	8.10	14.51	4.55
III	1990–91 to 1999–00	2.08	2.82	4.78
IV	2000–01 to 2009–10	12.23	9.02	9.44

Source Based on NSDP data provided by Central Statistical Organisation, New Delhi

manufacturing sector NSDP has been relatively high during period I. But, its position worsened in period II when Himachal Pradesh took the lead and it was followed by Haryana. Similar situation prevailed in period III. In period IV, there was an improvement and Punjab gained second position among the three states.

Looking across registered and unregistered segments, similar pattern is observed when Punjab's manufacturing sector performed well in period I followed by relatively worst performance in subsequent periods II and III. In period IV, the relative state of the performance remained same for registered segment but the unregistered segment recorded robust increase. Such relative state of under-performance depicts the sorry state of Punjab's manufacturing sector.

12.9 Key Concerns

In such comparative state of growth profile, it is evident that Punjab's manufacturing sector is experiencing tough times. In fact, most of the manufacturing enterprises in Punjab resemble the characteristics of informal enterprises which employ less than 10 workers. There is hardly any upgradation of technology in these units. Technology is largely exogenous and thereby a dearer option. As a consequence, the capital stock in these units remains largely obsolete. In such situation, these firms are trying to strive and survive through intensive and extensive usage of labour which adds to the vulnerability of the working class (Jain 2008, 2010b).

It is observed that the state government had an apathetic attitude to the woes of manufacturing sector. It did not provide adequate incentives for its better growth. At the same time, the Centre influenced the policy framework to the disadvantage of Punjab by way of giving special incentives to other congress-ruled states of Uttarakhand and Himachal Pradesh (Sharma 2014) which led to the shifting of industrial units to these states. Numerous pharmaceutical firms have shifted to Himachal Pradesh for availing tax benefits. Similarly, there has been a flight of big textile houses, viz. Vardhman, Nahar and Trident to Madhya Pradesh (Neel 2007). Recently, there are news for the shift of Ludhiana's bicycle industry, mainly to Bihar.

A glance at Punjab's industrial policy framework vis-à-vis Haryana, Gujarat, Maharashtra, Tamil Nadu and Karnataka reveals that all the states except Punjab are having very simple and straightforward norms for facilitating the ease of entry. All these states have considered very seriously the aspect of industrial growth and thus, they have offered various incentives. Similarly, they have also laid adequate emphasis on the development of infrastructure and human resources (Ahluwalia et al. 2007). It is also noteworthy that Punjab government has recently announced its new industrial policy. Most of the measures in this policy serve medium and large-sized units and it has remained mum over challenges faced by informal sector enterprises in competing business environs.

12.10 Strategy for Rejuvenating Punjab's Industrial Economy

There is a need to create a favourable economic environment at the policy level. The state should attract the large investors for setting-up mega projects. These projects due to their interlinkages with small firms would lead to the emergence of innumerable firms (of various levels) and it would be more economical to harness the economies of scale. In fact, the industrialists should be invited by the Chief Minister for having thorough discussion on setting-up new industrial ventures and there should be speedier clearance through single window system. The state may also think of inviting Punjabi diaspora for large-scale investment. Similarly, the state may consider the option of developing 'Special Economic Zones'.

Being an agricultural economy, there is a need to identify the major strengths. Its produces such as cotton, food grains, etc. has the potential of becoming a full-fledged industry. There is a need for undertaking high-value added activities in these industries. For this, Punjab may draw lessons from the successful experiences of various countries. In fact, there lies a large potential for developing the food processing industry. Earlier, the state in Punjab has invited large players such as PEPSI for making large investments. With some limitations, it has been a successful experience. The state should explore such avenues. In dairy sector, Amul's example is a classic one. While learning lessons from Gujarat, the state should promote the milk cooperatives.

Uninterrupted availability of electricity is a prerequisite for full capacity utilisation in the manufacturing sector. The state should make huge investments in strengthening the generation potentials. Similarly, there is a need for taking corrective measures at the distribution end. Regarding sales, it is observed that the state is cross-subsidising the agriculture sector by charging heavy tariff from the industrial sector. It is not conducive for healthy industrial development. Moreover, there is a need for promoting cogeneration and it should have attractive policy framework for buying surplus electricity. By drawing lessons from countries like Malaysia, the state may utilise the rice husk for electricity generation.

The state should institutionalise the skill development centres catering to the latest and practical needs of the industry. Given the fact that a large segment of the manufacturing sector in Punjab resembles the characteristics of informal enterprises, there is a need to develop a suitable policy framework for the promotion of these enterprises. It is often seen that the macro-economic policies tend to ignore and discriminate against the informal manufacturing sector. It should not happen rather these units should be provided incentives for improving their performance in various aspects like product quality, input usage, etc. An effort should also be made to facilitate these units against their problems linked with raw materials. Some policy mechanism can be thought of providing inputs to these units at reasonably right prices.

The availability of adequate credit is a major factor that mitigates the impact of risks posed by different problems. Most of the units in both rural and urban areas experience the inadequate availability of credit. Therefore, there is a need to improve the access of credit to these units. The availability of institutional credit at cheap rates should be ensured so as to protect these units from the clutches of usurious money-lenders in the informal credit markets. Smaller industrial units are left with the choice of meeting its needs through household savings. It has been generally held that smaller units, which are using household saving, do not take risk and expand their business. Therefore, there is a need for providing adequate financial support to these units.

It is noteworthy that the productivity of capital in Punjab has remained very low. There is a need to augment this. In fact, lower capital productivity is the result of obsolete technology, unreliable and inadequate supply of electricity and inadequacy of skilled manpower. Technology upgradation for small and tiny units is a substantive problem, which needs immediate solutions. The exogenous arrangements of technology are not only costly but they require continuous import of technology. Therefore, the technological development process needs to be endogenised. Cooperative R&D can be a possible choice where state should play a fundamental role to establish innovation institutions but small units should also contribute and work in close cooperation with the R&D units to solve the technology related problems. The continuous upgradation of technology may improve the quality of goods produced in unorganised industries.

Most of the small-scale units face the problem of marketing. They also face a considerable threat of competition from large firms so there is a need to support these units in this respect. The small manufacturing units should not be seen as competitors rather they should act complementary to the organised sector units with respect to access to markets, inputs, information and technology. There should be some effort at the macro level as well to raise the demand for their products. It is a widely supported fact that the poor people constitute a major group of buyers for the production of small-scale units so there is a need to design such policies that generate income for the poor and in turn, it would help in raising the demand for unorganised industry's production.

An effort should be made to augment the capabilities of the workforce by improving their access to education, training and health services. In addition, the small manufacturing units should be imparted necessary technical training and instruction in simple managerial techniques such as accounting and book keeping, marketing and technical know-how as these capabilities can yield great benefits at little cost.

Almost every worker in the small-scale manufacturing sector, unlike its counterparts in organised sector, faces insecurity of one kind or the other. There is a need to ensure some kind of security to these workers. Adequate transfer payments out of public funds are required to provide a safety net to these workers to protect them against occupational injuries and accidents, unemployment, work irregularity, etc. The self-employed workers working in the small and tiny units are incapable of generating sufficient surpluses for business expansion and decent living. Therefore, when the workers due to health problems or old age cannot work and earn the livelihood, then there is nothing to fall back upon. This brings in the issue of social security for the attention of the policy makers. Social security not only can solve the problems of old age, but will also allow the owners of small and tiny units to expand the size of the units by providing more labour who may work actively even in old age.

Above all, the availability of good infrastructure along with a non-corrupt, efficient administrative apparatus can be a major factor in facilitating these small manufacturing units towards their effort to emerge, compete and survive in a hostile economic environment. Good infrastructure-uninterrupted electricity and skilled manpower—is the precondition of any economic activity to flourish. It is the fundamental responsibility of the state to facilitate its provision. In fact, Punjab is deficient in both. Therefore, there is a need to tackle these problems on a priority basis. It would help in making small units more efficient and they would be able to compete in competitive business environments.

12.11 Concluding Remarks

Thus, this study outlines the process of evolution of the manufacturing segment in an otherwise agrarian state of Punjab. It also examines its growth performance over the period of time in both absolute and relative sense. Similarly, it raises the key concerns troubling the sustained growth of manufacturing segment in this state. It is interesting to notice that the industrial growth in the present-day Punjab is rooted in the wrecks of partition when the bare-foot entrepreneurs preferred to initiate small-scale manufacturing activities. Such initiatives were impressive as they were the need of those times but what is worrying is the fact that a large chunk of the manufacturing segment has remained small-scale in its nature which is highly uncompetitive. The small units are suffering from lack of access to technology, cheap credit and skilled manpower. There is a very limited use of ICT and the enterprises are mainly producing the third-class entrepreneurs. The state is virtually apathetic to the woes of small-scale enterprises. As a consequence, these enterprises in Punjab's manufacturing segment are at the verge of collapse. In such situation, the study suggests a set of policy measures that may play a crucial role in rejuvenating the industrial economy of the state.

References

Ahluwalia IJ, Chaudhuri S, Sidhu S (2007) Punjab industrial review. Study funded by the Department of Industrial Policy and Promotion, Government of India and United Nations Industrial Development Organisation

Ali I (1987) Malign growth? Agricultural colonization and the roots of backwardness in the Punjab. Past and Present 114(Feb.), pp. 110–132

Ali I (1988) The Punjab under imperialism, 1885–1947. Oxford University Press, Delhi

Anwar AA (1953) Effect of partition on industries in the border districts of Lahore and Sialkot, Punjab (Pakistan). Publication No. 105, Board of Economic Inquiry

Banerjee H (1982) Agrarian society of the Punjab, 1849–1901. Manohar Publications, New Delhi

Bhalla GS (1995) Agricultural growth and industrial development in Punjab, pp 67–112. In: Mellor JW (ed) Agriculture on the Road to Industrialization, John Hopkins University Press, Baltimore

Bharadwaj K (1987) Analytics of agriculture-industry relation. Econ Polit Wkly 22(19, 20 and 21): AN15–AN20

Calvert H (1936) The wealth and welfare of the Punjab, 2nd edn. The Civil and Military Gazette Ltd, The Mall, Lahore

Chitra VR (ed) (1948) Cottage industries of India (Guide book and symposium). Silpi Publication, Madras

Eapen M (2003) Rural industrialisation in kerala: reexamining the issue of rural growth linkages. Working paper no. 348, Centre for Development Studies, Thiruvananthapuram, Kerala (India)

Eltis W (1988) The contrasting theories of industrialization of Francois Quesnay and Adam Smith. Oxford Econ Papers 40(2):269–288

GoP (1950) Statistical abstract Punjab, 1947–50. Public Relations Department, Government of Punjab, Research and Reference Division, Punjab

GoP (1952) Punjab: industrial statistics of the Punjab, 1947–48 to 1950–51. Economic and Statistical Advisor to Government, Punjab, Chandigarh

GoP (1968) Statistical abstract Punjab, 1967. Economic Advisor to Government Punjab, Chandigarh

GoP (2013) Statistical abstract Punjab, 2012. Economic Advisor to Government Punjab, Chandigarh

Harriss B (1987a) Regional growth linkages from agriculture. J Dev Stud 23(2):275–289

Harriss B (1987b) Regional growth linkages from agriculture and resource flows in non-farm economy. Econ Polit Wkly 22(1/2):31–46

Hirschman AO (1958) The strategy of economic development. Yale University Press, New Haven

Hymer S, Resnick S (1969) A model of an agrarian economy with non-agricultural activities. Am Econ Rev 59(4):493–506
Islam MM (1997) Irrigation, agriculture and the raj: Punjab, 1887–1947. Manohar Publishers and Distributors, New Delhi
Jain V (2008) An inquiry into the growth dynamics of Punjab's urban unorganised establishments: a labour perspective. Int J Bus Emerg Mark 1(2):171–188
Jain V (2010a) Dynamics of insecurity in India's informal sector: a study of manufacturing in Punjab. Unpublished Ph.D. Dissertation submitted to Jawaharlal Nehru University, New Delhi
Jain V (2010b) Wageworkers' exposure to discrimination and work-related insecurity in Punjab's urban unorganised establishments: a social class analysis, pp. 339–366, In: Gill SS, Singh L, Marwah R (eds) Economic and environmental sustainability of the Asian region, Routledge (Taylor & Francis), London, NewYork and New Delhi
Kalecki M (1960) Unemployment in underdeveloped countries. Indian J Labour Econ 3(2):59–61
Kuznets S (1968) Towards a theory of economic growth with reflections on the economic growth of nations. Norton, New York
Latifi A (1911) The industrial Punjab: a survey of facts, conditions and possibilities. Longmans, Green & Co., Bombay
Mukherjee M (1985) commercialization and agrarian change in pre-independence Punjab, pp. 51–104. In: Raj KN, Bhattacharya N, Guha S, Padhi S (eds) Essays on the commercialization of Indian agriculture, Oxford University Press, Delhi
Neel Kamal (2007) Punjab industries have new address. The Times of India, Chandigarh October 29
Nurkse R (1961) Patterns of trade and development. Basil Blackwell, Oxford
Paustian PW (1930) Canal irrigation in the Punjab: an economic inquiry relating to certain aspects of the development of canal irrigation by the British in the Punjab. Columbia University Press, New York
Rai SM (1965) Partition of the Punjab. Asia Publications, Delhi
Rangarajan C (1982) Agricultural growth and industrial performance in India. International Food Policy Research Institute, Washington, DC
Ranis G, Stewart F (1993) Rural non-agricultural activities in development: theory and application. J Dev Econ 40(1):75–101
Saini BS (1975) The social & economic history of the Punjab: 1901–1939 (including Haryana & Himachal Pradesh). ESS Publications, Delhi
Sharma A (2014) Special incentives to neighbouring states may force Punjab industry to flee. Hindustan Times, Punjab Jan 21
Singh L (2005) Deceleration of industrial growth and rural industrialization strategy for Indian Punjab. J Punjab Stud 12(2):271–284
Singh L, Jain V (2007) Growth and dynamics of unorganised industries in Punjab. Int J Bus Glob 1(1):60–87
Tewari M (1998) Intersectoral linkages and the role of the state in shaping the conditions of industrial accumulation: a study of Ludhiana's manufacturing industry. World Dev 26 (8):1387–1411
Tewari M (1999) Successful adjustment in Indian industry: the case of Ludhiana's woolen knitwear cluster. World Dev 27(9):1651–1671
Thorburn SS (1983) Musalmans and money-lenders in the Punjab. Mittal Publications, Delhi
Vakil CN (1950) Economic consequences of divided india: a study of the economy of India and Pakistan. Vora & Co. Publishers Ltd., Bombay
Wolf L (1969) The green revolution in Punjab: a field trip. Econ Polit Wkly 4(26):A73–A82

Chapter 13
Service Sector and Economic Growth in Punjab

Inderjeet Singh

13.1 Introduction

As an economy moves from the lower to higher stages of development, there occurs a shift from simpler to more modern and complicated techniques of production on the one hand and from primary to secondary and/or to tertiary sectors on the other. The status, and pattern and growth of tertiary sector coupled with state-of-the-art technology have its own implications for the future development patterns of a system. Worldwide, in the majority of countries, the service sector share in GDP has crossed the 60 % mark and is appearing as an engine of economic growth.

Punjab, a state in northern India, has been a leader in Green Revolution for the past four decades. Punjab followed an agro-centric model of development that provided higher income levels to the people of the state and the much required food security to the whole country. Now the negative externalities of the model of development have started appearing. As one of the fallouts of this model of development, compared to some other states of the country, the service sector has not been able to catch up due to some inherent impediments in the system. The emerging service sector in the economy is an outcome of new policy regime and legacy the development model followed. To transform the economy from a stagnant to a vibrant one and making the service sector an engine of growth, analysis of growth and tertiarization is the need of the hour. *In this context, this chapter is an attempt to analyze the structure, pattern, and growth of the Punjab economy with special reference to the service sector.*

I. Singh (✉)
Department of Economics, Punjabi University, Patiala 147002, India
e-mail: inderjeetsidhu@rediffmail.com

L. Singh and N. Singh (eds.), *Economic Transformation of a Developing Economy*, India Studies in Business and Economics,
DOI 10.1007/978-981-10-0197-0_13

13.2 Coverage and Methodology

Keeping in view the broad objectives of the study, the secondary data has been used. Data have been obtained from various published and unpublished sources. Most of the published data has been drawn from various issues of Statistical Abstracts of Punjab. The data used in the empirical exercise, carried out in this study, relates to estimates of State Domestic Product at constant prices in 2004–05. The data pertain to the three broad sectors, that is, primary, secondary, and tertiary; and for the subsectors of the tertiary sector. Analysis covers the period from 1970–71 to 2011–12. The total period has been divided into three sub-periods. First, the launching of Green Revolution in the state, second, the period of social and political turmoil, and third, the recovery period. Wherever needed, appropriate price adjustment has been done.

13.3 A Synoptic Review of Theory and Empirics

Empirics on sectoral growth and performance analysis draw their origin from the dual economy model of Lewis (1954) and Hirschman (1958), which attempt to explain economic growth by examining the role and relationship between the traditional agricultural sector and the modern manufacturing sector. There exist two opposing schools of thought on the relationship between the service producing sector and economic growth (Glasmeier and Howland 1993). The *first school of thought* is of the view that the service producing sector can aid economic growth; and the *second* is of the view that the service producing sector should not be seen as independent of, nor is it a replacement for, the traditional goods producing sector such as agriculture, mining, and manufacturing.

The available evidence indicates that the service producing sector has dominated the goods producing sector in most of the developed economies; it accounts for about two-thirds of employment and output in many advanced economies such as Canada and Australia (Economic Council of Canada 1991). The relationship between the service producing sector and economic growth must be viewed in terms of both the size of the sector in economic activity and to productivity gains. Increasingly, the service sector is seen as the key to economic growth in a postindustrial economy. As per S&P report, the East Asian region will have trouble in maintaining the growth momentum over the long term, if it continues to rely primarily on traded goods due to stiff competition from China and India (Standard and Poor 2007). Compared to the goods producing sector, the service sector is less likely to be export oriented and hence less likely to be affected by slowdown in growth of a major trading partner (Mansell 1985).

There are a large number of studies on the Indian economy that have explored the service sector and economic growth nexus (Pradhan et al. 2006; Nagaraj 2010;

Rashmi Banga 2005). There are very few studies on analysis of tertiary sector in a predominantly agrarian economy (Sawhney 2007). This paper is an attempt to fill this gap.

13.4 Analysis

In contrast to the overall Indian economy and other states of the Indian union, Punjab has been one of the most prosperous states of India in the past; however, it is losing its prosperity due to various economic and noneconomic causes. The decade of the 1970s has been an onset of Green Revolution and setting on of vibrancy in the system. The period of the late 1980s and early 1990s was a period of social turmoil that led to an uncertain future for the state. Punjab faced a dual problem in the new policy regime: first, recovery from the dark past and second reorienting the system to compete, liberalize, and privatize.

13.4.1 Structural Change in Terms of Sectoral Shares

The growth pattern of different sectors of the economy is the best indicator of structural change in an economy. Sector-wise gross state domestic product for Punjab is presented in Table 13.1. The table is indicative of the fact that the contribution of the tertiary sector in gross state domestic product has been on the

Table 13.1 Sector-wise gross state domestic product for Punjab at constant prices (2004–05) in Rs. Crores

Year	Sector						Total GSDP	
	Primary		Secondary		Tertiary			
	Amount	Percent	Amount	Percent	Amount	Percent	Amount	Percent
1970–71	9088	46.55	3125	16.01	7311	37.44	19,524	100
1975–76	10,626	44.06	4038	16.74	9455	39.20	24,119	100
1980–81	13,015	41.30	5149	16.34	13,351	42.36	31,515	100
1985–86	18,035	43.56	7339	17.73	16,032	38.72	41,406	100
1990–91	21,459	41.28	10,332	19.88	20,191	38.84	51,981	100
1995–96	25,183	39.23	14,839	23.12	24,166	37.65	64,187	100
2000–01	29,396	35.46	19,912	24.02	33,581	40.51	82,888	100
2005–06	31,936	31.14	26,632	25.97	43,988	42.89	102,556	100
2010–11	35,267	23.88	45,441	30.77	66,963	45.35	147,670	100
2011–12	36,022	23.03	46,854	29.96	73,534	47.01	156,411	100
2012–13	35,899	21.82	48,511	29.49	80,115	48.69	164,525	100

Source ESO, Govt. of Punjab, various publications

rise in the recent past. The gross state domestic product that used to be merely Rs. 19.52 thousand crores in the year 1970–71, became Rs. 51.98 thousand crores in 1990–91 and touched the level of nearly Rs. 164.53 thousand crores in the year 2012–13. Over the past four decades, the gross state domestic product has grown by almost 8 times. At the disaggregate level, the GSDP from the primary sector that was Rs. 9.09 thousand crores in the year 1970–71, touched the level of 35.90 thousand crore in 2012–13, i.e., rose to an almost 4 times level. The secondary sector has grown; from Rs 3.13 thousand crores in 1981–82 it registered the level of Rs. 48.51 thousand crores in 2012–13, a rise of almost 15 times. The tertiary sector that stood at Rs. 7.31 thousand crore has reached the level of 80.12 crore in the same period, which is 11 times the initial period. *Structural change is indicative of the fact that, the secondary and tertiary sectors are fast growing sectors of the economy compared to the primary sector.*

Temporal and spatial variation in sector-wise shares is the simplest possible way to represent structural change in an economy. Sector-wise percentage shares in gross state domestic product at factor cost for Punjab is also presented in Table 13.1. Temporal data covering the last four decades is indicative of the fact that in the beginning of the decade of the 1970s, the share of the primary sector was 46.55 %, followed by the tertiary sector share as 37.44 % and the secondary sector share as 16.01 %, in that order. At the onset of the decade of the 1990s, the share of the primary sector came down to 41.28 % and this fall was shared by the secondary and tertiary sectors; the secondary sector share rose to 19.88 % and the tertiary sector share to 38.84 %. In the year 2012–13, the tertiary sector touched the level of 48.69 % share in gross state domestic product, the share of the primary sector was 21.82 and that of the secondary sector 29.49 %. *Hence, in terms of contribution to gross state domestic product, the primary sector is losing the share and both secondary and tertiary are gaining ground. The tertiary sector has become a dominant sector, however, in terms of national/other state comparisons, Punjab is far behind. Hence, the nature and composition of this tertiary sector needs to be explored in detail.*

In terms of net state domestic product (Table 13.2), the relative position of three sectors is not much different. In terms of contribution to net state domestic product, the primary sector is losing its share and the other two sectors are gaining ground.

Subsector wise shares of the tertiary sector in GSDP in Punjab (Table 13.3) are indicative of the fact that in the decade of the 1970s, the leading sector in terms of share has been the 'other services' (33.61 %), followed by 'real estate, ownership of dwelling and business services' (27.71 %) and 'trade hotels and restaurants' (26.55 %). In the decade of the 1980s, the subsector, 'other services', which included professional services and support services, started losing, in terms of share and the decline accelerated in all the following decades. The decade of the 1980s also registered the start of a perpetual decline in the share of subsectors, 'trade, hotels and restaurants' and 'real estate, ownership of dwelling and business services'. In the 1980s and the following decades, some sectors that showed a continuous improvement in terms of shares have been, 'transport, storage and

Table 13.2 Sector-wise net state domestic product for Punjab at constant prices (2004–05) in Rs. Crores

Year	Sectors						Total NSDP	
	Primary		Secondary		Tertiary			
	Amount	Percent	Amount	Percent	Amount	Percent	Amount	Percent
1970–71	8348	46.63	2788	15.57	6769	37.80	17,904	100
1975–76	9853	44.43	3519	15.87	8802	39.69	22,173	100
1980–81	11,987	41.48	4396	15.21	12,518	43.31	28,901	100
1985–86	16,850	44.28	6194	16.28	15,006	39.44	38,051	100
1990–91	20,480	42.56	8844	18.38	18,801	39.07	48,126	100
1995–96	23,808	40.86	12,563	21.56	21,903	37.59	58,274	100
2000–01	27,714	37.19	16,441	22.07	30,357	40.74	74,512	100
2005–06	32,510	33.90	22,966	23.95	40,426	42.15	95,902	100
2010–11	64,052	31.70	51,384	25.43	86,589	42.86	202,025	100
2011–12	71,801	30.88	58,031	24.96	102,692	44.16	232,524	100
2012–13	80,047	30.26	65,363	24.71	119,128	45.03	264,537	100

Source ESO, Govt. of Punjab, various publications

Table 13.3 Subsector-wise shares of tertiary sector in GSDP, Punjab

Year	Subsectors of tertiary sector						Total tertiary sector
	TSC	THR	B&I	RE	PA	OTH	
1970–71	4.02	26.55	2.43	27.71	5.68	33.61	100
1975–76	4.15	30.64	2.33	23.05	4.98	34.84	100
1980–81	4.28	31.87	3.12	21.70	8.10	30.93	100
1985–86	5.12	31.02	4.31	21.36	8.19	30.00	100
1990–91	6.11	29.48	6.78	18.84	11.15	27.64	100
1995–96	7.52	29.83	7.84	17.78	10.64	26.38	100
2000–01	11.04	29.50	10.09	14.56	11.92	22.90	100
2005–06	15.38	28.10	11.65	13.03	10.88	20.95	100
2010–11	14.63	25.27	16.96	10.68	10.66	21.79	100
2011–12	14.54	25.30	17.86	10.13	10.35	21.82	100
2012–13	14.22	25.45	18.68	9.73	10.14	21.76	100

Note Abbreviations used in the table are as follows
TSC Transport, storage and communication
THR Trade, hotels and restaurants
B&I Banking and insurance
RE Real estate, ownership of dwelling and business services
PA Public administration
OTH Other service
Source ESO, Govt. of Punjab, various publications

communication' and 'banking and insurance'. This has been basically due to the natural momentum of the subsectors and demand pull forces generated by the rising income levels in the state.

Table 13.4 Sector-wise percentage share of estimated workforce

Level	Sectors	Year				
		1983	1993–94	1999–00	2005–06	2011–12
Punjab	Primary	67.93	56.74	53.23	44.90	36.45
	Secondary	12.75	15.63	17.51	22.10	30.52
	Tertiary	19.32	27.63	29.26	33.00	33.03
	Total	100.00	100.00	100.00	100.00	100.00
India	Primary	69.03	64.67	60.41	58.00	49.44
	Secondary	13.76	14.83	16.85	18.80	23.72
	Tertiary	17.21	20.50	22.74	23.20	26.84
	Total	100.00	100.00	100.00	100.00	100.00

Source NSSO reports, various issues

Social turmoil in the state during the 1980s and the early 1990 decades put the economy into crisis. *Investors and entrepreneurs in trade, hotels, restaurants, real estate, ownership of dwelling and business services lost interest in the state and capital out-flight took place in decade of 1980s and earlier 1990s. Activities complementary to these services, the professional services and support services also followed the same path. Social turmoil period witnessed a sharp rise in the share of 'public administration' due to heavy public expenditure on police, paramilitary forces, and related enormous paraphernalia.*

13.4.2 Structural Change in Terms of Distribution of Workforce

Sector-wise distribution of workforce in Punjab in relation to India is presented in Table 13.4. Throughout the period under consideration, the primary sector continued to be the largest employer of workforce in India and as well as in Punjab. Because of negligible mining and quarrying, the primary sector in Punjab is basically the agricultural sector and allied sectors. In 1983, the percentage of workforce employed in the primary sector was 67.93 %. In the temporal dimension, it was 53.23 % in 1999–2000 and went down to 36.45 % in 2011–12. The decline in workforce employed in agriculture has been faster in Punjab compared to the all-India level, yet the primary sector continues to be the largest employer. Further, the services sector is the second largest employer and the secondary sector has the least share in the sector-wise distribution of workforce over the period 1983–2011. *During the period under consideration, Punjab experienced a greater shift in workforce to the nonagricultural sectors compared to the country as a whole. It dispels the commonly held myth that Punjab historically being an agricultural economy has not experienced a major shift of workers outside the primary sector.*

Table 13.5 Subsector-wise percentage share of estimated workforce

Subsector of tertiary sector	Year				
	1983	1993–94	1999–00	2005–06	2011–12
Trade, hotels and restaurants	6.17	10.45	13.05	13.46	13.57
Transport, storage and communication	3.41	3.56	5.10	5.28	5.38
Banking and insurance	0.91	1.07	1.25	1.56	1.63
Public Adm. and community services	7.88	11.57	9.01	9.86	10.23
Other services	0.95	0.98	0.85	2.84	2.49
Total tertiary	19.32	27.63	29.26	33.00	33.30

Source NSSO reports, various issues

Subsector-wise analysis of tertiary sector for different years (Table 13.5) shows that within the tertiary sector from the employment share point of view, all the sectors have picked up slightly in the post-social turmoil period. Presently, in terms of workforce share, 'trade, hotels and restaurants' subsector has the highest share followed by the subsectors, 'public administration and community services' and 'transport, storage and communication', in that order. Compared to 1983, the share of subsectors, 'trade, hotels and restaurants', doubled by years 1999–2000; after that it almost stabilized to around 13 %.

The pattern of workforce within the tertiary sector in Punjab is indicative of the fact that there has not been any drastic change in the percentage distribution of workforce in most of the subsectors within the tertiary sector. The largest share in the state income now comes from the services sector. From the point of view of employment, though the primary sector still has the maximum share in sector-wise workforce, the share of the tertiary sector in workforce has been increasing over time.

13.4.3 Economic Growth Trajectory and Tertiary Sector

Various curves fitted to long-term series state domestic product, as a function of time, show that the GSDP of Punjab follows the exponential trend ($R^2 = 0.997$). Hence the exponential curve of SDP and time is the best measure of long-term expected growth trajectory of the state. This expected trajectory can be compared with the actual SDP series trajectory to identify the critical time points in the development of the state. GSDP series in comparison to linear and exponential trends are presented in graph (Appendix Graph 13.1). The growth trajectory of the state shows that there have been three critical points and four periods in the development trajectory of the state: (a) the Green Revolution take-off period (up to 1980–81); (b) social turmoil period (1980–81 to 1994–95); (c) Recovery from social turmoil period (1994–95 to 2006–07); and take-off period (2006–07 onwards). Growth trajectory of NSDP series (Appendix Graphs 13.2 and 13.3) also follows the exponential trend. Plotting of long-term NSDP along with exponential trend of the same shows that social turmoil heat was realized by the NSDP in 1981–82 and take-off period by the year 2006–07. This is almost in consonance with what we identified with curve analysis of GSDP series. This periodic analysis of the data can help us to capture the finer dynamics of the system.

The long-term growth rate of state domestic product of Punjab has been 5.08 % per annum (Table 13.6). On the onset of Green Revolution in Punjab, the GSDP grew at the rate of 5.28 % per annum. As expected, the growth engine was the primary sector that grew at the rate of 6.07 % per annum. It was followed by the secondary (5.53 % per annum) and tertiary sectors (4.48 % per annum), in that order. In the social turmoil period, the growth rate of GSDP went down to 4.88 per annum and the growth of the secondary sector was the highest (7.04 % per annum) followed by the primary (4.65 % per annum) and tertiary sector (4.08 % per annum), in that order. During the post-social turmoil period the annual growth rate of GSDP touched the lowest level of 4.46; except for slight improvement in the tertiary sector, the rest of the system faced a slowdown. The slight improvement of the tertiary sector has been partly due to the pay commission hike during this period. The commonly held opinion is that, during social turmoil period, there was out flight of capital and labor from the state. The secondary sector, due to its very nature, could not wind up and ran overnight to another destination. Heavy fixed capital and tight networking of debtors and creditor did not allow the industry to migrate immediately; rather, it tried to adjust itself to disturbed period, by adjusting working hours, dis-saving and maintaining the system even at a heavy transaction cost. Industry faced a crisis on multiple fronts. Supplies on credit from other states got affected adversely and other state customers and suppliers curtailed visiting

Table 13.6 Sector-wise growth profile of GSDP and NSDP in Punjab economy

Period/item	Primary	Secondary	Tertiary	Total
GSDP				
Green revolution take off	6.07	5.53	4.48	5.28
Social turmoil	4.65	7.04	4.08	4.88
Post social turmoil	2.34	5.19	5.91	4.46
Recovery	1.40	6.62	9.10	6.37
All	3.65	6.76	5.40	5.08
NSDP				
Green revolution take off	4.50	5.80	6.13	5.36
Social turmoil	4.91	7.04	3.85	4.86
Post social turmoil	2.53	4.96	5.73	4.36
Recovery	12.93	13.91	16.61	14.74
All	4.79	7.27	5.95	5.76

Source Calculated from ESO publication, various publications

Punjab. Banking, insurance coupled with transport, and communication growth provided the required short run cushion to the industry to stay in the state. Another saving grace has been that due to tough state administration and adverse environment in the state unionism and the resulting strikes and lockouts were also negligible during this period.

The growth trajectory is indicative of the fact that the secondary sector tried to sustain the higher growth rate even during the social turmoil but got shaken due to prolonged disturbance; much of the slowdown came in the post-social turmoil period. On the other hand, the services by their very foot loose nature started withdrawing immediately, as soon as the disturbance started in Punjab. It is during the recovery period that the economy has registered a growth of 6.37 % per annum and industry and services registered an annual growth rate of 6.62 and 9.10 % respectively.

Within the tertiary sector, a look at the temporal behavior of subsectors (Table 13.7) is indicative of the fact that during the Green Revolution take-off decade, 'banking and insurance' grew at the rate of 9.41 % per annum and during disturbance period its growth rate was 10.05 % per annum. In the post-social turmoil period, it suffered a slight reduction in terms of growth rate. The same is the behavior pattern of 'transport, storage and communication'.

Hence, during social turmoil, the industry by its very nature did not fly out to other states immediately during the disturbance period, but it could not sustain in the legacy of the turmoil period for a long time. Service sector activities like banking, finance, insurance, transportation, and communication maintained their pace during and after disturbance and provided a short-term cushion to the struggling secondary sector. Due to social turmoil in the state, the public administration system grew fast. Services like trading, hotels, restaurants, professional, and supportive services reduced their operations or migrated out. Now the state had entered

Table 13.7 Subsector-wise growth profile of tertiary sector in Punjab

	Transport, storage and communication	Trade, hotels and restaurants	Banking and insurance	Real estate, ownership of dwelling and business services	Public adm.	Other services
Green revolution take off	6.37	7.93	9.41	1.76	7.31	4.69
Social turmoil	7.53	3.28	10.05	2.54	8.57	2.94
Post social turmoil	14.99	5.40	8.08	2.74	6.02	3.54
Recovery	7.21	7.73	15.51	4.32	8.58	10.21
All	9.52	4.96	10.83	3.10	7.52	3.88

Source Calculated from ESO publication, various publications

Table 13.8 Credit-deposit (C-D) ratio in Punjab

Years	CD ratio in Punjab
1980	38.6
1985	44.6
1990	45.5
1995	41.4
2000	39.4
2005	50.1
2009	65.5
2010	71.1

Source Statistical tables relating to banks in India, reserve bank of India (various issues)

into a higher growth trajectory and the tertiary sector and secondary sectors were leading the growth.

Effect of social turmoil is clearly visible on the banking sector. Credit is the backbone of tertiarization and the credit-deposit ratio (Table 13.8) is the best approximation of banking operations in a region. Although the credit-deposit ratio in Punjab improved a lot during the past decade, it remained slightly subdued in the decade of the 1980s and 1990s. It was just 38.6 % in 1980 and 71.1 % in 2010. So, in the social turmoil period credit also shied away from the region.

As per development economics, investment-GDP ratio is the best determinant of the growth and development of a region. Table 13.9 shows the ratio of investment to GDP in Punjab in comparison to all over India. During 1980–81, the investment-GDP ratio that was mere 15.6 %, rose to 21.6 % in 1985–86 and then to 24.2 % in 1989–90. Later, 1989–90 onwards, there was a continuous decline in the investment GDP ratio with minor exceptions. Investment-GDP ratio that was 20.6 % in 2001–02 went down and was 14.5 % in 2009–10. Throughout the period under consideration, it has been much lower than the national investment-GDP ratio. Presently, the national investment-GDP ratio is 2.5 times that of Punjab. *The Punjab model of development, with social turmoil further compounding its negative fallouts, led to either out-flight of capital or the capital shied away from it. This is what explains the cause for the poor industrial base and under-grown tertiary sector.*

13.4.4 Spatial Distribution of Tertiary Sector

Spatial distribution of the tertiary sector in relation to other sectors gives the nature and extent of tertiary sector development in a region. A look at Table 13.10 and Appendix Graph 13.4 shows that tertiarization in Punjab is not evenly distributed in the state. Districts like Moga, Sangrur, Barnala, and Ferozepur have a very low

Table 13.9 Investment-GDP ratio in Punjab in comparison to all India

Years	Investment GDP ratio (%), India	Investment GDP ratio (%), Punjab	Gap (%) (India–Punjab)
1980–81	15.3	15.6	0.3
1985–86	22.8	21.6	1.2
1989–90	25.0	24.2	0.8
1990–91	27.1	23.1	4.0
1991–92	23.6	22.0	1.6
1992–93	22.0	21.1	0.9
1993–94	22.4	22.4	0.0
1994–95	25.4	22.9	2.5
1995–96	26.6	30.9	−4.3
1996–97	24.0	18.9	5.1
1997–98	25.3	20.5	4.8
1998–99	23.3	20.1	3.2
1999–00	25.9	16.9	9.0
2000–01	24.3	20.6	3.7
2001–02	24.8	20.9	3.9
2002–03	25.2	16.2	9.0
2003–04	27.6	16.1	11.5
2004–05	32.7	19.5	13.2
2005–06	34.3	19.1	15.2
2006–07	35.5	19.9	15.6
2007–08	37.7	16.8	20.9
2008–09	34.9	15.4	19.5
2009–10	36.5	14.5	22.0
2010–11	38.2	15.1	23.1

Source Statistical abstract of Punjab, various issues

share of tertiary sector share in the district domestic product; it is 32.13, 33.66, 34.32, and 36.00 %, respectively. Amritsar has the highest level (51.00 %) in terms of tertiary sector share in district domestic product. It is followed by Roopnagar (49.82 %), Gurdaspur (46.43 %), and Jalandhar (45.90 %) in that order. *Spatial distribution of the tertiary sector shows that developed regions, with better economic and social infrastructure have a higher share of tertiary sector in domestic product and* vice versa. *Much of the development and resulting tertiary sector development has taken place in already developed regions and somehow, the backward regions, especially a major chunk of Malwa region, is still low on ladder of tertiarization.*

13.4.5 Linkage Analysis of Tertiary Sector

The shift in composition of SDP has led to a specific pattern of inter-sectoral production and demand linkages. The study of inter-sectoral linkages is the need of

Table 13.10 Spatial distribution of tertiary sector share in Punjab, 2010–11

Sr. no.	District	Sector			
		Primary	Secondary	Tertiary	Total
1	Gurdaspur	33.58	19.99	46.43	100
2	Amritsar	26.69	22.31	51.00	100
3	Tarntaran	41.72	18.62	39.67	100
4	Kapurthala	36.39	23.60	40.01	100
5	Jalandhar	22.49	31.61	45.90	100
6	SBS Nagar	26.34	39.06	34.60	100
7	Hoshiarpur	31.38	26.23	42.39	100
8	Roopnagar	27.86	22.32	49.82	100
9	SAS Nagar	26.78	30.26	42.96	100
10	Ludhiana	20.85	38.98	40.17	100
11	Firozepur	49.85	14.15	36.00	100
12	Faridkot	42.86	15.09	42.05	100
13	Mukatsar	46.24	12.85	40.91	100
14	Moga	32.75	35.12	32.13	100
15	Bathinda	43.65	15.77	40.58	100
16	Mansa	49.01	13.86	37.14	100
17	Sangrur	43.00	23.33	33.66	100
18	Barnala	45.53	20.16	34.32	100
19	Patiala	32.55	24.10	43.35	100
20	Fatehgarh Sahib	33.59	25.38	41.03	100

Source Statistical abstract of Punjab

Table 13.11 Sectoral linkages of tertiary sector, 2006–07

Sector	Backward linkage	Forward linkage
Primary	0.0253	0.03818
Secondary	0.2234	0.36024
Tertiary	0.1389	0.61213

Source Calculated from Singh and Singh (2011)

the hour so that the positive growth stimuli among sectors could be identified and fostered to sustain the economic growth momentum. The production linkages or backward linkages among various sectors of an economy basically arise from interdependence of sectors, for meeting their productive input needs. Output linkages or forward linkages give the pattern of output disposition among the sectors. The analysis of *backward linkages* (Table 13.11) is indicative of the fact that to produce one unit worth of output, in 1968–69, the *tertiary sector* required 0.0253 unit worth of input from the primary sector, 0.2234 from the secondary sector and 0.1389 from itself. That is, for input requirements the tertiary sector depended more on the secondary sector and on itself; while its dependence on the primary sector has been the least. Input dependence of the tertiary sector has been biased more toward the secondary sector than toward the primary sector. The demand linkages or *forward linkages* of *tertiary sector* have been the highest with itself, followed by the secondary sector. Its forward linkage with primary sector has been very weak. Analysis of linkages of tertiary sector is indicative of the fact that the emerging tertiary sector in the Punjab economy is loosely connected to the agricultural sector on the backward and forward fronts. This requires further in-depth disaggregate analysis, fortified with a wider database, to derive some finer conclusions regarding the viability of such a skewed pattern of linkages in an agrarian economy.

13.5 Conclusions

To sum, we can say, the poor developed tertiary sector has its roots in the social turmoil period of the late 1980s and early 1990s. Due to overemphasis on agriculture and because of the social turmoil, the required preconditions for the tertiary sector revolution could not be created. The state has lagged behind in the transition to service economy. There is ample scope to improve the economic growth via the tertiary sector growth, provided the proper human resource planning and integration of tertiary sector with commodity sector is done. In this context the following are the policy implications.

(a) Tertiary sector growth and its translation to higher per capita income growth is a function of human capital. The state with poor human capital needs to develop it and improve the efficiency of labor if the benefits of the tertiary sector-led growth are to be obtained.
(b) A massive and sustained investment in human resource development is the need of the hour. The education, health, and economic opportunities system needs to be revamped thoroughly.
(c) Economic infrastructure, especially related to transportation needs to be upgraded. In this regard, because of paucity of resources with the state, public–private participation needs to be explored.
(d) Special packages, in the form of technology parks and economic zones need to be perceived to attract corporate investment.
(e) Being an active border state and the food bowl of the country, some special Union budget allocations for improving the investment base are required.

Appendix Graphs

See Graphs 13.1, 13.2, 13.3 and 13.4.

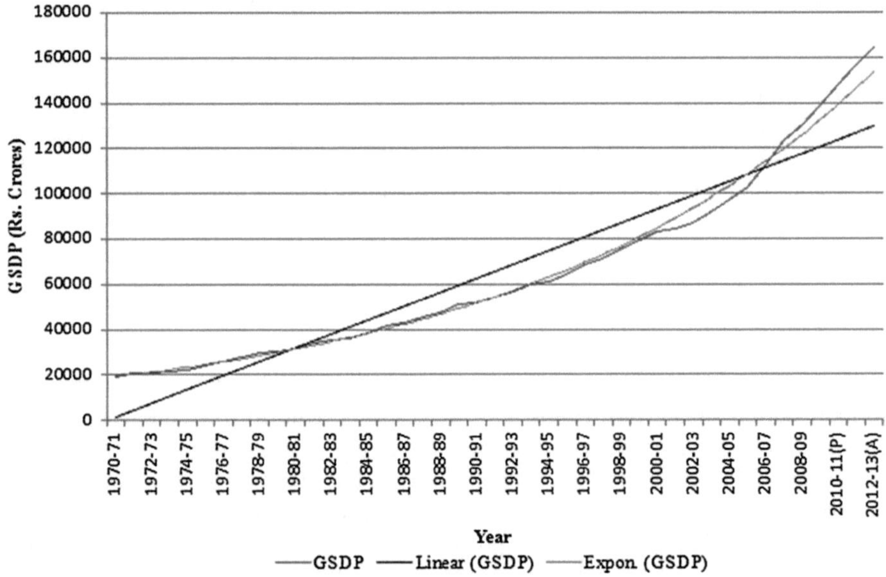

Graph 13.1 Growth trajectory of GSDP, Punjab

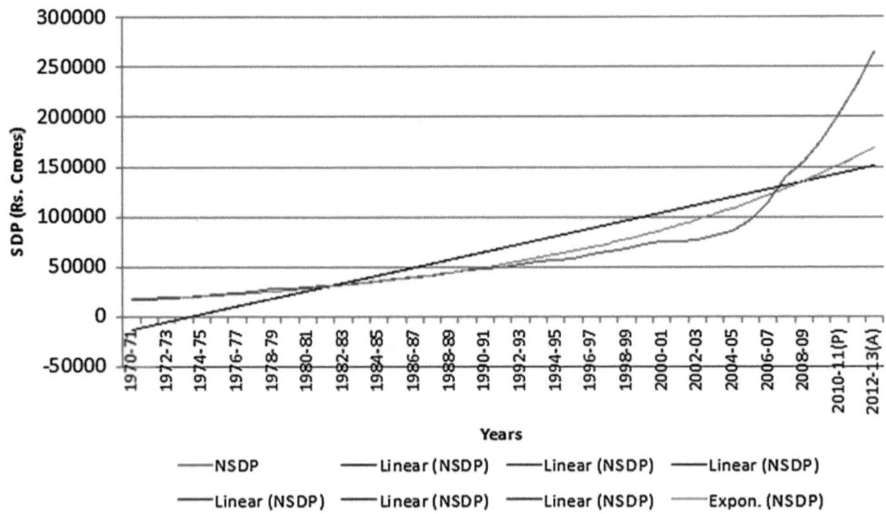

Graph 13.2 Growth trajectory of NSDP, Punjab

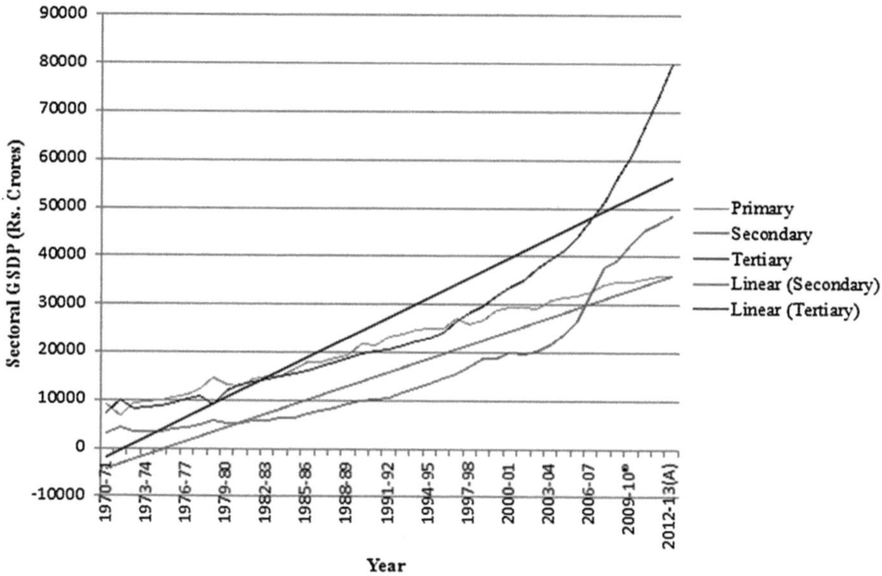

Graph 13.3 Temporal profile of sectors in Punjab

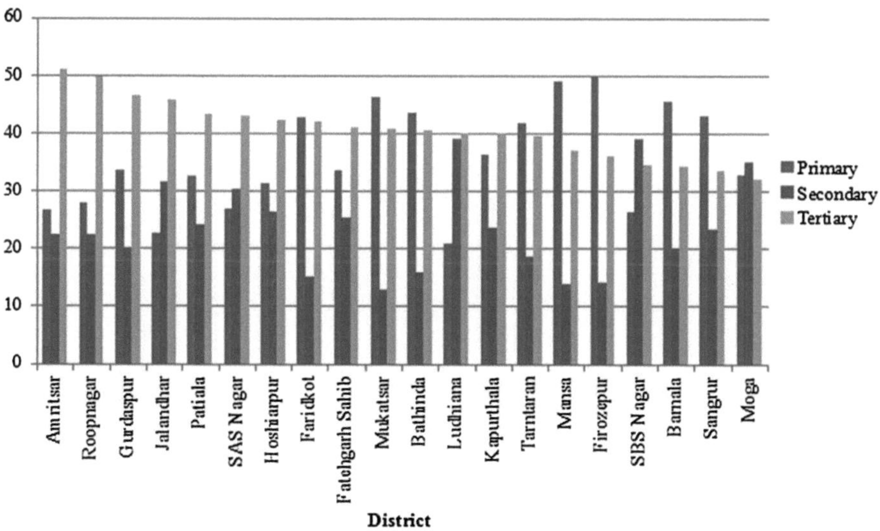

Graph 13.4 District-wise distribution of sector in Punjab, 2010–11

References

Banga R (2005) Role of service in growth process: a survey. Indian council for trade and international economic relations (ICRIER), working paper 159
Economic Council of Canada (1991) Employment in the service sector. Minister of Supply and Services, Ottawa
Glasmeier A, Marie H (1993) Service-led rural development: definitions, theories, and empirical evidence. Int Reg Sci Rev 16(1–2):197–229
Hirschmann AO (1958) The strategy of economic development. Yale University Press, New Haven
Lewis WA (1954) Economic development with limited supplies of labour. Manchester Sch Soc Sci 22:139–191
Mansell R (1985) The service sector and western economic growth. Can Public Policy 11(s1): 354–360
Nagaraj R (2010) Is service sector's output overestimated. Econ Polit Wkly 44(5):40–45
Pradhan JP, Sahu MK, Abraham V (2006) Rise of service sector outward foreign direct investment from Indian economy: trends, patterns, and determinants. GITAM J Manag 4:1
Sawhney U (2007) Growth of services sector in a predominantly agricultural economy of Punjab. Polit Econ J India 17(1–2):1–11
Sing I, Singh L (2011) Regional input output table for the state of Punjab. MPRA paper 32344, University Library of Munich, Germany
Standard and Poor (2007) Unfulfilled potential: the services sector in Southeast Asia

Part IV
Human Development in Punjab's Economic Transformation

Chapter 14
Critical Evaluation of Educational Development in Punjab

Jaswinder Singh Brar

14.1 Introduction

The state of Punjab holds a complex structure which encompasses comparatively higher level of economic growth and prosperity with moderate level of human resources more so when the latter being examined on the basis of universally accepted parameters of educational build up in any society. The state has been experiencing higher levels of per capita incomes with the big push being initially provided by its highly mechanized and commercialized modern agricultural sector. The state realized structural transformation relatively earlier compared to vast majority of other states with rise in the weight of industrial and service sectors in the state income. But, the state has not shown the same vigor and commitment in translating its economic advantage into better quality human resources by enhancing educational delivery mechanism. For example, in terms of overall literacy, the rank of Punjab among all the 35 states and union territories of the country was 15 from above during 2001. Notably, it slipped to the 21st position during 2011; and more so it was 24th in case of males' literacy and 18th in females' literacy (Census of India 2011). Further, as per DISE data, during 2011–2012, on the basis of Educational Development Index (EDI) the state stood at 32nd and 35th rank as far as 'Educational Outcomes' are concerned, respectively, for primary and upper primary levels of schooling though relatively better placed on other three components of EDI namely 'Access,' 'Infrastructure,' and 'Teachers' (DISE 2011–12).

The education sector of the state during the last about two decades under the national level adoption of new economic and educational dispensation witnessed drastic change and transformation. The private sector of huge variety and forms has

J.S. Brar (✉)
Centre for Research in Economic Change, Punjabi University,
Patiala 147002, India
e-mail: brar_jas@yahoo.co.in

L. Singh and N. Singh (eds.), *Economic Transformation of a Developing Economy*, India Studies in Business and Economics,
DOI 10.1007/978-981-10-0197-0_14

emerged in a big way in all the types and stages of education in a deregulated environment across the rural and urban locations and population settlements in the state. The dwindled sate interest because of plethora of factors has given serious jolt to the educational effectiveness of directly government controlled and backed educational institutions which have sizeable share in student enrollment. The under governance of educational sector has badly shaken the public interest in usefulness of availing of the government institutions for their wards. Resultantly, the households who can afford have started utilizing the services of private education service suppliers. The educational choices of households even for basic education got a deep connection with the affordability factor. The vertical split of education sector on the lines of institutions for under privileged and those of better off has affected the process of education formation in the state in a serious manner. Rest of the chapter in such a framework and perspective examines the educational progress of the state. The following Sect. 14.2 provides the details of educational progress of the state in terms of literacy indicators in the national context as well as that of in respect to other states. It also provides the rural and urban literacy scenario of the state including inter district variations. Section 14.3 gives information about the education levels among the workers including mean years of schooling. Section 14.4 deals with the enrollment patterns and levels. Section 14.5 profiles the most disturbing aspects of the education sector of the state by focusing upon the drop out and out of school children. Section 14.6 brings out the quality and performance issues by using suitable parameters. Section 14.7 sums up the discussion and analysis with concluding observations.

14.2 Comparative Literacy Progress

Literacy though being considered as a very crude and rudimentary yardstick of educational attainment, yet it throws enough light upon the educational happenings in a society historically placed in lower level equilibrium trap. Literacy being the direct product of formal education systems emanates from the spread of basic education in any politico-administrative set up. The continuous rise in the level of literacy over a specified period shows the growing involvement of larger number of persons in the ambit of schooling. The quicker progress of literacy has been considered more desirable for realization of numerous direct and indirect as well the short and long-term benefits associated with educational build up. The slower progress on educational front in fact implies simultaneous existence of more number of illiterate generations of populace. The societies which succeeded in attaining higher levels of literacy in relatively shorter span established their economic supremacy by overcoming problems of general backwardness and dogma.

The literacy progress in Punjab closely resembles and moves with the national scenario of literacy build up (Table 14.1). The literacy rate of the state was slightly on lower side to national average during 1971 and 1981 but crossed it marginally during 1991 onwards (Fig. 14.1). In both cases, i.e., Punjab and India, the literacy

Table 14.1 [a]Literacy rate in Punjab and India, 1971–2011 (%)

Literacy	1971	1981	1991	2001	2011
India					
(a) Persons	34.45	43.67	52.21	64.83	74.04
(b) Male	45.95	56.50	64.13	75.26	82.14
(c) Female	21.97	29.85	39.29	53.67	65.46
(d) Gap	23.98	26.65	24.84	21.59	16.68
Punjab					
(a) Persons	33.67	40.86	58.51	69.70	76.70
(b) Male	40.38	47.16	65.66	75.23	81.50
(c) Female	25.90	33.69	50.41	63.36	71.30
(d) Gap	14.48	13.47	15.25	11.87	10.20

Note [a]The measurement of literacy changed at national level. Therefore, literacy rate for census 1971 relates to population aged 5 years and above and for 1981, 1991, 2001, and 2011 for aged 7 years and above

Source Statistical Abstract of Punjab, ESO, Chandigarh (various issues)

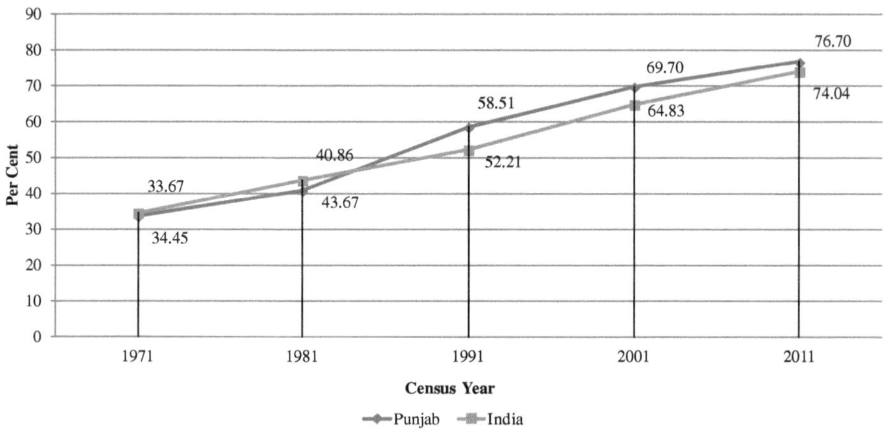

Fig. 14.1 Decadal literacy progress of Punjab and India, 1971–2011. *Source* based on data of Table 14.1

rates rose consistently during each and every census but at a slower pace as it took a very long period for literacy rates to show any worthwhile levels. In case of India as a whole, the literacy rate rose from 34.45 to 74.04 % over the period from 1971 to 2011. In case of Punjab, literacy rates rose from 33.67 to 76.70 % during corresponding years. This has been the case for both Punjab and India in case of all literacy categories reported such as male and female literacy. The gap in male and female literacy rates narrowed both in case of Punjab and India but it happened more at all India level as it declined from 23.98 to 16.68 % from 1971 to 2011. But in Punjab, the gap was 10.20 % during 2011. The slow pace of progress of literacy

Table 14.2 Literacy rate in Punjab and India according to NSSO survey rounds

Period	1993	1995–1996	1997–1998	1999–2000	2004–2005
Punjab	63.00	66.00	70.00	68.00	67.00
India	56.00	59.00	62.00	62.00	64.00

Source CSO (2011, Table 3.2, p. 74)

Table 14.3 Position of Punjab in states and UT according to literacy ranges, 2011

Literacy range (%)	States/UT	Number
a. >90	Kerala, Lakshadweep, Mizoram	3
b. 85–90	Tripura, Goa, Daman and Diu, Puducherry, Chandigarh, Delhi, Andaman and Nicobar Islands	7
c. 80–85	Himachal Pradesh, Maharashtra, Sikkim, Tamil Nadu, Nagaland	5
d. 75–80	Manipur, Uttarakhand, Gujarat, Dadra and Nagar Haveli, West Bengal, Punjab, Haryana, Karnataka, Meghalaya	9
e. 70–75	Orissa, Assam, Chhatisgarh, Madhya Pradesh	4
f. 65–70	Uttar Pradesh, Jammu and Kashmir, Andhra Pradesh, Jharkhand, Rajasthan, Arunachal Pradesh	6
g. 60–65	Bihar	1

Note Total number of states and union territories is 35
Source Census of India (2011), statement 23 (1)

in Punjab has also been corroborated by five rounds of NSSO data (Table 14.2) during the period from 1993 to 2004–2005.

In India, three units namely Kerala, Lakshadweep, Mizoram crossed the literacy mark of 90 % when the achieved literacy rates were clubbed into seven ranges of 5 % starting from 60 % to more than 90 % during 2011 (Table 14.3). Punjab falls into the middle category of 75–80 % with other nine states and union territories, viz., Manipur, Uttarakhand, Gujarat, Dadra and Nagar Haveli, West Bengal, Punjab, Haryana, Karnataka, and Meghalaya. Alternatively putting the matter, exactly 15 states and union territories occupied higher position than the literacy range to which the state belongs.

The perusal of literacy data over the period of 40 years from 1971 to 2011 substantiates the fact of slower pace of literacy build up in the state (Table 14.4). The level of literacy, in case of persons, for the state as a whole rose from 33.67 % during 1971 to 76.70 % during 2011. For males it rose from 40.38 to 81.50 % and for females from 25.90 to 71.30 % during corresponding years. The decadal progress happened to be on higher side during the period from 1991 over 1981 as compared to other periods. During this decade, the additions on percent basis points were 17.65 for persons, 18.50 for males, and 16.72 for females. This has also been true in case of rural and urban literacy rate both for males and females. But, on the other side, the gaps in literacy levels somewhat narrowed down over the study

Table 14.4 Literacy rate, Punjab, 1971–2011 (%)

Literacy	1971	1981	1991	2001	2011
Persons	33.67	40.86 (7.19)	58.51 (17.65)	69.70 (11.19)	76.70 (7.00)
Male	40.38	47.16 (6.78)	65.66 (18.50)	75.23 (9.57)	81.50 (6.27)
Female	25.90	33.69 (7.79)	50.41 (16.72)	63.36 (12.95)	71.30 (7.94)
Gap	14.48	13.47	15.25	11.87	10.20
Rural literacy					
Persons	27.60	35.20 (7.60)	52.77 (17.57)	64.72 (11.95)	72.45 (7.73)
Males	34.55	41.91 (7.36)	60.73 (18.82)	71.05 (10.32)	77.92 (6.87)
Females	19.58	27.63 (8.05)	43.85 (16.22)	57.72 (13.87)	66.47 (8.75)
Gap	14.97	14..28	16.88	13.33	11.45
Urban literacy					
Persons	48.10	55.63 (7.53)	72.08 (16.45)	79.10 (7.02)	83.70 (4.60)
Males	54.40	60.73 (6.33)	77.26 (16.53)	83.05 (5.79)	87.28 (4.23)
Females	40.80	49.72 (8.92)	66.13 (16.41)	74.49 (8.36)	79.62 (5.13)
Gap	13.60	11.01	11.13	8.56	7.66

Note Figures in brackets indicate decadal percentage basis differences
Source Statistical Abstract of Punjab, ESO, Chandigarh (various issues); and CSO (2011, Table 3.2, p. 73)

period as female literacy progressed at a higher rate than that of males in case of all literacy categories reported during 2001–2011.

Literacy progress of Punjab has also been viewed in terms of comparison of over period literacy rate of Punjab with that of all India and among the neighboring states of Haryana and Himachal Pradesh on the basis of respective literacy ratios (Table 14.5). The literacy ratios have been reported for six literacy categories: rural and urban person literacy, male literacy, and female literacy. In comparison to all overIndia, the state improved literacy at somewhat better rate in all categories shown here but for rural females particularly during the period of last two decades as literacy ratio declined from 1.43 (1991) to 1.24 (2001) to 1.15 (2011). The states of Haryana and Himachal Pradesh have been carved out from Punjab by its reorganization during 1966. As per 1971 Census, Punjab was better in terms of rural literacy than Haryana while the latter was having edge in urban literacy. But, Himachal Pradesh was having edge in terms of all literacy categories reported here with slightly lower literacy in case of rural females than of Punjab. Over all, Haryana made better progress in literacy of rural females than Punjab. It started with much lower female literacy than Punjab but reached near to it as literacy ratio declined from 2.12 (1971) to 1.11 (2011). However, Himachal Pradesh maintained its edge over Punjab in all literacy categories more noticeably in case of rural literacy as compared to urban literacy which in the two moved toward convergence.

But, the literacy progress viewed in terms of different sections of society presents a picture of gap and neglect (Table 14.6). The perusal of data pertaining to the deep division of society in terms of Scheduled Castes and Non-Scheduled Castes categories show that the former has considerably lower level of literacy than that of the

Table 14.5 Comparative progress of literacy of Punjab versus all India, Haryana and Himachal Pradesh (1971–2011) (ratio for specific categories)

Category	1971	1981	1991	2001	2011
Rural a. Persons	0.99 (1.27) [0.93]	0.98 (0.94) [0.72]	1.18 (1.06) [0.85]	1.09 (1.01) [0.87]	1.07 (1.01) [0.89]
b. Males	0.71 (1.06) [0.84]	0.84 (0.79) [0.67]	1.05 (0.94) [0.82]	1.00 (0.93) [0.85]	1.01 (0.96) [0.88]
c. Females	1.26 (2.12) [1.08]	1.27 (1.47) [0.78]	1.43 (1.35) [0.88]	1.24 (1.16) [0.88]	1.15 (1.11) [0.89]
Urban a. Persons	0.80 (0.94) [0.79]	0.83 (0.83) [0.72]	0.99 (0.98) [0.86]	0.99 (0.99) [0.88]	1.00 (1.01) [0.92]
b. Males	0.78 (0.92) [0.81]	0.79 (0.80) [0.73]	0.95 (0.94) [0.87]	0.96 (0.96) [0.90]	0.98 (0.98) [0.93]
c. Females	0.84 (0.98) [0.78]	0.88 (0.89) [0.71]	1.03 (1.03) [0.84]	1.02 (1.03) [0.87]	1.01 (1.04) [0.90]

Note 1. Figures are obtained by dividing the respective literacy rates of Punjab with that of India, Haryana and that of Himachal Pradesh
2. Figures in round brackets stand for Punjab to Haryana literacy ratio
3. Figures in round brackets stand for Punjab to Himachal Pradesh literacy ratio
Source Statistical Abstract of Punjab, ESO, Chandigarh (various issues) and Census of India (2011)

Table 14.6 Literacy rate of SCs versus non-SCs population, 2011

Group	Total	Rural	Urban
(a) SC population	64.81	62.98	69.78
(b) Non-SC population	82.07	77.91	87.70
Gap (a–b)	17.26	14.93	17.92
Males			
(a) SC population	70.66	68.94	75.30
(b) Non-SC population	86.34	83.08	90.65
Gap (a–b)	15.68	14.14	15.35
Females			
(a) SC population	58.39	56.47	63.66
(b) Non-SC population	77.28	72.24	84.29
Gap (a–b)	18.89	15.77	20.63

Source Calculated from two sources (1) Statistical Abstract of Punjab (2012), ESO, Chandigarh and (2) PCA (2011)

latter. As per 2011 Census, the literacy rates were 64.8 % in case of Scheduled Castes and 82.07 % of Non-Scheduled Castes with gap of 17.26 %. The gaps were found to be slightly on lower side for rural segments than their urban counterparts. But, on the other side, the literacy rate was highest in case of 'Non-SC Urban Males' (90.65 %) and lowest for 'SC Rural Females' (58.39 %). This shows that different sections of society stand at historically different stages of progress of literacy in the state. Notably, Scheduled Castes constituted 31.94 % of overall population of the state as per population census, 2011 (PCA 2011).

The inter-district literacy levels of state present interesting details with good degree of variation across all the 20 districts of state during 2011 (Table 14.7). The district of Mansa stands at the bottom with a literacy rate of 62.8 % compared to 85.4 % of Hoshiarpur; district with highest level of literacy. Moreover, as many as 10 districts (Moga, Firozpur, Muktsar, Faridkot, Bathinda, Mansa, Patiala, Tarn Taran, Sangrur, and Barnala) has literacy rate lower than the state average of 76.7 %. Further, Hoshiarpur occupies the top position both for males' literacy (89.9 %) and females' literacy (80.8 %) and that of rural males (89.48 %), rural females (79.56 %), and urban females (85.48 %). And, Mansa remained at the bottom in both males' literacy and females' literacy levels. However, in case of urban males, SAS Nagar tops the literacy scene by achieving 92.28 % literacy level. By comparing and contrasting all the seven categories of literacy reported here, it emerges that urban males of SAS Nagar (92.28 %) formed the most literate stock of the state with rural females of Mansa (52.47 %) the least indicating that the state has to tread long journey in order to bridge inter-location and inter-gender literacy gaps.

Table 14.7 District wise literacy among various categories in Punjab, 2011

	Persons	Males	Females	Rural males	Rural females	Urban males	Urban females
Gurdaspur	81.1	85.9	75.7	83.49	72.60	91.54	83.83
Kapurthala	80.2	84.6	75.4	82.15	71.80	88.95	82.22
Jalandhar	82.4	86.1	78.3	84.19	74.26	87.81	82.03
Hoshiarpur	85.4	89.9	80.8	89.48	79.56	91.61	85.48
SBS Nagar	80.3	86.2	74.3	85.94	73.32	87.03	78.12
Fatehgarh Sahib	80.3	84.5	75.5	83.15	73.42	87.56	80.47
Ludhiana	82.5	86.3	78.2	83.96	74.02	87.97	81.13
Moga	71.6	75.3	67.4	72.98	64.64	83.42	76.98
Firozpur	69.8	76.7	62.2	73.70	57.69	84.42	74.45
Muktsar	66.8	72.9	60.0	69.28	55.70	82.21	71.25
Faridkot	70.6	75.9	64.8	71.39	59.94	83.97	73.96
Bathinda	69.6	75.3	62.9	69.44	56.29	85.78	74.96
Mansa	62.8	68.4	56.4	64.74	52.47	82.20	70.85
Patiala	76.3	81.4	70.5	76.32	63.25	88.90	81.02
Amritsar	77.2	81.2	72.8	73.74	63.27	87.36	80.94
Tarn Taran	69.4	75.4	62.9	74.31	61.42	82.70	73.01
Rupnagar	83.3	88.9	77.2	88.23	75.15	90.77	82.92
SAS Nagar	84.9	89.2	80.0	85.37	73.65	92.28	85.10
Sangrur	68.9	74.2	62.9	71.37	59.42	80.60	70.49
Barnala	69.9	73.1	64.1	70.09	61.13	79.54	70.65
Punjab	76.7	81.5	71.3	77.92	66.47	87.28	79.62

Source Statistical Abstract of Punjab (2012), ESO, Chandigarh, Table 2.8

14.3 Education Levels

The actual levels of education attained by the labour force in any particular set up have been considered as the very strong method of measuring the economically relevant method of educational progress in any society. In fact, the externality of education in both the market and household domain essentially flows from the levels and types of education actually received by the growing stock of population particularly in the working age group. This age group comes in direct contact with the production process in the form of very active factor of production by handling all the economic activities in multiple ways. Table 14.8 provides education levels of population by using the National Family Health Survey data collected during 2005–2006 by locations and sex for various levels of education for the population aged 6 years and above. Importantly, 22.6 % of overall population of the state was not formally educated at all. The proportion for males was 20.7 % and for females 33.0 %. And, the proportion of those with less than 5 years of education was

Table 14.8 Residence and sex wise education level of population of Punjab, 2005–2006

S. no.	Level of education	Rural			Urban			Overall		
		Male	Female	Total	Male	Female	Total	Male	Female	Total
1	No education	25.2	37.9	31.4	13.6	24.0	18.3	20.7	33.0	22.6
2	<5 years complete	17.0	13.4	15.2	14.7	10.9	13.0	16.1	12.5	14.4
3	5–9 years complete	33.9	30.0	32.0	30.6	26.3	28.6	32.6	28.7	30.8
4	10–11 years complete	15.4	11.4	13.4	20.1	16.1	18.3	17.2	13.1	15.2
5	12 or more years complete	8.4	7.2	7.9	21.0	22.7	21.8	13.2	12.7	13.0

Note The data pertains to population age 6 years and above. The sum of first five rows may not be equal to hundred because of missing values/do not know response on-reporting by sampled respondent households
Source NFHS (2008, p. 30)

Table 14.9 Education levels of labour force (age 15+), usual status (PS+SS); both (rural and urban), 2007–2008

Education levels	Punjab	Haryana	Himachal Pradesh	Kerala	India
1. Not literate	27.67	28.97	21.90	5.39	34.53
2. Literate up to primary	21.28	22.98	25.50	24.45	24.72
3. Middle	12.99	13.99	12.90	32.63	16.72
4. Secondary	19.08	16.88	20.50	15.47	10.11
5. Higher secondary	8.79	8.59	9.90	4.49	5.21
6. Diploma/certificate	1.70	2.70	2.60	7.29	1.90
7. Degree and post graduation	8.49	5.89	6.70	10.28	6.81
Total (1–7)	100.00	100.00	100.00	100.00	100.00
Mean years of schooling	6.551	6.222	6.893	8.408	5.482

Source Planning Commission (2014)

14.4 %. Amazing to note that 13 % of population of the state falls into the category of those who had completed 'twelve and more years of education.' Moreover, as high as about 38 % of rural females were found to be without any education. The situation was reported to be worse in case of rural areas and females than their respective counterparts.

Table 14.9 provides the detailed break up of information of the labour force (age 15+) both for rural and urban areas in case of employment category called Usual Status for 2007–2008 for four states comprising Punjab, Haryana, Himachal Pradesh, and Kerala in overall India. Importantly, in such a framework, the position of the state of Punjab is slightly better than national average but considerably poor than that of Kerala. For the type of labour force reported here, as high as more than one fourth (27.67 %) was illiterate with comparable proportion of just 5.39 % in Kerala. Moreover, Kerala secured better rank by and large for all seven categories of education levels reported. The education levels attained by the labour force seems to be more skewed in case of Punjab, Haryana, and Himachal Pradesh as the

Table 14.10 Education level of head of farm households in Punjab, 2005–2006

Education attained	Agro-climatic zones				
	Semi-Hilly	Central	South-West	Overall	
Number of years in schools	7.0	6.1	5.4	5.9	
Percent of households with education of 12 years and more	0.0	7.6	3.5	5.5	
Education attained	Farm-size category (operational holdings in hectares)				
	Marginal (up to 1)	Small (1.01–2)	Semi medium (2.01–4)	Medium (4.01–6)	Large (above 6)
Number of years in schools	5.9	5.5	5.5	6.1	7.1
Percent of households with education of 12 years and more	4.7	4.0	3.2	8.0	9.7

Source Singh et al. (2007, Tables 3.1 and 3.3)

proportion of those falling in the category of not literate, literate up to primary and that of middle was found to be on higher side. However, these three states hold a better position so far labour force with secondary education is concerned. The perusal of education levels further establish the weak position of labour force so far getting of skills in the form of diploma and certificates in Punjab in particular as just 1.70 % of the labour force has been endowed with it. Kerala has given more attention toward such type of skills. This is also reflected by the data on Mean Years of Schooling attained by the labour force of these states. Here too, as obvious Kerala occupies the top slot with level of 8.408. Among the three neighboring states reported here, Himachal Pradesh has better position than that of Punjab and Haryana with respective levels of 6.893, 6.551, and 6.222.

Similarly, from Table 14.10 it is evident that the education levels of households engaged into farming were found to be low when measured in terms of years put into formal schooling both in case of Agro-Climatic Zones and size class of operational holding. The average number of years put into schooling by heads of farm households in overall was equivalent to 5.9 during 2005–2006. And, heads of households with education of 12 years and more was extremely low. It was nil in case of Semi-Hilly Zone, 7.6 % in Central Zone, and 3.5 % in South-West Zone; with overall level of 5.5 %. In the same way, the number of years of schooling by heads of farm households across the various size-classes of farmers was very low as follows: Marginal (5.9 years), Small (5.5 years), Semi-Medium (5.5 years), Medium (6.1 years), and Large (7.1 years). And, the proportion of heads of farm households having education of 12 years and more was too abysmal as reported herewith: Marginal (4.7 %), Small (4.0 %), Semi-Medium (3.2 %), Medium (8.0 %), and Large (9.7 %). Thus, the households engaged into cultivation in the form of marginal, small, and semi-medium size of operational holdings lack educational progress which is fundamental to transformation of rural economy. It is to be noted that out of 10,52,554 operational holdings in the state, the proportion of marginal, small, and semi-medium category of farmers, respectively, was 15.62, 18.57, and 30.83 %

during 2010–2011. The total number of these three categories was 6,84,385 with collective share of 65.02 % (SAP 2012, pp. 120–121). Thus, the huge proportion of farming community of the state has not reached that critical level of educational buildup which triggers the modernization of family economies by facilitating the entry of family members into off-farm and non-farm employment and livelihood.

14.4 Enrollment Rates and Patterns

Much has happened in the state so far the opening up of education sector to the private players is concerned. The structure of education sector changed drastically with the change in relative proportion of different types of service suppliers in the school sector. The private sector has made strong additions to the existing government controlled schools and government aided privately managed schools in the state. This comes up very clearly from the data put into Table 14.11. During 2008–2009, in case of primary, out of total enrollment the proportionate shares of government schools, aided private schools and private schools were 74.54, 5, and 20.46 %. At upper primary level, the corresponding shares were 74.23, 8.09, and 17.68 %. During elementary as a whole the respective figures were 74.42, 6.16, and 19.42 %. Thus, it indicates that about one-fifth of school enrolled students got associated with private schools in the state. Further, girl students constitute about 40 % of the total enrollment in private schools. The data are also the pointer to the rising and significant role of private sector in imparting education to the schools in the state.

The changed structure of schooling strongly affects the enrollment levels as growing addition of service suppliers increase the access at least by making the service availability at more locations. Table 14.12 provides the information for the state during 2004–2005 on the basis of Gross Enrollment Ratio for eight categories of student age groups which in fact correspond to different levels of education. Notably, the Gross Enrollment Ratios were quite on lower side in the state during 2004–2005. At primary level (6–11 years age group), Gross Enrollment Ratios were 74.49 % for boys, 80.52 % for girls, and 77.20 % in overall. In upper primary level, the corresponding figures were 63.78, 67.40, and 65.42 %. For full elementary stage, the levels were 70.30, 75.34, and 72.57 %, respectively. However, the Gross Enrollment Ratios declined considerably in case of secondary education level. Importantly, the enrollment ratio declined very steeply during the next stage of senior secondary. During Senior Secondary stage, the Gross Enrollment Ratios for the boys, girls and in overall were just 28.20, 27.48, and 27.87 %, respectively. During school education from I to X class, the respective ratios were 59.58, 63.01, and 61.13 %. Overall the Gross Enrollment Ratios indicates that the rate of enrollment were considerably on lower side than that of desired level.

The Gross Enrollment Ratio though indicates much about the state of education but it has one important limitation in that it refers to the enrollment of all the students in a particular stage of education irrespective of age of the student. That is

Table 14.11 Management-wise pattern of enrollment in Punjab, 2008–2009 (30 September)

Standard	Government	Private aided	Private unaided	Total
Primary (I–V)	1,247,180 (74.54) [47.20]	83,631 (5.00) [46.12]	342,399 (20.46) [40.43]	1,673,210 (100) [45.76]
Upper primary (VI–VIII)	749,040 (74.23) [47.62]	81,606 (8.09) [44.39]	178,395 (17.68) [40.26]	1,009,041 (100) [46.05]
Elementary (I–VIII)	1,996,220 (74.42) [47.35]	165,237 (6.16) [45.26]	520,794 (19.42) [40.37]	2,682,251 (100) [45.87]

Note 1 Figures in round brackets indicate the management wise percentage share of total enrolment
2 Figures in Square Brackets indicate the percentage share of girls in respective category
Source DISE (2008–09, Tables 3.5 (p. 45), 3.7 (p. 47), and 3.19 (p. 59))

Table 14.12 Gross enrollment ratio in Punjab for boys, girls and overall during 2004–2005

Standard	Boys	Girls	Total
1. I–V (6–11 yrs)	74.49	80.52	77.20
2. VI–VIII (11–14 yrs)	63.78	67.40	65.42
3. I–VIII (6–14 yrs)	70.30	75.34	72.57
4. IX–X (14–16 yrs)	50.21	52.97	51.47
5. XI–XII (16–18 yrs)	28.20	27.48	27.87
6. IX–XII (14–18 yrs)	39.17	40.10	39.60
7. I–XII (6–18 yrs)	59.58	63.01	61.13
8. HE (18–24 yrs)	9.40	11.23	10.24

Source MHRD (2004–05, Table 8, p. 61)

Table 14.13 Net enrollment ratio, Punjab versus India

Year	Primary		Upper primary	
	Punjab	India	Punjab	India
2005–06	51.78	84.53	37.68	43.14
2006–07	55.49	92.75	44.02	48.45
2007–08	53.02	95.92	42.10	52.55
2008–09	59.69	98.59	49.64	56.22
2009–10	63.05	98.28	52.21	58.29
2010–11	89.41	99.89	71.76	61.82

Source DISE (2011–12, p. 36)

why a different concept of Net Enrollment ratio has been used which excludes the students from measurement who do not belong to that age cohort. Such data for the state have been presented in Table 14.13. The perusal of data shows that the level of Net Enrollment Ratios further declined compared to Gross Enrollment Ratio. Moreover, the state has considerably lower ratios than that of all India both for primary and upper primary stage over the period of 6 years from 2005–2006 to 2010–2011. During primary stage, the Net Enrollment Ratio of Punjab was 51.78 % as compared to 84.53 % for India. Similarly, during upper primary stage the corresponding ratios were 37.68 and 43.14 % during 2004–2005. Moreover, the Net Enrollment Ratios improve consistently in case of all India average but not so in case of Punjab during primary stage. But, during upper primary stage the Net Enrollment Ratios improved to some extent in case of Punjab and crossed that of India. But, the fact which demand notice is that even during the year 2010–2011 the Net Enrollment Ratio at primary level in the state was 89.41 % indicating thereby that 10.59 % of the students of eligible age group were not enrolled in the various schools of the state. This turned out to be good number keeping in view the huge proportion of child population in the society of state particularly large proportion of weaker sections such as Scheduled Castes and marginal and small farmers in the state.

Table 14.14 Out of school children in Punjab, age group (6–14 years), January, 2008

District	Boys	Girls	Total	Percent of total	Percent share of girls
Amritsar	4349	4234	8583	8.54	49.33
Barnala	947	752	1699	1.69	44.26
Bathinda	3963	3093	7056	7.02	43.84
Faridkot	2061	1775	3836	3.82	46.27
Fatehgarh	598	462	1060	1.06	43.58
Firozpur	6401	6279	12,680	12.62	49.52
Gurdaspur	2236	2158	4394	4.37	49.11
Hoshiarpur	2246	1939	4185	4.17	46.33
Jalandhar	3424	2805	6229	6.20	45.03
Kapurthala	776	659	1435	1.43	45.92
Ludhiana	4446	3788	8234	8.20	46.00
Mansa	2743	2311	5054	5.03	45.73
Moga	2270	1820	4090	4.07	44.50
Mohali	843	807	1650	1.64	48.91
Muktsar	3381	2821	6202	6.17	45.49
SBS Nagar	517	382	899	0.89	42.49
Patiala	3788	3266	7054	7.02	46.30
Rupnagar	1420	1264	2684	2.67	47.09
Sangrur	3693	2926	6619	6.59	44.21
Tarn Taran	3463	3351	6814	6.78	49.18
Punjab	53,565	46,892	1,00,457	100.00	46.68

Source 1. SSA (2006–07, p. 68) and SSA (2007–08, p. 72)

14.5 Non-completion and Excluded

There are some estimates available about the number of children not enrolled in schools called out-of-school children. In case of Punjab as per data reported in Table 14.14 the number of out-of-school children was found to be high. During January 2008, the total number of such children was equivalent to 1,00,457. Out of these, the number and proportion of girls was 46,892 forming 46.68 % of total. Further, no district of the state was free from this problem as out-of-school children were found in each and every district. The number in absolute sense was the maximum in Firozpur (12,680) and minimum in SBS Nagar (899); comprising, respectively, 12.62 and 0.89 % of total. The huge number of out-of-school children in all the districts indicates the much complexity of public access problem of school systems of the state. It also indicate that the creation of public access simply in the physical sense will not solve the problem of non-availing of existing infrastructure. It is also obvious that overwhelming proportion of such children must be belonging to the households which have been deprived off from education due to multitude of factors.

Table 14.15 Drop-out-rate of students in Punjab, 1999–2000 to 2005–2006

Year	I–V			I–VIII		
	Boys	Girls	Total	Boys	Girls	Total
1999–00	24.12	19.99	22.17	25.71	21.33	23.66
2001–02	21.28	19.28	20.34	35.31	38.82	36.99
2002–03	26.37	24.07	25.29	33.71	31.67	32.75
2003–04	23.60	20.21	22.03	35.13	35.26	35.19
2004–05	27.42	19.91	23.96	32.64	34.82	33.67
2005–06	25.71	21.33	23.66	31.42	34.71	32.98

Source Figures for drop-out rates are based on: (1) *Economic Survey of Punjab* 1999–2000 and 2005–2006 (p. 17), ESO, Chandigarh; and (2) Figures for year 2006–2007 are based on *Economic Survey*, 2009–2010, ESO, Chandigarh, p. 97

Table 14.16 Drop out rate among SCs-students, 2007–2008

Standard	Boys	Girls	Total
I–VIII	43.87	42.58	43.27
I–X	63.79	66.34	65.00

Source Rao (2011–12, Table 10.13, p. 18)

The drop-out-rate among the students may be contributing to the ongoing problem of prevalence of large number of out-of-school children. The drop-out-rate of students in the state was quite on higher side over the period from 1990–2000 to 2005–2006 both for primary and elementary stages of education (Table 14.15). For example, in case of primary stage, the drop-out-rate actually increased from 22.17 to 23.66 % from 1999–2000 to 2005–2006. For boys, it increased from 24.12 to 25.71 %. The corresponding figures for the girls were 19.99 and 23.66 %. During elementary stage, the drop-out-rate too increased from 23.66 to 32.98 % over the period from 1999–2000 to 2005–2006. Amazingly, it had happened both in the case of boys and girls. More importantly, the drop-out-rate increased with the rise in the stage of education. The drop-out-rate was much higher during elementary stage as compared to primary stage. The existence of extremely higher level of drop-out-rate firmly establishes the fact that the system of education in the state operates at very lower level of efficiency and indulges in wastage of resources. The problem of drop-out-rate was found to be still more serious among the weaker sections of society (Table 14.16). For example, during 2007–2008, the drop-out-rate was as high as 43.27 % during the elementary stage of education. It was 43.87 % for boys and 42.58 % for girls. But, the drop-out-rate rose to extremely higher level in case of secondary stage of education. The drop-out-rate was 63.79 % for boys, 66.34 % for girls and 65 % in overall. It implies that in case of such category of students the proportion of those who complete a particular stage of education was substantially on lower side than those leave the cycle in between without completing that stage of education.

The high rate of dropping out from the schools apart from other reasons has also a deep connection with not joining the schools at right stage of life. This also leads

Table 14.17 Under-age and over-age children in schools of Punjab

Year	Under-age children		Over-age children	
	Primary	Upper primary	Primary	Upper primary
2009–10	10.28	5.90	11.32	16.22
2010–11	10.94	6.53	9.37	14.18
2011–12	10.94	7.43	9.63	13.62

Source DISE (2011–12, p. 29)

to adjustment with the peer group specific to that standard of study and activities. In the state, the number of under-age and over-age students was reported to be on higher side both during the primary and upper primary stages across the districts (Table 14.17). For example, in case of under-age-children, during primary stage, the proportion was as high as 10.28 % during 2009–2010 which rose to 10.94 during 2011–2012. And, during upper primary stage, the corresponding figures were 5.90 and 7.43 %. Similarly, in case of over-age-children, during primary stage, the proportions were 11.32 and 9.63 % during 2009–2010 and 2011–2012. And, during upper primary stage, the respective proportions were 16.22 and 13.62 %. Thus, by taking collective view of the situation in the form of students who falls beyond the education stage specific age-cohort either in the form of under-age or over-age the number of students who join at right age and progress smoothly comes down than depicted by normal enrollment figures. It implies that the education system has not been connected deeply with the educational requirements of the households especially those which face multiple deprivations. Interestingly the problem prevails even after launching of so many national and state level schemes related to schools in the form of infrastructure building, provision of stationery and books, providing of alternative and innovative teaching, various inclusionary measures, constitution of education development committees at village, school and block levels, girl-student-oriented policy programs, special teacher training and orientation programs and family specific initiatives. This brings to forth the under efficacy of the public resources put into basic education by the state and national level public authorities.

14.6 Quality and Performance

The spread and growth of education in a typical numerical sense though it is very crucial but is not sufficient to generate any meaningful impact in the system until and unless it embodied the recipient with good quality of education in the form of right package of reading, writing, numerical and other useful life skills and abilities. The challenge of providing of education of reasonably good quality seems to be far more serious than that of expanding education in a numerical mode as has been emerged as the primary objective in practice. Table 14.18 provides the information

Table 14.18 Performance of rural children, Punjab versus Haryana, Himachal Pradesh and India, 2009

STD	Percentage of children who can read			Percentage of children who can read english			Percentage of children who can do arithmetic		
	Category	Punjab	India	Category	Punjab	India	Category	Punjab	India
STD I	Letters or more	85.6 (85.0)	68.8 [76.8]	Capital letters or more	67.7 (72.5)	43.8 [65.8]	Recognize numbers 1–9 or more	82.7 (86.4)	69.3 [77.4]
STD II	Words or more	61.0 (75.4)	55.2 [64.5]	Capital letters or more	83.4 (92.4)	66.2 [86.2]	Recognize numbers 11–99 or more	59.5 (82.5)	54.6 [66.7]
STD III	STD I level text or more	51.0 (65.7)	46.6 [55.3]	Words or more	39.9 (63.5)	28.6 [47.3]	Subtract or do more	50.9 (66.1)	39.0 [53.0]
STD IV	STD I level text or more	75.5 (86.0)	67.4 [71.3]	Words or more	58.0 (84.5)	44.1 [60.5]	Subtract or do more	73.3 (84.4)	58.8 [68.1]
STD V	STD II level text or more	64.3 (73.2)	52.8 [65.8]	Sentences	34.5 (63.3)	25.7 [43.8]	Do division	48.9 (64.1)	38.0 [54.9]

Note Figures in round brackets stand for Himachal Pradesh and in square brackets for Haryana
Source Planning Commission (2014, p. 237)

Table 14.19 Results of school examination board (PSEB, Mohali), 2005

Category	High school (X)		Senior secondary (XII)	
	All students	SC-students	All students	SC-students
Boys	66.20	57.20	69.30	57.90
Girls	72.50	59.80	79.90	69.20
Total	69.00	58.40	74.40	62.90

Source MHRD (2004–05, Table 22)

pertaining to the performance of children in rural areas on the basis of testing of learning level in three domains, i.e., general reading ability, English reading ability and arithmetic doing ability. The performance in above three specified domains has been tested for the primary stage for each of the five standards from first to fifth in case of all India, Haryana, and Himachal Pradesh. Within each category, different set of activities have been tested by using specific tests. Punjab has no doubt secured higher position than that of India among all the categories and subcategories for all of the classes. The all India situation was found to be quite pathetic as learning levels were found to be quite on lower side. The reading and arithmetic ability was found to be miserably low. For example, just 25.7 % of children of Standard V could read English sentences. And, 38 % could do division and 52.8 % read. Importantly it has been the situation during 2009. In case of Punjab, under first category, i.e., percentage of children who can read English (sub category namely reading English capital letters), 67.7 % children of Standard I were found to have acquired this skill.

In case of mathematical ability, importantly 82.7 % of children of Standard I of rural Punjab could identify the numbers from 1 to 9. The remaining proportion of children, i.e., 17.3 % had not acquired such capability. Similarly, the large proportion of students was found to be deficient so far subtraction and division were concerned. In overall, students from Himachal Pradesh have performed much better than their counterparts of Punjab in testing of learning. Similarly, Haryana too reported its edge in large majority of cases than Punjab. The proportion of students who had not acquired basic skills pertaining to reading and arithmetic was high in state with long-term implications for promotion to higher classes and retention. The low level of learning outcomes defeats the basic purpose of education which involves the enhancement of cognitive skills of students by enhancing and fine tuning their basic reading, writing and numerical ability in order to endow with problem solving capabilities. This has also been corroborated by the analysis of examination results of students from the state for high and senior secondary levels. The perusal of data (Table 14.19) brings out this more vividly. It has been the case for all students as well as SC students during 2005. Of all the categories of results reported here girls performed better than those of boys both during secondary and senior secondary examinations. For example, in class X results, in case of all students the proportion of girls who passed the examination was 72.50 % compared to 66.20 % of boys. In higher secondary, the respective proportions were 79.90 and 69.30 %. It has also been the case as girls belonging to SC families has outperformed the boys belonging to such families. But, in overall the results from the category called overall students was on higher side as compared to SC students. It implicitly implies that the non-SC students' results were on quite higher side than their counterparts in the form of SC-students because inclusion of results from SC-students brings down the state average. This further implies that the state has not paid adequate attention to the education of students from weaker sections those have been suffering from multiple social and economic deprivations and depending more on government and low quality private schools with negligible support from their families because of economic hardship in the situation of lower incomes, vulnerability to income shocks, rising health care expenses and livelihood problems.

14.7 Summing up with Extended Observations

Educational progress though fundamental to economic growth and general prosperity has received comparatively subdued priority in larger part of the developing world. The educational systems remained preoccupied with plethora of structural constraints which essentially emanates from perpetual state apathy. The educational requirements of masses remained unfulfilled even by the existence of vast network of educational institutions. The public education systems gradually lost momentum in the situation of long drawn neglect. The state of Punjab though occupying higher levels of per capita incomes among the various states in the country has made comparatively moderate progress so far educating the masses is concerned (Brar 2002). The foregone analysis firmly establish the fact that the state has to do much more in order to mark its presence felt as a case of society with high quality of human resources. The state has to act both on the quality and quantity front to improve its position among other sates of the union as well as to reap benefits of quality education in the form of externality. From the overall and interstate analysis, it can also be described that the number of those without any worthwhile schooling was quite substantial posing formidable challenge for the growth process and development policy of the state and a pointer to the constrained reach of various schooling systems operating in the state.

The progress of literacy in the state has not only been tardy but is highly iniquitous in many respects such as locations, sexes, regions, districts, weaker versus other sections, etc. The neighboring state of Haryana and Himachal Pradesh performed better on literacy front than Punjab. The state of Haryana in particular recorded better progress of rural female literacy than their counter part in Punjab. The female literacy particularly in the rural areas and more so among the weaker sections has not progressed at a desired pace in the state which has reduced the overall literacy rate of state. The rank of the state on literacy front among the states actually slipped over the period instead of improving as was expected because of higher level of per capita state income. The state ranked at lower level in terms of indexing involving infrastructure, access, teachers and educational outcomes. The literacy progress of the state has essentially moved in close relation to national average. The general gaps over the period though narrowed in case of males and females but were found to be on higher side when literacy achievements were compared over the large spectrum comprising urban males of educationally advanced districts with rural females of educationally under achieved districts. The districts with lower level of literacy at the time of reorganization of state continuously remained at a lower level because of less improvement in rural and female literacy. The state has not adopted any specific policy toward such districts and sections of society in order to bring them at par with others with explicit thrust to overcome historically lower level of educational activity in such areas. The lower educational levels of general population and labor force were another area of concern. The low level of formal education among the farming households has become a big constraint in the transformation of rural as well as family economies of farmers possessing small, marginal and semi-medium size of holdings. The state lagged behind in imparting technical skills to labour force which is very much required in the present period of skill-intensive economic growth.

The school sector of the state shows certain very disquieting features and tendencies which points toward serious shortcomings such as prevalence of out-of-school children, high drop-out-rates, enrollment of under-age and over-age children, less than satisfactory examination results and lower level of net enrollment rates, etc. The lower level educational outcomes in the form of depressed level of reading and arithmetic ability reduce the actual worth of education. The enhancement of actual learning skills is basic to attain any sort of demographic dividend for the economy in transition. All these things firmly prove the fact that the extent of wastage and inefficiency of the school sector of the state has acquired alarming levels with serious repercussions for human capital formation of the state. The promotion of students into higher grades without sufficiently equipping them with the learning level prescribed for lower grades has been a major fault and formidable challenge for the education policy and system of the state.

The education sector has gotten divided into parallel streams with emergence of completely unregulated huge sized private sector. The state withdrawal has crippled the functioning of government institutions which ultimately turned out to be the institutions of those who cannot afford the high quality private institutions. The private sector is quite heterogeneous with large component of highly commercialized substandard institutions thriving without any worthwhile educational standards in the situation of extremely lower level of public confidence in the education provided by public sector institutions. The withdrawal of wards by the influential sections from public institutions in favor of private institutions has ended all sort of pressure on the state system to improve the public institutions. The situation became quite deplorable with the lack of collective pressure by those who depend upon public institutions for the study of their wards. The political process in the state has been embroiled in issues with weak connection with larger issues of public interest in the situation of low level of civil society assertions and lack of any organized pressure from those who need state schools. This has led to the decline in public expenditure on education in the state as proportion to state income and budgetary spending considerably during about last two decades. The education budget of the state shows serious imbalances in terms of high share of revenue account and non-plan account expenditure and extremely lowers levels of capital and plan account spending. The state budget has recorded lower growth in real prices during the last about two decades. Moreover, the education budget recorded lower growth than that of state income and budgetary spending. The compressed education budget ultimately turned out to be a salary budget leaving less for undertaking other activities. The state has been reported to spending less on education in the country on per student and per capita basis also (Mittar et al. 2002; Brar 2008). The exclusion of students from rural areas has also been the matter of great concern (Ghuman et al. 2009). The period of liberalization has not been found to be conducive for the development of the education sector of the state in terms of resources and other infrastructure (Gill et al. 2007). The education sector of the state has been attracting bad press on daily basis related to shortage of teachers, headmasters, untimely releasing of salaries and recruitment of large variety of teachers on contractual basis under varied and novel designations. The educational administration in the state lack critical edge because of unstated policy of keeping large number of posts of headmasters, principals, block and district level education officers vacant for any length of time. The state policy of bringing of large number of government schools under rural local bodies has not yielded any worthwhile results and ultimately they have been made the part of the cadre of education department of the state recently. The education sector has become a field for undertaking novel experiments in terms of ownership, financing, recruitment practices, admission norms, teaching of languages, promotion of students to higher classes, conduct of examinations, establishment of new schools, up gradation of existing schools, etc. The aided school sector in the state is actually on the verge of closure with non-filling of posts for the considerable period of time. The interventions in the form of central schemes during the recent past have solved to some extent the basic infrastructural problems only. But, the basic issues which jeopardized the governance of education sector of the state remained as it is. The growing clout of private players with active connivance of political class of the state has made the government schools totally dysfunctional. The efficient school teachers and headmasters of government schools have also been reportedly changed in many cases with the pressure of nearby private schools in order to get students from government schools. These developments strongly points toward the deepening of structural crisis of education sector of the state which could be corrected only by qualitative shift in the public policy of the state.

References

Brar JS (2002) Basic education, health care and economic growth in Punjab. Man and Development 24(1):51–63

Brar JS (2008) Public expenditure on education in Punjab: an evaluation (1992–93 to 2001–02). In: Dhesi AS, Singh G (eds) Rural development in Punjab: a success story going astray. Routledge, New Delhi, pp 333–50

Census of India (2011) State of literacy, Provisional population totals-India. Census of India, Director Census Operations, New Delhi, pp 98–136
CSO (2011) Selected socio-economic statistics-India. Government of India, Ministry of Statistics and Program Implementation, Central Statistical Organization, New Delhi
DISE (2008–09) Elementary education in government schools in Punjab. Sarva Shiksha Abhiyan Authority of Punjab, Chandigarh
DISE (2011–12) Elementary education in India-progress towards UEE, flash statistics. National University of Educational Planning and Administration (NUEPA), New Delhi
Ghuman RS, Singh S, Brar JS (2009) Professional education in Punjab: exclusion of rural students. Publication Bureau, Punjabi University, Patiala
Gill SS, Sukhwinder S, Brar JS (2007) Globalization and Indian state: a study of delivery of education, health, and agricultural extension services. National Foundation for India (NFI), New Delhi
MHRD (2004–05) Selected educational statistics. Ministry of Human Resources Development (MHRD), New Delhi
Mittar V, Singh SS, Brar JS (2002) Changing structure of education in Punjab: some issues and policy recommendations. Publication Bureau, Punjabi University, Patiala
NFHS (2008) National family health survey India, Punjab (NFHS-3). Ministry of Health and Family Welfare, Government of India, New Delhi
PCA (2011) Primary census abstract, state-dist Sc-2, census of India, New Delhi. www.censusindia.gov.in/2011/census/hlo/pca/pca-pdf/pca-crc-0300.pdf. Accessed 26 May 2014
Planning Commission (2014) Data book for use of deputy chairman. Planning Commission, Government of India, New Delhi. http://planningcommission.gov.in. Accessed 23 May 2014
Rao KH (2011–12) Rural development statistics. National Institute for Rural Development (NIRD), Hyderabad. www.nird.org.in/rural%20development%20statistics,%202011-12/rdsindex.html. Accessed 26 May 2014
SAP (2012) Statistical Abstract of Punjab. Economic and Statistical Organization (ESO), Punjab, Chandigarh, Publication no. 938
Singh S, Kaur M, Kingra HS (2007) Flow of funds to farmers and indebtedness in Punjab. Punjab State Farmers Commission, Government of Punjab, Chandigarh
SSA (2006–07) Annual report. Sarva Shiksha Abhiyan Authority of Punjab, Chandigarh
SSA (2007–08) Annual report. Sarva Shiksha Abhiyan Authority of Punjab, Chandigarh

Chapter 15
Economic Development and Emerging Health Scenario in Punjab: A Need for State Support and Accountability

Sukhwinder Singh

Economic development and health status of people living in a developing economy/region are closely correlated and reinforcing each other; although positive improvements in people's health status are largely dependent not only on the rising income, consumption and living standards, but also upon many other factors such as the access to adequate food, safe drinking water, proper housing, behaviour pattern, presence of robust public health care system, knowledge of diseases, treatment processes and cost of seeking treatment. It is true that the Punjab's economy during the decades of 1970s and 1980s had experienced impressive economic growth and steadily rising per capita income compared to all-India average and across all the major states. This has brought much acclaimed prosperity and affluence to the general masses in the state as the state was ranked number one in terms of per capita income till 2001–02 (Jain 2014). These remarkable achievements have been attributed to the state sponsored efforts, under which heavy amount of public investment in the agricultural related sectors such as the dams, canals, electricity, rural roads and credit facilities; and other social sectors such as the education and health services were made. Further, Punjab's economy stimulated by the public and private initiatives and enterprises progressed well in the industrial, business and services sectors also, especially of small-scale variety. On the social front, these activities contributed a lot in raising per capita income and health related indicators in the state; although many researchers stated that such achievements were iniquitous and exclusionary in nature (Jain 2014).

Till the 1980s, growth drivers of Punjab's economy were revolved around the new agricultural technology and the state efforts. After that, farm productivity in the state, having dearth of new innovations, reached a plateau and the farming sector has become an enterprise of diminishing returns (Singh 2013). Further, future growth potential of Punjab's agricultural sector having finite resources (land, water, seeds, etc.) has become a subject of debate; which could be answered with the help of 'limits to growth' propagated by Meadows's growth model (Meadows et al. 1972). It means

S. Singh (✉)
Centre for Research in Economic Change, Punjabi University,
Patiala 147002, India
e-mail: sohi42pbi@yahoo.com

L. Singh and N. Singh (eds.), *Economic Transformation of a Developing Economy*, India Studies in Business and Economics,
DOI 10.1007/978-981-10-0197-0_15

that the farming sector in the long run has a limited capacity to grow and unable to become a leading sector of the economy to bring out many desirable changes in the other vital sectors of economy. Further, the political turmoil of the 1980s pushed the Punjab state into severe resource crunch and non-responsive state administration to revive its growth agenda. Even, the Punjab's economy did not get any worthwhile benefits with the adoption of New Economic Policy in 1991 (NEP). In fact, growth of Punjab economy in the post-liberalization era, instead of getting momentum, has been slowed down. Facing a severe resource crunch, the state is seeking ways and means to trim/reduce public spending on many vital sectors of economy such as agriculture, education, health and other social welfare sectors. This has brought out a faster deterioration in the functioning of public services in Punjab, especially the education, health and agricultural extension services (Gill et al. 2010). High degree of rent-seeking behaviour of political and business elites had made the state's institutional framework and governance very weak and dysfunctional (Singh 2015).

In the light of these observations and policy changes, this chapter examines the nature and extent of economic slowdown, its impacts on emerging health scenario, and urgency of radical reforms in Punjab's health policy. The chapter is divided into five sections. Section 15.1 analyzes, in brief, how the economic slowdown and NEP parameters have impacted the Punjab's health sector. Section 15.2 examines the incidence and changing pattern of diseases in Punjab. Pattern of public expenditure on health services in the state has been discussed in Sect. 15.3. Section 15.4 deals with growing health infrastructure in the state, its non-functional and dismal performance. And, emerging consequences and public policy issues are set forth in Sect. 15.5.

15.1 Economic Slowdown, New Economic Policy and Health Sector

No doubt, Punjab economy had experienced an impressive growth rate during the decades of 1970s and 1980s of the twentieth century. For instance, average annual growth rate in state income was found to be 5.1 % during the decade of 1970 (1970–79) compared the all-India average of 3.6 % per annum (Table 15.1). During the Sixth Five Year Plan (1980–85), growth rate of Punjab economy was recorded at 5.3 % per annum compared India's growth rate of 5.3 % per annum. In the Seventh Five year Plan (1985–90), Punjab's growth rate of 6.0 % per annum was slightly higher than that of India's growth rate (5.8 %). After the 1991, however, annual growth rate of Punjab economy decelerated in all subsequent Five Year Plans. In the Eighth Five year Plan (1992–97), average annual growth rates of Punjab economy was 4.8 %, whereas it was 6.8 % in the case of Indian economy. Similarly, the economy of Punjab grew at 3.9 % per annum compared to national average growth rate of 5.5 % during the Ninth Five Year Plan (1997–2002). In the Tenth Five Year Plan (2002–07) and Eleventh Five Year Plan (2007–12), Punjab again recorded very lower average annual growth rates of 5.1 and 6.9 % compared to all-India's rates of 7.8 and 9.0 %, respectively. Further, the state has targeted to

Table 15.1 Average annual compound growth rate of Punjab economy versus Indian economy

Time/plan period	CGR in state income by sector (% per year)					
	State	Primary	Secondary	Tertiary	Overall	Base prices
1970–71 to 1978–79	Punjab	4.3	6.8	5.9	**5.1**	1970–71 = 100
	India	2.1	5.0	4.8	3.6	
Fifth Five Year Plan (1974–79)	Punjab	5.6	8.4	8.2	**6.8**	1970–71 = 100
	India	3.6	6.4	6.5	5.1	
Sixth Five Year Plan (1980–85)	Punjab	5.3	5.0	5.1	**5.3**	1980–81 = 100
	India	5.6	6.1	5.4	5.7	
Seventh Five Year Plan (1985–90	Punjab	5.2	8.7	5.2	**6.0**	1980–81 = 100
	India	3.6	6.5	7.4	5.8	
Eighth Five Year Plan (1992–97)	Punjab	3.1	7.1	5. 8	**4.8**	1993–94 = 100
	India	3.8	8.3	7.9	6.8	
Ninth Five Year Plan (1997–2002)	Punjab	1.9	4.9	5.8	**3.9**	1993–94 = 100
	India	2.2	4.6	8.1	5.5	
Tenth Five Year Plan (2002–07)	Punjab	2.3	7.7	6.0	**5.1**	1999–00 = 100
	India	2.7	9.4	9.4	7.8	
Eleventh Five Year Plan (2007–12)	Punjab	1.9	7.8	8.0	**6.9**	2004–05 = 100
	India	3.6	7.6	9.7	9.0	
Twelfth Five Year Plan (2012–17)[a]	Punjab	1.6	7.5	8.0	**6.4**	
	India	4.0	8.1	9.1	8.2	

[a]Target Growth Rate
Source GOP, Statistical Abstract of Punjab (Different Years) and GOI, Twelfth Five Year Plan 2012–17, Vol. I

grow at 6.4 % per annum against the national average of 8.2 % during the Twelfth Five Year Plan (2012–17).

This slowdown has also been found in its three subsectors: primary, secondary and tertiary sectors. For instance, the agriculture sector, which forms the backbone of Punjab economy, is suffering very seriously from this slowdown since the Eighth Five Year Plan (1992–97). The severity of agricultural crisis is manifested in the form of stagnating yields and diminishing returns to the farmers. This has pushed a large proportion of small and marginal farmers into debt trap (Shergill 2010) and many of them committed suicides (Gill and Singh 2006; Gill 2010). Mechanization of agriculture drastically reduced physical efforts as well as number of employment days in this sector. Intensive agriculture has also polluted the state's ecology—water, soils, flora and fauna—to a great extent. Poisoning of soils and water resources largely due to the high/intensive use of fertilizers, insecticides and pesticides have created several undesirable health problems such as the cancer, diabetes, blood pressure and heart ailments along with continuation of traditional water borne diseases (Shiva 1992; Khurana 2011).

Further, economic surpluses generated across the rural areas could not be invested in agroprocessing and other industrial activities. Instead, these surpluses through the banking mechanism were syphoned-off to other parts of the country.

Industrial incentives given to the neighbouring hill states further hit the industrial base of the state. Investment–GDP ratio in the state remained below 20 %—the lowest among the fourteen major states of India (CDEIS 2012). In the post-reforms, state could not devise a smart strategy to attract foreign direct investment (FDI) in the state despite having rich diaspora connections. In the national level policy making, Punjab state is now relegated to background and its economy has continuously been faced an economic slowdown (Singh 2015). Consequently, Punjab slipped down in terms of per capita income ranking across all major Indian states from the first rank in 1991–92 to the second rank in 1992–93 and sixth rank in 2009–10 (GOI 2013a, b). This has happened because in the era of globalization, Punjab economy has been experienced a slower growth rate than that of the fast growing states such as Haryana, Maharashtra, Kerala, Gujarat and Tamil Nadu, which have now overtaken the Punjab's per capita income. In 1999–2000, Punjab's per capita income was 61.4 % higher than that of the all-India average, which in 2009–10 had come down to mere 34.2 % more than all-India average. It means that in the post-reforms era, India's economy has entered into an accelerated growth path, but Punjab's economy has been facing a stagnating growth path.

Moreover, the NEP has been influencing India's health sector in many ways (Misra et al. 2003). In its true essence, the NEP means the growing economic interdependence of nation–states through the increasing volume and variety of cross-border transactions of goods/services, free movement of capital, people, ideas and knowledge, and more importantly, diffusion of new technology at an astonished speed (Gill et al. 2010), which, indeed, affects the people's health and health delivery system both positively and negatively through the direct/indirect mechanisms. Its positive impacts may be observed in the form of better health outcomes (more incomes, better living conditions, rising life expectancy, easy access to health technology/medicine, etc.). And, its highly deleterious impacts can be seen in rising treatment costs, high incidence of man-made diseases, irrational use of drugs/technology, elite-oriented health policies, stressful life, etc.

Directly, the global forces will influence a nation's health positively mainly through: (i) enhanced movement of pharmaceutical products, health personals and patients across the national boundaries; (ii) increased output of pharmaceutical products; (iii) medical tourism via the Internet and other information means; (iv) easy availability of new therapeutic and diagnostic techniques; and (iv) establishment of big corporate hospitals with five star medical facilities. Similarly, increasing mobility of people raises more chances of spreading/contracting diseases (e.g. bird flu) across the nation's borders (Gill et al. 2010). Further, it is feared that the globalization if accompanied by low allocation of public funds to the health sector will play havoc with the health of poor people in the developing countries (Baum 2001).

These forces also affect the people's health indirectly via the heightened industrial activities, depletion of natural resources, indiscriminate use of insecticides/pesticides, increasing environmental pollution (air and water pollution), unsafe/untreated disposal of industrial waste, etc. Moreover, high consumption of tobacco/alcohol, packed/frozen foods and aerated beverages has also affecting the people's health negatively. The emergence of high risk chronic and life style diseases such as the diabetes, cancer, heart disease, and other life style diseases (TB, HIV/AIDS, etc.) can be linked to the global economic policies (Mohan et al. 2011). For the resource-poor people, falling prey to these catastrophic diseases means more incidence of poverty and malnutrition of women/children in the family (Cornia 2001; Raman and Bjorkman 2009).

In India, with the adoption of NEP in 1991, integration of nation's economy to the global economy has become a reality. As a consequence, state funding to public health sector has relatively been decreased in India and across all states. The prescriptions of international funding agencies began to dominate India's health sector. The World Bank piloted health sector schemes/reforms initiated in India or elsewhere has been advocated the private sector initiatives, put more emphasis on the non-government bodies, and other forms of organization (PPP) in health sector delivery and management systems. In nutshell, these health sector reforms initiated in the country revolves around: curtailing public health investments, opening up of health care to the private sector, levying of users' charges, contracting out some services of public hospitals and relying upon purely technocentric public health interventions (Qadeer 2000).

It is also feared that this paradigm shift in health policy, especially cutbacks in public health funds, may adversely affect primary health care In India (Qadeer 2000). Further, in the absence of liberal federal funding, various diseases control programmes are being disrupted; family welfare programme began to focus on the reproductive health of married women only; and mothers'/children' health and nutritional needs largely being ignored across all states. Side by side, handing over the health care to the private players, without any regulatory mechanism, quality aspects in the diagnostic techniques and treating patients are seriously being compromised both in urban and rural settings (Banerjee and Duflo 2009; Das et al. 2012). In such a scenario, state governments are unable to fulfil their constitutional obligations and are adversely affecting the equity principle in accessing public health services by the poor (Baru 1998). Surprisingly, all these policy prescriptions are now being implemented in Punjab more vigorously (Singh 2005; Gill et al. 2010). It means that the poor who lack resources (income/employment, assets, etc.) could not afford very high out-of-pocket health expenditure, particularly when they seek indoor treatment from the private sector owned institutions.

15.2 Rising Incidence and Emergence of New Diseases in Punjab

As expected, an epidemiological transition has taken place in the state. It has been found that state's agriculture led growth has produced many undesirable impacts on state's environment and ecology, which in turn influenced the health and disease pattern in the state. Further, growing urbanization, industrial pollution, air pollution,

Table 15.2 Growing number of ailing persons and incidence of morbidity in Punjab

Region/area	Number of ailing persons (in thousands)			CGR per annum		Incidence of morbidity 2004–05 (per thousand persons)		
	1973–74	1995–96	2004–05	1973/74–1995/96	1995/96–2004/05	Male	Female	All
Punjab								
Rural	545.6	1047.1	2116.8	3.01	8.13	114	160	136
Urban	143.6	535.0	813.0	6.16	4.76	100	115	107
Combined	689.2	1582.1	2929.8	3.85	7.09	109	146	127
India								
Rural	20047.1	35407.4	63193.4	2.62	6.65	83	93	88
Urban	518.4	11085.3	24267.7	3.56	9.10	91	108	99
Combined	25185.5	46492.7	87461.1	2.83	7.27	85	97	91

Note Estimates of ailing persons were generated on the basis of prevalence rates from data given in NSSO (1980), NSSO (1998) and NSSO (2006)
Source Singh (2009)

slums and ageing population have also posed many serious health hazards that are adversely affected the health of people. In fact, unrestricted use of agrochemicals, increasing intake of dietary fats, physical inactivity, adverse lifestyles and other behaviour patterns (anxiety, stressful life, etc.) have not only raised the burden of new diseases in the state, but also put a large proportion of population in the risky zone of attracting many serious non-communicable diseases like diabetes, cancers, high blood pressure, strokes, cardiovascular diseases and accidents/injuries (IIPS 2007). Further, it has been observed that, like the developed countries, demographic transition has been appeared in the state (Bobadilla et al. 1993; Mosley et al. 1993), where chronic, non-communicable, degenerative (ageing) and man-made diseases began to dominate compared to the earlier dominance of malnutritious, infectious and childhood-related diseases. All these negative forces seem to be working in the state, when one can see a significant rise in number of illness episodes as well as new pattern of disease.

An assessment of NSSO data revealed (Table 15.2) that number of ailing persons in Punjab grew at the rate of 7.09 % per annum during 1995–2004 compared to 3.85 % per annum during 1973–1995. However, the pace of growth rates amongst ailing persons differ considerably both in the rural and urban areas. Whereas per annum growth rate across ailing persons in rural areas has been doubled: rose from 3.01 % during 1973–1995 to 8.13 % during 1995–2004, but annual growth rate across urban ailing persons decelerated: from 6.16 to 4.76 % during same periods. The data also showed that on an average, 127 persons per thousand people were found to be suffering from one or other ailments in Punjab during 2004–05. Incidence of morbidity was much more in rural Punjab (136 per thousand people) than that of urban Punjab (107 per thousand people). Further, prevalence of morbidity was significantly higher among females both in the rural (160 per thousand females) and urban (115 per thousand females) areas of state. Although male–female differentials in the morbidity rates were also prevailing in India as a whole, but male–female differentials in rural Punjab were almost three times high than that of India as a whole. Moreover, incidence of ailing persons was much higher in Punjab (127 per thousand people) than that of the country as a whole (91 per thousand people). The data clearly pointed out that number of ailing persons as well as incidence of morbidity has been increased over the time period in Punjab.

Further, it has been observed that general economic progress in the state yielded considerable improvements in living conditions of populace which in turn induced positive improvements in the life expectancy, mortality and fertility rates (Kumar 2011). In fact, morbidity load has been shifted from the younger to the older populations. It is also true that advancement in therapeutic science often postpones or averts death across the older people, but it does not cure the disease/s at all (Bobadilla et al. 1993). Along with environmental hazards, both demographic and epidemiologic transitions had showed emergence of new health problems such as chronic, non-communicable, ageing and man-made diseases (Mosley et al. 1993). The data also pointed out (Table 15.3) that leaving aside the mix group of diagnosed ailments, the respiratory/ENT diseases, unknown fevers, cardiovascular diseases, gastrointestinal infections, disorder of joints and bones and bronchial asthma emerged as the six top ranking ailments in the descending order of importance in Punjab. Together, these diseases cornered 54.27 % share of total ailments. These six top ranking diseases are followed by the accidents/injuries/burns, undiagnosed ailments, diabetes mellitus, gynaecological disorders, kidney/urinary tract infections, febrile illnesses, eye ailments, disabilities, neuro/psychiatric disorders, cancer/other tumours, dental problems and tuberculosis in terms of prevalence rate in Punjab.

Further, all those ailments that needed hospitalization were the accident/injury/burn victims, followed by the gastrointestinal diseases, unknown fevers, kidney/urinary tract infections, gynaecological disorders, cardiovascular diseases, bronchial asthma, neuro/psychiatric disorders, respiratory/ENT diseases and disorder of joints and bones. It is interesting to note that gastrointestinal diseases, cardiovascular diseases, respiratory/ENT diseases, bronchial asthma, disorder of joints and bones, unknown fevers and accidents/injuries/burns were eight important diseases that figured both in the top ten causes of outdoor ailments and hospitalization cases. It also showed that old set of communicable/infectious diseases (small pox, whooping cough, tetanus, polio, mumps, malaria, etc.) had declined rapidly, but another set of chronic non-communicable (cancers, cardiovascular diseases, diabetes, kidney disorders, pains in joints and bones) and man-made diseases (accident/injury/burns, psychiatric disorders, respiratory diseases, etc.) were went upward at an astonishing speed in the state. It means that the people in Punjab have been facing a new pattern of diseases as has been experienced in many developed countries of world (GOI 2005).

The NFHS-3 data for 2005–06 presented a mixed picture of disease pattern in the state. It showed that, during 2005–06, incidence of tuberculosis in the state was low as just 201 persons per lakh population were suffering from tuberculosis compared to overall figure of 445 persons per lakh people in India (IIPS 2007).

Table 15.3 Number of outdoor and indoor treated illness episodes by broad group, 2004–05

Ailment group	Number of treated ailment episodes								
	Outdoor			Indoor			Both		
	Number	% share	Rank	Number	% share	Rank	Number	% share	Rank
Gastrointestinal	181,488	9.05	5	55,540	10.55	3	237,028	9.36	5
Cardiovascular	215,970	10.77	4	31,168	5.92	7	247,138	9.76	4
Respiratory/ENT	290,662	14.50	2	19,165	3.64	10	309,827	12.24	2
Tuberculosis	9461	0.47	20	13,263	2.52	13	22,724	0.90	19
Bronchial asthma	91,825	4.58	7	29,247	5.55	8	121,072	4.78	7
Disorder of joints and bones	144,414	7.20	6	18,892	3.59	11	163,306	6.45	6
Kidney/urinary tract infections	19,896	0.99	18	35,576	6.75	5	55,472	2.19	12
Gynaecological disorders	30,510	1.52	13	32,407	6.15	6	62,917	2.49	11
Neuro/psychiatric disorders	21,413	1.07	16	20,463	3.89	9	41,876	1.65	16
Eye ailments	42,782	2.13	11	5531	1.05	18	48,313	1.91	14
Diabetes mellitus	71,758	3.58	9	10,843	2.06	15	82,601	3.26	10
Anaemia/malnutrition	10,696	0.53	19	9502	1.80	16	20,198	0.80	20
STD infections	5962	0.30	21	1943	0.37	21	7905	0.31	21
Febrile illnesses	45,085	2.25	10	4169	0.79	20	49,254	1.95	13
Unknown fevers	251,573	12.55	3	43,657	8.29	4	295,230	11.66	3
Disabilities	28,258	1.41	14	13,824	2.62	12	42,082	1.66	15
Dental problems	27,035	1.35	15	4320	0.82	19	31,355	1.24	18
Accidents/injuries/burns	34,602	1.73	12	74,872	14.22	2	109,474	4.32	8
Cancer and other tumours	21,314	1.06	17	11,434	2.17	14	32,748	1.29	17
Undiagnosed ailments	83,584	4.17	8	8469	1.61	17	92,053	3.64	9
Other diagnosed ailments[a]	376,257	18.77	1	82,409	15.65	1	458,666	18.12	1
Total	2,004,545	100		526,694	100		2,531,239	100	

[a]Includes all other diagnosed ailments

Source Derived from the data given in Singh (2009)

Further, incidence of diabetes, asthma and goitre/other thyroid disorders across the Punjabi women was found to be quite high compared to the Punjabi men. In the case of diabetes, 849 women compared to 802 men per lakh population were found to be suffered during 2005–06. Similarly, 945 women compared to 802 men per lakh population were suffering from the asthma. In the case of goitre/other thyroid disorders, 601 women compared to 241 men per lakh population were found to be suffering from such a common but easily preventable disease/s (IIPS 2007).

The NFHS-3 data also highlighted the widespread malnutrition in the state. The data revealed that a little less than one-half of women (48.8 %) aged 15–49 years were underweight/having thin body (18.9 %) or victims of overweight/obesity (29.9 %). Similarly, 20.6 % men aged 15–49 years were underweight or having thin body and another 22.2 % were overweight or with obesity features. Further, nearly one-fourth of children aged 6–59 months were showing malnutrition feature during 2005–06 (IIPS 2007). Moreover, 66.4 % children aged 6–59 months, 38 % women and 13.6 % men aged 15–49 years were found to be anaemic in the state during 2005–06 (IIPS 2008). It means that the Punjab state has also become a storehouse of many undesirable diseases such as the malnutrition related infectious/parasitic diseases on one side and non-communicable/life style diseases on the other.

Surprisingly, cancer has acquired endemic proportion in the state. In 2009, there were 7738 cancer patients in Punjab; of which 2576 patients (33.29 %) were found in five districts, namely, Mukatsar, Bathinda, Barnala, Mansa, and Faridkot (GOP 2012). The latest door-to-door Cancer Survey of 2013 identified 23,874 patients as confirmed/diagnosed cancer cases, and 84,453 persons were put in the category of suspected cancer cases (Table 15.4). Further, 33,318 cancer deaths were reported in the state during the last 5 years. Incidence of cancer disease measured per lakh population is very high: 90 patients in the case of confirmed/diagnosed cases and 319 patients in the case of suspected cancers cases. In the last 5 years, 18 people died each day in Punjab due to the cancer disease. Across different regions of Punjab, the Malwa region has recorded the highest incidence of cancer disease: 107 patients per lakh people in the category of confirmed/diagnosed cases and 390 patients per lakh people in the category of suspected cancers cases. Although there

Table 15.4 Number of cancer cases/patients and deaths in punjab by region, 2013

Region	Population surveyed (lakh)	Total number cancer cases/deaths			Cancer incidence (per lakh population)		
		Confirmed	Suspected	Deaths[a]	Confirmed	Suspected	Deaths[a]
Punjab	264.84	23,874	84,453	33,318	90.1	318.9	125.8
By Region							
Malwa	102.43	11,005	39,992	14,682	107.4	390.4	143.9
Majha	57.19	3700	20,648	5790	64.7	361.0	101.2
Doaba	50.51	4451	14,770	6890	88.1	292.4	136.4
Unclassified	54.71	4718	9043	5956	86.2	165.3	108.9
Total	264.84	23,874	84,453	33,318	90.1	318.9	125.8

[a]During Last Five Years

Source GOP (2013)

is no authenticated scientific evidence to suggest which factor/s is/are behind rising incidence of cancer disease in Punjab, yet the leading health professionals, academia and policy makers in the state generally attributed occurrence of cancer disease to the rising utilization of agrochemicals (insecticides, pesticides, etc.), presence of uranium, poor quality of drinking water, polluted environment, unhygienic living conditions and ageing of population.

15.3 Decreasing Public Health Expenditure in Punjab

Now the question arises whether the state has been allocating adequate public funds to tackle emerging disease pattern in Punjab. It is true that public health expenditure is a powerful instrument in the hands of state to improve health conditions of the poor (Walle and Nead 1995). Such expenditure also produces a number of externalities such as controlling population by reducing fertility and child mortality rates. As public health sector has to compete with other development sectors for public funds, it is interesting to examine its behaviour pattern over the longer period of time. An analysis of data revealed (Table 15.5) that, although the total expenditure on health services (in real terms at 1993–94 prices) has spiralled from Rs. 138.81 crore by the triennium ending 1980–81 to Rs. 713.78. crore by the triennium ending 2007–08, yet health sector's share out of total budgetary expenditure, development expenditure and state income has shown a decreasing share. For instance, health sector's share had remained around 9 % between the triennium ending period of 1980–81 and 1986–87. And after that, it decreased to 6.97 % by the triennium ending 1989–90, 5.46 % by the triennium ending 1992–93, 4.35 % by the triennium ending 1995–96; slightly rose to 5.48 % by the triennium ending 1998–99 and fell to 4.02 % by the triennium ending 2004–05 and 3.58 % by the triennium ending 2007–08.

Surprisingly, public health expenditure as a proportion of NSDP in Punjab never reached to 1 % for the most of years against the normative ratio of 3 % of national income. The share, instead of rising, has declined to the lowest ebb (0.62 %) by the triennium ending year of 2007–08. The analysis makes it clear that public health sector expenditure in the state has been decelerated over the time period, especially in the post-reforms period. In the absence of adequate public health funds, public health services provided by the state-run hospitals, CHCs/PHCs and dispensaries had become very weak. Many micro-level studies showed a poor utilization of public health infrastructure by the people in the state (Singh 1991, 2013b; Kumar 2011). Moreover, quality of infrastructure in public health institutions found to be unimpressive. Most rural patients felt shy and avoided to visit public health facility for getting treatment because they did not find it useful either due to non-presence of health staff or unfriendly environment (rude behaviour) or non-availability of medicines in the facility (Kumar 2011; Singh 2011). The poor people are pushed to unregulated private health care providers (RMPs, Hakims, faith healers, etc.). Inefficiency, low preference and rent-seeking behaviour of public heath servants

Table 15.5 Distribution of public expenditure in punjab by major heads (revenue account) (Figures in Rs. crores at 1993–94 prices)

Average for triennium ending year	Total expenditure (all heads)	Non-development expenditure	Development expenditure	Social services	Health and family welfare	Health and FW as % age of			Per capita expenditure Rs.
						Social services	Development expenditure	NSDP	
1980–81	1520.24	410.71	1109.54	625.73	139.81	22.34	12.68	1.08	87
	(100.00	(26.66)	(73.34)	(41.00)	(9.30)				
1983–84	1889.60	571.45	1318.14	741.97	172.42	23.24	12.95	1.29	101
	(100.00)	(30.67)	(69.33)	(39.00)	(8.98)				
1986–87	2383.50	837.89	1545.62	932.16	211.71	22.71	14.01	0.99	117
	(100.00)	(34.51)	(65.49)	(39.48)	(9.18)				
1989–90	2994.60	955.39	2039.17	1330.45	215.49	16.20	10.05	0.82	112
	(100.00)	(30.69)	(69.31)	(45.01)	(6.97)				
1992–93	4025.37	1365.99	2689.78	1153.73	223.34	19.36	7.83	0.75	110
	(100.00)	(31.28)	(69.67)	(28.25)	(5.46)				
1995–96	4686.01	2676.80	2009.18	1161.97	214.95	18.50	10.62	0.89	100
	(100.00)	(59.06)	(40.94)	(24.06)	(4.35)				
1998–99	5537.74	2697.89	2839.84	1476.69	292.82	19.83	10.98	0.91	124
	(100.00)	(50.14)	(49.86)	(27.65)	(5.48)				
2001–02	7044.19	4108.59	2935.60	1780.51	371.05	19.84	11.76	0.87	154
	(100.00)	(58.98)	(41.02)	(24.97)	(5.23)				
2004–05	9152.56	5395.67	3756.89	1992.08	371.73	18.66	10.12	0.81	147
	(100.00)	(60.24)	(39.76)	(21.67)	(4.02)				
2007–08[a]	19937.13	11601.50	8335.63	4013.78	713.78	17.78	8.56	0.62	260
	(100.00)	(58.19)	(41.81)	(20.13)	(3.58)				

[a]Expenditure data at current prices. *Note* Figures in parentheses are percent shares

Source **Statistical Abstract of Punjab**, (Various Issues), Economic Advisor to Government of Punjab

have become hallmark of public health sector in the state. Lack of political will and inadequate socio-economic movements, further, encourages the growth of unqualified health care providers, who are mushrooming in numbers in every hook and corner of the state. In the absence of monitoring and control, they indeed played with health of the people.

15.4 Pitfalls of Public Health Delivery System in Punjab

Punjab's public health delivery system has been operating at three levels: (i) at the primary level, (CHC, PHCs and dispensaries); (ii) at the secondary level, (district and tehsil hospitals); and (iii) at the tertiary level (hospitals attached with medical colleges and of centrally funded PGI). In large urban towns, public hospitals attached with the Medical Colleges are providing advance tertiary health care facilities. In medium/smaller towns and few larger villages, the state government runs an extensive network of districts hospitals, tehsil hospitals, CHCs and rural hospitals (RHs). Similarly, an extensive network of CHCs/RHs, PHCs and dispensaries have been serving the rural people. On paper, Punjab's public health care system looks alike an ideal model for delivering universal health care to all including the poor. Its comprehensive three tier design ensures that all households, rural and urban, are closer to a public health facility in the state. For instance, an average household in Punjab can access nearest public facility within 2 km distance; yet this system quite apparently failed to deliver. Widespread absenteeism amongst the health employees and non-accountability had reached nadir in the state. Now, a question arises, whether available the public health infrastructure in the state is adequate or any new reform was introduced over the time period?

15.4.1 Stagnated Public Health Infrastructure

Undoubtedly, public health facilities in Punjab were increased till the mid-1980s mainly due to increased allocation of central funds to state health sector and pro-rural policy of the state (Singh 2005). After that, public funds to the state health services have declined drastically and there was no appreciable increase in public health infrastructure in the state (Table 15.6). Instead, total number of hospitals decreased from 244 to 219 between the triennium ending periods of 1980–81 and 2007–08. On the other side, number of PHCs increased from 129 to 441, and of dispensaries from 1255 to 1453 during the same period. There were progressive decline in the proportions of rural hospitals from 43.77 % by the triennium ending 1986–87 to 35.10 % by the triennium ending 1995–96, and 33.33 % by the triennium ending 2007–08. The proportion of rurally located dispensaries also showed a marginal decrease (from 85.31 % by the triennium ending 1980–81 to 83.20 % by the triennium ending 2007–08), despite the more allocation of central

Table 15.6 Growth of health care infrastructure in Punjab

Average for triennium ending year	Type of health care infrastructure											
	All types of institutions					Population served per institution				Population served per bed		
	Allopathic					Allopathic			Non-A			
	H	PHC	D	CHCs	Total	H	D	Rural PHC[a]	H & D	Total	Rural	Urban
1980–81	244	129	1255	–	1630	0.67	0.13	1.13	0.36	854	1558	387
	(40.98)	(81.65)	(85.31)	–	(78.25)							
1983–84	256	130	1742	–	2137	0.68	0.10	1.13	0.33	802	1276	410
	(43.43)	(85.38)	(87.92)	–	(82.05)							
1986–87	264	143	1779	–	2187	0.70	0.10	1.06	0.33	811	1283	422
	(43.43)	(86.51)	(87.49)	–	(82.10)							
1989–90	250	362	1564	23	2199	0.78	0.12	0.40	0.32	814	1291	436
	(42.72)	(93.38)	(85.57)	(61.43)	(81.74)							
1992–93	210	441	1470	93	2213	0.98	0.14	0.34	0.33	841	1339	449
	(38.16)	(95.23)	(84.06)	(60.79)	(80.96)							
1995–96	208	446	1465	104	2223	1.05	0.15	0.35	0.34	873	1408	477
	(35.10)	(94.62)	(83.30)	(57.69)	(79.86)							
1998–99	208	444	1468	110	2229	1.16	0.16	0.37	0.38	954	1446	589
	(34.99)	(94.74)	(83.04)	(58.36)	(79.68)							
2001–02	216	441	1476	108	2240	1.13	0.16	0.39	0.38	957	1483	566
	(33.69)	(94.55)	(82.70)	(60.99)	(79.27)							
2004–05	219	441	1479	103	2242	1.17	0.17	0.40	0.40	1018	1555	624
	(33.33)	(94.33)	(82.56)	(62.14)	(79.13)							
2007–08	219	441	1453	117	2226	1.23	018	0.40	0.42	1025	1600	677
	(33.33)	(94.33)	(83.20)	(60.18)	(79.33)							

[a]Rural Population, Non-A means non-allopathic which includes Ayurvedic, Unani and Homoeopathic

H Hospital, *D* Dispensary, *PHC* Primary Health Centres, *CHC* Community Health Centres

Figures in parentheses are percent share of rural areas

Source Culled from the **Health Information of Punjab**, (Various Issues), Directorate of Health and Family Welfare, Government of Punjab, Chandigarh

funds to rural health under the Minimum Needs Programme started since the Fifth Five Year Plan (1974–79). This decrease in proportion of rurally located dispensaries is largely due to the upgradation of many rural dispensaries into CHCs/PHCs in the same area during 1984–2000 (Singh 2005).

Further, population served per institution did not showed a progressive decline. For instance, population served per hospital, which was 0.67 lakh during the triennium ending 1980–81, rose to 1.23 lakh during the triennium ending 2007–08. In the case of PHCs that are exclusively for the rural areas, a different picture has been emerged. Actually, due to a sharp increase in number of PHCs over the years, population served per PHC fell from 1.13 lakh persons during the triennium ending 1980–81 to 0.34 lakh during the triennium ending 1989–90, but rose to 0.40 lakh during the triennium ending 2007–08 (Table 15.6). Still, Punjab state is far away from the norms set by the Union Government in terms of population served per PHC (i.e. 30,000 populations per PHC). Similarly, population served per bed did not show any improvement in the state; instead this ratio rose to 1025 persons per bed during the triennium ending 2007–08. Population served per bed also showed wide variations across the rural and urban areas. In rural areas, a bed was for 1276 persons (410 persons in the case of urban areas) by the triennium ending 1983–84 but this ratio rose to 1600 persons (677 persons in the case of urban areas) by the triennium ending 2007–08. The analysis makes it clear that no effort was made by the state government to establish more beds in public owned health institutions of the state. In fact, indoor treatment facility has been deteriorated in the state-run institutions during the post-reforms period (Kumar 2011).

Moreover, one can observe many glaring deficiencies public health facilities in terms of non-presence of health staff, non-availability of health machinery, equipments, buildings and residential accommodation, particularly located in the rural areas. As the entire burden of health care (promotive, preventive and curative cares) in rural Punjab was fell on the rural CHCs/PHCs, which were not adequately equipped (Singh 1991; Kumar 2011) and suffered from rampant absenteeism of health staff (Chaudhury et al. 2006). In fact, an overwhelming majority of rural CHCs/PHCs even today are consultation clinics (OPDs). Hospitalization, trauma care and emergency services (indoor treatment) are almost non-existence in these institutions. At the micro-level, the data revealed no bed occupancy in all rural PHCs and dispensaries in Patiala district during 2008–09 (Office of Civil Surgeon, Patiala District 2009). These findings were also true in the case of other districts of Punjab.

Another dismal aspect is related to non-filling sanctioned post of doctors (specialists as well as generalists) and paramedical staff in public health institutions. Without adequate medical staff, one can imagine the working of these institutions. These posts are deliberately kept vacant by banning recruitment, which is largely due to the pressure of NEP-1991 and of severe resource crunch faced by the state in the post-1990s era. The data in Table 15.7 showed that about one-fifth of sanctioned posts (18.68 %) in state health department were lying vacant in 2005. Interestingly, one-sixth posts of medical officers (16.80 %) were also lying vacant, whereas a large numbers of qualified doctors as unemployed were available in the state.

Table 15.7 Position of doctors, paramedical staff and district health officers in Punjab, 2005

Name of post	Number of posts			% age of vacant posts
	Sanctioned	Filled	Vacant	
Medical officers[a]	4380	3644	736	16.80
Paramedical staff[b]	15,131	12,350	2781	18.38
District health extension officers/supporting staff[c]	278	121	157	56.47
Drivers	532	410	122	22.93
All posts	20,321	16,525	3796	18.68

Note [a]It includes Dental Doctors
[b]It includes Pharmacists, Ophthalmic Technicians, Radiographers, Laboratory Technicians, Staff Nurses, Lady Health Visitors, Supervisors, ANMs, MPWs (M/F), etc
[c]It Includes DMIEOs, District Drug Inspectors, Principal Tutors, Nursing Superintends, District Public Health Nurses, Food Inspectors, Block Extension Educators, Artist-cum-Photographer, etc
Source **Office of Director Health Services**, Department of Health and Family Welfare, Government of Punjab, Chandigarh

Similarly, more than one-sixth of sectioned positions of paramedical staff (18.38 %) and more than one-fifth posts of drivers (22.93 %) were kept vacant. Further, more than one-half of sanctioned posts of district level health extension officers (56.47 %) that provide a crucial link to maintain quality checks in health related fields were vacant. Due to not-filling of sanctioned posts of doctors, paramedical staff and district level health officers (supervisory and monitoring duty), efficiency of state-run public institutions reached a nadir in the state.

In the absence of health staff (doctors and paramedics), particularly in rural health institutions, the people are deprived of easily available, cost effective and good quality treatment supposed to be provided by these institutions at their door steps. Since the public health system in rural Punjab suffered from many weaknesses, one can observe mushrooming growth of quacks in rural areas that are playing havoc with the health of rural people, especially of the poor, by providing substandard treatment and charging exorbitantly high prices. Current dynamics of health care system revealed that still wide gaps were prevalent in the rural and urban health indicators and achievements. The data in Table 15.8 makes it clear that, though all these health indicators have shown positive changes over the time period, yet the rural–urban differences are clearly visible and remained static. For instance, during the triennium ending 2007–08, birth rate in Rural Punjab was 18.2 per thousand live births compared to urban Punjab' birth rate of 16.4 per thousand live births. Similarly, rural death rate was 7.7 per thousand compared to 5.9 per thousand people in urban Punjab during the same period. As regards the infant mortality rate, it was 46.7 per thousand live births and 34.7 per thousand live births in the rural and urban Punjab, respectively. It means that rural areas are lagged behind so far as the progress in health related indicators are concerned.

Table 15.8 Birth rate, death rate and infant mortality rate in punjab by location (rates per thousand)

Average for triennium ending year	Birth rate			Death rate			Infant mortality rate		
	Rural	Urban	Combined	Rural	Urban	Combined	Rural	Urban	Combined
1980–81	29.8	27.6	29.3	10.4	8.0	9.9	105.0	72.7	96.0
1983–84	30.8	28.7	30.3	9.8	6.9	9.1	84.7	57.7	78.7
1986–87	29.6	27.8	29.1	9.5	6.3	8.7	75.3	47.0	68.0
1989–90	29.1	27.5	28.4	8.8	7.0	8.3	66.0	55.7	63.3
1992–93	28.4	25.2	27.5	8.6	6.0	7.9	61.3	42.0	50.0
1995–96	26.6	21.8	25.3	8.3	5.9	7.6	59.0	37.7	54.0
1998–99	24.6	18.9	23.1	8.0	6.2	7.5	55.7	39.3	52.3
2001–03	22.4	18.6	21.4	7.7	6.1	7.3	56.0	38.0	52.3
2004–05	21.6	18.0	20.7	7.3	6.1	7.0	53.7	34.3	49.7
2007–08	18.2	16.4	17.6	7.7	5.9	7.0	46.7	34.7	42.7

Source **Health Information of Punjab**, (Various Issues), Directorate of Health and Family Welfare, Government of Punjab, Chandigarh

15.4.2 Weak Initiatives to Improve Health Infrastructure

The state government, despite being fully aware of these ground realities, did not initiate any planned effort to bring reforms in the public health infrastructure in the state since 1991. The only two initiatives, limited in scope, were taken to reorganize state health system in Punjab. **First initiative** is related to the corporatization of public health services in the state by establishing the Punjab Health Systems Corporation (PHSC) during the late 1990s. The PHSC has taken over only 154 public hospitals—ranging from district hospitals (17), subdivisional hospitals (45) to CHCs/PHCs (92). The main motives of the PHSC were to (i) upgrade the secondary health care system (on selective basis) and (ii) introduce the financing reforms, particularly levying of users' fee and contracting out many services to the private sector. This has been done with the help of World Bank loan of Rs. 422 crores. This has generated a debate and created many suspicions in the minds of intellectuals, policy makers, and health employees, and also among the general public of the state. Many of them fear that it is the implementation of the IMF-World Bank's prescriptions of commercialization and corporatization of health services in the state. Their doubts/fears came true with the introduction of users' charges for every service provided by these institutions and contracting out a part of services provided by the PHSC-owned institutions by allowing the establishment of private diagnostic facilities at these institutions' premises. On the other hand, however, the state government's defence in setting up the PHSC is resting on three counts: **One**, it will upgrade the secondary health care system in the state with the World Bank assistance, which is in bad shape and dire need of funds; **Two**, corporation will have inherent flexible mechanism of taking needy decisions that will otherwise take too much time state bureaucratic set up. Further, it is possible for the corporation to govern their employees in a better way and offer various incentives/rewards on the basis of their performance; and **Three**, it will improve the utilization of public health services by attracting more patients on one hand, and generate internal funds at the institution level through the users' charges for further improvement or expansion of health services on the other.

Second initiative related to improving rural health delivery system in the state under NRHM started in 2005–06. Under this initiative, (i) liberal public funds were made available to upgrade rural health care infrastructure; and (ii) decentralization in the decision-making and administrative control was introduced by handing over 1310 rural dispensaries to district level PRIs (Zila Prishad) in the state. Nearly Rs. 1300 crore were spent by the Punjab government during the last 6 years, i.e. 2005–06 to 2010–11. And, state government has upgraded infrastructural facilities in almost all CHCs (115 out of 116) and 211 PHCs (43.6 %; out of 484) up to 2010–11. In the case of SHCs, service providers (Qualified Doctor) were appointed on the contract assignments @ Rs. 3.50 lakh per year per dispensary. Out of Rs. 3.50 lakh contract money, a service provider is responsible for hiring one pharmacist, one peon and maintaining the basic sanitation and other facilities in dispensary him/her self. On an average, one SHC headed by a service provider served 10 villages. As per initial reports, this contract system has been working very well; service providers are now available to the rural patients during specified hours as their attendance has been monitored by the village Panchayat. A tenfold increase in the number of outpatients has been recorded in these dispensaries. Institutional deliveries have also increased in the rural hospitals/PHCs/CHCs. Absenteeism among the health staff has been reduced. However, the critics point out that an administrative decentralization is no panacea for the basic ills of rural health delivery system in the state, which requires aggressive public health interventions, state support and efficient personnel. For success of decentralization in context of Punjab, it needs a process of devolution of powers, not just the delegation of responsibility by the state to the periphery. Actually, the former involves sharing of decision-making powers and control over the resources, not just the administrative decentralization or shifting the responsibility of resource mobilization, which often has a negative impact, especially on the poor living in the periphery (rural areas).

15.5 Low Efficiency of Public Health Sector

As already reported, there was no major rise in number of public health institutions and beds in the state since the 1990s. Besides, rising rent-seeking behaviour of health sector employees, weak monitoring mechanism and administration apathy during the militancy (1980–95) had attributed directly to low efficiency and low utilization of public health facilities by the patients. An assessment of bed occupancy ratio—a better measure to judge efficiency of any public health services—has shown a very dismal picture. For instance, district hospitals, which were

Table 15.9 Bed occupancy ratio in Punjab by type of hospital

Year	Type of hospital								
	District	Tehsil	Women	T.B	50 beded	30 beded	25 beded	PHC	Whole state
1980	97.4	79.5	79.9	82.2	–	–	–	–	–
1985	100.6	100.5	72.2	77.2	–	–	–	–	–
1990	91.6	65.7	37.3	74.3	50.8	16.3	R-26.5	20.5	63.9
1991	89.2	68.0	39.6	67.6	59.9	17.3	18.2	13.3	54.6
1993	80.8	61.3	40.9	59.4	62.4	12.1	14.5	22.3	46.6
1994	84.6	62.8	38.4	55.6	60.3	14.7	16.7	18.3	48.3
1995	87.9	63.9	37.3	54.4	61.7	16.2	18.7	13.5	44.2
2001	58.1	District hospitals of PHSC							58.3
2005	57.0								na
2007	63.3								na

Source Health Information of Punjab (earlier Health Statistics Punjab), Directorate of Health and Family Welfare Punjab, Chandigarh (various issues)
+ The Tribune, August 12, 2001

overcrowded with the patients (bed occupancy ratio was more than 100 %) during the 1970s (Singh 2005), had shown a downward trend in the utilization of beds for indoor treatment (Table 15.9). A sharper downward trend in bed occupancy ratio was observed in the tehsil hospitals, hospitals exclusively for women and tuberculosis patients. The 30-beded, 25-beded and PHCs that were mostly located in rural areas had shown abysmally low level of bed occupancy. Interestingly, 17 district hospitals taken over by the PHSC did not shown any impressive improvements in the bed occupancy ratio, as it was 58.1 % in 2001, 57.0 % in 2005 and 63.3 % in 2007. Even the hospitals attached with state medical colleges providing tertiary care had also witnessed low bed occupancy, mainly due to the reduced funding, deterioration in quality care and high user' charges since May 1999. Consequently, the patients affording medicare prefer to get medical treatment from the private hospitals/nursing homes, which have already been grown in leaps and bounds in the state (Singh 2005; Kumar 2011).

Two micro-level studies based on primary data (Singh 1991; Kumar 2011) concluded that a large majority of people suffering from different types of diseases in Punjab preferred, instead of nearest public health institutions, going to private hospitals/clinics for treatment even from the untrained persons (called quacks in popular parlance). These studies highlighted that nearly one-third of patients (32.78 % in 1991 and 33.24 % in 2011) used public health centres, and the remaining two-third patients (67.22 % in 1991 and 66.76 % in 2011) preferred to get treatment either the private hospitals/nursing homes or the private clinics (Table 15.10). Regarding to quality of private health facility, the data revealed two interesting trends. First, a very small proportion of rural patients in 1991 (1.41 %) preferred private hospital/nursing homes, whereas 18.16 % of rural patients in 2011 got treatment from such hospital/nursing homes. Second, an overwhelming majority of rural patients who preferred private clinics were treated by unqualified health

Table 15.10 Distribution of patients preferred treatment by type of diseases/illnesses and health centre—1991 and 2011

Type of health institution	Number of patients by type of disease/illness					
	1991			2011		
	Chronic diseases	Communicable and other diseases	Total	Chronic diseases	Communicable and other diseases	Total
Public sector						
Hospital	33 (17.74)	49 (8.28)	82 (10.54)	36 (23.84)	83 (40.10)	119 (33.24)
PHC/CHC/SHC	25 (13.44)	148 (25.00)	173 (22.24)			
Sub total	58 (31.18)	197 (33.28)	255 (32.78)	36 (23.84)	83 (40.10)	119 (33.24)
Private sector						
Hospital/nursing home	8 (4.30)	3 (0.51)	11 (1.41)	37 (24.84)	28 (13.53)	65 (18.16)
Clinic	120 (64.52)	392 (66.22)	512 (65.81)	78 (51.66)	96 (46.38)	174 (48.60)
Of which unqualified[a]	57[a] (47.50)	207[a] (52.81)	264[a] (51.56)	38[a] (48.72)	69[a] (71.88)	107[a] (61.60)
Total	186 (100.00)	592 (100.00)	(778) (100.00)	151 (100.00)	207 (100.00)	358 (100.00)

[a]It shows number of patients opted for private clinics owned by unqualified (Quacks) health personnel
Figures in brackets are percentages
Source Singh (1991), Kumar (2011)

persons. For instance, out of 65.81 % patients treated in private clinics during 1991, more than one-half patients (51.56 %) got treatment from unqualified health persons; whereas out of 48.60 % patients treated in private clinics during 2011, a little more than three-fifth patients (61.60 %) got treatment from unqualified health persons.

Another study by Paul et al. (2004) also confirms these findings. The study found that, although the rural respondents of more than three-fifths surveyed villages (62 %) in Punjab had reported easy access of public health facilities (near to home), yet nearly one-fourth of households (24 %) preferred public health facility for treatment of minor ailments (cough, cold, fever, wounds, loose motion, etc.). And, in the case of major ailments (surgery, fractures, complicated deliveries, strokes, etc.), a little more than two-fifths households (42 %) went to public health facility for treatment and the rest preferred the private health sector (Paul et al. 2004). Free/cheap treatment and easy accessibility were the main causes behind the preferences of surveyed villagers for utilizing public health services. However, only a small proportion of rural households (less than 3 %) that preferred public health institutions for treatment were fully satisfied with the service (Paul et al. 2004). Many other studies conducted in other states of India had similar conclusions (Banerjee et al. 2004; Hammer et al. 2007; Chaudhury et al. 2006).

15.6 Emerging Consequences and Public Policy Issues

The study clearly unravelled that the positive linkages and impacts of rising economic prosperity in Punjab on peoples' health and general well-being during the last few decades of development. It also demonstrates how an overemphasis on agricultural development put constraints on the future economic development of the state in the long run; how its ecology and environment has been deteriorated and polluted; and how the economic slowdown, in the absence of state support, adversely affected health status of the poor masses. It highlights that the moment global forces gained importance in India; public expenditure allocated to Punjab's health sector instead of rising has been reduced. In fact, it remained abysmally low (less than 1 % of NSDP against normative ratio of 3 %). And, no visible expansion and quality improvements were seen in state's public health infrastructure, except the upgradation of secondary health care (establishing PHSC in late 1990s) and rural health centres (NHRM since 2005–06). Thus, under the garb of health sector reforms, cutbacks in public expenditure, donor driven priorities, technocentric public health interventions and increasing reliance on private sector for solving health care problems have become the hallmark of new health strategy. Further, in the state, inadequate allocation of funds to other social sectors (education, rural development, social security, labour welfare, etc.) reduced additional intersectoral state supports to the health of poor people. In such a scenario, people living at subsistence levels (BPL) are becoming more vulnerable to ill-health/diseases and have a weak voice in the system.

The poor and vulnerable sections of society who lack resources (income/employment, assets, etc.) could not afford very high out-of-pocket health expenditure, particularly of the private sector's indoor treatment. When a serious illness/injury/disease strikes in such households, many of them do not seek treatment or delay treatment; and those who seek treatment do face financial hardships or fall into indebtedness or collapse ultimately. Many research studies convincingly demonstrated that ill-health in rural areas has become a major cause of indebtedness (Singh 1991; Kumar and Singh 2010; Singh 2010; Kumar 2011; Singh 2011). Moreover, emerging disease patterns—rising cases of cancers, blood pressure, heart diseases, diabetes, accidents, multiple addictions, violence, etc.—have posed many serious socio-economic problems for the poor who want to get rid of such diseases. A pro-poor health insurance such as the RSBY with much wider scope and official accountability did not working efficiently in the state.

Already, there are reports about gross underutilization and inefficiency in the working of public health services in the state. Truly, high absenteeism along with the absence of essential medicines, diagnostic facilities, first-aid kits and proper buildings, these health care institutions, particularly in rural areas, are acting primarily as the consultation clinics or first-aid centres. This has created a mistrust amongst the beneficiaries and led to rapid growth of private health services. Side by side, the rich and middle income groups, who become health conscious or capacity to pay, began to patronize private hospitals/nursing homes. This led to the establishment of many good private hospitals in the state. Already, 2174 health care facilities with 22,337 beds were working in Punjab's private health sector (PPCB 2012). Many of these hospitals and doctors have very good reputation in providing quality health care in the state. Such hospitals and doctors have the capacity to attract medical tourism in the state, which should be encouraged in the state.

This demand–supply mis-match in Punjab's health sector has been filled by growing number of private hospitals/nursing homes and clinics in the urban areas which are generally concentrated on low risk surgeries and other cases. In rural areas, one can find the mushrooming growth of unqualified health persons that are providing substandard treatment by charging comparatively high prices. Moreover, ever growing private health sector is largely unmonitored and unregulated, with no norms with regard to quality or price of treatment in the state. National Health Policy 2001 also did not suggest any necessary steps to regulate fee, bed charges and standard of treatment provided by the private health institutions. Further, inequities in income may lead to differential access as well as utilization pattern of health services in the state. In the future, these trends, if not regulated/controlled, will seriously jeopardize the human resource development, formation of human capital, its maintenance/improvements and future economic growth in the state.

It is, therefore, suggested that the state should urgently take a long-range view of the economic agenda to follow and integrate it to health policy and other components of state's development strategy. For this, state's economic agenda must be put on the rails by removing undesirable resource crunch and other growth impediments at the earliest. Similarly, state health policy should concentrate on three parameters: (i) raising the demand for 'improved health'; (ii) improving the quality of public health services; and (iii) making the health system more accountable to the users, particularly to the poor.

Acknowledgments The author thanks lavishly the editors of book for their invaluable and critical comments on the first draft of the paper. The errors, if still remaining, are mine.

References

Banerjee A, Duflo E (2009) The experimental approach to development economics. Annu Rev Econ 1:151–178

Banerjee A, Deaton A, Duflo E (2004) Health care delivery in rural Rajasthan. Econ. Polit. Wkly 39(9):944–949

Baru R (1998) Private health care in India: some characteristics and trends. Sage Publications, New Delhi

Baum F (2001) Health, equity, justice and globalization: some lessons from the people's health assembly. J Epidemiol Commun Health 55(9):613–616

Bobadilla JL, Frenk J, Lozano R, Frejka T, Stern C (1993) The epidemiologic transition and health priorities. In: Jamison DT, Mosley WH, Measham AR, Bobadilla JL (eds) disease control priorities in developing counties. Oxford University Press, New York, pp 51–63

CDEIS (2012) Rejuvenation of Punjab economy: a policy document, prepared by Centre for Development Economics and Innovation Studies (CDEIS). Punjabi University, Patiala. http://www.punjabiuniversity.ac.in/cdeiswebsite/index.html
Chaudhury N, Hammer J, Kremer M, Muralidharan K, Rogers HF (2006) Missing in action: teachers and health worker absence in developing countries. J Econ Perspect 20(1):91–116
Cornia GA (2001) Globalization and health: results and options. Bull World Health Organ 79(9):834–841
Das J, Hammer J, Sanchez-Paramo C (2012) The impact of recall periods on reported morbidity and health seeking behavior. J Dev Econ 98(1):76–88
Gill A (2010) Punjab peasantry: a question of life and debt. In: Deshpande RS, Arora S (eds) Agrarian crisis and farmer suicides. Sage Publications, New Delhi, pp 293–311
Gill A, Singh L (2006) 'Farmers' suicides and response of public policy: evidence, diagnosis and alternative from Punjab. Econ Polit Wkly 41(26):2762–2768
Gill SS, Singh S, Brar JS (2010) Globalization and Indian State: education, health and agricultural extension services in Punjab. Aakar Books, New Delhi
GOI (2005) Report of the national commission on macroeconomics and health. Ministry of Health & Family Welfare, Government of India, New Delhi
GOI (2013a) Economic survey 2012-13. Oxford University Press, New Delhi
GOI (2013b) Twelfth five year plan 2012-17, vol I. Sage Publications India Pvt. Ltd., New Delhi
GOP (2012) State programme for prevention and control of cancer, State Health Systems Resource Centre, Department of Health and Family Welfare, Government of Punjab, Chandigarh
GOP (2013) Punjab state report on cancer awareness and symptom based early detection compaign-2013. Department of Health and Family Welfare, Government of Punjab, Chandigarh
Hammer J, Aiyer Y, Samji S (2007) Understanding government failure in public health services. Econ Polit Wkly 42(40):4049–4057
IIPS (2007) National family health survey (NFHS-3) 2005-06, India. International Institute for Population Sciences (IIPS) and Macro International, Mumbai (India) and Maryland (USA)
IIPS (2008) National family health survey (NFHS-3) 2005–06, Punjab. International Institute for Population Sciences (IIPS) and Macro International, Mumbai (India) and Maryland (USA)
Jain V (2014) Affluence, vulnerability and social security evidence from Punjab. In: Singh Inderjeet, Singh Sukhwinder, Singh Lakhwinder (eds) Punjab's economic development in the era of globalisation: essays in honour of R.S. Ghuman. L.G. Publishers & Distributors, New Delhi, pp 248–272
Khurana MR (2011) Agrarian crisis in Punjab and the way-out. In: Shergill HS, Gill Sucha Singh, Singh Gurmail (eds) Understanding north-west Indian economy. Serials Publications, New Delhi, pp 36–108
Kumar K (2011) State, market and utilization pattern of health services: a study of Punjab. Unpublished Ph. D. Thesis, Department of Economics, Punjabi University, Patiala
Kumar K, Singh S (2010) Health infrastructure and utilization pattern in rural Punjab: emerging public policy issues. J Econ Soc Dev 6(2):79–96
Meadows DH, Randers J, Behrens WW III (1972) The limits to growth: a report for the club of Rome's project on the predicament of mankind. Universe Books, New York
Misra R, Chatterjee R, Rao S (2003) India health report. Oxford University Press, New Delhi
Mohan S, Reddy KS, Prabhakaran D (2011) Chronic non-communicable diseases in India: reversing the tide. Public Health Foundation of India. www.phfi.org. Accessed on March 2014
Mosley WH, Bobadilla JL, Jamison DT (1993) The health transition: implications for health policy in developing countries. In: Jamison DT, Mosley WH, Measham AR, Bobadilla JL (eds) Disease control priorities in developing counties. Oxford University Press, New York, pp 673–699
Paul S, Balakrishnan S, Gopakumar K, Sekhar S, Vivekananda M (2004) State of India's public services, benchmarks for the states. Econ Polit Wkly 39(9):920–933
PPCB (2012) Annual report of bio-medical waste management status 2012. www.ppcb.gov.in/environment_standred.php. Accessed in March 2014

Qadeer I (2000) Health care systems in transition III, India, Part I: the Indian experience. J Public Health Med 22(1):25–32

Raman AV, Bjorkman JW (2009) Public Private partnership in health care in India: lessons for developing countries. Routledge, London

Shergill HS (2010) Growth of farm debt in Punjab. Institute for Development and Communication (IDC), Chandigarh

Shiva V (1992) The violence of green revolution: third world agriculture, ecology and politics. Zed Books, London

Singh S (1991) Development and use of health care services in rural areas: a case study of Punjab. Unpublished Ph. D. Thesis, Department of Economics, Punjabi University, Patiala

Singh S (2005) Rural health infrastructure in Indian Punjab: some issues, challenges and policy prescriptions. In: Singh Gopal, Chauhan RK (eds) South Asia Today. Anamika Publishers & Distributors (P) Ltd, New Delhi, pp 380–403

Singh S (2009) Dimensions, determinants and economic burden of ill health in rural Punjab. Unpublished Ph. D. Thesis, Department of Economics, Panjab University, Chandigarh

Singh ND (2010) Rural health care and indebtedness in Punjab. Econ Polit Wkly 45(11):22–25

Singh VJ (2011) Financing of health expenditure in rural Punjab: a study of indoor patients. Unpublished M. Phil. Thesis, Department of Economics, Punjabi University, Patiala

Singh N (2013) State's economy: a case of arrested growth. Hindustan Times October 10

Singh S (2013b) Rural health in Punjab: in shadow of state neglect. In: Ghuman RS, Singh Sukhvinder (eds) Rural local self-government in India: some developmental experiences. Centre for Research in Rural and Industrial Development (CRRID), Chandigarh, pp 161–180

Singh L (2015) Resurrecting Punjab's economy. Hindustan Times, January 06, Chandigarh

Walle VD, Nead K (1995) Public spending and the poor: theory and evidence. The Johns Hopkins University Press, Baltimore

Part V
External Factors in Punjab's Economic Development

Chapter 16
Unpacking the "Diaspora-Development" Mantra: Does Punjabi Diaspora Have the Potential to Contribute to the Rejuvenation of Punjab's Economy?

Shinder S. Thandi

16.1 Introduction: A Success Story Going Astray?[1]

Punjab has historically been an important and strategic state. It is rich and highly productive and fertile agricultural resources tempted many a foreigner to conquer it. Throughout the Mogul, Sikh and British rule periods Punjab remained one of the most prosperous regions in the Indian subcontinent. The British invested heavily in developing its agriculture and communications infrastructure which both boosted commerce and trade and globalised Punjab and the Punjabi imagination, to the envy of other Indian states. In spite of the tragedy of partition and the second partition in 1966, in the post-independent period too, Punjab remained supreme as the number one region and contributed significantly in ensuring India's food security. Economic development of Punjab trickled down to the poor, directly contributing to an impressive record not only in poverty alleviation but also in improving other human development indicators. Using the Tendulkar methodology introduced in 2004–05 and NSSO consumption survey data, Punjab's poverty level during 2009–10 stood at 15.90 % compared with India's 29.8 % and Punjab appears to be on course to achieve the Millennium Development Goal of poverty level of 11.41 % by 2015 (ESO 2013, p. 140).

However, as we entered the twenty-first century the situation began to change and the successful Punjab model based largely around agriculture came under considerable strain. Furthermore, globalisation of the Indian economy, beginning in haste with the reform process of the early 1990s, tended to have accelerated

[1]I borrowed this title from a recently published comprehensive book on Punjab's economy edited by Dhesi and Singh (2007).

S.S. Thandi (✉)
Global and International Studies, University of California,
Santa Barbara CA 93106-7065, USA
e-mail: thandi@global.ucsb.edu

L. Singh and N. Singh (eds.), *Economic Transformation of a Developing Economy*, India Studies in Business and Economics,
DOI 10.1007/978-981-10-0197-0_16

Punjab's decline rather than rejuvenating it, in sharp contrast to the case in many other states. The political leadership in Punjab appeared not to have shown the vision, capability, or the political will to respond to opportunities offered by globalisation or to arrest Punjab's relative decline (Gill 1988; Singh and Singh 2002; Dhesi and Singh 2007; Sawhney 2012; Aiyer 2012).

In terms of its demographics, as a prosperous state, Punjab has experienced considerable amounts of both in and out migrations, the latter both to other Indian states and overseas. The out or overseas migration history is well known and we will assess its implications in more detail in part 2. In-migration was largely a new phenomenon which involved large numbers, especially with the onset of the green revolution in the 1970s. Presently, migrant labour has emerged as a prominent feature of Punjab's labour force in both agriculture and industry. For example, it would not be an exaggeration to say that Ludhiana's manufacturing success has largely been driven by migrant labour where almost two-thirds of the industrial workers were migrants (Mehra and Singh 2014; Pais and Yoshifumi 2014). In-migration, just as overseas migration, has had profound effects on Punjab' polity and society and there has been considerable discussion on the nature of the effects and possible long-term consequences. In recent years, especially in the context of relative economic decline of Punjab, the discourse continues to be framed largely in negative terms. Migrants are blamed for the rise in crime, for adulterating Punjabi culture, for changing the balance in Hindu–Sikh religious identities and for changing the voter balance in certain constituencies (Kaur et al. 2011). There is a dire need for studies which comprehensively identify and assess the net contribution of inward migration in sustaining Punjab's prosperity since the onset of green revolution.

The increased population pressure, compounded by in-migration has inevitably put a great strain on Punjab's natural resources. All types of resources have become overexploited and overstretched leading to environmental damage and raising important questions about loss of biodiversity and future sustainability (PSCST 2007). In addition to the rise in overall population, the socio-economic composition of the population has also changed which brings its own problems. Given the increased competition over resources, more and more Punjabi communities resorted to invoking identity politics in the 1990s to gain greater access (Kumar and Kumar 2002; Jodhka 2005). The failures of the main political parties to deliver on their promises have turned many, especially marginalised groups, to strategically mobilise their own social and cultural capital to gain greater access. Thus over the past two decades issues of caste, class, language and religious identities assumed greater importance in the political discourses on Punjab and India in general (Ram 2007; Jodhka and Mahajan 2012).

In the new globally connected world, the economic well-being or ill-being of Punjab has a direct impact on national and global perceptions and behaviour of all stakeholders, be they resident or non-resident Punjabis, state actors, peasants, migrants, borrowers, investors or philanthropists. This paper is divided into two parts, corresponding to the two main research questions being answered: the causes of relative economic decline of Punjab and the potential for diaspora Punjabis to arrest it. Thus first part provides an overview and a critical evaluation of the major narratives relating to the relative decline of the Punjab economy. These capture discourses on broader socio-economic and political processes including issues relating to agrarian crisis, resource sustainability, lack of industrialisation, nature of centre–state relations and the quality of economic and political governance. Given these narratives, the second part of the paper will then explore the significance of the diaspora-development nexus as applied to Punjab and assess whether the Punjabi diaspora at this juncture has the potential to arrest the decline of Punjab. The paper will conclude by assessing future prospects for diaspora contribution to transform Punjab's economy and polity.

16.2 Part 1: Why Punjab's Relative Decline?

The Punjab state is at a critical juncture in its process of socio-economic transformation. Available evidence suggests that the conventional characterisation of Punjab as predominantly an agricultural or agrarian state needs serious reconsideration. Certainly, in terms of contribution of agriculture to Punjab state's well-being, usually measured by its contribution to the State Domestic Product (SDP), agriculture's contribution has diminished significantly, from around 40 % in the heyday of the 1970s to around 15 % today. Whilst the role of agriculture has clearly declined, it is, however, not clear what Punjab is transforming into given that the historical pattern of structural change with the industrial sector leading the way, has not materialised either. We seem to be witnessing a rapid growth in tertiary sector activities with no strong lead taken by any one specific sectoral activity. With continuing stagnation in agriculture and no obvious lead sector, there is certainly a constraint on Punjab's overall growth rate relative to economic growth in competitor states. As a consequence, this had the inevitable effect of pushing Punjab down the ranking order in terms of per capita income. A state which took pride in being "*unonumero*" for so long has now slipped to sixth or seventh position today. We need to note that this is happening during a period when the Indian economy as a whole has been booming because of rapid liberalisation and globalisation and India's rising global prominence both economically and politically. Has the successful Punjab model run out of steam? Has Punjab submitted to and became consumed by the forces of globalisation rather than managing them better and take advantage of the opportunities it offers? Table 16.1 highlights the relative change in Punjab's ranking as measured by per capita income over the past two decades. It clearly re-enforces the point that Punjab's growth performance has lagged behind both India's and of its main competitor states in the post-reform period.

Table 16.1 Punjab's comparative performance against top 10 states over the past decade (per capita income at constant 1993–94 prices)

States	Per K income (2000–01)	Rank (2000–01)	10th Plan (2002–06)			11th Plan (2007–12)[a]			Per K and rank in 2009–10 (in 2004–05 constant prices)
			Growth rate	Per K income (2006–07)	Rank (2006–07)	Growth rate (target)[c]	Per K income (2011–12)[b]	Rank (2011–12)	
Punjab	15,071	1	5.72	17,864	4	5.9	22,112	7	43,5398 (6)
Maharashtra	14,207	2	8.76	19,680	2	9.1	27,508	3	57,458 (1)
Haryana	13,882	3	9.62	18,881	3	11.0	28,126	2	55,214 (2)
Tamil Nadu	12,994	4	7.21	15,908	6	8.5	22,672	6	46,823 (4)
Gujarat	12,489	5	10.44	21,062	1	11.2	32,394	1	49,030 (3)
Karnataka	11,939	6	9.41	16,256	5	11.2	25,545	4	37,464 (8)
HP	11,085	7	8.49	15,133	8	9.5	22,016	8	40,690 (7)
Kerala	10,174	8	9.42	15,803	7	6.4	23,826	5	46,511 (5)
Arunchal P	10,301	9	5.73	10,960	11	9.5	13,284	12	n/a
Andhra P	10,195	10	5.33	13,071	10	6.4	19,258	10	36,345 (9)
All India (States only)	10,308		8.04	14,009		9.0	19,553		33,731

[a]Projected
[b]Projected
[c]The actual growth rates in 2007–08, 08–09, 09–10 and 10–11 were 9.2, 6.55, 7.84 and 7.78 %, respectively, indicating that the final outcome in 2012 is unlikely to be seventh place ranking
Source Government of Punjab, Department of Planning, Economic and Statistical Organisation (2011)

16.2.1 Narratives on Punjab's Decline

Major narratives on Punjab's decline can be categorised under the following four broad subheadings:

- Declining Role of Agriculture;
- Punjab as a Border State and Militancy of the 1980s;
- Indian Federalism and Centre–State Relations;
- Economic and Political Governance.

16.2.1.1 Declining Role of Agriculture

Historically, a major barometer of health of Punjab's economy has always been the performance of the agricultural sector. The green revolution of the mid- to late 1960s and continuing through the following two decades, ushered in enormous gains both for the farmers (admittedly unevenly among them) and the non-farm sector. Punjab's total food grain production grew from 70 lakh metric tonnes in 1970–71 to 214 lakh metric tonnes in 1996–97 and to 290 lakh metric tonnes by 2011–12, although the rate of growth has slowed down in recent years (ESO 2013, p. 142). As the regional agrarian economy thrived, it also provided an impetus for small- and medium-sized industries to develop and expand to mainly service agricultural activities. However, the green revolution began to run out of steam in the 1990s and Punjab's agriculture thereafter began to stagnate, as evidenced by near stagnant growth in crop yields and productivity in the major crops of wheat, rice and maize (Govt. of India 2013).[2] At the same time, other Indian states did not stand still. Over time, as the green revolution technologies diffused to other states, their agricultural performance also saw spectacular gains and as a consequence the Indian state's dependence on Punjab for surplus food production and procurement began to diminish. Although Punjab can still be characterised as the breadbasket of India, because it is still the single largest contributor, dependency on Punjab continues to decline as seen in its falling contribution to the Central Pool in wheat and rice procurement. For example, Punjab's relative contribution to the Central Pool in wheat fell from 73 % in 1980–81 to 38.7 % in 2011–12 and in rice it halved from 45.3 to 22.1 % over the same period (ESO 2013).[3] These are not insignificant trends and will have long-term implications.

Besides enhancing Punjab's role as the breadbasket of India, the green revolution, however, also left a number of other legacies, the ramifications of which are

[2]According to the Economic Survey of India, yields of wheat, rice and maize have stagnated at around 4,000 and 4,000 between 2005–2006 and 2011–12.

[3]However, despite this relative decline Punjab still remains the single largest contributing state. Data taken from various issues of *Economic Survey of Punjab*, Government of Punjab, Economic and Statistical Organisation.

still being worked out in Punjab: environmental damage to soil and water caused by accentuation of the wheat–paddy rotation cropping pattern, growing level of landlessness as marginal farms lose viability, increased levels of farmer indebtedness and farmer suicides. Some of these negative consequences are discussed in greater detail below.

Green Revolution and Its Environmental Impacts

It has now become clear that the process through which agriculture has transformed over the last three decades imposed tremendous constraints on further growth and sustainability of rural livelihoods. Intensification of land use resulting in perpetuation of the wheat–rice cropping pattern has not only crowded out other forms of food or cash crop cultivation but also resulted in several detrimental environmental impacts that are worth noting. First, a lot of evidence points to a long-term fall in Punjab's water table, a decline of between 5 and 15 m between over the last 20 years and not helped by subsidies to electricity (Humphreys et al. 2010, p. 8). The intensive wheat–rice cultivation has resulted in a serious disturbance of the ground water table, resulting in water shortages in most districts but waterlogging in some others. Moreover, the general depletion of the water table in large parts of Punjab, where water usage is outstripping water recharge, is considered so serious, it forced the government to place 83 of the 138 development blocks in Punjab in the "dark" category where the annual recharge is only between 85 and 100 % and totally inadequate, leading to a fall in the water table by between 30 and 40 ft in these blocks. The situation appears to be particularly acute in the central and south-eastern districts of Punjab with falls of up to 5 m. Falling water table has one important short-term and one long-term consequence. In the short-term, many households need to have their submersible hand pumps re-bored to a deeper level for them to lift water. This is an additional expenditure which some households find difficult to undertake. For farmers who use tube wells or submersible water pumps for irrigation, this is a considerable expense as the bore has to go down as deep as 200 ft from the previous 90–120 ft. This extra but necessary expenditure may require the farmer to finance this investment through a loan, adding to their overall debt. The above effects have been relatively widespread in Punjab over the past 5–10 years. Over the longer term, if present levels of usage continue, water will fast become even more of a scarce resource and it may only be a matter of time before it becomes rationed and punitive charges are levied. Many consumers in urban areas already pay and over time this practice will also spread to rural areas.

Second, the intensity of combined usage of water, fertilisers and pesticides, the so-called magic formula for getting the best out of high-yielding miracle seeds, has resulted in soil degradation and contamination which has not only resulted in "tired-out soil" and near stagnant productivity but has also entered the food chain and animal feed with lethal consequences on well-being. In fact, in one cotton-growing Malwa district of Punjab, infamous for its "cancer train to Rajasthan"—because reliable diagnostic or treatment facilities are not available locally—residues of excessive pesticide and insecticide use, without any health or safety considerations, has already claimed over 33,000 lives.[4] The warning signs of the catastrophic environmental damage have been there for some time but were largely ignored until recently.

Third, intensive and extensive rice cultivation, with water-filled paddy fields lying almost adjacent to or surrounding village housing, has lead to the re-emergence of water-borne diseases such as malaria and dengue which had been largely eradicated. In addition to the above environmental impacts, various other forms of air and water pollution have also been reported and there is continuing loss of biodiversity with certain species of trees, birds and other wildlife disappearing from Punjab's landscape.[5]

The above environmental impacts have generated a vigorous academic debate and positions appear to be clearly divided along two diametrically opposed lines: that Punjab must remain specialised as this offers the Punjab peasantry risk-free and secure livelihoods under current central government pricing and procurement policies; and that Punjab must diversify its cropping pattern if agriculture is to survive as an occupation and retain viability and sustainability in the long run. Such heated academic debates have fortunately generated some positive action and agricultural diversification is now generally promoted by the state and central governments and water management and innovative rice plantation and cultivation methods have been promoted but unfortunately wheat–paddy rotation still reigns supreme today. It remains to be seen whether agriculture, the traditional sustainer of livelihoods, will also become the destroyer of livelihoods under prevailing conditions.

Agrarian Crisis, Indebtedness and Farmer Suicides

In the case of Punjab, historically there has always been an observed relationship between the peasantry and debt.[6] There is no doubt that the total farm debt has gone

[4]There is growing evidence that high level of pesticide residues in soil and water in many Malwa villages which, along with excessive tobacco and alcohol use, contribute to more than average incidences of cancer. Studies show that Punjab has 90 cases per 100,000 of cancer patients compared with the Indian average of 80. In the Malwa region the figure rises to 107.4 but in the Muktsar district it is even higher at 136.3 per 100,000. Over 33,000 deaths were identified up to end of 2014. For some studies, see (CSE 2005; Thakur et al. 2008; The Hindu 2013; The Tribune 2014a, b).

[5]In 2007 the Punjab State Council for Science and Technology provided a comprehensive and detailed report on all aspects of environmental damage and loss of biodiversity in Punjab. See PSCST (2007) for details.

[6]During British colonial times several books by administrators highlighted this facet of Punjabi peasant life, especially as captured in the travelogues of Calvert and Darling. For a recent historical study which revisits the Punjab peasantry and debt question under British rule, see Sohal (2012).

up manifold and according to a recent study by Shergill it rose from Rs 5,700.91 crore in 1997 to Rs 13,829.32 crore in 2008 and household debt (at 1997 constant prices) has grown almost three times in the same period—rising from Rs 52,000 to Rs 1.39 lakh per household (Shergill 2010). Because farmer debt is growing faster than the rise in farm incomes, the absolute debt burden has grown with an alarming rise in outstanding debt. Shergill in his study argued that 72 % of farmers were under debt to various stakeholders such as commission agents, private moneylenders, commercial banks and cooperatives. More recent estimates, based on NSSO data, suggest that the total farmer debt in Punjab is the largest of all Indian states and stood at over Rs 35,000 crores (ESO 2013, p. 150). The debt burden facing small and marginal farmers is the most acute as their capacity to payback is very limited (Gill 2009). The causes of this rising debt are varied and although most of the borrowing appears to be for productive purposes, there is an increasing tendency, especially among some categories of farmers to use borrowing to fund excessive use of alcohol and drugs, to overspend on social ceremonies like marriages, engage in lengthy litigation and on paying travel agents to send their sons overseas in the hope that they will find a well-paying job.

Not surprisingly, the unfolding agrarian crisis in Punjab discussed above has lead to the emergence of an extensive academic literature on identifying and analysing the causes of the agrarian crisis, rise in farm sector debt and increased incidences of farmer suicides. Although growing agrarian crisis and farmer distress culminating in suicides, is an all-India phenomenon, and the Punjab situation is nowhere as desperate as that in states such Karnataka, Madhya Pradesh and Maharashtra, nevertheless it has emerged as an important debating point in discussions on the Punjab model, especially when considered in combination with other dimensions of Punjab's poor performance. The major studies, mainly focusing on the four troubled districts of Mansa, Moga, Bhatinda and Sangrur, with the latter two being the worst affected, point to a number of general but interrelated factors which include increasing cost of agricultural inputs, declining productivity and shrinking incomes which all combine to increase the severity of indebtedness especially among the small and marginal farmers (Jaijee and Sidhu 2011; Iyer and Aora 2010). These studies make two important points: the problem of farmer distress has increasingly worsened over the last 10 years and the issue is particularly acute in the district of Sangrur, followed by Bhatinda, both known for their intensive cotton cultivation. Ironically, the latter debt-ridden district, Bathinda, is also home to the Badal dynasty. Apparently, the fate of the marginal farmers and agricultural labourers in this district is not acknowledged as an issue, or it is not considered an important enough problem for something to be done about it.

The actual number of farmer suicides in Punjab is difficult to estimate, not least because of the interrelationship between the factors involved. There are methodological and other issues too in enumerating the number of total deaths and estimates continue to vary wildly. One of the difficulties relates to ways of categorising deaths. Are farmer suicides really a new phenomenon, as earlier they could have easily been "hidden" under different categories of rural deaths or is this a new "political" category which developed out of a growing awareness about a national phenomenon popularised by left-oriented academics and the media as they highlighted the downside of India's unquestioning embrace of globalisation? The scale of the problem and state-level generalisations are also difficult to identify. Gill, an eminent Punjab economist, commenting after reviewing the various studies on farmer suicides argued that studies which estimated total deaths based on average deaths in one or two of the high population density blocks (of a district) are likely to overestimate the number of suicides of small and marginal farmers and agricultural labourers. Incidentally, the latter category receives little attention due to many of them belonging to non-landed castes. Writing in 2005 Gill stated "there is no systematic study as yet conducted in Punjab to cover all districts of the state to arrive at accurate estimates of such suicide cases" (Gill 2005, p. 233).

Of course some of these small and marginal farmers and agricultural labourers who are in a debt trap find it difficult to manage, leading to acute distress, with many taking their lives. However, identifying the causes of farmer suicides is not an easy task as the decision is likely to be based on several interrelated factors and these are likely to vary from district to district and time to time. Some of the most common variables identified, in addition to the problem of debt, include family disputes, crop failure, loss of status, alcohol and drug abuse, mental problems and low level of education (Shiva et al. 2000).

It is interesting to note that it took some considerable time, including a 2002 directive by the Punjab and Haryana High Court, to persuade the Punjab government, first to acknowledge that there was a problem in Punjab and then to set up a quick enquiry to identify the nature and scale of the problem and finally to negotiate with the Centre to come up with a Relief and Rehabilitations Package similar to that offered to other states facing similar problems. Punjabi farmers were eventually offered relief but it was too little and in many cases too late (Sharma 2013). Finally, the Chief Minister of Punjab, Parkash Singh Badal, maybe as a fallout of the recent Lok Sabha elections, where a new party, the Aam Aadmi Party made spectacular gains and had made farmer suicides an election issue, set up an expert committee, to be led by the Chairman of the Punjab State Farmers Commission, GS Kalkat, to formulate a comprehensive policy to prevent suicide by farmers (The Tribune 2014a, b).

16.2.1.2 Punjab as a Border State and Militancy of the 1980s

Punjab's relative industrial backwardness is often blamed on it being a landlocked, mineral-less and a sensitive border state. It is further argued that its status as a border state acted to both fuel militancy and prolong its duration. Taken together, both translated into low levels of domestic private sector investment and even lower levels of foreign direct investment. In terms of attracting Foreign Direct Investment (FDI), relative to other Indian states, Punjab's record has been abysmal with the state attracting less than 0.6 % of total inward FDI to India since the start of liberalisation in 1991–1992 (DIPP 2011). Undoubtedly, part of Punjab's poor performance can be blamed on the impact of militancy in the 1980s and its legacy which deterred both domestic as well as foreign investments in the state and in fact may have caused some capital flight (Bal 2005). The World Bank (2004) described the economic cost of militancy in the following stark ways:

> The impact of militant activities on growth was swift, widespread and, in some cases, permanent: The industrial growth rate halved, from 8 to 4 %: and the growth rate of services sector decelerated as well, and fell by half, between 1987/88 and 1992/93. Even the agricultural growth rate plummeted from around 6 % year to around 2 % during this period due to decline in long term investment associated with the uncertainty surrounding the militancy activities. Our calculation shows that the output loss suffered by Punjab on account of militancy activities could be as large as 13,000 crores in today's prices (equivalent to 29 % of today's GSDP).

But militancy ended in the early 1990s and we cannot keep on blaming the subsequent poor performance of over 20 years on militancy. In any case Punjab politics has never enjoyed such a stable and golden age in the last 15 years with three consecutive full-term governments and with the current Akali-led government enjoying almost two full terms.

In concluding this section, whilst Punjab may have the disadvantages of being a border state and suffering a prolonged period of militancy which in turn affected investor behaviour, it would be wrong to explain away Punjab's problems using this narrative. This would not explain, for instance, why other border states, whether in South Asia or elsewhere and which are equally disadvantaged, tend to do better and have not suffered from the same fate as Punjab.

16.2.1.3 Indian Federalism and Nature of Centre–State Relations

It has been argued, most forcefully by Pritam Singh that Punjab's development problems, especially the state's overdependence on agriculture and its lack of industrialization, largely stem from the nature of the Indian federal set-up designed towards the project of Indian nation-building at the time of independence and the specific form of centre–state relations this generates (Singh 2008). These centre–state relations work against the interests of Punjab and Punjabis in several ways. First, the Indian state or the Centre generally perceives Punjab as primarily an agrarian state which is crucial for providing food security to India in its overarching quest for cementing Indian nationalism. Through appropriate use of agricultural pricing and procurement policies, Punjab is expected to provide both relatively cheap and plentiful supplies of food grains to the central pool. Second, the Indian State's project of promoting equitable development through redistributing central government grants and financial assistance from highly developed richer states such as Punjab to poorly developed ones like Bihar has disadvantaged Punjab in terms of central allocation of financial resources (Vasishtha and Singh 2004).[7] This would also partly explain why public sector investment in Punjab is negligible compared with other Indian states such as Gujarat and Maharashtra. Third, since Indian federalism works through highly centralised organisations such as the Planning and Finance Commissions, regional aspirations remain suppressed due to limited autonomy and lack of decentralisation in decision-making, thwarting the project of Sikh/Punjabi nationalism. This leads to political tension as competing nationalisms clash. And finally given the constraints under which Punjab is forced to operate, the nature of its economic development is distorted with continuing dependency on agriculture with only limited industrialization. Singh concludes "Punjab's development pattern cannot be understood unless one situates it in the context of Indian federalism, India's development path and the troubled history of relations between the Punjabi Sikhs and the Delhi-based central powers in general and the post-1947 Indian nationalist state in particular" (Singh 2008, p. 166).

Singh's approach is novel and refreshing in that he contextualises the patterns of Punjab development within the wider federal set-up and Indian development strategy, rather than the more micro or regional-centric approaches used by other scholars. However, whilst this narrative may provide a useful framework for explaining Punjab's pattern of development between 1966 and 1991, the time period studied by Singh, it may be limited in explaining Punjab's post-1991 relative decline when greater autonomy was offered to states by liberalisation. In the post-1991 period Singh's argument does begin to weaken and given that major constraints were removed in 1991 (when a "historic break" occurred), why does Punjab, instead of experiencing rapid industrialization, actually undergoes decline in its relative position in the economic league table of Indian states? The important question then seems to be why were other similar, economically developed states, in a better position than Punjab to take advantage of the new environment offered by liberalisation and globalisation? It is a pity that Singh's book, although published in 2008, does not offer any commentary on this phenomenon, especially in terms of exploring post-1991 legacies. It can thus only offer us, at best, a partial understanding of Punjab's current predicament.

In the absence of a significant experience of large-scale industrialisation in the post-1991 liberalisation period—Punjab still remains dominated by SMEs which constitute 90 % of the industrial sector of Punjab—and with Punjab now fully open

[7]Centre–State Fiscal Transfers is a thorny and controversial issue in India and much has been written about reform and shrinking fiscal space for subnational states. To simplify, the assistance to Punjab from the Centre comes in four different forms; share of central taxes, normal central assistance, special central assistance and centrally sponsored schemes. Each has its own criteria for distribution and this is believed to favour relatively poorer states. For example, the Finance Commission's criteria for devolving central taxes to states is based on population, area, fiscal capacity, distance and fiscal discipline which tends to be biased against more developed states and according to the Punjab's Economic and Statistical Organisation, Punjab's share of central taxes fell from 2.45 % in 1970–75 to 1.39 % in 2010–15 (ESO 2013). Others have argued that level of extent of political representation and bargaining power at the Centre also has an effect. For the latter argument, see Vasishtha and Singh 2004.

Structural Change in the Punjab Economy and Sectoral Contribution to State Domestic Product 1980-2013(in 2004-2005 constant prices)

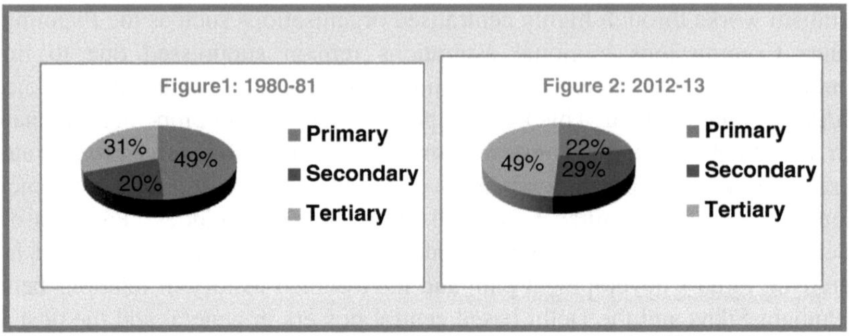

Source: *Economic Survey of Punjab* (2013)

Fig. 16.1 Structural change in the Punjab economy and sectoral contribution to state domestic product 1980–2013 (in 2004–2005 constant prices). *Source* Economic Survey of Punjab (2013)

to global companies, Punjabis have ended up consuming a very large proportion of both domestically produced consumer goods and imported consumer goods. This massive growth in "consumerism" is manifested in the rapid growth in transportation, distribution and warehousing and financial services which have become the leading components of the tertiary sector. Figure 16.1 shows the structural changes in Punjab's economy over the past 30 years. It illustrates agriculture's diminishing share in SDP and the rise of the tertiary sector, at 44 %, to emerge as the largest sector. It helps to re-enforce the point that Punjab has transformed from being a "production"-based economy to one based on "consumption". Needless to say, the growth in middle class consumption, especially of consumer goods—cars and SUVs, cable/satellite TV, refrigerators, CD and DVD players, PCs and laptops, mobile phones and tablets, ceiling fans, air-conditioning units, washing machines, etc.—has lead to a massive demand on energy, contributing further to generate acute power shortages.

In the regional political domain, however, Singh's diagnosis of the problem is more clearly articulated by the leadership of Shiromani Akali Dal (SAD), a Sikh party which has ruled Punjab (in coalition with the BJP as minor partner) for 12 out of the last 15 years. For SAD, every problem faced by Punjab has its roots in discrimination by the Centre, whether it is lack of industrialization, financial burden caused by fighting militancy or agricultural diversification. Given that the recent election has resulted in an outright BJP majority in Parliament, it would indeed be interesting to see how this will affect Centre's attitude towards Punjab's development needs.

On a related issue, although there is ample research which examines state-level performance, literature which examines intra-regional performances and inequalities, especially between the three main subregions of *Malwa*, *Majha* and *Doaba* is very limited. Cursory analysis of the subregions suggests that economic inequalities have worsened with Malwa remaining the most backward, despite having elected to office many Chief Ministers, including Badal, and other very prominent politicians.[8] In response to Malwa's domination in political decision-making, critics have, with some justification, often alleged economic discrimination against Manjha and Doaba as Malwa seemed to have more projects sanctioned by both the state and central government in recent years. In reality though many of these projects have failed to take off or were never completed and Malwa still remains the most underdeveloped region of Punjab and also suffers from the acute agrarian problems discussed above. This relative backwardness can be seen in many sectors such as in the number of medical institutions, education, roads and general infrastructure. The Punjab development model, especially in the non-agricultural sectors, seems to be based on strengthening the growth pole surrounding five major cities: Amritsar, Jalandhar, Ludhiana, Patiala and Bathinda. The scale of industrial development in some smaller industrial towns such Asron, Kurali, Mohali, Nabha, Moga, Phagwara, Goraya and Batala is negligible to have an overall impact on Punjab's economic growth. And when one moves inland, away from the cities and small towns of most districts, there is hardly any evidence of industrial development. Furthermore, situation in the border villages is even worse as they are lagging behind markedly despite various schemes to upgrade them. Thus it is imperative that rejuvenation policies for Punjab must address both state-level relative decline and growth in intra-regional inequalities.

16.2.1.4 Economic and Political Governance—Growing Fiscal Distress

Punjab is often characterised as a "rich state with poor government" due to the health of state's public finances. One would think that a rich and buoyant state would be able to generate sufficient tax revenues to keep up with rising expenditures or at least demonstrate an element of fiscal prudence and responsibility. On the contrary, Punjab has emerged as one of the most profligate and indebted states amongst the top 10 states of India and its fiscal deficit has continued to mushroom. Punjab currently has total accumulated debt of Rs. 69549 crore which is 30.40 % of the GSDP and expected to go up to Rs. 78,000 crore by the end of 2011–12 and with net borrowing at Rs. 8923 crore.[9] An examination of the causes of the deficit indicates that on the revenue side there is inadequate effort on collection of tax revenues and widespread tax evasion and where revenues could be raised, for example urban property taxes or through water and electricity charges, political constraints get in the way. Populist sops in the form of heavy subsidies to both urban and rural elites means that the political status quo and vote banks remain

[8]Apparently, village Badal, the home of the Badal family, is highly developed and can be seen as an oasis in an otherwise undeveloped region.

[9]Government of Punjab (2011) press statement as of 31/3/2011.

unchallenged. On the expenditure side, centrally mandated salary increases to an ever growing bureaucracy, pensions, interest payments on accumulated debt, subsidies to poor performing public undertakings, perks to politicians and public employees, personal gifts and grants which perpetuate feudal style political patronage by politicians, especially by the CM himself such as in the "*sangat-darshan*" programme, all contribute towards widening the fiscal deficit. Salary increases mandated by the Pay Commissions, pension payments and interest payments on accumulated debt alone constitute a very large proportion of state expenditure, in some years making up 70 % of collected revenues.

The Punjab State has generally tried to shift the blame on rising debt on expenditure incurred in fighting militancy during the 1980s and early 1990s and has regularly appealed for debt forgiveness but the Centre has refused to write off all the debt, presumably because the Centre does not see any real intent on the part of Punjab government to demonstrate fiscal prudence or responsibility, despite having passed the Fiscal Responsibility and Budget Management Act in 2003. However, we need to be fair in not laying all the blame on Punjab governments. A plan to bring down the fiscal deficit through consolidation to 3 % of GSDP by 2014–15 has been agreed with the various Finance Commissions but we wait and see if the targets on deficit reduction will be met (ESO 2013).

One important consequences of fiscal irresponsibility is that very little is left over for development expenditure on schools, higher education, hospitals and primary health facilities and community development. Whilst some of these facilities are now beginning to be provided by the private sector—maybe that is the hidden agenda—it is shameful that in large parts of the rural areas, state provision of basic services is either highly inadequate or has continued to deteriorate.

In this first part of the paper, we have used four dominant narratives which shed light on the relative economic decline of Punjab: stagnation in agriculture; Punjab as a border state coupled with role of militancy in the 1980s; Indian federalism and the nature of centre–state relations and political and economic governance. The overall relative economic decline of Punjab is matched by political and social corrosion of state institutions. The private sector (read wealthy families from the ruling elites from both Punjab and outside) is expanding its tentacles in all spheres of public life and the issue of corruption and accountability are matched by counter allegations of the same, leaving the common man helpless and a silent witness.[10] There is almost a collapse in the moral and ethical dimensions of public policy. The academy has responded by highlighting the issues and has proposed positive policies to move forward but these often fall on deaf ears because acknowledging them would involve taking proactive action and showing decisive leadership. How ironical that the demise of Punjab as a top state has happened in a period of unparalleled political stability in its post-independent history. Three successive full-term governments would have been a dream in the 1960s and 1970s but instead

[10]This context may help us to understand why in the recent Lok Sabha election the Aam Aadmi Party surprisingly won four seats—in fact the only wins for the AAP anywhere in India.

it has turned into a nightmare and prospects for a sustainable future on current trends look bleak indeed—unless radical changes occur as a result of recent parliamentary elections.

16.3 Part 2: Does Punjabi Diaspora Have the Potential to Contribute to the Rejuvenation of Punjab's Economy?

16.3.1 The Diaspora-Development Nexus

The closing decades of the last century have seen diasporas entering the centre stage of global affairs. Such is the importance attached to diasporas, there are now regular government-sponsored and multilateral agency conferences focusing on different dimensions of the potential contribution of diasporas to homeland development. These vary in scale and scope, for example focusing on the potential contribution of diasporas in the economic, financial, cultural, health, social and political spheres. Diaspora finance, such as remittances, bank deposits, diaspora bonds and non-resident Foreign Direct Investment, provides important sources of development funds as well as improving foreign exchange reserves. Governments and multilateral agencies are increasingly promoting innovative policies for active engagement with diasporas. The earlier dilemma posed to nation states and which dominated policymaking for several decades, perceived diasporas as "Janus faced" and a potential threat to national security (Kapur 2007, 2010). The new perception, however, increasingly views diasporas largely as agents of development (Merz et al. 2007; Brinkerhoff 2009; UNCTAD 2012). Certainly, state rhetoric and intent is there in terms of leveraging the diaspora but whether the potential is being realised or could be fully realised by nation states is a matter of some contention.

The academy too, initially, struggled in identifying roles and impacts of diasporas but there has been a fundamental shift in thinking about diaspora's potential contribution over the last two decades. Academic discourses shifted from viewing diasporas as potential liabilities—because they can fund extremism, communalism, separatism and perpetuate inequalities—towards perceiving them as strategic assets which can bring positive contribution to the homeland, but only if the right mix of policies are adopted. The last decade has seen a proliferation in research which regurgitates the positive diaspora-development mantra (Merz et al. 2007; Brinkerhoff 2009; Kapur 2010). Figures 16.2 and 16.3 capture the essence of latest thinking on diaspora's potential contribution to development through two lenses. Figure 16.2 identifies the four types of diaspora capital which have the potential to bring about socio-economic transformation of the homeland. Each of these "capitals" makes a contribution at different levels of the homeland economy, resulting in potential transformation. Figure 16.3 highlights the three major channels through which diasporas can raise the productive capacity and capability of the homeland,

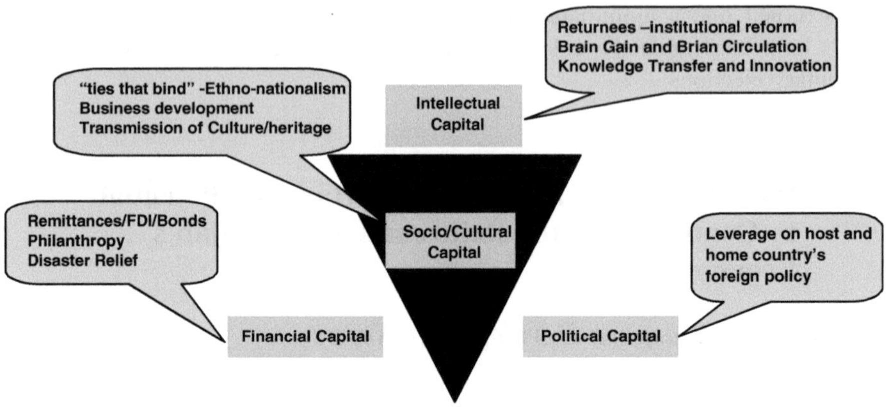

Fig. 16.2 The 4 C's of diaspora capital

through assisting with better utilisation of productive resources, enhancing entrepreneurial capabilities and via developing production linkages. The concepts and issues raised in these two frameworks need to be viewed as complementary as they both represent different dimensions of diaspora contribution.

In the Punjab case, financial capital is the most tangible and visible contribution with overseas remittances historically playing an important role (Thandi 1994). Diaspora philanthropy has also emerged as a valuable micro-level contribution especially in the health and education sectors (Thandi 2007; Dusenbery and Tatla 2010). Unfortunately, other forms of diaspora financial capital, such as FDI and diaspora bonds have little presence in Punjab with the Punjab government so far shying away from issuing special diaspora bonds, unlike the Indian and Sri Lankan governments (Ketkar and Ratha 2007). Further, thus far there is only scant evidence of diaspora contribution in the forms of social/cultural and intellectual capital and, if anything, evidence points to a negative contribution of the former with some small sections of the Sikh diaspora funding the Khalistan movement. There is some evidence of leverage of political capital but its effects are felt largely in the political rather than the economic domain. Taken together, the relative lack of almost all forms of diaspora capital mean that production linkages fail to develop and diaspora's potential contribution towards raising productive capabilities remains highly restricted.

Concluding on diaspora finance, family remittances still remain the most popular and important form of diaspora capital. Although philanthropic or community remittances have also become popular in the last couple of decades, their impact remains at the microeconomic level and their potential could be further maximised.[11] The most disappointing aspect of the Punjab case is lack of mobilisation

[11]For instance according to one estimate, annual remittances to Punjab are as high as US$2 to US $3 billion, which amount to a significant 12–18 % of Punjab's gross state domestic product (World Bank 2004, p. 21).

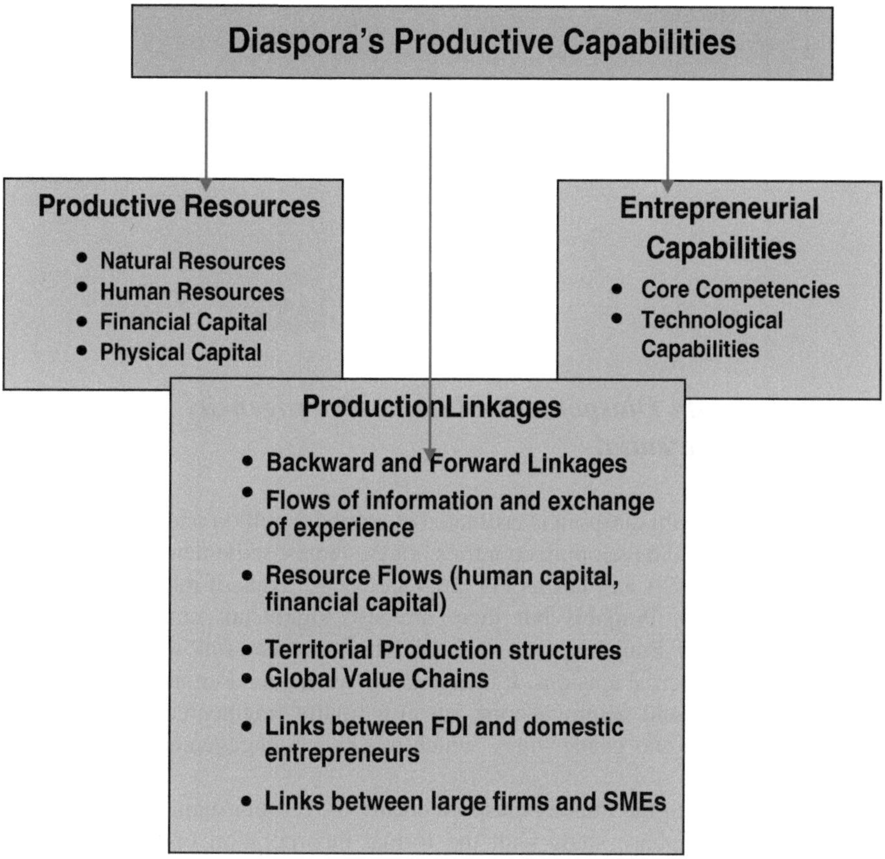

Fig. 16.3 Diaspora's contribution to raising productive capacity. *Source* Adapted from UNCTAD (2012, p. 27)

of diasporan foreign direct investment which remains almost conspicuous by its absence and constitutes a failed story relative to other migrant-sending states of India such as Gujarat, Kerala and Karnataka. The very little NRI FDI that has flowed in has been in the IT, real estate and education sectors and is generally only of small scale.

So why has the promise of Punjabi diaspora failed to translate into reality? What explains the lack of constructive engagement? To answer these questions we need to turn to the patterns of emergence, evolution and characteristics of Punjabi diaspora and Punjab's diaspora engagement policies.

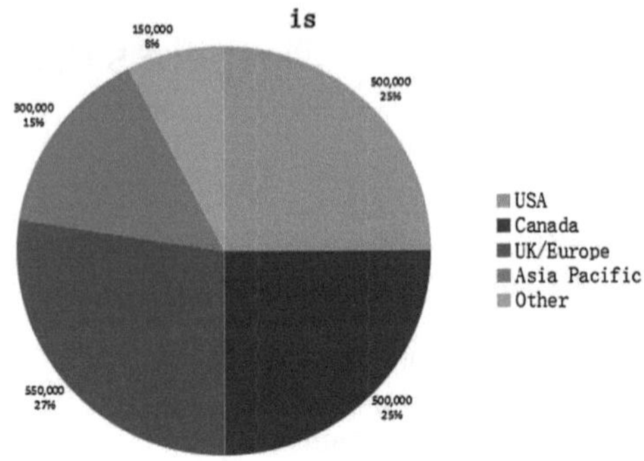

Fig. 16.4 2 Million global Punjabis. *Source* Thandi (2014, p. 43)

16.3.2 Punjabi Diaspora: Evolution, Heterogeneity and Potential

Currently, the Punjabi diaspora is estimated at around 2 million and is spread across many developed and developing countries but the largest settlements—almost 75 % —are in Canada, USA and UK as Fig. 16.4 shows. In terms of religion, the largest component is Sikh Punjabis but there are also significant numbers of Hindu Punjabis and *Dalit* Punjabis, many of the latter are also followers of the Sikh tradition despite internal tensions. It is argued below that the Punjabi diaspora is not only very diverse and heterogeneous but also highly fragmented along religion, region, class, caste and gender lines, which makes any engagement with it highly problematic.

The emergence of the Punjabi diaspora occurred over four main and overlapping phases. The early phase starts with the formal incorporation of Punjab into the British Empire in 1849 which also coincides with the latter's expansionist phase, especially east of India. Although many went abroad as part of imperial duties in South-east Asia, there were also a considerable number of fare paying migrants looking for an adventure and opportunity abroad, venturing as far as Latin America and the Pacific coast around Vancouver. The second phase starts in the post-WW2 period, which proved to be critical in the evolution of the modern Punjabi diaspora. Mass migration occurs to the UK and then Canada and on a more limited extent to the USA, especially after immigration controls became more relaxed in North America from the mid-1960s. The third phase starts with rise of the construction boom in newly rich Gulf States in the early 1970s with different types of Punjabis readily supplying both skilled and unskilled labours. Punjabi *dalits* and artisans were particularly prone to take advantage of the new employment opportunities offered in the Gulf States and other oil-rich Arab states in general. The final phase starts with the ending of the Cold War which opened up new land and sea routes to different geographical regions of Europe. As a consequence new communities of significant size have emerged in southern mainland Europe especially in Italy, Greece and Spain, adding greatly to those already settled earlier in Germany (Thandi 2012, 2014). This phase also sees a significant increase in new migration associated with militancy in Punjab where migrants are travelling to North America or Europe, legally or illegally, to escape violence in Punjab and claim political asylum or refugee status.

Thus, by the close of the last century there had emerged a significant global presence of Punjabis in many parts of the globe, especially in territories erstwhile occupied by the British and in the heart of the Empire itself. These Punjabis varied in terms of their districts of origin in Punjab, in terms of their religion, caste and socio-economic backgrounds. One common characteristic, however, was their overwhelmingly rural character. In diaspora locations, whilst their Punjabi regional identity united them and lead them to share many common cultural and political organisations, festivals and customs, however, fissures began to develop leading to social and caste differentiation over the longer term. In some diaspora locations such as the UK, diversity and heterogeneity continue to be perpetuated over time. We can clearly see this differentiation among Punjabi communities in terms of segregated or caste-based places of worship, festivals, neighbourhoods, social and kinship relationships. Unfortunately, even a significant percentage of philanthropic giving to Punjab has also become caste- and religion-specific. Table 16.2 provides estimates of the number of global Punjabis, their major characteristics and nature of their engagement with the homeland.

Given the lengthy period of settlement, family reunion and consolidation, diaspora communities in the more developed countries have become relatively wealthy with a substantial growth in the number of Punjabis engaged in professional, business and entrepreneurial activities in their adopted countries. Although still small in number relative to the total size of the overseas Punjabi community, businessmen and entrepreneurs wield considerable economic and political power in their host countries and have the potential to play an active part in their homeland development too, given the right conditions. In fact all members of the community have the potential to contribute through many channels discussed in Sect. 16.3.1. The reason why actual contribution is very different from the potential contribution is discussed below.

16.3.3 Constraints to Positive Engagement in Punjab

There are several specific constraints which can be identified in explaining Punjab's lack of success in developing a constructive engagement with its diaspora. The first and foremost constraint is related to the character of Punjabi diaspora as discussed in Sect. 16.3.2. Not only is it economically, socially and politically fragmented, it also offers limited potential in terms of contributing to Punjab's development, for example lack of a critical mass of skilled and talented migrants and established entrepreneurs who may have the potential to contribute through intellectual capital. Although Punjabi enterprise is thriving in many diaspora locations, it is largely small-scale offering limited opportunities for transnational investment and trade. In any case, the more powerful industrialists and entrepreneurs do not see Punjab as a

Table 16.2 Global Punjabi diaspora—salient characteristics

Country	No. of Punjabis	Characteristics	Type of engagement
UK/Europe	550,000	Largely second or third generation Majority rural Sikh Jats from *doaba* region Also significant number of Hindus, Ramgarhias and Ravidassias Highly politicised and caste-conscious	Remittances Philanthropy Small-scale industrial investments Investment in rural and urban real estate, e.g. purchase of land plots and apartments
USA	500,000	Limited number from "old" migrants but largely second generation Mostly post-1960s with a mixture of both unskilled/semi-skilled and professionals Mixture of rural and urban origins Significant number of vocal post-1984 migrants Highly politicised with wide support for "human rights agenda"	Remittances Philanthropy Small-scale industrial investments Investment in rural and urban real estate, e.g. purchase of land plots and apartments
Canada	500,000	Limited number from "old" migrants but largely second generation Mostly post-1960s with a mixture of both unskilled/semi-skilled and professionals although former greater in number Largely from rural areas especially doaba region Significant number of vocal post-1984 migrants Highly politicised with Sikh Jats most vocal especially in Vancouver and Surrey, BC	Remittances Philanthropy Small-scale industrial investments Investment in rural and urban real estate, e.g. purchase of land plots and apartments
Asia and Pacific	300,000	Constitutes "old" and "new" diasporas Old diasporas in places such as Fiji, Thailand, Malaysia and New Zealand—fifth or sixth generation Old diaspora but rapidly developing relatively new diaspora in Australia	Limited remittances
Other	150,000	Old and new—largely in Africa, Latin America, Middle East	Remittances
Grand total	2,000,000		

Source Thandi (2014, p. 45)

place to earn high returns and tend to either invest in other parts of India or world. A classic example is Swaraj Paul, head of Caparo Industries who originally migrated from Jalandhar. Although the group has made many investments in India, Punjab has not figured in the plans. Even highly successful, wealthy and large landowners in California such as Didar Singh Bains or the Tut brothers, have shown little interest in investing in Punjab agriculture or in agroprocessing industry which has been crying out for foreign investment. Further, many of the Punjabi entrepreneurs engaged in trade in ethnic goods, especially food, tend to be importers of commodities—rice, pulses, spices, canned vegetables, etc., rather than exporters. Thus, even if Punjabis showed a greater homeward orientation and patriotism, given their limited scale and scope, their ability to contribute effectively will be fairly limited in rejuvenating the Punjab economy. Punjabi diaspora's fragmentation also makes implementation of outreach policies more challenging as their "one size fits all" character will not appeal to all kinds of Punjabis, particularly as more and more of them are born abroad (ONS 2012).[12]

As mentioned previously, an important characteristic of overseas Punjabis is their overwhelming rural origins, with many having an agrarian mindset rather than an industrial, business or ICT background. Despite business success among some diasporan Punjabis and the emergence of a sizable professional class among second- and third-generation Punjabis, they lack critical mass of financial, social and intellectual capital (as described in Figs. 16.2 and 16.3) and these act to constrain the flow of both the quantity and quality of all forms of diaspora capital to Punjab. Paradoxically therefore, for Punjab, incentives and mechanisms which increase the flow of family remittances or philanthropic giving may have a greater chance of success than the oft-hyped NRI contribution through foreign direct investment (Thandi 2007; Dusenbery and Tatla 2010; Thandi 2010). A further possibility, which has already yielded some success, for example in the case of Indo-Canadian trade and investment, is the potential role that diaspora-based Punjabi politicians can play in improving bilateral economic relations (Slessor 2013). But that too faces serious constraints as discussed below.

There are two additional points related to characteristics of overseas Punjabis which are noteworthy. First, in locations where empire or pioneer Punjabis migrated in the early part of the twentieth century, their fifth or sixth generation children have largely lost touch with their Punjabi roots and thus may not have any regular connection with Punjab, except occasional visits in connection with heritage tourism. To them, Punjab is a foreign environment and not necessarily the place they want to do business in. In such a context Punjab government's outreach policies are hardly going to attract their attention. Second, given that the largest component of Punjabi, especially Sikh diaspora—and those settled in UK, Canada or USA—is post-mid-1960s, and with a significant number post-1980s, their relationship with Punjab has become problematic, particularly given the volatile

[12]For example the 2011 UK census reported that 56 % of the UK Sikh population was born in the UK (ONS 2012).

political situation in Punjab in the 1980s. Many still feel a deep sense of alienation from both India and Punjab especially over Operation Bluestar of June 1984 and inability of the Indian state to bring closure to the anti-Sikh violence which erupted in Delhi in the aftermath of the assassination of Indira Gandhi in November 1984. This deep sense of injustice is reflected, for instance, in one Sikh advocacy group, *Sikhs for Justice*, attempting to indict both the Chief Minister of Punjab, Parkash Singh Badal and Sonia Gandhi, leader of the Congress Party, to a USA court for alleged gross human rights violations. However, farcical this may sound or whether we see these as cheap political stunts by the Sikh advocacy group, these actions have wider support or at least there are no significant countervoices against this form of advocacy. This alienation is also seen in the significant diasporic support for the release of "political prisoners" like Bhullar and Rajoana.[13] More recently, the release of UK government classified documents under the 30 year rule which revealed that the British government gave military intelligence assistance in planning Operation Bluestar some months before the army assault on Darbar Sahib in early June 1984 has reopened old wounds. These revelations have estranged many British Sikhs from the UK Conservative Party and created further tensions with Punjab-based parties who were party to discussions leading up to Operation Bluestar. I give these examples as symptoms of a deeply troubled relationship between significant segments of the Punjabi diaspora which probably has the greatest potential to contribute positively to Punjab's development. Given this prevailing context, it makes little sense to regurgitate the diaspora-development mantra for Punjab.

The second factor relates to the importance of creating strong networks of emigrants engaged in the business of diaspora finance, including diasporan philanthropy. At present the most successful forms of diaspora finance are coming from individual or family remittances and from village-level philanthropic associations, some aided by Punjab government's matching grant schemes. Recent research has indicated that private and community-oriented financing is also important in promoting equitable rural development, especially in the *doaba* region (Singh and Singh 2007; Sidel 2007; Thandi 2010; Sahai et al. 2011). In addition to the Punjab government courting only wealthy Punjabis, who may make promises to invest in Punjab, it needs to strengthen wider networks so that more investment flows into trade and industry of the whole region. Evidence from other states of India such as Kerala, Tamil Nadu and Gujarat suggests that promotion of investment in specific sectors such as health or education or by identifying industrial clusters may be a more effective strategy to harness the talent of overseas-based businessmen and professional migrants. Unfortunately, Punjab is deficient on a number of fronts which prevent potential foreign investors from taking advantage of

[13]It is noteworthy that on 28 February 2013, after a petition organised by *Kesri Lehar*, and with support from the Sikh Federation, both UK-based Sikh organisations, initiated the British government to have a one and half hour parliamentary debate on the death penalty in India. The petition was largely based on Sikhs' opposition to the unjust treatment of Bhullar and Rajoana. For details of the debate, see Daily Hansard (2013).

positive externalities, for example lack of industrial and IT sectors which would generate agglomeration economies, sound infrastructure, lack of a pool of skilled and educated manpower, assistance in business start-ups for NRI returnees and investor-friendly and transparent decision-making. It is reasonable to assume that the very factors which constrain FDI inflows into Punjab are also responsible for limiting NRI investment and even Punjabi domestic investment.

The third failure relates to the lack of an infrastructure that would facilitate effective communication channels between diaspora communities and their homeland. The Internet offers an enormous potential for leaders in the homeland and diaspora communities to exchange and share information relatively instantly and cheaply. Such information can pertain to business and investment opportunities, skill shortages, databases on diaspora-based and homeland experts, progress reports on ongoing or new philanthropic projects, organisations offering opportunities for social and cultural exchanges and briefings on new multilateral initiatives on diaspora engagement. In Punjab, some token initiatives have been introduced to offer this facilitation but they remain largely undeveloped, under-resourced, and politicised. As regards the latter, for instance, whenever Shiromani Akali Dal or Congress Party politicians have visited abroad, their appeal remains limited exclusively to within their own political party circles, community or personal networks thereby excluding some Punjabi groups such as the Punjabi Hindus or dalits. Further, the highly politicised and fractious Punjab NRI Sabha has hardly made any inroads into identifying and assessing the contribution of all sections of the Punjabi diaspora to Punjab's economy let alone engage in any outreach activities abroad (Thandi 2000). Punjabi pluralism abroad needs to be matched by a multipronged pluralist diaspora policy which is inclusive in approach.

The fourth failure in leveraging the diaspora has been lack of incentives and innovative mechanisms for luring migrant investment. These include not only liberalisation of key sectors not currently open to NRIs but also liberalisation of financial flows. Recent incentives such as offering matching state grants are also part of this strategy—and Punjab has in the past introduced these for NRI village modernisation projects—but this need to be expanded and fully embraced and complemented through larger budgetary allocations and dedicated administrators rather than revolving ones to develop credibility, sustainability and trust.[14] Further, too often the incentives are geared towards promoting inflows but neglect the fact that incentives are also required for reversal of flows if the migrants deem it necessary. Appealing to the Punjabi migrant's sense of cultural or ethnic identity or patriotic loyalty will not work if the migrant's perception is that the incentives on offer are not transparent or are discretionary and unfair. In certain cases there may also be a role for offering non-financial incentives, for instance high-profile awards which acknowledge the migrant's contribution to the economic well-being of the

[14]In this regard the role of Hometown Associations in contributing to economic development in some Mexican and other Central American countries is worth considering and replicating. For an assessment, see Orozco and Welle (2009).

region or in their country of adoption. The recent honouring of high-profile individuals at *Pravasi Bharatiya Divas* at national and state functions has acknowledged this requirement but these need to be promoted in a non-politicised and non-communitarian way to ensure credibility. The NRI Sabha and the Punjab Chamber of Commerce were seen as potential vehicles for promoting this activity but their limited powers and politicisation have rendered them relatively toothless in garnering wider appeal among overseas Punjabi communities.

However, it needs to be acknowledged that recent Punjab governments have become more proactive in introducing some aspects of the above policies, but often it has been the case of too little, too late—thus not generating a great deal of commitment and trust amongst the Punjabi diaspora communities. One should not be very surprised, therefore, that despite the hype, Punjabi migrant response, especially in terms of diaspora investment, has been very disappointing. The continuing perception of Punjab as a state with poor governance, lacking transparency in decision-making, having a meddlesome bureaucracy means that potential diaspora-based investors shy away.

16.3.4 Mobilisation Strategies—Is There a Way Forward?

It has been argued above that largely due to structural characteristics of the Punjabi diaspora, there are formidable barriers to it playing a constructive role in Punjab's development. However, three out of the four reasons discussed above point to shortcomings in effective engagement and mobilisation policies of successive Punjab governments, leading to a failure in making Punjabi diaspora a true partner in the home country's development process. Agunias and Newland (2012) in Fig. 16.5 highlights four fundamental principles on which to lay the foundations of a successful diaspora engagement policy: identifying goals and capacities, mapping diaspora geography and its assets and skills, taking actions which create relationship of trust between diaspora communities and governments of both host and home countries and finally mobilising all stakeholders, including diasporas, to contribute to sustainable development. Although the model outlined above shows different stages in developing an effective partnership, they are in fact interactive and need to be developed simultaneously with focus on continuous capacity building and feedback on different processes. The balloons on each side represent the actions required at each element of the engagement strategy. Applying this to the Punjab situation, whilst some of the actions have already been taken at the central or state level, many others are crucially missing, making the actions seem ad hoc, arbitrary, incoherent and incomplete which indicate an absence of strategic thinking and a long-term strategy.

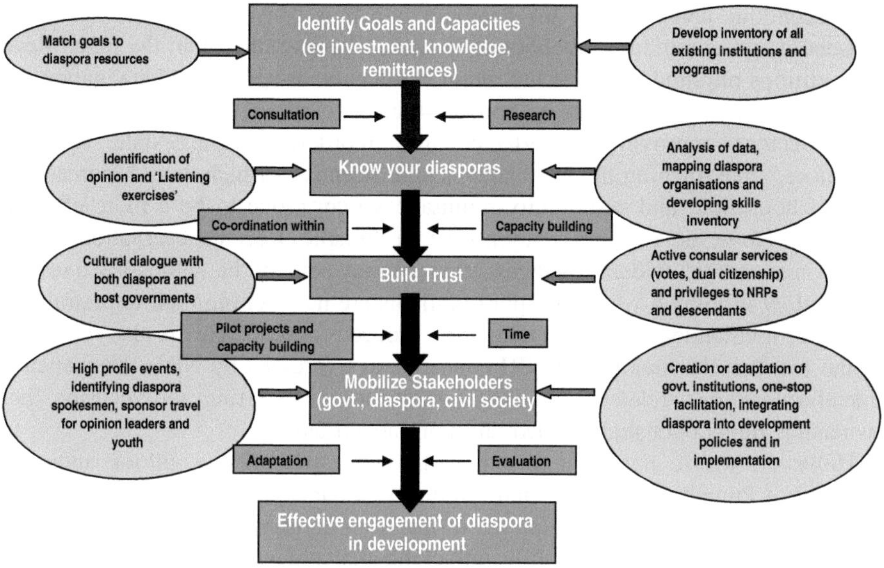

Fig. 16.5 A road map for diaspora engagement. *Source* Adapted from Agunias and Newland (2012, p. 8)

16.4 Conclusions

In this paper, we have presented two contrasting narratives and dimensions of the contemporary Punjab predicament. In the first part, we discussed in some considerable detail major explanations which diagnose the demise of Punjab from its erstwhile status as the most dynamic state in the country. These diagnoses have several policy prescriptions, some of which are beginning to be implemented in Punjab with limited success, such as, for example diversification of agriculture. The second part introduced the new diaspora-development mantra which has now emerged as conventional wisdom among multilateral institutions and governments that have large diasporas. Various policies have been implemented by both Indian and Punjab governments to woo and leverage the diaspora to enable it to contribute more effectively to host land development. This part also discussed the emergence of the Punjabi diaspora, its great diversity and heterogeneity and placed particular emphasis on the various constraints that limits its potential contribution to homeland development.

Having examined in detail, both Punjab's specific development problems and various constraints on potential contribution by the Punjabi diaspora, we conclude that there is a significant disconnect between the causes of malaise of the Punjab economy and the capacity and capability of the Punjabi diaspora to potentially contribute in ending this malaise. Thus, diaspora's overall potential in helping to rejuvenate the Punjab economy are at best very limited and largely relate to microeconomic-level effects, for example boosting consumption and sustaining household and community livelihoods in rural villages rather than the macro-level interventions required to tackle the major challenges of agricultural stagnation and diversification, investment in agroprocessing, developing a strong and dynamic SME sector, improving governance and reordering centre–state relations. Therefore, strengthening the mechanisms and incentives which would increase the flow of household and community remittances may prove to be a more effective approach. However, even this may not be sustainable. Recent observations, albeit based on anecdotal evidence, suggests that we may actually be witnessing a reverse capital flow in Punjab where diaspora Punjabis are now selling their ancestral land and other non-landed assets and taking the proceeds abroad. This is also reinforced by the fact that the majority of NRI concerns, as expressed by NRIs themselves at annual *sammelans*, relate to challenges they face in asserting and securing their ownership rights over their landed and non-landed assets.

However, we do not want to end with such a pessimistic outlook about the potential of Punjabi diaspora's contribution to Punjab's economy. There can be no doubt about the existence of potential, as has been demonstrated in many countries around the world, but successfully unlocking that potential is a different matter. A large number of preconditions need to be established and nurtured—as suggested in the road map outlined in Fig. 16.5—before a more productive partnership can occur. Improving the nature of regulatory framework and promotional policies and developing new and innovative *apolitical* outreach policies, altering perceptions of corruption, bureaucracy and indifference may be essential prerequisites for successful engagement. Some of these, of course, will only happen over time through a dedicated, multipronged approach that begins to develop a genuine partnership between the government of Punjab and Punjabi diaspora. But that is only one side of the story. As Sikhs comprise the largest component of the Punjabi diaspora and arguably have the greatest potential to contribute, eliminating the current trust deficit and alienation between them and the Punjab and Indian governments assumes greater importance. Thus, the largest responsibility inevitably falls on the Punjab government and the Indian state to try harder to bring about closure to the victims and survivors of 1984 and work towards reconciliation.

References

Agunias DA, Newland K (2012) Engaging the Asian Diaspora. Issues in Brief. November 2012, Migration Policy Institute

Aiyer SSA (2012) Why Punjab has suffered long. Steady Decline. Financial Express. 9th November

Bal G (2005) Violence, migration and entrepreneurship: Punjab during the Khalistan movement. Econ Polit Wkly, September 3

Brinkerhoff JM (ed) (2008) Diasporas and development: exploring the potential. Lynne Rienner, London

Brinkerhoff J (2009) Creating an enabling environment for diaspora's participation in homeland development. Int Migr 50(1):75–95
CSE (2005) Analysis of pesticide residues in blood samples from villages of Punjab. Centre for Sciences and Environment, New Delhi
Daily Hansard (2013) Death Penalty (India). http://www.publications.parliament.uk/pa/cm201213/cmhansrd/cm130228/debtext/130228-0002.htm. Accessed 1st July 2013
Department of Industrial Policy and Promotion (2011) SIA Newsletter. June
Dhesi, Autar and Singh, Gurmail (eds) (2007) Rural Development in Punjab: A Success Story Going Astray. (Delhi: Routledge India)
Dusenbery Verne A, Tatla Darshan S (eds) (2010) Sikh Diaspora Philanthropy in Punjab: global giving for local good. Oxford University Press, New Delhi
Economic and Statistical Organisation (2013) Economic Survey of Punjab 2012-13 (Economic Advisor, Government of Punjab)
Gill SS (1988) Contradictions of Punjab model of growth and search for alternative. Econ Polit Wkly 23(42):2167–2173
Gill A (2009) Punjab peasantry: a question of life and debt. J Punjab Stud 16(1):71–87
Gill, Sucha S (2005) Economic Distress and Suicides in Rural Punjab, Journal of Punjab Studies, Vol 12. No 2, Fall, pp 219–238
Government of India (2013) Economic survey of India 2012-13
Govt of Punjab (2011) Department of planning, economic and statistical organisation
Humphreys E, Kukal SS, Christen EW, Hira GS, Singh B, Yadav S, Sharma RK (2010) Halting the groundwater decline in North-West India-Which crop technologies will be Winners?' In: Sparks DL (ed) Advances in agronomy, vol 109, pp 155–217. Academic Press, San Diego, CA
Iyer KG, Arora S (2010) Indebtedness and farmer suicides. In: Dashpande RS, Saroj Arora (eds.) Agrarian crisis and farmer suicides (New Delhi, Sage), pp 264–291
Jaijee, Inderjit Singh and Sidhu, A (2011) Debt and Death in Rural India: The Punjab Story, (Delhi: Sage Publications)
Jodhka SS (2005) Return of the region: identities and electoral politics in Punjab. Econ Polit Wkly XL(3):224–230
Jodhka SS, Gurpreet M (2012) Religions, democracy and governance: spaces for the marginalized in contemporary India. Econ Polit Wkly XLVII(1):45–52
Kapur D (2007) The Janus face of diasporas. In: Merz Barbara J, Chen Lincoln C, Geithner Peter F (eds) Diasporas and development. Harvard University Press, Cambridge, pp 89–118
Kapur D (2010) Diaspora, development and democracy: the domestic impact of international migration from India. Princeton University Press, Princeton, NJ
Kaur B, Singh JM, Garg BR, Singh J, Singh S (2011) Causes and impact of labour migration: a case study of Punjab. Agricul Econ Res Rev 24, Conference Number, pp 459–466
Ketkar SL, Ratha D (2007) Development finance via diaspora bonds: track record and potential. Paper presented at the migration and development conference at the World Bank, Washington D.C. May 23
Kumar A, Kumar S (2002) Punjab: assembly elections—decline of identity politics. Econ Polit Wkly XXXVI(15):1384-1342
Merz, Barbara J, Chen, Lincoln C, Geithner, Peter, F (ed.) (2007) Diasporas and Development, Harvard University Press, Cambridge, USA
Mehra S, Singh G (2014) Migration: a propitious compromise. Econ Polit Wkly 49(15):24–29
Office of National Statistics (2012) Ethnicity and religion in the UK Census, London
Orozco M, Wellie K (2006) Hometown associations and development: ownership, correspondence, sustainability and replicability in web anthology on migration remittances and development. Res Perspect March 2009
Pais J, Yoshifumi U (2014) Migrant workers in Ludhiana. In: Shuji U (ed.) Industrial clusters, migrant workers and labour markets in India, Chap. 2. London Palgrave Macmillan
Punjab State Council for Science and Technology (2007) State of Environment Punjab—2007, Chandigarh
Ram R (2007) Social exclusion resistance and Deras. Econ Polit Wkly XLII(40):4066–4077

Sahai P S, Chand K, Kumar P, Sahai T (2011) Study of Indian diaspora with particular reference to the State of Punjab, Centre for Research in Rural and Industrial Development, Chandigarh, February

Sawhney U (2012) Subnational reforms and public policy issues in Punjab. J Punjab Stud 12(1):49–66

Sharma V (2013) CAG finds major lapses in farmer debt waiver scheme. The Tribune 5th March

Shergill HS (2010) Growth in farm Debt in Punjab 1997-2008. Institute for Development and Communication, Chandigarh

Shiva V, Afsar H, J Ashok, Manish P (2000) Seeds of suicide: the ecological and human costs of globalisation of agriculture. Research Foundation for Science, Technology and Ecology, New Delhi

Sidel M (2007) Focusing on the State: Government responses to diaspora giving and implications for equity. In: Merz Barbara J, Chen Lincoln C, Geithner Peter F (eds) Diasporas and development. Harvard University Press, Cambridge, pp 25–54

Singh P (2008) Federalism, nationalism and development: India and the Punjab economy. Routledge, New Delhi

Singh L, Singh S (2002) Deceleration of economic growth in Punjab: evidence, explanation and a way out. Econ Polit Wkly 37(6):579–586

Singh G, Singh S (2007) Diaspora philanthropy in action: an evaluation of modernisation of Punjab villages. J Punjab Stud 14(2):225–248

Slessor S (2013) Looking at long-term relationships. The Tribune 28th May

Sohal SS (2012) Credit, rural debt and the Punjab peasantry (1849–1947) Guru Nanak Dev University, Amritsar

Thakur JS, Rao BT, Rajwanshi A, Parwana HK, Kumar R (2008) Epidemiological study of high cancer among rural agricultural community of Punjab in Northern India. Int J Environ Res Public Health 5(5):399–407

Thandi SS (1994) Strengthening capitalist agriculture: the impact of overseas remittances in rural central Punjab in the 1970s. Int J Punjab Stud 1(2):239–270

Thandi SS (2000) Vilayati Paisa: some reflections on the potential of diaspora finance in the socio-economic development of Indian Punjab. Int J Punjab Stud 7(2):323–342

Thandi SS (2007) Evaluating the potential contribution of the Punjabi diasora to rural development. In: Dhesi, Autar, Singh, Gurmail (eds.) Rural development in Punjab: a success story going astray, pp. 446–459. Routledge, New Delhi

Thandi SS (2010) Diasporas and development: can diaspora finance and philanthropy deliver human development in Punjab. In: Ghuman RS, Brar JS (eds.) Globalization and change: perspectives from Punjab: essays in honour of Prof. Gill, pp. 366–386. Rawat Publications, New Delhi

Thandi SS (2012) Migration and comparative experiences of Sikhs in Europe: reflections on issues of cultural transmission and identity 50 years. In Jacobsen, Knut A, Myrvold K (eds.) Sikhs across borders: transnational practices of European Sikhs, pp. 11–35. Bloomsbury Academic, London

Thandi SS (2014) The Punjab paradox: understanding the failures of diaspora engagement diaspora studies 7(1) January–June

The Hindu (2013) Cancer Records 33,318 Deaths in Punjab Special Correspondent. 29th January

The Tribune (2014a) Cancer hospital welcome, Editorial. 1st January

The Tribune (2014b) 4th June

UNCTAD (2012) Least developed countries report 2012: harnessing remittances and diaspora knowledge to build productive capacities. UNCTAD, Geneva

Vasishtha G, Singh N (2004) Patterns in centre-state fiscal transfers. Econ Polit Wkly XXXIX (45):4897–4903

World Bank (2004) Resuming Punjab's prosperity: the opportunities and challenges ahead. Washington

Chapter 17
How Centre–State Relations Have Shaped Punjab's Development Pattern

Pritam Singh

17.1 Introduction

Capitalism since its inception has been a globally interconnected system in varying degrees at different points in its evolution. Different countries and regions of these countries are incorporated into this system in varying manners depending upon a range of variables of which the nature of national state intervention into the country's/region's economy is a critical one. In understanding Punjab's development pattern, the nature of the Indian state's intervention in the Indian economy as a part of the global capitalist economy and the uneven impact of this intervention on different regions of India is of key importance. Singh (2008b, 2009a) examines this by focussing on the nature of Indian federalism as the chief institutional mechanism through which the central Indian state intervenes into the national and regional economies.

The development literature attempts, though not wholly satisfactorily, to deal with this issue of global, national and regional interactions in the making of global, national and regional economies by classifying different forces shaping an economy of any country/region as external versus internal (see Cypher and Dietz 2009). The main external forces from the angle of a national economy can be identified as: the history of colonialism, the pattern of world trade and investment, and the currency exchange rate fluctuations, etc. The main internal forces can be identified as: resource endowment, class structure, sociocultural values and practices, quality of human skills and the levels of labour productivity. The development process can be seen as being shaped by the interaction between the politico-economic forces external to the country/region and the internal matrix of forces, although too often what appears to be internal has also been shaped by the external and, conversely,

P. Singh (✉)
Department of Accounting, Finance and Economics,
Oxford Brookes University, Oxford, OX33 1HX, UK
e-mail: psingh@brookes.ac.uk

L. Singh and N. Singh (eds.), *Economic Transformation of a Developing Economy*, India Studies in Business and Economics,
DOI 10.1007/978-981-10-0197-0_17

the degree of influence of the external forces is also considerably dependent upon the internal mix of forces. In this paper, we limit ourselves to an exploration of the impact of one set of external forces upon Punjab's development path, i.e. the set of institutions that can be legitimately categorised as Centre in India's federal structure. The structure of Centre–State relations shaped by the mode of engagement of the Centre with the Punjab economy becomes a key external force in the making of the Punjab economy. Any impact of the changes in the global economy on Punjab economy is also filtered through the institutions controlled and managed by the Centre.

The overwhelming feature of Punjab's development has been its strong reliance upon the agricultural sector, although there has been some change more recently as we discuss this later in the paper. Two events of historical significance, which can be categorised as external forces and have shaped the direction of Punjab's economic development towards an agriculturally oriented pattern of development in the last 165 years, are:

(i) The British annexation of Punjab, which had existed as a sovereign State from 1799 to 1849 under the rule of Maharaja Ranjit Singh and his feuding successors, as a part of the growing power of the expanding British colonial empire.
(ii) The emergence of an independent Indian nation state in 1947 with the key role assigned to the Centre in shaping the economic policy of the new nation state.[1]

Both the British colonial State and the Indian national State come in the category of external forces impinging upon the development process in Punjab. A good account of the development process during the Ranjit Singh era still needs to be constructed but it is reasonable to state that whatever might be the rights or wrongs of the development process then, it was dictated by the inner logic of the Ranjit Singh regime. This changed with the colonial annexation of Punjab—its economy got subjugated to the needs of the British Empire. 1947 brought an end to that colonial empire but its replacement by a post-colonial state brought an institutionalised structure that subjugated Punjab and other states in the Indian union to the policy designs of this new state that was highly centralist in its decision-making processes (Government of India 1967, 1987, 1988; Singh 2016) .

Both the British colonial State and the Indian national State pursued economic policies in Punjab that were in consonance with the respective needs of those two regime types and in both cases, as we demonstrate below, these policies contributed to the development of the agricultural sector, and to the relative neglect of the non-agricultural sectors in Punjab. The development of Canal Colonies during the British colonial rule and the introduction of the Green Revolution strategy by the

[1]Kessinger (1974) is a very fascinating long-range historical micro-level study of rural change in Punjab. The strength of this study is its timescale, which covers both the regime types (colonial and national) but its weakness is that by focusing on only one village, it is unable to address the issues concerning the macro-level development trends in Punjab economy and society.

independent Indian State are the two high watermarks of the respective economic policies followed in Punjab.

I have very briefly discussed below the role of the colonial state in contributing to the agrarian-oriented development pattern. This discussion has been kept deliberately brief since the focus of my argument is on the role played by the post-colonial Indian State, particularly post-1966. The purpose of this brief discussion is twofold: one, to provide a historical background to the role of the Indian nationalist State in Punjab's economic development; and two, to point out the continuity in the agriculturally oriented economic policy of two different regime types in Punjab.

17.2 Historical Roots of the Agrarian-Oriented Development Pattern in Punjab: The Colonial Period

Punjab was incorporated into the British Empire in 1849. Within a few decades of the consolidation of the British rule in Punjab, the colonial administration initiated an ambitious programme of canal irrigation networks in Punjab. This came to be popularly known as the Canal Colonies programme, because it involved the settlement of the Punjabi peasants from the East Punjab (i.e. the post-1947 partition Indian Punjab) into the areas of West Punjab (i.e. the post-1947 Pakistan Punjab) where the canal networks had been developed (Ali 1999). Soldiers retiring from the army were also given land grants in these colonies. These soldiers came predominantly from a peasant social background, and these land grants were seen both by the peasants and the colonial administration as the best economic award for military service to the Empire. The development of these irrigation networks and canal colonies was one of the most impressive developmental projects that the British Empire had undertaken in India. The colonial administration had three interlocking aims behind this massive project: (i) to increase agricultural output for the maximisation of land revenue returns; (ii) to facilitate military recruitment from the peasantry by making military service an economically attractive route to land acquirement; and (iii) to create a loyal political base in the countryside for the British rule (Bal 1986; Ali 1999; Mazumdar 2003). This politico-economic development strategy generated long-term favourable conditions for an agriculturally oriented pattern of development in Punjab (Singh 1993). The implications of this British strategy for Punjab's agriculturally oriented pattern of development become clearer if we compare this strategy with that adopted in some of the coastal provinces, such as the Bombay Presidency (the present Maharashtra, Gujarat region), the Madras Presidency (the present Tamil Nadu region), and the Calcutta Presidency (the present Bengal region), which favoured some degree of industrialisation in these regions (Bharadwaj 1982). Undoubtedly, the internal geographical conditions of Punjab and the coastal provinces were an important contributory factor in these differentiated patterns of development. However, the externally governed politico-economic strategy of British colonial rule played a decisive role in interacting with internal conditions to generate the pattern of development in these regions. This was especially so in the case of Punjab (Ali 1999; Singh 1993).[2] It demonstrated the power of the State in engineering a development path. This development path had contradictory features: it led to a highly developed agriculture sector and the neglect of non-agricultural sectors.

Talbot (1988, 1991) has extensively examined the role of the colonial State in strengthening rural-oriented politico-economic structures in Punjab. Similarly, Fox (1985), in a controversial and provocative work, argues that "the British… in their model province, the Punjab… distorted agrarian conditions and classes in the interests of the capitalist world system and… foreign rule" (p. 11). He calls Punjab's agriculture "mainly a colonial manufacture" (p. 11). In a retrospective study, Malik (1995) throws light on the long-term implications of the colonial State policy for inter-sectoral and intra-sectoral imbalances and distortions in the Pakistani Punjab economy. He argues that "…the canal-fed areas—even after almost a century, have remained totally different in their economy and resultant outlook from the *barani* region where people have generally opted for soldiery and similar other professions" (p. 9) and that "industrial and urban development has been equally confined to certain specific regions leading to a number of grievances from western and northern Punjab—retarding the urban-based mainstream political movement" (p. 10). The contradictory nature of the development path engineered in Punjab by the colonial administration has been best demonstrated by Ali (1999), when he argues that the coexistence of development and underdevelopment in Punjab was a logical culmination of the colonial policy of developing Punjab merely as an agrarian region. He gives a very succinct description of the consequences of this colonial policy: "From 1885 on, the economy of the Punjab began to be reshaped by the unprecedented extension in agricultural production brought about by canal colonisation" (p. 5). The focus of Ali's thesis of this development coexisting with underdevelopment perhaps emerges best when he argues that Punjab "experienced economic growth" as a result of this colonial policy "and yet remained backward or even… acquired through the very process of growth further structural resistance to change… That continued backwardness was entrenched because of, rather than in spite of, economic change" (p. vii).[3]

[2]Dependency theories of development have pioneered research on the role of external structures on shaping the development pattern of an economy. This approach revolutionised research on the role of imperialism and colonialism on thwarting development in the colonies. Andre Gunder Frank played the most important role in theorising and articulating the dependency school of development. His most celebrated paper is Frank (1966). Bhusal and Singh (2011) have analysed the developmental constraints faced by Nepal by referring to the external constraints on Nepal's development.

[3]Singh (2008b, 2009a) has coined the term "rich but not developed" to characterise the contradictory nature of Punjab's development experience after 1947 which witnessed a rise in per capita income accompanied by structural unbalance in its economy.

Having given some flavour of the agriculturally oriented path of development pursued in Punjab by the colonial State, I would now focus on the role of the Indian State in continuing and deepening this agrarian-oriented path of development in Punjab after 1947, and especially after 1966.

17.3 The Agrarian-Oriented Path of Development in Punjab After 1947 and the Politico-Economic Agenda of the Indian Nationalist State

The overarching politico-economic goal of the post-colonial Indian state was to mould the diversities of India into one Indian nationhood through ideological, political, economic and military means. Every policy initiative was supposed to be subordinated to or at least compatible with this overarching goal. I have identified four main guiding principles of the economic policy of the independent Indian nationalist State which fitted in with this overarching role (Singh 2008b, 2009a): economic self-reliance, political non-alignment, balanced regional development, and the reduction of socio-economic inequalities.[4] The goals of economic self-reliance and political non-alignment reflected foreign policy concerns, and the goals of reducing regional and social inequalities reflected domestic policy objectives. These goals were not necessarily all mutually compatible, nor were they all successfully pursued. For example, to illustrate incompatibility between some of these goals, one could argue that the goal of economic self-reliance required faster economic development of Indian economy as a whole which, in turn, could require focussing on relatively more developed regions to increase India's international competitiveness. Prioritising the development of already developed regions to meet the goal of economic self-reliance would thus lead to sacrificing the goal of balanced regional development. However, in spite of such possible incompatibilities, the common ideological thread running through these policy goals was the building of a unified Indian nationalism. A unified Indian nationhood was considered a prerequisite to the building of a strong Indian nationalist state, and this strong Indian nationalist state was perceived as necessary to keep India united as a territorial and political entity (Singh 1999, 2016). Economic self-reliance was aimed at providing economic muscle to the pursuit of independence in domestic and foreign

[4]The limitations of space here do not allow me to elaborate fully on all the components of this formulation. Some useful references for further study are: Chandra (1966) on historical background; Bettelheim (1968), Johnson (1979) and Chakravarty (1989) on self-reliance; Prasad (1989), especially Chap. 11, and Bagchi (1988) on regional development; and Bhagwati (1992) on poverty reduction. Bardhan (1989), Khilnani (1999) and Desai (2005) also take up some of these themes. Khilnani's account highlights the importance of the goals of self-reliance and political sovereignty in the Nehruvian strategy of development. For a discussion on this issue in the context of the importance of the public sector versus the private sector in alternative paradigms of development in India, see Ram Mohan (2005).

policy design by the nationalist State. Political non-alignment was aimed at making the best possible use of the Cold War rivalry to pursue the goal of making the new nation state as strong as possible—economically and politically—by seeking economic cooperation and support of both the rival superpowers of that time (USA and Soviet Union). The domestic goals of reducing regional and socio-economic inequalities were aimed at developing the self-identification of the economically weaker regions and social groups with Indian nationhood.

Central to the goal of achieving economic self-reliance and political self-dependence, was the goal of food self-sufficiency. Every independent nation, especially an insecure one such as India that was just emerging out of the colonial shadow, aims to be food self-dependent.[5] Even in the 1960s, i.e. nearly 15 years after independence, India was dependent on US food aid, provided under Public Law 480 programme of the US administration (Shenoy 1974).[6] The overriding concern of the Indian nationalist state in introducing the Green Revolution strategy in Punjab and some districts of other states was to achieve the goal of self-reliance through food self-sufficiency, and thus avoid "the humiliation of accepting the conditions of US food aid" (Dantwala 1985, p. 115).[7] PL 480 food aid was cut off following the outbreak of the 1965 armed conflict between India and Pakistan. In the context of the Cold War at that time, the US foreign policy was pro-Pakistan as a counterweight against the pro-India policy of Soviet Union. The American state tried to use India's food dependence for political blackmail during the 1965 Indo-Pak conflict (Shenoy 1974). The political goal of non-alignment and national self-reliance hinged crucially on achieving self-sufficiency in food output availability (Chaudhuri 1971; Dantwala 1976; Frankel 1978; Dutt 1984; Chakravarty 1989; Dhar 1989). The vulnerability of the Indian State was further enhanced by the fear of food riots, as a result of the decline in domestic food production brought on by the 1965–1967 drought (Patnaik 1975, pp. 76–77; Sims 1988, p. 38; Jeffrey

[5]Similar to India, China also had, since the Maoist take over in 1949, the goal of food self-reliance as central to its economic policy design but has now abandoned that goal as a result of its now increased global economic muscle and self-confidence. Hornby (2014, p. 10) reports: "China has given up one of its most sacred tenets and in effect abandoned its policy of being self-sufficient in grain…Under the new rules the country will prioritise the supply and quality of meat, vegetables and fruits, all of which require less land than bulk grains and create more agricultural jobs. That in turn should lead to increased imports from countries with sufficient space to grow grain—including the US, Australia, Canada and Ukraine, a recently favoured destination for Chinese agricultural investment".

[6]According to Johl (2005), "In the mid-1960s, the country was importing huge quantities of foodgrains. In 1964–65, India imported around 13 million tonnes of foodgrains".

[7]M.L. Dantwala was a leading Indian government economic policy planner. See also Dantwala (1976). Prasad (2005), an Indian Economic Service officer who worked in the Planning Commission and the various key central government economic ministries, captures the gravity of the situation: "The need to increase foodgrains production was so urgent that the HYV [High-Yielding Varieties] Programme was implemented in suitable areas with the help of farmers who could afford the package deal. According to M.L. Dantwala, *the Government had to grow more food as quickly as possible, irrespective of where it was grown and by whom*" (p. 53, italics added).

1994, p. 79). If the domestic pressure to match food supply with rising domestic demand required *some* increase in food output, the foreign policy compulsions required not *simple* increase in food output but *substantial* increase to attain food self-sufficiency.

This necessitated a massive policy shift at the national central level. From the Second Five-Year Plan (launched in 1956) onwards, the national central policy was heavily oriented towards the industrialisation of the country (Chakravarty 1989). The shift from a pro-industry policy to a pro-agriculture policy was therefore a national imperative to achieve the goal of increased foot output for food self-reliance. This shift was symbolised by the increased power of the then Food and Agriculture Minister C. Subramaniam in the economic policy decision-making process and by the introduction of the Green Revolution strategy in the mid 1960s.[8] Subramaniam was himself acutely aware of the historical role he was playing in pushing a policy shift (Subramaniam 1979, 1982).[9] Swaran Singh was replaced as the food and agriculture minister by C. Subramaniam in 1964 because Singh was seen as complacent in pursuing the strategy of increasing food output (Singh 1973, p. 113).

The Green Revolution strategy involved using high-yielding varieties of seeds on irrigated land, and the application of fertilisers, insecticides and pesticides. In using this package of irrigation–seeds–fertilisers, the strategists aimed at a quick increase in crop production (Randhawa 1974). N. Srinivasan, a Professor of Political Science at Delhi's Indian Institute of Public Administration, argued at a very high level conference in Delhi in 1970 that the survival of Indian nationhood was dependent upon an increased agricultural output brought about by "the application of science and technology". He emphasised therefore that the development of agriculture and crop production must take "the highest priority in our plans" (Srinivasan 1972, p. 128). Two other eminent political scientists (Iqbal Narain and P.C. Mathur) also highlighted the importance of "intensive agricultural development" for attaining the "national objective of securing self-sufficiency in

---

[8]C. Subramaniam, when questioned about why the Green Revolution policies were adopted when they were, replied, "Our political survival was dependent on food production" (Kohli's interview with C. Subramaniam, Madras, March 11, 1979 quoted in Kohli (1989, p. 78). Similarly, Indira Gandhi, who was the Prime Minister at that time, later commenting on the adoption of the Green Revolution strategy, noted, "When it [the "Green Revolution" strategy] had been evolved, it was a question of sheer survival: It was hardly time to think of anything except increasing production". (*Hindustan Times*, April 19, 1968 quoted by Kohli 1989). Ali (1999) points out that political survival was also the main motivating force behind the British colonial State's intervention in Punjab agriculture: "Ultimately it depended on the State structure whether it wished to utilise the potential of colonisation for economic development or distort it for purposes of its own survival. One of the roots of underdevelopment in the Punjab lay in the fact that the latter option was adopted" (p. 23).

[9]Subramaniam was awarded India's highest civilian honour, the Bharat Ratna (Jewel of India), in 1998 in recognition of his historic contribution to the country's success in achieving the goal of food self-sufficiency. When he died on 7 November 2000 at the age of 90, he was widely hailed as the "father" of the Green Revolution (The Economist 2000).

food grains" (Narain and Mathur 1963, p. 122). Even the advocates of the earlier policy of emphasis on industry started seeing the national benefits of increased food output for Indian industry. The view that continuing low levels of food production by increasing food prices would lead to high wage costs, with adverse consequences for industrial profitability, was accepted even by pro-industry policymakers and turned them into grudging supporters of the shift towards pro-agriculture policy (Ahluwalia 1985; Chakravarty 1989; Dhar 1989; Nayar 1989).

Looking at Table 17.1, we can see that, in the allocation of the Indian State's resources to the agricultural sector, the marked priority was a quick increase in crop production.

The policy shift adopted by the central policy planners "reflected not only economic interests, but also *the interests and hopes of the political authorities in securing their power by facilitating rapid gains in food production*"[10] (Kohli 1989, p. 75, italics added). The specific politico-economic conditions of the time when the

[10]On the policy shift, see Chakravarty (1989) and Dhar (1989); on details of the politico-economic pressures on the Indian State, see Sims (1988) and Frankel (1978). It is interesting and instructive to note that if self-sufficiency and quick rise in food production dictated Indian nationalist State's intervention in Punjab agriculture, self-sufficiency and quick rise in horse and camel production for militaristic imperial needs was one of the key objectives that dictated the colonial State's intervention in Punjab agriculture. Ali (1999) writes:

> The central Government [The British colonial government] stressed the need to make India independent of overseas supplies of horses, and to create a readily available reserve of country-bred animals for an emergency. It pointed out that Jhelum colony had become the most important area for imperial horse breeding in India, but the numbers produced were still inadequate to meet the annual requirements of British cavalry regiments stationed there. It therefore wanted as large an area as possible to be devoted to horse and mule breeding in the new [Lower Bari Doab] colony (pp. 30–31).
>
> Ali points out that in its communications with the provincial Punjab government, "The Government of India expressed concern over the increasingly insecure foreign sources of cavalry remounts. In Argentina, Australia, Canada and the United States the production of riding horses was said to be rapidly declining" (p. 31).
>
> Ali further points out that in the "two large colonisation projects, Jhelum and Lower Bari Doab" where horse-breeding operations dominated "... *the aim was to make India a self-sufficient producer of cavalry horses*". He shows that the needs of the Colonial State led to distortions in the developmental pattern of Punjab's agriculture. "In a period when the horse was being rapidly displaced as a military animal by technological change, the British in South Asia began diverting extensive agricultural resources for its production and upkeep" (p. 135, italics added).
>
> Ali also describes the preferential treatment given by the Colonial State to the Bilochis, the camel-owning tribe, over the Janglis, the cattle-owning tribe in order to encourage breeding and upkeep of camels which was "an animal of much importance to military transport" (pp. 123–129).

Table 17.1 Breakdown of percentage share of total agricultural outlay in 3rd and 4th Five-Year Plans

	3rd plan (1961–66)	Draft 4th plan (1969–74)
Crop production	11.5	21.3
Major irrigation	37.3	28.6
Minor irrigation	15.3	15.4
Community development	16.5	7.7
Miscellaneous	19.4	27.0

Source Government of India, Planning Commission, *Five-Year Plans* [Third, and draft Fourth Plan (New Delhi, 1969) respectively] quoted by Kohli (1989, p. 74)
Note There was a period of "plan holiday" from 1966 to 1969 when, due to the conditions of 1965 Indo-Pakistan War, drought and food shortages, the Five-Year Planning process was abandoned and three ad hoc Annual Plans (1966–67, 67–68, 68–69) were adopted

Green Revolution strategy was adopted "reflected and contributed to the specific pattern of state intervention in India's deliberate development" (Kohli 1989, p. 77).

In order to fulfil their nationally decided objectives, central policy planners deemed Punjab to be the most natural and suitable choice for the introduction of the Green Revolution strategy. Historically, Punjab was a relatively better irrigated State, and the forcibly migrated peasantry from the canal colonies after the 1947 partition had accumulated a rich experience of managing irrigated agriculture.[11] Nair (1961) highlights the positive contribution of these refugee peasants to agricultural development in Punjab, and Randhawa (1974) argues that the Sikh religion of the Punjab peasantry made Punjab the best choice for launching the Green Revolution in India. According to him:

> There is no doubt that the Sikh farmer is the best farmer in India. Sikhism is a faith which brought about a social revolution in north India five centuries ago…It liberated people from the ancient Brahmanical system which looked to the past for its Golden Age. The new faith promoted dignity of labour and exhorted its followers to earn their living by manual work. …Above all, it gave new dignity to agriculture which was declared as the best of professions (pp. 33–34).

[11]Large sections of the Punjabi peasantry, from the districts that constitute the present Indian Punjab, had been incentivised during the colonial period to migrate to the canal colony districts. Ali (1999) points out that "In terms of population densities… the canal colonies had a profound impact on demographic levels in the Western Punjab" (p. 61). Percentage rises well above the provincial average for 1891–1941 were recorded in the districts of Jhang, Lahore, Layallpur, Montgomery, Multan, Shahpur and Skeikhupura. Migration took place from high population density districts, such as Amritsar, Jullundur and Ludhiana to the low density canal colony districts. By 1941, the canal colony districts could no longer be regarded as the sparsely populated districts that they were in the nineteenth century.

Malcolm Darling, an administrator during the colonial period, had done a pioneering study of the Punjab peasantry in the early 1920s and had paid similar kind of glowing tributes to the farming skills of the Jat Sikh peasantry (Darling 1947).[12]

I have not come across any written evidence that suggests that Indian policy planners took into consideration the sociological and religious characteristics of the Jat Sikh peasantry in arriving at the decision to introduce the Green Revolution strategy in Punjab. There is some evidence to suggest that some of the policy planners were aware of the historical background of the Punjab peasantry, and would have viewed it as another factor in favour of introducing the Green Revolution strategy in Punjab, in addition to the objective material conditions prevailing in Punjab agriculture (e.g. irrigation sources and potentialities) (Randhawa 1974).[13]

As a key component of its Green Revolution strategy, the Central government played an active interventionist role in the setting up of the Punjab Agriculture University in Ludhiana, to support research into farming techniques for the purpose of raising food output in Punjab (Randhawa 1974). This centrally directed and assisted research into agronomical practices (cropping pattern, efficient doses of fertilisers, use of insecticides/pesticides, water use, high-yielding varieties of seeds) was aimed at increasing the food yield per acre, and played a key role in raising the total food output in Punjab (Sims 1988; Chadha 1986).

The increase in food output that resulted from the introduction of the Green Revolution strategy was hugely impressive and made India food self-sufficient for

[12]Religion has played a very complex role in the agrarian economy of Punjab and, in more recent decades, in influencing the nature of politico-economic relationships between Punjab and the Centre. I have analysed elsewhere how the Green Revolution strategy gave impetus to capitalist modernisation of Punjabi economy and rural society. The process of commodification accelerated by capitalist penetration into agriculture generated many forms of cultural degradation which, in turn, provoked religious revivalism. The growth of religious revivalism sharpened the conflict between Punjabi/Sikh nationalism and the Centre eventually resulting in the bloody confrontation at the Golden Temple in June 1984, assassination of India's prime minister Mrs Gandhi who had ordered the attack on the Golden Temple, genocidal revenge attacks on the Sikhs in Delhi and many other north Indian towns, and the emergence of a decade long Sikh insurgency and state-led anti-insurgency campaign resulting in deaths of thousands of Punjabi youth at the most prime and productive years of their lives. This violent phase in Punjab damaged the prospects of industrialisation of Punjab and pushed Punjab deeper into agriculturally oriented development path. See P. Singh (1987, 2010a Chap. 6 on the relationship between rural capitalism and the emergence of religious revivalism), and Singh (2008b, 2009a) on distortions in Punjab's development path. There is a discernible vicious circle involved here. The Centre's need to achieve food self-sufficiency leads to introduction of Green Revolution in Punjab which by accelerating capitalism in Punjabi rural society provokes religious revivalism. This religious revivalism partly the result of Centre's agrarian policy in Punjab grows into violent confrontation between Punjab and the Centre which then leads the Centre to follow repressive policies in Punjab to suppress separatist militancy resulting in social and economic instability that hinders the process of economic development in Punjab. In other words, Centre's own policies in Punjab become the cause for repression in Punjab. The perception of having been wronged fuels the appeal of religious militancy. See Singh and Purewal (2013) for socio-economic examination of the continuous appeal of religious rebels such as that of Bhindranwale, the militant icon.

[13]In an interview with me in the UK, Professor S.S. Johl reiterated this observation.

the first time in its history. Lakdawala, once a Deputy Chairman of India's Planning Commission, recounting the importance of planning in India's development, highlighted that "Its [India's] foodgrains production has reached a stage where it can meet the effective demand of its teeming population…without the need to replenish them [government food stocks] through imports" (Lakdawala 1987, p. 3). The total foodgrain production in 1960–1961 was 82 million tonnes, which increased to 108 million tonnes in 1970–1971, 130 million tonnes in 1980–1981, and 175 million tonnes in 1990–1991 (Gill 1993, p. 1). It had more than doubled in a time span of 30 years.

The consequences of the Green Revolution strategy for Punjab's overall economic development in independent India have not proved to be very different from those of the Canal Colonies strategy during the British colonial rule: primarily, a structural imbalance in the economy, with a developed agrarian sector coexisting with a backward non-agrarian sector. The common point between the two very different historical situations, which deserves special consideration because it has remained almost completely unconsidered in the scholarly work on Punjab studies, is the absence of autonomy for Punjab to chart its own economic priorities and strategy of development in correspondence with its own resource endowments and its own stage of economic transition. In the first situation, the colonial rulers and the imperialist bourgeoisie initiated a strategy of development (Canal Colonies) in correspondence with their own global and local politico-economic and military objectives; and in the second situation, the Indian nationalist political leadership which controlled power at the centre initiated a strategy of development (Green Revolution) suited to their own historical agenda of achieving food self-sufficiency in order to deal with domestic and foreign policy exigencies. The point I am making is not that the colonial and the Indian nationalist strategies did not generate any gains for Punjab's rural economy. On the contrary, I am suggesting that Punjab's rural economy benefited significantly in terms of increase in agricultural output and incomes. Nonetheless, what I am trying to highlight is that these two strategies (Canal Colonies and Green Revolution), through their overreliance upon agriculture, reinforced an agriculturally oriented pattern of development and contributed to creating structural impediments for the transition of Punjab's economy towards non-agricultural sectors.

The biggest damage to Punjab as a consequence of these agrarian models of development was (and is) the "ruralisation" of Punjab—even of its bourgeoisie. Imran Ali characterises this class and the post-Canal Colony development process thus:

> Agricultural expansion tied this class more closely to the values of agrarian society, thereby weakening the impetus to diversify its economic activity. Agricultural expansion did not produce a social base conducive to rapid change, indeed, the reinforcement of the existing class structure created, through the very process of economic growth, a situation that was hostile to an economic transformation" (Ali 1999, p. 242).

His description also echoes some of the post-Green Revolution development processes in Punjab. In his well-documented study, G.K. Chadha observes that, "In the post-Partition period, in Indian Punjab, there was a steady shift of power from the urban bourgeoisie to the rural elite… *the development of agriculture has been the first priority with each successive government in the state*" (Chadha 1986, p. 28, emphasis original).[14] He observes further that, "It is perhaps ironic that the investible surpluses of rural Punjab have been used to the advantage of agriculture and allied activities only; a 'modern industrial culture' has never emerged directly out of rural enterprise" (Chadha 1986, p. 34).[15] However, what is missing in Chadha's study is an examination of the role of the Central government's strategies in shaping the choices of the state-based governments in Punjab—that is, towards agrarian-oriented policies in Punjab's economy, politics and culture.

The familiar joke that Punjab has no "culture" but only "agriculture" captures popular perceptions regarding the consequences of the agrarian models of development introduced in Punjab by the British colonial State and the Independent Indian nationalist State.

17.4 The Economic Structure of Punjab: Its Inherent Weakness

A comparison of the economic structure of Punjab, India and the advanced industrial capitalist economies until the early 1990s (as depicted in Table 17.2) before the impact of the new economic policy regime introduced in July 1991, shows that the Punjab economy was still locked in agrarian dependence, and had not undergone the normal process of economic transition from the agrarian sector to non-agrarian sectors that the Indian economy as a whole (albeit with unevenness between the states) was undergoing and the advanced industrial economies [i.e. OECD countries] had dramatically undergone.

The ranking of the Indian states in the post-independent period in terms of per capita income is often used to project a better economic profile for Punjab. Apart from several fundamental methodological objections to this method of comparing economic performance, the alleged "better" economic profile of Punjab in these terms hides the reality that Punjab owes this status primarily to its agrarian-oriented development path. From column 2 of the Table 17.3, it can be observed that in 1949–1950, West Bengal had the highest per capita income and Punjab (including Haryana) had the second highest. In 1960–1961, Maharashtra had the highest, W. Bengal the

[14]Though Singh (1983) also emphasises the slower growth of industry in Punjab in comparison with its agriculture, he provides a slightly favourable view of the role of the Punjab state government in its effort to develop Punjab's industrial sector (pp. 46–48).

[15]In Pakistani Punjab also this anti-industry ruralisation pressure has been observed in the Punjab–Centre conflict there. Farhan Bokhari (1991) in his report "Punjabi farmers seek new deal" (Financial Times, London, 5.11.91) wrote, "Pakistani Federal government may find it increasingly difficult to sell its agricultural policy to Punjab… Mr. Mohammad Azad Cheema, a provincial legislator and secretary-general of the Chamber of Agriculture in Lahore, says that the government must provide new incentives to agriculture, under the same terms as to the industrial sector".

Table 17.2 Share of agricultural and non-agricultural sector in GSDP/NNP/GDP (Punjab, India, OECD countries)

	Punjab (SDP)			India (NNP)				Advanced industrial econ. (GDP)	
Years	1970–71	1980–81	1992–93	1961	1971	1981	1991–92	1960	1994
Agricultural	58.37	48.20	46.92	49.34	42.76	35.52	28.4	6	2.1
Non-agri.	41.63	49.80	53.08	50.66	57.24	64.48	71.6	94	97.9

Source
(i) For Punjab (1970–1971) (Government of Punjab, 1987); for Punjab (1980–1981 and 1992–1993) and India (1991–1992), *Economic Survey of Punjab* 1993–94, Economic Adviser to Government of Punjab, Chandigarh, p. 45
(ii) For India (except for 1991–1992, for which see (i) above) V.K.R.V. Rao, *India's National Income, 1950–1980: An Analysis of Economic Growth and Change* (Delhi, 1982) quoted by Chakravarty (1989, p. 125)
(iii) For advanced industrial economies, OECD data cited by Griffiths and Wall (1997, p. 8)

second highest and Punjab the third highest. Only since 1970–1971, after the Green Revolution strategy had been introduced, has Punjab had the highest per capita income among the *major* Indian states (Goa has had the highest per capita income, if we consider *all* the states, for the decade of 1980s).[16]

More recent data shows that if we look at the per capita income of the states for the year 2009–2010 at 2004–2005 prices as the basis, Delhi (with Rs. 100,050) and Goa (with Rs. 96,885) are at the top and Punjab's per capita income (Rs. 42,752) is below many states' including Maharashtra (Rs. 57,458), Haryana (Rs. 54,884), Gujarat (48,511), Tamil Nadu (Rs. 46,692), Kerala (Rs. 45,908) and Himachal Pradesh (Rs. 43,305).[17] Although the Green Revolution did push up Punjab's relative per capita income status in its early phase, the agrarian-oriented development path in Punjab based on it is handicapped in sustaining long-term growth. It has eventually led to decline in Punjab's status among the Indian states to the ninth place in terms of per capital income criterion.

17.5 The Saturation Crisis of Punjab Agriculture

The analysis of the data on various aspects of Punjab's agriculture suggests that the potentiality of Punjab's agriculture to sustain further development of the Punjab economy is almost exhausted. Although the share of the primary sector in the state's GDP has come down from nearly 47 % in 1992–93 (see Table 17.2) to 32.67 % in 2004–05 and 24.14 % in 2010–11, it still is the main source of livelihood for the rural population in the state that constitutes 62.51 % of Punjab's

[16]Government of Punjab (1992, p. 116) and Economic and Political Weekly Research Foundation (1995, p. 3323).

[17]Government of Punjab (2012) has a coloured diagram between pages 134 and 135 providing this data.

Table 17.3 Per capita income of Indian states at current prices (Rs.)

	State (1)	1949–50 (2)	1960–61 (3)	1970–71 (4)	1980–81 (5)	1984–85 (6)	1985–86 (7)	1986–87 (8) (Prov.)
1	Andhra Pradesh	229	275	585	1,358	2,039	2,205	2,333
2	Assam	–	–	535	1,221	2,037	2,068	2204
3	Bihar	200	215	402	943	1,513	1,643	1802
4	Gujarat	X	362	829	1,967	2,952	2,775	3223
5	Haryana	XX	327	877	2,361	3,230	3,748	3925
6	Himachal Pradesh			651	1,530	2,216	2,636	2908
7	Jammu and Kashmir			548	1,455	2,111	2,270	2344
8	Karnataka	186	296	641	1,454	2,189	2,264	2486
9	Kerala	234	259	594	1,385	2,104	2,140	2371
10	Madhya Pradesh	255	252	484	1,181	1,699	1,960	2020
11	Maharashtra	273[a]	409	783	2,244	3,177	3,549	3793
12	Manipur	–	–	390	1,382	2,218	2,383	2533
13	Orissa	188	217	478	1,173	1,671	1,954	1997
14	Punjab	334[b]	366	1070	2,620	4,103	4,536	4954
15	Rajasthan	173	284	651	1,220	2,050	2,106	2150
16	Tamil Nadu	229	334	581	1,324	2,173	2,514	2732
18	Uttar Pradesh	262	252	486	1,272	1,284	2,003	2146
19	West Bengal	353	390	722	1,643	2,576	2,767	2988
	All India	246 for 1950–1951	306	633	1,627	2,477	2,721	2974

Source Column (2) and (3) Prasad (1989, p. 110)
Columns (4) to (8) *Statistical Abstract of Punjab 1988* (Government of Punjab 1989, pp. 106–107)
[a]Gujarat and Maharashtra
[b]Haryana and Punjab (Punjab acquired its new territorial status after 1966)

total population (Government of Punjab 2012, p. 145). This indicates that a shrinking sector in terms of its share in the state's GDP, has to still support majority of the state's population. There is very little scope to further increase agricultural production because almost the entire cultivable area has been brought under cultivation and irrigation, and the intensity of cultivation has reached its highest peak. These limits had been already reached by the early 1990s and the situation has become more precarious since then. According to the *Economic Survey of Punjab 1990–1991*, published by the Economic Adviser to the Government of Punjab, over 84 % of Punjab's geographical area was under cultivation (Government of Punjab 1990–91, p. 45). The *Economic Survey of Punjab 1993–94* pointed out: "Since 96 % of the cultivable land was under plough during 1991–92 there is limited scope to bring more area under cultivation in future" (Government of Punjab 1993, 1993–94, p. 55).[18] The fact that the forest area was only about 5.65 % of the total area in

[18]See also Johar and Singh (1983, pp. 11–12) and Dhillon (1990, p. 5) for observations regarding area under cultivation.

Punjab (in the Kapurthala district the forest area was as low as 1.04 % of the district's total area) further highlighted the extremely limited possibility of any further extension in the area under cultivation (Government of Punjab 1992, p. 258).[19] With the figures for cropping intensity having reached as high as 175.7 %, the highest in the country, any further increase in the area under cultivation (even through intensive cultivation) was extremely limited (Government of Punjab 1990–91, p. 45). A very high proportion of this cultivated land was irrigated. According to the estimates made by the Directorate of Land Records (Punjab), on the intensity of irrigation in Punjab, the percentage of gross irrigated area (of the total gross cropped area) had reached as high as 95 %, and in Kapurthala district it was 100 %. Except for the two semi-hilly districts of Hoshiarpur and Rupnagar, where this figure was 64.1 and 65.5 % respectively (thus indicating some possible scope for expansion of irrigation potentialities), in all the remaining districts this figure was above 93.3 % (in Ludhiana, Sangrur and Jalandhar, it was 99.8, 99.6 and 99.1 % respectively).[20] The overall figure for percentage of gross irrigated area out of the total gross cropped area has further increased from 95 % in 1992 to 98 % in 2010–2011 and 73 % of this total irrigated area is irrigated by 13.82 lakhs tube wells (Government of Punjab 2012, p. 145). This overuse of ground water is creating a potentially very dangerous ecological situation that can lead to exhaustion of the potentially renewable source of water.[21]

Profit margins on major Punjab crops have been shrinking primarily because the institutions of Central regulation over agriculture allowed the Centre to exercise a decisive role in determining agriculture input and output prices.[22] A number of studies conducted in the 1970s and 1980s suggest an overall pattern, whereby a large majority of the farmers in Punjab were either running into deficit or else making only a small profit. According to a survey conducted by the RCPI (Revolutionary Communist Party of India), "the small farmers were running annually a per capita loss of Rs. 125 whereas the farmers with land between 5 and 10 acres were producing a per capita profit of Rs. 1200".[23] According to another study pertaining to the years 1976–1977 and 1977–1978, the marginal and small farmers' households were annually running into an average deficit of Rs. 1513.17 and Rs. 1648.17 respectively (Azad 1980, p. 306). In 1982, it was noted that 24 % of the small farmers and 31 % of the marginal farmers in Punjab lived below the

---

[19]Even of this "forest" area, most of it was a manmade plantation of eucalyptus. See Kang (1982, p. 198).

[20]Government of Punjab (1992, p. 214).

[21]As per Dynamic Ground Water Resource Report of Punjab of 2004 (cited in Government of Punjab 2012, p. 146), the utilisation of water is more than its recharge rate, due to which 103 blocks of the state have been declared as overexploited, 5 blocks as critical, 4 as semi-critical and only 25 blocks as safe.

[22]See: Gill and Singhal (1984) and H. Singh (1987, p. 32), Sarkaria Commission Report (Government of India 1988, pp. 442–44).

[23]RCPI *Punjab Da Kisani Masla* (in Punjabi) [The Question of the Peasantry in Punjab], March 13, 1984, quoted by H. Singh (1987, p. 33).

poverty line (Bhalla and Chadha 1982, p. 870). If we use the categorisation employed by the All India Report on Agricultural Census 1980–81 (i.e. marginal farmers: below 1 ha and small farmers: 1–2 ha), then by 1985–1986, 23.55 % of all operational holdings in Punjab were marginal and 19.08 % were small. Only about 6.75 % were "large", i.e. above the 10 ha size.[24] The All India Report on Agricultural Census 2005–06 (cited in Government of Punjab 2013, pp. 122–123) shows that 13.4 % were marginal, 18.2 % were small, 31.9 % were semi-medium (2–4 ha), 29.4 % medium (4–10 ha) and 7.1 % were large (10 ha and above), indicating a further decline of the share of marginal and small farmers (combined) from 42.63 % in 1985–1986 to 31.6 % in 2005–2006. Within a time span of 20 years, this decline in the share of marginal and small farmers suggests that many in this category have been forced to sell their land and become depeasantised. Most observers of Punjab's agrarian economy agree that by the end of the 1980s it had reached a "saturation point."[25] The situation since then has further deteriorated (Bawa and Raikhy 2000, Dhesi and Singh 2008).

The diversification of crops was recommended (see Johl 1986) and was widely viewed as a strategy to get Punjab agriculture out of its saturation crisis. There was certainly some merit in these recommendations, since they recognised that the food-dependent agrarian economy of Punjab had a bleak future, and that an alternative framework for the future of Punjab's economy needed to be developed. However, there was one fundamental weakness with this recommendation for the diversification of the cropping pattern in Punjab. There were very limited potentialities of changing the cropping pattern in Punjab, since the Centre had overwhelming control over the pricing and marketing of agricultural products (especially food products). The Centre still needed Punjab to continue producing food crops and contributing to the Central food procurement stock. Therefore, the Central government did not develop any incentive structure to encourage Punjabi farmers to move away from the wheat–rice cropping pattern in Punjab.[26]

---

[24]Computed from the data provided in Tables 6.16 and 6.18 in the *Statistical Abstract of Punjab, 1991* (Government of Punjab 1992, pp. 175–177).

[25]Government of Punjab (1990–91, p. 39). Also see papers on Punjab agriculture by Gill (1983), Johar and Singh (1983), Johar and Raikhy (1983), Grewal and Rangi (1983) and Johar and Khanna (1983); for the views of a senior Punjabi administrator with special interest in Punjab agriculture, see Gill (1987).

[26]Shergill (2012) argued that, while the present cropping pattern in Punjab (especially the growing of rice, which requires intensive water use) might have serious environmental consequences in the long run in the form of decline in water table, the shift away from these food crops especially rice would economically be damaging for the Punjab peasantry. His argument against growing non-food crops such as cotton and sugar cane is that apart from the technological advantage in growing rice over these non-food crops, there is no price incentive and marketing facility for non-food crops. B.P. Singh has in correspondence with me disagreed with Shergill's views. Singh believes that, in the interests of sustainability, Punjabi farmers should move away from food crops (especially rice) even if it means short-term economic losses. Shergill (2013) contends that soil fertility, in fact, has improved under green revolution. Despite serious differences in the approaches of these two serious and well meaning scholars, about the feasibility and desirability of the diversification of Punjab's crops, both allow their analysis to remain confined within the sphere of

Another serious, perhaps even more fundamental, criticism of the strategy of diversification of crops is that such a strategy will reinforce the agrarian-dependent character of the Punjab economy. This does not mean that some limited initiatives such as encouraging dairy farming do not have some potential from the viewpoint of lessening Punjab agriculture's overreliance upon wheat–rice combination. Such initiatives may increase the income of the farming community in the short run, and that possible gain is not something to be lightly dismissed in the context of deteriorating economic conditions of the small peasantry that has pushed this peasantry into debt and suicides (Sidhu and Jaijee 2011).[27] However, despite the importance of such initiatives as indicated here, they are not substantive enough to change the agrarian-oriented development pattern of Punjab economy. There are indeed lessons to be learnt regarding the potential of dairy farming from New Zealand and Scandinavian economies especially Denmark but a mechanical comparison of such economies with Punjab must be avoided because Punjab's location within the confines of a federal economy forces economic compulsions on Punjab such as being subjected to the food self-sufficiency and food security strategic objectives set by India's central government. New Zealand and Denmark as sovereign states do not have to undergo the pressure of adapting to such externally inspired objectives. These nation states use the power of their sovereignty when dealing with changes taking place in the global economy that have possible repercussions for them. In spite of several limitations that globalisation imposes on sovereign states, the nation states still play a critical role in engaging with and sometimes defying the forces of globalisation in fashioning their economic policies to their national needs (Desai 2013; Singh 2008a, 2009a, 2010b, 2014).

The embedded nature of agrarian orientation in Punjab economy, therefore, raises the question of possible transition paths for the Punjab economy.

17.6 Potentialities of Economic Transition in Punjab

The only way that Punjab can keep up and improve its rate of economic growth, which is also compatible with the requirements of environmental sustainability, is to make a transition towards a non-agrarian economic structure. Punjab can move

(Footnote 26 continued)

agriculture sector and do not investigate the possibilities of non-agrarian future for Punjab that would change the terms of discourse on cropping patterns.

[27]I wish to pay homage to Aman Sidhu who is a co-author of this important book written by her illustrious father, Inderjit Singh Jaijee, who has worked tirelessly over the years to document the debt-related farmers' suicides in Punjab. Aman died in a tragic car accident along with her daughter Anahat in 2006. I had the opportunity to meet Aman and know her passion for academic study of the economic, social and psychological misery of the Punjab peasantry. We explored the possibilities of her being my student. At the time of her death, she was working for her doctorate on the subject of rural suicides at Panjab University Chandigarh's Sociology department.

out of its present poverty-stricken footloose small-scale industrial sector (see Pandit 1978, 1985) to a modern developed industrial sector and a thriving tertiary sector through massive central public sector investment in Punjab and/or a massive inflow of private capital (Indian or non-Indian). There is very little likelihood of this happening within the existing framework of Centre–State relations. The transition to a non-agrarian economic structure also requires a dramatic shift in the agricultural policy followed within the State. The important components of the agriculture policy—cropping patterns, pricing of agricultural products and marketing of agricultural products—will have to be refashioned in order to articulate with the needs of industrial and tertiary sector development in the state. However, the state government has very limited power to reshape these components of the agricultural policy within the constraints of Centre–State relations in agriculture.[28] This does not mean that a state government such as that in Punjab bears no responsibility for what happens in the sphere of the economy. It is true that the policies pursued at the state level have also contributed to Punjab remaining attached to agriculturally oriented policies. However, this needs to be visualised in the larger context of centralisation of economic powers in India which have weakened the state political leadership's capacity for imagination, innovativeness and initiative. The damaging impact of centralisation in creating a political culture of dependence and shirking responsibility have far reaching implications which are not easily visible and, therefore, difficult to quantify.

There are no easy ways of challenging centralisation and offering solutions. There has to be a radical challenge to the centralist bias in India's constitution, which provides the legal framework for the centrally oriented policies that thwart the initiative of the states to pursue policies that respond to their resource endowments and requirements for economic transition (Singh 2005, 2007, 2008a, 2009a, 2016). This requires the building of a coalition of forces that pursues a new path of economic and political decentralisation that is in tune with the needs and aspirations of the states. This requires a visionary leadership that has the intellectual and moral resources to build a country wide mass movement that can reverse the destructive path of centrally directed development pursued in India since independence. There has been a constant struggle at different levels between the forces of centralisation and decentralisation in India right from the period of independence and, in this struggle; the forces of centralisation have been victorious until now through a combination of ideological, legal/constitutional, political, economic and military strategies (Singh 1999, 2002, 2005, 2007, 2008a, 2009a, 2015). However, the future is not closed and it is not "the end of history". New historical possibilities can emerge (Singh 2008b, 2009b, c) and the political forces in Punjab need to proactively engage with the political process in India to steer the change towards decentralisation for the sake of opening possibilities of development pattern in Punjab that is conducive to the internal needs and agendas of Punjabi people.

[28]For a more detailed discussion of the constitutional and policy centralism in agriculture policy in India, see the chapter on agriculture in Singh (2008b, 2009a).

The change in the economic policy regime at the Centre since 1991 has had contradictory implications for decentralisation and centralisation of the Indian economy and polity. In one domain i.e. negotiating foreign capital investment, the states have acquired more powers than they had before but major levers of economic policy (industrial policy, agricultural policy and, in the new context of the globalisation of the economy, monetary and fiscal policy that have acquired more traction) are still controlled by the Centre (Guhan 1995; Singh 1993, 2008a, 2009a). Some weakening of the planning mechanism has transformed the mode of operation of the Centre's intervention in the economy, it has not weakened its powers to initiate policy changes and regulate and control the economy. Even more significant from the viewpoint of its impact on Punjab, the interstate competition for inward investment both by Indian and foreign capital has meant that the already more industrialised states such as Maharashtra, Gujarat, Tamil Nadu and Karnataka have been able to attract more capital than the industrially backward states such as Punjab. The accumulated effect of the agriculturally oriented pattern of development in Punjab shaped by the Centre during the planning era has been to further reinforce industrial backwardness in Punjab in the new era of economic reforms and globalisation. The continuing politico-economic need of the Indian state to acquire and maintain food security keeps Punjab integrated into the central policy design that requires Punjab to remain focussed on remaining a food-dependent agrarian economy.

Decentralisation, if it does take place even in a limited fashion, throws new challenges in dealing with the external pressures of global capitalism. However, there is no single way to engaging with the forces of global capitalism. There are pluralities of paths, and individual states have a high degree of manoeuvrability in dealing with the forces of globalisation (Desai 2013). Many examples of Latin America countries such as Bolivia, Ecuador, Uruguay and Venezuela are demonstrating the possibilities of alternative paths of development while engaging and challenging the forces of global capitalism. One most significant aspect of these alternative paths of development is that they are emphasising the need for environmental sustainability along with economic development. The environmental degradation in Punjab is directly related to the Central policy of maximising food output from Punjab. The aim of maximisation of food output is the main contributor to the environmentally damaging policies of the state governments in Punjab regarding the subsidy to use electricity and especially water for irrigation. The deepening crisis of environmental degradation in Punjab heightens the need for pursuing a sustainable and decentralist path of development.

17.7 Conclusions

Punjab's development process in the last 165 years is the product of Punjab's economy being subjected to the strategic objectives of those external actors/agents who ruled over Punjab and who were not motivated by the requirements of the development path Punjab needed to pursue for sustainable development.

The strategic politico-economic goals of the British Rule in Punjab led this province to be developed on an agrarian-oriented development path. The Central government policies in India after independence (especially in the 1960s) reinforced this agrarian-oriented path of development in Punjab. The national goal of self-reliance in food availability played a key role in initiating the policy of Green Revolution in Punjab. The pattern of agricultural output in Punjab shifted crucially towards two food items: wheat and rice. The Punjab economy increasingly became a food-dependent agrarian economy and the process of economic transition towards non-agricultural sectors remained neglected throughout the 1980s. In the last over two decades, though agriculture's share in the state's GDP has declined, the dependence of the majority of the state's population for livelihood still remains on agriculture.

For Punjab to come out of this centrally governed path of development, it needs to join a coalition of forces that can fashion a new decentralised path of development in India that corresponds to the internal developmental needs of Punjab and other Indian states while simultaneously responding to the changes in the global economy in accordance with their own needs, requirements and compulsions. The international experiences of countries especially in Latin America that have defied the forces of global capitalism and have bravely embarked on to the path of sustainable development can be role models for environmentally damaged Punjab while recognising simultaneously the limitations of Punjab being able to pursue policies which sovereign states in Latin America have been able to pursue.

References

Ahluwalia I (1985) Industrial growth in India. Oxford University Press, Delhi

Ali I (1999) Sikh Settlers in the Western Punjab during British rule. In: Singh P, Thandi SS (eds) Punjabi identity in a global context. Oxford University Press, New Delhi, pp 139–151

Azad NS (1980) Small peasantry in Punjab: an analysis of production conditions. Ph.D. thesis, Punjabi University, Patiala

Bagchi AK (ed) (1988) Economy, society and polity: essays in the political economy of Indian planning. Oxford University Press, Calcutta

Bal SS (1986) British administration in the Punjab and its aftermath. Guru Nanak Dev University, Amritsar

Bardhan P (1989) The political economy of development in India. Basil Blackwell, Oxford

Bawa RS, Raikhy PS (eds) (2000) Punjab economy: emerging issues. Guru Nanak Dev University, Amritsar

Bettelheim C (1968) India independent. MacGibbon & Kee, London

Bhagwati J (1992) India's economy: the shackled giant. Unpublished version of the Radhakrishnan Lectures, Oxford
Bhalla GS, Chadha GK (1982) Green revolution and small peasant: a study of income distribution. Econ Polit Wkly VI(47):2363–2365
Bharadwaj K (1982) Regional Differentiation in India: a note. Econ Polit Wkly XVII(14–16):605–614
Bhusal LN, Singh P (2011) Exploring the role of external factors in the development process: a study of the role of India and China in Nepal's development. Millennial Asia Int J Asian Stud 2 (1):163–186
Bokhari F (1991) Punjabi farmers seek new deal. Financial times, 5th Nov
Chadha GK (1986) The state and rural economic transformation: the case of Punjab 1950–85. Sage Publications, Delhi
Chakravarty S (1989) Development planning: the Indian experience. Oxford University Press, Delhi
Chandra B (1966) Rise and growth of economic nationalism in India: economic policies of Indian national leadership, 1880–1905. Peoples Publishing House, New Delhi
Chaudhuri P (1971) India: objectives, achievements and constraints. In: Chaudhuri P (ed) Aspects of Indian economic development. George Allen and Unwin, London, pp 17–91
Cypher JM, Dietz JL (2009) The process of economic development, 3rd edn. Routledge, London
Dantwala ML (1976) Agricultural policy since independence. Ind J Agric Econ 31(4)
Dantwala ML (1985) Technology, Growth and Equity in Agriculture. In: Mellor J, Desai G (eds) Agricultural change and rural poverty. John Hopkins University, Baltimore, pp 110–123
Darling ML (1947) The Punjab peasant in prosperity and debt, 4th edn. Oxford University Press, Bombay (First published in 1925)
Desai M (2005) Development and nationhood: essays in the political economy of India. Oxford University Press, New Delhi
Desai R (2013) Geopolitical economy: after US hegemony, globalization and empire. Pluto, London
Dhar PN (1989) The Indian economy: past performance and current issues. In: Lucas R, Papanek G (eds) The Indian economy: recent developments and future prospects. Oxford University Press, Delhi, pp 3–22
Dhesi AS, Singh G (eds) (2008) Rural development in Punjab: a success story gone astray. Routledge, Delhi
Dhillon SS (1990) Economic aspect of Punjab problem. In: Bulletin of the Christian Institute for Religious Studies, Batala, vol 19, no. 1
Dutt S (1984) India and the third world. Zed Books, London
Economic and Political Weekly Research Foundation (1995) National Accounts Statistics of India, 6: Net State Domestic Product. Economic and Political Weekly, 23 December, 30(50):3321–3328
Fox RG (1985) Lions of the Punjab: culture in the making. University of California Press, Berkeley and Archives Publishers, Delhi
Frank AG (1966) The development of underdevelopment. Monthly review, September
Frankel F (1978) India's political economy, 1947–77. Princeton University Press, Princeton
Gill KS (1983) Agricultural Development in Punjab. In: Johar RS, Khanna JS (eds) Studies in Punjab economy. Guru Nanak Dev University, Amritsar, pp 1–10
Gill MS (1987) Needs of Punjab economy. The tribune, 10th June
Gill KS (1993) A growing agricultural economy: technological change, constraints and sustainability. Oxford & IBH Publishing Co, New Delhi
Gill SS, Singhal KC (1984) Farmers' agitation: response to development crisis of agriculture. Econ Polit Wkly 19(40):1728–1732
Government of India (1967) Report of the study team on centre-state relationships, vol 1. The Administrative Reforms Committee, Delhi
Government of India (1987) Commission on centre-state relations report, Part II. Government of India Press, Nasik

Government of India (1988) Commission on centre-state relations report, Part I. Government of India Press, Nasik
Government of India (1990) Economic survey 1989–90. Ministry of Finance, New Delhi
Government of Punjab (1987) Statistical abstract of Punjab 1986. Economic Advisor to the Government of Punjab, Chandigarh
Government of Punjab (1989) Statistical abstract of Punjab 1988. Economic Advisor to the Government of Punjab, Chandigarh
Government of Punjab (1990–91) Economic survey of Punjab 1990–91. Economic Advisor to the Government of Punjab, Chandigarh
Government of Punjab (1992) Statistical abstract of Punjab 1991. Economic Advisor to the Government of Punjab, Chandigarh
Government of Punjab (1993) Statistical abstract of Punjab 1992. Economic Advisor to the Government of Punjab, Chandigarh
Government of Punjab (1993–94) Economic survey of Punjab 1993–94. Economic Advisor to the Government of Punjab, Chandigarh
Government of Punjab (2012) Economic survey of Punjab 2011–12. Economic & Statistical Organisation, Government of Punjab, Chandigarh
Government of Punjab (2013) Statistical abstract of Punjab 2012. Economic Advisor to the Government of Punjab, Chandigarh
Grewal SS, Rangi, PS (1983) Imbalances in growth of Punjab agriculture. In: Johar RS, Khanna JS (eds) Studies in Punjab economy. Guru Nanak Dev University, Amritsar, pp 47–64
Griffiths A, Wall S (1997) Applied economics, 7th edn. Addison Wesley Longman, London
Guhan S (1995) Centre and State in the Reform Process. In: Cassen R, Joshi V (eds) India: the future of economic reforms. Oxford University Press, Delhi
Hornby L (2014) Beijing abandons grain self-reliance. The financial times, London, Feb 12
Jeffrey R (1994) What's happening to India? Punjab, ethnic conflict and the test for federalism, 2nd edn. Macmillan, London
Johar RS, Khanna JS (eds) (1983) Studies in Punjab economy. Guru Nanak Dev University, Amritsar
Johar RS, Raikhy PS (1983) Agricultural productivity in Punjab—an analysis of inter-district variations. In: Johar RS, Khanna JS (eds) Studies in Punjab economy. Guru Nanak Dev University, Amritsar, pp 36–46
Johar RS, Singh P (1983) Agricultural development in Punjab. In: Johar RS, Khanna JS (eds) Studies in Punjab economy. Guru Nanak Dev University, Amritsar, pp 11–35
Johar RS, Khanna JS, Raikhy PS (1983) Industrial development of Punjab—a study in characterisation, case for, and constraints. In: Johar RS, Khanna JS (eds) Studies in Punjab economy. Guru Nanak Dev University, Amritsar, pp 150–177
Johl SS (1986) Report of the expert committee on diversification of agriculture in Punjab. Unpublished Government of Punjab document
Johl SS (2005) Food and agriculture: sow right for a rich harvest. In: India: the tasks ahead, special supplement. The tribune, Chandigarh, 24th Sept
Johnson BLC (1979) India: resources and development. Heinemann Educational Books, London
Kang DS (1982) Environmental problems of the green revolution with a focus on Punjab, India. In: Barratt R (ed) International dimensions of the environmental crisis. Westview Press, Colorado, p 1982
Kessinger T (1974) Vilyatpur 1848–1968. University of California Press, Berkeley
Khilnani S (1999) The idea of India. Penguin, London and New Delhi
Kohli A (1989) The state and poverty in India. Cambridge University Press, Cambridge and New York
Lakdawala DT (1987) Lessons of planning. Oxford University Press, Delhi
Malik I (1995) Identity formation and Muslim party politics in the Punjab, 1897–1936: a retrospective analysis. Mod Asian Stud 29(2):293–323
Mazumdar RK (2003) The Indian army and the making of Punjab. Permanent Black, Delhi

Nair K (1961) Blossoms in the dust: the human dimension in Indian development. Gerald Duckworth, London

Narain I, Mathur PC (1963) Union-state relations in India: a case study in Rajasthan. J Commonwealth Polit Stud 2(2):120–140

Nayar BR (1989) India's mixed economy. Popular Prakashan, Bombay

Pandit ML (1978) Some less known factors behind the industrial change in Punjab and Haryana. Econ Polit Wkly XIII(47):1935–1940

Pandit ML (1985) Industrial development in the Punjab and Haryana(domination of footloose industries). BR Publishing Corporation, Delhi

Patnaik P (1975) Imperialism and the Growth of Indian Capitalism. In: Blackburn Robin (ed) Explosions in a subcontinent. Penguin, London, pp 51–78

Prasad P (1989) Lopsided Growth: political economy of Indian development. Oxford University Press, Bombay

Prasad CS (2005) India: economic policies and performance, 1947–48 to 2004–05: year-wise economic review of the Indian economy since independence. New Century Publications, New Delhi

Ram Mohan TT (2005) Privatisation in India: challenging economic orthodoxy. Routledge Curzon, London

Randhawa MS (1974) Green Revolution. Vikas Publishing House, Delhi

Shenoy BR (1974) PL-480 and India's food problem. East West Press, Delhi

Shergill HS (2012) Why area under rice will not be reduced in Punjab? (unpublished)

Shergill HS (2013) Improvement in soil fertility in Punjab under green revolution: the evidence and the mechanisms. J Agric Dev Policy 23(1):18–30

Sidhu A, Jaijee IS (2011) Debt and death in rural India: the Punjab story. Sage Publications, Delhi

Sims H (1988) Political regimes, public policy and economic development: agricultural performance and rural change in two Punjabs. Sage Publications, Delhi

Singh SP (1973) Centre-state relations in agricultural development. Vikas Publishing House, Delhi

Singh A (1983) Industrialisation, employment and basic needs in a fast-growing agrarian state: a study of the Indian Punjab. World employment program research working paper, International Labour Organisation

Singh H (1987) Emergence and growth of Bhartiya Kisan Union in Punjab. M.Phil thesis, New Delhi: Jawaharlal Nehru University

Singh P (1987) Two facets of religious revivalism. In: Singh G (ed) Punjab today. Intellectual Publishing House, Delhi, pp 167–179

Singh P (1993) Political economy of the British Colonial State and the Indian Nationalist State and the agrarian-oriental development pattern in Punjab. Indo-Br Rev XXI(1):97–110

Singh P (1994) Federal financial arrangements in India with special reference to Punjab. Aust J Dev Stud 9(3)

Singh P (1999) Capital, state & nation: reflections with respect to Punjab. Int J Punjab Stud 6 (1):85–99

Singh P (2002) Political economy of nationalism: minority left and minority nationalisms vs majority left and majority nationalism. Int J Punjab Stud 9(2):287–298

Singh P (2005) Hindu Bias in India's "Secular" constitution: probing flaws in the instruments of governance. Third World Q 26(6):909–926

Singh P (2007) Political economy of centralisation in India: some critical notes from a decentralist perspective. In: Nayak B (ed) Nationalizing crisis: the political economy of public policy in contemporary India. Atlantic Publishers, Delhi, pp 17–45

Singh P (2008a) Political economy of the 'third front' in India. Contemp South Asia 16 (4):465–469

Singh P (2008b) Federalism, nationalism and development: India and the Punjab economy. Routledge, London (paperback edition 2009)

Singh P (2009a) Federalism, nationalism and development: India and the Punjab economy. Routledge, Delhi (special Indian reprint)

Singh P (2009b) The left and the third front. Econ Polit Wkly XLIV(12):8–11

Singh P (2009c) Regional nationalism. Econ Polit Wkly XLIV(17):4
Singh P (2010a) Economy, culture and human rights: turbulence in Punjab, India and beyond. Three Essays Collective, Delhi
Singh P (2010b) Food crisis as a part of the crisis of global capitalism. In: Ghuman RS, Singh S, Brar JS (eds) Globalization and change. Rawat Publications, Jaipur, pp 87–102
Singh P (2014) Russian ban: a blessing in disguise? Imported food contributes to growth in transport and gas emissions. The tribune, Chandigarh, 11 August
Singh P (2016) (forthcoming) Capital, state and nation in Indian federalism: with special emphasis on Punjab'. In: Mohanty M, Sebastian G (eds) Class and its intersectionalities Aakar Books, Delhi
Singh P, Purewal NK (2013) The resurgence of Bhindranwale's image in contemporary Punjab. Contemp South Asia 21(2):133–147
Srinivasan N (1972) Centre-state relations in the field of agricultural development. In: Jain SN, Kashyap SC, Srinivasan N (eds) The union and the states. National Publishing House, Delhi, pp 110–129
Subramaniam C (1979) The New strategy in Indian agriculture: the first decade and after. Vikas, New Delhi
Subramaniam C (1982) A blueprint for Indian agriculture. The Indian express, 11 April
Talbot I (1988) Punjab and the Raj, 1849–1947. Manohar, Delhi
Talbot I (1991) British rule in the Punjab, 1849–1947. J Imperial Commonwealth Hist XIX (2):203–221
The Economist (2000) Chidambaram Subramaniam: Obituary, 18 November

Part VI
Fiscal Policy of Punjab in Comparative Perspective

Chapter 18
Public Finances and Development: The Case of Punjab

Tapas K. Sen

18.1 Introduction

The Twelfth and Thirteenth Finance Commissions identified the state of Punjab as among the three that are fiscally stressed, the other two being West Bengal and Kerala. This was based on mainly two indicators of fiscal health—indebtedness and trends in fiscal balances. Between the three states, Punjab has had the highest levels of per capita income until the middle of the last decade, while West Bengal has had relatively low levels of per capita income for the entire decade. While it is perhaps not surprising for a state with low levels of per capita income to exhibit chronic fiscal imbalance and high levels of indebtedness resulting from large public expenditure obligations in the absence of adequate private purchasing power and low levels of revenue collections, the fiscal stress in a relatively high-income state like Punjab is somewhat puzzling.

The states in India generally rely heavily on sales tax/VAT for revenues, supplemented by revenues from a few other taxes like state excise (primarily levied on alcoholic beverages), stamp duty (primarily collected on the basis of transactions in the real estate sector), and taxes on motor vehicles. Thus, the tax structure of states essentially targets the uses of funds, which has the advantage of including in the tax base the net inflow of funds from outside the state economy over and above what is included in the Gross State Domestic Product (GSDP), which is generally taken to be a proxy for the broad revenue base. Punjab is generally believed to receive significant amounts of remittances, which should actually allow it to raise revenues more than proportional to its GSDP. There can be leakages from the tax base also if significant parts of GSDP escape taxation; for example, transactions leading to eventual exports, interstate transactions not amounting to sale (branch transfers), or

T.K. Sen (✉)
National Institute of Public Finance and Policy, 18/2 Special Institutional Area,
New Delhi 110067, India
e-mail: tapas.sen@nipfp.org.in

L. Singh and N. Singh (eds.), *Economic Transformation of a Developing Economy*, India Studies in Business and Economics,
DOI 10.1007/978-981-10-0197-0_18

significant amounts of 'trade diversion' (direct purchases by the state taxpayers outside the state). While no firm data are available on these potential avenues for leakage, these are believed to be of similar significance as in other states, or even smaller, given that Punjab is not a mineral producing state where such leakages are substantial. On the expenditure side, the relatively high level of per capita income and low levels of poverty should reduce the pressure on the state government for large expenditures on social services and welfare, and on poverty alleviation. This is because larger private incomes allow its citizens to pay for private supply of various services to a greater extent than in a state with low private incomes, the dependence on public supply being greater in the latter. Fiscal problems of Punjab are thus not easily explained, and merit a closer look.

Further, the relative deceleration of growth of the state economy is a matter of concern. Table 18.1 clearly shows that during the previous decade, the rank of Punjab in terms of per capita income among general category states of India has

Table 18.1 Index of per capita NSDP/GSDP (constant prices) of selected states

States	1961–62[a]	1970–71[a]	1981–82[a,b]	1990–91[a,b]	2001–02	2005–06	2010–11
High-income states							
GOA	N.A.	162.2	210.6	223.7	234.7	310.8	287.4
GUJ	116.1	125.7	122.7	118.3	108.6	138.8	148.0
HAR	100.9	135.1	145.7	151.8	152.7	156.2	162.7
MAH	124.5	123.7	145.1	151.5	132.8	156.3	164.4
PUN	115.0	161.9	170.4	168.8	155.0	131.1	123.2
Middle-income states							
APR	87.7	88.9	89.3	80.3	102.7	105.7	108.5
KAR	95.6	101.7	93.7	95.2	103.8	112.6	111.0
KER	79.9	92.0	90.5	83.2	123.4	133.9	135.9
TND	101.5	95.1	93.7	99.3	117.8	131.2	140.7
WBL	118.1	115.2	100.8	95.0	102.7	87.1	88.9
Low-income states							
ASM	98.6	90.2	79.9	68.3	74.7	65.5	60.0
BIH	67.9	62.5	58.1	52.7	35.8	29.8	32.4
JRD					62.3	66.9	63.7
MPR	74.5	75.1	82.3	73.8	69.9	61.2	60.8
CHG					72.8	71.2	71.0
ORS	74.7	88.8	73.3	68.5	63.8	69.9	65.7
RAJ	90.0	89.2	76.3	81.3	83.1	74.7	76.0
UPR	76.7	74.4	78.0	72.8	57.7	51.7	47.8
India[c]	100.0	100.0	100.0	100.0	100.0	100.0	100.0

[a]3-year averages centred on the year mentioned
[b]Index of per capita GSDP used for these two periods only
[c]All-India per capita NDP/NNP
Source Chaudhury (2000) for the first four data columns, and computed on the basis of data from CSO for the last three (Annexure I)

slipped from second to seventh.[1] Among various contributory factors, the possibility of persistent poor health of the state's finances imposing a constraint on the growth prospects of the state cannot be altogether ignored. Even with a relatively high level of per capita income, the importance of government expenditures, particularly capital formation, cannot be overlooked; the examination of a possible link between the fiscal trends and the comparative deceleration of growth of the state's economy may therefore be of immediate policy interest.

Keeping these considerations in view, this paper makes a preliminary attempt at examining the state finances of Punjab to identify proximate reasons for the persistence of fiscal problems of the state and to assess whether specific features of public finances of the state have failed to provide the necessary impetus to the economic growth of the state.

18.2 Role of State Governments in Indian Federal System

An important issue in this context that links public finance and economic growth at the state level in India is: how important is the role of states in promoting economic growth? Can the state governments adopt policies that will encourage growth substantially enough to make a difference? Unless the answer is in the affirmative, the link between public finances and socio-economic development will be rather tenuous in the sense that mere availability of additional resources will not lead to any development of a state. That fiscal policy in general can impact economic growth has been demonstrated in several cross-country studies (Barro 1990; Easterly and Levine 2001; Gregoriou and Ghosh 2009). More specifically, the idea that public expenditures of the right kind can push up growth is as old as Lord Keynes and his concept of multipliers. But there is an additional issue involved in the present context—in the specific case of the federal setup of India; do the states have in their arsenal fiscal policy instruments that can provide a fillip to growth? Conceptually, the answer should again be in the affirmative; both taxation and expenditures by state governments should potentially influence growth in their jurisdictions through encouragement to private investment by improving profitability, and by providing better infrastructure and social environment to reduce costs of production and improve productivity.[2] There are not too many empirical

---

[1]It may be noted that Table 18.1 is based on data that are not comparable for any state over time, because the basic data are taken from different series with varying base years.

[2]The causation runs the other way round also: there are studies on growth and its impact on the size of the public sector beginning with the well-known 'Wagner's law'. However, it is entirely likely that lags would be involved in the causation running from public expenditures to growth, which may not be the case for the converse causation. In the Indian context, a casual regression with panel data for 16 selected states covering the period 2001–02 to 2010–11 indicates per capita public expenditures rising with per capita GSDP, but with a decreasing slope. The estimated regression is: $PCPUBEXP = -848.34 + 0.2434467(PCGSDP) - 0.0000009(PCGSDP^2)$, with the

studies on this topic in India, but the few that there are (e.g., Lall 1999) suggest ample scope for state fiscal policies to play a role in promoting economic growth.[3]

18.3 Overview of Punjab State Finances

The broad indicators of fiscal situation of the state—revenue and fiscal deficits and overall liabilities—indicate that it has improved since the first 3 or 4 years of the last decade (Fig. 18.1). At the start of the reference period till 2003–04, revenue and fiscal deficits were in the range of 3–5 and 5–6.5 % of GSDP. The year 2006–07 saw the lowest levels of revenue deficit (surplus of 1.6) and fiscal deficit (0.48) as percentages of GSDP. Total liabilities had started declining earlier since 2004–05, and have been declining steadily, ending at just over 30 % staring from almost 40 % of GSDP in 2000–01.[4]

Although fiscal deficits have been reasonably controlled even after 2006–07,[5] it is the revenue deficit that gives some reasons for concern, for it has remained above 2 % of GSDP after 2006–07, contributing about 70 % of the fiscal deficit, and thus leaving little scope for capital expenditures. The immediate task before the Government of Punjab therefore is to bring it down to the level of zero as required by the Finance Commission/FRBM legislation for the year 2014–15; this would allow the capital expenditures (including net lending) to rise to 3 % of GSDP, almost a doubling of its current level. The tight control on fiscal deficits has had the desired effect of causing a steady decline in total liabilities as a ratio of GSDP; it may be pertinent to note that a level of 25 % (as against the present 32 %) of this ratio has been considered manageable in general by the Finance Commission. However, apart from the accounted liabilities, outstanding guarantees amounted to Rs. 58,102 crore against total liabilities of Rs. 92,543 crore in 2012–13. These guarantees given by the state government to facilitate loans by public enterprises, local bodies, co-operative banks and societies are contingent liabilities that pose a

(Footnote 2 continued)

nominal values of the variables considered. Both the explanatory variables are statistically significant. This result accords well with the expectation that the share of the public sector in state GSDP will fall as per capita GSDP rises.

[3]It is of interest to note that according to several empirical studies, the composition of public expenditure matters; results generally indicate a higher impact of revenue (current) expenditures on growth compared to the negligible or even negative impact of capital expenditures. Even so, researchers are unwilling to draw the implication that infrastructure does not matter, because it flies in the face of a priori reasoning. In all probability, the insignificance of capital expenditures is a result of (a) too little capital expenditures to show any impact and (b) non-consideration of appropriate lags in the posited relationship.

[4]For a comparative analysis of trends in fiscal aggregates, see Sen and Dash (2013).

[5]The Finance Commission prescribed level of fiscal deficit during the period 2010–2013 was 3.5 % of GSDP, and the state kept the actuals below that level. The prescribed level for the next two years is 3 % of GSDP.

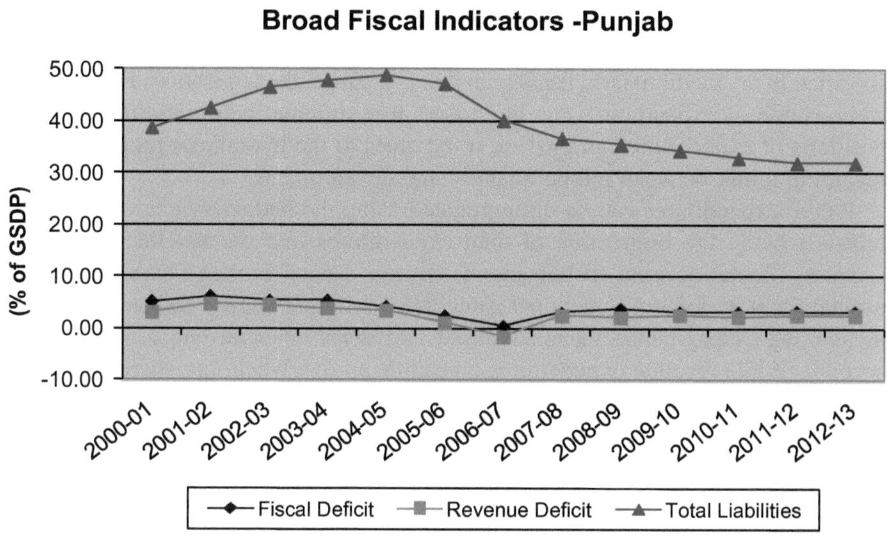

Fig. 18.1 Broad fiscal indicators-Punjab

financial risk for the state government; this risk is brought home by the fact that most of the beneficiaries are not even paying up the prescribed guarantee fees to the state government.

In any case, the steadily declining ratio of liabilities to GSDP has already started a virtuous circle of lower interest payments as a result of lower level of liabilities, which in turn should help in controlling revenue and fiscal deficits and thus further reduction in the total liabilities ratio. But for this to happen, it must be ensured that the reduction in interest payments is not neutralised by increase in other non-productive revenue expenditures or slackening revenue effort.

Even when revenue deficit is identified as the target variable for adjustment, it must be remembered that it is the balance of the revenue account of the budget, and both revenue receipts and expenditures can affect its level. Hence, it is necessary to go into some details of both sides to assess the prospects for adjustment on both sides and form an idea of the possible extent of the same. This is attempted in the next two sections.

18.4 Expenditure Trends

An examination of public expenditures requires an assessment of both levels and composition. The total expenditure levels are not unduly high in Punjab compared to some other states; but its revenue expenditures are relatively high when compared to other high-income states.[6] Given the requirements of FRBM legislation, expenditures are now constrained by the revenue receipts because the level of fiscal deficit is specified in the medium term fiscal path that is a part of the legislation. However, the composition of expenditures can be looked at in different ways, and these decompositions of expenditure can provide some clues to the hypothesis proposed above regarding a link between public finances and development.

Public expenditures can be disaggregated using the budgetary classification, the broadest being the bifurcation of total expenditures into the revenue and capital account. Capital account disbursements in turn can be broken down into capital expenditures on various functional categories and other capital disbursements that include debt repayments, loans advanced and other financial outgo in the capital account. While revenue expenditures constitute an overwhelming share of the total expenditures in Punjab, they are rather large relative to many other states in India. But the level of capital expenditures is inordinately low, crossing 1.5 % of GSDP in only 1 year during our entire reference period of 2000–01 to 2012–13 in 2006–07 (Fig. 18.2). Obviously, capital formation in the public sector is commensurately low, and an extended period of low capital formation in the public sector can adversely affect the availability of both physical and social infrastructure. This, in turn, is quite likely to have dampened growth prospects of the state economy to some extent. Clearly, a reallocation of public expenditures in favour of capital expenditures is needed, so that the level of revenue expenditure is reduced and that of capital expenditures increased. This would also be what is required in terms of fiscal prudence legislation: reduction in revenue expenditures would bring the revenue deficit closer to the required level of zero, leaving fiscal deficit (which is only a little higher than the required level of 3 %) unchanged.

The classification of revenue expenditures by functional groups also points to certain reforms needed. Figure 18.3 presents the four groups of revenue expenditures on (i) general, (ii) social and (iii) economic services, and (iv) transfers to local bodies and other institutions.

It can be seen that general services account for the larger share of revenue expenditures (50 % or more, except in 2012–13), partly because of interest payments included in it. However, steadily falling interest payments since 2002–03 (from 4.18 % of GSDP in 2002–03 to 2.40 % in 2012–13) do not seem to have adversely affected the share of general services significantly, except in 2011–12 and 2012–13. Even the present share is too large a proportion of revenue expenditures merely to ensure perpetuation of the government machinery. Social and economic services account for at best 28 and 23 %, respectively over the entire reference period. As a result, developmental expenditures (on economic and social services)

[6]The annual publication of Reserve Bank of India on state finances for 2013–14 shows the revenue expenditure to GSDP ratio to be persistently high compared to all other high-income and middle-income states on an average during the periods 2004–08, 2008–10 (only West Bengal has a higher ratio), and 2010–13 (only Goa and Karnataka have higher ratios) (Table IV.4.10 A, p. 45). This could be possibly because of greater vote-catching populist expenditures in Punjab compared to other states, something noted in several earlier studies.

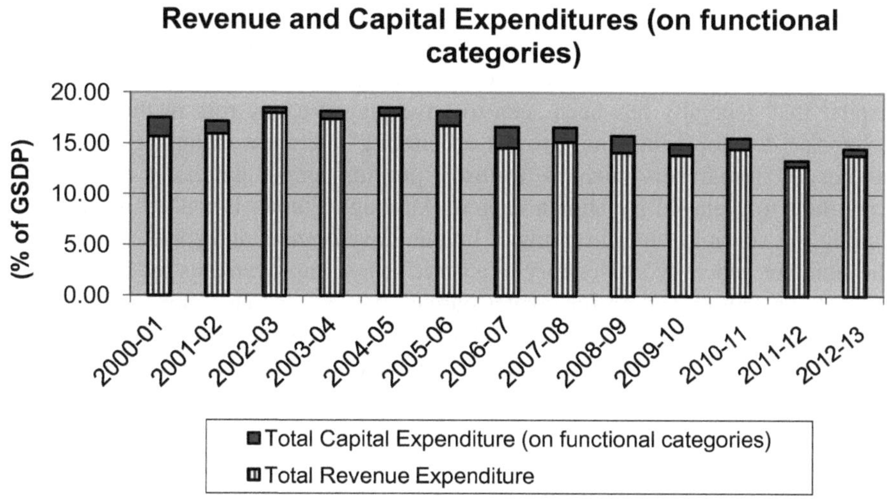

Fig. 18.2 Revenue and capital expenditures (on functional categories)

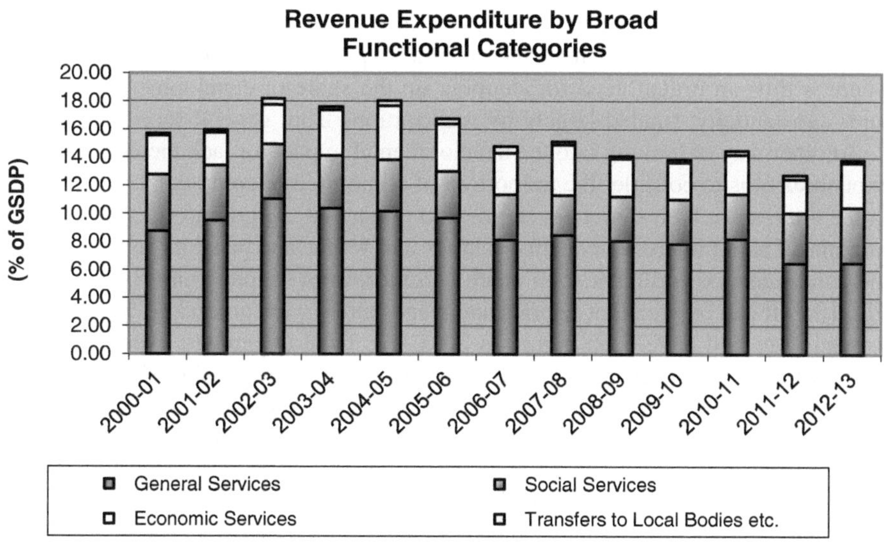

Fig. 18.3 Revenue expenditure by broad functional categories

are less than 50 % of total revenue expenditures, except in 2012–13. In order to curtail revenue expenditures, general services appear to be the obvious candidate; such a step would also automatically boost the shares of social and economic services. As a ratio of GSDP, developmental revenue expenditure has been relatively low in Punjab (RBI study of state finances, 2013–14), and probably needs some augmentation.

In the case of social services, by their very nature, the bulk of the public expenditures are on revenue account, so the low proportion of revenue expenditures for social services implies a lower priority of the government for building up human capital that generally has been seen to have played a key role in the process of economic development. The 'growth accounting' literature including well-known studies by researchers such as Denison provide ample empirical basis to the important role played by human capital. Although Punjab is ranked at number 2 among the states in India in terms of human development and social indicators of the state are generally satisfactory in a static sense, improvements in the indicators are not substantial, calling for greater public intervention. This, however, does not necessarily call for large doses of additional government expenditure; judicious reallocation and small doses of additional expenditure in key areas may suffice. In economic services including most of the infrastructure services in the state domain, the low share reflects a low priority attached to repairs and maintenance of physical assets created by the government through previous capital expenditures (rather small, as observed already), particularly when it is observed that a significant part of the revenue expenditures on economic services are accounted for by poorly designed and targeted subsidies. The likely end result would be poor quality and effectively smaller supply of publicly created infrastructure to support the economy and its continued development. Once again, there could be a need for rationalisation of these expenditures and small incremental expenditures in identified key areas. There is thus an urgent need for stepping up the share of developmental expenditures substantially, funded largely by reallocations from general services.

Another way of looking into the developmental impact (or lack thereof) of public expenditures is to consider the proportion of committed or contractual expenditures in the total, since their direct developmental impact on the ground is expected to be minimal. Taking interest payments, salaries and wages and pensions as constituting the committed expenditures, their share in total revenue expenditures is depicted in Fig. 18.4. It can be seen that salaries and wages alone were around 40 % of revenue expenditures and have been higher in 2011–12. Total committed expenditures (as defined here) have been 65–70 % of revenue expenditures, rising significantly in 2011–12, mainly on account of higher share of salaries and wages, but falling a little in 2012–13. The financial problems associated with unfunded pensions are gradually assuming serious proportions, as the widening band showing the share of pensions confirms. This is likely to pre-empt even larger amounts of resources in the coming years, and the state must prepare a plan to finance these based on reasonably accurate estimates of this liability for future years. In any case, the graph clearly shows that after reaching a plateau in 2007–08 and 2008–09, the share of total contractual expenditures have been rising to reach a level of more than 70 % of total revenue expenditures in 2011–12 (though it fell a little in 2012–13), leaving less than a mere 30 % for expenditures addressing actual augmentation of quality and quantity of publicly supplied services at the discretion of the government—there is only a limited amount of flexibility available. To correct this over the medium-to-long run, the government must try and limit its wage bill—it cannot do anything about pensions, and interest payments have been falling anyway, but have not prevented the

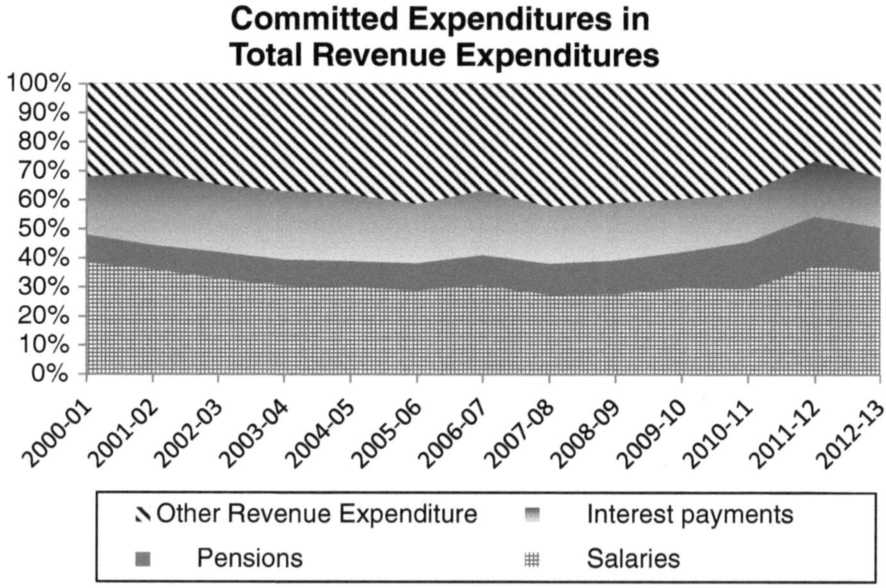

Fig. 18.4 Committed expenditures in total revenue expenditures

share of total contractual expenditures from rising. Coupled with the need to reduce the share of general services, it points towards a rationalisation of employees (the figures indicate an overstaffing of secretariat/general supervisory and support staff) to improve the 'teeth-to-tail' ratio. This would be even more important given the expected salary revisions in 2016 at the central level that is certain to have its repercussions on the states. It may even be necessary to limit pay revisions as much as possible.

Subsidies constitute another large element of revenue expenditures of Punjab, the bulk accounted for by the power subsidies. While all the subsidies are not necessarily defensible, the power subsidies have been a major drain on the state. This, of course is linked to the overall financial health of the state owned power utilities, which is not particularly good. There is an urgent need to clean up the books of these utilities once for all, and then require them to be financially self-reliant; the present trend of annual patch-ups and covering up the poor state of their balance sheets need to be halted. Further, the unbundling and corporatization of the Punjab State Electricity Board legislated in 2010 will realise its full benefits only when the accounts are cleaned up once for all by securitizing all long-term liabilities on the books at the time of the reorganisation, all further financial transactions are transparent and due financial accountability is demanded from the new power utilities. In particular, subsidies from the government have to be clearly accounted for, and treatment of pending government debt liabilities clearly specified as per policy decisions made or to be made.

Table 18.2 Revenue receipts—Punjab (percentage of GSDP)

	2000–01	2005–06	2006–07	2009–10	2010–11	2011–12	2012–13
Total revenue receipts	12.56	15.62	16.18	11.22	12.17	10.12	11.24
Total tax revenue	7.52	9.40	8.33	7.18	8.76	8.64	9.34
Own tax revenue	6.55	8.27	7.09	6.10	7.42	7.27	7.92
Shared taxes	0.96	1.13	1.23	1.09	1.34	1.37	1.42
Total non-tax revenue	5.04	6.21	7.85	4.04	3.41	1.48	1.90
Own non-tax revenue	3.93	4.18	6.09	2.86	2.35	0.54	0.92
Grants from centre	1.11	2.04	1.76	1.17	1.06	0.94	0.97

Source Finance accounts—Punjab, various issues and ESO, government of Punjab

18.5 Revenue Receipts

In general, states in India rely heavily on taxes to raise revenues; the low-income states and the special category states are favoured in the distribution of central transfers to cater to fiscal equalisation and socio-political considerations, making them more reliant on central transfers than other states. Punjab does not belong to either category and must substantially rely on its own revenues. Table 18.2 reflects this in terms of actual trends in revenue receipts.

It can be seen that total revenue receipts rose sharply between 2001–01 and 2006–07 (when it peaked) from 12.56 of GSDP to 16.18 %, but dropped sharply thereafter falling to a low of only 10.12 %. The changes are largely ascribable to own non-tax revenues, more specifically to miscellaneous general services and even more specifically to state lotteries.[7] In that sense, while tax revenue figures are comparable across the years, non-tax revenues are not. For the latter, the figures relating to the period 2010–12 are better indicators of revenue mobilisation than any other year over the reference period because of the absence of any substantive revenue from lotteries.[8]

As the table shows, the bulk of the revenue receipts (tax and non-tax) are raised by the state itself (8.84 % of GSDP in 2012–13); transfers from the centre account for less than 25 %. Within own revenues, tax revenues constitute the lion's share

[7]Because of the accounting practice that credits the revenue receipts with all receipts from state lotteries in gross terms rather than net (with all outgo for the same included in revenue expenditures) of expenditures, and with gross numbers being quite large, changes in policy regarding state-run lottery can cause large shifts in trends when only revenue receipts or revenue expenditures are considered.

[8]The non-tax revenue figure for 2012–13 also reflects a large one-time credit relating to unclaimed deposits, making it non-representative.

Table 18.3 Tax-GSDP ratio of selected states (percentage)

State	Average of 1999–2002	Average of 2010–13
Andhra Pradesh	7.27	7.94
Bihar	4.24	5.04
Chhattisgarh	6.38	8.03
Goa	6.80	7.29
Gujarat	7.74	7.48
Haryana	7.78	6.67
Jharkhand	4.85	4.77
Karnataka	8.18	9.91
Kerala	7.81	8.40
Madhya Pradesh	5.49	8.33
Maharashtra	7.49	7.36
Odisha	5.16	5.94
Punjab	*6.73*	*7.55*
Rajasthan	6.14	6.36
Tamilnadu	8.63	10.17
Uttar Pradesh	5.45	7.40
West Bengal	4.22	4.84

Source Computed on the basis of data from finance accounts of concerned states and from the Planning Commission

with 7.92 % of GSDP in 2012–13. This ratio has fluctuated somewhat over the years, but the 2012–13 level represents the second highest level during the entire reference period. The highest ratio was achieved in 2005–06 (8.27 %), higher than the 2012–13 level by 0.35 % point. This level of tax revenue mobilisation cannot be termed satisfactory, although it cannot be called as poor either. Table 18.3 provides a comparative picture of own tax mobilisation by selected states of India and the change therein over the years, to assess the direction of change in Punjab vis-à-vis other non-special category states. It can be seen from the table that there has been some improvement in the relative performance of Punjab in raising taxes from the years 1999–2002 to 2010–13, as also an increase in the tax-GSDP ratio. This indicates a change in the desired direction, because additional revenue mobilisation through both tax and non-tax sources is an important part of the fiscal reforms needed, as stressed earlier.

The own tax to GSDP ratio of Punjab remains below that of better-performing southern states of Andhra Pradesh, Karnataka, Kerala and Tamilnadu, and also Chhattisgarh and Madhya Pradesh in the period 2010–13. In the earlier period, the ratio was lower than even some other states like Gujarat, Haryana and Maharashtra, but the same has fallen significantly in these states (marginally in Maharashtra) while Punjab has managed to raise its ratio significantly, resulting in Punjab exhibiting a higher tax-GSDP ratio than these three states. It should also be noted that a part of the tax revenue remains off-budget in Punjab—part of the tax on agriculture through the market (*mandi*) fees does not enter the Consolidated Fund.

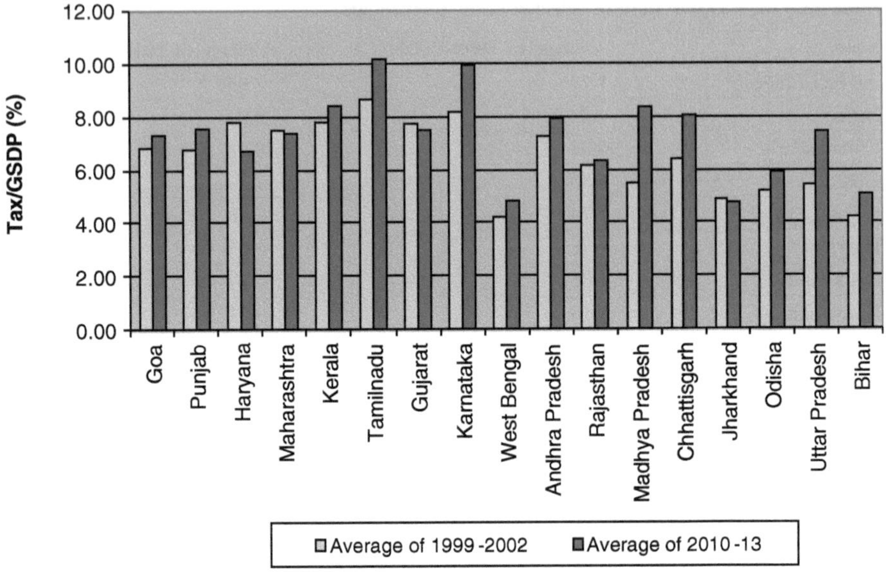

Fig. 18.5 Tax ratios of selected states

With this included, the tax ratio in Punjab (and other states like Haryana that have sizeable collections from this source) would rise to some extent.

In this context, it is interesting to examine the possibility of a systematic relationship between tax ratio and income level (as represented by per capita NSDP). To this end, Fig. 18.5 represents tax ratios of the selected states arranged in descending order of per capita income (average of 2010–13). Any systematic relationship should show up as a broadly rising or falling trend in tax ratio in the diagram.

Clearly, the diagram does not indicate any pattern except a rising trend towards the middle (for the latter period in particular), but even that pattern is vitiated by the low tax ratio of West Bengal bang in the middle. More rigorous statistical examination with regression estimates of tax ratio as a function of per capita NSDP (PCNSDP) also do not reveal any pattern, with the coefficients of PCNSDP not statistically significant. The overall regression results also do not indicate any significant explanation of tax ratio by the level of PCNSDP of the selected states.[9]

[9]The estimated cross-section regression for the averages of 1999–2002 is:

Tax/GSDP = 4.91 + 0.0000378(PCNSDP); R^2 = 0.2808.
(2.42)

For the latter period of 2010–13, the estimated regression is:

Tax/GSDP = 6.55 + 0.0000165(PCNSDP); R^2 *= 0.0758.*
(1.11)

Table 18.4 Tax revenues in Punjab, (percentage of GSDP)

	2000–01	2005–06	2006–07	2007–08	2009–10	2010–11	2011–12	2012–13
Own tax revenues	6.55	8.27	7.09	6.50	6.10	7.42	7.27	7.92
Sales tax/VAT	3.54	4.26	3.80	3.51	3.84	4.42	4.31	4.64
State excise	1.77	1.44	1.08	1.22	1.06	1.05	1.06	1.17
Motor vehicle tax	0.45	0.40	0.37	0.33	0.28	0.29	0.33	0.35
Stamps and registration fees	0.57	1.54	1.42	1.03	0.79	1.02	1.19	1.02
Land revenue	0.01	0.01	0.01	0.01	0.01	0.01	0.01	0.01
Other taxes	0.21	0.62	0.42	0.40	0.12	0.64	0.37	0.73

Source As in Table 18.2

As such, the southern states (and even more strongly, Madhya Pradesh) demonstrate the possibility of further increasing the tax ratio by at least 1 percentage point in Punjab. This is another urgent task that the Punjab government faces, because to eliminate the current levels of revenue deficit, a significant part of the burden of adjustment has to be borne by the receipts side, given that there would be limits to controlling revenue expenditures.

Tax revenues being the main source of own revenue receipts of Punjab (this is the case in most other states of India too), it is of interest to examine the trends in tax revenues by major components. Although a detailed analysis of taxes is beyond the scope of this paper and requires detailed information on tax structure and administration, a comparison across the years can possibly point to apparent weaknesses or slackening effort. Table 18.4 provides the necessary information.

As is commonly seen in Indian states, sales tax/VAT collects bulk of the tax revenues in Punjab. Immediately upon the introduction of VAT in 2005, there was a jump in collections (possibly related to processing of setoffs), which fell back to roughly pre-VAT levels in the next year. The sales tax system has suffered from continuing uncertainties regarding the introduction of Goods and Services tax (GST), and the final form of the same. As such, now is probably not a good time for unilateral reforms in the sales tax system—such a measure must await the actual introduction of GST. All the same, the last 3 years of our reference period have seen a substantive increase in tax collections from sales tax/VAT, hitting the peak level during the reference years in 2012–13, which is encouraging.

A mild increase in collections from stamp duty and registration fees can be observed, clearly related to the real estate boom in the state, though 2005–06 and 2006–07 remain the peak collection years. The relatively subdued collections in more recent years despite rising property values indicate possibilities of additional revenues from this source with tighter administration. In this context, the recent trend in Indian states has been that of lower rates and better representation of market value of real estate in the tax base. The latter is usually achieved through a statutory recognition of market values as represented by regularly updated 'register values' maintained by the concerned department as the tax base in cases of suspected undervaluation. Also, closing legal loopholes that permit taxpayers to classify conveyance as something else to reduce tax liability has also paid dividends in several states.

Collections from state excise have fallen substantially, with no apparent reason. This phenomenon needs a closer examination to locate the causes and identification of corrective measures. Motor vehicle taxes have always been relatively low in Punjab, and there has been some slippage in collections even from the 2000–01 levels in terms of collections under this tax as a ratio of GSDP. A thorough examination of this tax, and an informed reform of the system [sp] based thereupon is probably long overdue. Collection from land revenue is next to nothing, despite land being the scarcest resource in Punjab. For a rational land-use pattern, a paradigm change in the land revenue system (perhaps coupled with changes in the surprisingly light property tax system) may be called for. Finally, the state must explore the possibility of introducing one or more of the unused taxes that it can levy (e.g. profession tax, although a part of the state government employees being located in Chandigarh, a Union Territory serving as the state capital for both Punjab and Haryana, does complicate matters).

The low level of revenues from non-tax revenues point to possibilities of augmenting the state's resources through these sources, but it is impossible to be more specific on this without a detailed examination of the potential sources. In general, the relatively high per capita income of the state should make it possible to levy/raise proper prices for public services and/or user charges. This includes not only the administrative departments of the state government, but also the various state government agencies that draw upon the budget for subsidies for continued operation. Augmenting the resources of local bodies by empowering them to raise selected additional revenues would also benefit the state finances with reduced liability for support. Perhaps it is time the government set up a high level committee to examine different sources of revenue (other than sales tax) with a view to raise substantial additional revenues on a sustainable basis. The improving, but still only medium-level overall tax-GSDP ratio indicates that this should be possible.

18.6 State Public Sector Undertakings

One of the strategies for providing support to economic development of a state by its government involves setting up public sector undertakings tasked with attending to specific sectors. The reasons for doing it through public undertakings rather than its own departmental structure can vary, but a common reason is the granting of some degree of autonomy in the functioning of the undertaking. Public enterprises can be part of an administrative department, or can be more independent; public sector undertakings are set up with a corporate structure. These undertakings are allowed to raise revenues and make their own investment decisions. The added autonomy is expected to facilitate their functioning without all the constraints within which the departmental structure operates, and improve developmental prospects in the designated area that each public enterprise covers.

In Punjab, the aggregate size of the public sector enterprises is significant with their turnover accounting for more than 10 % of GSDP. They include joint stock companies as well as statutory corporations (there are four in Punjab). Unfortunately, poor financial viability has effectively caused almost half of the government companies to become non-functional. Further, few of the remaining can boast of healthy financial status and an ability to function without regular infusion of funds from the state government. Instead of promoting the development of the state, the public undertakings have in general become a burden on the state budget.

The lion's share of the state government's investment in public undertakings (equity and long-term loans) is accounted for by the power sector. The former Punjab State Electricity Board—now unbundled and corporatized—accounts for more than 80 % of the total government investment in public undertakings. Unfortunately, the dependence on government subsidies (mainly for the distribution companies) continues, thus eroding the autonomy. The total budgetary outgo for public undertakings in various forms was as much as Rs. 3690 crore in 2010–11. Moreover, it shows an increasing trend. Budgetary outgo is sometimes supplemented by loan write-offs, conversion of loan into equity, as also state government guarantees for loans availed by the public undertakings (outstanding guarantees are contingent liabilities). Overall annual losses in public enterprises have come down since 2005–06, but they are still substantial at about Rs. 1500 crore, with the accumulated loss at over Rs. 12,000 crore (2010–11).

The state government set up in 2002 the Directorate of Disinvestment in the Department of Finance to oversee the closure, privatisation or reform, as the case may be, of public sector undertakings. There are a large number of public undertakings that are non-functional but still exist in the legal sense. These urgently require decisions regarding their fate. Besides, other undertakings, even if functional, may require one of the three above-mentioned actions. These have to be identified and the appropriate course of action decided. Essentially, if the intended service is not provided in a desired manner by any public undertaking, there is no reason to continue supporting it with scarce public resources. The overall developmental impact of the public undertakings has dwindled to insignificance, if they ever were significant, many of them not even providing the service to supply which they were set up to any significant extent.

18.7 Imperatives for Fiscal Reform

An analysis of state finances based on broad trends in budgetary data can be of only limited help in chalking out a reform program. Even so, it can be of use in identifying some areas of weakness for closer examination and corrective measures based on more informed and detailed assessment. This was the limited purpose of the present paper, and even the admittedly broad analysis of state finances identifies certain reform priorities. These can be recapitulated as follows:

- While fiscal deficits require only a small adjustment, revenue deficits require a much larger adjustment to be brought down to the zero level required by the FRBM legislation. The scale of adjustment required suggests that both revenue receipts and revenue expenditures have to share the burden of adjustment.
- In the revenue expenditures, a sharp reduction in expenditures on salaries and wages and in general services is called for; both of these can be achieved by cutting down secretariat and non-field level staff as much as possible while simultaneously keeping a lid on salary and wage rates.
- In particular, the state has to prepare for likely increases in pension payments and unavoidable salary revision; for the former, a reasonably accurate estimation of the future pension burden at existing rates (salary revision would also revise pensions, in all probability) is necessary.
- Subsidies, particularly power subsidies, need to be rationalised; this cannot be accomplished without a complete overhaul of the finances of the power utilities that is overdue. This may involve some short-term financial instability given the state of the balance sheets of the power utilities, but this ought to be beneficial in the long run if a more transparent and cleaner financial system in the power utilities is insisted upon.
- Capital expenditures on actual building up of assets and revenue expenditures on maintenance and repairs of the existing assets have to be augmented to reverse the slackening of economic growth.
- Additional resource mobilisation through both tax and non-tax sources is now a priority task; to achieve this in a rational manner, it is probably time to examine various potential sources of revenue (other than sales tax) in detail. This would call for setting up a high level official committee for the purpose.
- Rationalisation of public sector undertakings including closures where merited, has to be expeditiously undertaken.

The discussion of state finances above has also thrown up possible linkages with the state's development process, and ways of eliminating possible negative impacts. It must be realised, however, that economic development of a state is a product of multiple factors, of which state policies including financial policies constitute a subset. It is incumbent upon the state government to at least pursue policies—both financial and other—of its own that maximises their positive impact.

References

Barro R (1990) Government spending in a simple model of endogenous growth. J Polit Econ 98(5):103–125

Chaudhury S (2000) Economic growth in the states—four decades. Money & Finance October–December 45–69

Easterly W, Levine R (2001) It's not factor accumulation: stylized facts and growth models. World Bank Econ Rev 15(2):177–219

Gregoriou A, Ghosh S (2009) On the heterogeneous impact of public capital and current spending on growth across nations. Econ Lett 105(2009):32–35

Lall Somik V (1999) The role of public infrastructure investments in regional development: experience of Indian states. Econ Polit Wkly 34(12):717–725

Sen TK, Dash SK (2013) Fiscal imbalances and indebtedness across indian states: recent trends, working paper 119, National Institute of Public Finance and Policy, New Delhi

Chapter 19
Strategy for Fiscal Stability and Revitalizing the Economy of Punjab

Upinder Sahwney

The economy of Punjab was leading India's development journey up to the turn of the present century. Punjab was one of the fastest growing states of India in the 1970s and the 1980s. Data (statistical abstracts, GOP) show that when the average compound annual growth rate (CAGR) of gross national income in India was 4.08 % in 1985–86, gross state income grew at a CAGR of 7.88 % in Punjab; when it was 1.20 % in India in 1991–92, it grew at 5.09 % in Punjab but when during the Eleventh Five-Year Plan (2007–12) gross national income in India grew at 8.03 % per annum, it grew only at 6.73 % in Punjab The state had the highest per capita income in the country up to 2003–04 when it started faltering. Punjab lost its 'numero uno' position gradually as its pace of growth slowed down during the 1990s and in 2005–06 it was at the third position in terms of per capita income amongst the major Indian states and in 2010–11 slipped to the seventh position (GOP 2012–13). The rate of growth of Punjab economy is much slower than the all-India growth rate as mentioned above, even though the poverty ratio in the state is only 15.9 % compared to 29.8 % in India. However, a matter of concern is the higher unemployment rate per thousand according to the 66th round of national sample survey organization (NSSO) in Punjab, which was 42 % compared to only 25 % at the all-India level. The level of urbanization in Punjab is much higher than the country as a whole. 37.5 % of the population of Punjab lives in urban areas compared to only 31.2 % in India. The proportion of the scheduled caste (SC) population in the state is 31.9 % compared to the all India average of 16.64 %. The literacy rate in Punjab (75.84) is about the same as the all-India average (74.04). Keeping in view the high rate of unemployment, the proportion of the SC population as also the high rate of urbanization, the state government has a huge responsibility with respect to social welfare/social security provision, civic amenities and the need for creating employment opportunities.

It is imperative to boost investment, create infrastructure, and provide citizen centric services in Punjab. All this requires adequate public funds and a sound fiscal position of the state government to carry out development. Punjab has been expe-

U. Sahwney (✉)
Department of Economics, Panjab University, Chandigarh, India
e-mail: us18.econ@pu.ac.in

L. Singh and N. Singh (eds.), *Economic Transformation of a Developing Economy*, India Studies in Business and Economics,
DOI 10.1007/978-981-10-0197-0_19

riencing fiscal deterioration since the beginning of the 1980s. There are several reasons for the faltering performance of the Punjab economy in the post-reform period when other states of India began to perform better than before; prominent among them is the fiscal imbalances faced by the economy over a long period of time. The fiscal crisis is a manifestation of various political, economic and administrative failures of the government during the decade-long civil strife in the 1980s when the administration was non-functional, ineffective and non-accountable. Enough effort was not made by the elected governments since the early 1990s to put the economy back on the path of economic development; attributing the deteriorating fiscal situation of the 1990s to the decade of political strife in the state. This is one of the causes for fiscal crisis but other factors accentuate the problem further.

19.1 Fiscal Imbalances in Punjab

The 3 key indicators needed to analyse the fiscal performance of a government are the gross fiscal deficit (GFD), revenue deficit (RD) and primary deficit (PD). The deficits in the government accounts represent the gap between its receipts and expenditure. The deficit indicators (Tables in Appendix 1) of the state show that Punjab has had a high fiscal deficit since the beginning of the 1980s. The first year when Punjab had an RD (1984–85), FD was 5.73 % of GSDP and further increased to 7.90 % of GSDP in 1987–88. Revenue deficit indicates the excess of revenue expenditure over revenue receipts and must be zero at all times. RD in Punjab has never been zero since the mid-1980s. Thereafter, FD, RD and PD all kept fluctuating but FD consistently declined over the first few years of the 2000s and was the least, i.e. 2.44 % of GSDP in 2005–06 when RD was only 1.14 % of GSDP. Primary deficit also fluctuated significantly over the study period. Between 2006–07 and 2011–12 all the 3 indicators have shown a rising trend pointing towards worsening of Punjab state finances once again. The nature of deficits is an indicator of the prudent fiscal management of the government. The absence of a consistent decline in the deficits in Punjab finances brings out the fact that fiscal management in Punjab has not been sustainable over a long period of time.

According to the *White Paper on State Finances* (GOP 2002), the factors that adversely impacted the state's fiscal situation during the 1990s are ever-increasing salaries and wages of the employees, mounting debt burden, heavily subsidized social and economic services, slow growth of revenue and loss making public sector undertakings (PSUs). All this was compounded by the lagged effect of terrorism on the growth of the State. This adversely affected the buoyancy in tax revenue. During the prolonged spell of President's rule in Punjab, no additional resource mobilization measures were taken. The state had to incur a huge expenditure on paramilitary forces to combat terrorism. The GOP in the late 1990s followed the populist path and allowed free power to the farm sector and also abolished octroi. Vast losses incurred by Punjab State Electricity Board (PSEB), low irrigation charges, uneconomic transport fares all combined to produce unduly low returns on decades of past investments, which in turn adversely affected further investments in infrastructure and also hurt the required expansion in education, health and other social services.

19.1.1 Committed Expenditure of the Government of Punjab

Committed liabilities of the governments are that part of the non-plan expenditure which the government has to pay without an option of avoidance and government cannot shirk from its obligation to incur this expenditure. Such expenditure includes the salary and pension liabilities, interest payments, subsidies and expenditure incurred on administrative services. This expenditure is non-developmental in nature and due to its rigid and inevitable nature it drains a major share of the government revenues. The share of the committed expenditure in total revenue receipts and expenditure is very large in Punjab (Tables in Appendix 2). Committed expenditure increased continuously since 1980–81 to reach nearly 72 % of revenue receipts (RR) in 1998–99 and nearly 50 % of revenue expenditure (RE). Thereafter it declined for several years and was 41.62 % of RR and 39 % of RE in 2005–06. It started increasing again and committed expenditure of GOP was more than 60 % of revenue receipts and 48 % of revenue expenditure in 2011–12. If the share of committed expenditure is large it implies that most of the government resources are drained towards non-plan and non-developmental commitments with lesser amount left to be spent on development and effective service delivery in the state.

Interest payments are an important component of committed expenditure (Tables in Appendix 3). Ratio of interest payments to revenue receipts was only about 11 % in 1980–81 which increased continuously and was above 40 % in 1998–99. Thereafter this ratio started declining and was only slightly above 15 % in 2009–10, only to rise again to nearly 24 % in 2011–12. Interest payment to revenue expenditure ratio was 11.27 % in 1980–81 but increased to more than 27 % in 1998–99. Thereafter it varied between 20 and 25 %, which reflects that the state is spending a high proportion of its revenue expenditure on interest payment. This implies that for most of the years a substantial part of revenue receipts and expenditure were spent on servicing the debt.

Subsidies are another component of committed expenditure that pose a huge burden on the public exchequer. The data on subsidies are analysed only for the last 10 years, i.e., from 2002–03 to 2011–12 as the data prior to that are not available in a consistent manner (Tables in Appendix 4). Subsidies as a proportion of RR and RE almost doubled during the decade. The ratio of subsidies to RR was the highest in 2004–05 and the ratio to RE was the highest in 2007–08 and declined thereafter. The power sector accounts for almost the entire amount of subsidy in Punjab. The burden of power subsidy is becoming unmanageable for the state. Even after unbundling of PSEB, no steps have been taken to rationalize the expenditure and augment resources by imposing user charges for power consumption on well-off farmers in the agriculture sector of the state.

The ratio of outstanding liabilities (OL) of the state to GSDP as also to revenue receipts has increased persistently since 1980–81, which further corroborates the fact that the state has been under fiscal stress for a long time now. RBI (2014) brings out the fact that Punjab has ranked in the bottom five states having the highest OL/GSDP ratio in the past two decades (Tables in Appendix 5). The ratio of outstanding liabilities to GSDP was 17.39 % in the beginning of the 1980s and increased to 48.78 % in 2002–03. Similarly, the outstanding debt to revenue receipts ratio of Punjab increased from 153.87 % to a whopping 400.16 % 2001–02. Thereafter it remained more than 300 % for most of the years in the recent past and did not show any signs of a consistent decline over the last 10 years.

State governments also stand guarantees for loans raised by PSUs and other state institutions. In the event of inability of the organization to repay the loan and interest thereon, the guarantee can be invoked and the state has to bear the burden of the loan. In the case of Punjab, the government has been standing guarantees for loans indiscriminately and without assessing the repayment capability of the organization. Since the PSUs in Punjab are sinking into a debt trap, it is almost certain that the liability of loans generated will devolve upon the state government in the near future. The ratio of outstanding debt including guarantees has been worked out only for the period 2002–03 to 2011–12 because of non-availability of data on guarantees prior to that. This highlights that the actual liabilities of the state are much higher than observed without including guarantees. The ratio to GSDP has been much higher than the one brought out without including guarantees, even though it has declined over the years from more than 65 % in 2002–03 to nearly 50 % in 2011–12.

The ratio of debt to GSDP, which is still above 32 %, shows that the state is excessively dependent on the debt sources to finance its expenditure needs. After 2006–07 this ratio declined continuously even though the debt increased substantially in absolute terms. Most of the increase in debt can be attributed to an increase in the committed expenditure of the GOP as a result of interest liability and the pay revision on the recommendations of the fifth and sixth Central Pay Commission awards. Implementation of the awards raised the fiscal deficit of Punjab dramatically and so also the debt. Increased debt leads to higher payments for servicing the debt apart from the principal in the form of interest payments and most of the revenue generated by the state is spent on debt servicing.

The ratio of interest payments to revenue receipts clearly shows that from 2002–03 to 2004–05 around 30 % of the revenue receipts were spent on servicing the debt which later declined but still nearly one-fourth of the revenue receipts are spent on interest payments. Interest payment to revenue expenditure ratio has also varied between 23 and nearly 20, which reflects that the state is spending a high proportion of its revenue expenditure on interest payment. In their study Rangarajan and Prasad (2012) categorized the states as High Debt Stressed whose debt/GSDP ratio lies between 30 and 50 and the ratio of interest payment to revenue receipt is between 15 and 25. Accordingly, it is clear that Punjab can be categorized as a debt stressed state and the fiscal situation of the state needs some concrete action by the government to make its public debt sustainable.

The severity of the fiscal stress is further highlighted by the number of days that Punjab was availing of ways and means advances (WMA) and was in overdraft (OD) with the RBI. In the first half of the 1990s the State's OD increased from 6 days during 1992–93 to 26 days during 1994–95, while the number of days that it was availing WMA went up from 5 to 20. After 1995–96, however, there was a sharp increase and during 1998–99 the number of days the state was in overdraft went up to 225 with the state availing of WMA on 130 days. Thus, there were only 10 days in the entire year when the state had a positive cash balance (Sawhney 2005). According to the RBI annual report 2012–13 (Appendix 6) the Punjab Government has used the WMA facility on 232 days during 2012–13. It also availed of special WMA on 233 days in the year. This special facility comes against the pledge of government securities. This was the highest utilization by any state. The interest on both types of WMA is linked to the repo rate of the RBI. Punjab had also taken an overdraft on 139 days. OD comes at an additional 2 % points (currently at 9.25 %). For a state government to remain that long in overdraft mode is indicative of some structural problems. The financial management of the state is extremely detrimental to its fiscal health going by the steadily increasing recourse to WMA/OD over the past few years.

19.1.2 Utilization of Borrowings for Repayments

The Government of Punjab utilizes most part of the borrowed funds for the repayment of the previous debt of the government and only a small proportion is left for investment in capital/development projects in Punjab. Table 19.1 gives a view of this situation, which indicates that in fresh government borrowings, during the last 5 years the share of debt repayment has been continuously increasing leading to a decline in the available borrowed funds for capital expenditure.

The analysis of the borrowed funds of the state shows that the share of repayment of fresh loans has increased substantially from 34.83 % in 2007–08 to 60. 17 % in 2011–12. This indicates the inability of the state government to repay the loans from its own sources and its increasing dependence on borrowed funds indicating that the economy of Punjab is in a debt trap. It is evident from an overview of the state finances in Punjab that the state has been continuously facing fiscal crisis and is heavily dependent on borrowed funds for meeting its general governance needs and development obligations.

Table 19.1 Utilization of borrowings for debt repayment (Rs. crores)

Year	Borrowings	Debt repayment
2007–08	6050.64	2107.65 (34.83)
2008–09	6432.25	2288.52 (35.58)
2009–10	10107.84	5308.36 (52.52)
2010–11	10934.37	5952.88 (54.44)
2011–12	14870.88	8947.23 (60.17)

Source: Report of the Comptroller and Auditor General of India, various issues

Note: Figures in parenthesis are percentages

19.2 Fiscal Reform Programme

In pursuance of the decision of the GOI to provide assistance to the state governments in order to strengthen their financial situation, the Government of Punjab signed a memorandum of understanding (MOU) with the GOI. The agreement reached between Ministry of Finance, GOI and Government of Punjab is termed as Fiscal Reform Programme for Punjab. According to this agreement, the Ministry of Finance would provide immediate assistance to help the state government get out of the overdraft. The assistance comprised permitting state governments to carry out market borrowing immediately and on priority basis, making advanced devolution and releases of Central Plan Assistance and WMA. These releases and permission were conditional in that the state government would raise its internal resources and agree to undertake time-bound action on the reform programme. The MOU stated that in order to increase revenues and reduce expenditure, the state government would draw up an implementation plan, giving details of the various actions, the agencies responsible for carrying out these actions and a time frame within which the actions would be completed. The MOU listed certain measures for improving the fiscal situation. These were reduction in non-plan revenue expenditure, reduction in subsidies through improved cost recovery for both social and economic services, withdrawal of tax incentives to industries, disinvestment, reform of tax regime and improvement in management of public debt.

However, even after signing the MOU, progress towards fiscal consolidation in Punjab leaves a lot to be desired. The action taken report submitted by the Government of Punjab to the GOI in November 2000 indicated a lack of headway made on this front. The Punjab government continued to face financial problems. Non-plan expenditure, which was to be reduced by 5 % in 1999–2000 from its level in 1998–99, actually increased by 7 % during that period. The government took certain policy initiatives in the state budgets of 2000–01 and 2001–02. The fiscal measures spelt out in these budgets included rightsizing the government, rationalization of tax structure, compression of non-productive expenditure and revision of user charges. The institutional reforms announced included the constitution of Public Expenditure Reforms Commission and Public Sector Disinvestment Commission, preparation of MOU with the Government of India on power sectors reforms and notification of State Electricity Regulatory Commission.

Despite the set of measures announced by the government towards fiscal reforms, Punjab continued to face a severe financial crunch. Faced with the precarious situation, the Punjab government had been using the guarantee route for solving its liquidity problems. In the process it impaired its own solvency. The change of government in the state in February 2002 and the subsequent announcement of the various budgetary and fiscal reforms provided yet another opportunity for fiscal consolidation. Realizing the gravity of financial crises the government brought out a *White Paper on the State's Finances* in March, 2002. The government committed itself to correcting institutional factors leading to economic and financial distortions. The most important step in this direction was the enactment of the *Fiscal Responsibility and Budget Management Act* (FRBMA) in May 2003. The state government signed another MOU with the Ministry of Finance, GOI on July 23, 2003 to achieve fiscal sustainability in the medium term.

19.2.1 Fiscal Responsibility Legislation in Punjab

Fiscal consolidation in India was initiated with some seriousness only after adopting the target-based fiscal rules in the form of fiscal responsibility legislations (FRLs). The Government of India enacted the FRBMA in 2003 after which all the state governments followed suit and enacted FRLs at the sub-national level. Punjab was one of the first to enact the FRL at sub-national level in the form of Punjab Fiscal Responsibility and Budget Management Act (PFRBMA), 2003, which stated that it is, "An Act to provide for the responsibility of the State government to ensure inter-generational equity in fiscal management and long-term financial stability by achieving sufficient revenue surplus, containing fiscal deficit and prudential debt management consistent with fiscal sustainability through limits on the State government borrowings, debt and deficits, greater transparency in fiscal operations of the State government and conducting fiscal policy in a medium-term framework and for matters connected therewith or incidental thereto" (Punjab Gazette 2003).

The PFRBMA, 2003 has been amended twice, first in 2005 and again in 2011. The second amendment was made to bring the fiscal indicators in line with the fiscal roadmap of the Thirteenth Finance Commission which stated that, "we recommend that the states' enactment/amendment of their FRLs incorporating the above targets should be conditionality for release of all state-specific grants". Keeping these recommendations in view, PFRBM Act, 2003 amended the targets for the deficit indicators as well as for debt levels and state guarantees. Table 19.2 has been prepared on the basis of the amendments to PFRBMA, 2003 as brought out by the Government of Punjab from time to time.

19.2.2 Compliance of the PFRBMA

Implementation of the PFRBM Act 2003 was considered as a deterrent to the imprudent fiscal behaviour of the state government, which would bring books of the state in balance. The original PFRBM Act 2003 provisioned that the ratio of revenue deficit to revenue receipts should be reduced by 5 % points compared to the previous year and containing the rate of growth of fiscal deficit to 2 % per annum in nominal terms until the fiscal deficit is brought down to 3 % of GSDP (Table 19.3).

The table shows that the state had achieved the target of revenue deficit and it declined from 29.35 to 24.56 % in 2004–05 and further 7.32 % in 2005–06. Fiscal deficit also reduced during this period but the reduction in 2004–05 was less than 2 % as mandated by the Act and the target was not achieved in 2004–05; however,

Table 19.2 PFRBM Act and its amendments

Parameters	PFRBM Act and amendments		
	PFRBMA 2003	PFRBM (Amendment) Act, 2005	PFRBM (Amendment) Act, 2011
Fiscal deficit	Containing the rate of growth of fiscal deficit to 2 % per annum in nominal terms until the fiscal deficit is brought down to 3 % of GSDP	To reduce the fiscal deficit from 2005–06 to bring it down to 3 % by the year 2008–09	To reduce the fiscal deficit 2010–11 3.5 % 2011–12 3.5 % 2012–13 3.5 % 2013–14 3.0 % 2014–15 and onwards 3.0 %
Revenue deficit	Reduction in revenue deficit as percentage of total revenue receipts, by at least 5 % points, from the previous year	To reduce the revenue deficit from 2005 to 06 to bring it down to 0 % of GSDP by the year 2008–09 and surplus thereafter	To reduce the revenue deficit 2011–12 1.8 % 2012–13 1.2 % 2013–14 0.6 % 2014–15 0 % 2014–15 onwards (+)
Debt	Cap the ratio of debt to GSDP at 40 % to be achieved by 2006–07	To bring the ratio of debt *including contingent liabilities* to GSDP down to 28 % within a period of 5 years from 2005–06 to 2009–10	To bring down its debt as percent of GSDP by 2010–11 42.5 % 2011–12 41.8 % 2012–13 41.0 % 2013–14 39.8 % 2014–15 38.7 %
Outstanding guarantees	Cap outstanding guarantees on long term debt to 80 % of revenue receipts of the previous year	Unchanged	Unchanged

the state government succeeded in achieving it in 2005–06. Target of debt/GSDP ratio was to be reduced to 40 % but the state failed to achieve this target. The guarantees were capped to 80 % to the previous years' revenue receipts and the state government achieved this target successfully (Table 19.4).

In exercise of the powers conferred by Section 7 of the Act, as amended, the state government framed the Punjab Fiscal Responsibility and Budget Management Rules in December 2006 with the sole target "to reduce the fiscal deficit from the financial year 2005–06 so as to bring it down to 3 % of GSDP by the year 2009–10".

The target of fiscal deficit was achieved for the period 2005–06 to 2007–08 but later fiscal deficit started rising again and targets of the 2008–10 period were not

Table 19.3 FRBMA compliance status of the state (2003–04 to 2005–06)

Year	RD/RR (reduce 5 %)		FD (reduce 2 % in nominal terms)		Debt/GSDP		Guarantees/RR	
	Target	Achieved	Target	Achieved	Target (%)	Achieved	Target (%)	Achieved (%)
2003–04	↓ by 5 %	29.35	4313	4880	40	47.53	80	110.58
2004–05	↓ by 5 %	24.56	4227	4036	40	48.61	80	73.19
2005–06	↓ by 5 %	7.32	4143	2656	40	47.07	80	64.10

Table 19.4 FRBMA compliance status of the state (2005–06 to 2011–12)

Year	GFD/GSDP		RD/GSDP		OL/GSDP		Guarantees/RR	
	Target	Actuals	Target	Actuals	Target	Actuals	Target	Actuals
First Amendment of PFRBMA 2003 in 2005								
2005–06	3.5	2.44	↓	1.14	↓	55.22	80	64.10
2006–07	3.5	3.46	↓	1.38	↓	51.21	80	82.04
2007–08	3.5	3.01	↓	2.50	↓	43.73	80	65.58
2008–09	3.0	3.84	0	2.22	↓	50.22	80	134.47
2009–10	3.0	3.12	Surplus	2.66	28	51.18	80	160.75
Second Amendment of PFRBMA 2003 in 2011								
2010–11	3.5	3.15	2.9	2.33	41.8	32.96	80	182.03
2011–12	3.5	3.28	1.8	2.63	41.0	32.12	80	165.58
2012–13	3.5	3.18	1.2	2.52	41.0	31.41	80	221.48

achieved. After the second amendment of the Act, targets were revised for the state fiscal deficit and it remained within the limit in 2010–11, 2011–12 and 2012–13, which indicates that the state government complied with the targets of the Act.

Revenue deficits do not present a very encouraging picture. The PFRBM (Amendment) Act, 2005 provisioned that revenue deficit should decline continuously from 2005–06 and it should be in surplus by the end of the year 2008–09. The state failed to comply with these targets completely and revenue deficit never reduced for the 2005–10 period. In fact RD continued to increase during this period. The second amendment of the Act in 2011 prescribed a limit of 2.9 % for 2010–11 and the state was able to achieve this target, but it again failed in 2011–12 and 2012–13 to keep the revenue deficit within the prescribed limit of 1.80 % and 1.20 % respectively. It was 2.63 % in 2011–12 and 2.52 % in 2012–13, much higher than it was mandated by PFRBMA as amended in 2011.

PFRBM (Amendment) Act, 2005 prescribed that outstanding debt including guarantees should decline over time and by the end of 2009–10 it should be 28 % of GSDP. The state government never achieved this figure during 2005–10, except for 2007–08 when it remained more than 50 % to GSDP. This showed that the state had absolutely failed to achieve the debt targets of the Act. The second amendment of 2011 did not clearly prescribe whether debt included contingent liabilities or not and it fixed the target of 41.8 and 41.0 % for the years 2010–11 and 2011–12 and 2012–13 respectively. If the contingent liabilities of the state are excluded then the debt/GSDP ratio remained around 32 % and the targets have been met.

The cap on long-term guarantees was fixed at 80 % of the revenue receipts of the previous year and it remained unchanged in both the amendments. The state complied with these targets until 2007–08 but after that guarantees showed a very steep rise and guarantees as percent to revenue receipts doubled in 2008–09 to 134.47 % from 65.58 % in 2007–08. This ratio increased continuously and in 2010–11 it reached 182.03 %. However, in 2011–12 this ratio declined to 165.58 % but remained more than double the limit of 80 % prescribed by the Act. In 2012–13 this ratio increased significantly to 221.48 which is nearly three times higher than the prescribed limit and will make the task of fiscal consolidation in Punjab even more arduous.

The analysis of fiscal imbalances of Punjab state shows that the fiscal performance of the state is not up to the mark and except for the fiscal deficit targets the state had failed to achieve the targets recommended in its FRL. The state had achieved the debt targets in past 2 years but the share of contingent liabilities has been excluded from the total debt. If contingent liabilities are included in the total outstanding debt the picture changes completely and debt including contingent liabilities was 50.74 and 49.75 % of GSDP for the years 2010–11 and 2011–12 respectively.

In view of the mounting debt/outstanding liabilities of GOP, it is pertinent to look into the debt management efforts of the state.

19.3 Debt Management in Punjab

In India sub-national debt is managed by the central government, Finance Commission of India and Reserve Bank of India apart from the respective state governments. The Finance Commission has made significant efforts to improve the fiscal health of state governments and to bring the debt to a sustainable level. Debt sustainability and debt relief issues have been considered since the time of the Second Finance Commission but from the Ninth Finance Commission onwards the issue has gained more importance, when it became mandatory for the Commission to review the debt position of the states as a whole and suggest corrective measures. Reports of various Finance Commissions have suggested measures to improve sub-national finances that include debt consolidation and rescheduling at lower interest rates, rescheduling of loans without lowering of interest rates, moratorium on interest payments and repayments, debt write-off, debt relief linked to fiscal performance, etc. To ease the debt burden of states, the central government implemented various measures in the early 2000s. Debt Swap Scheme (DSS) was introduced in 2002–03 to lessen the burden of interest payments of the states. Another measure, in the form of Debt Consolidation and Relief Facility (DCRF), was recommended by the Twelfth

Finance Commission. Punjab has benefitted from both these reform measures and it helped to mitigate the debt burden of the state to some extent.

19.3.1 Debt Swapped Under Debt Swap Scheme (DSS)

Under the debt swap scheme (DSS) for states offered by the Government of India, loans from the centre bearing coupon rates in excess of 13 % were swapped against small savings proceeds and open market borrowings (OMB). The scheme was in operation for a period of 3 years, i.e. from 2002–03 to 2004–05 and Punjab has benefitted by swapping loans worth Rs. 5359 crores during this period to lower interest rate loans from open market and small saving funds. This scheme did not help to reduce the stock of debt rather it merely changed the composition of debt by swapping high interest loans for lower interest loans, thus reducing the interest burden of the state government. Table 19.5 shows debt swapped under DSS in the case of Punjab.

19.3.2 Debt Consolidation and Relief Facility

The Twelfth Finance Commission recommended debt consolidation and relief facility (DCRF) which included debt consolidation and debt write-off. This facility was available for only those state governments that had enacted the Fiscal Responsibility and Budget Management Act (Table 19.6).

The facility of debt consolidation was provided for consolidating central loans issued to state governments by the Ministry of Finance until March 31, 2004 and outstanding as on March 31, 2005 into fresh loans for 20 years to be repaid in 20 equal instalments carrying a lower interest rate of 7.5 %. Repayments due from states during the period 2005–06 to 2009–10 on these loans were eligible for write-off. During a period of 5 years the total relief for Punjab amounted to Rs. 970 crores, which includes both debt and interest relief.

It is pertinent to mention here that the GOP did not initiate any measures on its own to either manage its debt or reduce the borrowings.

Table 19.5 Debt swapped under debt swap scheme (Rs. crores)

Year	AOMB	SSL	Total
2002–03	717	275	992
2003–04	1440	1013	2453
2004–05	1280	634	1914

AOMB Additional open market borrowings. *SSL* Small savings loans

Source RBI State Finances: a Study of State Budgets, various issues

Table 19.6 Debt and interest relief under DCRF for Punjab (Rs. crores)

Year	Debt relief by central government	Interest relief
2005–06	64	131
2006–07	68	134
2007–08	86	125
2008–09	153	110
2009–10	–	99
Total	371	599

Source RBI State Finances: a Study of State Budgets various issues

19.4 Strategy for Rejuvenation and Fiscal Stability in Punjab

The evaluation of state finances of Punjab clearly brings out that Punjab is a highly debt-stressed state and is borrowing mainly to repay its earlier debt, thereby undermining the capacity of the state to create new assets or improve the quality of service delivery in the state. The committed expenditure of the state is colossal and the populist policies of the government have further aggravated the severity of fiscal imbalances. Consequently, from the point of view of sound financial management, such fiscal profligacy must not be ignored and encouraged further. The onus of all this rests with the successive governments of Punjab over the past two decades and the GOP is mainly responsible for fiscal consolidation and arrest further downslide of the economy. There are many tough decisions that the GOP needs to take in order to turn around the economy. There is a need to adopt a multi- pronged strategy to reverse the fiscal distress and restore the lost glory of the state–revenue augmentation and expenditure rationalization besides several other measures. The government cannot afford to lose more time in mere rhetoric, the action on the ground has to be visible in terms of improvement in fiscal condition of the state and availability of fiscal space for carrying out the development activity and improving the service delivery in Punjab.

19.4.1 Revenue Augmentation

Effective, transparent and accountable tax administration is the first step that the Government of Punjab should aim at as there are huge leakages in the case of taxes like stamp duty, excise and value added tax (VAT). It is almost impossible to estimate the extent of tax evasion in the state but there is surely undervaluation of taxable goods and services. This problem can be effectively tackled through e-governance and computerization of all government transactions and efficient machinery for tax administration. A strong political will is required to weed out dishonest, corrupt and inefficient manpower. Similarly, abolition of Octroi in Punjab has been a populist policy. There are also certain other areas where revenue augmentation is possible but the main hindrance is the conflict of interest of the policy makers in the state. Many people, across party lines, in Punjab happen to be at the helm of policy making as also the owners of private commercial transport, schools, colleges, hospitals, etc.

One of the major sources of non-tax revenue for any government should be the return on investment of public funds made in the PSUs. The state level public enterprises (SLPEs) in Punjab generate negligible resources. On the contrary these enterprises are a huge burden on the state exchequer. The administrative and establishment expenses of most of the SLPEs in Punjab are much higher than their contribution to the state fisc, thereby undermining the justification for their existence. Disinvestment of SLPEs must be effectively implemented so that some resources that are lying locked up in loss making public enterprises may be made available for development and social welfare in the state.

Revenue in Punjab can be augmented to a significant extent by energizing the economy, i.e. boosting economic activity in all the three sectors of the economy. Revival of the agricultural sector is of paramount concern as more than half the workforce in Punjab is still dependent on agriculture. Creation and strengthening of agri-infrastructure and investment in R&D in agriculture are prerequisites for turning around this sector in the state. This requires huge public funding. The strength of an economy lies in utilizing its potential in the manufacturing sector. Punjab has a huge potential for small and medium enterprises (SMEs) to flourish. The scope of agro-industrial development in Punjab, which has often been discussed but never seriously pursued through a concrete policy, must be converted into reality. If a consistent state policy is followed, without bureaucratic hurdles and red-tapism, SMEs can contribute to the turnaround of the state economy. An investor friendly regime, quick decision making, uninterrupted power supply and clean administration are prerequisites for any investment in Punjab. Finally, there is a huge scope of growth of services sector in the state. The real estate sector is the only subsector in which any investment is visible, even though, information technology (IT) and IT enabled services (ITeS) have a tremendous potential in Punjab. The perception of corrupt and inefficient state machinery needs to be firmly dispelled from the minds of the investors in order to attract both domestic and foreign investment. The GOP has initiated a movement to attract investment in the state recently by promising proper infrastructure and investor friendly policies and incentives. An investment to the tune of Rs. 65,000 crores has been promised by corporate houses during an event "Progressive Punjab Investors Summit" organized by the GOP in December 2013, where the state government showcased the opportunities for investment in Punjab. Another event "Progressive Punjab Agriculture Summit" was organized in February 2014 in which farmers, researchers, policy makers and other stakeholders participated in order to discuss the future of agriculture in Punjab and the need for diversification, research and development, etc. It remains to be seen to what extent these two events actually translate into investment in different sectors of the economy. Strengthening the investment in all sectors of the economy will result in increased economic activity resulting in enhanced revenue collection in the long run. This kind of effort is likely to give sustainable results.

19.4.2 Expenditure Rationalization in Punjab

A large part of the expenditure of GOP is non-developmental in nature. Therefore, the funds for service delivery and infrastructure development in the state are inadequate, which has serious long-term implications for social and economic development of the state. The subsidies, which are a large chunk of committed expenditure, need to be pruned and only the most desirable ones need to be retained. Desirability is subjective, therefore, it is suggested that the economic condition of the target population must be taken into account before dispensing any economic benefits and all general subsidies must be done away with. This is mainly applicable in the case of all types of farm subsidies—power, irrigation, inputs, etc. A careful and item-wise analysis of various heads must be taken up to see wherever it is feasible to impose user charges without harming the interest of the marginalized sections of the society. Although there is a very strong case for power subsidy in Punjab as its withdrawal may increase the cost of food grains, yet it has to be a targeted subsidy. This must be provided only to small and marginal farmers. Subsidies must follow a simple formula, i.e. social gain + economic gain must be greater than the cost.

Also, power sector losses need to be minimized through proper metering and controlling transmission and distribution (T&D) losses. The notional privatization of Punjab State Electricity Board in the form of unbundling into two separate entities, Punjab State Power Corporation Limited and Punjab State Power Transmission Company, has not changed the work culture to any meaningful extent. The power sector in Punjab needs major reforms even after unbundling. Except for providing clean balance sheets for the new entities created, it has failed to infuse real corporate culture by appointing professionals at the helm of affairs, with the powers to take independent decisions and not allowing any political interference. Effective power sector reforms will go a long way in helping fiscal consolidation in Punjab as most of the subsidies are accounted for by the power sector.

Huge amount of public resources are locked up in loss making public enterprises in Punjab. All the SLPEs that have been recommended for closure/winding up by different disinvestment commissions of Punjab from time to time must be wound up at the earliest so that their establishment costs can be curtailed. There are certain areas where both government departments and public enterprises exist to carry out the same functions, e.g. the Department of Social Welfare and the Punjab State Scheduled Castes Welfare Corporation serve the same purpose. Similarly, the Department of Food and Civil Supplies as well as the Punjab Foodgrain Corporation and MARKFED are engaged in procurement of food grains in Punjab. Therefore, there is a dire necessity for restructuring the government departments in order to cut down on expenditure. Another area where the government can reduce its contingent liabilities is the guarantees extended by the state government for loss making SLPEs. There is no justification for increasing the fiscal liability for organizations that do not contribute anything to the state economy.

A significant part of the expenditure of GOP is committed not only in the form of interest payments and subsidies but also salaries and pensions. Salaries and wages eat away a major part of expenditure incurred on education and health. Punjab pays the highest salaries to its bureaucrats, teachers, doctors and other employees in the country. However, absenteeism amongst teachers and doctors in the state as also the lack of adequate infrastructure and basic needs such as medicines in hospitals, blackboards and chalk in schools has eroded the productivity in these sectors. The quality of expenditure on education and health in the state needs to be improved in a significant manner.

19.4.3 Other Measures

Articles 266 and 283 of the Constitution of India provide that all receipts of the state should be credited to the Consolidated Fund of the State and withdrawal of money therefrom should be regulated by law made by the legislature of the state. Accordingly, fees/cess levied through acts of legislature of the state and sale proceeds of government lands should be credited to the Consolidated Fund of the State. There are several extra-budgetary funds like the Cattle Fair Fund, the Punjab Education Development Fund, the Punjab Infrastructure Development Fund and the Punjab Infrastructure Fund, etc., where income on account of fees in cattle fairs, cess on sale of liquor, beer, petrol, and agricultural produce and sale proceeds of lands are not credited to the Consolidated Fund of the State which results in reduction of availability of revenue. Mandi (market) fees and rural development cess are collected by the Mandi Committees and retained by the Mandi Board and Rural Development Board, respectively. These proceeds are meant to be utilized for building infrastructure in the Mandis and rural areas. However, in the absence of a rigorous system of transparency and accountability, the proceeds have been used in an unauthorized and sub-optimal way. As reported by comptroller and auditor general of India (CAG), not only are certain receipts not available for public expenditure but money is also irregularly disbursed by politicians for populist purposes in the state without prior identification and assessment of the requirement of funds. These funds are not subject to scrutiny by the CAG. These should be made a part of the Consolidated Fund of the State, thereby raising the amount of state revenue. Their utilization also must be subjected to auditing as other budgetary receipts and expenditure. This will instil discipline in expenditure and improve the quality of resource allocation in the state.

19.5 Wrap Up

The economy of Punjab has experienced a definite deceleration in the past two decades, which became evident in its falling rank in terms of per capita income amongst Indian states since the beginning of the present century. There has been a structural flaw in the development pattern of Punjab, i.e. a lack of diversification of the economy and emphasis only on the growth and development of the agricultural sector (Singh 2009). Also, fiscal imbalances have afflicted the state in the past three decades and fiscal reform measures taken up after the enactment of Fiscal Responsibility Legislation did not have a lasting effect. In fact, debt sustainability is a major challenge before the Government of Punjab. The situation is not irretrievable, only the government has to put its act together. A multi-pronged strategy is required to revitalize the state economy as also restore its lost glory. On the one hand, fiscal reform measures are required to be implemented in order to enforce discipline in the management of state finances in Punjab, on the other, overall economic development has to be taken up in all sectors of the economy.

There is a huge potential for the revival of the agricultural sector and rural economy of the state. Agro-industrial development requires a push by way of providing an enabling environment through creation of adequate and sector-specific infrastructure. A recent study (Shergill 2013) shows that nearly 6.28 lakh non-agricultural enterprises of 66 different types are working in rural Punjab. As per Census 2011 and the 66th round of NSSO (2009–10) about 38.35 % of rural workers are engaged in various rural non-agricultural activities. Therefore, the GOP must systematically work towards identifying non-agricultural rural activities/enterprises which have a high labour absorptive capacity and gives attractive remuneration to encourage people to participate in those works. The focus has to be on skill development for identified activities, provision of institutional finance, establishment of marketing link with urban centres, etc. More importantly, there is a dire necessity of public funding of research both in rural agricultural and non-agricultural activities in order to improve their quality and returns from those activities. Further the linkages between all three sectors of the economy are very important.

Fiscal imbalances in the state, to a great extent, have been the result of lack of transparency and accountability (Sawhney 2005). Non-transparent tax concession, quasi-fiscal subsidies and off-budget spending all contribute to such imbalances. Fiscal transparency requires a high degree of fiscal marksmanship. It also consists of a transparent regulatory framework, open public procurement and employment practices, a code of conduct for officials and published performance audits. Restoration of financial discipline calls for bringing in all extra-budgetary transactions into the Consolidated Fund of the State. The application of funds outside the consolidated fund should be subjected to the same rigours as the budgeting process through appropriate auditing mechanisms and periodic reviews. A restructuring of government expenditure needs to focus on its functional aspects and eliminate programmes that are no longer relevant. A reduction in subsidies by increasing user charges for services delivered is another step towards fiscal consolidation. Unless the state's finances are looked at in totality on a continuous basis and come up for close scrutiny in the legislature and outside, it will be difficult to ensure adequate transparency and accountability.

There are a few facts about Punjab that must be kept in mind whenever the economy of the state is evaluated or studied. Punjab shares a live border with Pakistan and had to bear the brunt of not only two wars—1965 and 1971, but also a decade-long civil strife in the state. This eroded the power of GOP to mobilize resources in the state which also resulted in a huge debt on account of forces engaged to maintain peace in Punjab. The industrial development in Punjab was progressing fairly well prior to the 1980s, but the state witnessed not only lack of future investments but also a flight of capital. After political stability was attained in Punjab, the neighbouring state of Himachal Pradesh (HP) is competing away the investment from the state on account of special incentives offered to investors, HP being given the status of 'Special Category State' by the GOI. Punjab cannot afford to offer any more sops to any sector in view of its precarious financial situation in order to counter the incentives offered by H.P.; to that extent the economy of Punjab is suffering.

The share of Punjab in central taxes and grants as recommended by successive finance commissions has declined from 2.2 % (Fourth FC) for present Punjab to 1.147 % as per the recommendations of the Eleventh FC. It, however, increased marginally as recommended by the Twelfth and Thirteenth FCs. Also, the criterion adopted for sharing of taxes based on growth performance of the states has been discriminatory towards better performing states like Punjab. Punjab has been the food bowl of the nation and its precarious financial health ought to be a matter of concern for the national government. This places a responsibility on the Government of India to take cognizance of these facts and come out with a special package for Punjab in order to supplement the effort of the State government towards fiscal consolidation and overall growth and development of the State.

The Government of Punjab cannot wait for the Government of India to help it out of the crisis but has to make a concerted effort to revive the state economy and correct fiscal imbalances. The state has to seriously pursue the fiscal reform programme towards achieving fiscal consolidation and generation of quality infrastructure and competitive environment. The success of the entire reform programme depends on how far the government is able to resist the temptation for populist measures. If the government continues to succumb to the populist political pressure, the fiscal crisis in Punjab will only deepen. The state machinery has to be made accountable through strong governance reforms and adoption of e-governance. The recent efforts of the Government of Punjab towards attracting investment in all 3 sectors of the state must be translated into practice. In order to achieve the desired goals political will to translate ideas into practice and administrative competence are imperative. The ruling elite owe this to the hard-working and enterprising people of Punjab.

Note: Tables in annexures are based on RBI State Finances: A Study of Budgets, various issues, unless specified otherwise.

Appendix 1

See Table 19.7.

Appendix 2

See Table 19.8.

Table 19.7 Deficits in Punjab state finances (1980–81 to 2011–12) (percent)

Year	1980–81	1981–82	1982–83	1983–84	1984–85	1985–86	1986–87	1987–88	1988–89	1989–90	1990–91
GFD/	3.18	2.99	2.77	3.58	5.73	5.95	3.29	7.90	5.91	5.35	6.58
RD/GSDPGSDP	−0.36	−1.06	−1.56	−0.81	0.11	−0.07	−0.86	1.87	1.73	1.30	2.88
PD/GSDP	1.95	1.75	1.50	2.36	3.91	4.41	1.62	6.59	4.36	3.98	4.82
Year	1991–92	1992–93	1993–94	1994–95	1995–96	1996–97	1997–98	1998–99	1999–00	2000–01	2001–02
GFD/GSDP	5.04	4.76	4.94	5.22	3.53	3.31	5.09	6.78	4.76	5.23	6.23
RD/GSDP	2.11	2.42	2.54	2.17	1.17	3.07	3.05	4.72	4.06	3.13	4.75
PD/GSDP	3.46	3.20	1.49	1.58	−0.32	−0.38	1.29	2.62	0.83	2.09	2.24
Year	2002–03	2003–04	2004–05	2005–06	2006–07	2007–08	2008–09	2009–10	2010–11	2011–12	
GFD/GSDP	5.35	5.42	4.17	2.44	3.46	3.01	3.84	3.12	3.15	3.28	
RD/GSDP	4.56	3.95	3.50	1.14	1.38	2.50	2.22	2.66	2.33	2.63	
PD/GSDP	1.18	1.30	0.06	−0.98	0.18	0.05	1.03	0.59	0.72	0.85	

Table 19.8 Committed expenditure (CE) of the government of Punjab (1980–81 to 2011–12) (percent)

Year	1980–81	1981–82	1982–83	1983–84	1984–85	1985–86	1986–87	1987–88	1988–89	1989–90
CE/RR	23.24	24.01	23.79	24.12	29.83	27.44	30.09	28.19	31.10	35.11
CE/RE	24.00	26.45	27.34	25.85	29.54	27.60	32.36	24.24	27.03	31.27

Year	1990–91	1991–92	1992–93	1993–94	1994–95	1995–96	1996–97	1997–98	1998–99	1999–2000	2000–01	2001–02
CE/RR	40.49	24.43	49.52	54.32	40.20	47.08	49.52	51.11	71.79	65.18	49.46	60.96
CE/RE	31.75	21.63	40.32	44.02	35.26	43.32	39.82	41.43	49.28	47.75	39.60	42.82

Year	2002–03	2003–04	2004–05	2005–06	2006–07	2007–08	2008–09	2009–10	2010–11	2011–12
CE/RR	56.08	54.59	50.03	41.62	47.00	46.90	48.61	49.73	51.09	60.46
CE/RE	41.88	42.20	40.17	38.78	42.57	39.12	40.98	40.20	42.87	48.00

Appendix 3

See Table 19.9.

Table 19.9 Interest burden of the government of Punjab (percent)

Year	1980–81	1981–82	1982–83	1983–84	1984–85	1985–86	1986–87	1987–88	1988–89	1989–90	1990–91
Interest payments/RR	10.92	10.83	10.69	10.24	16.31	12.56	13.53	11.46	13.49	13.00	16.80
Interest payments/RE	11.27	11.94	12.28	10.98	16.15	12.64	14.56	9.85	11.72	11.58	13.17
Year	1991–92	1992–93	1993–94	1994–95	1995–96	1996–97	1997–98	1998–99	1999–00	2000–01	2001–02
Interest payment/RR	9.71	14.75	31.8	23.47	28.74	29.34	29.11	40.25	35.31	24.99	35.59
Interest payments/RE	8.6	12.01	25.77	20.59	26.44	23.59	23.6	27.64	25.87	20	25
Year	2002–03	2003–04	2004–05	2005–06	2006–07	2007–08	2008–09	2009–10	2010–11	2011–12	
Interest payment/RR	31.02	30.58	28.84	21.9	24.72	23.53	23.67	15.15	19.98	23.94	
Interest payments/RE	23.16	23.64	23.15	20.4	22.39	19.63	19.95	12.25	16.76	19.00	

Appendix 4

See Table 19.10.

Table 19.10 Subsidies of the government of Punjab (2002–03 to 2011–12) (percent)

Year	2002–03	2003–04	2004–05	2005–06	2006–07	2007–08	2008–09	2009–10	2010–11	2011–12
Subsidy/RR	6.93	11.2	15.81	9.28	9.25	15.7	13.55	13.17	12.6	12.26
Subsidy/RE	5.17	8.65	12.69	8.64	8.37	13.1	11.42	10.65	10.58	9.73
Year	2002–03	2003–04	2004–05	2005–06	2006–07	2007–08	2008–09	2009–10	2010–11	2011–12
Power subsidies to total subsidies	97.78	99.26	99.40	98.54	91.69	94.27	92.73	98.16	96.98	99.53

Source CAG reports, various issues

Appendix 5

See Tables 19.11 and 19.12.

Table 19.11 Outstanding liabilities (OL) of the government of Punjab (1980–81 to 2011–12) (percent)

Year	1980–81	1981–82	1982–83	1983–84	1984–85	1985–86	1986–87	1987–88	1988–89	1989–90	1990–91
OL/GSDP	17.39	17.72	18.1	19.81	21.47	26.12	26.95	30.40	32.70	32.73	37.45
OL/RR	153.87	154.47	152.04	165.07	192.49	212.22	217.4	265.12	283.68	308.78	357.84
Year	1991–92	1992–93	1993–94	1994–95	1995–96	1996–97	1997–98	1998–99	1999–00	2000–01	2001–02
OL/GSDP	35.60	36.25	35.95	36.40	36.36	35.34	36.76	39.15	39.62	41.19	44.88
OL/RR	218.81	341.73	331.83	234.94	270.78	280.45	281.91	379.13	356.32	328.07	400.16

Year	2002–03	2003–04	2004–05	2005–06	2006–07	2007–08	2008–09	2009–10	2010–11	2011–12
OL including guarantees/GSDP	65.48	61.12	57.78	55.22	51.21	43.73	50.22	51.18	50.74	49.75
OL/GSDP	48.78	47.53	48.61	47.07	40.23	36.52	35.35	34.32	32.96	32.12
OL/RR	362.43	352.74	340.91	301.42	303.71	290.03	296.73	305.91	270.86	317.33

Table 19.12 Ranking of Punjab vis-a-vis other states—OL/GSDP[a]

Year	Punjab	Highest	Lowest	Year	Punjab	Highest	Lowest
1991	4	Goa	Tamil Nadu	2003	3	Bihar	Jharkhand
1992	4	Goa	Karnataka	2004	5	Bihar	Jharkhand
1993	5	Bihar	Maharashtra	2005	2	Bihar	Jharkhand
1994	4	Bihar	Maharashtra	2006	5	Bihar	Chhattisgarh
1995	4	Bihar	Maharashtra	2007	6	Uttar Pradesh	Chhattisgarh
1996	4	Bihar	Maharashtra	2008	5	Uttar Pradesh	Chhattisgarh
1997	5	Bihar	Maharashtra	2009	5	West Bengal	Chhattisgarh
1998	4	Bihar	Tamil Nadu	2010	5	West Bengal	Chhattisgarh
1999	4	Bihar	Tamil Nadu	2011	3	West Bengal	Chhattisgarh
2000	3	Bihar	Tamil Nadu	2012	3	West Bengal	Chhattisgarh
2001	4	Bihar	Jharkhand	2013 (R.E.)	3	West Bengal	Chhattisgarh
2002	5	Bihar	Jharkhand	2014 (B.E.)	2	West Bengal	Chhattisgarh

[a]No.1 being the highest indebted state

Appendix 6

See Table 19.13.

Table 19.13 WMA and OD of GOP

Year	2004–05	2005–06	2006–07	2007–08	2008–09	2009–10	2010–11	2011–12	2012–13
WMA	268	22	–	19	21	128	132	177	232
OVERDRAFT	115	–	–	–	–	29	13	26	139

References

Government of Punjab Report of the Comptroller and Auditor General of India on State Finances, various issues, Chandigarh

Government of Punjab Statistical Abstract of Punjab. Various issues, Chandigarh

Government of Punjab (2012–13) Economic Survey. Chandigarh

Government of Punjab (2002) White paper on the state's finances. Department of Finance, Chandigarh

Government of Punjab (2003) Fiscal responsibility and budget management act, 2003. Punjab Government Gazette, Chandigarh

Rangarajan C, Prasad A (2012) Managing State Debt and ensuring solvency: the Indian experience. Policy research working paper no. 6039, Economic Policy and Debt Department, The World Bank, Washington DC

Reserve Bank of India (2014) State finances: a study of budgets, various issues, Mumbai

Sawhney U (2005) Fiscal Reforms at the sub-national level: the case of Punjab, working paper 26, National Institute of Public Finance and Policy, New Delhi

Singh P (2009) Federalism, nationalism and development. Routledge, London

Shergill HS (2013) Growth of non-agricultural enterprises in rural Punjab. Institute for Development and Communication, Chandigarh

Part VII
Perspectives on Rejuvenation of Punjab Economy

Chapter 20
Peasant Movement and Rejuvenation of Punjab's Economy

Sucha Singh Gill

The revival of dynamism of the Punjab economy is going to be multi-dimensional in nature. In this effort multiple sections have to be involved. Peasantry is one of such sections and it has been most adversely affected and the major part of it is under stress. The involvement of peasantry in this process, especially for building fresh dynamism in agriculture is possible through their organizations. A consensus can be built on acceptable agrarian agenda. For the last three decades several attempts have been made in the name of diversification of agriculture but the efforts have not been successful. One of the reasons for diversification not taking off has been lack of involvement of peasant organizations in arriving at an acceptable agenda of agrarian change. In order to understand this, a genesis has to be made of the derailment of the vision or perspective of agrarian agenda commonly developed by peasant movement during 1970s and 1980s. The paper attempts to relate the new agricultural policy of the government, peasant vision and emerging agrarian situation in the state. The paper is organized into four sections and the first section covers agricultural crisis in the state. The second section deals with the new policy programme and non acceptance by the farmers. The third section discusses the vision of farmers' movement and its derailment and also brings out the barriers in the implementation of this vision. The last section attempts at synchronization of the agrarian agenda with the farmers' interests, which can be achieved by the farmers' organizations by combining the strategy of struggle and reconstruction.

20.1 Nature of Agrarian Distress

Agricultural production system is affected by cultivated ecosystem and social productive system. A cultivated ecosystem consists of gardens, ploughable lands, meadows, pastures forests. This depends on external factors such as water supply

S.S. Gill (✉)
Centre for Rural and Industrial Development (CRRID),
Sector 19A, Madhya Marg 160019, Chandigarh, India
e-mail: gsuchasingh@gmail.com

L. Singh and N. Singh (eds.), *Economic Transformation of a Developing Economy*, India Studies in Business and Economics,
DOI 10.1007/978-981-10-0197-0_20

and drainage. Thus, the rainfall, flow of water in streams, the ground water resources and their quality, temperature, quality of soil, etc. are important for agricultural production but are general external factors for production raised by the farmers. The social productive system is composed of internal resources consisting of human resources (labour power, knowledge, know-how), productive implements and equipment and living resources such as cultivated plants and animals (Mazoyer and Eroudart 2008, pp. 48–49). The agrarian system is the expression of historically constituted and geographically localized type of agriculture composed of a cultivated ecosystem and a social productive system. The working of the agrarian system cannot be understood without taking into consideration the external exchanges such as upstream activities, rainfall, flow of water in the rivers and activities of internal resources affecting ground water resources and their quality, replenishment of fertility of soil, availability of productive implements and equipment, labour power, knowledge and know-how of producers/farmers. Given the internal resources in an agrarian system, the changes in the extent of external exchanges in an ecosystem such as the rainfall, flow of water in rivers and temperature affect agricultural production. These changes are popularly associated with occurrence of droughts or floods and extreme weather conditions. These changes are very common and are associated with weather cycles, affecting agricultural production. In countries like India where the level of monsoon determines rainfall, the flow of water in rivers and also the ground water resources, agriculture is rightly described as 'gamble in the monsoon'. The fluctuation in the agricultural production and consequently, the income of the farmers and agricultural labour depends considerably on rain gods. It is in this sense that agricultural production system and generation of income of the farmers is quite different from income generation in other sectors of the economy. Indian farmers and agricultural labourers have been facing periodic cyclical stress due to excessive rainfall (floods) or shortfall of rainfall (droughts) causing falls in their income. This is well documented in reports of Famine Commission in the British period.

The distress to population engaged in agriculture by vagaries of weather and furies of nature is compounded by the system of surplus extraction from agriculture by the state and other sections of economy. In the medieval period followed by British Colonialism, land revenue was the major source of income of the state. Along with the land revenue, the tenants were burdened with extraction of rent by the landlords, generally consisting of one-half of the produce of the land. This rent has been, now, replaced by cash rent in areas of modern agriculture in India. The introduction of modern technology with the arrival of green revolution in the mid 1960s, market risks have become very serious. The new technology based on motorization, mechanization, mineral fertilizers, special selection of seeds, crop specialization has made agriculture highly dependent on the market both for input (machinery, labour, chemical inputs, fuel, seeds) acquisition as well as output disposal. The output being seasonal, there is no regular flow of cash, but agricultural producers are required to spend continuously on input acquisition. This makes them dependent on borrowing, both for agricultural production as well as for domestic consumption. The borrowed amount creates interest liability along with the principal amount which has to be cleared at the time of crop harvest. Crop failure or major reduction in the yields due to natural calamities push farmers in distress and unpaid debt further adds to increased liability along with the fresh crop loans. Even in the absence of natural calamities, market failures such as sudden fall in prices due to glut of production (in case of commercial crops especially vegetables and fruits) also add to the woes of the farmers. The contrast with the nature of market like monopoly or monopolistic competition in other sectors, agriculture faces monopsony or monopsonistic market structure. Thus, neither price fixation of agricultural produce nor fixation of input prices is within the control of the farmers. The other sectors because of monopsony structure in input market have mechanisms of lowering input prices or (upward) flexible output prices due to monopoly in output market to make necessary adjustments to maintain their margins. This mechanism is not available to agriculture and farmers (peasants) remain at the mercy of the market conditions.

In view of frequent natural calamities and often break down of market clearance and crash of prices, there is no effective distress redressal mechanism for the population engaged in agriculture. Agricultural producers are not unionized (except in few pockets) and their distress remains unarticulated and unredressed. The levers of powers of the state both at the level of Union Government and State Governments are pulled by those who have dominant interests in non-agricultural activities. Agriculture is a state subject; poor fiscal health of states adds to the difficulties in redressing the economic distress. Rampant corruption leads to inefficiency and apathy of the government machinery which enables non eligible or affluent sections to corner whatever little financial benefits are given by the government. For instance, only 6 % of power subsidy reached the small and marginal farmers in Punjab who constitute 34 % of the total farmers. Same is the case with other subsidies in agriculture on fertilizers and other inputs (Sukhal 2014, p. 84).

In the recent past especially after neo-liberal reforms, the role of the state has diminished giving greater role to the private sector and free play to market forces. The three areas which have affected farmers seriously need special mention. They are rural education, rural health and agricultural research/extension services. In the pre reform period these services were provided by the state either at very nominal prices or free of cost.[1] With the arrival of the economic reforms they have been opened to private sector. Instead of strengthening these services in the state sector and allowing healthy competition, they were allowed to collapse by not appointing staff in vacancies caused by retirees, by withdrawing financial support for the

[1]The delivery of social services provided by the government began to crumble during the phase of terrorism and political strife in the state of Punjab. There was change in the outlook of administration from development-oriented to law- and order-oriented administration. During the long spell of President's rule, there was degeneration of governance leading to impairing of capacity to collect taxes. The restoration of civil administration in 1992 in the state was accompanied by the introduction of neo-liberal economic policy, which worked to withdraw the state from the provisioning of social services and created a bigger role for private players in health, education and extension services in agriculture (Gill et al. 2010, pp. 116–118).

equipment for teaching/tests and labs. They were virtually made non functional. On top of it monitoring of the staff was also withdrawn leading to collapse of rural education, rural health and agricultural research/extension services in the public domain (Gill et al. 2010, pp. 116–124). This led to the proliferation of such sub standard services in private sector but at exorbitant prices. This has become a major mechanism of transfer of resources from agriculture to non-agriculture sector. This is in addition to the market-related processes of value transfers from agriculture to non-agriculture sectors. The share of the consumer prices reaching farmers is around 53 % in case of paddy, 77.00 % for wheat, 67.00 % for cotton, 42–47 % for vegetables and 20–25 % for fruits in Punjab (Raul 2001, pp. 132–134). The forward trading by big companies in these crops in the recent years has further reduced the share of the producers in consumer prices.[2] The greater role of the market and reduced role of the state has increased the margins of the intermediaries.

Agriculture and allied activities, which form the backbone of economy of the state, are suffering from serious crisis. The crisis is manifest in the form of stagnating production and per hectare yields. In fact, the state has exhausted the potentials of new (green revolution) technology among the major crops by achieving above 83 % of the potential yield level in case of rice and Bt. Cotton and above 90 % in wheat (Sidhu and Singh 2011, p. 29). Besides, this technology has brought disastrous economic, environment and social consequences. Commercial agriculture with intensive farming techniques has added in costs at a rate higher than that of output prices reducing the diminishing per hectare income for the farmers/peasants (Ghuman 2002, pp. 141–42; Sidhu and Johl 2002, pp. 22–25). This has made a large proportion of small and marginal farmers unviable (Kalkat Committee 2013, p. 5). This has pushed a large number of them in debt trap (Shergill 2010, pp. 69–74). In addition, commercial agriculture has weakened traditional social ties and community support to the peasants. The pauperized peasants and agricultural labourers and those involved in debt trap have resorted to suicides (AFDR 2000, pp. 10–15; Gill 2004, pp. 219–237; Gill and Singh 2006, pp. 2762–2768; Gill 2010, pp. 292–311; Iyer and Manick 2000, pp. 264–291). The commercialized capitalist agriculture has intensified the process of depeasantization of pauperized peasantry and their land is being transferred to more prosperous, middle and big (rich) farmers through mechanism of reverse tenancy, mortgage and sale deeds. An exhaustive study (Singh et al. 2009, pp. 585–602) on differentiation of peasantry and process of throwing peasantry out of agriculture covering 40 villages from the state brings out that 10.9 % of the farmers have left agriculture between 1990 and 2008. Majority of them (63 %) left agriculture between 2000 and 2008. Those who left cultivation, 21.7 % of them have become labourers and mostly belonged to small and marginal category of farmers. Those who became

[2]This is based on experience of Reliance Fresh in case of Kinnow fruit in 2010–11 and companies engaged in diversification of crops in basmati rice, sunflower, hyola, peas, carrot, sweet chilly, winter maize, etc. in 2003–04. The author had done such a study on crop diversification and contract farming (Gill 2004). This experience has been repeated in the basmati rice in the current year (September–October, 2014).

entrepreneur/commission agents largely belong to upper/rich category of farmers. The land leased out or mortgaged/sold by the farmers leaving agriculture has gone to middle and bigger (rich) farmers. The differentiation process and commercial nature of contracts have weakened community sense in the rural/agricultural economy. The poor among the farmers leaving cultivation are lacking skills and expertise to join new occupations. They, therefore, have no option but to become casual labourers and face unemployment. Mechanization of agricultural operations has reduced the labour absorption capacity of agriculture (Gill 2002, pp. 56–68).

The green revolution also has very disastrous consequences for both farmers and environment in the state. The bio-diversity has been destroyed and replaced by mono cropping culture. There has been massive soil depletion leading to deficiency in micro nutrients, over exploitation of ground water resources,[3] poisoning of soil and water resources due to high/intensive use of insecticides and pesticides. This has also created several health problems like cancer, diabetes, blood pressure and heart ailments along with continuation of traditional water-borne diseases (Shiva 1989, pp. 69–80; Khurana 2011, pp. 48–76).

20.2 Policy Programme and Non Acceptance by Farmers

The cropping pattern in the state began to be dominated by wheat–paddy rotation in Punjab after the green revolution. This generated imbalances in production pattern, difficulties in marketing and problems associated with input supply in agriculture production. The intensive cultivation of land with wheat–paddy rotation led to greater use of water pumped out by tube wells which disturbed the water balance in the state. The water table began to lower in large parts of the state every year. This cropping pattern also led to deterioration of the soil health, multiplication of pests and diseases, intensive use of commercial energy and deterioration of overall agro-eco-system of the state. These changes led to stagnation of farm income and slowdown of productivity growth of the major crops. The government of Punjab appointed an Expert Committee under chairmanship of Dr. S.S. Johl in 1985 to examine the problems of agriculture and make suggestions on the diversification of agriculture in Punjab. The Committee submitted its report in May 1986. The Committee recommended that 20 % of the area presently under wheat and paddy should be diverted to other crops such as sugarcane, rapeseed, mustard, arhar, moong, cotton and soya bean provided pricing and procurement support is provided on the pattern of wheat and paddy. The promotion of cultivation of fruits, vegetable, commercial forestry and dairying was also recommended. It was suggested that for perishable commodity production of fruit, vegetables and milk, processing facilities

[3]The over exploitation of groundwater has been compounded by the state government policy to provide free electricity to tube wells since 1997 and also the policy of free canal water and its greater supply to southern Punjab, which has changed water balance in the state leading to steep fall in water table in central Punjab and water logging in southern Punjab.

have to be developed in the producing areas in private or cooperative sectors. Several recommendations were made to improve quality and productivity of new crops/commodities involving research to improve technology and improvement in sanitation and health of animals (in dairying). The committee suggested contract farming with the processing plant providing seeds and extension services to the farmers who entered into agreement to supply the agricultural produce grown on their farms (Johl Committee I 1986, pp. 42–52, 61). Several years after the committee report, the state could not move towards diversification of agriculture; rather area under wheat and paddy had increased.

Government of Punjab appointed another Committee on Agriculture Policy and Restructuring in 2002, under the chairmanship of Dr. S.S. Johl, which submitted its report in October 2002. The Committee observed that farmers "see no viable alternatives that will provide them with more or even equal returns with certainty in market clearance. Therefore, the farmers have per force continued producing wheat and rice crops in the state" (Johl Committee II 2002, pp. 11–12). The Committee recommended that one million hectare of area currently under wheat and paddy crops be shifted to other recommended crops and farmers will be paid Rs. 12,500 per hectare (Rs. 5,000 per acre) as compensation/subsidy for shifting to the new crops/commodities as suggested by Johl Committee II. It was worked out that along with subsidy to farmers, some administrative cost would also be required and subsidy bill will add to Rs. 1,250 crore per year. This was suggested to be paid by the Government of India as it will not have to procure the wheat and paddy on one million hectares of cultivated land in Punjab (Johl Committee II 2002, p. 106). This proposal was submitted to the Government of India which did not accept it. The state government launched a massive diversification of agriculture campaign during 2003 to which farmers responded by increasing the area under paddy. Although the government involved several private companies such as Tata Rallies, Mahindra, Shubhlabh, Pepsi Foods and Advanta India for contract farming of new suggested crops like hyola, barley, winter maize, durum wheat, sunflower, spring corn, basmati rice, kharif corn, guar gum, castor/jastropha, groundnut, vegetables and horticulture produce, the experience of the farmers with the contracting companies worked to the disadvantage of the farmers. After first year of bitter experience with the private companies they did not cultivate the new crops and reverted back to wheat–paddy rotation. Although the government has been appealing for diversification of crops by raising the issues of declining water table, deteriorating soil health and increasing pollution caused by burning of rice straws, farmers are not listening to such appeals and are continuing with the established cropping pattern. The existing cropping pattern has been contributing to the deterioration of agro-eco-system and also leading to lower per acre returns. Consequently, some farmers (especially small and marginal farmers) are becoming unviable leading to their exit from farming. Worried over the emerging agrarian crisis, the Government of Punjab appointed a "Committee for Formulation of State Agriculture Policy" in 2012 under the chairmanship of Dr. G.S. Kalkat. This committee submitted its report in March 2013. The committee has tried to prepare a road map for future agriculture in the state with measures for the optimal use of resources for improvement of the economy of the farmers. Like two Johl Committees, this Committee has recommended that 1.2 million hectares out of 2.8 million hectares area currently under paddy cultivation be replaced by maize, cotton, sugarcane, soya bean, pulses, groundnuts, etc. This is higher than the area to be shifted out of wheat–paddy rotation by the two earlier Committees. The new crops and commodities are the same. In addition to the crops mentioned above, the new commodities suggested include vegetables and fruits in horticulture and dairy products. Kalkat committee also underlines like Johl Committees that diversification is possible if support to the new crops in the form of minimum support price (MSP) and market, storage is provided on the pattern of wheat and paddy. For horticulture crops, dairy/animal husbandry procurement and processing with cold chains is mentioned as a necessary condition along with considerable improvement in production technology, procurement and marketing institutions. This committee like Johl Committee II wants financial support from the Government of India but with corpus fund of Rs. 5000 crore for price support operation of diversification. Although Kalkat Committee differs in detail in the suggestions for diversification, in essence suggestions are common and reasoning is similar to those of Johl Committees. This committee is equally worried about soil and water conservation and deterioration of agri-eco-system in the state. A step ahead of Johl Committees, this committee has come out openly in favour of genetically modified (GM) crops in the state.

After 1 year of the submission of Kalkat Committee, nothing much has happened in the state. No major initiative has been announced by the state government. Given the past experience of the working of the present government and its fragile financial position, one cannot expect drastic initiatives from it. More than the government, the response of the farmers is equally important. In the absence of establishment of MSP and procurement of mechanism of the new/suggested crops, the farmers are continuing with the wheat and paddy crops for which MSP and procurement had been established since 1965–66.

Punjab farmers are historically progressive and they have been very quick to accept the new technology, production practices and related changes in agriculture. But they are not accepting the changes in cropping pattern recommended by the three expert committees, which submitted their reports during the last 28 years. This needs some discussion. At the face of it there appears some disconnect between expert thinking and farmers' thinking. The experts are taking long view of agriculture especially depleting water table, falling quality of soil and deteriorating overall agro-eco-system of agriculture while farmers are concerned with the immediate level of production and profitability from farming. At practical level the farmers' unions (various factions of BKU) and experts are no longer interacting while preparing their reports. There is wide difference in their perspectives. This is the reason that the experts are not in a position to understand the deep structure of problems of the farming community. There is common running thread in the three reports of the expert committees. This is related to the theoretical basis of the recommendations of these committees.

All the three reports are based on the theoretical foundations of neo-liberal market framework. The solutions are expected to take place through market forces with private traders, processors of the agricultural produce and suppliers of inputs that are the main players. The farmers are considered as not only takers of new policy but also as passive community of recipients of market outcomes. It is not visualized as a community with some organized/collective strength. In practice even if the farmers are divided into several organizations rallied around particular group of leadership, yet their collective strength exerts considerable amount of pressure on the government for free supply of electricity and canal water for irrigation. They have the capacity to change the governments. Without engaging the farmers' organizations and putting them on board, the cropping pattern cannot be changed in the state. This is a difficult but most important task to engage the farmers' organizations for achieving changes in the agricultural practices and cropping patterns in the state. At the same time,the implementation of the major recommendations of various committees demand to establish MSP for new crops along with the assured market clearance mechanism comparable to wheat and paddy crops. This necessary condition for diversification of agriculture has not been attempted by any government during the last 28 years. This has created a mismatch between the needs of ecological conditions and requirements of the farming community. Several farmers tried to cultivate the new suggested crops at their own level or in response to the government initiatives in collaboration with private companies through contract farming but got bitter experience in the form of low income. Had the government established MSP and the assured market clearance mechanism, crop diversification could have taken off much earlier. This has led to credibility loss of the experts and the government programmes are treated by the farmers as rhetoric.

20.3 Vision of Farmers' Movement and Its Derailment

The present phase of farmers' movement in the state began to take shape in the early 1970s and emerged as a powerful vehicle of social mobilization by the latter part of the decade. As the movement matured its leaders began to articulate the vision of the future of farmers. The union produced a historical document (in Punjabi), the English title of which can be read as *Bhartiya Kisan Union: Historical Facts* (1985) which carried vision of the farmers' movement in Punjab. The BKU (Bhartiya Kisan Union) has been publishing a journal titled *Kisan* for many years printing on the back pack of the each issue the major objectives of the union displaying the vision of the movement.

BKU, Punjab visualized, in consonance with BKU India, that there has been urban bias in the development process within the country. The major political parties have been responsible for creating imbalance between the rural and urban development. This imbalance can be corrected by mobilization of rural population under BKU for pressurizing the government to adopt alternative strategy of development favouring the rural areas. The BKU conceived that under the alternative strategy, the farmers have to be involved in trading and processing activities along with the production of crops and milk, meat, vegetables, fruits, etc. The BKU pleaded with the farmers to diversify from cultivation to trading and processing of agricultural produce. The BKU leadership set up a company in 1987, the Punjab Kishan Kheti Udyog Limited. The objective of this company was to supply agricultural inputs directly to the farmers. The BKU held the view that the farmers could obtain remunerative prices if there is massive expansion of agro-processing in the state. Along with agro-processing undertaken by the farmers and their companies, the BKU leadership campaigned in favour of agro-processing by private sector including MNCs like Pepsi Company. The BKU believed that the burden of population on agriculture could be reduced by developing agro-processing industries and locating them in the rural areas. BKU planned to set up such industries in the rural areas and reserve 75 % jobs for local village residents. The BKU made efforts to set up sugar mills, milk plants, plywood units at its own level with support from Punjab state industrial development corporation (PSIDC). Thus the BKU wanted to integrate agricultural production activities with marketing and processing/manufacturing activities on its own. They supported involvement of big private companies in agro-processing with location in the rural areas and also favoured jobs for the local residents of the villages. The BKU not only stood for diversification of agriculture through introduction of new crops but also diversification of economic activities and expansion of non-farm employment in the rural areas. In order to make the rural population eligible for jobs in non-farm activities, the BKU stood for improvement of rural education and reservation of seats in professional colleges for students from the rural areas. The BKU wanted to end exploitation of farmers and free rural administration and governance of corruption. In order to save its leaders from corrupt electoral politics, the BKU decided that office bearers of the union would not contest elections for state assemblies and parliament. The members of political parties could become members but could not hold any office of the BKU. The BKU members and leaders could contest elections for village panchayats as well as those of cooperative societies and other such organizations. Such a vision of BKU could make it a best suited organization in implementation of diversification programme suggested by various committees. But this has not happened in the state. The attempts by the BKU to set up processing plants faced serious difficulties at the level of bureaucracy. In cooperative sectors they were not allowed to manage a cooperative sugar mill when BKU had support of the majority of the shareholders. The bureaucracy supported by political leadership came in their way. The BKU also could not get financial support from the bureaucracy controlled PSIDC. The state government did not adopt Model Cooperative Act proposed by the Planning Commission to free the cooperatives from the clutches of bureaucracy (Gill 1995, pp. 195–211).

When the BKU was struggling to introduce innovations in the reorganization of production, marketing and processing activities, a tussle began between top leadership for supremacy. This led to the first split in the BKU in 1989. This was the time when the BKU leadership began to move closer to one or other political party/group. The second split in the BKU came in 1994. Later on several BKU splinter groups have separated from the parent organization but operating under the same name but with separate identity in the name of their leaders. This led to dilution of the vision and derailment of agenda of the farmers' movement. Now all factions of the BKU and other farmers' organizations operate on the agenda of higher MSP of wheat and paddy and subsidy on (free) electricity. Occasionally they raise the issue of farmers' suicides and compensation to the victims' families. This has not only weakened the movement but also incapacitated it for innovative thinking and initiatives (Gill 2000, pp. 356–77). The split in the movement was explicitly on an ideological basis. One section of the movement led at national level by Sharad Joshi and within the state by Balbir Singh Rajewal and Bhupinder Singh Mann supported WTO and free movement of agricultural commodities nationally and internationally while another section led at the national level by Mohinder Singh Tikait and within the state by Ajmer Singh Lakhowal and Pishora Singh Sidhupur opposed WTO and favoured restricted movement of agricultural commodities. The latter faction wanted retention of MSP and did not support opening up of Kisan companies for agro-processing or marketing of agricultural produce. The farmers' movement based on the BKU is explicitly non-party farmers' mobilization. The movement keeps distance from political parties and does not contest elections to legislation assemblies or the Parliament. This distance from political parties creates conditions that it can organize agitations but cannot be part of the ruling party/parties to influence shaping of agricultural policy. The BKU movement has less potential to mobilize support of the ruling political parties at national or Punjab level to implement its vision of agricultural and rural transformation. The political parties in the state (both Akali Dal and Indian National Congress) are now dominated by the politicians who have dominant interests in occupations which are non-agricultural. The ruling politicians have strong interests in transport, hotel, real estate and business (trading and storage) and declining interest in agriculture. This is a barrier which needs to be crossed if agrarian agenda and vision of the BKU is to be implemented. There is a pressing need to integrate farmers' agenda with the agenda of the ruling political parties in the state which draws strong electoral support from the rural areas especially from the farming communities but deliver very little to the farming communities. As yet BKU on its own as a movement is not in a position to influence the political parties' agrarian agenda at practical level. This has to be done to achieve smooth agrarian transformation. Either political parties are forced to adopt the agrarian agenda of the BKU or made to exit the political scene. This would require very strong mobilization and unity among the different sections of the BKU especially at the time of elections and change in the perspective of the BKU on the political processes in the state.

20.4 Synchronization of Agrarian Agenda with the Farmers' Interests

Any policy programme for a target group can succeed if it meets short and long term requirements and promote interests of that group. If vision of that group comes in conflict with the policy programme, a serious hurdle comes into existence for such a programme. As discussed in the earlier section the programme of diversification of agriculture of the state has been on the agenda of the various governments since 1986 but it has not received a favourable response from the farming community. Except for very few enterprising individual farmers, the farmers of the state continue to grow traditional crops, i.e. wheat and paddy or wheat–cotton rotation. In order to break the cycle of mono cropping culture and introduce new crops, the synchronization of farmers' vision and the vision of policy planners of the government and officials involved in the programme is necessary. All the three committees appointed by the government of Punjab at different points of time have recommended that for successful of introduction of the new crops the introduction of MSP and mechanism for assured market clearance on the pattern of wheat and paddy crops were the necessary conditions for success of crop diversification in the state (Johl Committee I 1986; Johl Committee II 2002; Kalkat Committee 2013). But the state government has not been able to meet these necessary conditions. The introduction of the new crops faces three risks, i.e. (i) market clearance risk, (ii) price risk, and (iii) income risks. The small and marginal farmers and to some extent the middle farmers cannot afford to take these risks. The government could not establish free and compulsory crop insurance scheme for the new crops. At the same time, the government could not create disincentives in the form of some tax or withdrawal of free electricity and canal water for the traditional crops. Consequently, the farmers do not accept the recommendations of the committees appointed by the government and perceive them as unfavourable to the farming community. In fact the lack of adequate financial support from the state government has been the single largest factor in the non adoption of this programme. In fact, the last two committees (Johl Committee-II 2002; Kalkat Committee 2013) have recommended that the Government of India provide some package of support to the state government to implement this programme. The Government of India has not provided the requisite financial amount to support the implementation of this programme. The state government could not implement this package of programme because of its poor financial health. This is due to political populism to continue with unsustainable subsidies and lack of political will to collect taxes in the state.

It is unfortunate that none of the committees have looked very closely the vision of the farmers' movement articulated in the mid-1980s (BKU 1985). In this vision farmers are put at the centre of the whole discussion of the transformation of the rural economy. It is envisioned that the farmers of the state have to be involved in marketing and processing of agricultural produce in addition to the agricultural production. The suggested modes have been farmers' group organization. It could be farmers' cooperatives or farmers' companies. Incidentally, this has also been recommended by the Planning Commission in the Twelfth Five Year Plan. It has been recommended by the Working Groups set up by the Agriculture Division of the Planning Commission "Existing group activity takes many forms depending on the purpose. From low tiers of formal cooperative structure in credit, marketing, dairy and fishery, extending to self-help groups (SHG), farmer clubs, joint liability groups (JLG) and, more recently, to producer companies. For simplicity these can be termed as farmer producer organizations (FPO)" (Planning Commission 2012, Vol. II, p. 21). This can be seen as an extension of the thinking of the Report Agrarian Reforms Committee of the Congress (1949). This committee recommended that for non viable holdings cooperative joint farming and for landless agricultural labourers collective farming on the surplus land distributed among them (AICC 1949, pp. 9–10). In Indian context viability of holdings has been a perpetual part of the debate on the issues of agriculture. In the context of revival of Punjab's economy, viability of holdings is an important question as depeasantization of small and marginal holdings has already begun (Singh et al. 2009, pp. 585–602). The involvement of farmers' organizations is suggested at three levels. One, they have been consulted in the formulation of strategy for agriculture development. They can provide very useful insights into the problems and possibility of the agriculture. Secondly, at practical level, the farmers can be easily involved in proposed agrarian programmes through their organizations as farmers have sufficient confidence in their organizations and recommendations made by them. On the contrary, they do not evince such confidence in the officials of the government. Thirdly, the farmers cannot be involved in the marketing and processing individually but collectively. This is a critical area of developing linkage between agriculture and industry. The farmers' collective strength can be tapped and this is possible through their organizations.

It is only through this that a programme of diversification of agriculture which seems not taking off today can be made successful. At the same time, farmers of the state can be made partners in sharing the prosperity of the economy. The processing of agricultural produce is necessary for building linkages between agriculture and industry. This can generate a lot of employment both for skilled and unskilled labourers. It can also tap capital resources from banking and other financial institutions for transformation of the rural economy. The challenge of the institution of the commission agent known as *arhtiya* which is a great barrier to progress in agriculture and which sucks the resources of the poor farmers can be met only through the collective strength of the farmers. It is through the collective or joint entities of the farmers that extraction of resources from the farmers by the middlemen (arhtiya) can be checked and the collective or joint energy of the farmers can be released for rural development and progress of agriculture. The farmers' organization can be the instrument to put farmers in the centre for revival of productive forces in agriculture, rural transformation and maintenance of balance in agro-eco-system. A large amount of non-farm employment can be created through agro-processing, which can provide off-season employment and income to the rural population. FPOs can arrange low interest loans for joint activities and energize local initiatives in the rural areas. The state government must initiate steps to promote FPOs so that farmers can be involved in formulation and implementation of agrarian programmes. This is a very critical issue ignored so far in most of the policy programmes in agriculture. It is imperative that the ruling political parties get awakened to the task of adopting proper agrarian agenda in the larger interest of the economy and society in the state. At the same time various factions of the BKU have to rise to the occasion, forge unity among the farmers' organization and force the ruling parties to awaken to the agrarian agenda. They will have to move along with agrarian agitations to agrarian reconstruction where farmers are engaged in the production of agricultural produce, its marketing and processing. In this task at certain level, farmers' organizations have to work in cooperation with the government officials and seek support from the government. They have to work on the basis of strategy of struggle and reconstruction.

Acknowledgments Sincere thanks are expressed to anonymous referee for comments on the earlier draft of the paper.

References

AFDR (2000) Suicides in rural Punjab: a report (in Punjabi). Association for Democratic Rights, Ludhiana

AICC (1949) Report of the congress agrarian reforms committee. AICC, New Delhi

BKU (1985) Bharatiya kisan union: historical facts. BKU, Ludhiana

Ghuman RS (2002) World trade organization and indian agriculture with special reference to Punjab. In: Johl SS, Ray SK (eds) Future of agriculture in Punjab. CRRID, Chandigarh

Gill A (2010) Punjab peasantry: a question of life and debt. In: Deshpande RS, Arora SA (eds) Agrarian crisis and farmers' suicides. Sage Publications, New Delhi

Gill SS, Singh S, Brar JS (2010) Globalization and Indian state. Aakar Publications, New Delhi

Gill A, Singh L (2006) Farmers' suicides and response of public policy: evidence, diagnosis and alternatives from Punjab. Econ Polit Wkly 41:2762–2768

Gill SS (2004) Contract farming hurts farmers. The Tribune, Chandigarh

Gill SS (2002) Agriculture crop technology and employment generation in Punjab. In: Johl SS, Ray SK (eds) Future of agriculture in Punjab. CRRID, Chandigarh

Gill SS (1995) The farmers' movement and agrarian change in the green revolution belt of North-West India. In: Tom B (ed) New farmers' movements in India. Frank Cass, Ilford and Portland

Gill SS (2000) Agrarian change and farmers' movement in Punjab. In: Harish P, Judge PS (eds) Social movements in Punjab. Rewat Publications, Jaipur

Iyer G, Manick MS (2000) Indebtedness, impoverishment and suicides in rural Punjab. India Publishers and Distributors, New Delhi

Johl Committee I (1986) Report of expert committee on diversification of agriculture in Punjab. Government of Punjab, Chandigarh

Johl Committee II (2002) Agricultural production pattern adjustment programme in Punjab for productivity growth: a report. Government of Punjab, Chandigarh

Johl SS, Sidhu RS (2002) Three decades of intensive agriculture in Punjab: socio-economic and environmental consequences. In: Johl SS, Ray SK (eds) Future of agriculture in Punjab. CRRID, Chandigarh

Kalkat Committee (2013) Agriculture policy for Punjab. Government of Punjab, Chandigarh

Khurana MR (2011) Agrarian crisis in Punjab and the way out. In: Shergill HS, Gill SS, Singh G (eds) Understanding North-West Indian economy. Serial Publications, New Delhi
Mazoyer M, Eroduart I (2008) A history of world agriculture: from neolithic age to the current crisis. Cornerstone Publications, Kharagpur
Planning Commission (2012) Twelfth five year plan 2012–17, vol II. Government of India, New Delhi
Roul C (2001) Bitter to better harvest: post-green revolution agricultural and marketing strategy for India. Northern Book Centre, New Delhi
Shergill HS (2010) Growth of farm debt in Punjab: 1977-2008. IDC, Chandigarh
Shiva V (1989) The violence of green revolution: ecological degradation and political conflict in Punjab. Research Foundation for Science and Ecology, Dehradun
Sidhu MS, Varinder PS (2011) Problems and prospects of agriculture in Punjab. In: Shergill HS, Gill SS, Singh G (eds) Understanding North-West Indian economy. Serials Publications, New Delhi
Singh K, Sukhpal S, Kingra HS (2009) Agrarian crisis and depeasantization in Punjab: status of marginal farmers who left agriculture. Indian J Agric Econ 64(1)
Sukhpal S (2014) Problems of arhtiyas (middlemen commission agents) viz-a-viz farmers in Punjab. Department of Economics and Sociology, PAU, Ludhiana

Chapter 21
Breaking the Mould: Thoughts on Punjab's Future Economic Development

Nirvikar Singh

21.1 Introduction

The economy of Punjab state in India offers an interesting case study. On the one hand, Punjab has been for decades—and remains—one of India's better-off states. Because of this relative position, the state tends not be included in the primary focus of national programs meant to reduce poverty or spur economic development. On the other hand, Punjab's relative position in rankings of India's states by output per capita has declined rapidly in recent years. This decline has been accompanied by environmental problems and symptoms of deep social malaise. As will be argued in this chapter, Punjab is facing a multidimensional crisis that requires urgent attention.

This chapter provides somewhat of an overview of Punjab's crisis, through an analysis of the dynamics of Punjab's economic development as shaped by its political economy, its social dynamics and exogenous events since independence.[1] I will argue that one can understand both Punjab's success in certain areas of agriculture and its subsequent relative decline in terms of the interaction of these factors. I will then use this historical analysis to provide an assessment of Punjab's future economic development, in terms of the structural changes that are needed, and how these can be encouraged or implemented by policy makers within the constraints of its current political–economic equilibrium.

[1]Other papers in this volume provide detailed analyses of specific sectors of the Punjab economy, institutional and societal factors, and particular policy issues. Overall, this volume seeks to provide inputs that can help in arriving at a consensus on policy measures for the revival and rejuvenation of Punjab's economy. A brief document that tackles a similar set of issues is Centre for Development Economics and Innovation Studies (2012).

N. Singh (✉)
Department of Economics, University of California, Santa Cruz, 1156 High Street, Santa Cruz, CA 95064, USA
e-mail: boxjenk@ucsc.edu

L. Singh and N. Singh (eds.), *Economic Transformation of a Developing Economy*, India Studies in Business and Economics,
DOI 10.1007/978-981-10-0197-0_21

To understand the specific case of Punjab's economic development, it is useful to lay out some broader ideas about what drives development. One of the key debates has been that of State versus Market, partially clarified by the demise of the Soviet model and the success of China's shift towards greater market orientation. There are still differing views, however, of the relative merits of 'governing the market' (e.g., Wade 1990) compared to 'enabling the market.' More specifically, the standard economic arguments for public intervention in certain areas have not changed. These areas can include basic health, nutrition and education, as well as the provision of law and order, property rights protection, and arm's length regulation of industries where market forces alone may not guarantee efficient competition. A less clear-cut boundary for the government's role lies in the realm of industrial policy, and recent attempts to make a case for industrial policy (e.g., Rodrik 2006) have been quite cautious in their claims.[2] To quote Rodrik:

> What I understand by "industrial policy" is not an effort by the government to select particular sectors and subsidize them through a range of instruments (directed credit, subsidies, tax incentives, and so on). The critics of industrial policy are correct when they argue that governments do not have adequate knowledge to pick "winners." …[I]ndustrial policy is more appropriately conceived as a *process* whereby the state and the private sector jointly arrive at diagnoses about the sources of blockage in new economic activities and propose solutions to them. Industrial policy requires the government to take an ex-ante stand neither on the activities to be promoted nor on the instruments to be deployed. It simply requires it to build the public-private institutional arrangements whereby information on profitable activities and useful instruments of intervention can be elicited.

Aside from the State-versus-Market debate, another strand of economic analysis has sought to understand the development process in terms of the interplay of interests and institutions (e.g., Acemoglu et al. 2005; Rajan and Zingales 2006). For example, the quality of both market and governance institutions shapes the possibilities of economic development, while institutions may themselves be circumscribed by the power of different interest groups. The design and working of industrial policy, for example, may depend on the precise nature of the interests and institutions within and around which such a policy will operate. Another, less precise driver of outcomes is a third 'I', namely ideas.[3] Changing ideas may be the first step in improving the quality of institutions, or overcoming sub-optimal interest-group equilibrium. This triad of ideas-interests-institutions will be particularly helpful, in trying to describe a feasible positive path for the future of Punjab's economy.

---

[2]A detailed discussion of different concepts of industrial policy and their applicability to the experience of India and China is in Kaur and Singh (2013).

[3]In a work specifically examining the Green Revolution in Punjab, my co-author and I introduced a different set of three 'I's': infrastructure, information and incentives (Singh and Kohli 2005).

21.2 How Punjab Got Where It Is

One can begin by noting some very basic characteristics of Punjab. The facts of its geography—simultaneously a fertile agricultural plain and a frontier region—have continued to shape its politics and economics for centuries.[4] This geography helped to create a particular kind of society, simultaneously heterogeneous and egalitarian, prone to innovation as well as conflict. This assertion is not meant to suggest any kind of simple determinism here, merely to note some factors that make Punjab unique within the Indian context. More specifically, one can also highlight historical events such as the British investment in the canal colonies, which represented an early example of public action to boost the local economy for national gain, and the rise of the Arya Samaj in Punjab in the late nineteenth century, including its explicit attack on Sikhism, the region's distinctive religion.[5] These and other events of the colonial—and to a lesser extent, Mughal—period continued to have an impact on the trajectory of Punjab's politics and economics, but the subsequent discussion will focus on post-independence happenings.[6]

The post-independence story is at once complex and understandable. To summarise the Punjab experience after independence, what the state possessed in relative abundance was human capital. Many Sikhs, in particular, moved from areas such as the canal colonies to eastern Punjab, bringing their farming experience with them. Non-farmers such as traders and other entrepreneurs also brought their skills and social networks. Political and administrative institutions were less developed, since they had to be redesigned and reconstructed for an independent country, but by the mid-1950s, public investment was taking place in dams, canals, electric power, rural roads and market towns.[7] This laid the foundation for the Green Revolution of the 1960s, fueled by technological innovation. In addition to the previous public investments, agricultural extension as a public good or service played a role as well. Public procurement reduced the market risks faced by farmers. Developments in agriculture had implications for ancillary light manufacturing and services, which also developed. Other light manufacturing such as woollen textiles and bicycles grew as well, spurred by rising purchasing power, though there was not any significant technological innovation in these products, and manufacturing equipment typically came from elsewhere.[8]

Private enterprise and initiative, both on and off the farm, played a role in Punjab's post-independence economic progress. But the underlying drivers of change were technological and political, and this can be seen in the precise pattern

[4]A useful collection of articles on the geography of Punjab is in *Journal of Punjab Studies* (2004).

[5]On the role of the Arya Samaj, see Jones (1973, 1976).

[6]An excellent account of Punjab's history in the Sikh period is Grewal (1998).

[7]See Singh and Kohli (2005), Nair and Singh (2014), and the references therein, for more details of this account of the Green Revolution in Punjab.

[8]Punjab's experience of industrial development is well documented in Jain (2016) and the references therein.

of development. In agriculture, Partition had provided somewhat of a clean slate in terms of the influence of vested interests versus ordinary individuals. Most critically, the Green Revolution in Punjab was of great importance to the national government, seeking to avoid the political embarrassment of emergency food imports. The agriculture sector saw an alignment of interests at different levels of the polity. Furthermore, it created new business opportunities, in the provision of inputs for farmers, as Green Revolution farming required more sophisticated production methods. On the other hand, in industry, the national government's control of location and investment decisions, and the strategic fears associated with Punjab's frontier position (as well as its Sikh population), limited total investment.[9] A government-dominated banking system also had implications for the way in which agriculture and industry developed. Punjab did see the rise of some new industrial families, but not to the extent of becoming significant driving force of the state economy.

The Green Revolution, combined with the lack of broader industrial development, created a potentially unstable situation. Inequality rose, partly as a natural consequence of growth, but partly as a result of unequal access to inputs such as credit. The power of middlemen who provide credit, access to inputs, and a channel for quick sale of produce, also increased in this period—though moneylenders had always been a powerful group, even in the pre-independence canal colonies.[10] Even though the local economy was not absorbing enough labour from agriculture, armed services recruitment provided a safety valve, as it had done for decades, and emigration to the West became an additional avenue for surplus rural labour. If circumstances were different, this might have been a reasonably long-lasting steady state, but many factors intervened.

The 1966 division of Punjab into Punjab and Haryana, while increasing the autonomy of the Sikhs as a small religious and language minority within India, actually weakened their position in the larger national political game. Haryana became an explicit bellwether for political competition throughout the Hindi-speaking belt of Northern India, rather than a sub-region of Punjab that competed for resources and control within the larger state. At the same time, inter-caste and rural–urban political competition within the new smaller state of Punjab remained fierce, with the ruling Congress party not willing to cede control to a regional party.[11]

The 1970s brought further difficulties. The Green Revolution did not bring any additional innovation to Punjab, so that the gains began to be second order in magnitude, and subject to sharply diminishing returns. Global energy prices rose,

[9]An early analysis of the Green Revolution was Frankel (1971); see also Bhalla and Chadha (1983), Singh (2001).

[10]A classic early account of peasant indebtedness in Punjab is Darling (1928). Post-Green Revolution credit markets have been analysed in Gill (2000, 2004, 2016). A more general discussion of the power of intermediaries in Indian contexts is Harriss-White (2003).

[11]There are many different accounts and analyses of the history presented here: for example, see Deol (2000), Singh (2008), Chima (2010), Thandi (2016), Singh (2016).

and access to water and electric power became increasingly critical for successful farming. Both the domestic and international political and economic environment became less favourable. There was a negative reaction to the social change that economic growth and the project of national integration (stressing Hindi or English in the language dimension, and "secularism" or Hinduism in the religious sphere) were wreaking in Punjab. The 1970s saw two oil shocks, the national Emergency declared by Indira Gandhi, and the Soviet invasion of Afghanistan. Drugs and guns began to flood that part of the South Asian region. The two safety valves for excess labour—emigration and military service—began to be choked off, for completely different reasons, but at about the same time.

In this scenario, political competition in Punjab was myopic at best and malevolent at worst. A focus on extending the fruits of the Green Revolution by trying to preserve access to adequate water contributed to political conflict, but this was overshadowed by other forces. In particular, bundling a specific issue of inter-state water-sharing with larger issues of federalism only fed the increasing paranoia of the national leadership of the time. Worse still, economic change in Punjab, because of its distorted patterns, but also because of the nature of modernisation that accompanies such change, was producing a religious backlash, harking back to the period of Arya Samaj and Singh Sabha conflict, but in a more violent form. This cultural and religious instability unfortunately became a tool of political competition as well.

Meanwhile, subsidies for water, electric power and fertiliser created huge distortions in input use and cropping decisions. Water intensive crops such as rice and sugar cane expanded in acreage, and created new lock-in effects for farmers to go with those for wheat under the public distribution system (PDS). Sugar mill owners, providers of inputs on credit, and middlemen in the *mandis* all gained power and influence. Groundwater began to be pumped at alarming and unsustainable rates, as surface irrigation became less and less adequate. In the 1980s, Punjab descended into political and social chaos, with militant violence, brutal repression, and a complete suspension of normal politics.

When the Indian government began to liberalise the economy in 1991, its recent history meant that Punjab was among the worst placed of the richer states to benefit from this change. The removal of controls on industrial licensing did not create positive incentives to invest in the state. Agriculture, which might have benefited from decontrol, remained heavily regulated, and dominated by the production of grains for the PDS. State politics did not stabilise (or perhaps normalise is a better word) until the middle of the 1990s, and over a decade without state-level elected government created a situation where corruption and rent-seeking were prevalent throughout the layers of government. Top-level corruption is pervasive in India,[12] and in many other successful economies, but the most severe problems arise when

[12]This statement is based on anecdotal evidence and journalistic reports, since it is difficult to document such activities. The recent arrest of J. Jayalalitha in Tamil Nadu illustrates the pervasiveness and size of the problem all over India, not just in Punjab.

there is a free-for-all in the sphere of such activities, as opposed to monopolisation of corruption at the top (Shleifer and Vishny 1993). Arguably, this corruption free-for-all was a major factor in the failure of efforts to create a software industry in Mohali, just before the turn of the millennium, precisely when several areas of southern India were seizing that opportunity.[13]

The attempt to create a software industry in Punjab was also somewhat limited. It did not represent a fundamental rethinking of the pattern or future trajectory of the state's economic development. More effort was still focused on issues of agriculture. Certainly, since the 1980s, there had been considerable attention paid to diversification in agriculture (Johl 1985). There had also been concerns raised about environmental degradation (Singh 1991) associated with the Green Revolution technologies and, more importantly, the nature of their application in the specific context of Punjab (e.g., the manner in which fertiliser and water were being used, and the choice of crops). Attempts to create a food processing industry were also ongoing. Yet none of these concerns or attempts made a significant dent in the overall pattern of economic activity in Punjab. Institutions, interests and ideas were all trapped in the status quo situation.

21.3 Breaking Punjab's Mould

The metaphor used in the chapter title is that of a mould: whatever is poured in that mould takes on its shape. If that is the case, making something new requires breaking the mould, not just pouring more into the existing shape. If that is the case, focusing on reviving or transforming agriculture will not be the solution to the problem of Punjab's economy. That is not to say that agriculture should be neglected. Indeed, the current patterns of production will lead to disaster in as little as a decade. In October 2013, Rahul Gandhi gave a political speech in Punjab, in which he was quoted as saying, "Punjab gives food to India…the country cannot stand without it."[14] He related Punjab's role in feeding the PDS to the feasibility of the Right to Food effort of the ruling coalition. This rhetoric only hardens the mould that is trapping Punjab's economy, and the policies that underlie it will only accelerate looming disaster. So it is certainly the case that Punjab's agriculture needs to be reoriented away from a doomed role as India's breadbasket: this will involve attention to issues such as credit markets, agricultural extension, supply chain infrastructure, water-saving technologies and much more.[15] But these are defensive measures that will be too small and too slow to halt environmental

---

[13]For a discussion of Punjab's earlier attempts to create a software industry, see Singh (2008).

[14]See Express News Service (2013) for an account of this speech, including the quote.

[15]For recent analyses of problems and solutions for Punjab's agricultural economy, see Singh (2013), Munjal Institute for Global Manufacturing (2013a, b), and the majority of chapters in this volume.

disaster and its attendant possibility of social disruption. Nor will they provide the transformation that Punjab's economy needs to continue growing and absorbing labour.

What is to be done? Given Punjab's social and economic structures, its size and geographic position, it is not a great candidate for large-scale labour intensive manufacturing. Hence, a China-style transition is probably not feasible, even less than in the rest of India.[16] Instead, Punjab has some chance of succeeding as a place for flexible mass-customised production. An analogy might be to northern Italy, which thrived in this role for decades, though it is now suffering from lack of cost competitiveness, especially for goods such as consumer appliances. But Italy is already a relatively rich country, and its comparative advantage has shifted even more to high-end design.[17] Another possibility might be Germany's *mittelstand* of family-run engineering firms.[18] This model raises issues of whether Punjab's people have the right skills, and I return to that issue later in the chapter. A third example is the Swiss niche in watch making, which has survived over the years by adapting to technological change that made watches a commodity—the Swiss moved upscale, and emphasised design and status, avoiding to some extent the problem now faced in Italy. The Swiss comparison is also interesting from the perspective of geography, society, and Switzerland's ability to straddle a range of sectors, including finance and high-value-added agricultural products as well as certain manufactures. My suggestion, therefore, is that Punjab needs to develop a strategic vision of what manufacturing and service niches the state can realistically fill in the global and national economic systems.[19] Japan, South Korea, Taiwan and China have all had strategic visions to some degree, though implementations have varied greatly by time, place and circumstances.[20]

What should shape a strategic vision? The famous example of Japan's strategic intent from 1950 onward of building a world-class automobile industry is useful to recall: the idea was to develop expertise in a production process that maximised knowledge spillovers and a product for which demand would grow over time.[21] In a different, more recent context, China's latest five-year plan emphasises the support of seven "Strategic Emerging Industries," including biotechnology, new materials,

---

[16]For a discussion of Indian manufacturing, see Sharma and Singh (2013). Kaur and Singh (2013) also provide some analysis and comparison with China.

[17]One useful recent analysis of Italy's competitiveness is Tiffin (2014). Putnam (1993) provides a classic analysis of the origins of long-standing differences between northern and southern Italy, in terms of social capital.

[18]For example, see *The Economist* (2014), Rattner (2011) and Linnemann (2007).

[19]The Swiss example, unlike the East Asian cases described subsequently in the chapter, is not one of strategic vision. Weder and Weder (2009) include democracy, decentralisation, competition, flexible labour markets and immigration among factors that helped Switzerland's early economic growth.

[20]For example, see Amsden (1989), Wade (1990), Kaur and Singh (2013).

[21]This understanding of the Japanese experience does not require accepting a strong version of the role of industrial policy, as famously articulated by Johnson (1982).

and energy conservation and environmental protection.[22] The Japanese example, as noted earlier, is one which requires large scale, and an additional barrier is that the scope for becoming a global manufacturer is more limited now (Rodrik 2008) than it was 50 years ago. China, as well, is developing its strategic vision at a national scale, and from a more advanced base than Punjab, so it is not an ideal role model. Nevertheless, there is a general lesson in these examples, that a strategic vision is important—it has to be tailored to the circumstances, but not limited by them.

It is useful to provide an example of a possible vision for Punjab. A sector where global as well as national demand will only increase, due to demographics as well as income effects, is health care. This sector covers a wide range of products and services: for example, electronic medical devices for monitoring and testing, prosthetics, generic pharmaceuticals, certain classes of surgical procedures, and even ayurvedic health and beauty products.[23] This is not a complete, or even necessarily the "right" list, but the choice of health care is suggested by the increasing world demand for health products and services, in an analogy to the Japanese vision of 1950. This particular list is not too ambitious, and does not involve substantial leapfrogging, but it could be extended to include more complex products and services, including those which involve biotechnology. But there are also possible links to Punjab's existing agricultural economy, in the case of ayurvedic health and beauty products, or possible connections to existing expertise in light manufacturing, in the case of prosthetics or simple medical devices. There are also differences from the Japanese case, in that the example is based on an entire sector, with a wide range of products and services, as a possible focus for growth, rather than an individual product—the automobile. Of course, automobile production was conceived of as a gateway to a set of skills for a wide range of engineering-intensive products. Medical devices might be an analogue, in that they cover a range of complexity, though again the category represents a broader set of uses than the case of automobiles for personal transportation.

In any case, the purpose of the example is not to chart a specific direction for the Punjab economy, but to illustrate the suggested framework for thinking about how to break the current mould that traps both thought and action. It is important to note that there are two possible paths for the government. One is to pick sectors—possibly very broadly defined—for potential support, as in the example I have just given of the health sector. The second is to work broadly to improve the business investment climate. As quoted earlier, Rodrik (2006) backs away from the targeting approach to industrial policy, arguing that the government cannot pick winners, but merely create mechanisms for public–private interactions on what activities might be profitable and worth encouraging through policy action. In an earlier analysis of South Korea and Taiwan (Rodrik 1995), he argues that they were able to pick

[22]See Kaur and Singh (2013) for details of the Chinese case.

[23]Of course Kerala has established itself as an international provider of ayurvedic health services, combined with tourism. However, the global market is sufficiently large, and Punjab is sufficiently different in what it can offer in this sphere.

winners by following the previous trajectory of Japan, but at the same time he emphasises that the success of these two economies was based on government overcoming coordination failures that resulted from externalities in investment. Specifically, "while the rate of return to coordinated investments was extremely high, the rate of return to individual investments remained low" (Rodrik 1995, p. 78). This illustrates how the second, broader approach to industrial policy can be conceptualised. However, one can argue that the East Asian case illustrates the value of both approaches. Governments took measures that subsidised and coordinated private investment, but in doing so, to the extent that they chose particular sectors or industries for these policies, one can argue that they still picked winners, albeit in a different sense than the usual use of the term.

One need not be dogmatic about the role of government in this context. There is no reason why industry and government together cannot identify specific opportunities for future growth. However, there is an argument that existing business interests may have distorted incentives for such identification, and to the extent to which such interests influence government policy, lock-into a long-run sub-optimal equilibrium may be difficult to avoid.[24] This is one of the problems facing Punjab.[25] The coordination failure approach of Rodrik can be conceived of as including the need to provide an appropriate environment for doing business: indeed, one can think of this provision as reducing an implicit tax on investment, rather than providing a subsidy. This, in turn connects to other issues of political economy, in addition to the influence of vested interests. Rodrik (1995) provides a discussion of why the political economy of South Korea and Taiwan worked, whereas it has not done so in other countries, and that will be an important issue to consider for Punjab.

The political economy of Punjab is the most challenging aspect of breaking the mould that constrains its future development, involving a complex interplay of interests, institutions and ideas. Before turning to this central challenge, there is one other critical element of a future growth story to be highlighted. I suggested earlier that Punjab's human capital was well-suited for overcoming the disruption of partition, and the Green Revolution was also supported by the strength of this resource—in addition to investments in public infrastructure. However, Punjab's human capital is no longer adequate for future growth.[26] Indeed, an important part of Rodrik's argument for how government policy worked in South Korea and Taiwan is that a necessary precondition was the relative abundance of skilled labour, achieved prior to the increase in physical investment that was triggered by overcoming coordination failures. From this perspective, Punjab's policy failure in the 1970s included an inadequate attention to human capital development. One of

[24]This is the point of the Rajan and Zingales (2006) analysis.

[25]To some extent, this is a generic problem, and affects India as a whole, not just Punjab. Crony capitalism, which is related to this problem of vested interests, also creates distortions in business investment, but can be based on social or family ties, rather than solely on the influence of money.

[26]An overview of the status of education in Punjab is provided by Brar (2016).

the problems, of course, was that in this period, at the national level, it seemed that India was producing more college graduates than it could absorb into the labour force, and devoting excessive resources to higher education.[27] Global economic stagnation, a stifling of domestic industrial investment and misallocation of resources within each segment of the education sector were all contributory factors to this situation. However, Punjab had its own special problem of political conflict that also served to affect both access to, and the benefits of education.

India's information technology (IT) boom led to several southern states greatly expanding engineering education. The opportunity to serve a large global market also created jobs for engineers across a range of specific disciplines—computer science or computer engineering graduates were a minority of those who were employed by India's new software industry. Punjab, emerging from a decade and a half of turmoil, lagged in training students with the necessary skills for these new jobs, and those with the skills sought the better opportunities of Bangalore, Hyderabad and the National Capital Region.[28] At this juncture in Punjab's economic development, investments in education required are across a range of sectors, not just engineering and IT. Agricultural science, biological and life sciences, and manufacturing technology are examples of areas where Punjab can build human capital capabilities, by expanding and upgrading higher education in the state. Essentially, human capital investment has to match market needs, in particular demand niches, whether for consumer products or industrial goods. Hence, this investment needs to be shaped by the strategic vision for the state's future development, which will determine what kinds of jobs will be available. Furthermore, industry in the state needs to help in formulating a strategy for building human capital. The Indian School of Business (ISB) campus in Mohali is an example of how things might progress, with specialised institutes for manufacturing, health care, infrastructure and public policy, funded by state business interests.

Clearly, the ISB is an elite private institution that will serve a small minority of the country's—let alone the state's—students. At the other end of the spectrum is the Punjab Technical University, with as many as four hundred thousand students across India, served through an eclectic mix of decentralised institutional arrangements. In the middle lie the traditional universities, such as Panjab University and Punjabi University, with centers of excellence, but also hampered by legacy models of education delivery and institutional and financial arrangements. Achieving the requisite scale, agility and quality in Punjab's higher education provision quickly enough will require importing individual and organisational expertise. National-level liberalisation of entry by foreign education providers should be seized on proactively by Punjab's industry and its government. Such providers, with established brands, have an incentive not to behave as fly-by-night operators, but do not need to be Ivy League or other elite institutions. Mohali,

[27]Kapur and Mehta (2008) provide an overview of Indian higher education that discusses these issues.

[28]See also Singh (Singh 2008a, b).

Punjab's hill areas, and the fading but still palpable grandeur of the former princely states of Patiala and Nabha provide possibly attractive physical locations for new education facilities.

In some ways, the argument for developing higher education facilities in Punjab is independent of the state's future economic development in other dimensions—higher education can be a growth sector by itself, serving a national or even global student body. The situation of Massachusetts, in the United States, is instructive, with its plethora of colleges and universities. Of course, some of those institutions also provide the human capital for other dimensions of economic development, with the Massachusetts Institute of Technology being the prime example. The relatively recent growth of a cluster of biotech companies in Cambridge, Massachusetts, in an area still filled with former factories and warehouses from the nineteenth century, is illustrative of the possibilities at the high end of the higher education spectrum.[29]

Now I turn to the political economy of Punjab. I have argued that national politics has had a baleful, even malignant impact on the trajectory of the state. But the state's own fault lines, rural versus urban, Sikh versus Hindu, and others, more variegated, have also contributed. The evolution of the state's political coalition in the last decade is of interest here. Most obviously, the alliance of the main Akali Dal party and the Bharatiya Janata Party (BJP), dating back to the national emergency, and cemented by the Congress party's role in brutal repression in the state, represents a significant step forward. It provides an opportunity to balance different interests within the state government, rather than reducing politics to polarisation. The greater influence of the capitalist industrial families of Punjab, rather than just small traders, may approximate what Evans (1995) called "embedded autonomy" in the context of South Korea's experience.[30] It is perhaps too soon to tell whether Punjab's rulers can achieve the balance of coherence and connectedness captured by the idea of embedded autonomy, rather than continue in their path so far, which has been one of crony and family capitalism. In some sense, the issue is whether a

---

[29]For example, see Nelsen (2005).

[30]To quote Evans (1995, Chap. 1): "The internal organization of developmental states comes much closer to approximating a Weberian bureaucracy. Highly selective meritocratic recruitment and long term career rewards create commitment and a sense of corporate coherence. Corporate coherence gives these apparatuses a certain kind of "autonomy." They are not, however, insulated from society as Weber suggested they should be. To the contrary, they are embedded in a concrete set of social ties which binds the state to society and provides institutionalised channels for the continual negotiation and renegotiation of goals and policies. Either side of the combination by itself would not work. A state that was only autonomous would lack both sources of intelligence and the ability to rely on decentralised private implementation. Dense connecting networks without a robust internal structure would leave the state incapable of resolving "collective action" problems, of transcending the individual interests of its private counterparts. Only when embeddedness and autonomy are joined together can a state be called developmental. This apparently contradictory combination of corporate coherence and connectedness, which I call "embedded autonomy," provides the underlying structural basis for successful state involvement in industrial transformation.

more fundamental coordination failure—that of the ruling elite—can be overcome before the coordination failure at the level of the economy can be tackled.

There are several other issues that arise in considering the political equilibrium and its economic consequences. First, the Akali–BJP alliance has the potential to marginalise the Congress, attenuating the incentive effects of electoral competition.[31] Of course, the examples of South Korea and Taiwan show that policies to support development can precede democracy. In such cases, one has to identify another motivating force, such as security, ideology, national pride, and so on. What this can be in the Punjab case is somewhat problematic. Fault lines of identity exist in ways that were not salient in the various East Asian successes. While (in contrast to the traditional Arya Samaj) the BJP has been willing to put aside its Hindutva agenda to access political power (Brass 2005), the shadow of that agenda always remains, and is expressed in ways that can be uncomfortable for the Sikh community, which remains a tiny minority in India despite having a slender majority in Punjab.

Given the history of Punjab in the late nineteenth century, when the founder of the Arya Samaj launched an attack on the founder of Sikhism, and the role of Hindu ideologues in the conflict of the 1970s and 1980s, where Bhindranwale ultimately became the center of conflict, it will be important for the ruling coalition in Punjab to deal squarely with concerns about erosion of identity, tradition and heritage.[32] Indeed, these issues would be problematic even in the absence of Hindutva, with influences from Western hip-hop to Bollywood and Hollywood challenging the traditional order. In this complicated scenario, the obvious approach of government support of religiosity on multiple fronts (something the national government has also indulged in) does not get to the roots of the challenge. The focus of this chapter is economics and politics, and so one cannot get to grips with the entire complexity of the societal issues that are and will be associated with modernisation, but this range of issues needs to be made explicit, and the main actors who should be involved (including religious and other civil society leaders) need to be identified.

The issue of identity does have some bearing on more immediately addressable problems of political implementation of a transformative strategy for Punjab's economy. I have stressed the need for breaking out of the existing economic mould. But, just as Punjab was not well placed to take advantage of economic liberalisation, there is a danger that some groups within Punjab will be left out of the state's economic transformation, if and when it occurs. This danger is a strong argument for pushing access to good quality, skill-oriented higher education throughout Punjab, particularly the rural areas of the west and south of the state. From this perspective, concentrating educational developments around Chandigarh would be a mistake. Educational centers in places like Talwandi Sabo and Tarn Taran would

[31]Interestingly, voters in Punjab gave the Aam Aadmi Party its only seats in Parliament in the last general election, of May 2014, seeing it as a new alternative to the Akali–BJP coalition.

[32]A useful analysis of issues of Sikh identity in the contemporary context is Gupta (1996).

provide regional outreach as well as symbolic significance. Secondly, while I have argued that agricultural diversification and infrastructure development will not provide the needed engine for Punjab's future growth, there is a strong political economy case for investments on this front, from the perspective of making sure that rural Punjab and its inhabitants are not left out of future economic development.

21.4 Conclusion

This conclusion attempts to summarise the main arguments of this chapter, and also notes a few additional nuances. I have argued that Punjab needs a strategic vision for future economic development. This process requires government and industry to jointly take a proactive role in mapping possible futures and feasible pathways. Feasibility requires managing potentially conflicting political interests, and these are driven by broader societal and cultural concerns, in addition to material interests. A critical precondition for any form of development is accelerated investment in human capital at several levels, from basic skill acquisition to world-class higher education. This chapter has not given attention to fiscal policy,[33] or to details of how the government can create the right kind of business environment or affect private sector incentives for positive outcomes,[34] but some of these are topics for further research. I have also not discussed the details of how infrastructure needs to be upgraded, particularly in cities and towns that will need to serve as growth poles in the state's economic transformation.[35]

The goal of this chapter has been to provide a conceptual framework for thinking about Punjab's future economic development, recognising the roles played by society, culture and history in determining where Punjab is today. To change the interplay of interests and institutions in shaping economic development, one needs to refresh one's ideas, and that is what I hope this chapter has contributed to doing. I want to end by stating that the choice for Punjab is not between stagnation and growth, or between stasis and transformation. The alternative to a fundamental and rapid transformation of Punjab's economy is collapse and chaos, since the core of the current economy is built around an economic system that will end in total environmental collapse in a decade or shortly thereafter.[36] Hence, there is an urgency to addressing Punjab's situation that is absent for many other regions of

---

[33]On Punjab's fiscal situation, see Sawhney (2014) and Sen (2014).

[34]For example, see Accenture (2014) for an overview of the Indian situation, including state-level case studies.

[35]A discussion of such issues for India can be found in Nandi and Gamkhar (2013).

[36]In particular, see Lall (2009a, b) for a discussion of Punjab's groundwater problem and possible solutions.

India, or indeed, the world. In microcosm, of course, Punjab's environmental challenge is one that the whole world faces, on a global scale, and with a somewhat longer timeline for action.

Acknowledgments This chapter is based on my keynote address delivered at the international conference, Rejuvenation of Punjab Economy, held at the Centre for Development Economics and Innovation Studies, Punjabi University, Patiala, March 21–23, 2014. I am grateful to Professor Lakhwinder Singh, director of the Centre for the opportunity. I have also drawn on and expanded some of the ideas first presented in Singh (2013a, b).

References

Accenture (2014) Best practices to improve the business environment across India, May 1. Department of Industrial Policy and Promotion, Ministry of Commerce, Government of India, New Delhi

Acemoglu D, Johnson S, Robinson JA (2005) Institutions as a fundamental cause of long-run growth. In: Aghion P, Durlauf SN (eds) Handbook of economic growth, vol 1A. Elsevier BV, Amsterdam

Amsden A (1989) Asia's next giant: South Korea and late industrialization. Oxford University Press, New York

Bhalla GS, Chadha GK (1983) Green revolution and the small peasant: a study of income distribution among Punjab cultivators. Concept Publishing Company, New Delhi

Brar JS (2016) Critical evaluation of educational development in Punjab, this volume

Brass PR (2005) Language, religion and politics in North India. Cambridge University Press, Cambridge

Centre for Development Economics and Innovation Studies (2012) Rejuvenation of Punjab economy: a policy document, July. Department of Economics, Punjabi University, Patiala

Chima JS (2010) The Sikh separatist insurgency in India: political leadership and ethno nationalist movements. Sage Publications, New Delhi

Darling M (1928) The Punjab peasant in prosperity and debt. Humphrey Milford Oxford University Press, London

Deol H (2000) Religion and nationalism in India: the case of the Punjab. Routledge, London

Evans P (1995) Embedded autonomy: states and industrial transformation. Princeton University Press, Princeton

Express News Service (2013) 10 things you should know about Rahul Gandhi's speech in Punjab, 10 Oct. http://archive.indianexpress.com/news/10-things-you-should-know-about-rahul-gandhis-speech-in-punjab/1180883/. Accessed 11 Oct 2013

Frankel F (1971) India's green revolution: economic gains and political costs. Princeton University Press, Princeton

Gill A (2000) Rural credit markets: financial sector reforms and the informal lenders. Deep and Deep Publishers, New Delhi

Gill A (2004) Interlinked agrarian credit markets: case study of Punjab. Economic and Political Weekly 39(33):3741–3751

Gill A (2016) Agricultural credit in Punjab: have policy initiatives made a dent in informal credit market? this volume

Grewal JS (1998) The Sikhs of the Punjab (revised edition). Cambridge University Press, Cambridge

Gupta D (1996) The context of ethnicity: Sikh identity in a comparative perspective. Oxford University Press, New Delhi

Harriss-White B (2003) India working: essays on society and economy. Cambridge University Press, Cambridge
Jain V (2016) Manufacturing sector in Punjab: evolution, growth dynamism, key concerns and rejuvenation strategy, this volume
Johl SS (1985) Diversification of Punjab agriculture. Government of Punjab, Chandigarh
Johnson CA (1982) MITI and the Japanese miracle: the growth of industrial policy, 1925–1975. Stanford University Press, Stanford
Jones KW (1973) Ham Hindū Nahīn: Arya Sikh Relations, 1877–1905. J Asian Stud 32(3): 457–475
Jones KW (1976) Arya dharm: hindu consciousness in 19th-century Punjab. University of California Press, Berkeley
Journal of Punjab Studies (2004) Special issue on geography of Punjab. Spring 11(1):1–100
Kapur D, Mehta PB (2008) Mortgaging the future? Indian higher education. India Policy Forum 4. Sage Publishers, New Delhi 2007–08:101–158
Kaur I, Singh N (2013) China, India, and industrial policy for inclusive growth. China Econ Policy Rev 2(1):1375001-1–27
Lall U (2009a) Punjab: a tale of prosperity and decline. http://blogs.ei.columbia.edu/2009/07/28/punjab-a-tale-of-prosperity-and-decline/. Accessed 10 Oct 2014
Lall U (2009b) Punjab: less water, more money, Parts 1–3. http://blogs.ei.columbia.edu/2009/10/13/punjab-less-water-more-money-part-1/. Accessed 10 Oct 2014
Linnemann C (2007) Germany's Mittelstand: an endangered species?. Deutsche Bank Research, Frankfurt July 6
Munjal Institute for Global Manufacturing (2013a) Inefficiencies in agriculture supply chain in Punjab and opportunities for IT interventions. Indian School of Business, Mohali
Munjal Institute for Global Manufacturing (2013b) Analysing the potential of increase in acreage for kinnow, maize, wood, turmeric and moong as per the draft agriculture policy for Punjab-2013. Indian School of Business, Mohali
Nair KN, Singh G (2014) Some issues concerning the role of technological and institutional changes in the growth and transformation of agriculture in Punjab, this volume
Nandi S, Gamkhar S (2013) Urban challenges in India: a review of recent policy measures. Habitat International, New Delhi 39:55–61
Nelsen L (2005) The role of research institutions in the formation of the biotech cluster in Massachusetts, December. Massachusetts Institute of Technology. http://web.mit.edu/lis/Nelsen.pdf. Accessed 10 Oct 2014
Putnam R (1993) Making democracy work: civic traditions in modern Italy (with Robert Leonardi and Raffaella Y Nanetti). Princeton University Press, Princeton
Rajan R, Zingales L (2006) The persistence of underdevelopment: institutions, human capital or constituencies? CEPR discussion paper 5867. Centre for Economic Policy Research, London
Rattner S (2011) The secrets of Germany's success. Foreign Affairs 90(4):7–11
Rodrik D (1995) Getting interventions right: how South Korea and Taiwan grew rich. Econ Policy 10(20):53–107
Rodrik D (2006) Industrial development: stylized facts and policies, in industrial development for the 21st century: sustainable development perspectives. In: O'Connor D (ed), UN-DESA, New York, pp 7–28
Rodrik D (2008) Is export-led growth passé? project syndicate. http://www.project-syndicate.org/commentary/is-export-led-growth-pass. Accessed 10 Oct 2014
Sawhney U (2016) Strategy for fiscal stability and revitalizing the economy of Punjab, this volume
Sen TK (2016) Public finances and development: the case of Punjab, this volume
Sharma S, Singh N (2013) Information technology and productivity in Indian manufacturing. India Policy Forum 9, 2012–13. SAGE Publishers, New Delhi, pp 187–229
Shelifer A, Vishny R (1993) Corruption. Quart J Econ 108(3):599–617
Singh G (1991) Environmental deterioration in India: causes and control: with special reference to Punjab. Agricole Publishing Academy, New Delhi

Singh H (2001) Green revolutions reconsidered: the rural world of contemporary Punjab. Oxford University Press, New Delhi

Singh L (2013) Vision for economic development in Punjab. Paper presented at conference, Re-Building Punjab, March 29–30. University of California, Santa Cruz

Singh N (2008a) Crossing a chasm: technologies, institutions and policies for developing a regional IT industry. In: Saith A, Vijayabaskar M, Gayathri V (eds) ICTs and Indian social change: diffusion, poverty and governance. Sage Publications, New Delhi, pp 192–218

Singh N (2013a) Reflections on the future of Punjab's economy: arrested development. Lecture delivered at Punjabi University, Patiala Oct 10

Singh N (2013b) The Punjab paradox, financial express, 21 Oct. http://www.financialexpress.com/news/the-punjab-paradox/1185014

Singh N, Kohli DS (2005) The green revolution in Punjab, India: the economics of technological change. J Punjab Stud 12(2):285–306

Singh P (2008b) Federalism, nationalism and development: India and the Punjab economy. Routledge, London

Singh P (2016) How centre-state relations shape Punjab's development pattern, this volume

Thandi SS (2016) Unpacking the 'Diaspora-Development' mantra: does Punjabi diaspora have the potential to contribute to the rejuvenation of Punjab's economy? this volume

The Economist (2014) German lessons: Many countries want a Mittelstand like Germany's. It is not so easy to copy, Schumpeter column, 12 July. http://www.economist.com/news/business/21606834-many-countries-want-mittelstand-germanys-it-not-so-easy-copy-german-lessons. Accessed 10 Oct 2014

Tiffin A (2014) European productivity, innovation and competitiveness: the case of Italy, 9 May. IMF Working Paper No. 14/79, International Monetary Fund, Washington, DC

Wade R (1990) Governing the market: economic theory and the role of government in East Asian industrialization. Princeton University Press, Princeton

Weder B, Weder R (2009) Switzerland's rise to a wealthy nation: competition and contestability as key success factors. UNU-WIDER Research Paper No. 2009/25, World Institute for Development Economic Research, Helsinki

Index

L. Singh and N. Singh (eds.), *Economic Transformation of a Developing Economy*, India Studies in Business and Economics,
DOI 10.1007/978-981-10-0197-0

MIX
Papier aus verantwortungsvollen Quellen
Paper from responsible sources
FSC® C105338

If you have any concerns about our products,
you can contact us on
ProductSafety@springernature.com

In case Publisher is established outside the EU,
the EU authorized representative is:
Springer Nature Customer Service Center GmbH
Europaplatz 3, 69115 Heidelberg, Germany

Printed by Libri Plureos GmbH
in Hamburg, Germany